Las Vegas

timeout.com/lasvegas

Published by Time Out Guides Ltd, a wholly owned subsidiary of Time Out Group Ltd.
Time Out and the Time Out logo are trademarks of Time Out Group Ltd.

© Time Out Group Ltd 2007
Previous editions 1998, 2000, 2001, 2003, 2005, 2007.

10 9 8 7 6 5 4 3 2 1

This edition first published in Great Britain in 2007 by Ebury Publishing
A Random House Group Company
20 Vauxhall Bridge Road, London SW1V 2SA

Random House Australia Pty Limited 20 Alfred Street, Milsons Point, Sydney, New South Wales 2061, Australia
Random House New Zealand Limited 18 Poland Road, Glenfield, Auckland 10, New Zealand
Random House South Africa (Pty) Limited Isle of Houghton, Corner Boundary
Road & Carse O'Gowrie, Houghton 2198, South Africa

Random House UK Limited Reg. No. 954009

For further distribution details, see www.timeout.com

ISBN 10: 1-84670-017-5
ISBN 13: 978184670 0170

A CIP catalogue record for this book is available from the British Library

Printed and bound by Firmengruppe APPL, aprinta druck, Wemding, Germany

The Random House Group Limited makes every effort to ensure that the papers used in our books are made from trees
that have been legally sourced from well-managed and credibly certified forests. Our paper procurement policy can
be found on www.randomhouse.co.uk.

Time Out Guides Limited
Universal House
251 Tottenham Court Road
London W1T 7AB
Tel + 44 (0)20 7813 3000
Fax + 44 (0)20 7813 6001
Email guides@timeout.com
www.timeout.com

Editorial

Editor Will Fulford-Jones
Deputy Editor Charlotte Thomas
Consultant Editor James P Reza
Listings Editor Miranda Morton
Copy Editors Edoardo Albert, Ismay Atkins
Proofreader Tamsin Shelton
Indexer Sam Le Quesne

Managing Director Peter Fiennes
Financial Director Gareth Garner
Editorial Director Ruth Jarvis
Deputy Series Editor Dominic Earle
Editorial Manager Holly Pick

Design

Art Director Scott Moore
Art Editor Pinelope Kourmouzoglou
Senior Designer Henry Elphick
Graphic Designer Gemma Doyle
Junior Graphic Designer Kei Ishimaru
Digital Imaging Simon Foster
Ad Make-up Jodi Sher

Picture Desk

Picture Editor Jael Marschner
Deputy Picture Editor Tracey Kerrigan
Picture Researcher Helen McFarland

Advertising

Sales Director Mark Phillips
Advertising Sales Manager (North America) Rani Vavilis
International Sales Consultant Ross Canadé
International Sales Executive Charlie Sokol
Advertising Assistant Kate Staddon

Marketing

Group Marketing Director John Luck
Marketing Manager Yvonne Poon
Sales & Marketing Director, North America Lisa Levinson

Production

Group Production Director Mark Lamond
Production Manager Brendan McKeown
Production Controller Caroline Bradford
Production Coordinator Susan Whittaker

Time Out Group

Chairman Tony Elliott
Financial Director Richard Waterlow
Time Out Magazine Ltd MD David Pepper
Group General Manager/Director Nichola Coulthard
Time Out Communications Ltd MD David Pepper
Time Out International MD Cathy Runciman
Group Art Director John Oakey
Group IT Director Simon Chappell

Contributors

Introduction Will Fulford-Jones. **History** Will Fulford-Jones (*Stealing from the rich, The best-laid plans* Deke Castleman; *Don't fence me in* Gregory Crosby). **Las Vegas Today** David Surratt. **Architecture** Phil Hagen (*What's that?* Matt Weatherford). **The Juice** Dayvid Figler. **Land of the Free** James Reza. **Gambling** Deke Castleman. **Casinos & Hotels** *reviews* Will Fulford-Jones, Phil Hagen, Amy Schmidt; *gambling* Deke Castleman; *additional research* Michael T Toole (*Meet the regulars* Matt Weatherford; *The curse of the lamp* Phil Hagen; *Don't look down* Dayvid Figler; *Going to extremes* Deke Castleman). **Sightseeing: Introduction** Will Fulford-Jones. **The Strip** CM Buford (*Stealth mountain* Deke Castleman; *Get around* Matt Weatherford). **Off-Strip** Will Fulford-Jones. **Downtown** Dayvid Figler (*Lighting up the past* Phil Hagen). **The Rest of the City** Emily Richmond (*Play the silver ball* Dayvid Figler). **Restaurants & Buffets** Will Fulford-Jones, Phil Hagen, Al Mancini, James P Reza, Amy Schmidt (*Going to extremes* Deke Castleman; *Drink up* Phil Hagen). **Bars & Lounges** Kate Silver (*It's all in the mix* Phil Hagen; *Going to extremes* Deke Castleman). **Shops & Services** Amy Schmidt (*Pony up!, Take a seat* Anne Kellogg; *It's a man's world* Phil Hagen). **Festivals & Events** Beverly Bryan (*Back to the future* Deke Castleman). **Adult Entertainment** James P Reza. **Casino Entertainment** Will Fulford-Jones, Julie Seabaugh (*Elvis hasn't left the building, Coming soon?* Matt Weatherford; *They say the neon lights are bright* Emily Richmond). **Children** Phil Hagen. **Film** Mike Prevatt (*Screen tests* Geoff Carter). **Galleries** Erika Pope. **Gay & Lesbian** Mike Prevatt. **Music** PJ Perez (*Stars in your eyes* Dayvid Figler). **Nightclubs** PJ Perez (*Hey Mr DJ* Mike Prevatt). **Sports & Fitness** Kate Silver. **Theatre & Dance** David Surratt (*No pain, no gain* PJ Perez). **Weddings** Beverly Bryan (*Driving me crazy* Renée Battle). **Trips Out of Town: Getting Started, Day Trips, Arizona, California** Will Fulford-Jones. **Nevada** Will Fulford-Jones; *Reno, No fear of failure* Deke Castleman. **Utah** Will Fulford-Jones. **Directory** Will Fulford-Jones.

Maps john@jsgraphics.co.uk, except page 331, used by kind permission of the Regional Transportation Commission of Southern Nevada.

Photography Jonathan Perugia, except: page 12 Bettmann/Corbis; pages 17, 33 (middle), 301 Heloise Bergman; page 18 Underwood & Underwood/Corbis; page 21 SuperStock; page 22 Darrin Bush/AP/PA Photos; page 33 (top) Elan Fleisher; page 35 Rex Features; page 37 KM Cannon/AP/PA Photos; pages 215, 296 Getty Images; page 221 Tomasz Rossa (photography) & Thierry Mugler (costumes); page 227 Isaac Brekken; page 229 Frank Bauer; page 232 Tomas Muscionico; page 241 United Artists/The Kobal Collection/Suzanne Hanover; pages 292, 294 Will Fulford-Jones. The following images were provided by the featured establishments/artists: pages 31, 113, 207, 224, 231, 235, 262, 268, 269.

Illustrations pages 72, 93, 109 Elliot Elam.

The Editor would like to thank Nyx Bradley, Ros Sales and all contributors to previous editions of *Time Out Las Vegas*, whose work forms the basis for parts of this book.

Contents

Introduction

The best time to arrive is at night, in a plane that flies over the Strip before landing at its southernmost extremity. The street is at its most dramatic after dark, several billion bulbs beckoning partiers, gamblers and lost souls into the casinos they illuminate. But, more than that, it's then that the city's monstrous sprawl is most visible from the air, little lights spreadeagling into what was desert scrub less than a generation ago.

The growth of Las Vegas over the last two decades, since Steve Wynn planted the roots of a revolution and opened the Mirage hotel in 1989, has been an archetypally American miracle. There's no reason for the city to have survived its troubled early beginnings, when bust invariably followed boom and new settlers were quick to unsettle and move elsewhere. By rights, this should be a ghost town, like so many of the mining settlements and gold rush cities that ringed it.

And yet a century after its founding, Las Vegas continues to expand. A combination of persistence, greed, marketing savvy and dumb luck has elevated this inhospitable desert outpost into a mammoth cash cow, its milk provided by an astonishing 40 million visitors a year. But it's also the fastest growing residential area in the US, slouching ever further into the valley in which it sits. Only from above is it really visible just how mammoth Las Vegas has become.

The sea change came in the 1990s, when Las Vegas Boulevard – aka the Strip, the most preposterous four-mile thoroughfare in the country – was virtually rebuilt from scratch by developers who saw potential in what had been a fading vacation town. Themed casinos, luxury hotels and outlandish resorts sprung up along the street, doubling the number of hotel rooms here in next to no time. It was an audacious and expensive gamble, but it paid off: visitor numbers soared and the city boomed like never before.

Las Vegas spent the early part of the 21st century consolidating its success, but another swell of construction has since engulfed it. A few old stagers (the Stardust, the Desert Inn, the New Frontier) have bitten the dust in a series of cacophonous demolitions. In their place will stand a slew of skyscraping, wallet-emptying residential condo developments, each one standing as priapic testament to the city's status as one of the most fashionable and luxurious in the country.

Low rollers are always welcome here. But with glamour-packed nightclubs and upmarket restaurants now overshadowing glum lounges and all-you-can-scoff buffets, modern-day Las Vegas continues to surf a wave that simply refuses to break. Many outside observers are waiting for the bust to follow this most extraordinary of booms, but don't bet on it happening any time soon.

ABOUT TIME OUT CITY GUIDES

This is the sixth edition of *Time Out Las Vegas*, one of an expanding series of more than 50 Time Out guides produced by the people behind the successful listings magazines in London, New York and Chicago and a variety of other cities around the globe. Our guides are all written by resident experts who have striven to provide you with all the most up-to-date information you'll need to explore the city or read up on its background, whether you're a local or a first-time visitor.

THE LOWDOWN ON THE LISTINGS

We have tried to make this book as easy to use as possible. Addresses, phone numbers, websites, bus information, opening times, admission prices and credit card details have all been included in the listings, as have details of other selected services and facilities. However, businesses can change their arrangements at

any time. Before you go out of your way, we strongly advise you to phone ahead and check opening times and other particulars. While every effort and care has been made to ensure the accuracy of the information contained in this guide, the publishers cannot accept responsibility for any errors it may contain.

PRICES AND PAYMENT

Our listings detail which of the five major credit cards – American Express (AmEx), Diners Club (DC), Discover (Disc), MasterCard (MC) and Visa (V) – are accepted by each venue in the guide. Many businesses will also accept other cards, as well as travellers' cheques issued by a major financial institution.

The prices we've listed in this guide should be treated as guidelines, not gospel. Fluctuating exchange rates and inflation can cause prices to change rapidly, especially in shops and restaurants. If prices vary wildly from those we've quoted, ask whether there's a good reason, then please email to let us know. We aim to give the best and most up-to-date advice, so we want to know if you've been badly treated or overcharged.

THE LIE OF THE LAND
Many visitors find Las Vegas an easy city to negotiate, if only because they rarely leave Las Vegas Boulevard (aka the Strip). However, there is a sizeable city beyond the bright lights of its main road.

To make both book and city easier to navigate, we've divided Las Vegas into areas and assigned each one its own chapter in our Sightseeing section. For consistency, the same areas have been used in addresses throughout the guide; we haven't included an area name in the addresses of businesses located on the Strip. Although these area designations are a simplification of Las Vegas's geography, we hope they'll help you to understand the city's layout. An overview map on page 334 illustrates these areas. For more on finding your way around the city, *see pp120-121*.

Advertisers

We would like to stress that no establishment has been included in this guide because it has advertised in any of our publications and no payment of any kind has influenced any review. The opinions given in this book are those of Time Out writers and entirely independent.

The back of this book contains maps of Las Vegas, along with a full street index. The street maps start on page 327; on them are pinponted the locations of all casinos and hotels (❶), restaurants (❶) and bars (❶) featured in the guide. For all addresses throughout the book, we've given both a cross-street and a map reference, along with details of the most convenient bus route.

TELEPHONE NUMBERS
The area code for Las Vegas is 702. All phone numbers listed in this guide take this code unless stated. The country code for the US is 1. For more on telephones and codes, *see p315*.

ESSENTIAL INFORMATION
For all the practical information you might need for visiting Las Vegas, including visa, customs and immigration information, details of the local transport network, a listing of emergency numbers and a selection of useful websites, turn to the Directory at the back of this guide (*see pp306-318*).

LET US KNOW WHAT YOU THINK
We hope you enjoy *Time Out Las Vegas*, and we'd like to know what you think of it. We welcome tips for places that you consider we should include in future editions and take note of your criticism of our choices. You can email us at guides@timeout.com.

There is an online version of this book, along with guides to over 100 international cities, at **www.timeout.com**.

Time Out
Travel Guides

Worldwide

All our guides are
written by a team of
local experts with a
unique and stylish
insider perspective.
We offer essential tips,
trusted advice and
honest reviews for
everything you need
to know in the city.

Over 50 destinations
available at all good
bookshops and at
timeout.com/shop

Time Out
Travel Guides

USA

Time Out
Boston

Time Out
California

Time Out
Chicago

Time Out
Las Vegas

Time Out
Los Angeles

Time Out
Miami
& the Florida Keys

Time Out
New York

Time Out
San Francisco

Time Out
Washington, DC

**Available at all good bookshops
and at timeout.com/shop**

PHOTO CREDIT: ELAN FLEISHER

Time Out
Guides

In Context

Features

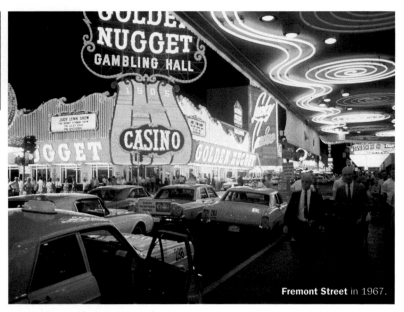

Fremont Street in 1967.

History

The self-made city that gambled on its own success.

Around 25,000 years ago, at the tail end of the last ice age, the large valley in which Las Vegas now sits was partly under water. Glaciers were retreating from the mountains that ring the Las Vegas Valley; the glacial run-off fed a vast lake, 20 miles wide and thousands of feet deep. The lake's outlet was a river known now as the Las Vegas Wash; it flowed for only 40 miles, but was larger than any other river in the western United States. At its mouth, the Wash was swallowed by the monster waterway that had been carving the Grand Canyon for a couple of hundred million years, later named the Colorado River. The Strip was built at what was once the deepest part of the lake.

Palaeo-Indians lived in caves near the lake's shoreline, which shrank as the climate changed gradually from cold and wet to warm and dry. The first Las Vegans shared the tule marsh at the edge of the lake with prehistoric horses, giant ground sloths,

American camels and massive condors, and hunted big Pleistocene mammals (woolly mammoth, bison, mastodon and caribou) as early as 13000 BC. Little is known about these early inhabitants. However, from 5,000 years ago, a clearer picture of the local prehistoric people begins to emerge.

Hunter-gatherers known as Archaic Indians introduced a culture that evolved over four millennia. The area they occupied was by then desert, although spring water bubbled to the surface and flowed down the Las Vegas Wash (now a creek) to the canyon-carving Colorado River. Even so, it wasn't until the first centuries AD that signs of civilisation sprang up in and around Nevada's southern desert. By AD 500, they had evolved into an organised people: hunting with bows and arrows, making pottery, mining salt and trading with their neighbours. They also refined their building techniques, and constructed their dwellings with adobe walls.

Three centuries later, the Anasazi tribe was cultivating beans and corn in irrigated fields, living in 100-room pueblos, fashioning artistic pots and mining turquoise. Mysteriously, they disappeared from the area around 1150: perhaps due to disease, drought, overpopulation or war, though no one really knows for sure. A large Anasazi village was discovered in 1924; parts of it are now preserved at the Lost City Museum in Overton, north-east of Las Vegas.

Southern Paiutes, hunter-gatherers more like Archaic Indians than the Anasazi, claimed the abandoned territory, but they never regained the advanced elements of their predecessors' society. For the next 700 years, the Paiutes remained semi-nomadic, establishing base camps of movable 'wickiups' (similar to tepees), cultivating squash and corn at the springs and creeks, and travelling seasonally to hunt and harvest wild foods. A frequent stopover on their travels was the Big Spring, the centre of a lush riparian habitat. Now known as the Las Vegas Springs Preserve, it opened as a park, visitor attraction and educational facility in 2007.

MEXICANS AND MORMONS

The first white men to enter the region, arriving in the early 19th century, were Mexican traders, who travelled along the Old Spanish Trail blazed by Franciscan friars to connect Spanish-Catholic missions scattered between New Mexico and the California coast. In 1830, three decades before the Civil War, Antonio Armijo set out from Santa Fe to trade goods along the trail. An experienced scout in his party by the name of Rafael Rivera found a short cut via the Big Spring, and became the first non-native to set foot on the land. He named the area Las Vegas, or 'the Meadows'.

By the time John C Fremont, a surveyor and cartographer for the Army Topographical Corps, passed through the Las Vegas Valley in 1845, the Old Spanish Trail had become the most travelled route through the Southwest. With Big Spring providing the only fresh water within a day's march, the area had become a popular camping spot. Having settled at the shore of the Great Salt Lake a few hundred miles further north-east, Latter-Day Saints also regularly passed through Las Vegas on their way to Los Angeles. Indeed, by the early 1850s, Mormon pioneer parties, wagon trains and mail carriers travelling between central Utah and southern California stopped at Big Spring with such frequency that Church elders decided to colonise the area.

In 1855, a party of Mormon missionaries was dispatched from Salt Lake City to establish a community at Las Vegas that would serve the travellers on the trail and convert the Paiute

people. The missionaries erected a fort, dug irrigation ditches, cultivated crops and even managed to befriend some Indians. But the rigours of domesticating a vast desert proved beyond them. Crops failed and rations were meagre. Timber had to be hauled from the nearest mountainsides, 20 miles away.

Even so, the mission might have succeeded had the colonists not located deposits of lead nearby. The discovery attracted miners from Salt Lake City, whose need for food, lumber and shelter taxed the colonists' already inadequate supplies to breaking point. Despite the miners' vociferous objections, the colonists petitioned Salt Lake City to be recalled, and the mission was abandoned in 1858. A small remnant of the Mormon fort survives as the oldest standing structure in Las Vegas.

OD GASS AND HELEN STEWART

Soon after the Mormons abandoned Las Vegas, prospectors picked up where the lead miners left off and discovered that the ore averaged a rich $650 per ton in silver. A small mining boomtown mushroomed in the desert around Big Spring. Miners who arrived too late to get in on the action fanned out from the settlement and found gold along the Colorado River, about 50 miles south-east of Las Vegas.

> **'Eager settlers, Los Angeles speculators and East Coast investors were all gambling on the prosperity of yet another western railroad boomtown.'**

One of the gold-seekers, Octavius Decatur Gass, saw a more enticing opportunity: homesteading the well-watered valley. Craftily, Gass appropriated the Mormon fort in 1865, using the lumber to build a ranch house and utility shop. He dug irrigation canals, planted grain, vegetables and fruit trees, and ran cattle on a chunk of land known as Las Vegas Ranch. Over the next ten years, Gass expanded his land and water holdings, assumed civic duties and helped other homesteaders get established.

However, Gass's ambition eventually got the better of him. In financial trouble by the 1870s, he took a loan from Archibald Stewart, a rich rancher from the mining boomtown of Pioche. When, in 1881, Gass couldn't repay the loan, Stewart foreclosed on it and took over the Las Vegas Ranch, expanding the property until he was shot dead in 1884 after an argument with a ranch hand from a neighbouring spread.

Stealing from the rich

For a large chunk of Las Vegas's colourful history, even the most accomplished thieves and robbers shied away from stealing from the casinos. Security surrounding the cashier's cage was thought to be virtually impenetrable; on the few occasions that a robber did make it out with the money, the police were usually close behind. And if the thieves somehow managed to elude the cops, a few heavies quietly employed by the casino would track them down and turn them into coyote bait.

Over the last couple of decades, however, the city's casinos have been the target of thieves and armed robbers pulling a variety of jobs, from the quiet to the brazen. On average, the Las Vegas police deal with between 15 and 20 casino robberies a year; it may not sound like many, but the yields can be huge.

In the mid 1990s, Vegas casinos were subjected to a rash of armed robberies by LA gangs. Talk about audacious: the robbers entered the casinos in great numbers, submachine pistols clearly visible, and vaulted the counter into the cashier's cages. As they fled, they sprayed around a few rounds of ammo for good measure. However, most of the gang-bangers were caught; it was even reputed that the cash was recovered still bundled in straps bearing the names of the casinos from which it was taken.

Inside jobs aren't quite as public and messy, and the well-planned ones can be lucrative. One of the best known and most successful of all inside heists took place in 1992 at the now-defunct Stardust. A cashier

in the sports book managed to stuff $500,000 of cash and chips into a duffel bag while the other employees were busy taking bets on a big game; he then walked out of the casino with the loot, never to be seen or heard from again. How did he do it? The strongest theory is that he worked with a confederate to whom he surreptitiously passed the money. But no one knows for sure.

The most lucrative casino theft in recent Vegas history amounted to the perfect crime. On the morning of 1 October 1993, an armoured truck operated by the Loomis security firm pulled into Circus Circus, the first stop of the day for guards dispatched to fill the city's ATMs. But as two of the guards went into the casino to load the machines, the truck's driver sped away.

By the time police had figured out what was going on, it was too late. Heather Tallchief, a 21-year-old with no prior criminal record, had driven the truck to a garage; here, she met her lover, a career criminal named Roberto Solis who is believed to have planned the elaborate heist. The duo emptied the truck of $3 million in cash and boarded a chartered Lear Jet to Denver, later travelling to Miami and the Cayman Islands. At all times, the duo remained one step ahead of their pursuers, eventually vanishing into the ether. So it came as some surprise when, after 12 years on the run, Tallchief returned to the US from her new home of Amsterdam and turned herself in, whereupon she was sentenced to five years in prison. Solis remains at large.

Stewart's wife Helen ran the ranch for the next 20 years, buying up more acreage, making a living in the livestock business, and running a resort for nearby ranchers and a campground for travellers on the Mormon Trail.

The San Pedro, Los Angeles & Salt Lake Railroad arrived in 1903, its planned route running through the heart of the ranch. Thanks to its strategic location and plentiful water, Las Vegas had been designated a division point for crew changes, a service stop for through trains and, eventually, a site for maintenance shops. Ready to retire, Mrs Stewart sold most of her 2,000-acre site for $55,000, but deeded ten acres to the Paiutes, who'd been reduced to living on the edge of town through government largesse. For this and other civic-minded deeds, Stewart is considered the First Lady of Las Vegas.

In preparation for the land sale, Stewart hired JT McWilliams to survey her property. The canny McWilliams discovered and immediately claimed 80 untitled acres just west of the big ranch, planned a town site and began selling lots to a steadfast group of Las Vegas 'sooners' (the earliest speculators on the scene). In late 1904, two railroad construction crews, one from the north-east and one from the south-west, converged on Las Vegas Valley. And then, in January 1905, a golden spike was driven into a tie near Jean, Nevada, 23 miles south of Las Vegas, ceremonially completing the railroad.

GAMBLING ON PROSPERITY

McWilliams's settlement, known as Ragtown, was one of a long line of boomtowns that had been erupting across Nevada over the preceding 50 years. On the day the first train travelled through Big Spring on its route between Salt Lake City and Los Angeles, Ragtown's saloons, banks and tent hotels teemed with settlers, speculators, tradesmen and itinerants. But the San Pedro, Los Angeles & Salt Lake Railroad had other plans for the fledgling settlement. It organised a subsidiary, Las Vegas Land & Water, to build its own town.

Officials laid out the town site, scraped the scrub from 40 square blocks and staked 1,200 lots. The new town site of Las Vegas received national publicity and demand for the land was high, with prospective buyers coming by train from Los Angeles ($16 return) and Salt Lake City ($20). Competition for locations proved so overwhelming that the railroad scheduled an auction, pitting eager settlers against Los Angeles real estate speculators and East Coast investors. All were gambling on the prosperity of yet another western railroad boomtown.

The auction was held on 15 May 1905 at the intersection of Main and Fremont Streets, on the site of today's Plaza Hotel in Downtown. The bidding quickly inflated the price of choice lots to more than double their listed values. The locals over in Ragtown grumbled about the railroad tactic of encouraging out-of-town investors to heat up the prices. But when it was over, nearly 1,000 lots had been sold for the grand total of $265,000, which was $195,000 more than the railroad had paid for the entire Las Vegas Ranch only three years earlier.

The proud new property owners immediately searched out the stakes marking the boundaries of their lots and erected makeshift shelters on them. Ragtowners rolled their possessions over to the new Las Vegas on horse- and ox-drawn wagons. What remained of the first town site burned to the ground four months later, and the first Las Vegas building boom followed.

SETTLING IN

In stereotypical western fashion, the first structures to go up were saloons and brothels, built in the designated nightlife and red light district on Block 16 between Ogden and Stewart and 1st and 2nd Streets (now the parking lot at Binion's). Hotels, restaurants, banks and shops were erected along Fremont Street; railroad and town administrative offices, a school, a post office and two churches surrounded the core. The railroad company built the infrastructure: gravel streets and plank sidewalks, water service and sporadic electricity. Houses went

An early settler showing off his very welcome water supply in 1895.

up along the residential streets of the eight-block-long and five-block-wide town; supplies arrived daily by train. By New Year's Day 1906, some 1,500 pioneers were calling Las Vegas home. However, the initial boom was short-lived. Barely a year passed before the railroad town managers showed their true colours, concerned first with operating the main line and last with servicing the town. Their refusal to extend pipes beyond the town site stunted growth, forcing the rural dwellers to dig wells and tap into the aquifer. Fires, conflicts and the usual growing pains of a young settlement slowed the influx of new residents, reducing both property values and optimism. The heat, dust and isolation contributed to the consensus of discomfort.

A rare bit of good news arrived in 1909, when the Nevada Legislature created Clark County in the south of the state (it was named after William Clark, the chairman of the San Pedro, Los Angeles & Salt Lake Railroad) and named Las Vegas as its seat of government. Two years later, the railroad gave the town a boost when it opened a shop designed to help maintain the steam locomotives, passenger coaches and freight cars along the line. Hundreds of jobs were created at a single stroke; by the time the shop was fully staffed, the population of Las Vegas had doubled to 3,000. Telephone service arrived, with the first phone (taking, of course, the number '1') installed at the cigar counter in the lobby of the Hotel Nevada (now the Golden Gate). And in 1915, big town generators began supplying electricity to residents 24 hours a day.

But for the next 15 years, everything went downhill. The railroad found itself losing business to car and truck traffic, and workers were laid off. Union Pacific bought up the San Pedro, Los Angeles & Salt Lake Railroad, relegating it to the status of a small siding on a vast nationwide network. Measures brought in by Union Pacific severely inhibited the town's growth; when it then closed the railroad maintenance shops, locals were driven to leave town in search of work. Las Vegas would have dried up and blown away by the late 1920s if it hadn't been for a monumental federal dam-building project gearing up nearby.

THE HOOVER DAM

The 1,450-mile Colorado River had been gouging great canyons and watering lush valleys for aeons, when the US government became determined to harness its flow in the service of irrigation, electricity, flood control and recreation. The Bureau of Reclamation began to consider damming the Colorado in 1907, eventually narrowing down the choice of

locations for the dam to two canyons east of Las Vegas. In 1930, six years after the site for it had been selected, Congress appropriated the $165 million necessary to build the Boulder Dam.

Anticipation of the dam project began to fuel noticeable growth in the railroad town. By the time construction began in 1931 (the name change, from the Boulder Dam to the Hoover Dam, was announced at the spike-driving ceremony), a long-distance phone service, a federal highway linking Salt Lake City to Los Angeles and regular air-passenger services had arrived. The population soared to 5,000, with thousands more passing through Las Vegas en route to the soon-to-be-tamed river.

'Backroom illegal gambling had long been the norm for the libertine frontier state of Nevada.'

Even today, the building of the Hoover Dam is mind-boggling in its immensity. The nearest power plant was 200 miles away in southern California; wires had to be strung all the way from it in order to supply electricity. Some 5,000 workers had to be hired, and an entire town (Boulder City) was built to house them and their families. Most dauntingly of all, the mighty Colorado River itself had to be diverted simply for the project to begin. It took 16 months to hack four diversion tunnels through the canyon walls before the river could be routed around the construction site. Only then could work begin on what would eventually become one of the man-made wonders of the world.

Some five million buckets of concrete were poured into the dam over a two-year period. When it was completed in 1935, Hoover Dam stood 656 feet (200 metres) wide at its base, 49 feet (15 metres) thick at its crest, 1,358 feet (414 metres) across and 794 feet (242 metres) tall. After the diversion tunnels were closed, it took a further three years to fill Lake Mead. At 109 miles long, reaching a depth of 545 feet (166 metres), it's the largest man-made lake in North America. The legacy of the dam has been monumental, endowing Las Vegas with the power and the water it needed to fulfil its early promise.

THE NEW BOOM

In 1931, another event occurred that was to have long-lasting implications for Las Vegas: the statewide legalisation of wide-open casino gambling. Backroom illegal gambling had long been the norm for the libertine frontier state of Nevada. But when legislators gave gambling their blessing (along with easy divorces, no-wait marriages, prostitution and championship

Don't fence me in

'Still a Frontier Town!'

The tag line dreamed up in the 1940s by the J Walter Thompson Agency in Los Angeles, in order to promote a dusty little gambling town halfway between the City of Angels and the City of Saints (Salt Lake City), was an appealing one. The fact that Las Vegas had never actually been a frontier town – watering hole and railroad stop would be more accurate – was no bar to the creation of a quintessential cowpoke to go along with the Chamber of Commerce's PR campaign. Thus was born Vegas Vic, a long and lanky cartoon with a strong chin and a welcoming glint in his squinty eye. Decked out in dude-ranch finery, a cigarette dangling from his lips, Vic beckoned the weary traveller to fun and sun in the desert.

However, Vic would likely be forgotten if not for his incarnation as that most powerful of Vegas icons: the neon sign. Translated by the Young Electric Sign Company into 48 feet (15 metres) of metal and glass, Vegas Vic became the unofficial mayor of Fremont Street when he was installed on the façade of the Pioneer Club in 1947 (the current version dates from 1951). Motors moved Vic's arm, his thumb out like some sort of demented hitchhiker, while a hidden loudspeaker boomed out, every few minutes or so, a welcome to the rubes: 'Howdy, Podner!'

Vic's monotonous greeting got on everyone's nerves after a few years, most famously actor Lee Marvin's. While in town working on a Western, Marvin leaned out of his hotel window, across the street at the Mint, and shot poor Vic full of arrows. It seems Vic's voice was interfering with a particularly heavy hangover. Vic was soon silenced; a few years later, when the mechanism in his arm gave out, the Pioneer Club's owners didn't bother to fix it.

They didn't need to. By then, Vic, in his gaudy wide-brimmed hat, yellow-checked shirt, red 'kerchief and blue jeans, was a signature part of Downtown. It's a measure of his fame that when the Fremont Street Experience canopy was built in 1995, he wasn't removed but merely lowered a few feet, giving him the appearance of a giant stuck in a low-ceilinged room. Long before then, though, he'd been joined on Glitter Gulch by Vegas Vicky, a neon cowgirl with entirely different assets.

Sadly, Vic and Vicky were doomed to enjoy each other only from afar: they literally work different sides of the street. Vic now presides over the Pioneer Club in name only, the casino having long since been replaced by a souvenir shop, while Vicky crowns the newly renovated Topless Girls of Glitter Gulch strip joint. Vic and Vicky might not be remnants of an 'Old West' Vegas that never was, but they're cherished relics of the honky-tonk town of the last century, at the moment when the final frontier of glitz, glamour and gambling was about to be crossed forever.

The building of the **Hoover Dam**...

boxing matches), the transformation of Las Vegas from a railroad company town into a casino company town began in earnest.

Casino operators migrated in droves to the only state in the union where they could ply their trade without risking arrest; vice-starved visitors followed. The bars and casinos moved a block, from the shadows of Ogden Street to the more inviting Fremont Street. The ladies of the night stayed behind at Block 16, but lights began to brighten the gambling joints along Fremont, soon nicknamed 'Glitter Gulch'.

Las Vegas also enjoyed widespread publicity from the building of the dam. By 1935, when 20,000 people saw Franklin D Roosevelt preside over the Hoover Dam dedication ceremony, word was beginning to get around that this little town by the dam was a slice of the authentic Wild West, with legal casinos, legal prostitution and legal everything else. Temptation led to prosperity, which in turn led to construction. Three new casinos were built at the start of the 1940s: the El Cortez in Downtown, and the Last Frontier and El Rancho on the Los Angeles Highway, a stretch of road that would eventually come to be known as the Strip.

With the nation preparing for World War II, the federal government took over a million acres north of Las Vegas for use as a training school for military pilots and gunners. Between 1940 and 1945, the Las Vegas Aerial Gunnery School trained thousands of pilots, navigators, bombers and gunners, then shipped them to the front in Europe or the Pacific. The school eventually expanded to three million acres. And in 1942, Basic Magnesium, one of the largest metal-processing factories in the country, was built halfway between Las Vegas and Boulder City. At the peak of production, 10,000 workers were processing millions of tons of magnesium, a newly developed metal used in the manufacture of bomb casings, aeroplane components and flares. To house them, an entire town was built: Henderson, Las Vegas's first next-door neighbour. During the war years, its population doubled from 8,500 to 17,000.

THE MOB AND THE BOMB

As much as the war brought economic benefits to Las Vegas, it also gave a boost to organised crime throughout the US, as the black market in scarce consumer goods resulted in handsome profits for those savvy enough to sell them. But while the masters of the underworld were making a decent wage all over the US, they looked upon Las Vegas as the Promised Land. Flush with cash from bootlegging during

... and the end result.

Prohibition and black market trading during the war, gangsters from all over the country stood poised to invade Nevada with money, management and muscle. All they needed was someone to raise a torch and show them the way. Enter Benjamin 'Bugsy' Siegel: tall, handsome and fearless, and partnered by the most powerful criminal bosses in the country.

Siegel elbowed into and bowed out of several casinos during the early 1940s, until her finally settled on the Flamingo. He insinuated himself into the management (which, contrary to popular myth, already existed), then so terrorised the team that they fled for their lives and left him with the unfinished joint. Siegel knew nothing about building a casino; construction ran $4 million over budget. What's more, he wasn't around long enough to enjoy its spoils: less than six months after the doors opened in December 1946, Siegel was assassinated in his girlfriend's Beverly Hills mansion.

Thus began 20 years of the Italian-Jewish crime syndicate's presence in Las Vegas, and ten years of the biggest hotel-building boom the country had ever seen. Black money from top Mob bosses, along with their fronts, pawns, soldiers and workers, poured in from the underworld power centres of New York,

New England, Cleveland, Chicago, Kansas City, New Orleans, Miami and Havana. Between 1951 and 1958, 11 major hotel-casinos opened in Las Vegas, nine on the Strip and two Downtown. All but one was financed by dirty cash.

Eventually, a full 25 years after gambling was legalised in Nevada, the state and federal governments woke up to the questionable histories of the people who were in charge of the largest industry in Las Vegas. In every other state in the country, they were considered criminals; in Vegas, they'd successfully bought power, influence and respectability. The war between the police and the gangsters began, but it was overshadowed by an event that cast the town in a very strange light.

When the federal government went looking for a vast tract of uninhabited land on which to perfect its nuclear weapons, it found one at the Las Vegas Aerial Gunnery School. Just 70 miles north-west of the city, the Nevada Test Site went on to host roughly 120 above-ground nuclear test explosions, about one a month for a decade. Thousands of guinea-pig soldiers were deployed near the explosions, purposefully exposed to the shockwaves so medical teams could measure the effects of the radiation.

A few locals worried about which way the wind blew. However, most of the 65,000

The best-laid plans

If you hadn't noticed, Las Vegas is all about excess. You won't be able to move in the city without bumping into the world's largest this, the world's most luxurious that or the world's most expensive other thing. But for all the visions of grandeur that come to fruition, there are twice as many delusions that never make it past the planning stage.

Some of these plans are good ideas that, for whatever reason, can't find the financing or the favours required for lift-off. Some are heavy on hype yet light on logic, tossed out by hucksters hoping to make a quick buck. Others are so absurd that they don't stand a chance. And still others are such hopeless pipe dreams that even normally respectful TV reporters can't help sniggering between the lines.

Perhaps the biggest and most symbolically foolish of these fantasies was Moon, a 250-acre, $5-billion, 10,000-room lunar-themed mega-resort announced with much fanfare in 2002. Michael Henderson, the pitchman for this lunacy, poured every imaginable amenity into his plans, probably figuring he might as well throw it all against the wall and see what stuck. But despite the promise of a zero-gravity simulator and a 'crater wave pool', Moon disappeared almost immediately from the local radar screen. From the start, it had as much chance of being built in Las Vegas as it did of opening on the moon itself.

Following behind Moon in terms of unrealised scope are the various figments of the imagination that have dogged the old El Rancho property. After plans for the $1-billion Starship Orion hotel-casino were lost in space in 1996, several ill-conceived incarnations of Countryland USA (1997-99) came and went. The lot was subsequently slated for casinos modelled on London, one of three such proposals down the years, and San Francisco, a theme favoured at various times

by no fewer than four teams of Vegas developers. Both fell by the wayside, but ground has at long last been broken on the plot; the 4,000-room, Miami Beach-themed Fontainebleau is expected to open in 2009.

Some developers simply don't seem to have done their research. Desert Kingdom (1994) was the name of a proposed hotel planned for 34 vacant acres next to the Desert Inn and aimed purely at high rollers. The plans called for 3,500 rooms, which was only about 3,000 rooms in excess of the number of high rollers around at the time; the project was quietly but quickly cancelled. Just up the Strip in 1999, promoter extraordinaire Bob Stupak floated a proposal for the Boat, a 1,200-cabin, *Titanic*-themed hotel and timeshare complex complete with an iceberg-shaped mall. Naturally, it sank without a trace.

Other failed adventures have come with celebrity endorsements. The World Wrestling Federation bought Debbie Reynolds' hotel-casino (originally the Paddlewheel, now the Greek Isles) for $10.6 million in 1998 and pinned its hopes on a $100million, 1,000-room resort with a wrestling theme. They sold it a year later. The site now occupied by the Palms was once tagged as the home of Desert Winds (1993), an $87-million, 400-room fantasy themed after the ill-starred musical Jackson family, and for Sound Stage, a 1,000-room project launched by Black Entertainment Television in 1997. Other off-the-wall plans that never left the drawing board included casinos themed after Bugsy Siegel (1998), Elvis Presley (1999 and 2006) and even Gen X (2000). But none were quite as absurd as Winter Wonderland, a chilly casino centred around a climate-controlled dome where it snowed every day. Only in Vegas? Happily not.

Las Vegans seemed to revel in the notoriety that radiated from the tests. The boosters had a ball, marketing everything from 'atom burgers' to pictures of Miss Atomic Blast, and the openings of several casinos were scheduled to coincide with blasts. People had picnics atop the tallest buildings in town, looking across at the mushroom clouds. The Nuclear Test Ban treaty in 1962 drove the explosions underground, where 600 tests were held in the following three decades. But the reputation remained.

THE DIATRIBE

The Mob, the bombs, the gambling and the general naughtiness of Las Vegas attracted plenty of heat from the rest of the United States, most of it magnified by the media. A steamroller of criticism levelled the town's reputation, turning it into a national scandal. Known as 'the Diatribe', this systematic attack remains the greatest ever public castigation of an American city. The assault coloured Las Vegas's image for 30 years.

At the same time, though, people flocked to the town, proving the old rule about all publicity being good publicity. These pilgrims found that a strange thing happened at the Nevada state line: criminals who crossed it were suddenly accorded the status of legitimate businessmen, while the good citizens of the rest of the country suddenly became naughty boys and girls. These were the glamour years, when you didn't go out in Las Vegas after dark if you weren't wearing a suit or a cocktail dress. Crap shooters rolled the bones elbow-to-elbow with hit men. Mafia pit bosses had the 'power of the pencil' to hand out free rooms, food and beverages at their discretion, and the comps flowed as easily as the champagne.

'Scandals erupted at the casinos at which the Mob was entrenched.'

During this period, Frank Sinatra, Dean Martin and Sammy Davis Jr performed in the Copa Room at the Sands, then invaded lounges around town. Joining the likes of Shecky Greene, Buddy Hackett and Louis Prima on stage, the Rat Pack became iconic fixtures of the new, high-rollin' Vegas. Many locals and visitors who were around from the early 1950s to the mid '60s still pine for these lost years.

The end of the Diatribe can be traced back to the arrival of multi-millionaire Howard Hughes. Smuggled under cover into town in November 1966, the tycoon settled into the ninth floor of the Desert Inn, from where he cultivated his eccentricities and planned his assault on the city. When the management at the Desert Inn threatened him with eviction, reputedly because they wanted to reserve his penthouse for high rollers, he dug $13 million from his bank account and bought the hotel. Over the next few years, Hughes went on to spend $300 million in the city, buying five casinos (including the Sands), an airline and the KLAS TV station, the latter purely so he could control the all-night programming he obsessively watched.

The publicity generated by his spending spree turned around the town's reputation: no longer was the town run by the Mob. Between 1968 and 1973, another dozen casinos opened, many of them run by respected companies that had previously been careful not to touch the crime-riddled town with a bargepole. It took a little while for various task forces to hound the old gangsters into oblivion; one scandal after another erupted at the older casinos at which the Mob was still entrenched. But eventually, in the mid 1980s, the city's casinos were free of any discernible Mob involvement.

THE NEW LAS VEGAS

In November 1989, a maverick 47-year-old businessman by the name of Steve Wynn opened a 3,000-room, $650-million pleasure palace in the heart of the Strip. The size, elegance and price tag of the Mirage stunned the old guard in Las Vegas. But the phenomenal enthusiasm with which the public greeted the it, not to mention the $1-million-a-day profits that resulted, galvanised the industry, and changed both the look and the culture of Las Vegas. The forlorn old casinos, with their scruffy buffets and dowdy lounges, were soon replaced by sophisticated resorts, complete with impressive restaurants, high-budget shows and plush new lounges. A new breed of vacationer, more moneyed than at any point since the 1960s, came to see them.

There was plenty to see. The Excalibur, a family-friendly, medieval-themed casino-resort, opened in June 1990, followed in 1993 by the pyramidal Luxor, the pirate-technic Treasure Island and the 5,005-room MGM Grand, at the time the world's largest hotel. The Hard Rock Hotel brought some glamour back to the town when it opened in 1995; the 1,257-foot (383-metre) Stratosphere Tower, the opulent Monte Carlo

The glamour years: Vegas in the 1960s.

Steve Wynn. *See p21.*

and the pop art New York New York all opened between April 1996 and January 1997. Another wave of construction crested in October 1998 with the opening of the $1.6-billion Bellagio, then the most expensive hotel ever built. The $1-billion Mandalay Bay, all hipness and whimsy, followed six months later, with the $1.5-billion Venetian and the $760-million Paris Las Vegas making their debuts in September 1999. Then, in August 2000, came the Aladdin.

While these major casinos went up, others came tumbling down. The building boom of the 1990s was accompanied by the spectacular implosion of a number of key casinos. Between October 1993 and April 1998, the Dunes, the Landmark, the Sands, the Hacienda and the old Aladdin were all levelled, to be replaced by the Bellagio, a parking lot, the Venetian, Mandalay Bay and the new Aladdin (now Planet Hollywood) respectively. Implosions in 2001 and 2004 finally levelled the Desert Inn; on its site stands Wynn Las Vegas, which in 2005 became the first major casino to arrive on the Strip in a half-decade. And in 2007, nearly 50 years after it opened, the Stardust was blown up. Locals mourned the loss of these icons, but many turned up to watch the last rites.

21ST-CENTURY VEGAS

Despite the fact that the town already has more than 130,000 hotel rooms and 17 of the 22 largest hotels on earth, Las Vegas continues to grow. After a slight blip post-9/11, visitor numbers in Las Vegas have now reached record levels. An astonishing 39 million people, around ten per cent of them from abroad, visited the city in 2006, spending untold billions in the process. Many people check out Sin City once just to see what all the fuss is about, but millions more become regulars, attracted by the agreeable climate, the big-budget shows, the swanky hotels, the increasingly excellent food, the fashionably nightlife and, of course, the chance of instant riches.

Indeed, many have relocated to the world's greatest boomtown. Las Vegas is the largest American city to have been founded in the 20th century, and has also been its fastest growing major metropolitan area for more than a decade. Two building booms are ongoing in Las Vegas: one that will add yet more hotels to the city's roster, and another that's adding a welter of hyper-expensive condo towers to the Strip skyline. The city celebrated its 100th birthday in mid 2005, a century during which it developed from a desolate railroad town to the glamour capital of the world. Heaven only knows what the next ten decades will bring.

▶ For more on **new buildings**, *see pp30-31.*
▶ For more on the **Hoover Dam**, *see pp278-279.*

Key events

c800 Anasazi civilisation begins to develop in the southern Nevada desert.
c1150 The semi-nomadic southern Paiute tribe claim territory abandoned by the Anasazi.
1830 Rafael Rivera discovers a short cut via Big Spring while on the trading route from Santa Fe. He names the area Las Vegas (meaning 'the Meadows').
1845 The surveyor John C Fremont visits the Las Vegas Valley. By this time, Big Spring has become a popular camping spot on the well-travelled Old Spanish Trail.
1855-58 Mormon missionaries from Salt Lake City establish a short-lived community at Las Vegas. Lead is discovered in the area.
c1858 Silver ore and gold are discovered, prompting the sudden growth of a mining boomtown around Big Spring and along the Colorado River.
1865 The old Mormon fort is appropriated by OD Gass and redeveloped as the Las Vegas Ranch.
1881 The Las Vegas Ranch is taken over by Archibald Stewart, who expands the property until his death in 1884.
1884 The Las Vegas Ranch is managed and developed by Stewart's widow Helen.
1903 Helen Stewart sells most of the Las Vegas Ranch to the San Pedro, Los Angeles & Salt Lake Railroad. JT McWilliams claims 80 acres of land west of the Las Vegas Ranch and sells them as lots of a planned town site, known as Ragtown.
1905 The Salt Lake City to Los Angeles railroad is completed at Jean, Nevada. A subsidiary of the railroad company auctions 1,000 lots for a new town site across the tracks from Ragtown. Four months later, Ragtown burns to the ground.
1905 The new town of Las Vegas begins to develop with a nightlife district on Block 16 (today's Downtown).
1909 Las Vegas is made the seat of the newly created Clark County, prompting a mini-boom in the town.
c1915-30 Union Pacific buys up the San Pedro, Los Angeles & Salt Lake Railroad, leading to economic decline in Las Vegas.
1924 Two canyons east of Las Vegas are chosen as the site of an ambitious new project to dam the Colorado River.
1931 Gambling is legalised in Nevada, prompting an influx of casino operators into Las Vegas and the development of Fremont Street (soon nicknamed 'Glitter Gulch') as the main nightlife area. Construction begins on the Hoover Dam, with Boulder City established to house the workers.
1935 President Roosevelt and 20,000 others attend the Hoover Dam dedication ceremony.
1940 US government takes over a million acres of Nevada desert to the north-west of Las Vegas to train soldiers for World War II.
early 1940s Three major casinos are built: the El Cortez in Downtown, and El Rancho and the Last Frontier on the Los Angeles Highway.
1946 Construction of Benjamin 'Bugsy' Siegel's Flamingo casino.
1947 Bugsy Siegel is shot dead in Beverly Hills. For the next 20 years, the Mob dominates gambling in Las Vegas.
1951-58 Eleven major hotel-casinos open in Vegas; ten of them are funded by the Mob.
1951-62 Around 120 nuclear bombs are detonated above ground over the Nevada Test Site, north-west of Las Vegas.
1960-61 The legendary Rat Pack perform in the Copa Room at the Sands casino.
1962 First Limited Nuclear Test Ban Treaty prohibits atmospheric nuclear explosions.
1962-92 800 nuclear devices are detonated underground at the Nevada Test Site.
1966 Millionaire Howard Hughes takes up residence at the Desert Inn, buying up six casinos and stimulating a new boom. A dozen new casinos are built in the next seven years.
1967 Stunt motorcyclist Evel Knievel tries and fails to jump over the fountains at Caesars Palace.
1989 Steve Wynn opens the Mirage, the first major hotel-casino to be built for 16 years.
1990-2000 Myriad new resorts are built on the Strip and beyond it, from the medieval-themed Excalibur in 1990 to the Aladdin in 2000. The town undergoes a new lease of life and the population of Clark County almost doubles from 770,280 in 1990 to 1,425,723 a decade later.
1995 The Fremont Street Experience opens.
1999 Oscar Goodman is elected mayor.
2001 The Palms opens for business.
2005 As the town celebrates its centenary, Steve Wynn opens Wynn Las Vegas, the Strip's most luxurious property yet.
2006 Construction begins on MGM Mirage's CityCenter development.
2007 The Stardust is demolished.

Las Vegas Today

A swish new Vegas aims to ditch the showgirls and sequins.

In the wee small hours of 13 March 2007, a crowd of tourists and locals gathered just west of Las Vegas Boulevard, a safe distance from the evacuated and spotlit Stardust hotel. After several minutes' worth of fireworks exploded above them, a further pyrotechnical display attached to the hotel's 32-storey west tower traced the enormous digits of a ten-second countdown. And then, at 2.33am, a formerly indispensable piece of the Las Vegas skyline slouched and sank to an upsurge of dust, cheers and cries. 'Bye-bye, Stardust: thanks for the memories!'

It was a memorable moment, but hardly a unique one. The 16-storey Boardwalk fell in 2006, as did Bourbon Street and Castaways. Two years earlier, the Desert Inn's St Andrews Tower came down; as, for that matter, did its Palms Tower, just seven years after it went up. Its short lifespan wasn't even a record for the city: a week before the Stardust's demolition, a nine-storey employee parking garage at Wynn Las Vegas met its demise at the tender age of four. The grand total: 14 implosions in 14 years. Like a temperamental tyke at the beach,

levelling one sandcastle to make room for another, the city has been cashing in its less lucrative architecture for bigger and better ideas, and it's stepping up the effort daily.

ALTERED STATES

Change may be a constant in Las Vegas, but it's not the only one. While the landscape goes through endless metamorphoses, the core Vegas concept – bring your money and go nuts – stays the same. This is still the neon eruption sought and easily found by all who care to spend a few days in a hyperkinetic, if carefully regulated, den of iniquity. Slot machine exposure still starts in the baggage claim area at McCarran Airport. Hookers still flourish under the thinnest of 'escort service' veils. And in the majority of bars, there's still no such thing as last call.

What's changed most about today's Vegas is a matter of scope. No longer fully satisfied with its 'adult Disneyland' identity, this century-old frontier town now wants to grow up into a world-class city. It's an aspiration reflected not only in what's rushing to fill the vacuum left by all these vanishing buildings, but in the new images sported by a number of the ones that are still standing. The de-theming of the Strip is well under way.

When Treasure Island got a makeover back in the yesteryear of 2003, its owners reasoned that too much yo-ho-ho and Jolly Roger might not be the most sophisticated way to draw an adult market that, they now realised, was a better bet than the family crowd they'd been courting with diminishing success. The strategy worked; and, like any casino-led innovation that works here, it immediately got adopted by its originator's rivals. In April 2007, after a long time in limbo, the Aladdin became Planet Hollywood, but a more sophisticated Planet Hollywood than its restaurant-only siblings across the world. At the same time, the Luxor was formulating plans to close two of its Egyptian-themed gift shops and nix the Sphinx out front, while New York New York is apparently planning to ditch its Coney Island-themed kids' arcade for a new ultralounge.

In fact, there's been no bigger swing in Vegas's image than in its nightlife. See-and-be-seen dance clubs and so-called ultralounges have become screamingly popular over the last few years, ever since someone realised that 20,000 square feet of casino space without slots could still yield big profits if it was tricked out with state-of-the-art lighting effects, sturdy cover charges and wallet-draining bottle-service policies that bring with them the kind of air of exclusivity that only money or celebrity can buy. As such, casinos now market ethereal, monosyllabically named joints – Jet, Light, Tao, Rain, Tryst, Pure, Mist et al – as aggressively as they hawk their poker rooms.

ONE FOR ALL

The concerted revamping projects on the Strip are made a good deal easier by the fact that all the hotels just mentioned, with the exception of Planet Hollywood, are now owned by the same corporation. On the Strip's four-mile Monopoly board, the MGM Mirage group is in the lead. After buying the Mandalay Resort Group in 2005, a deal initially rejected by competitors due to antitrust concerns, the MGM Mirage group expanded their portfolio of properties to encompass the MGM Grand, the Bellagio, the Mirage, Mandalay Bay, the Luxor, New York NewYork, the Excalibur, the Monte Carlo and Circus Circus. In other words, about half the Strip.

While MGM Mirage is now responsible for roughly 50 per cent of the Strip's 75,000 hotel rooms, Harrah's controls around half the remainder in the shapes of Caesars Palace, Paris Las Vegas, the Imperial Palace, the Flamingo, Bally's and its namesake resort. In early 2007,

the firm announced plans to acquire seven new parcels of land… shortly after accepting a $17.9 billion buyout by two private equity firms.

If it appears over the top, it's really just a reflection of changes in the country at large. The dizzying number of deals that have lit up the Vegas business pages are all part of a tightening food chain that closely follows a national trend toward dry, megacorporate entities. It seems a particularly heartbreaking compromise for a town built on a foundation of libertarianism that bordered, at times, on anarchy. Bugsy Siegel at least had a face.

Even so, Bugsy likely never envisioned anything like CityCenter, one of a slew of ambitious new projects being built on the ruins of not-so-ancient Vegas. An MGM Mirage venture, the $7.4billion, 68-acre project will feature a 60-storey resort and casino, two additional boutique hotels (plans call for a total of around 5,000 guestrooms), multiple condo and condo-hotel towers, immeasurable amounts of retail space, theatres, spas and a parking garage with room for 7,500 vehicles. It'll also have its own power plant and fire station, making CityCenter a semi-autonomous community in an unincorporated township (the Strip) within a larger, sprawling desert outpost that's struggling to address some far less flashy concerns of its own.

TROUBLE AT HOME

Population numbers and property values are booming in Las Vegas. So, simultaneously, are the city's problems with substandard education, pollution, homelessness, addiction and even suicide: although high visitor numbers may skew the statistics a little, all are issues in which this tourist-distracted city ranks among the worst in the nation. Nevada was 45th in the US in per-pupil education expenditure in 2005; five years earlier, the state clocked the highest teen pregnancy rates in the nation, though a prevention-through-education campaign has since helped a little. Social ills abound, and what the future holds for cavalier Las Vegas is anyones guess. For now, it remains far more interested in continued growth through visitor revenue than in reaching out to its own.

New residents arriving from all over the world eventually become deeply familiar with a key truth that isn't so visible from hotel balconies: Sin City is less about sin than it is about moral disinterest. The 'Good luck!' you'll hear when buying chips at the cashier's cage is offered indiscriminately but not really insincerely. What's more, it might as well be applied just as aptly to life after the craps table. Vegas is home to thousands who came, lost, lost again and stayed in town to win, but are still waiting

Life on the street

During his speech at the grand opening of the upgraded Fremont Street Experience in 2004, Oscar Goodman was all smiles. But as the mayor rhapsodised about how everyone is welcome at the Downtown pedestrian mall, he interrupted himself, and a pained look crossed his face. 'Except,' he muttered, 'for the bums.'

No tirade followed; Goodman went right back to his message of hospitality to all. But it was both a telling and a prescient moment. In July 2006, the city passed legislation making it a misdemeanour to give food to any of the estimated 15,000 homeless in a city park, after a local activist began distributing

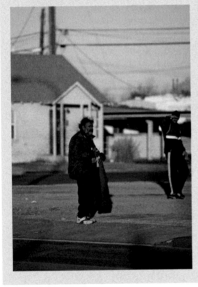

spaghetti, soup and sandwiches six times a week. After a challenge from the American Civil Liberties Union, a federal court struck down the ordinance as unconstitutional.

One month later, it was made illegal to sleep within 500 feet (152 metres) of human urine or faeces. Three homeless men were arrested and jailed for the offence in November the same year, two months after the law had been repealed. One city attorney explained that it had been passed by mistake; the men were ultimately awarded $45,000 in a wrongful arrest lawsuit settlement.

City Hall's legislative success at eliminating the homeless from Las Vegas has thus far been limited, but the message is clear: 'No home? No mercy.' All local governments tend to be skittish about the effect of the visible unwashed on tourism revenue, but Las Vegas appears positively petrified. On top of his legal initiatives and his characterisation of homeless advocates as 'enablers, crying like bleating sheep', Goodman even issued a proposal that all homeless should be shipped to an abandoned prison 30 miles away.

The mayor has mentioned that city shelters do exist, and that they often have empty beds. Critics say this doesn't take into account the apprehension many substance-addicted and mentally ill homeless have toward shelters, and lament a lack of city funding for addressing the problem more humanely. In a town where only 36 per cent of voters supported a tax increase of one per cent per $100 of property (a tax increase for the average homeowner of $3,000 a year), such funding may be hard to find. Meanwhile, Goodman won a third term in 2007 with 84 per cent of the vote, suggesting that most Las Vegans aren't too troubled by the city's hard line when it comes to dealing with those having the least fun.

in a land where all those ready diversions are more compelling than ever, yet by no means fun. To those who visit with plenty of cash and a sense of when to give the debauchery a rest, good luck. To all others… well, good luck.

WHERE ALL THE LIGHTS ARE BRIGHT
With the arrival of high-budget stage shows, world-class dining options and even an outpost of the Guggenheim, 21st-century Las Vegas is very different to the showgirls-and-steaks scene of days past. The streets just off the Strip are also morphing constantly and dramatically,

with condo construction galore all over the city (*see pp28-34*). But it's Downtown where the real changes are being set in motion, or so waggish mayor Oscar Goodman would have you believe. Goodman has made the revitalisation of Downtown one of his top priorities; after several false dawns, the collaborative efforts of local business owners and Goodman's Office of Business Development are at long last starting to reap rewards.

For years, Downtown was something of a shambles, a cluster of seen-better-days casinos frequented by seen-better-days gamblers that was overshadowed in every way by the mega-resorts on the Strip. After a rocky few years following its 1995 opening, the light-show canopy above casino-lined Fremont Street now regularly attracts tourists to Downtown. But it's also, at this point in time, fairly old news.

To the south, in a square roughly bounded by Charleston Avenue, Las Vegas Boulevard, Wyoming Avenue and the railroad tracks, an arts district is gradually emerging, brought to life once a month by the increasingly popular First Friday block party. Controversial proposals for the area from a Michigan-based developer that call for a 73-acre hotel, casino and condo redevelopment remain on the drawing board, at least for now. North-east of here (just south-west of the Fremont Street Experience), construction on the Union Park development is under way; among its additions will be the Lou Ruvo Brain Institute, the city's first Frank Gehry-designed building.

There are further changes just across Las Vegas Boulevard from the Fremont Street Experience, where the rather stolidly named Fremont East Entertainment District is coalescing around the retro-chic Beauty Bar. Since opening in 2004, it's been joined by similar nightspots such as the upscale Downtown Cocktail Room. Comedy clubs, music venues and art galleries are also in the plans for what the city hopes will be a Strip-alternative haven for locals and tourists alike. And all over the area, condo towers are shooting from imagination to drawing board to vacant lots.

As Fremont East takes shape, out-of-towners may well find what a growing number of locals want them to find: a relatively authentic urban entertainment nook where their presence is welcome but not desperately needed. Las Vegas is a service economy town full of bartenders, cocktail servers, dancers, pit bosses and other workers whose job it is to keep visitors from so-called real cities happy. The trouble is that it doesn't offer much in the way of real-city decompression areas where that workforce can retreat at quitting time. Most simply punch out and head back to a suburban sea of stuccoed, monochrome housing that, while fast and functional, doesn't do much for a strange young town's social development. The new Downtown aims for a way to feel 'real' in a city where, on the whole, the word itself tends to lose meaning.

In any case, Las Vegas is feeling some real growing pains as it booms – the kind felt by any city faced with challenges of planning, corruption control, and the building of an infrastructure that can support what's coming as it comes. The question seems to be whether Las Vegans can overcome a peculiar and ironic handicap in the process. How does a town like this learn to take care of itself while putting the tourists first at all costs? Building and revitalisation efforts in any city are typically high-risk, especially without the insurance of another thousand video poker screens to fund it. But until the gambling capital of the US can bring itself to make that bet, the world-class reputation it craves might remain a mirage.

New York New York. *See p31.*

Architecture

Vegas is growing up. And up and up…

The Las Vegas Strip has always been a movie set of sorts. With each new era, relics of the greatest hits in oasis-style hospitality make way for a fresh backdrop and new stars. Just as the mid-century modernist Dunes was imploded for the sake of the opulent **Bellagio**, so the Treasure Island that helped launch the theme-happy family era in Vegas was repackaged into the younger, sexier **TI**. The trend in Las Vegas has always been for disposable or mutable architecture; this is a city more likely to tear down its laurels than rest on them. Along the Strip, it's survival not so much of the fittest but of the tallest, the biggest and the boldest.

The next era in Vegas architecture seems set to throw things off cycle. While some of the town's history will inevitably vanish, what's going up – high up – are attractions that are more dense, more metropolitan and even a little more green. For a change, they're also being built to last.

The most significant new exponent of the new era in Vegas construction, and the most expensive privately funded development in the US, is MGM Mirage's $7-billion **CityCenter** complex of buildings, currently sprouting up on the 76 acres between Bellagio and the Monte Carlo. When it's complete, theoretically by 1 November 2009, the complex will hold a modern, five-building community of 2,400 condos, punctuated by Pelli Clarke Pelli's 60-storey, 4,000-room hotel-casino. The highlights, at least on the plans, are Helmut Jahn's two 37-storey Veer Towers, which will lean a striking five degrees in opposite directions. A theme is conspicuous by its absence; instead, CityCenter will be a model of large-scale contemporary urban architecture, with a number of sleek towers and eco-friendly credentials.

More evidence of this mini-metropolitan movement can be found at the northern end of the Strip, where **Echelon Place** is going up on the old Stardust casino lot. Boyd Gaming's plan calls for four hotels; among them will be the Asian-glam Shangri-La and the Hollywood-chic Mondrian, both boutique-style resorts and neither themed. President Robert Boughner neatly summed up the project and the new Vegas attitude. 'Echelon, in terms of architecture, is more about designing a building that will evoke an emotion. A theme doesn't evoke an emotion; it evokes a cheap thrill.'

Meanwhile, the City of Las Vegas (with help from Newland Communities) is working on its own urban core on a long-barren Downtown railroad lot formerly known as the 61 Acres but now renamed **Union Park**. Marquee projects here include the Frank Gehry-designed **Lou Ruvo Brain Institute** and David Schwarz's **Smith Center for the Performing Arts**; they'll eventually be joined by a new city hall, a couple of boutique hotels and the 57-storey World Jewelry Center. On adjacent land, the vast **World Market Center** (*see p211* **Take a seat**) continues to take shape, with two buildings open and five more on the way.

The cityscape isn't only developing aesthetically: Las Vegas has also finally got out of the starting blocks in the green movement. Around 20 projects in the area have registered for the US Green Building Council's LEED certification, among them a sustainable TV campus (Vegas PBS) and a neighbourhood of luxury holiday homes (Enchantment Way). Even CityCenter is getting in on the act, striving to be the largest project to be LEED-certified. But the granddaddy of all green projects is the **Las Vegas Springs Preserve** (*see p146*), a central park with seven structures with LEED Platinum potential that are both built to be sustainable and designed to teach sustainability to visitors.

With such high-profile urban and urbane projects in the pipeline, Vegas is adopting a more refined appearance. But those who hanker after the decadent ol' days will still find plenty to dazzle. The 64-storey gold-and-white **Trump International Hotel & Tower** is due to open in 2008 across the Boulevard from Steve Wynn's bronze-and-tan **Wynn Las Vegas**, standing taller, gaudier and somehow even shinier than its neighbour. Wynn has his encore planned: a second, 2,000-room tower due for Christmas 2008. Meanwhile, his neighbour Sheldon Adelson is playing the Palazzo card with a 3,000-room tower resort that will complement his Venetian casino-resort by early 2008.

In 2009, former Mandalay Resorts boss Glenn Schaeffer may just trump them all on the north Strip. Schaeffer is overseeing what could be one of the most architecturally significant hotel-casinos in modern Vegas: the **Fontainebleau**, which draws heavily on the style of Morris Lapidus (who designed the original in Miami Beach in the 1950s). It'll be interesting to see the level of its influence over the town.

THE EARLY DAYS

Although Las Vegas has been a popular resort town for more than half a century, the way in which its hotels are designed has altered hugely

down the years, as much thanks to social change as by any direct design imperative. The old Vegas was a Mafia-controlled demimonde, a place in which men gambled wearing jackets and ties while being watched by women clad in diamonds and ballgowns. Back then, gambling was illegal in much of the US. But now that it's permitted in 48 of the 50 states, and now that the industry is controlled not by the Mob but by big business, the town has reinvented itself.

From World War II onwards, when the town's expansion began to take hold, Las Vegas developed its own distinctive style, a dazzlingly vulgar cocktail of expressionist modern architecture and monumental neon signs that illuminated stretches of desert on Las Vegas Boulevard. A key figure in this development was Wayne McAllister, a pioneering southern Californian architect whose influence over modern Vegas is perhaps greater than that of any other designer. It was McAllister who built the cowboy-flavoured **El Rancho**, the first ever themed resort on what's known as the Strip, back in 1941. A decade later, he constructed the original **Sands**, the Rat Pack's casino of choice, and also had a hand in the **Desert Inn**.

'For casino moguls, Europe equals sophistication.'

The town's smaller hotels were, if anything, even more exotic, and in some cases positively space-age. Many were products of the automotive age, built to dazzle and attract passing drivers. At the original Mirage, built in 1952, swimmers could be seen through portholes on the street-front side of the pool; indeed, the motel became better known as the **Glass Pool Inn**, as it was rechristened more than three decades after it opened. In 1961, Paul Revere Williams' **La Concha Motel** drew attention for its zinging concrete lobby, the design of which aped the form of a shell.

Modern Vegas has upped the scale and sophistication of its resorts, adding shops and amusements to create vast complexes replicating the kind of walk-through fantasies popularised by Disney. The kaleidoscope of neon that was once the city's trademark has been dwarfed by themed resorts approximating all kinds of cities, countries and (the key word here) experiences. As a result, little remains from the 1950s and '60s. As the town unsentimentally continues to cut ties with its past, most of the properties mentioned in the preceding pair of paragraphs have been destroyed in the name of progress. The sole survivor is the old La Concha lobby,

High lights

At the zenith of Las Vegas's upward thrust a few years back, it was said that nearly 140 high-rise projects were submitted to local planning departments. Today, only about two dozen of those are getting off the ground. The city's once-keen speculators sold their suddenly more valuable land, mismanaged their deals or simply gave up after construction costs went through the roof. Such are the growing pains of a maturing metropolis.

In many cases, it was probably for the best. Many of the proposed structures looked ugly in their original renderings (one even resembled a giant electric shaver), and by no means all of the entrepreneurs were taken seriously. However, some plans had serious consequences. Developers demolished the Algiers, one of the Strip's old treasures, to make room for the proposed Krystle Sands resort. Its cancellation led its home-buyers to file a lawsuit against developers; the site has since been purchased by the owners of Turnberry Place.

The historically low-rise Vegas Valley won't, then, grow as high as expectations once promised. However, its buildings are showing a clear skyward trend, thanks in part to the cost of land (which, on the Strip, is reputedly going for up to $30 million an acre) but also due to a new desire that the town should look and feel more urban. Progress has been steady: the 14 towers that were under construction in mid 2007, most of them along the Strip or Downtown, will yield more than 6,600 units.

The trend for building up can be traced back to the construction in 1996 of the 1,100-foot (335-metre) **Stratosphere**, the largest freestanding structure west of the Mississippi. But on the Strip, resorts have slowly been pushing upwards for years; even **New York New York**'s scaled-down cityscape boosted Vegas's skyline in the 1990s. When some casino operators started heading for the skies, older resorts had to follow suit (the cartoonish **Caesars Palace** addition, for instance) or perish (the late and not especially lamented **Boardwalk**). The most recent growth spurt among resorts was headed by the 50-storey **Wynn**, which opened in 2005, and the whopping 64-storey **Trump Tower** across the street.

The next generation is taking urban residential concepts to a new level, with MGM Mirage's multi-tower **CityCenter** project (on the old Boardwalk site) and Boyd Gaming's five-tower **Echelon Place** (replacing the Stardust) due to arrive in the next few years. This Manhattanisation of the city actually first surfaced off the Strip, with the construction of high-end condo community **Turnberry Place** in 2001. In the course of just five years, four 40-storey residential towers sprang up east along Paradise Road, with the new Turnberry

salvaged in 2007 and scheduled to be rebuilt Downtown by the Neon Museum (*see p141* **Lighting up the past**).

ENTERTAINMENT ARCHITECTURE

The earliest gambling joints on what became the Strip had a western flavour. The **El Rancho**, which opened in 1941, and the **Last Frontier**, which followed a year later, took as their themes nostalgia for the Old West. A few years down the line, Benjamin 'Bugsy' Siegel helped create the **Flamingo** (*see p78*) in 1946, an LA Moderne-style tropical paradise. With variations, this style reigned during the adults-only, post-war years. But when Jay Sarno built his instantly sensational, pseudo-Roman **Caesars Palace** (*see p68*) in 1966, and followed it two years later with the camp **Circus Circus** (*see p89*), the die was cast.

After a relatively quiet few years, the stakes in the theming game escalated with the work of Steve Wynn, without whom Vegas would look very different. In 1989, Wynn opened the South Seas-themed **Mirage** (*see p73*), which melded the upmarket stylings of Siegel's Flamingo with the fantasy of Caesars and the mass appeal of Circus Circus and became the Strip's first mega-resort. Then, four years later, the entrepreneur delivered the Caribbean-inspired **Treasure Island** (*see p87*) just next door. The same period saw the construction of the riotous, candy-coloured **Excalibur** (1990; *see p90*), the agreeably preposterous **Luxor** (1993; *see p80*) and the ugly but enormous **MGM Grand** (1993; *see p81*). However, it was Wynn's duo that really reversed the downward spiral of Las Vegas during the early 1980s.

Casino bosses have since gone in for even more extravagant design. Where once the properties were signed by fizzing neon, the theming is now so wild that the casinos introduce themselves. The Egyptian-themed

Towers due to add another two 45-storey towers across the street (one in 2007, the second in 2008). And on the west side of the Strip (Harmon Avenue & I-15), the twin aqua-blue **Panorama Towers** soar 30 storeys tall, with a third building on the way.

The city's most dramatic skyscraping, however, will come with the mammoth

Union Park project, a new 61-acre urban core that's being built on an old railway yard in Downtown. The highest structure in the development looks likely to be the 57-storey **World Jewelry Center**, slated for completion in 2010. Reaching to a height of 815 feet (248 metres), it'll be the new tallest building. But for how long?

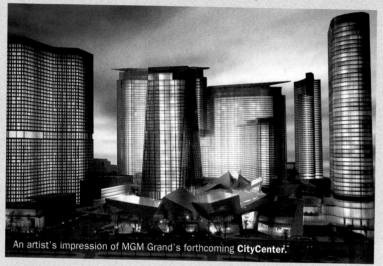

An artist's impression of MGM Grand's forthcoming **CityCenter.**

Luxor is, from street level, a vast black glass pyramid guarded by a squatting sphinx; the hotel, casino and sign are integrated into one structure, so the building itself is the sign. **New York New York** (*photo p28*; *see p84*) represented theming at its most fully realised when it opened four years later with a mini-Grand Central Station, a half-size Statue of Liberty and 12 jaunty, 1:3-scale skyscrapers mimicking the Manhattan skyline. And in 1999, **Paris Las Vegas** (*see p74*) dropped a half-size replica of the Eiffel Tower on to the Strip. It looks tongue-in-cheek and it is, but the attempts at authenticity are touching; although the tower is welded together, cosmetic rivets have been positioned in the appropriate places.

Paris Las Vegas is one of several recent resorts that have taken their cues from across the Atlantic. For casino moguls – and, arguably, for middle Americans who make up the greater part of Vegas's custom – Europe equals

sophistication. With that in mind, it's no surprise that two of the Strip's most luxurious and expensive resorts have carefully realised European themes.

The first to open was the $1.4-billion **Bellagio** (*see p68*), an Italianate theme park for high-rolling grown-ups built by Wynn in 1998. The property is fronted by an eight-acre imitation of Lake Como; inside, marble is conspicuous in both the lobbies and the rooms. The basic trefoil tower structure is hardly innovative, but there are imaginative moments within, among them the glass anemones by sculptor Dale Chihuly on the lobby ceiling, the extravagant conservatory and the lake's dancing fountains. The Sands, meanwhile, was replaced in 1999 by the **Venetian** (*see p75*), which links the Rialto bridge to the Doge's Palace and piazza San Marco. Within it lies the Guggenheim Hermitage Museum, completed in 2001 to designs by Dutch architect Rem Koolhaas.

Other developments in Vegas's casinos have come with the expansion of its shopping scene from negligible to extensive. One of Las Vegas's most stunning themed environments, the **Forum Shops** at Caesars Palace (1993; *see p191*), set a trend that's since been emulated at Paris Las Vegas, the Venetian and Planet Hollywood. This cod-Roman shopping street, complete with trompe l'oeil sky and lighting that simulates the transition from dawn to dusk, showed casino moguls that malls could be money-spinners, and also introduced convincing aged walls and styrofoam sculptures to a city that had previously been quite happy with cheerfully silly evocation. The mall's expansion in 2004 brought another only-in-Vegas innovation: spiral escalators.

AFTER DARK

Aiming for younger, more upscale and more urbane customers, the gaming kings of Las Vegas have hired some of the world's top architects and designers to create swanky new restaurants, nightclubs and lounges inside their casinos. It's here that you'll find some of the city's more exciting design touches. Not all are original, granted; some restaurants have been described as 'New York-style', while a few nightclubs are keen to play up their European origins or their retro fittings. But there's vibrancy here, not to mention excess.

The **Palms** resort (*see p98*), which opened in 2001, has been at the forefront of the movement towards a cooler kind of ostentation. Three of its venues deliver it in spades: **Rain** (*see p258*), a nightclub and concert venue with a lounge, an elevated dancefloor and (the Vegas touch) light fixtures that shoot fire; **Ghostbar** (*see p183*), where the similarly retro edge would make Austin Powers feel at home; and the **N9ne** steakhouse (*see p169*), where coloured lights wash the ceiling. Other casinos have been getting in on the act, most recently the Beatles-themed, Cirque du Soleil-created **Revolution** lounge at the Mirage (*see p180*).

Not every ode to modernity sits on the Strip. At 3rd and Ogden Streets in Downtown, the owners of the currently-shuttered Lady Luck casino have opened a handsome locals' favourite called **Triple George** (*see p171*), complete with adjoining, brick-walled piano bar. Next door is George's little brother **Sidebar** (*see p184*), a quaint, stylish hangout that wouldn't look out of place in San Francisco. Plans for the new **Fremont East Entertainment District**, due for completion in summer 2007, will bring wider, more pedestrian-friendly sidewalks and retro signage to the area, with smartly designed venues such as the **Downtown Cocktail Room** and the **Griffin** (for both, *see p184*)

teasing a hip, metropolitan vibe out of some gritty old structures. And all without a single slot machine in sight.

NON-RESORT ARCHITECTURE

Attention was first drawn to the city's public architecture in the late 1980s with Charles Hunsberger's ambitious and controversial library-building programme. Using a range of architects with a view to making each of the nine libraries adventurous and unique, the programme was an attempt to create, without precedent, a Las Vegas 'high' architecture style. Characterised by earthen forms, variegated concrete and sandy stone, pyramids, cones and dry desert landscaping, the libraries can be seen as an effort to reflect and adapt to the harsh environment of the Mojave desert; the **Sahara West Library & Las Vegas Arts Museum**, the **West Charleston Library** and the **Summerlin Library & Performing Arts Center** (for all, *see p312*) are perhaps best examples. This trend reached its extreme with the **Clark County Government Center** (*see p33* **What's that?**).

> ### 'There's little evidence of planning, just an ugly checkerboard of "leapfrog" development.'

Other lively buildings also welcome visitors, and perhaps even inspire them. The tech-savvy **Lied Library** at UNLV, for example, is a concrete, steel and glass structure with towering cast windows and a massive, inviting lobby. And the first structure visitors are likely to notice is the sleek Terminal D at **McCarran International Airport**. Having announced its authority with steel and glass, the terminal incorporates both past (Googie-style graphics, vintage passenger planes) and future (exposed steel trusses, hangar-high ceilings, large glass windows). While you're here, look out for the airport's award-winning new control tower, a robot-like structure crowned with what (intentionally) looks like a policeman's cap.

One of the most visible additions is Downtown's **Lloyd D George Federal Courthouse** (333 Las Vegas Boulevard South). Designed by Dwarsky & Associates of LA, with a keen emphasis on security in the wake of the 1995 Oklahoma City bombing, the plaza is raised above street level, and the building itself has a blast-resistant wall of windows facing Las Vegas Boulevard. Nearby is the **Regional Justice Center**, an award-winning complex designed by Tate Snyder Kimsey that consolidated the operations of the municipal,

What's that?

Most of the landmarks in Las Vegas are pretty easy to identify. That massive, concrete phallus? The Stratosphere. The white castle with the candy-coloured turrets? The Excalibur. The big bronze hotel with Wynn scripted on the side? You get the idea. However, some of the eye-catching structures on the city's horizon aren't so easily identifiable, not least because they take no part in the gambling industry.

North of the Strip and just east of I-15 is the **Clark County Government Center & Regional Transportation Commission Building** (600 S Grand Central Parkway). The facility looks more like a new-age campus than a municipal space, with plenty of outdoor seating and a round amphitheatre at the centre. The exteriors have Indian symbols embedded in them, and one structure is a pyramid. It's impressive in a way that makes locals wonder how many of their tax dollars were spent on it. But more to the point, where the heck do you pay your parking fines?

Huddled amid the Strip casinos, the Fashion Show Mall (*see p193*) is a high-end shopping centre with a Neiman Marcus and a Saks Fifth Avenue. What visitors notice first, though, is the bewildering silver UFO suspended 128 feet (39 metres) above the sidewalk. Spreading to an impressive diameter of 480 feet (146 metres), it's called the **Cloud**. People expect it to take off into outer space or dazzle them; it does neither, but it does create shade for pedestrians, giving them less incentive to head into the mall's air-conditioned bubble. And its columns contain screens and speakers that broadcast videos and images from inside the mall. After all, entertainment is so very hard to find here...

Located close to Downtown on the east side of the I-15, the massive **World Market Center** (*see p211* **Take a seat**) is comprised of two huge buildings with nondescript names. Building A is a rectangle with a hemispherical cut-out, while Building B looks like someone squashed together two grey municipal buildings. They're stylish structures, but the dearth of windows betrays their purpose. Roughly 1,500 furniture and home design companies show their wares over an area of 2.6 million square feet (240,000 square metres), the equivalent of more than 15 MGM Grand casinos. Proof, were it needed, that Las Vegas's capacity for overkill goes beyond its hotels.

Clark County Government Center.

The Cloud at Fashion Show Mall.

World Market Center.

justice and state supreme courts into 'one user-friendly courthouse'. One of these more friendly uses is the Marriage License Bureau, which has its own entrance as well as a small courtyard and canopy of trees for happy snappers.

Yet despite growing aspirations, these public buildings represent a few bright points in an architectural desert. Non-resort Las Vegas is still defined by endless one- and two-storey stucco-and-Spanish-tile tract houses and monotonous shopping centres, convenience stores and fast-food restaurants. There's little evidence of planning, just an ugly checkerboard of 'leapfrog' development spreading in all directions.

Downtown is re-emerging as a residential locale, especially within the delightful, historic 160-home **John S Park neighbourhood** east of Las Vegas Boulevard South and north of Charleston Boulevard. However, on the whole, living close to the centre is still seen as undesirable in a city where roads have not yet become permanently gridlocked. Affluent and middle-class families prefer residential enclaves built around golf courses and artificial lakes on the edge of the valley; on the Strip, high-rise condo structures such as **Turnberry Place** at the north end and **Park Towers** at the south appeal largely to jetsetters here for six weeks a year. One of the latest such statements comes in the shape of the two sleek **Panorama Towers**, perched near the Strip alongside Interstate 15.

Supplementing its gated neighbourhoods, Las Vegas has gone one step further – as usual – with 'master-planned' communities, town-sized swathes of privately owned land on which management companies create entire societies (housing in several price brackets, business and commercial districts, retirement complexes, schools, parks, even hospitals). Residents sign up to the community's rules and, in theory, settle back to enjoy their suburban utopia.

The most carefully planned of such communities was **Summerlin** (*see p145*). With its abundance of parks, sports fields, tennis courts and trails, not to mention its proximity to Red Rock Canyon, it's favoured by outdoorsy urbanites and disdained by those who thrive on an independent lifestyle. (You want to paint your house green? Forget it.) People have continued to buy into what has become the new American Dream; similar planned communities include **Seven Hills** and **Anthem**, both in Henderson, and **Aliante** in north Las Vegas. However, the latest breed, among them **Inspirada** near Anthem and **Kyle Canyon** in the north-west, have at least attempted to incorporate 'new urbanism' to counteract ills such as the lack of pedestrian destinations.

Of all the structures here, there's one you absolutely can't miss. The quirk? It's not a building, not in Las Vegas and not designed by an architect. Conceived by engineer John Savage and built as part of Roosevelt's public works programme, the monumental **Hoover Dam** (*see p18*) on the Colorado River is a marvel of human ingenuity. Utterly utilitarian, with art deco touches, it has the grandeur and permanence missing from most buildings in Vegas. What's more, completed in 1935, it's older than almost anywhere else in the city.

John S Park neighbourhood.

Meyer Lansky (third from right) and pals. *See p36.*

The Juice

In Vegas, it's a fine line between influence and corruption.

Early in the campaign for the national mid-term elections in 2006, Senate minority leader Harry Reid found himself under the spotlight in DC. One morning, the Democratic senator for Nevada awoke to find himself the subject of an accusatory story in the *Washington Post*; 'Reid Accepted Free Boxing Tickets While a Related Bill was Pending,' read the report. Yet Reid's constituents at home, especially those in southern Nevada where he was born and raised, merely shrugged. Out here, one person's bribe is merely another's 'comp', and all the nuance in between is part of the vocabulary of corruption endemic throughout the development of Las Vegas as a modern city.

So when Reid accepted ringside seats from the state agency that regulates the sport, despite the fact the agency had a bill pending before the Senate at the time, locals were quick to dismiss any allegations of impropriety. This was clearly just a courtesy comp to someone with power; or, in Vegas parlance, 'juice'. (As it later turned out, Reid voted squarely against the agency that gave him the tickets.) Comps? Juice? Allowable bribes? Is this proof of a lower

standard of morality in Las Vegas government? Throughout history, the answer has been as jumpy as a roulette ball during a particularly lively spin around the wheel.

BUILDING ON QUICKSAND

Even the creation of the state of Nevada in 1864 was a bit of a spirited horse trade. Aware that this great land mass was rich in minerals and speculative investment potential, powerful people lobbied to shape the state from the territory in which it rested. Capitalising on Abraham Lincoln's desire to add another non-slave state to the union, Nevada's forefathers aligned themselves with the president. In so doing, they cannily gave themselves a head start in the race to wield power over what did soon become the union's newest entry.

By the beginning of the 20th century, the doors were open for all sorts of outsiders to reinvent themselves in Nevada and help shape the future of Las Vegas. None was more successful than Montana native William Clark, considered by many to be the founding father of Vegas; not for nothing does the county in which the city sits now bear his name. Clark was no stranger to allegations of corruption, having been caught red-handed trying to buy a seat on the Montana legislature in 1899. But such behaviour didn't stop voters from electing him to the Senate in Montana two years later. And nor, in 1905, did it prevent Clark from manoeuvring himself and his family into control over the San Pedro, Los Angeles & Salt Lake Railroad, which was set to run through Las Vegas, and then over the city's water supply and its plum plots of land. Clark's power enabled him to extract or extort huge fees from anyone who wanted to venture into the uncharted future of Las Vegas.

Four decades later, another corrupt force controlled the ways and means of Las Vegas in the form of the shadow government known as the Mob. This period, which ran for longer than the city dared admit, has long been romanticised by popular culture. However, it's also remembered fondly by old-timers who curiously long for 'the days when the Mob ran things', conveniently forgetting the killings and the thefts associated with what was, in reality, one of the darkest chapters in the town's past.

'Ample scandals, continued profit-skimming and ceaseless brutality fuelled a spectre of corruption.'

At the time, the growth of Las Vegas was directly linked to the interests of 'businessmen' with nefarious pasts in faraway towns. Benjamin 'Bugsy' Siegel didn't come up with the idea for the Flamingo hotel, stealing both the concept and the property from a fellow named Billy Wilkerson, but he saw it through in such a way as to lay the foundations for what Las Vegas later became. And when the amateurish mobster met the wrong end of a .30-caliber bullet in 1947 (a hit that was reputedly ordered by fellow mobster and former ally Meyer Lansky (*photo p35*), who later went on to run the Desert Inn), Siegel also inadvertently set in place the rules for how such power and influence was won and lost.

It's a moot point whether the mafia actually ran the town. However, it's certain that there was at least a tortured co-existence between the bad guys and the government, necessary to ensure that the Bugsy-styled resorts would keep on rolling, keep on drawing and, most crucially, keep on earning. To those ends, eventually became respectable in Las Vegas high society and in local philanthropic circles. At the same time, the ample scandals, continued

profit-skimming and ceaseless brutality fuelled a spectre of corruption that lasted until the last identifiable organised crime boss was ostensibly driven from power over any local entity.

Originally known in Las Vegas as the man behind the Desert Inn, Morris 'Moe' Dalitz was long tagged as a gangster and racketeer. Tied in many accounts to the Cleveland Mob, Dalitz was also rumoured to be tight with the likes of corrupt union leader Jimmy Hoffa and Nevada senator Pat McCarran, whom he persuaded to fight an oppressive federal tax on sports betting (McCarran won the battle). Several hotels, not to mention one of the first major hospitals in Las Vegas, were built with Teamster pension money secured through Dalitz's connections. But if there was corruption afoot, no one seems to have cared in the wake of Las Vegas's emergence as a major city. And after selling the Desert Inn to Howard Hughes in the 1960s, Dalitz successfully reinvented himself as a beloved benefactor to many local charities and religious organisations.

ALL 'GOOD' THINGS COME TO AN END

Ralph Lamb, the town's tough-as-nails sheriff from 1962 until 1980, had a reputation for literally slapping around the good fellas if they stepped out of line, and effectively put a speed bump in front of the gangsters. But the kind of violence depicted in popular books of the time such as *The Green Felt Jungle*, and in later movies like Martin Scorsese's *Casino*, escalated to eye-catching levels, and federal intervention soon loomed on the horizon.

By the 1970s, a culture of what is known in other cities as corruption had established a chokehold on Las Vegas. Even good ol' Sheriff Lamb was the subject of an investigation after allegations of financial wrongdoings. Absolved of all charges but bruised to such a degree that he lost his bid for re-election, Lamb was far from the last public official accused of exchanging favours for cold hard cash. But as Roger Foley, the US District Court judge who acquitted Lamb, put it , 'Many fringe benefits come to a public official which may be accepted along with the honest discharge of duty.' Foley was merely explaining a philosophy on which many in power here have long relied, but this greyest of lines has nonetheless landed many a modern-day government official in hot water.

Since the 1980s, innumerable allegations of public corruption have been thrown around in the city, mostly involving the development of land or other business opportunities that have arisen in this modern-day boomtown. In 1991, for example, Las Vegas mayor Ron Lurie didn't stand for re-election amid accusations

Dirty work

Once upon a time, the Crazy Horse Too strip club in Las Vegas was famous less for its notorious alumni, among them future porn diva Jenna Jameson, than for its Teflon-like resistance to law enforcement. For more than a decade, cops struggled to lay a finger (easy now) on the joint, despite long-standing rumours that it was tied to organised crime. The club was dogged by allegations of disreputable business practices; one customer received a $10 million settlement in a plea deal after he was left paralysed from the chest down, reputedly following an argument about the accuracy of his bar tab.

Still, the Crazy Horse Too continued to strut its stuff until a fateful day in 2003, when strapping FBI agents, clad in blue windbreakers and armed with semi-automatic weapons, stormed the joint during business hours. The sight of high-heeled dancers clutching their sweaty dollars to cover their naked breasts is indelibly etched in the minds of anyone who caught the seemingly endless replays on the evening news in the weeks following the raid.

Upon raiding the Crazy Horse Too, local government officials were shocked to learn that lap dancing, liquor sales and the exchange of untaxed money took place within these allegedly regulated businesses. In the end, a complicated plea bargain plucked the property from owner Rick Rizzolo (pictured), who was convicted on the relatively trifling charge of tax evasion. With the plea bargain, all parties avoided a trial at which the issue of the influence of organised crime over Las Vegas strip clubs, or at least over this one Las Vegas strip club, might once and for all have been settled.

Rizzolo lay low in 2007, having apparently sold the club to local businessman Mike Signorelli. However, his name was never far from the headlines, and a cloud continued to hang over the operation. When Signorelli and his lawyer Jay Brown applied for the reinstatement of the liquor licence that had been removed from the club in the wake of Rizzolo's conviction, the local police strongly objected. 'A reasonable person,' sighed a police-issued statement that was reported by the Las Vegas Review-Journal, 'could draw the conclusion that Signorelli is simply running the business for Rizzolo, who is forbidden to do so.' The council unanimously approved the alcohol licence regardless.

However, while the Crazy Horse Too continues to trade, the fallout from the raid resulted in a number of efforts to control more tightly the licences of existing clubs. Many local club owners now have to jump through hoop after hoop just to keep their businesses open. It's yet to be seen if the legal campaign contributions made by strip club owners will stop quicker than a dancer in a VIP room upon learning the credit card has been maxed out.

(which he denied) that he had profited from insider information regarding land development when he was a city councilman. Similar controversies have been caused by what's been termed the 'revolving door principle', with private sector jobs provided by businesses to the politicians who once regulated them.

ASK AND THOU SHALT RECEIVE

Former county commissioner Yvonne Atkinson Gates resigned in 2007 to spend more time with her family and her business, at roughly the same time that police were investigating whether she misused campaign funds to the benefit of her family. The allegations, which she refuted, were just the latest in a long line of complaints about her ethical behaviour during her long tenure as one of the gatekeepers of areas that included the Strip. Gates's most notorious escapade involved her plan to open her own businesses in casinos that, at the time, she was responsible for regulating. At the 1997 hearings at which she was reprimanded by the state's Ethics Commission, it was learned that the embattled Gates had placed her reputation on the line for a string of frozen daiquiri concessions. Of *course*.

Where she'll land no one knows, but perhaps she'll take a leaf from the book of retired Las Vegas mayor Jan Jones. During her two terms in office, Jones was sometimes accused by her detractors of being too friendly to the casino industry. After stepping down from the rigours of government in June 1999, Jones stepped up four months later into a vice-president position with Harrah's, one of the major players in Nevada gaming. Still, at least Jones waited a while before mailing her résumé to the private sector: county commissioner Lynette Boggs McDonald briefly served in a paid capacity on the board of directors of a local casino chain while she was serving the public on the Las Vegas City Council. Boggs McDonald, incidentally, lost her bid for re-election in 2006 amid allegations, which she denied, that she received favourable treatment from a developer whose interests she had previously supported on the council.

Of course, there are gifts, and there are *gifts*. In 2005, ten lawmakers (affiliated to both parties) accepted comped tickets to a sold-out Rolling Stones concert from former attorney general and latterday lobbyist Frankie Sue del Papa. The freebies were granted on behalf of Del Papa's client Ameriquest, a national mortgage-lending firm that at the time was dogged by allegations of financial irregularities. When the propriety of such largesse was questioned, the concertgoers borrowed a page from boxing fan Harry Reid and maintained that in Las Vegas, there's a difference between freebies and bribes.

The distinction baffles the outside world, but it's nonetheless one that the local populace are happy to make. Comps in Las Vegas are dispensed for many reasons and purposes: as a sign of respect, as a gesture of friendship, as a motivational tool to ensure a full house or as a way to unload something that might otherwise go unused. 'Influencing the recipient' hardly makes the list, although comps are also often distributed with the hope that good karma payback will someday land the giver a similar comp. That said, it's telling that none of the Rolling Stoners were ousted from office in the next election; indeed, some were elevated to higher office. Apparently, sometimes you can always get what you want.

NAKED CITY

Not everyone was as lucky. Take the four former Clark County commissioners who were recently stung in what may be the granddaddy of all corruption probes, salaciously dubbed 'Operation G-Sting' by the local media because of its strip club connections. Although one of the commissioners had retired by the time the investigation moved into full swing, two were seeking higher office at the time; only after they lost their respective races were indictments pinned on them.

With favours, cash and even sex proffered in exchange for votes, Operation G-Sting is a textbook tale of political corruption. In this case, bribes bought an easing of regulations hampering 'free speech' (lap dances) in clubs, and a limiting of competition for one well-heeled strip club owner. The bottom fell out for the accused only after years of surveillance, with the realisation that key witnesses would be prepared to testify for the prosecution in exchange for favourable treatment at trial. Using portions of the federal Patriot Act, the FBI came down with a vengeance on the former officials, resulting in the kind of corruption trial hitherto unseen in the city's history. After months of testimony and cross-examination, the Department of Justice was able to secure convictions on its targets, resulting in substantial prison time and extensive fines.

Whether the success of Operation G-Sting signals the end of the road for the culture of corruption and allowable fringe benefits in Las Vegas remains to be seen. Then again, now that the probe has essentially concluded, some have suggested that the hours of wiretapped conversations contain evidence of dubious influence-peddling that stands completely apart from the ever-shady world of strip clubs. Early indicators reveal it might have something to do with land development, the legacy of Las Vegas corruption from the town's very beginnings.

Land of the Free

Is Las Vegas losing its libertine streak?

Long before the Disneyfication of excess became the city's calling card, Las Vegas packaged and sold, if not entirely embodied, an atmosphere of freewheeling libertarianism. From its mid-1800s mining and Mormon settlement years right through until the end of the 20th century, it prided itself on being a true western city, one that went far beyond a basic American sense of liberty and extended to extreme notions of freedom of choice, individual rights and, especially, personal privacy.

Las Vegas was the quintessential western outpost. The town was watered by natural springs, yet socially and physically isolated by hundreds of dusty miles from anywhere; surrounded by mountains ripe (if not rich) with minerals yet challenged by efforts to extract them; populated by a small but hardy group of Native Americans but willing to displace them for financial gain. It was every man for himself, and that's how the settlers liked it… as long as the money and the liquor were flowing.

Having been settled by Mormon missionaries in the 1850s, Las Vegas was a different roll of the dice from other Wild West towns. By design

(and sometimes, incongruously, by government intervention), Las Vegas neither dried up and blew away like nearby Goldfield, nor grew into an international cosmopolitan crossroads like San Francisco. Instead, it became the longest standing, largest example of old-school western freedom, one that would hold dear its libertine roots until the turn of its own centennial.

DRAWING THE BOUNDARIES

As in other frontier towns planted far from what pioneers saw as the overreaching shadow of the federal government, gambling and prostitution were an accepted (if not officially endorsed) part of daily life in Vegas. Alongside legal prostitution, gambling was unregulated and openly tolerated until 1909, when it was briefly criminalised to appease a national movement that all but swept it away. But in the face of declining mining revenues, the law was short lived. In a direct effort to boost the struggling state's bottom line, the Nevada legislature officially legalised gambling in 1931.

And herein lies a clue. If one can point to any reason as to how and why Nevada evolved as such an unharnessed state, it's the cycles of boom and bust. Discover valuable minerals within a day's trot of Big Spring? *Boom.* Suffer the harsh realities of life in the Mojave Desert? *Bust.* Here comes the railroad: *boom*! There goes the railroad and here comes the Depression: *bust*! So let's build a dam, legalise gambling, make it easier to get married (and divorced), pour liquor 24 hours a day; hell, let's put the favourite vices of the American frontiersmen on a pedestal and celebrate a lifestyle built around them. *Boom boom boom*!

As the east coast struggled to balance the spirit that spawned it with the needs of its ever-growing, ever-challenging urban populations, Las Vegas fashioned itself as the nation's last bastion of freedom, a frontier town teetering on the edge of both yesterday and tomorrow. Forget silver and gold, agriculture and industry: the one at-hand resource Las Vegas had to sell was freedom. Come as you please, leave your past behind and embrace the vices of greed, gluttony and sex in a town that not only was built upon them but upholds them as virtues.

TAKE IT TO THE LIMIT

It wasn't all boosterism. For those who lived here in its early days, which one can count as lasting until the late 1970s, Las Vegas offered a unique combination. In 1970, a mere 273,000 people called the city home while 6.8 million visitors streamed through it, making Vegas an energetic fantasmagoria at the weekends and a small desert town during the week. Those who lived here reaped more than mere financial rewards: they came to live within and embody its spirit of freedom and privacy. In a nutshell, it was a kind of conservative libertarianism: you have the right to do what you want as long as it doesn't hurt me, but I also have the right to not have to hear about it and, thus, not be socially responsible for you or to you.

Out of such an attitude came some of the unusual realities of life in Las Vegas: gambling in grocery stores, liquor on tap around the clock, and unavoidable sex, from billboard ads to waitress outfits. Speeds were posted as 'unlimited' on roads to Reno, minors drank in casino bars with little hassle, and respectable civic figures bought gasoline with casino chips. Relatively unskilled workers made barrels of money in the service industries; at the other end of the scale, corporations were formed with anonymous owners and money was shielded and transferred with no outside knowledge of where it came from and where it was going.

Aware that their neighbours might be showgirls or stickmen (or, more nefariously, mobsters or corrupt politicians), Las Vegans lived under a frontier philosophy that combined

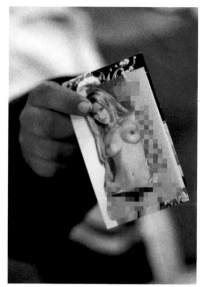

live-and-let-live with don't-ask-don't-tell. They built homes on lots ringed by block walls and kept their secrets and those of their neighbours well tended. The philosophy is illustrated by the Mormons, who wielded (and continue to wield) great power in law offices, banks and local government, yet did daily business with the city's purveyors of sin. The money kept flowing, into one pocket and out the other.

This era spawned the longtime local's lament, part reality and part romanticism: *Things were better when the Mob ran the place.* Underworld figures reputed to be behind the casino operations were reinventing themselves as good Samaritans with deep pockets, but were also credited with keeping crimes against the average citizen at a low rate. Just as crucially, they sat at the top of the food chain at a time when most Las Vegans, straight and crooked, were never more than one step removed from a casino job. Fortunately, there was more than enough money to go around.

MOVING DAY

As time marched on, the Mob was vanquished, once-glorious casinos fell into disrepair and the city became a caricature of itself. But Las Vegas rebounded and reinvented itself again, and again, and again. Shiny new resorts, high-class shopping, star chefs? *Boom boom boom*! Las Vegas was reawakened not as a shady little outpost of freedom and sin but as a relatively respectable world-renowned resort town. Something had to give.

Perhaps most responsible for the change in the city's character was the unimaginable success of Las Vegas as a place to live, a by-product of its continued success as a place to visit. With more hotels and casinos came more visitors, and the need for more workers to serve them. As labourers with little or no skill flocked to the city, eager to capitalise on the cash flow of what had by now morphed in name from the 'casino industry' to the 'service industry', cultural commentator Kurt Andersen tagged Las Vegas as 'the Detroit of the 21st century'.

'For most visitors, the mere idea of reckless freedom was enough.'

In 2003, the ratio of annual visitors to permanent residents remained steady at the 1970 figure of 25-to-1. The difference? There were 35.5 million visitors that year, and they required 1.65 million residents to serve them. Las Vegas was no longer capable of behaving like a small town with too much money. The cash was no longer as easy to get as before, and neither were the jobs. And amid the growth, the infrastructure – roadways, social services and so on – started to buckle. The urban challenges from which Las Vegas had long escaped were banging down its doorway. And so freedom, its most valuable resource, had to be rationed.

As the now-infamous 'What happens here, stays here' ad campaign was launched around the dawn of the 21st century, some new arrivals in the city started to cry foul. *What kind of image is this for my family?* Many of these folks, often transplants from California, were accustomed to what some would call a more socially responsible government culture. And yet longtime Las Vegans looked on in disbelief as expats who moved to suburban enclaves such as Summerlin and Green Valley did so without realising just how pervasive the so-called culture of Las Vegas was. They didn't know what they were getting into until they were in it. The uproars – about neighbourhood casinos, about naughty billboards, about taxicabs carrying ads for strip clubs – got louder, and the jaws of old-timers dropped ever lower.

During this time, state gaming regulators started cracking down on casinos for a variety of offences, most notably the behaviour of their nightclub patrons and the portrayal of those clubs in ads. The most famous incident occured in 2004: two years after the Hard Rock agreed to pay a fine of $100,000 to the Gaming Control Board after officials investigated allegations of 'overt sexual activity' in its

nightclub, the casino forked over further fines totalling $300,000 to the GCB following a racy billboard advertising campaign. The Las Vegas Convention & Visitors Authority's canny ad campaigns seemed to recognise that for most visitors to the city, the mere idea of reckless freedom was enough.

NO SMOKE WITHOUT FIRE
The shift in the city's social culture manifested itself dramatically in 2006. Gambling, drinking and smoking have long existed symbiotically here; some folks even say they rarely find themselves participating in one activity without the other. But, spearheaded by anti-smoking groups and lobbyists, a battle over the pervasiveness of smoking in Las Vegas eventually went to a ballot, hung on the idea of protecting children from second-hand smoke.

The regulations squeaked by, eliminating smoking from grocery stores and anywhere – restaurants, cafés, bars – that served prepared food. The hitch? Casinos with full gaming licences and strip clubs were exempt from the law, a kink that highlighted the way in which the new Las Vegas and the new Las Vegans intend to confine the city's traditional libertarian culture to its tourist areas.

By the middle of 2007, challengers from the old guard had won a small victory. As the inherent difficulties of enforcing the anti-smoking law made headlines, so they were stripped of their criminal penalties. Some local taverns openly flaunted the regulations by continuing to serve food while turning a blind eye to smoking patrons. Even so, local company Herbst Gaming, which derives its income primarily from the slot machines it operates in grocery and convenience stores, reported a net loss of $3.9 million for the first quarter of 2007, as opposed to a profit of $17.2 million in the first quarter of the previous year. The firm attributed the change to the new smoking regulations.

Las Vegas is definitely undergoing a shift in its culture, but is it much different from the wholesale reinventions it has undertaken in the past? All had one goal in mind: to protect the cashflow and maintain Nevada as an economically healthy state. Perhaps selling a watered-down, packaged version of the libertarian ideal that built Las Vegas is the answer; perhaps it's not. Meanwhile, the 'real' city changes its own course, maturing and demanding ever more cosmopolitan experiences, as well as a government far more responsive (some would say invasive) than ever before. What happens tomorrow, however, is anyone's guess. For it's always all about the money in Las Vegas, and it takes a lot of it to take care of two million people.

Gambling

Put your money where your mouth is.

The old and oft-told joke runs that no one in Las Vegas ever got rich through gambling except the owners of the casinos. For many people, it's a gag that's a lot funnier at the start of their trip than it is at the end. Gambling built Las Vegas, and the fact that the city is still expanding at record speed is proof enough that the novelty of the pastime is as bright as it's ever been.

Sorry to shatter your dreams, then, but if you're thinking that you'll walk away from Las Vegas set up for life, you'd best think again. However, if all you're after is a little fun, having filed your gambling budget under 'entertainment' and prepared yourself for manageable losses, you're in the right place. And you'll certainly have more fun if you know a little about the games you're playing. While the games staged by the casinos aren't especially complicated, a little knowledge will help your money last a good deal longer than it otherwise might. Indeed, play your cards right and you may even end up ahead. But don't bet on it.

HOW CASINOS MAKE MONEY

Before learning how to play the games, it's wise to get acquainted with the casinos' angles on them. There are four ways for the casinos to generate gaming revenue: the *house edge*, favourable rules, commissions and dumb players.

● The *house edge* is the difference between the *true odds* of an event occurring and the odds used for payouts. For example, in double-zero roulette, there are 38 possible winning numbers. If the casino paid *true odds*, it would pay off a winning number at 37:1 (for a total of $38, including your $1 bet). Instead, the casino pays off a winning number at 35:1. Calculating the *house edge* from this scenario is simple.

First, imagine placing a $1 bet on every possible number in double-zero roulette, a

> ▶ All terms in *italics* throughout this chapter are defined in **The gambler's lexicon**, for which *see p46*.

total wager of $38. No matter which number wins, you'll receive a payout of $36: winnings of $35 at the 35:1 payoff, plus your original $1 bet. The difference between the *true odds* payout and the actual payout is $2, money that goes directly into the house's pocket. To calculate the *house edge*, simply divide the money kept by the house (2) by the money that the house would have paid on *true odds* (38). This calculation shows a *house edge* of 5.26 per cent, which means that the house expects to keep 5.26¢ of each dollar bet at a roulette table.

The *house edge* varies from game to game, and even within each game. Casinos love it when gamblers keep playing for hour after hour, because the *house edge* grinds its little takeout from every dollar wagered. The law of averages favours the casino.
● The rules for casino games are structured to favour the house. The best example is blackjack, where the dealer gets to play his hand last. Should a player *bust* beforehand, the dealer wins by default. Even if the dealer ends up *busting* later, the player loses and the house wins.
● Commissions are collected by the house in a few table games. In poker, the house serves as dealer but doesn't play a hand. To make money, the house takes a percentage of every *pot*, a sum of money that's called the 'rake', or charges players a flat fee of $5 to $7 per half-hour of play. In baccarat, the house takes five per cent of all winnings from bank bets.

● Be they drunk, superstitious, careless or ill-informed, dumb gamblers are a boundless source of funds for the smart house. Why else do casinos offer gamblers free drinks? Alcohol is wonderful for loosening inhibitions, such as the inhibition against losing next month's rent, but it also causes sensible players to make stupid mistakes. An example: although the *house edge* in blackjack has been calculated at around two per cent, casinos expect a win (or 'hold') of 15 to 20 per cent of the total amount of money brought to the table (the *drop*), due entirely to the incompetence of the players.

BETTING LIMITS AND MINIMUMS
At every table game, there's a sign detailing the minimum (and often maximum) allowable bet. At blackjack, it might be $5 to $500. Casinos expect players to bet towards the low end of the limit. This separates players by class, so a big player seeking a speedy $500-a-hand game doesn't have to endure poky play from a piker betting five bucks each time. *High rollers* can bet at higher-than-posted limits if the house is willing to 'fade' (cover) them. In roulette, the minimum means the sum total of all bets that an individual gambler can place in one round; in other words, if the table has a $5 minimum, you can make it with five $1 bets. But in blackjack, if you play two hands at once, you must bet the minimum on each.

ETIQUETTE

Before you lay down your money, always note the minimum-bet requirement, usually posted on a sign in the far left corner. If you don't want to embarrass yourself, don't toss out a red ($5) *chip* on a $100-minimum table. Similarly, don't put a quarter into a dollar slot or video poker machine; the coin will pass through the thing and clank into the hopper, alerting the other players that you're a novice. That said, most machines no longer accept coins; only bills and cashout tickets will pass muster.

Table games have strict rules about when players can touch *chips* or cards, rules that exist to discourage cheats. Many blackjack games are dealt face up and players never touch the cards. Once you make a bet, never touch the *chips* you've laid down; if you're 'splitting' or doubling down in blackjack, push out a new pile of *chips* but don't touch the original bet. This rule is to discourage 'past posting', a scam by which cheats sneak more *chips* on to their bet after peeking at their cards.

Only handle dice with one hand. The pit bosses, the dealers and the other players will all get very nervous if you touch the dice with

two hands, or make a fist around them with one hand so they can't be seen. Blow on them, shake them and turn them so your favourite numbers are up, but don't hide them for a second. That's how dice cheats use sleight of hand to get loaded dice into a game of craps.

All told, it's best for novice gamblers to stand back at first and watch the action; after a few minutes, you'll get the hang of the procedures. If you need to be corrected, the dealer will do so gently and unobtrusively. And don't worry if it happens: the other players at the tables have all been corrected at one time or another. They didn't step up to a crap table for the first time knowing everything about the game.

You must be 21 to gamble. If you're under 21 and start winning (or hit a jackpot that requires you to sign tax forms), your *chips* or jackpot will be confiscated and you'll be tossed out of the casino faster than you can say, 'But…'. You may even be turned over to a Gaming Control Board agent. The lower your age and the higher your bet, the bigger the trouble.

Most casinos subscribe to the old tradition that cameras are unwelcome, and it's wise to leave your SLRs and camcorders in your room, your car or your backpack. If you're discreet, or even if you ask permission, you can sometimes get away with taking photographs in casinos, particularly at the Excalibur and Harrah's. On the other hand, wherever you go in a casino (except the toilets), you'll be watched by *eye in the sky* cameras and taped for posterity. Nowhere on earth is Big Brother busier than in a casino; make sure you behave accordingly.

MONEY, MONEY, MONEY

To play table games, you'll need *chips*. However, in some games, you can throw down a bill for your first plays; in blackjack, for example, it's usually fine to play with cash, though any winnings will be paid as *chips*. You can buy *chips* at the table in a process called a *buy in*; you can also buy *chips* at the *cage*. Chips can only be redeemed at the *cage*.

Chips are like currency in the casino within which they're issued. However, due to problems with counterfeiting, casinos rarely honour each others' *chips* for gambling unless, as is the case with the MGM-operated Mirage and TI (for example), they're under the same ownership. It's sometimes possible to exchange sub-$100 denominations from other casinos for house *chips* at the *cage*.

Most modern slot and video poker machines have bill slots that change greenbacks into credits. If you don't want to use it, or if you only have bills in denominations not accepted by the machine, press the 'Change' button.

Sucker bets

Just when you think you know the rules, Las Vegas changes the games. Take blackjack, for example. Many gamblers know that a blackjack game dealt from a single deck offers savvy players the best chance to win. Now, however, many casinos have made a seemingly minor change to the single-deck rules hoping players don't notice that it's no longer the best version of 21, but quite easily the worst.

A few years ago, single-deck blackjack was only available in the high-roller salons, with most of the low-limit games dealt from four or even six decks. In the last few years, however, single-deck tables have become more common than fake breasts at Mandalay Bay. This should be good news for gamblers. However, in the process, the payoff for *natural* 21s has been lowered in many casinos from 3:2 to 6:5; in other words, hitting a blackjack on a $10 bet will win you only $12 where it used to net $15. Doesn't sound like much of

a difference? Think again. The rule change is so bad that the casino's profit is several times higher than at the city's worst six-deck shoe game, and up to eight times more than at a regular single-deck game.

Keen-eyed Europeans will also notice that the odds have been shifted out of their favour on the roulette wheel. In many European casinos, the wheel has only a single green '0'. However, in the US, there's also a double zero ('00') on the wheel; that one little extra green spot tips the *house edge* from 2.7 per cent to 5.26 per cent. Check before you play.

Finally, avoid almost anything called a 'side bet', extra bets beyond the basic wager at table games. They include jackpots for making certain hands at Let it Ride and three-card poker, or being dealt your first two cards of the same suit at blackjack. Don't waste your money: the casinos aren't charities, so there's no reason to give until it hurts.

This activates a light on top of the machine, which summons a roving change person.

Most casinos are converting to cashless machines (also known as 'ticket in/ticket out', or TITO). You play the machines by putting a regular bill in the slot; however, when you're ready to cash out, the machine dispenses not cash but a ticket detailing your total credits. You can either take the ticket and feed it into another machine, or redeem it for cash at the *cage*. Be very careful with the tickets, and be sure to redeem them before leaving the casino: some expire in 30 days. And don't leave a TITO machine for even a moment: someone will almost certainly press the 'Cash Out' button, grab the ticket and run.

LEARNING TO GAMBLE

If you want to study before arriving, you'll find hundreds of books on everything from baccarat to video poker. For recommendations, *see pp317-318*, though you're generally safe with anything published by **Huntington Press** (3665 S Procyon Avenue, Las Vegas, NV 89103, 1-800 244 2224, www.shoplva.com). There are numerous software programs available, as well as a slew of instructive websites (*see p318*). The **Gamblers Book Club** (*see p194*) and the **Gamblers General Store** (*see p203*) are both excellent resources.

Many of the large casinos offer free hands-on lessons at table games. The instructors, usually informative and personable sorts, will take you

through the playing procedures and etiquette one step at a time, but they almost certainly won't warn you about sucker games and bets: after all, they're paid by the casino. Lessons are usually held in the late morning during the week, when the casino is at its quietest; some are followed by open low-minimum 'live' games for punters who want to celebrate their new-found skills under casino conditions.

When you're ready to join a game, first stand back and watch the action for a while in order to pick up the rhythms and routines. (However, don't stand too long behind blackjack tables, as most bosses will suspect you of 'back counting' the deck in order to slip in a bet at the most advantageous time.) Choose a table with the lowest possible minimum, so that you're not risking $100, $25 or even $10 a hand at a game you're playing for the first time. Downtown casinos and locals' casinos tend to have lower minimums than the casinos on the Strip.

MAKING THE MOST OF IT

There are plenty of ways to make the most of your money, many of them set up by casinos in an attempt to draw customers. Most popular among them are the casino's *players clubs* (*see p60*): they cost nothing to join, and the points you accrue on them can be redeemed for rooms, food and cash.

Always ask for *comps* when you play table games. As soon as you make a bet, call over a floorman and ask: 'How long do I have to play

The gambler's lexicon

ante a small bet that players must place into the *pot* before a hand of poker is dealt.

bankroll your total gambling budget.

Black Book a list, kept by the State Gaming Control Board, of people barred from casinos due to cheating or a link to organised crime.

boxman casino executive who acts as the umpire in a game of craps.

bust a blackjack hand exceeding 21.

buy in exchange cash for casino *chips*.

cage the cashier, where *chips* and tokens are converted into cash and credit is established.

carousel a group of slots that are often connected to a joint *progressive jackpot*.

change colour swapping *chips* for ones of a higher or lower denomination.

checks another word for *chips*.

chips tokens issued by casinos and used, instead of cash, for table games.

colour up exchange small denomination *chips* for larger denomination *chips*.

comps 'complimentaries', anything from free cocktails to 'RFB' (room, food and beverage). Their value is calculated by the gambler's average bet, multiplied by the time spent playing, multiplied by the *house edge*. To qualify, you must be a *rated player* or belong to a *players club*.

credit line amount of credit a gambler is allowed.

croupier casino employee who controls the action in games of baccarat and roulette.

drop total funds, including *chips*, cash and *markers*, gambled at a table or a machine.

edge see *house edge*.

European wheel a roulette wheel with a single '0' position, which gives players better odds. Most wheels in Vegas have '0' and '00'.

even money a bet that pays back an amount equal to the bet itself. In other words, if you win on a $5 bet, you receive your $5 stake plus a $5 win.

eye in the sky casino surveillance systems.

face cards jacks, queens and kings; also known as 'pictures' or 'paint'.

funbook a booklet of vouchers (meal deals and the like) or match-play coupons (only valid in conjunction with cash).

George dealer-speak for a good tipper.

grind joint a casino with low table minimums and low-denomination slot machines.

high roller gambler who bets at least $100 per hand on a table game, and plays $5 slots.

hit in blackjack, to take another card.

hole card blackjack dealer's face-down card.

house edge the percentage difference (retained by the casino) between the *true odds* and the actual payout.

inside bet in roulette, betting on a single number or small combination of numbers.

to get a buffet *comp*?' He or she will look at your bet and tell you. Play for as long as he or she indicates, then head off and eat yourself silly. And look for coupons in *funbooks*, free coupon booklets handed out in front of many casinos. Two-for-one, three-for-two and seven-for-five coupons on *even money* bets give gamblers a huge *edge* over the house at blackjack, craps and the like.

While the casinos can help you make your money last, you can also help yourself. Play slowly, for one thing: you're better off exposing your *bankroll* to the *house edge* for 50 hands an hour at a busy table than 100 hands an hour playing one-on-one against the dealer, or pulling the handle on a slot machine for 400 spins an hour rather than running at double-time by hitting the spin button like a lunatic.

To ensure you have gambling funds for your whole trip, it's a good idea to divide your money into 'session' portions. Lost an entire portion quickly? End of session. Don't dig into your remaining *bankroll* until it's time for the next session. Always keep an eye on your coins, cash, tickets and *chips*; watch for 'rail thieves' when you're at the crap table; and ensure back-to-back slot machines have a plastic or metal guard between them to prevent 'reach through' thievery.

TIP TALK

Las Vegas is a town that runs on tips. This goes particularly for casino dealers, who are paid little more than the minimum wage. Every shift of dealers combines and divides their tips, which make up the bulk of their pay. Giving tips (or *tokes*, as dealers call them, short for 'tokens' of appreciation) is smart, as a happy dealer is your friend. Dealers can assist players in a number of ways: they can slow down the pace of the game (extremely useful when you're playing for *comps*), create a sociable atmosphere, and even deal a little deeper in the deck, critical for card counters.

You can *toke* the dealer as you leave the table. However, while they appreciate the tip, it won't gain you any help while you're playing. A better method is to *toke*

juice power and influence; who you know.

layout diagram on the playing table that marks the area of the game.

loose a term used to describe a slot machine that pays out frequently. Casinos compete in claiming that their slots are the *loosest*.

low roller gambler who bets at low-minimum slot machines, usually in *grind joints*.

marker IOU signed by a *rated player* to obtain *chips* and paid off with *chips* or cash.

natural in blackjack, a two-card total of 21; in baccarat, a two-card total of eight or nine.

outside bet in roulette, betting outside the single-number *layout*: on black or red, on odds or evens, on the first, second or third 12 numbers as a group, etc.

pit area behind the gaming tables reserved for casino employees.

pit boss casino executive who oversees the gambling action from inside the pit.

players club clubs for slots and video poker players where members accrue points as they play; these can then later be redeemed against meals, gifts, cash and other perks.

pot the bets accumulated while playing a hand of poker.

progressive a slot or video poker machine on which the jackpot increases as more coins are played. A *linked progressive* is a group of machines networked to share their jackpot.

push in blackjack, where the dealer and player(s) have the same un-*busted* hand. No money changes hands.

rated player player whose gambling is assessed by the casino and is thus eligible for *comps*.

shill casino employee who plays at empty tables (with house money) to encourage visitors to join the action.

shoe container for decks of cards from which card games are often dealt.

shooter the player who throws the dice in a game of craps.

stand in blackjack, to refuse another card.

stiff someone who doesn't tip, one of the worst insults in Las Vegas; also refers to blackjack hands totalling 12-16.

tight used to describe a slot machine that is perceived to pay out infrequently.

toke a tip for a casino employee, often given in the form of a bet on their behalf.

true odds real chances of winning on any game as opposed to the money actually paid out by the casino.

underlay a bet that's higher than strict probability suggests is wise.

up card the blackjack dealer's face-*up card*.

vigorish also 'vig'; see *house edge*.

whale big-money gambler prepared to wager at least $5,000 a hand at high-stakes games.

immediately after a big win; this way, the dealer knows you're thinking of him or her and could start to help you. Don't bother *toking* if the dealer is rude, creepy or unco-operative. In fact, don't even play there: just get up and move on to another table.

The best way to show your appreciation is to place a bet for the dealer alongside your own wager. If you win, the *toke* is paid off at regular odds and the dealer takes the winnings. If you lose, the house wins the *toke*, but the dealer will still appreciate the gesture. In blackjack, you can place a *chip* outside the line surrounding your wager circle, but if this *toke* bet wins, it has to be scooped up by the dealer right away. Alternatively, if you're riding a hot streak, place the dealer's *toke* next to your bet within your wager circle. If you win, you can let the *toke* ride (continue to the next deal): it's yours until you give it to the dealer. Just tell the dealer the extra bet is a *toke*. Note, though, that some dealers resent it if you let their *tokes* ride, and have a take-the-money-and-run attitude.

The Games

Baccarat

Long viewed as an obscure, weirdly ritualised game for *high rollers*, baccarat ('ba-cuh-rah') is a table game with a small *house edge*. Up to 15 players sit around the *layout* and bet on BANK, PLAYER or TIE. Dealers lay out two hands of two cards each, titled PLAYER and BANK. The object is for each hand to total as close to nine as possible. *Face cards* and tens count as zero and any total over nine is reduced by eliminating the first digit (for instance, 15 is valued as five). Players have no control over whether to 'draw' or 'stand'. Dealers follow a strict set of rules to determine if they must 'hit' either hand with a third card.

If PLAYER or BANK bets win, the house pays at *even money*. Since the rules determine that BANK wins slightly more often, the house retains a five per cent commission on all BANK

The best Baccarat

If you can fade the minimums, the **Mirage** (*see p73*) has the most elegant baccarat pit in town, complete with a mini-buffet for the players. For mini-baccarat, try the **Gold Coast** (*see p116*), which has six tables with $10 minimums.

winnings. Even with the commission, the house holds only a 1.17 per cent *edge* on BANK bets and 1.36 per cent on PLAYER bets. (The TIE bet should be avoided. It pays off at eight to one, but since the *true odds* are about 9.5:1, the *house edge* equates to a whopping 14 per cent.)

The rhythm of baccarat is leisurely and the mood subdued. In fact, it's rarely necessary for players to speak. Baccarat *pits* are usually secluded behind velvet ropes or in high-limit rooms, which often come complete with small buffets that lend an air of exclusivity. However, if you can handle the minimum (often $100), you're welcome to join the action. Casinos catering to low-end gamblers tend to ignore baccarat, but high-end casinos hold it dear for good reason: it's very profitable. The Mirage has estimated that as much as ten per cent of its annual revenue comes from baccarat.

MINI BACCARAT

Mini baccarat is a low-stakes version of the game played in the main *pit*, usually near the blackjack tables. It's a good introduction: the rules are the same but the bets are lower. As it attracts fewer players, the pace of the game is faster.

Bingo

It might not be posh, but bingo is a gambling stalwart in Vegas, especially in neighbourhood casinos: the game is played in the same way as it is all over the world. The *house edge* is slightly better than the similar keno (*see p52*), though it's hard to pin it down to a precise figure since so much depends on the variety of the game and its payout. The one advantage bingo has over keno is that bingo numbers are called until a player wins. By contrast, a million keno games can go by without anyone hitting the big jackpot.

Blackjack (21)

Blackjack is by far the most popular table game in the casinos. The reasons are obvious: it's easy to play, the basic strategy slims the *house edge* to nearly zero, and dozens of books claim the house can be beaten with card counting.

THE BASICS

After placing their bets, everyone at the table is dealt two cards. Single- and double-deck blackjack (games played with either one deck or two decks shuffled together) are dealt from the dealer's hand; for multiple-deck blackjack, the decks are combined and placed in a *shoe*, from which the dealer pulls cards. *Face cards* count as ten; aces can count as one or 11. (A hand in which an ace is counted as 11 is known as a 'soft' hand; for example, an ace and a six is called 'soft 17'.) Each player competes against the dealer's hand by trying to get as close as possible to a total of 21 without exceeding it (or *busting*). The game moves clockwise around the table; the player sitting on the right as he or she faces the dealer is the first to play. The first of the dealer's cards is dealt face up (the *up card*), with the second dealt face down (the *hole card*).

First, check your cards. If you want an extra card, ask to *hit*; when satisfied with your total, you *stand*. After all players have *stood* or *busted*, the dealer reveals his or her *hole card* and plays the hand according to fixed rules: he or she must *hit* totals of 16 or less and must *stand* on 17 or above. (The rules vary if the dealer has soft 17, with some casinos requiring dealers to *hit* and others to *stand*; the players' *edge* is increased by 0.2 per cent for the latter.)

Once the dealer has *stood* or *busted*, the hands are compared; players who beat the dealer are paid off at *even money*. Ties between the house and player are a *push* and no money changes hands; dealers indicate a *push* by knocking gently on the *layout*. If a player is dealt an ace and a ten-value card, it's considered a *natural* blackjack (also known as a 'snapper'); unless the dealer's *up card* is an ace or a ten, indicating a possible blackjack, the player is immediately paid at 3:2. Watch out for games (often single-deck or low-limit) where *naturals* pay only 6:5; *see p45* **Sucker bets**.

ETIQUETTE
With the crucial exception of the dealer's *hole card*, almost all multi-deck blackjack games are dealt with the cards face up. In these games, players never touch the cards, but instead indicate *hit* or *stand* with hand motions. This reduces the potential for misunderstandings between the player and the dealer, and also makes it easier for disputed plays to be reviewed on security videos. For a *hit*, players hold one hand palm down above the felt and brush their fingers toward them. To *stand*, players hold their hand the same way, but with the fingers straight outward, and move it right and left.

Single- and double-deck games are almost always dealt face down, and players hold their own cards. Always hold them with one hand only; it makes the dealer and the *eye* nervous if you cup them with both. *Hitting* is indicated by scratching the cards towards you on the *layout*, while *standing* is indicated by sliding the cards face down under the *chips*.

Though blackjack sets each player's hand against the dealer's, most players view the game as everyone against the dealer. Their goal is to make the dealer *bust*, which means payoffs for all players still in the game. These folks don't take kindly to people playing stupidly ('splitting' tens or *hitting* a 14, say, against a dealer's six), especially if the offending party sits in the last seat on the left (known as 'third base'), since they feel those cards should have gone to the dealer. In truth, it doesn't really matter, since on average, a player's good decisions cancel the bad decisions. However, many gamers focus only on the bad decisions, which is why novices shouldn't sit at third base.

BETTING
There are four ways in which players can alter their bets after the cards have been dealt: 'doubling down', 'splitting', 'insurance' and 'surrender'. Splitting and doubling down

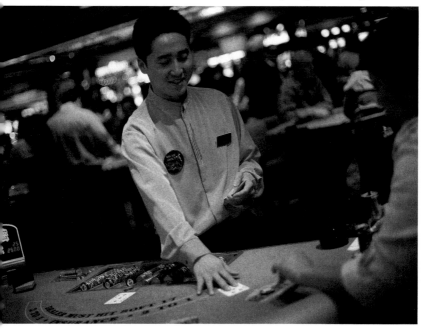

aggressively are the secrets to winning at basic strategy blackjack, as they give players the chance to press their bets when they're holding a strong starting hand.

● When a player 'doubles down', he or she makes another bet equal to the original and receives one (only one) more card. It's the choice move when you've got a total of nine, ten or 11 and the dealer shows a weak card such as a six; for full advice, *see p51* **Blackjack strategy**. You can double down only if you haven't already taken a *hit*.

● 'Splitting' is an option when players are dealt two cards of the same value. An additional bet equal to the original bet is put out and the cards are split, with each played as a separate hand. It's to the player's advantage to double down or split each of the post-split hands, though some casinos limit what you can do. Check the strategy chart (*p51*) for more advice.

● 'Insurance' is a side bet offered when the dealer has a possible blackjack (in other words, when the dealer is showing an ace or ten-value card). An insurance bet is limited to 50 per cent of the original bet and is lost if the dealer doesn't have a blackjack. If he or she does have a blackjack, insurance pays at 2:1, making the whole bet into a *push*.

Despite the word's connotations, insurance is a sucker bet. Unless you're a card counter and can calculate the odds of a blackjack, there's no reason to take insurance, even if you're holding a *natural* 21. If you're holding a *natural* and the dealer is calling for insurance bets, you can take

even money on your bet. If you don't take *even money* and the dealer has a two-card 21, it's a *push*. If the dealer doesn't have 21, your *natural* is paid at 3:2 (again, don't play 6:5 games; *see p45* **Sucker bets**).

● 'Surrender' is an obscure but useful rule that's not in effect everywhere. It permits players to fold and sacrifice half their bet as long as they haven't played their hand. This is an excellent way to drop out and minimise losses when dealt weak cards. If used correctly, it increases the player's *edge* by 0.2 per cent.

CARD COUNTING

Card counting is a technique whereby a player visually tracks exposed cards and mentally keeps a running total to determine if the deck is positive or negative. In the simplest count, the ten-value cards and aces are valued at –1, while cards numbered two to seven take a value of +1; the eights and nines have no value. If the running total is positive, players have an advantage and should raise their bets.

Does it work? Yes, but only if you devote weeks of practice, are cool under the pressures of casino play, and develop camouflage skills so that the house doesn't know you're counting. Although card counting isn't against the law, casinos frown upon it, and 'back off' (forbid card counters from playing blackjack) or 'bar' (kick them out of the casino) any player that they suspect of using the practice. Counting cards is a gruelling discipline at which most fail. However, successful card counters, especially high-stakes players, are among the few gamblers who beat the casinos at their own game.

If you're not among the handful of people who have perfected this dark art, it's best to stick to basic strategy. At its simplest level, this entails memorising a chart that contains the answer to every decision in blackjack, based on your first two cards and the dealer's *up card*. You can usually bring the chart to the table and check it as you play, as long as you don't slow down the game. For the chart, *see p51*.

The best Blackjack

More or less every casino on the Strip will claim to be the best place to play this most popular of table games. However, you're better off heading Downtown, where you'll find the best combination of good rules, low minimums, easy *comps* and tolerant dealers. (There's nothing worse than Strip dealers looking down their noses at you: they're minimum-wage card dealers, for cryin' out loud.)

If you just want to play on the cheap, you'll find $2-$5 blackjack on the Strip at **Slots-a-Fun** (2880 Las Vegas Boulevard South, 734 0410), and Downtown at the **Western** (899 Fremont Street, 384 4620), just west of Las Vegas Boulevard. **El Cortez** (*see p106*) is among the few casinos that offer $5 minimum single-deck blackjack that pays 3:2 for a *natural*.

Craps

Fast, furious and enormously confusing, craps is an action-filled dice game that terrifies most novices. It can also be hugely exciting: if you hear a roar of excitement while wandering through a casino, it's probably coming from a craps table. The players cheer, curse and scream, dice and *chips* fly across the table, and everybody roots for different numbers. Fortunes can be won and lost in minutes, which is why craps is worshipped by a subculture. It's confounding, but by sticking to a few smart bets, players can enjoy a boisterous game with a *house edge* as low as one per cent, and occasionally lower.

THE BASICS

Craps is played on a large table surrounded by a low, padded wall, with a rail for *chips* on top and, outside, a shelf for the ever-present drinks. The game is staffed by between one and four casino employees, and there's room for 12 to 14 players to belly up to the table.

The *layout* is divided into three sections. The two at each end are identical, but in the centre is an area reserved for special wagers known as 'proposition bets'. A game starts with dice being offered to a new *shooter* by the 'stickman', the dealer located mid-table who's holding the stick. This first roll of the dice is known as the 'come out roll'. (Each player will be offered the dice at some point, though it's common to refuse.) The *shooter* must throw two dice in such a way that they bounce off the table's far wall.

Basically, players bet on which numbers the *shooters* will throw, and in what order they will appear. The *shooter* must place a bet before his or her first throw, and traditionally chooses PASS. Those betting with the *shooter* are known as 'right' bettors, while those betting against the *shooter* are called 'wrong' bettors.

BETTING

There are four basic wagers known as 'line bets' marked on the *layout*: PASS, DON'T PASS, COME and DON'T COME (the DON'T bets are for wrong bettors). Players bet on the PASS or DON'T PASS lines. If the dice show seven (statistically the most likely roll) or 11 on the come out roll, PASS bettors win at even odds and DON'T PASS bettors lose. If the *shooter* throws a total of two or three, DON'T PASS wins and PASS loses. If the dice show 12, PASS bettors lose and it's a 'push' (or tie) for DON'T PASS bettors. Rolling two, three or 12 is known as 'crapping out'. If any other number is thrown (four, five, six, eight, nine or ten), that number becomes the 'point'.

Once a point is established, the *shooter* keeps rolling, attempting to repeat the point before rolling a seven (known as 'sevening out'). In this context, the point and seven are the only numbers that count: all PASS and DON'T PASS bets ride until the 'point' is hit or the *shooter* sevens out. If the *shooter* hits the point, PASS bettors win and DON'T PASS bettors lose. If the *shooter* tosses a seven, DON'T PASS bettors win, PASS bettors lose and the *shooter* relinquishes control of the dice. The shortest roll a *shooter* can have is two throws, hitting a point on the come out roll followed by a seven;

Blackjack strategy

Dealer's up card

If you have a total of	2	3	4	5	6	7	8	9	10	A
2-8	H	H	H	H	H	H	H	H	H	H
9	H	D	D	D	D	H	H	H	H	H
10	D	D	D	D	D	D	D	D	H	H
11	D	D	D	D	D	D	D	D	D	D
12	H	H	S	S	S	H	H	H	H	H
13-16	S	S	S	S	S	H	H	H	H	H
17-20	S	S	S	S	S	S	S	S	S	S

Dealer's up card

If you have an ace	2	3	4	5	6	7	8	9	10	A
A+2	H	H	D	D	D	H	H	H	H	H
A+3	H	H	D	D	D	H	H	H	H	H
A+4	H	H	D	D	D	H	H	H	H	H
A+5	H	H	D	D	D	H	H	H	H	H
A+6	D	D	D	D	D	H	H	H	H	H
A+7	S	D	D	D	D	S	S	H	H	S
A+8	S	S	S	S	S	S	S	S	S	S
A+9	S	S	S	S	S	S	S	S	S	S

Dealer's up card

If you have a pair	2	3	4	5	6	7	8	9	10	A
2s	Sp	Sp	Sp	Sp	Sp	Sp	H	H	H	H
3s	Sp	Sp	Sp	Sp	Sp	Sp	H	H	H	H
4s	H	H	H	H	H	H	H	H	H	H
5s	D	D	D	D	D	D	D	D	H	H
6s	Sp	Sp	Sp	Sp	Sp	H	H	H	H	H
7s	Sp	Sp	Sp	Sp	Sp	Sp	H	H	H	H
8s	Sp	Sp	Sp	Sp	Sp	Sp	Sp	Sp	Sp	Sp
9s	Sp	Sp	Sp	Sp	Sp	S	Sp	Sp	S	S
10s	S	S	S	S	S	S	S	S	S	S
As	Sp	Sp	Sp	Sp	Sp	Sp	Sp	Sp	Sp	Sp

H=*hit*; **S**=*stand*; **D**=double down; **Sp**=split

Players should consider 'surrendering':

- with hard 13-16 against dealer's A
- with hard 14-16 against dealer's 10
- with hard 15-16 against dealer's 9

But if all that's too much to memorise, at least remember the following five golden rules:

- *stand* on 17-21, but always *hit* soft 17
- *stand* on 12-16 against dealer's 2 to 6, but *hit* on 12-16 against dealer's 7 to A
- always split 8s and aces, but never split the 'F's, (4s, 5s and *face cards*)
- double down on 10s and 11s against the dealer's 2 to 9
- never take insurance

in this situation, wrong bettors win. But if he or she avoids 'sevening out', the *shooter* can roll forever, and right bettors can rack up big bucks. Every time the 'point' is hit, the whole game is reset and the next throw is a fresh 'come out roll'. However, all the side bets, such as COME bets, remain in play.

COME and DON'T COME bets represent an optional second layer of betting that runs concurrently with the original layer. They're similar to PASS and DON'T PASS bets, with exactly the same set of outcomes (an immediate win, lose or 'push', or the establishment of a 'point'), but they can only be made on throws subsequent to the come out roll. For instance, say the *shooter* establishes a point of four; on the next roll, you make a COME bet. (If you want, you can enter the game with a COME/DON'T COME bet at any time during a hand without having previously made a PASS or DON'T PASS bet.) The next roll is nine, so nine becomes your 'point'. If that throw had yielded seven or 11, you would have won immediately, and the DON'T COME bets would have lost. If the dice had totalled two, three or 12, your COME bet would have lost. And if the *shooter* had hit his number, the COME bets ride, awaiting a seven or a repeat of the come point.

TAKING THE ODDS

If a player sticks to the four 'line' bets outlined above, the *house edge* is only about 1.4 per cent. But even that tiny amount can be further reduced with the use of the 'odds' bet, a wager where the house holds an *edge* of, believe it or not, zero. Unsurprisingly, these are the only

such wagers in the casino, which is doubtless the reason why the *layout* of a crap table doesn't mention them at all.

Once a point is established, any player with a line bet can back up that wager with an 'odds' bet, placing the bet behind the original 'line' bet on the craps *layout*. This allows players to increase their bet midstream. In a game with single odds, the maximum odds bet equals the line bet. That alone slashes the *house edge* from about 1.4 per cent to 0.85 per cent. Some casinos offer double odds, triple odds, 10x or even 100x odds, all of which reduce the *house edge* even further. A few offer different odds on specified points. Anyone making line bets in craps should take, at the very least, single odds on every bet made. It's worth attending a lesson to learn how to make the most of this tactic.

THE REST OF THE TABLE

Smart players stick to line and odds bets, but action junkies need more. For them, the table offers another world of wagers, none of which is worthwhile. Granted, some bets offer an *edge* only slightly worse than line bets. But most of the one-roll proposition bets are simply horrific.

For instance, the ANY 7 proposition bet has a stunning *house edge* of 16.67 per cent, the worst *edge* of any game wager apart from keno and the Money Wheel. Don't waste time on it. Instead, stick to right and wrong betting with line bets pressed with odds and you'll get more than enough action. A straightforward odds-effective play is to bet the minimum stake on PASS and bet the same amount on two COME bets, taking odds on both (double or triple, if they're offered and you can afford it).

The best Craps

Don't bother heading to **Binion's** (see p106): after 50 years as the best crap joint in town, it's now just average. Instead, try **Casino Royale** (see p89) for 100x odds, **Main Street Station** (see p105) for 20x odds, or the **California** (12 Ogden Street, 1-800 634 6255), which has five tables in a dedicated pit. If you hold the dice at the latter for at least an hour, you're inducted into the Golden Arm Hall of Fame and get your name on a plaque hanging on the wall on the pedestrian overpass.

On a budget? Head to **Slots A Fun** (2880 Las Vegas Boulevard South, 734 0410) for dollar craps with 3x odds. **El Cortez** (see p106) and **Sam's Town** (see p117) offer $1 minimums, the latter with 20x odds.

Keno

This lottery offshoot is the worst bet in the casino, with an appalling *house edge* of 25 to 40 per cent. You might as well climb to the top of the Stratosphere and throw your money into the wind. At least you'll have a nice view.

As with an old-style lottery or bingo, keno involves a ticket (or 'blank') containing 80 numbers, on which players circle as many as 15 or 20 numbers. When the game starts, 20 numbers are selected at random (ping-pong balls are blown from a 'goose' into a pair of 'arms') and displayed on screens around the casino. If your numbers are picked, you win. If not, you lose. (Get used to the second option.) The greater the proportion of your numbers picked, the higher the payback. Remember that, if by some remote chance you win at keno, you must claim your money before the next game begins or you will forfeit your winnings.

There are many variations for keno, but none makes the *edge* even remotely acceptable. Worst of all, payouts for keno in no way reflect the *true odds* of your bet, since they're capped at an arbitrary figure. For instance, your chances of selecting nine numbers and hitting all of them are 1,380,700:1. Your payout for such a feat? Usually no more than $250,000 on a $2 bet. Here's another fun fact: if two players hit the big jackpot at the same time, they have to split the cash. The only way to win at keno is never to play it.

Money Wheel or Big Six

It makes sense to be wary of a game that's been imported to casinos from the morally challenged world of carnivals. That's the case with the Money Wheel (aka Big Six), the grandchild of spin-the-wheel games loved by carnies everywhere.

The game is simple. A large, ornate wheel is mounted vertically a few feet above the floor. On it are 54 evenly spaced slots. Two show joker or house symbols; the other 52 are divided into $1, $2, $5, $10 and $20 denominations. There are usually 24 $1 slots and only two $20 slots. A *layout* in front of the wheel has squares matching those denominations. Players put cash or *chips* on the squares of their choice, and the wheel spins. When it stops, bettors who selected the correct denomination win, with the payoff determined by the dollar value of the winning slot. A $20 symbol pays off at 20:1; a $1 symbol pays off at *even money*. House or joker symbols pay off at 40:1, sometimes 45:1. As you might guess, the casino holds a serious *edge*, ranging from 11 per cent for a bet on the $1 symbol to 25.9 per cent on the joker. Don't be a sucker.

Poker

From the casino's point of view, poker isn't a good bet. In poker, gamblers bet against each other, not the house. A casino employee merely deals, acting as the cashier. The house's income is limited to a percentage taken from each *pot*,

The best Keno

The least of all the keno evils might be the **Gold Coast** (*see p116*) or the **Silverton** (*see p115*): the *house edge* on the eight-spot tickets here is a 'mere' 25 per cent, better than the 30 per cent edge at most other joints (but still awful odds).

or a seat rental of $5 or $7 per half-hour. This small sum is the main reason why many casinos opted out of the game in the 1990s.

However, thanks to the explosion in the popularity of poker over the past few years, many casinos are getting right back into it. Almost every month, a casino either opens a new poker room, expands an old room or reopens a closed one. The entire state of Nevada had 701 poker tables in 2005; in 2006, Las Vegas alone had a total of 809 tables. Statewide poker revenues for 2006 amounted to $161 million, a whopping 61 per cent increase from 2004. Another telling statistic: in 2002, 631 players competed in the $10,000-buy-in World Series of Poker, the granddaddy of all gambling tournaments, with the winner taking home a first-place prize of $1.1 million. Four years later, the player pool had grown more than tenfold to 8,000, with tournament winner Jamie Gold taking home a cool $12.5 million.

Blame television, which has cottoned on to the camera-friendliness of the game to dramatic effect. TV networks such as ESPN, Fox and even NBC now televise poker tournaments, celebrity matches, one-on-one showdowns and even dramas based on the game. Online poker is also growing at an amazing rate: a whole new generation of poker players are training on their computers for the big games and tournaments. However, while poker has arrived as a national pastime, it still has a way to go before overtaking blackjack as the biggest grossing table game in town. Whereas poker netted casinos $161 million in 2006, the same year saw blackjack yield an astonishing $1.38 billion.

PLAYING IN VEGAS

To join a poker game in a Las Vegas casino, just sit in an empty seat and *buy in* (which usually costs ten times the minimum or maximum bet, depending on the game) with *chips* or cash. If there's no space at any of the tables, put your name on a waiting list. The traditional rules that everyone knows are in effect for poker in Las Vegas: the most popular games are Texas hold 'em and seven-card stud, but many casinos in town have recently been experimenting with variations.

In Texas hold 'em, each player is dealt two cards face down, before five common cards are pitched up on to the *layout* for the table. The first three common cards appear together (this is called the 'flop'), followed by the fourth card (the 'turn') and the fifth card (the 'river'). Players determine their best five-card hand from the seven cards available to them. In seven-card stud, players get two cards face down and one face up, followed by three cards face up and a final card face down. Again, players then put together the best hand from their own seven cards.

Both of the above games have numerous rounds of betting and raising, so for all but the lowest-stakes games, a hefty *bankroll* is crucial. For games with betting limits, posted signs indicate the smallest and largest bet allowable (usually in the form '$5/$10'). In a limit game, you'll need a *bankroll* of at least 20 times the maximum bet. There are also *pot*-limit games, which means raises can go as high as the *pot*, and no-limit games, in which raises can go as

high as the largest *bankroll* on the table. In all games, no matter the stakes, players are not allowed to bring more money to the table once a hand is dealt. If a player goes 'all in', betting all his or her money, and he or she can't match another player's raise, a side *pot* is formed for those who wish to continue betting. The all-in player is limited to playing for the main *pot*.

Explaining poker strategy here is impossible. Besides the complexities of the game itself, much of poker is psychological. Reading other players and bluffing are a huge part of the process; if you didn't know this already, you'll learn the first time you sit down in a card room. If you're not a seasoned poker player, be very careful of high-stakes games, which can be populated by sharks (sometimes operating in teams). They've learned the main casino secret: it's easy to take money from amateur gamblers. If you're a novice, stick to low-stakes games, which are usually straightforward and friendly.

The best Poker games

You might as well play pin the tail on the Caribbean stud donkey: most casinos in Las Vegas deal the game with low minimums, *progressive jackpot*s and bad odds. However, the **Golden Nugget** (*see p104*) in Downtown Vegas has had the fastest *progressive* meter for a couple of years. For Let it Ride, try **O'Shea's** (3355 Las Vegas Boulevard South, 697 2711): many see it as the best place to play this high-*house edge* game, due to the low minimums required.

CARIBBEAN STUD
Caribbean stud is a rather dumb game with a *house edge* of 5.27 per cent, just a hair worse than double-zero roulette. Sitting around a table with a *layout* similar to blackjack, players put out a single *ante* and receive five cards face down. The dealer also gets five cards, though one is dealt face up. At this point, players either fold (and lose their *ante*) or 'call' by adding a bet that's twice their *ante*. All players then reveal

their cards. If the dealer doesn't 'qualify' with at least an ace and king in his or her hand, all players win *even money* for their *ante* and the call bets are returned. Should the dealer's hand qualify, each player's hand is compared against the dealer's. If the player wins, the *ante* is paid at *even money* and the call bet qualifies for a 'bonus' payout based on the hand. Bonus payouts range from *even money* for a pair to 100:1 for a royal flush (most of the payouts are lower than those found in Let it Ride; *see below*).

The maximum bonus payout in Caribbean stud is usually capped somewhere between $5,000 and $60,000, so make sure your bet is no higher than it needs to be to win that amount. For example, if the bonus payout is capped at $5,000, your *ante* should never be above $25: this would make your call bet $50 and so a 100:1 payout would hit the $5,000 ceiling exactly. The simple math? Divide the maximum bonus payout by 200. Your *ante* should never exceed that figure.

For a side bet of another dollar per hand, Caribbean stud poker also offers players the chance to hit a *progressive jackpot* with payoffs based on the quality of their hand. A royal flush wins 100 per cent of the jackpot, while a flush gets a mere $50. The fact that jackpots have been known to go up to $5 million tells you something about how often a royal flush occurs.

LET IT RIDE

Let it Ride offers the unusual feature of allowing players to take back two thirds of their wager. Players bet three equal amounts and are dealt three cards face down. Two common cards are then dealt, also face down. At this point, players can pull back one of their bets by signalling to the dealer (don't touch your *chips*). When the first common card is turned over, players can withdraw their second bet. The final common card is then shown and payouts are made according to a fixed schedule, ranging from *even money* for a pair of tens or better to 1,000:1 for a royal flush. As you might guess, the payouts are way below *true odds*. For instance, the odds against drawing a flush are 508:1, but the payout is eight to one. Overall, the house holds about a four per cent *edge*, if players make all the right decisions.

The biggest lure of Let it Ride is that players compete against the cards, not each other, so it's more appealing to amateurs. Also, the option to withdraw two thirds of the bet gives players the illusion that their money is lasting longer than it might in other games. However, don't be fooled: the *house edge* grinds down almost everyone in the end. And since it's basically five-card stud, it can be a long time between winning hands.

Poker dos and don'ts

DO...

Know the rules If you don't know how to play, attend a poker class at a casino and learn the basics, or learn at one of the many free poker websites. When in doubt at a game, ask the dealer, not the other players.

Be ready Pay attention. When it's your turn to act, do so with alacrity. A surefire way to raise the hackles of other players is to drag down the game with long deliberations. But don't jump the gun, either. Always wait until it's your turn before acting.

Handle your chips properly Stack your *chips* in such a way that other players and dealer can tell what you're betting. 'Splashing' *chips* into the *pot* is rude and disruptive. Also, push your *chips* out in one move; 'stringing' your bets a few at a time is a bad move.

Ask for comps All players get free drinks. You can swipe your player's card to track your time; you usually get about a dollar in *comp* value for every hour. However, not all casinos use this system; be sure to ask how to get food *comps* and room discounts for your play.

DON'T...

Be an asshole Most of the problems that crop up at a poker table are due to bad or uncouth behaviour. Don't use foul language. Don't abuse other players. Don't hit on other players. Don't throw temper tantrums. Lose graciously and win graciously.

Blurt Don't be the peanut gallery at the table. Speculating on hand possibilities or, worse, talking about cards you just mucked can lead to all kinds of unfair advantages and recriminations. Likewise, after you've mucked your hand, stay out of it. You can inadvertently provide too much information to players still in the hand by reacting to the community cards.

Eat at the table or smoke at a non-smoking table The main problem with bringing food to a poker table is that the cards get greasy. And lighting up in a non-smoking area is one of the easiest ways to get beat up in a poker game, either verbally or physically. Even at smoking tables, there's no smoking at the seat on each side of the dealer.

PAI GOW POKER

Pai gow poker – not to be confused with pai gow, a Chinese game that utilises tiles – is played with a 53-card deck, a standard deck plus a wild joker. Players get seven cards, which they assemble into a five-card hand and a two-card hand. The five-card hand must score higher than the two-card hand. The object is to beat both the banker's hands. The banker wins all hands that tie; if a player wins only one hand, it's a *push*. The house or any player can be the banker. Winning hands are paid at *even money*, minus a five per cent commission.

If it sounds intimidating, don't worry; the dealer will help you arrange your cards in such a way as to maximise your two hands. Once you've watched a few hands, it's easy to get the hang of it. Pai gow poker is a lot slower – and friendlier – than blackjack or mini-baccarat, so it's a good game to play if you want to relax, socialise, or play as few hands as possible in a given period of time (more *comps*, less risk).

Roulette

Roulette doesn't have much of a fan club in the US. That's partly due to the calm nature of the game: Americans want action and speed when they gamble, and roulette gives them neither. Another reason is a subtle but crucial change in the US version. In Europe, roulette wheels typically have 36 numbered slots and one zero slot. On most American wheels, there are two zero slots (marked as zero and double zero). That change alone nearly doubles the *house edge* to 5.26 per cent, as compared to 2.7 per cent on single-zero wheels.

Roulette is simple to play. The wheel is mounted horizontally and a matching table *layout* serves as the betting area. All numbers are coloured red or black except for the zero and double zero, which are green. Players place their *chips* on the *layout*, before a ball is launched on to a spinning wheel. The ball comes to rest in a slot, and the winners are paid off at set odds. To minimise confusion about who made which bet, each player receives individually coloured 'wheel' *chips* when they *buy in*; these *chips* can only be used at the roulette table.

The easiest wager is a straight-up bet, where the player drops a *chip* on a single number. (Apparently, 17 is the most popular, due both to its central location and to the fact that James Bond bets it in the movies.) If the ball settles on your number, the bet will be paid off at 35:1. You can also make bets on groups of numbers: on lines separating numbers, on rows of numbers, or in special areas denoting odd or even, red or black and so on. In this way, a single bet covers anywhere

The boys in the bubble

NASCAR racing meets the World Series of Poker in the Poker Dome Challenge, the world's only high-speed high-tech MTV-generation arena-poker competition. Played in a custom-designed, sound-proofed glass bubble, this is spectator poker taken to an almost illogical extreme. Spectators can see into the bubble in which the game is taking place, and can follow every aspect of it on video screens, but the players can't see or hear anything outside the game itself.

The main TV monitor for the audience shows the whole table, while each player has two dedicated smaller screens. One of those projects a constant close-up, while the other reveals the player's hole cards and chip counts; the screens also display his or her heart rate. The chips are embedded with radio-frequency identification (RFID) sensors, so the chip counts are updated after every bet. And the cards themselves contain RFID sensors, which means that the spectators know the cards in the big blind before the player. Players have a mere 15 seconds to

check, bet, call, raise or fold; if they fail to do so before a series of red lights have flashed, they forfeit the hand.

The first season of the **Poker Dome Challenge** tournament began in May 2006 and ran for 43 weeks. Having qualified for one of the 216 available spots by winning daily freeroll tournaments at mansionpoker.net, six players faced off in a game of Texas hold 'em each week for a $25,000 prize. The winner of each of these 36 preliminary rounds took home $25K and advanced to one of six semi-finals. The six semi-final winners then went forward to the million-dollar final, eventually won by a 40-year-old mortgage clerk from Iowa named Rodel Tuazon.

During its first run, Poker Dome Challenge aired on FSN (Fox Sports Net) on Sundays at 11pm, and the second season looks likely to occupy a similar time slot. However, audience tickets are available for the recordings, which are held at 5pm on Saturdays and/or Sundays: go to TVTickets.com and scroll down the list to 'Poker Dome Challenge'.

from two to 18 numbers. Needless to say, the more numbers covered by the wager, the lower the payoff. For instance, betting odd or even pays *even money*.

The variety of wagers makes roulette an interesting game, especially if you like the languid pace. However, the odds are tough. Your best bet is to find a casino with a single-zero wheel – these come and go on occasion – and try to look elegant while losing.

Slot machines

Slot machines were once shunned by 'real' gamblers, patronised only by their bored wives and girlfriends or first-time casino goers who

The best Roulette

Single-zero roulette wheels come and go with some frequency in Las Vegas, but the best bet for the past couple of years has been the **MGM Grand** (*see p81*), which at any given time can have up to three wheels with a 2.7 per cent *house edge*. Several other casinos have single-zero wheels, but they're often either closed or have outrageous minimums.

Cheapskates unafraid of double-zero roulette should head for **El Cortez** (*see p106*) Downtown, or **Casino Royale** (*see p89*) on the Strip. Tokens are a mere quarter, making this a cheap way to have fun.

knew nothing more about gambling than how to drop coins into a slot. How times have changed. These days, they're the most popular and profitable part of the entire casino industry, so much so that some smaller casinos offer nothing but slots and video poker (*see p61*).

Novice gamblers prefer slots because there's little to learn and no pressure from dealers or other players. Put in money, pull the handle (or, more often nowadays, press the spin button) and in a few seconds, you're either a winner or a loser. Simple. What's more, jackpots can reach millions of dollars. But there is a downside, and a big one. Slots give the house an *edge* from two to 25 per cent, often making them one of the worst bets in the casino. And your chance of hitting a million-dollar jackpot is… well, what's the tiniest unit of measurement you can imagine? Smaller than that. Way smaller.

The basic slot machine in Las Vegas accepts a maximum of either two or three coins; some take four or five, some just one, and a new breed of slots is now able to take hundreds of coins, including pennies. Each coin beyond the minimum increases the payout proportionally (twice as much for two coins, triple for three) should a winning combination appear. In most cases, the winnings on betting the maximum number of coins are exponentially higher; almost always, the posted jackpot can only be won by betting the maximum number of coins on the winning pull/spin. What's more, many machines have multiple pay lines; on these machines, an added pay line is activated each time another coin is wagered. Always check the pay tables at the top of the machine.

Modern slots usually have a coin counter that displays your credits. Instead of coins crashing into the stainless-steel bin, wins are registered as credits. There's usually a bill changer on the machine: players can simply slide in a $20 bill, for example, and $20 worth of credits appear on the counter. Bets are made by pulling a handle or pressing a 'Spin' button. When you're done, hit the 'Cash Out' button and one of two things will happen. In older machines, coins equal to the unused credits will drop into the bin; the casino provides plastic cups to carry coins to other machines or the cashier. However, most slots these days are 'coinless'; when you hit 'Cash Out', you'll receive a voucher that can be redeemed at a ticket machine, a change booth or the *cage*, or fed into another slot machine and used as credits.

Slots fall into two categories: non-*progressive*, aka regular, and *progressive*. Regular slots have fixed payouts, which are posted on the front of the machine. *Progressive* slots offer a fixed payout schedule, but also offer the chance to hit a huge jackpot. This jackpot, funded by a percentage of every coin wagered, grows continuously until somebody wins it. A meter above the machines displays a running total of the current jackpot.

Many *progressive* slots are linked to form a system that feeds the jackpot. These machines might be from one *carousel* in a single casino, with a jackpot that resets at $1,000 and grows

from there, or spread across casinos state-wide, yielding multi-million-dollar jackpots. With literally hundreds of machines in the system, jackpots can reach astronomical levels. The Megabucks *linked progressive*, for example, consists of more than 700 machines; the world record slot jackpot of nearly $40 million was hit in March 2003 at the Excalibur by a 25-year-old computer programmer. Though rare, these payouts are well publicised, not least because they make excellent bait.

NEW SLOTS

A few years ago, video machines with oversized screens, multiple games and other gimmicks were all the rage. Today, a new generation of slots is being developed. New machines are more interactive and look a lot like video poker; on these slots, you'll be able to make choices about which symbols to hold or discard, based on a certain internal and intuitive logic. Slots are more fun to play today than they were even ten years ago, when they were still primarily 'one-armed bandits'; table-game players derisively referred to them as the 'idiot pull'.

However, these machines still won't line your pockets. Slot (and video poker) machines now account for upwards of 65 per cent of total casino revenues, which means that they take in twice as much revenue as all other casino games combined. Of the $12.6 billion won by Nevada casinos in 2006, $8.3 billion – just under 66 per cent – came from slots and video poker.

HOW SLOTS WORK

Modern slots are controlled by a computer chip called a random number generator, which churns out strings of numbers regardless of whether the game is being played. Pulling the handle (or pressing the spin button) on a machine releases the reels and selects one of these numbers. Each number corresponds to a certain set of symbols on the reels, which determines the outcome. The force of the pull has nothing to do with the point at which the reels stop rotating.

Regulating the payout amounts to computer science. By adjusting the random number generator, a slot technician can make a machine *tighter* or *looser*. In the old days, slots often had a built-in *edge* of 20 to 30 per cent, but the players flocked to the machines with the higher returns. Casinos did the sums and realised it was better to get five per cent of a lot than 30 per cent of nothing; hence, most Vegas slots now return between 92 and 95 per cent of the *drop* (less on nickel machines), leaving the *house edge* at between five and eight per cent. In 2006, $138 billion was bet on slots in Nevada; the casinos' win of $8.3 billion equates to an overall hold of six per cent.

Certain casinos boldly advertise 98 or 99 per cent payouts, but the small print is crucial. In such circumstances, the payout is usually 'up to 99 per cent', which could mean that a single machine on the floor might be set at 98 or 99 per cent, if that. Short of running 2,000 to 5,000 plays through similar machines and comparing payouts, there's no way to find out which slots are set *tight* or *loose*. Payout percentages are supposedly verified by the state Gaming Control Board, but it rarely checks unless a casino advertises something truly absurd.

The real advantage for the house comes with the constant repetition of slot plays. For instance, say that a player with $50 starts betting $1 per pull on a quarter machine, via four 25¢ bets per pull. Sometimes the player wins and those winnings are reinvested: the *drop* might only be $50, but if they're playing at a reasonable speed, they could end up giving the casino $240 of action every hour. The six per cent *edge* is enough for a slot machine to retain about $14 an hour (six per cent of $240), a hold equal to more than a quarter of the original *bankroll*. With a little less luck, that money could vanish even faster. And over time, even an *edge* of half of one per cent grinds down players, which is why so many of them stumble away from machines empty-handed. That and the fact that the payout percentage factors in the big and seldom-won jackpots.

SLOT TIPS

Slot jockeys say non-*progressive* machines are *looser* (the technical term for this is 'hit frequency') than *progressive* machines, though payouts are smaller (again, the technical term is 'average payback'). Non-*progressive* machines that give smaller top payouts are reportedly *looser* than those that give large top payouts. Similarly, among *progressive* machines, those with smaller jackpots hit more often. In fact, the amount of your bet that goes to the *progressive jackpot* is an indication of payout frequency. According to one executive, if the amount is less than one per cent, the *progressive* machine is likely to have more non-jackpot winners. If three to five per cent of every bet goes towards the *progressive jackpot*, the game is seriously weighted toward fewer large payouts.

It gets more complicated. Machines with high hit frequencies pay out small amounts. Those with low hit frequencies pay out less frequently overall, but when they do pay out, each return is higher. And there's no correlation between hit frequency and average payback: hit frequency can be high while average payback is low and vice versa, or both can be low or high. Of course, none of this information is posted in a casino, so players are mostly flying blind. Some believe that slots placed near doorways and aisles are *looser* than others. And one casino executive has said that house machines, those with the casino's name and logo on them, are more generous than non-house-brand slots.

The only recommendation that makes any sense is that if you're going to play the slots for big money, bet the maximum number of coins on each pull. That way, if lightning strikes and you're a winner, you'll get the

The best Slots

Reliable statistics on whose slots are the *loosest* are notoriously rare. A survey of the city's nickel slots carried out by Michael Shackleford for the *Las Vegas Advisor* in 2002 ranked the **Palms** (93.42 per cent payback; *see p98*), the **Gold Coast** (92.84 per cent; *see p116*) and the **Sahara** (92.81 per cent; *see p92*) as the top three casinos, and **Mandalay Bay** (87.51 per cent; *see p71*), the **Bellagio** (87.42 per cent; *see p68*) and the **Venetian** (86.66 per cent; *see p75*) as the three worst. But things may well have changed since then, and dramatically at that.

biggest payout possible. Avoid pumping cash into slots in non-casino locations such as convenience stores, which have a *house edge* one step below thievery. And, of course, never put a nickel into a slot machine without first having inserted your *players club* card into the reader. As long as you're playing the house's favourite game, you might as well get a bit of your play returned in the form of cashback or *comps*.

Slots can only pay out so many coins at any one time, so if you hit a monster jackpot, stay put and wait for an attendant to arrive. If you walk away, someone might claim your prize. The attendant will inform you of your tax obligations. US citizens need to fill out IRS paperwork on slot wins of more than $1,200; the tax situation varies for non-nationals.

PLAYERS CLUBS

Virtually every casino has a *players club*, the main aims of which are to keep track of a customer's slot and video poker play and to retain customer loyalty by providing rewards in the form of points that can be redeemed for hard cash or merchandise. Many clubs offer introductory gifts such as free buffets, bonus points, rebates on losses or other perks to get your name on the dotted line.

All *players clubs* issue their members with an ID card, which should be inserted into the slot or video poker machine to allow the machine's computer to track the amount of play. Points awarded by the computer are then redeemable for cash or for *comps* in the casino's restaurants and at the shows. Members also

qualify for discounts in the resort's shops, for reduced room rates, and for tickets to parties, barbecues and special tournaments.

Players club benefits change frequently. You can get an idea of what the various clubs are offering by checking out the Las Vegas Advisor, or the 'Best Bets' section of the Friday edition of the *Las Vegas Review-Journal* newspaper. All it takes to join a *players club* are a picture ID and a few minutes at the slot booth. Some casinos even have roving recruiters who'll sign you up at the machine. Membership is always free.

Sports betting

Thanks in no small part to Frank 'Lefty' Rosenthal, the casino executive whose life was dramatised in the movie *Casino*, betting on sports in Vegas is now a cult all of its own. Almost every casino has a sports book, at which money is gambled on countless aspects of the outcomes of pro sports and college games. They're lively and passionate places on big game days, such as Sundays during the football season; even if you're not betting, they're often good places to watch the action. Whatever sports wagers you make and wherever you make them, remember that cellphones and two-way communicators are prohibited in or near the sports books, a policy that's strictly and universally enforced.

Glance up at the vast boards and you might think that sports betting here is tough to understand. It's not, but it is hard to beat the system and come away rich.

THE MONEY LINE

Most of the sports on which you can bet (baseball, boxing, football, hockey, basketball) offer 'money lines', which lay the odds on the favourite or take the odds on the underdog. Take the following baseball-related example:

Boston Red Sox   + 145
New York Yankees   – 160

This means that you must bet $16 on the Yankees to win $10 (plus your stake back). However, you need bet only $10 on the Red Sox to win $14.50. The favourite team is always the one with the '–' prefix, with the underdog denoted by '+'. (Unlike in European sports, the home team is always listed second.)

OTHER BETS

There's a large variety of bets in the Vegas sports books. Here, though, are two of the more common ones. Both of them even the odds so that punters can make a 'straight bet', which here means putting up $11 to win $10 (plus your $11 stake back). In team games, one popular bet is on the margin of victory, or the 'point spread'. Take, for example, these odds for the 2007 Super Bowl.

Indianapolis Colts   – 7
Chicago Bears

This means that the Colts were favoured to beat the Bears by seven points. Everyone favouring the Colts on the point spread was betting on them to win by more than seven points, while everyone favouring the Bears was betting on either a Bears victory or a Colts win by fewer than seven points. The game ended Colts 29, Bears 17. The Colts won the game and also covered the point spread, meaning that everyone who bet on them won. If the Colts had beaten the Bears by exactly seven points, it's a *push*, and all money is refunded.

Another popular bet is to gamble on the total number of points scored in any given game. The casino advertises the total number of points they think will be scored in the game, and gamblers decide if they think the actual number will be higher or lower. This is known as the 'over/under'; like the point spread, this pays off at 10:11 odds. As above, if the outcome matches the casino's prediction, it's a *push*, and all bets are refunded.

Video poker

This electronic cousin of live poker enjoys a huge following in Las Vegas. Although a video poker machine resembles a slot machine and is typically located on the slot floor, it is an entirely different beast. Make no mistake about it: video poker is a game not of chance but of skill. If played perfectly, the *house edge* can often be flattened to zero or even pushed into the negative, which means a return to players of more than 100 per cent. Casinos can only afford to operate their machines in this way because perfect play is the province of the merest handful of experts, those people who use powerful computer programs to work out strategies that are accurate to within ten thousandths of a percentage point.

A video poker screen displays a five-card hand of draw poker, with every deal coming from a freshly shuffled 52-card deck. Buttons allow the player to hold or replace the dealt cards. After the draw, the game pays off according to a payout schedule listed on the screen. A pair of aces might pay *even money*, while a royal flush usually pays out at a rate of 4,000:1. Most basic poker rules are in effect as far as hand rankings go (minus 'kickers', or unpaired or unsuited high cards, on all but one or two variations), but the psychological angle is jettisoned. You're playing against a machine that doesn't respond to bluffing, so the quality of your hand is everything.

There's no way to summarise basic strategy for video poker, partly because it's extremely complex and partly because the game comes in so many different varieties. Each variety of video poker has its own unique characteristics such as wild cards and bonus options, giving rise to different pay tables and different strategies. You can buy video poker strategy

The best Sports betting

The 'super books' in the giant Strip casinos are the most popular in town, especially those at **Caesars Palace** (*see p68*), the **Mirage** (*see p73*) and **Bellagio** (*see p68*). Some, the Mirage included, have individual TV monitors on the seats; the book at the **Imperial Palace** (*see p80*) has individual monitors and tiered seating for the big screens.

Two books stand out. The **Las Vegas Hilton** (*see p97*) has the original 'Super Book'. The manager is a proposition-bet freak; he puts up wild prop bets year-long, and posted 250 of them for the 2005 Super Bowl. The **Palms** (*see p98*) also likes its props and sometimes attracts players with reduced *vig* (bet $10.50 to win $10).

cards (Huntington Press produces a good set), which allow you to make the right decision on every hand; in essence, you'll be playing computer-perfect strategy.

The most basic variation of video poker is 'Jacks or Better' (JoB), which plays most like five-card stud (no wild cards) and pays out on pairs of jacks or better. The strategies for JoB are pretty much intuitive for anyone who already knows how to play poker, but some rules have to be learned: for example, you never hold a kicker (a high-value card to be held along with a pair); you never draw to a four-card inside straight (for example, you're holding 3, 4, 6, 7 and you're looking for a 5); and you always go for a royal flush if you hold four of the cards required for it, even if it means sacrificing a flush, a pair or a straight in the process.

As with slots, it's wise to play the maximum number of coins, as this greatly increases the top payout for a royal flush. Another tip: be sure to play 'full-pay' games as opposed to their 'short-pay' brethren. For instance, in JoB, the full-pay version returns 9:1 on a full house and 6:1 on a flush; it's called a '9/6' machine. On the short-pay version, it's sliced to 8/5, 7/5 or even 6/5. The only reason to play a short-pay version of JoB would be if it was connected to

a *progressive jackpot* or paid off on a pair of tens or better. However, 8/5 Bonus, with extra payouts for four-of-a-kind, is a different animal, as are Double Bonus, Double Double Bonus, Triple Bonus and Double Triple Bonus variations. Then there's Joker Poker, plus many different varieties of Deuces Wild.

Video poker players should consult the books and reports on the market that detail proper play for sample video poker hands. There are excellent computer programmes available that tutor players in strategies. Casinos don't mind if you refer to strategy charts while playing, but they draw the line at laptops. Since it's impossible to absorb the tactics for all the possible variations at once, we recommend you study and master strategy for JoB, then, as you feel more comfortable, move on to more complex and rewarding games such as the full-pay Deuces Wild and Double Bonus varieties.

The latest varieties of machine to become all the rage in Las Vegas are multi-play machines, such as Triple-Play, Five-Play, Ten-Play, 50-Play and even 100-Play. Here, three, five, ten, 50 and 100 hands of video poker are dealt at the same time from the equivalent number of decks, requiring three, five, ten, 50, and 100 times the bet. The twist is that only the cards in the bottom hand are displayed on the deal. When you hold cards from the hand, the held cards appear in all the upper hands; when you draw, all the hands' cards are filled in around the held cards.

In Spin Poker, when you discard cards, the open spots spin like slot reels. Heads Up Poker, meanwhile, combines live poker with video poker. You're dealt five cards and you bet the hand. The machine responds by calling, raising or folding (and sometimes bluffing). You play out the video poker hand, but you still have the live hand to be resolved.

The best Video poker

In general, the best pay schedules and *comp* systems on 25¢ video poker in Las Vegas are at the locals' casinos; the **Silverton** (*see p115*) and the **Palms** (*see p98*) are widely regarded as the best of the bunch.

Casinos
& Hotels

Bellagio. *See p68*.

LIGHTS, CAMERA, PLANET HOLLYWOOD.

planet hollywood™
RESORT & CASINO · LAS VEGAS

planethollywoodresort.com

Casinos & Hotels

Stay a while, play a while...

And still it changes, and grows, and improves. Six decades ago, Vegas was framed around Downtown, a raffish cluster of buildings that provided little more than lairy gaming arenas and a few scruffy bedrooms. In the 1940s, a number of large resorts opened several miles away on deserted highway, spurring a boom that saw the city reinvent itself as a swanky resort town. After a decade of the doldrums, in 1989, Steve Wynn opened the **Mirage** (*see p73*) and inspired an eight-year regeneration of Las Vegas Boulevard, during which period a dozen casinos were built from scratch. And in 2005, after a spell when work was limited to expansion of existing casinos rather than the construction of new operations, Wynn returned with **Wynn Las Vegas** (*see p76*), raising the bar once again for aspiring casino operators and prompting yet more improvement works among his rivals.

The industry is always building something new: a 1,000-room tower, a 4,000-seat theatre, a 100-unit shopping mall (the latest trend). And hotel-casinos that don't expand are quick to change; it's a case of adapt or die. If you've not been to Vegas for four or five years, the changes will be noticeable. But even if you were here six months ago, you'll still see something new.

Staying in Las Vegas

Though you could plump for an alternative – a motel, a hostel, even an RV park – the majority of visitors to Las Vegas stay where the action is: a hotel-casino. These often-vast complexes, which line the Strip and clutter Downtown, are where most tourists spend upwards of 90 per cent of their time. All have casinos, restaurants, bars and assorted entertainments, alongside other amenities that range from the predictable (pools, malls) to the truly exceptional (zoos, rollercoasters). And all, of course, have guestrooms, from the 100 or so offered at the **Golden Gate** (*see p108*) to the 6,000-plus at the **MGM Grand** (*see p81*).

Visitors to Las Vegas once spent very little time in their gaming-subsidised guestrooms, which is why rooms in hotel-casinos built before 1989 are small-ish. But during the 1990s, casino moguls realised the value of providing guests with a nice place to sleep: rooms in newer hotel-casinos are brighter and more capacious. Phones, TVs (with cable) and air-conditioning are standard in rooms within Las Vegas hotel-casinos, which all offer free parking. Beyond that, it's a crapshoot.

Catch sight of some rare desert greenery at the **Bellagio**. *See p68.*

WHERE TO STAY

The vast majority of visitors stay on the three-mile stretch of Las Vegas Boulevard South that runs from the Mandalay Bay resort north to the Sahara, aka the Strip. Most never leave it. The Strip is where you'll find almost all the city's most glamorous, upscale and eye-catching resorts, as well as a number of its best bargains. If you want to stay on the Strip, remember it's a long (and, in summer, debilitating) hike from one end to the other. It's not enough simply to stay at a property with a Las Vegas Boulevard South address; the street number is also crucial.

The range of properties on the Strip is not as huge as it was a half-decade ago: most historic mid-century hotels and motels have been levelled in the name of progress. However, there's still variety. Note that while some hotel amenities are off-limits to non-guests, many others are open to everyone (bars, restaurants, clubs, shows). Access to spas, for which see p206, varies by hotel; most are open to the public, but a few limit access to their own guests.

There are, of course, hotels in other parts of town. A handful of big resorts are located just off the Strip, chief among them the **Hard Rock** (see p96) and the **Palms** (see p98). **Downtown**, the hub of Las Vegas until the 1950s, can't compete with the Strip in the glamour stakes, but you'll find bargains galore. Near the Convention Center sit hotels aimed squarely at the business traveller. And although the Station casinos are chiefly frequented by locals, a few of them – chiefly **Sunset Station** (see p117), **Red Rock Resort** (see p112) and **Green Valley Ranch** (see p111) – are well worth investigating.

RATES AND RESERVATIONS

Las Vegas has more rooms than anywhere in the world: roughly 130,000 in total, with the numbers still rising. However, with 40 million visitors a year, it needs them. Some weeks, bargains abound in even the poshest properties; at other times, you'll need to book way ahead if you want to avoid sleeping in your car.

Rates fluctuate wildly depending on the date: the same room can quadruple in price from one night to the next. You'll often find exceptional deals midweek and/or during off-season, when $200 rooms can go for a quarter of their rack rate. At weekends, though, prices skyrocket, and a two-night minimum is in effect almost everywhere. Steer clear of major conventions, too; we've listed these on pp109-110, but for a full list, see www.lvcva.com.

The best **Casinos & hotels**

For unrestrained luxury

Wynn Las Vegas (see p76) and the **Bellagio** (see p68) are the Strip's most upscale hotels, but the Mansion and the Skylofts at the **MGM Grand** (see p81) are also super-smart.

For unadulterated fun

The city that never sleeps comes to the city that never sleeps in the shape of **New York New York** (see p84).

For Sin City on a budget

The best deals are off the Strip. Downtown, try the **Golden Nugget** (see p104) or the **Vegas Club** (see p110); elsewhere, the **Station casinos** (see pp116-118) offer great rates.

For hyperhip nightlife

Don't let the ubiquity of Paris Hilton put you off: the **Palms** (see p98) just about edges the **Hard Rock** (see p96) and the **MGM Grand** (see p81) in the after-hours stakes.

For cheap thrills

Ride the rollercoasters at the **Sahara** (see p92) or the **Stratosphere** (see p93).

For fabulous food

Caesars Palace (see p68), the **MGM Grand** (see p81) and the **Venetian** (see p75) are the three best bets for a memorable meal.

For a game of poker

Binion's (see p106) has the history and the **Rio** (see p100) has the World Series of Poker, but the **Bellagio** (see p68) has the best players and the biggest pots.

For new Vegas

Look no further than the slew of soon-to-open resorts: the **Palazzo** (see p75), **Encore** (see p76) and **Trump International** (see p95).

For old Vegas

Vegas doesn't get much older than the **Golden Gate** (see p108): built in 1906, it's holding its own amid the Downtown changes.

For escaping the action

The **Artisan** (see p102), the **Four Seasons** (see p95), **Thehotel at Mandalay Bay** (see p95), the **Platinum** (see p101) and the **Ritz-Carlton, Lake Las Vegas** (see p118) all lack casinos.

For one night in a double room, expect to pay $40-$100 in a budget hotel-casino, $70-$200 in a mid-range operation, and $150 and up in a first-class property. In addition to these basic rates, rooms are subject to hotel tax (11 per cent Downtown, nine per cent elsewhere). You can book either by phone or online with almost every property in the city.

Playing in Las Vegas

Depending on the time and location, the action on Vegas's casino floors can be fast and furious, as slot players hammer 'spin' buttons, blackjack players celebrate 21s and crap players whoop it up in the dice pit. The scene is played out to the soundtrack of clinking glasses, rattling chips, tinkling coins and the electronic arpeggios of slot machines. It's overwhelming.

Still, with the nationwide spread of gambling, the experience has been dumbed down from the high-rolling James Bond image, and there's little required etiquette: common sense and common courtesy should see you through. Any outfit will do, from shorts to a dinner jacket, though you may want to carry a watch (clocks are conspicuous by their absence) and a sweater (the air-con is always cranked to the max).

Playing in Las Vegas is no longer just about gambling: casino attractions have evolved with the times. The circus acts at **Circus Circus** (*see p89*) and the dancing fountains at the **Bellagio** (*see p68*) remain, but resorts have also embraced adulthood. Nightclubs are all the rage, though you'll need to win big at the tables if you want to really enjoy yourself within their swanky confines.

About this chapter

This section is divided geographically, with each area subdivided into hotel-casinos and non-casino properties. The majority of the hotels are either right on the **Strip** or very close to it (a loose area that we call **Off-Strip**), and range from the incomparably luxurious to the hopelessly dissolute. In **Downtown** Las Vegas, the properties are smaller, less Disneyfied and cheaper. Casinos in the **Rest of the City** appeal more to locals than visitors, but compensate for their lack of frills with a full array of gambling and good-value eating options.

> ❶ Green numbers given in this chapter correspond to the location of each hotel on the street maps. *See pp333-336.*

LISTINGS INFORMATION

The address we've given for each casino is its main entrance. This is the place to arrive whether you're on foot or in a car. Here you'll find the valet parking (for hotels that offer it) and directions to self-parking: some casinos have extra entrances at the side and/or round the back. These can be essential if you don't want to spend hours stuck in traffic driving along the choked up Strip.

Each hotel-casino review has four headings: **Accommodation**, a survey of the guestrooms; **Eating & drinking**, where you'll find details on each hotel's bars and restaurants (many of these are also reviewed elsewhere; follow the cross-references for fuller critiques); **Entertainment**, detailing the main shows and lounges (again, follow the cross-references for more information); and **Gambling**, which provides an overview of the gaming facilities. Reviews of non-casino hotels are shorter for one key reason: there's less to review.

At the end of each review, we have detailed the property's key **Amenities** and the specific range of **Gambling** it offers. Bear in mind that table minimums are subject to change and can rise at night.

The Strip

Almost two thirds of the hotel rooms in Las Vegas are on the Strip, the stretch of Las Vegas Boulevard between the 'Welcome to Fabulous Las Vegas' sign and Sahara Avenue. Furthest south are **Mandalay Bay** (plus the **Four Seasons Las Vegas** and **Thehotel at Mandalay Bay**) and the **Luxor**. A little north, at the junction of Tropicana Avenue, are four large casinos: the **Tropicana**, the **Excalibur**, **New York New York** and the **MGM Grand**. The **Monte Carlo** is just north of NYNY, just by the massive construction site that will eventually become CityCenter (*see pp28-31*).

The centre of the Strip has the biggest cluster of hotel-casinos: **Planet Hollywood** and **Paris Las Vegas** are followed to the north by **Bally's**, the **Bellagio**, **Barbary Coast** and **Caesars Palace**, all at the junction with Flamingo Road; it's the liveliest corner of the city. Slightly further north, past the **Flamingo**, the **Imperial Palace**, **Harrah's**, **Casino Royale** and the **Venetian**, is the intersection with Spring Mountain/Sands Avenue, home to **Treasure Island**, the Fashion Show Mall and **Wynn Las Vegas**. North of here is the new **Trump International**, **Circus Circus**, the **Riviera** and, a long block north, the **Sahara**.

Hotel-casinos

Expensive

Bellagio
3600 Las Vegas Boulevard South, at W Flamingo Road, Las Vegas, NV 89109 (reservations 1-888 987 6667/front desk & casino 693 7111/www. bellagio.com). Bus Deuce, 202/self-parking Las Vegas Boulevard South/valet parking Las Vegas Boulevard South or W Flamingo Road. **Rooms** 3,933. **Rates** $159-$859 double. **Credit** AmEx, DC, Disc, MC, V. **Map** p336 A7 ❶

Since the Spa Tower opened at the Bellagio in 2005, the property seems to have paused for a breather. Sure, it's added the Adam Tihany-designed **Club Prive**, a high-limit gambling lounge that spotlights unbelievably rare spirits and world-class cigars. Granted, it's redone the poker room, and all the suites in the original tower will start getting a makeover by the end of 2007. And yes, there are more Picassos coming to the fine art gallery in 2008. Otherwise, though, why tamper with a winning formula?

The Bellagio continues to evoke a supersized, all-American Italian villa, complete with an eight-acre lake fronting the Strip, a lush garden conservatory that changes with the holidays and an elegant pool area that's been reimagined as a formal Italian garden. And it remains the archetypal playground for the well-heeled adult, with high-minded, grown-up entertainment in the form of posh restaurants, a tiny but tony promenade of boutiques, and Cirque du Soleil's most sophisticated show. The expanded spa in the Spa Tower features a salon, a fitness centre and even a one-chair barbershop; it's a lavish perk available only to guests, as is access to the renowned Shadow Creek golf course. But the most eye-catching attraction is the signature fountain, which, in the afternoons and evenings, shoots water into the air to a variety of different soundtracks. The sidewalk on the Strip in front of the hotel offers superb views, as do the Bellagio's lakefront restaurants and bars. *Photo p65.*

Accommodation
Bellagio's 3,933 rooms are large and beautifully furnished. The beds all have Serta mattresses, and the spacious, marble-floored bathrooms come with deep-soaking tubs and private-label amenities. Flat-screen TVs (27-inchers), electronic drapes and well-stocked minibars are standard. The Presidential suites atop the Spa Tower are ultra-modern; and the nine luxury villas, outfitted with gold fixtures, Lalique crystal accents, butler service, gyms, steam rooms, kitchens and private pools, are open to anyone willing to fork out $6,000 a night. The hotel's TV network simulcasts the fountain show music, so you can listen in your room as you watch the water.

Eating & drinking
The Bellagio has Vegas's best collection of superstar chefs under one roof. The roster starts with Julian Serrano's French/Mediterranean **Picasso**
(*see p161*), decorated with paintings by the eponymous artist. Lovers of steak head for **Prime** (*see p156*), Jean-Georges Vongerichten's superior chophouse, while those after seafood seek out **Michael Mina** (*see p165*). For Italian, try Todd English's **Olives** (*see p156*) or the circus-themed **Osteria del Circo**; the latter is overseen by Manhattan restauranteur Sirio Maccioni, who also owns the more formal **Le Cirque** (*see p158*) next door. In the Spa Tower, you'll find the serene **Sensi** (*see p162*), in which Martin Heierling serves Asian, Italian, grilled and seafood delicacies, and **Pâtisserie Jean-Philippe** (*see p161*), where a tri-coloured chocolate fountain (milk, white and dark) hints at the sweet sensations held within. The glitterati enjoy the upscale comfort food at **Fix** (*see p155*), while those looking for casual fare can check out the 24-hour **Café Bellagio**. The best drinks are served at **Petrossian**, named several times as one of America's best hotel bars by the hospitality industry's *Santé Magazine*.

Entertainment
A cast of dancers, musicians, clowns, acrobats, divers, swimmers and aerialists takes to the watery stage in **O** (*see p232*), a breathtaking spectacle from Cirque du Soleil. Catch cover bands at the **Fontana Bar** (*see p188*), a lounge with great cocktails and superb fountain views. For late-night fun, check out the pretty crowds sipping pricey martinis at **Caramel** (*see p179*) or gyrating at **Light** (*see p257*).

Gambling
The Bellagio's casino draws celebs such as Ben Affleck and Drew Barrymore, but its ostentatious luxury verges on vulgar: the upholstery, carpets and striped canopies are a clash of colours and patterns. As you might expect, table limits are higher than at most Strip properties: minimums are often $25-$50 and it's difficult to find even $10 blackjack. Still, the race and sports book is one of the most comfortable in town, and the poker room has replaced Binion's as the mecca for pros, sharks and big-time players.

Amenities *Bars (7). Business centre. Concierge. Disabled-adapted rooms. Gym. High-speed internet (ADSL $11.95). No-smoking floors. Pools (outdoor). Restaurants (19). Room service. Spa. TV: pay movies.* **Games** *Baccarat ($100-$15,000); Big Six; blackjack ($10-$10,000); Caribbean stud; craps (3x, 4x, 5x; from $5); casino war; Let it Ride; mini baccarat ($25-$15,000); pai gow poker; pai gow tiles; poker (39 tables); roulette (single & double zero); three-card poker.*

Caesars Palace
3570 Las Vegas Boulevard South, at W Flamingo Road, Las Vegas, NV 89109 (reservations 1-866 227 5938/front desk & casino 731 7110/www.harrahs. com). Bus Deuce, 202/self-parking & valet parking Las Vegas Boulevard South or S Industrial Road. **Rooms** 3,349. **Rates** $140-$920 double. **Credit** AmEx, DC, Disc, MC, V. **Map** p336 A7 ❷

When it was announced in 2005 that the powerful Harrah's group was set to take over Caesars Palace, many Vegas observers feared that the chain would

Caesars Palace.

denude the place of all its sass and turn it into Just Another Strip Resort. It hasn't happened yet. While the Bellagio is perhaps the epitome of new Vegas luxury, Caesars remains an icon of classic Sin City decadence, a meld of affluence, kitsch and glamour that continues to be a compelling sight more than four decades after its 1966 opening.

The resort remains a monument of sorts to ancient Greece and Rome, with miles of gold decor, marble columns, arches and colonnades, manicured gardens and copies of Greek and Roman statuary. These days, though, it's more about elegance than the kind of camp instilled in it by legendary founder Jay Sarno, at least in theory.

It's an enormous place, spread over a bewildering, labyrinthine casino floor and up into a variety of different towers. It's only getting bigger too. An additional tower is planned for the not too distant future, bringing the total room count to almost 4,500. But the existing towers have been kept in good shape by a recent renovation, dragging the design of the rooms into the 21st century.

Key to Caesars' continuing allure is the 4.5-acre Garden of the Gods pool area, a San Simeon-like peach with four mosaic pools, marble statuary, fountains and mini-throne lifeguard stands. A section of it, by the Venus pool, is set aside for topless sunbathing. While the pool draws a crowd only in summer, the ever-expanding **Forum Shops** (*see p191*) pulls visitors year-round. Fashioned, in true Vegas style, after an ancient Roman streetscape, the mall contains an unmatched range of shops, many of them not found anywhere else in the city. Other selling points include the luxurious **Qua Baths & Spa** (*see p208*) and the **Venus** salon; guests also get access to **Cascata**, the resort's golf course in Boulder City. *Photos p69.*

Accommodation

You'd expect a certain level of variety in a hotel this huge, and so it proves. The standard rooms (billed as 'Classic') are expansive and well maintained, but they aren't decorated in an especially inspiring fashion. If you've got a little cash, it's worth splashing for the 'Deluxe' rooms in the Augustus and Palace Towers, recently upgraded with high-tech facilities and stylishly modern design. The suites are fancier still: some have circular beds, in-room saunas, wet bars, living/dining rooms, home theatres, wine grottos, and even steam and workout rooms.

Eating & drinking

Top of the tree are **Bradley Ogden**'s chic regional American eatery (*see p155*), high-end French spot **Restaurant Guy Savoy** (*see p161*), and **808**, Jean-Marie Josselin's Euro-Asian-Pacific Rim restaurant. The Vegas edition of Bobby Flay's Manhattan-based, Southwestern-slanted hotspot **Mesa Grill** (*see p155*) looks great but promises more than it delivers; you're better off visiting **Rao's** (*see p161*), another New York import. Other options include the Japanese-oriented **Hyakumi**; the **Empress Court**, for upscale Chinese; **Café Lago**, the prettiest coffeeshop on the Strip; and the 24-hour **Augustus Café**.

There are also a number of excellent eateries in the Forum Shops, among them Florida's **Joe's Seafood, Prime Steak & Stone Crab** (*see p165*), Santa Monica's **Boa Prime Grill** and Manhattan's ridiculously pricey **Il Mulino**. Alternatives include **Sushi Roku**, straightforward Italian eaterie **Trevi** (*see p162*), and two Wolfgang Puck spots, Asian restaurant **Chinois** and trend-setting **Spago** (*see p156*). For casual fare, try **Stage Deli**, where portions and prices are both huge.

Entertainment

Celine Dion's five-year run in the purpose-built, 4,100-seat Colosseum comes to an end in December 2007; from February 2008, she'll be replaced by **Bette Midler** (*see p230*). **Elton John** (*see p230*) should be here through the end of 2008, performing his greatest hits-packed *Red Piano* show 50 times a year; other semi-regular headliners include comic **Jerry Seinfeld**.

The most notable nightlife option, and one of the most fashionable in the entire city, is the perpetually celeb-packed **Pure** (*see p258*), a South Beachian spot part-owned by Dion, Shaquille O'Neal, Andre Agassi and Steffi Graf; included in it is the burlesque-oriented **Pussycat Dolls Lounge**, which does pretty much what you might expect. The **Shadow Bar** (*see p181*) offers flair bartenders and silhouetted beauties bumping and grinding behind backlit scrims; for old-time Caesars Palace kitsch, there's the enduring **Cleopatra's Barge**. In summer, there's the **Venus Pool Club**. Also on site are the **Seahorse Lounge**, serving high-end cocktails in a room dominated by a giant aquarium, and the 24-hour **Galleria Bar**. And in the Forum Shops, there's **OPM** (*see p257*).

Gambling

Few casinos offer the limits or the atmosphere of Caesars; when there's a big fight in town, limits on the main floor can go through the roof. The sports book is one of the liveliest spots to watch the action, and accepts some of the biggest bets. You get a good view of the baccarat pit, an intimate nook where huge wagers are common. And for the boldest of slot players, the $500 machine, with a $1 million jackpot, uses gold-plated tokens. (Caveat: it pays a winning spin of only two $500 coins; for every other payback, the machine locks and an attendant hand-pays, for tax-paperwork purposes.) The high-limit slots are in the Palace Casino near the main entrance; blackjack pits and slots in the Forum Casino offer slightly lower limits. There's also a Pussycat Dolls themed area.

Amenities Bars (7). Business centre. Concierge. Disabled-adapted rooms. Gym. High-speed internet (ADSL $11.99). No-smoking floors. Pools (outdoor). Restaurants (10). Room service. Spa. TV: pay movies. Games Baccarat ($100-$15,000); Big Six; blackjack ($5-$10,000); Caribbean stud; casino war; craps (3x, 4x, 5x; from $10); keno; Let it Ride; mini baccarat ($25-$5,000); pai gow poker; pai gow tiles; poker (40 tables); roulette (single zero & double zero); Spanish 21; three-card poker.

Mandalay Bay.

Mandalay Bay

3950 Las Vegas Boulevard South, at W Hacienda Avenue, Las Vegas, NV 89119 (reservations 1-877 632 7800/front desk & casino 632 7777/www. mandalaybay.com). Bus Deuce, 104, 105/self-parking & valet parking W Hacienda Avenue. **Rooms** 2,791. **Rates** $109-$509 double. **Credit** AmEx, DC, Disc, MC, V. **Map** p336 A9 ❸

Not only do the suits at MGM Mirage know not to mess with a good thing, they also know how to make it better. There's no finer example of this skill than the South Seas island-themed Mandalay Bay, one of the Strip's most luxurious resorts. At its heart has always been an 11-acre water park with a sandy beach, a wave pool, a lazy river, two additional pools and a jogging track set in lush green foliage, plus the **Moorea Beach Club**, a limited-access South Beach-esque retreat that transforms into a sultry hotspot on warm-weather weekend nights. But a recent $30-million expansion added a three-storey, climate-controlled, glass-fronted casino on the sand, where guests can enjoy beachside gambling, casual dining or sun-worshipping. Book one of the decked-out Villas Soleil, where you and 15 pals can take advantage of your own wet bar, MP3 player, flat-screen TV and private third-level pool.

The interior is just as impressive. An understated oasis of water features, lush foliage, huge aquariums and island architecture, it encompasses a sensuous spa, a classy collection of restaurants, a pair of wedding chapels, several theatres and the kid-friendly

Shark Reef aquarium (*see p125*). **Mandalay Place**, a nice sky-bridge mall that connects the hotel with the Luxor, contains a number of upscale boutiques and restaurants, a chic barber and even Forty Deuce, a 'back-alley striptease lounge'. The convention facilities are among the city's best.

If all this doesn't work for you, there are two other hotels accessible from Mandalay Bay. A corridor off the lobby leads to the **Four Seasons** (*see p95*), which has its rooms on floors 35 to 39 but is run as a separate operation. Meanwhile, **Thehotel at Mandalay Bay** (*see p71*) is an all-suites, casino-free tower that eschews the island theme entirely.

Accommodation

All the 2,791 guestrooms and suites at Mandalay Bay were remodelled in 2007 with a contemporary look and additional amenities: lofty pillow-top beds with triple sheeting, 42-in plasma-screen TVs, iPod docks and high-speed net access. Bathrooms come with 15-in LCD TVs and giant tubs. Larger suites command excellent views of the Strip or the surrounding mountains and come with wet bars.

Eating & drinking

Mandalay Bay is unusual among the major resorts on the Strip in that it locates many of its eateries in a 'restaurant row' away from the casino, so you can dine without seeing – or, just as crucially, hearing – so much as a single slot machine. The new boîte on the block is Michael Mina's **Strip Steak** (*see p157*), the first steakhouse by a chef previously known for his seafood. Other noteworthy spots include Hubert Keller's **Fleur de Lys** (*see p160*); Charlie Palmer's **Aureole** (*see p153*); Wolfgang Puck's **Trattoria del Lupo**; and Mary Sue Milliken and Susan Feniger's nouveau Mexican **Border Grill** (*see p164*). **China Grill** and **Shanghai Lily** serve Asian fare; **Rumjungle** is a Brazilian rodizio and rum bar/nightclub (*see p258*); and **Red, White & Blue** is a decent but too-pricey café.

You'll have to venture into the casino to sample the Cajun cooking at **House of Blues** (*see p250*), upstairs from the music venue. Try Sunday's soul-stirring Gospel Brunch or, if you can, the super-exclusive **Foundation Room**, which serves dinner to members and VIPs amid deluxe furnishings on the top floor. Ringing the casino are the nice 24-hour **Raffles Café**, the **Noodle Shop** and **J-Pop**, where music and sushi are the order of the evening. Over at Mandalay Place, carnivores can have theirs with lettuce and tomato at the **Burger Bar** (*see p155*); also here are **RM Seafood** (with two dining rooms, R-Bar-Café and the more intimate restaurant RM; *see p165*) and **Chocolate Swan**.

Entertainment

The 12,000-seat **Mandalay Bay Events Center** (*see p251*) has a schedule of boxing events and concerts, but a better choice is the rather more acoustically reliable **House of Blues** (*see p250*), which features a concert roster rivalled only by the Pearl at the Palms. When the weather's warm, the hotel produces the Bay Rock Concert series on the beach. The hotel's resident show, imported from London but tweaked for Vegas, is featherweight Abba-fest **Mamma Mia!** (*see p231*), which will end its five-year run in summer 2008.

Leaving aside **Mix** at Thehotel at Mandalay Bay (*see p257*), Hollywood import **Forty Deuce** (*see p257*), over in Mandalay Place, is the hottest nightclub, though **Rumjungle** (*see p258*) draws a young, pretty crowd with pounding Latin beats, and the vodka selections at **Red Square** (*see p180*) remain impressive. There's piano music in the casino's **Orchid Lounge** and, on weekends (6-8pm), at Charlie Palmer Steak inside the Four Seasons.

Gambling

The 135,000sq ft (12,500sq m) casino is airier than many, with 2,400 machines (including nickel video slots that take up to 45 or 90 coins), but you have to hunt for good video poker machines. Table games, 122 of them, include blackjack, roulette, craps, Let it Ride, Caribbean stud, pai gow poker and mini baccarat. You'll also find a poker room where you can get your fix of seven-card stud and Texas or Omaha hold 'em. The race and sports book has 17 large screens, enough seating for some 300 sports fans, a bar and a good deli.

Meet the regulars South Strip

South Strippers stay at the newest hotels and happily pay a fortune for the privilege, as long as they can tell everyone how much they spent. They dress in black silk shirts, shades, Rolex watches and uncomfortable handmade shoes by Ferragamo or Manolo.

Their days start late, usually after noon. Then they hit the pricey shops at the Bellagio and Caesars to buy more silk shirts. Afterwards, they visit their hotels' tropical swimming pools, but not to swim: getting wet would ruin their hair. When the regular pool won't do, they pay extra to gain access to the 'European' bathing sections, where the ladies show off their surgeons' latest creations.

For dinner, South Strippers go some place where the sommelier and chef know their names and the tasting menus cost more than the price of a Hyundai. They pick up the tab before heading on to the balcony to smoke genuine Cuban cigars. After dinner, they might spend a couple of hours playing black-chip blackjack and roulette.

Once the clock strikes midnight, they'll change into a new silk shirt and head over to a trendy ultralounge like Tabu, Revolution or Light. They never wait in line; that's for chumps who don't know how to tip bouncers. They're pleasantly surprised that a bottle of Absolut costs $250 (hey, that's less than a silk shirt!), and that they only have to buy two to get table service. As the sun rises, the South Stripper returns to his penthouse suite with a new-found friend, then sneaks away to call Citibank and ask for an increase in his credit limit.

Fishing for comps: the 20,000-gallon aquarium at the **Mirage**.

Amenities *Bars (10). Business centre. Concierge. Disabled-adapted rooms. Gym. High-speed internet (ADSL $11.99). No-smoking floors. Pools (outdoor). Restaurants (21). Room service. Spa. TV: pay movies.* **Games** *Baccarat ($100-$15,000); blackjack ($10-$15,000); Caribbean stud; craps (3x, 4x, 5x; from $10); keno; Let it Ride; mini baccarat ($25-$15,000); pai gow poker; pai gow tiles; poker (10 tables); roulette (single zero & double zero); three-card poker.*

Mirage
3400 Las Vegas Boulevard South, between Spring Mountain & W Flamingo Roads, Las Vegas, NV 89109 (reservations 1-800 374 9000/front desk & casino 791 7111/www.mirage.com). Bus Deuce, 105, 202, 203/self-parking Spring Mountain Road/valet parking Las Vegas Boulevard South. **Rooms** 3,044. **Rates** $109-$699 double. **Credit** AmEx, DC, Disc, MC, V. **Map** p335 & p336 A6 ❹

With its Polynesian village decor, lush landscaping, lagoon-like pool and waterfalls, the $650-million Mirage set the standard for modern resorts when it was opened by Steve Wynn in 1989. But in much the same way that the likes of the Tropicana and the Flamingo were left standing at the gate when the Mirage welcomed its first guests, so the Mirage was in turn overtaken by its sassier competitors, who shrewdly realised that there was money to be made from a younger, more fashionable generation.

However, changes are afoot. Not in the guestrooms themselves, at least not yet. And not so much in the main public areas, which retain their longstanding island-paraside theme. But by vastly improving the hotel's dining options, introducing nightclubs and lounges aimed squarely at the under-thirties rather than the over-forties, and replacing the

Christmas-camp Siegfried & Roy with a vibrant Beatles-based show, the owners have pepped things up no end. The Mirage might not look like a different resort, but it certainly feels like one.

For all that, many of the old favourites remain. The mocked-up volcano at the front is no more realistic than it ever was, but its hourly shows (evenings only) remain a draw. Also still here are the 90ft rainforest atrium filled with fresh and faux palm trees and orchids, the much-imitated 20,000-gallon aquarium behind the registration desk, and the **Secret Garden & Dolphin Habitat** (*see p129*). And do make time to stop by the gorgeous pool area, which comprises a series of blue lagoons, inlets and waterfalls, plus two islands exotically landscaped with various palm trees and tropical flowers.

Accommodation
The redecoration of the Mirage in 2002 freshened the colour scheme from pale pastels to deeper cranberries, greens and yellows, with cane furnishings and crown mouldings. Several years on, the slightly stuffy design is somewhat at odds with the type of crowds that the hotel is trying to draw to its bars and restaurants, but the rooms are kept in good shape.

Eating & drinking
The ongoing regeneration here has taken hold of the catering. The **Samba Brazilian Steakhouse**, surf 'n' turf favourite **Kokomo's** and **Cravings**, hardly 'the ultimate buffet experience' but good nonetheless, have all survived. However, they're been joined by some eye-catching newcomers. Chief among them is **Japonais** (*see p162*), imported via Chicago and New York, and the swanky **Stack** (*see p157*), which places American cuisine into a tapas-style menu.

Fantastico! Gondola rides and *carnevale* costumes at the **Venetian**.

Other options include **Onda**, a smartish Italian restaurant; Chinese-oriented **Fin** (*see p158*); the almost forcibly casual **California Pizza Kitchen**; and, from New York, the **Carnegie Deli** (*see p164*).

Entertainment

The big show at the Mirage is one of the biggest and best in the city: **Love** (*see p231*), Cirque du Soleil's surprisingly successful reinvention of the Beatles' back catalogue. The show peddled by mediocre singer/impressionist **Danny Gans** (*see p227*) is virtually an antique by comparison, but he's a likeable enough personality. Gans's show is supplemented by a roster of irregular headliners: chiefly comedians, among them **Dana Carvey** and **Jay Leno**.

The nightlife here has received a not-before-time overhaul of late, and the changes have made a huge difference to the atmosphere throughout the Mirage. The Cirque-designed **Revolution Lounge** grabs the headlines, with its novel interactive tables and moreish speciality cocktails; however, the putative Beatles theme doesn't extend as far as the soundtrack, which (with the exception of a BritPop themed Thursday) tends towards polite house. Things are a little livelier at chi-chi **Jet** (*see p157*), a little mellower at the wine lounge at **Onda**, and a little breezier at the poolside **Dolphin Bar**.

Gambling

The Mirage has nearly 100 blackjack tables, most dealt from six-deck shoes. Minimums are high: $10 for 21, craps and roulette, $25 for mini baccarat, $100 for baccarat. You can find a good game of poker at any hour; since many players are tourists, the action, both on the low- and high-limit tables, is plentiful. For a break, check out the high-limit slots. If you're polite, and it's not too busy, an attendant might offer you some freshly sliced fruit, normally reserved for players who insert $100 tokens five at a time (their generosity truly knows no bounds). The Red, White & Blue slot offers a $1 million jackpot.

Amenities Bars (5). Business centre. Concierge. Disabled-adapted rooms. Gym. High-speed internet (ADSL & wireless $12.99). No-smoking floors. Pools (outdoor). Restaurants (14). Room service. Spa. TV: pay movies. Games Baccarat ($100-$15,000); Big Six; blackjack ($10-$10,000); Caribbean stud; casino war; craps (3x, 4x, 5x; from $10); keno; Let it Ride; mini baccarat ($15-$15,000); pai gow poker; pai gow tiles; poker (30 tables); roulette (single zero & double zero); Spanish 21; three-card poker.

Paris Las Vegas

3655 Las Vegas Boulevard South, at E Flamingo Road, Las Vegas, NV 89109 (reservations 1-877 603 4386/front desk & casino 946 7000/www. harrahs.com). Bus Deuce, 202/self-parking & valet parking Las Vegas Boulevard South or Audrie Street. **Rooms** 2,916. **Rates** $109-$499 double. **Credit** AmEx, DC, Disc, MC, V. **Map** p336 A7 ⑤
What happens when the City of Lights collides with the City of Light? Versions of Paris's greatest monuments cut down to size, all-you-can-eat crêpes at

the buffet, reasonably polite waiters, ancient Rome across the street… and, of course, the lights never go out. If only the real Paris could be so accommodating. Even the French love Las Vegas.

To say that this huge resort in the heart of the Strip is one of the town's most eye-catching is to do its effervescent absurdity a rank injustice. Its reproductions of Parisian landmarks start with the 34-storey hotel tower modelled after the Hôtel de Ville, and also take in the Louvre, the Paris Opéra, the Arc de Triomphe and, of course, the half-scale replica of the Eiffel Tower, built using Gustav Eiffel's original plans, that plunges into the casino. The theming continues within, with French-themed restaurants, shops and even, though you'll need to look closely, the casino. It may seem rather sub-Disney at first glance, but it's by no means all haw-hee-haw cliché: you can also get a massage in a mock-Balinese spa, sun yourself by the rooftop pool or take in one of Broadway's biggest recent hits.

Accommodation

The smallish guestrooms are comfortable, prim and stately, decorated in rich Regency style; some are furnished with canopied beds and armoires. The spacious marble bathrooms are outfitted with vanities, a make-up mirror and soaking tubs.

Eating & drinking

Paris Las Vegas doesn't do too badly at living up to its theme city's culinary reputation, albeit without the breadth of styles you'll find at the Venetian or the Bellagio. Along with **JJ's Boulangerie** and **La Creperie**, serving sandwiches and delicious sweet and savoury crêpes, and the quaint **Le Village Buffet** (*see p177*), which features regional cuisine from five French provinces, the hotel has the **Eiffel Tower Restaurant** (*see p160*), located on the tower's 11th floor, and the bustling **Mon Ami Gabi** (*see p160*), a streetside brasserie serving classics such as steak frites. **Les Artistes Steakhouse** has a menu of rotisserie-style meats, fish and poultry, while **Ah Sin** is a chic place with patio dining that serves Thai and Chinese dishes along with Korean barbecue and sushi. Most ridiculous of all? **Le Burger Brasserie**, putatively a French take on American classics. Hmm.

Entertainment

If Paris Las Vegas's strolling mimes leave you unenthusiastic, there's a variety of ways to spend the night wisely (or otherwise). The major show here is **The Producers** (*see p232*), the latest in a longish line of Broadway and/or West End imports to try their luck. If we all ignore hypnotist **Anthony Cools**, who performs six shows a week, perhaps he'll go away. A better bet is **Risqué** (*see p258*), a nightclub where old-world France meets contemporary Asian-tilted lounge, complete with house music and dessert bar. Downstairs there's dance music under sparkly lights among the shady faux trees of **Le Cabaret**. And there are decidedly non-French duelling piano singalongs in **Napoleon's** (*see p180*), a champagne and cigar bar.

Gambling

Three of the Eiffel Tower's four legs plunge into the casino, which is smaller, noisier and more energetically crowded than most. The 100 table games and 2,000-plus slot machines are not as budget-friendly as they used to be, though there are still plenty of 25¢ slots. The race and sports book has big TVs and 'pari-mutuel' betting on horse racing. Theming is rampant, from Monet-influenced carpets and Paris Métro-style wrought-iron canopies above the games to security guards in gendarme uniforms. Check out the LeRoy Neiman paintings in the high-limit pit.

Amenities *Bars (6). Business centre. Concierge. Disabled-adapted rooms. Gym. High-speed internet (ADSL $10.99). No-smoking floors. Pool (outdoor). Restaurants (11). Room service. Spa. TV: pay movies.* **Games** *Baccarat ($100-$15,000); Big Six; blackjack ($5-$10,000); Caribbean stud; casino war; craps (3x, 4x, 5x; from $5); Let it Ride; mini baccarat ($15-$5,000); pai gow poker; poker (10 tables); roulette (single zero & double zero); Spanish 21; three-card poker.*

Venetian & Palazzo

3555 Las Vegas Boulevard South, between Sands Avenue & E Flamingo Road, Las Vegas, NV 89109 (reservations 1-877 883 6423/front desk & casino 414 1000/www.venetian.com). Bus Deuce, 105, 203/ self-parking & valet parking Las Vegas Boulevard South or Koval Lane. **Rooms** *Venetian 4,049. Palazzo 3,025.* **Rates** $179-$559 suite. **Credit** AmEx, DC, Disc, MC, V. **Map** p335 & p336 B6 **⑥**

Sheldon Adelson's Venetian manages the neat trick of recreating the city of canals in the desert. To-scale replicas of the Rialto Bridge, the Doge's Palace and the Campanile are rendered with affection, and the singing gondoliers and itinerant 'street' performers in St Mark's Square perform with gusto and a wink. It's less tacky than you might expect.

Attractions here are, with the arguable exceptions of Andrew Lloyd Webber's *The Phantom of the Opera* and the adjacent **Madame Tussaud's** (*see p129*), pretty cultured. Designed by Rem Koolhaas, the **Guggenheim-Hermitage Museum** (*see p244*) offers artistic selections from home and abroad, while the **Grand Canal Shoppes** (*see p191*) is a meandering mall with flowing canals and faux façades that curve around to St Mark's Square. Another key draw is the **Canyon Ranch SpaClub**, which offers a full range of spa services along with movement and wellness classes, a climbing wall and a café. The resort connects to the **Sands Expo** (*see p309*); indeed, the Venetian pulls in much of its business from conventioneers, especially midweek.

Not one to rest on his laurels, Adelson will unveil the adjacent $1.6-billion **Palazzo** in late 2007 or early 2008. Aiming for an upper-crust Beverly Hills feel, the resort will feature a new mall, the **Shops at Palazzo** (*see p191*), connected to the Venetian via the Grand Canal Shoppes and anchored by Barneys department store. Directly above it will be 300 condo units that are expected to sell for $1,500-$2,000 per sq ft, the Strip's priciest residential offerings.

Accommodation

The standard suites (there are no regular rooms) at the Venetian are far larger than the Vegas norm. The sumptuously appointed suites underwent renovations during 2007, no doubt to keep them on a par with the Palazzo. The 12-storey Venezia Tower atop the car park has rooms that are similar to those in the original tower, but that now come with some extra amenities (private elevators, complimentary newspaper delivery, access to the secluded Italian-style pool garden and arboretum). For more exclusivity, the tower's top five floors contain an old world drawing room-style lounge and speciality baths.

Eating & drinking

Where to begin? The Venetian's restaurant roster reads like a Who's Who of top chefs. Thomas Keller (of French Laundry fame) oversees stellar brasserie **Bouchon** (*see p158*); Wolfgang Puck and Emeril Lagasse respectively run the San Francisco-style café **Postrio** (*see p156*) and the **Cajun Delmonico Steakhouse**; Joachim Splichal's **Pinot Brasserie** (*see p161*) brings a lighter taste of French cuisine; and Tom Moloney's **AquaKnox** (*see p164*) serves Californian cuisine. This being ersatz Venice, there's plenty of Italian food: Piero Selvaggio's dual rooms **Valentino** (*see p162*) and the **Grill at Valentino**; **Zeffirino**, a Genoan-style seafood restaurant with a fan club that includes Pavarotti; and **Canaletto**. New arrivals include **Tao** (*see p166*), an Asian bistro related to the fashionable New York restaurant-club; Mario Batali's **B&B Ristorante** and **Enoteca San Marco**; and **David Burke**'s signature American restaurant. Less pricey options (it's all relative) include **Noodle Asia** for pan-Asian noodle dishes, Hong Kong dim sum and vegetarian specialities; the excellent 24-hour **Grand Lux Café**; and **Taqueria Cañonita**.

Entertainment

The Venetian has improved its night-time entertainment options, ditching the tiresome Lord of the Dance in favour of the **Blue Man Group** (*see p230*) and all-round entertainer **Gordie Brown** (*see p227*). **Phantom** (*see p232*) moved into the old Guggenheim Las Vegas space in the spring of 2006 to wild acclaim; when the Palazzo opens, it'll host Broadway hit **Jersey Boys**.

After numerous attempts at starting a nightclub scene stalled at the gates, the Venetian finally hit the bullseye with **Tao** (*see p166*), a pan-Asian boîte, nightclub and rooftop lounge that entertains thousands on weekends. For more lounge and less club, check out the sizzling minimalist **V Bar** (*see p181*).

Gambling

In the casino, the 140 table games include blackjack, craps, Caribbean stud, Let it Ride and pai gow. The casino's 2,600 slots are weighted toward reel games, with a large mix of $1 machines. For the player with pull, there are high-denomination machines – $5, $25 and $100 – in the casino's high-limit salon, which also includes a baccarat pit and 12 table games (blackjack starting at $10,000 a hand).

Wynn Las Vegas.

Amenities Bars (3). Business centre. Concierge. Disabled-adapted rooms. Gym. High-speed internet (ADSL $10). No-smoking floors. Pools (outdoor). Restaurants (18). Room service. Spa. TV: DVD (selected rooms)/pay movies. Games Baccarat ($100-$15,000); mini baccarat ($25-$10,000); Big Six; blackjack ($10-$5,000); Caribbean stud; casino war; craps (3x, 4x, 5x; from $10); keno; Let il Ride; pai gow poker; pai gow tiles; poker (39 tables); roulette (double zero). Gambling lessons (craps 11am Mon-Fri; roulette noon Mon-Fri; blackjack 12.15pm Mon-Fri).

Wynn Las Vegas & Encore

3131 Las Vegas Boulevard South, between E Desert Inn Road & Sands Avenue, NV 89109 (reservations 1-888 320 9966/front desk & casino 770 7000/ www.wynnlasvegas.com). Bus Deuce, 203/self-parking & valet parking Las Vegas Boulevard South or (Tower Suites) Spring Mountain Road. **Rooms** *Wynn Las Vegas 2,716. Encore 2,034.* **Rates** *$199-$699 double.* **Credit** *AmEx, DC, Disc, MC, V.* **Map** *p335 & p336 B6* ❼

Before he'd even finished building his namesake hotel, Steve Wynn was, true to form, already planning an addition to it. However, Encore has since morphed into rather more than a mere addendum: when it opens in 2009, the $2-billion project will be another full-scale resort, complete with new restaurants, bars and nightclubs. Wynn, after all, can't let himself be outdone by fellow mogul Sheldon Adelson and his neighbouring Palazzo (*see p75*). But in the meantime, Wynn Las Vegas has more than enough diversions to keep visitors busy.

Known as the man who brought Vegas entertainment curbside, Wynn went against his own convention and designed this resort from the inside out. Luxury is everywhere, as you'd expect from a casino that cost somewhere in the region of $2.7 billion. On the far side of the faux mountain (*see p130*, **Stealth mountain**), the Lake of Dreams fuses light, water, horticulture and architecture into a multimedia experience. The garden-themed **Spa at Wynn** (*see p208*) houses 45 treatment rooms, a beauty salon and a fitness centre, while the 18-hole golf course (designed by Tom Fazio) is overlooked by 36 fairway villas.

The exclusivity extends to the **Wynn Esplanade** mall (*see p192*), where you'll find the crème de la crème of high-end fashion designers, including Louis Vuitton, Christian Dior, Oscar de la Renta and Brioni. If you can't fathom the thought of a hire car, there's also Penske Wynn Ferrari Maserati, Nevada's only factory-authorised Ferrari and Maserati dealership. The gallery, which featured paintings from Steve and Elaine Wynn's personal collection, is no longer open, but there are still several notable works of art hanging in the hotel's common areas.

Accommodation

The large and lavish (naturally) guestrooms offer floor-to-ceiling windows, signature Wynn beds with 320-thread-count European linens, a seating area with a sofa and ottomans, a dining table and chairs, flat-screen LCD TVs, spacious bath areas and bedside drapery controls. The suites set a new Vegas standard: some have their own massage rooms, VIP check-in areas, private pools and dining rooms. Don't even get us started on the villas.

Eating & drinking

Though Wynn has been partly responsible for the onslaught in Vegas of absentee celebrity chefs who slap their names on the marquees but mainly leave the cooking to others, the restaurants here are all run by the chefs whose names they bear. The signature spot is **Alex** (*see p158*), run by Alessandro Stratta; other options include **Daniel Boulud** (*see p159*), Eric Klein's **SW Steakhouse**, Mark LoRusso's **Tableau** (*see p157*), Stephen Kalt's **Corsa Cucina** (*see p161*) and Paul Bartolotta's **Bartolotta Ristorante di Mare** (*see p164*). There's more casual food at Asian bistro **Red 8** (*see p165*), the poolside **Terrace Pointe Café** and the sumptuous **Buffet**. **Parasol Up** and **Parasol Down** (*see p180*), the hotel's lobby bars, offer everything from tea to cocktails.

Entertainment

Erstwhile Cirque du Soleil producer Franco Dragone was called on to design **Le Rêve** (*see p233*), named after the Picasso masterpiece that was initially the inspiration for the hotel itself. It was recently revamped, but it still includes the same aerial acrobatics for which Dragone is known. Monty Python's **Spamalot** (*see p233*) is the other show here. The seductive **Lure** (*see p257*) serves as Wynn's version of the ultralounge; **Tryst** (*see p260*) is his answer to the nightclub scene.

Gambling

As you might expect, the action at Wynn is both sophisticated and decidedly pricey. Blackjack minimums start at $15, with a few single-deck games that pay the reduced 6:5 for naturals; hotel guests can also play 21 poolside at the Cabana Bar. Crap minimums are similar to blackjack. A single-zero roulette wheel is usually open in the high-limit room, though the minimums are dear. The slots run the gamut from pennies to a $5,000 machine. Amazingly, Wynn has tried to attract local video poker players with full-pay machines at higher denominations (very rare), though the schedules change unexpectedly; check the *Las Vegas Advisor* for their comings and goings. The keno lounge is one of the most comfortable in town.

Amenities *Bars (6). Business centre. Concierge. Disabled-adapted rooms. Gym. High-speed internet (ADSL $11.95; wireless in lobby). No-smoking floors. Pool (outdoor). Restaurants (18). Room service. Spa. TV: DVD (suites only)/pay movies.*
Games *Baccarat ($100-$15,000); Big Six; blackjack ($15-$10,000); Caribbean stud; casino war; craps (3x, 4x, 5x; from $10); Let it Ride; mini baccarat ($50-$10,000); pai gow poker; pai gow tiles; poker (26 tables); roulette (single & double zero); Spanish 21; three-card poker.*

Moderate

Bally's

3645 Las Vegas Boulevard South, at E Flamingo Road, Las Vegas, NV 89109 (reservations 1-877 603 4390/front desk & casino 967 4111/www. harrahs.com). Bus Deuce, 202/self-parking & valet parking Las Vegas Boulevard South or E Flamingo Road. **Rooms** 2,814. **Rates** $99-$459 double. **Credit** AmEx, DC, Disc, MC, V. **Map** p336 A7 ❺

A classic, Dan Tanna-esque *Vega$* experience can still be had at the grande dame of the Strip's Famous Four Corners. Though now owned by Harrah's, Bally's has stayed true to its Hollywood roots, albeit probably because management simply hasn't got around to renovating yet. The garish 8 miles of ostentatious looping neon, part of a multi-million-dollar 'grand entry' that delivers tourists to the hotel's elegant porte cochère, is pretty ugly, but Bally's retains its classic appeal inside. Amenities include an oversized, heated pool with private cabañas; eight flood-lit tennis courts next to a pro shop where you can sign up for lessons (it's one of the last hotels on the Strip with tennis courts); a full-service health club; and access to the Caesars-owned Cascata golf course. The Bally Avenue Shoppes house one-off boutiques.

Accommodation

The good-sized standard rooms are decorated with a West Coast casual elegance of bright velvet couches offset by muted earth tones. Of the 2,814 rooms, 265 are suites: the one- and two-bedroom Grand Suites, each with a huge jetted tub and wet bar, are slightly more contemporary. The 22nd Club offers access to private concierge services, free breakfast and evening cocktails with gorgeous Strip views.

Eating & drinking

The restaurant selection is like the rest of the resort: a throwback to old-school subtlety. It's no surprise that the best place to eat is an all-you-can-scoff affair: Sunday's **Sterling Brunch** (*see p177*), a spectacular linen-and-champers buffet for which booking is necessary. **Al Dente** offers contemporary Italian food, and the New England-style **Steakhouse** does grilled beef and seafood right. The only new addition: Yuk Sing Wong's **Asia**, serving regional specialities such as Hong Kong won ton soup and Szechwan shrimp. Along with the **Big Kitchen Buffet** (*see p177*), there's a host of casual spots for sushi, ice-cream, sandwiches and Italian fast food, plus cocktails at the sport-and-slots bar **Sully's** and the Mexican-slanted **Tequila Bar**.

Entertainment

For an old-school Vegas show experience, **Jubilee!** (*see p231*) is just the ticket: beautiful showgirls reprising world-famous production numbers with lavish sets and spectacular choreography (topless on the late run). A rotating line-up of local acts plays the **Indigo Lounge** (*see p188*).

Gambling

The casino is a large, rectangular space, an inviting atmosphere of soft lighting and art deco accents with 65 table games and 2,100 slot machines. Among them are 'champagne' $1,000 slots, with a top payout of a cool mil. Not surprisingly, you'll find all the latest creations from machine-maker Bally, including laserdisc versions of craps, roulette and blackjack; all are excellent practice tools before heading to the actual tables. The buy-ins at the tables start at $10 with an occasional $5 single-deck 6:5 21 game, though many players wager far more than the minimum. The video poker is pretty pitiful, but the sports book, on the lower level, is as classy and technically advanced as those at the Bellagio and the Hilton, and it's only crowded on big-game days.

Amenities *Bars (5). Business centre. Disabled-adapted rooms. Gym. High-speed internet (ADSL $10.99). No-smoking floors. Pool (outdoor). Restaurants (12). Room service. Spa. TV: pay movies.* **Games** *Baccarat ($100-$15,000); blackjack ($5-$3,000); Caribbean stud; casino war; craps (3x, 4x, 5x; from $5); keno; Let it Ride; mini baccarat ($15-$5,000); pai gow poker; poker (9 tables); roulette (double zero); Spanish 21; three-card poker.*

Flamingo

3555 Las Vegas Boulevard South, at E Flamingo Road, Las Vegas, NV 89109 (reservations 1-888 902 9929/front desk & casino 733 3111/www. harrahs.com). Bus Deuce, 202/self-parking & valet parking Las Vegas Boulevard South or Audrie Street. **Rooms** 3,626. **Rates** $90-$450 double. **Credit** AmEx, DC, Disc, MC, V. **Map** p336 A7 🟢
The Flamingo is the Strip's sleeping giant. Its location at the heart of the action couldn't be better; and thanks to its beginnings under Bugsy Siegel, its name is virtually legendary. But while its competitors at Caesars and the Bellagio across the street are

raising their game in an attempt to draw new crowds, the Harrah's-owned Flamingo seems content to coast along in third gear, happy to milk a gradually ageing clientele who apparently aren't interested in what the competition might be able to offer them.

Behind the signature pink neon sign, the resort is huge, with six guestroom towers. Hidden between them is the resort's centrepiece: a lush 15-acre tropical pool area with waterslides, waterfalls and jungle-like foliage enveloping four distinct pools (including Bugsy's oval-shaped original). Also outdoors are four tennis courts and an assortment of wildlife, including (yes) flamingos. So far so good, then, but the interior of the Flamingo is markedly less impressive, wedged some time in the 1980s and unable or unwilling to escape. The new Go guestrooms are a sign that change may be on the horizon, but it's going to be a long and difficult job.

Accommodation

The standard rooms at the Flamingo are smallish, fairly basic and profoundly old-fashioned, despite a relatively recent renovation. All of which makes the new Go guestrooms a surprise. Designed in a more modern style and done out with flat-screen TVs, iPod-friendly hi-fis and wireless access, they're more inviting than you'd expect from either the other rooms or, for that matter, the rest of the resort.

Note that while room rates at all Vegas properties vary from night to night, the differentials at the Flamingo are spectacular even by local standards. Guestrooms can be ridiculously cheap during the week and outrageously expensive at weekends.

Eating & drinking

The gastronomic revolution that's enlivened Vegas vacations over the last decade or so has yet to reach the Flamingo. Aside from a 24 hour coffeeshop and the inevitable buffet, visitors can choose from Italian (**Ventuno**), steaks and seafood (**Steakhouse 46**) or sushi and teppanyaki (popular chain **Hamada of Japan**). None disgrace their surroundings, but when your signature restaurant is **Jimmy Buffet's Margaritaville** (*see p180*), a theme bar-restaurant decorated in colours loud enough to blind from 50 paces, perhaps a rethink is in order.

Entertainment

Her chart career having gone on hiatus, singer **Toni Braxton** (*see p230*) shipped into the Flamingo for a residency in 2005, which was extended until late 2007 after it was well received by critics and audiences. The 10pm slot is held down by **George Wallace** (the comedian, not the segregationist former governor of Alabama; *see p228*), a reliably funny man who seems to have found a gig for life. Further laughs are provided by **Second City** (*see p234*), a satellite branch of the Chicagoan improv troupe; late at night, its theatre is home to burlesque shows.

Gambling

The casino area, though a bit claustrophobic and loud, offers you a real chance to survive: crap and blackjack minimums are a reasonable $5 outside prime time. It's tougher to come out ahead in the slot area: none of the 2,100 machines are considered loose (after all, the last renovation cost $130 million). You'll also find a lively card room, a keno parlour, and a race and sports book.

Amenities *Bars (5). Business centre. Disabled-adapted rooms. Gym. High-speed internet (ADSL $10.99, web TV $9.99). No-smoking floors. Pools (outdoor). Restaurants (9). Room service. Spa. TV: pay movies.* **Games** *Baccarat ($10-$5,000); Big Six; blackjack ($5-$3,000); Caribbean stud; craps (3x, 4x, 5x; from $5); keno; Let it Ride; mini baccarat ($10-$5,000); pai gow poker; poker (14 tables); roulette (double zero); three-card poker. Gambling lessons (craps 11am Tue-Sat).*

Harrah's

3475 Las Vegas Boulevard South, between Sands Avenue & E Flamingo Road, Las Vegas, NV 89109 (reservations 1-800 214 9110/front desk & casino 369 5000/www.harrahs.com). Bus Deuce, 105, 203/ self-parking & valet parking Koval Lane. **Rooms** 2,667. **Rates** $60-$450 double. **Credit** AmEx, DC, Disc, MC, V. **Map** p336 A6 ⑩

This middle-of-the-road, middle-of-the-Strip resort might not have the same cachet as most of its neighbours, Caesars Palace and the Venetian among them, but its parent company is one of the most powerful in town. The acquisition in 2005 of the Imperial Palace, which sits between Harrah's and sibling property the Flamingo, might have been the catalyst for recent change. The 35-year-old resort still plays the tired Mardi Gras theme, but fresh entertainment options, new eateries and just-renovated guestrooms have injected the property with a little spirit.

Accommodation
The guestrooms and suites in Harrah's three towers are comfortable and festive. Many have minibars, some have jetted tubs. The new deluxe rooms have updated decor and amenities.

Eating & drinking
There are no celeb chefs or brand-name chains here; all the restaurants are suitable for casual or smart-casual diners. If you're all dressed up, you'll feel most at home at the **Range Steakhouse** with its nice views of the Strip. Your next best bets are **Penazzi Italian Ristorante** and the **Oyster Bar at Penazzi** for Italian recipes, and **Ming's Table**, the gourmet restaurant formerly known as Asia, for crispy roast duck. Casual diners flock to remodelled buffet **Flavors** and the **Café at Harrah's**, which serves standard coffeeshop fare.

Entertainment
Veteran Strip headliner **Rita Rudner** (*see p228*) moved here from New York New York relatively recently, and continues to draw crowds. But the best option is the family-friendly afternoon magic show delivered by the hugely likeable **Mac King** (*see p228*). Budd Friedman's famous **Improv** comedy club (*see p234*) brings in fresh comedians each week. And you can listen to live country music in **Toby Keith's I Love this Bar & Grill** (*see p180*) or be dazzled by the flair bartenders in the **Carnaval Court** (*see p188*).

Gambling
Harrah's has a wide selection of table games, including Caribbean stud, Let it Ride and casino war. Most blackjack games are dealt from the shoe, but

Harrah's, the heart of operations for one of the Strip's biggest corporations.

higher limits – at least $25 minimum – are dealt from hand-held decks. Beware the single decks, which have lower limits but pay a measly 6:5 for naturals. Occasionally, gracious pit bosses will bring out the European single-zero roulette wheel for high rollers. For lively action, take a seat in the cosily compact poker room, while the race and sports book offers booths and table seating.

Amenities *Bars (7). Business centre. Disabled-adapted rooms. Gym. High-speed internet (ADSL $11.95). No-smoking floors. Pool (outdoor). Restaurants (8). Room service. Spa. TV: pay movies.* **Games** *Baccarat ($25-$10,000); blackjack ($10-$5,000); Caribbean stud; craps (3x, 4x, 5x; from $5); keno; Let it Ride; mini baccarat ($15-$5,000); pai gow poker; poker (15 tables); roulette (single & double zero); three-card poker.*

Imperial Palace

3535 Las Vegas Boulevard South, between Sands Avenue & E Flamingo Road, Las Vegas, NV 89109 (reservations 1-800 634 6441/front desk & casino 731 3311/www.imperialpalace.com). Bus Deuce, 105, 203/self-parking & valet parking Las Vegas Boulevard South. **Rooms** 2,640. **Rates** $66-$370 double. **Credit** AmEx, DC, Disc, MC, V. **Map** p336 A6 ⑪

You don't have to be royalty to stay at this Oriental-themed hotel, in fact, with the Stardust's demise, there should be even more demand for an on-Strip property where rates often drop into double digits.

The monorail station on site helps you get around to the hipper places, but the resort does offer a few reasons to stay. The main attraction is the **Auto Collections** (*see p129*), which has more than 200 antique, classic and special-interest vehicles on display and for sale. You can even get your photo taken with an old car for free. Speaking of which, the IP's venerable *Legends in Concert* is still thriving. Indeed, it's spilling over into the remodelled casino, where, at the Dealertainers Pit, you might find Michael Jackson or Cher, primed to belt out a song from behind the blackjack table.

Accommodation

All guestrooms, from small standard rooms through to the King Suite, recently received much-needed facelifts. Certain rooms come with a jacuzzi-driven 'luv tub'. The best penthouse suites have one or two bedrooms and an extra-large living room.

Eating & drinking

There are restaurants to satisfy most basic cravings, from the **Burger Palace** to the **Pizza Palace**, plus a couple of decent buffets in between. Head to the fifth floor for fancier places: **Embers** (steak), the **Cockeyed Clam** (seafood), **Fireside** (barbecue) and **Ming Terrace** (pan-Asian). The **Rockhouse** has a mean daiquiri bar, rock music, and free shots poured 24-7 by the Rockhouse Dancers. The IP recently added the **Madhouse Bar**, a frathouse saloon by Jeff Beacher (of Beacher's Madhouse infamy) where scantily clad servers produce 'bottle service' of mini beer kegs.

Entertainment

The long-running **Legends in Concert** tribute show (*see p227*) features good-to-excellent impersonations of a variety of singers (Madonna, Shania) and classic Vegas performers (Liberace, Elvis). From April to October, the pool transforms into a luau scene, with food and a Polynesian revue. Inside at **Tequila Joe's**, guests dance to DJs nightly.

Gambling

Thanks to its high-traffic location, the casino is always busy, though that doesn't necessarily mean it's particularly favourable. Typical central-Strip blackjack rules and video poker paybacks gouge the first-time tourist; the rest of the games gouge the sucker, no matter how experienced. 'Dealertainers' in the IP's party pit impersonate Madonna, the Blues Brothers, Elvis and other pop stars while pitching cards and rockin' out to the loud music. If you have to fade the bad odds, this is a fun place to do it.

Amenities *Bars (8). Business centre. Concierge. Disabled-adapted rooms. Gym. High-speed internet (wireless $9.99). No-smoking floors. Pool (outdoor). Restaurants (9). Room service. Spa. TV: pay movies.* **Games** *Big Six; blackjack ($10-$500); Caribbean stud; casino war; craps (3x, 4x, 5x; from $3); keno; Let it Ride; pai gow poker; roulette (double zero); three-card poker. Gambling lessons (blackjack 9am daily; roulette 10am daily; craps 11am daily).*

Luxor

3900 Las Vegas Boulevard South, at W Hacienda Avenue, Las Vegas, NV 89119 (reservations 1-888 777 0188/front desk & casino 262 4102/www.luxor.com). Bus Deuce, 104, 105/self-parking & valet parking Reno Avenue. **Rooms** 4,407. **Rates** $69-$599 double. **Credit** AmEx, DC, Disc, MC, V. **Map** p336 A9 ⑫

Second only to New York New York in terms of the absurdity of its exterior, the Luxor impresses on scale long before you've set foot inside it. While some casinos limit theming to the interiors, leaving the buildings as smart but not altogether memorable towers, the 30-storey glass pyramid housing much of the Luxor makes one hell of a first impression. At night, a high-intensity light shoots skywards from the top; visible in space, it's also a beacon to a swarm of insects and bats during warmer months.

The homage to ancient Egypt continues inside, but to a far lesser extent than it did when the casino opened in 1993. The campiest elements of the theming evaporated a number of years ago, but even more Egyptiana was mummified during a still-ongoing renovation that began in 2006, lending credence to rumours that the casino may rebrand itself as the Pyramid. The enjoyably silly **King Tut Museum** (*see p125*) remains, but the theming around the pool has been toned down, and several of the hotel's Egyptian-slanted bars and restaurants have gone.

Altogether, the Luxor is something of a casino in flux. Even so, it's still a likeable place to spend a few days, not least because its **Games of the Gods** arcade and **IMAX cinema** (*see p242*) are as appealing to kids as the bustling casino floor is to adults.

MGM Grand.

Accommodation

Only around half of the hotel's 4,407 guestrooms are actually located in the pyramid. These Strip-fronted rooms offer great views and are accessed by special elevators called 'inclinators', which rise, like enclosed ski lifts, at an angle of 39°. However, there are compensations if you don't get hooked up with a pyramid room: the guestrooms in the towers, just behind the pyramid, are larger, and were refurbished in 2006.

Eating & drinking

The eating options here are best described as reliable. The **Luxor Steakhouse** and the **Pharaoh's Pheast** buffet both have good reputations and are probably the best bets in the casino. Elsewhere, the **Backstage Deli** apes New York Jewish food as only an Egyptian-themed casino in Nevada can, while **Fusia** offers upmarket Asian dishes. Burgers, pizzas and expensive coffees are available at the food court. However, a slew of new bar and restaurant openings are promised for 2007; among them are **Aspen 702**, a steakhouse backed by micro-celebs Nicky Hilton and Nick Lachey, and a couple of putatively stylish lounges.

Entertainment

After the Blue Man Group moved to the Venetian in 2005, the Luxor struggled to fill the gap. *Hairspray* came and went in the blink of an eye, leaving supremely dislikeable prop comic **Carrot Top** (*see p227*) as the main act. However, in 2008, misspelt TV magician **Criss Angel** will launch a new show, compiled with the inevitable assistance of Cirque du Soleil. Late-night entertainment is provided by the underdressed dancers of the **Fantasy** revue (*see p226*). In late 2007, überhip Los Angeles club **LAX** will set up its first outpost inside the casino.

Gambling

The massive casino, decorated with hieroglyphics and ancient artefacts, is filled with the latest high-tech slot and video poker machines. Expect $10 minimums at blackjack and craps, higher on weekends. For poker players, the card room offers weekend action so lively that Cleopatra herself would have been impressed. Take a few minutes to walk the perimeter of the circular casino and get your bearings; if you can't identify landmarks, you'll wind up going in circles.

Amenities *Bars (3). Business centre. Concierge. Disabled-adapted rooms. Gym. High-speed internet (ADSL & wireless $11.99). No-smoking floors. Pool (outdoor). Restaurants (6). Room service. Spa. TV: pay movies.* **Games** *Big Six; blackjack ($10-$10,000); Caribbean stud; casino war; craps (3x, 4x, 5x; from $5); keno; Let it Ride; pai gow poker; poker (14 tables); roulette (single zero & double zero); three-card poker. Gambling lessons (poker 2pm daily).*

MGM Grand

3799 Las Vegas Boulevard South, at E Tropicana Avenue, Las Vegas, NV 89109 (reservations 1-877 880 0880/front desk & casino 891 7777/www.mgm grand.com). Bus Deuce, 201/self-parking Las Vegas Boulevard South, Koval Avenue or E Tropicana Avenue/valet parking E Tropicana Avenue. **Rooms** 6,852. **Rates** $109-$499 double. **Credit** AmEx, DC, Disc, MC, V. **Map** p336 A8 ⑬

There is a spa here, of course. Not to mention a pool, a convention centre and a kid-friendly animal attraction (the popular **Lion Habitat**, for which *see p125*). However, the MGM Grand really comes alive after dark, when this immense resort is at its vibrant, buzzing best.

The best guides to enjoying London life

(but don't just take our word for it)

'More than 700 places where you can eat out for less than £20 a head... a mass of useful information in a geuinely pocket–sized guide'

Mail on Sunday

'Armed with a tube map and this guide there is no excuse to find yourself in a duff bar again'

Evening Standard

'I'm always asked how I keep up to date with shopping and services in a city as big as London. This guide is the answer'

Red Magazine

'Get the inside track on the capital's neighbourhoods'

Independent on Sunday

'A treasure trove of treats that lists the best the capital has to offer'

The People

Rated 'Best Restaurant Guide'

Sunday Times

Available at all good bookshops and timeout.com/shop from £6.99

100% Independent

For a time, the largest hotel on earth (with, it should be said, one of the ugliest exteriors) aimed itself squarely at families. When Vegas fashion started to move back towards the adult market, the MGM was by no means quickest to react. However, it's since thrown itself into the grown-up market with commitment and smarts, building an unlikely but deserved reputation as one of the liveliest resorts on the Strip. Billing itself as 'Maximum Vegas' takes the point a bit far, but there's little doubt that the MGM balances the needs of cash-happy big spenders, easy-going middle Americans and youthful club kids as well as any resort in the city. *Photo p81.*

Accommodation

The 5,044 rooms (including 751 increasingly plush suites) in the main building are mostly done out with art deco-styled furnishings, designed to evoke back-lot bungalows from Hollywood's glamour age. They manage it pretty well, too, though you suspect Clark Gable and Louise Brooks would sooner be down the street at the Wynn. A fourth-floor guest services desk functions as an additional concierge, a massive plus in this huge hotel.

However, the real luxury is elsewhere on the lot. First to arrive was the Mansion, which contains 29 handsomely appointed and even more handsomely priced villas. In 2005, the hotel added 51 Skylofts, vast and chic two-storey accommodations designed by Tony Chi that remain among the town's more fashionable temporary addresses. And then there's the Signature, a luxurious condo-hotel development with three 576-suite towers. Rooms have jacuzzi tubs and balconies; guests also get access to private pool areas, among other perks.

Eating & drinking

Quietly, steadily and with great savvy, the MGM Grand has spent the last ten years reinventing its once-moribund dining to the point where it now contains the best and most varied range of restaurants in the city. Many casinos make the 'something for everyone' claim about their eating options; the MGM comes closer than any to fulfilling the brief.

You can't move here for all the celebrity chefs, or at least the assistants who quietly do their bidding for them. The flagship operation is **Joël Robuchon** (*see p160*), devised by the notoriously inventive French chef; those diners unable to stretch to the $360 16-course tasting menu may prefer the fractionally more casual **L'Atelier de Joël Robuchon** (*see p158*). Among the high-end options are Tom Colicchio's **Craftsteak** (*see p155*), where the focus is on meat, fish and fowl from small farms; **Fiamma** (*see p161*), an Italian trattoria imported from New York; Japanese restaurant **Shibuya** (*see p162*) and the all-Chinese **Pearl** (see p158); and two Michael Mina operations, Californian-style eaterie **Nobhill** (*see p156*) and seafood haven **Seablue** (*see p165*).

Other star names with a toe in the MGM's restaurant pool include Cajun specialist Emeril Lagasse (**Emeril's**) and Wolfgang Puck (at the laid-back **Wolfgang Puck Bar & Grill**; *see p157*), both of

which are very good options. Meanwhile, **Diego** (*see p164*) deals in excellent Mexican food, while there's slightly more casual fare at the **Rainforest Café** (*see p236*), Colicchio's '**Wichcraft** (*see p157*), the **Stage Deli** and the **Grand Wok & Sushi Bar**, which shares a kitchen with the 24-hour coffeeshop. The buffet is one of the best on the Strip.

Like its nightclubs **Studio 54** and **Tabú** (*see p258*), the MGM's bars tend towards the hipper end of the scale. The splashiest is **Centrifuge** (*see p179*), with a large central bar upon which dancers sometimes do their thang. **Zuri**, a cigar bar of sorts, and the open-plan **Rouge** are more sophisticated options.

Entertainment

The entertainment options at the MGM are led, as is fast becoming customary in Las Vegas casinos, by Cirque du Soleil. The fourth Cirque production to launch in the city, **Kà** (*see p231*) is a spectacular, high-concept piece of dramatic fluff that plays in a vast theatre accessible towards the rear of the main casino floor. The other full-time resident piece is **Crazy Horse Paris** (*see p225*), an adult show that nonetheless aims at a rather different audience than the Crazy Horse Too strip club on Industrial Road.

The 740-seat Hollywood Theatre hosts perhaps half a dozen acts on regular rotation for runs of anywhere from a week to a month. Ticket prices are high, but you're paying a premium for the privilege of seeing such big names as David Copperfield and Tom Jones in intimate confines. Intimacy isn't a word generally associated with the 16,800-seat **MGM Grand Garden Arena** (*see p251*), which stages a mix of concerts (the Police, Rush, Justin Timberlake and the like) and sporting events (boxing, ultimate fighting).

The nightlife here is strong and relentlessly fashionable. **Studio 54** (*see p258*) lacks the cocaine, celebrities and gay hookers that defined the New York original, but it's still a popular spot. **Tabú** (*see p258*) continues to consolidate its reputation as the Strip's coolest lounge, though you'll pay for the privilege of sitting in it. Diego hosts **Vida!**, a Latin club, every Friday and Saturday.

Gambling

The MGM has four gaming areas (Entertainment, Hollywood, Monte Carlo and Sports) in which you'll find all the games, including Spanish 21. It's the largest casino in Las Vegas and boasts hundreds of tables. Table minimums can go down to $10 on weekdays, but most are higher; in the pit, you'll find $25 minimums and $15,000 maximums. There's also a large race and sports book with floor-to-ceiling screens, one of the best poker rooms in town, and 3,700 slots, from a nickel to $500.

Amenities *Bars (7). Business centre. Concierge. Disabled-adapted rooms. Gym. High-speed internet (ADSL & wireless $11.99). No-smoking floors. Pool (outdoor). Restaurants (18). Room service. Spa. TV: pay movies.* **Games** *Baccarat ($100-$15,000); Big Six; blackjack ($10-$10,000); Caribbean stud; casino war; craps (3x, 4x, 5x; from $5); keno;*

Let it Ride; mini baccarat ($25-$15,000); pai gow poker; pai gow tiles; poker (22 tables); roulette (single zero & double zero); Spanish 21; three-card poker.

Monte Carlo

3770 Las Vegas Boulevard South, between W Harmon & W Tropicana Avenues, Las Vegas, NV 89109 (reservations 1-888 529 4828/front desk & casino 730 7777/www.montecarlo.com). Bus Deuce, 201/self-parking & valet parking Rue de Monte Carlo. **Rooms** *3,002.* **Rates** *$49-$599 double.* **Credit** AmEx, DC, Disc, MC, V.* **Map** *p336 A8* ⓮

Modelled after the Place du Casino in (of course) Monte Carlo, this handsome but low-key resort will either be an appealing, mid-range option or, like the hotel's star magician Lance Burton, a master of deception, depending on your point of view. The many attractive features, not least of which is the impressive exterior architecture (twin archway entrances, a big streetside fountain), suggest this $344-million resort might be on the same page as, say, the $1.4-billion Bellagio. The truth is that the Monte Carlo successfully appeals to those after an approximation of high style at low prices.

Next to its neighbours, the Monte Carlo isn't an especially charismatic option, less energetic than New York New York and nothing like as fashionable as the MGM Grand. Still, its lack of flash and filigree is just what its admirers like about the hotel, which seems very popular with business travellers. The casino floor is about as mellow as they come, thanks to the bright lighting and high ceilings, and the rooms are simple and familiar. Attractions include not rollercoasters or animal shows but a waterfall-filled pool area and outdoor tennis courts. The front desk's picture windows look over the verdant water park, giving the best lobby view in town. *Photo p88.*

Accommodation

The Monte Carlo's tri-tower set-up contains 3,002 rooms, including 259 suites. The standard rooms exhibit a comfortable, vaguely old-world feel, with cherrywood furniture and plump furnishings. The decor gets progressively more opulent the further up the price scale you climb.

Eating & drinking

The Monte Carlo's signature eaterie is **André's** (*see p172*), the sole Strip location of André Rochat's venerable Downtown establishment. The name of the spacious, industrial-styled **Monte Carlo Brewpub** has been a little misleading since it stopped brewing its own beer, but never mind. There's also a steakhouse (**Blackstone's**), a casual Italian trattoria (**Market City Caffè**), the requisite 24-hour coffeeshop and buffet, and the **Dragon Noodle Company**.

Entertainment

The family-friendly nature of the resort is emphasised by the nightly presence of wholly traditional, entirely unthreatening and disturbingly charisma-free magician **Lance Burton** (*see p228*). Those who missed Prince at the Rio may get some comfort from

covers band **Purple Reign**, who perform in the Brewpub, while in **Houdini's Lounge** a pianist plays nightly from Thursday to Sunday.

Gambling

There are plenty of $5 blackjack tables and many 5¢ opportunities among the 2,200 slots, and a bright, casual atmosphere. Players appreciate the details: stools with backs at every machine, wide walkways throughout the casino and even single-zero roulette. The Monte Carlo attracts brisk traffic from neighbouring casinos, but the tables never seem crowded. Players stand a better chance of landing a one-on-one blackjack game with the dealer than at most Strip resorts.

Amenities *Bars (3). Business centre. Concierge. Disabled-adapted rooms. Gym. High-speed internet (ADSL $11.99). No-smoking floors. Pool (outdoor). Restaurants (8). Room service. Spa.* **Games** *Baccarat ($25-$15,000); Big Six; blackjack ($5-$3,000); Caribbean stud; craps (3x, 4x, 5x; from $5); keno; Let it Ride; mini baccarat ($10-$5,000); pai gow poker; pai gow tiles; poker (9 tables); roulette (single & double zero); three-card poker. Gambling lessons (craps 11am daily).*

New York New York

3790 Las Vegas Boulevard South, at W Tropicana Avenue, Las Vegas, NV 89109 (reservations 1-866 815 4365/front desk & casino 740 6969/www.nyny hotelcasino.com). Bus Deuce, 201/self-parking Las Vegas Boulevard South or W Tropicana Avenue/valet parking W Tropicana Avenue. **Rooms** *2,023.* **Rates** *$69-$549 double.* **Credit** AmEx, DC, Disc, MC, V.* **Map** *p336 A8* ⓯

So good they named it twice? Well, yes, as it goes. The most audacious, preposterous example of hotel theming in Las Vegas – and, for that matter, perhaps even the world – remains a thrilling success more than a decade after it welcomed its first guests. Built at a cost of $460 million, it's been called the largest piece of pop art in the world.

A mini-New York Harbor, complete with tugboats, a scaled-down Brooklyn Bridge and a giant Statue of Liberty, looms over the Tropicana/Strip intersection. Above it, the resort's skyline includes a dozen of the Big Apple's most famous landmarks, among them the Empire State Building, the Chrysler Building and the New Yorker Hotel but not the World Trade Center; the hotel was themed after 1950s New York, long before the twin towers were built. Inside, along with representations of Times Square, Central Park, Greenwich Village and Wall Street, you'll find every New York cliché in the book: a Broadway subway station, graffitied mailboxes, steam rising from manhole covers… It sounds silly, but it's tremendous fun, and seems to inspire visitors to act as if they were out on the East Coast: it's got energy like no other casino floor in town.

The resort's greatest trick, one that New York City has yet to achieve, is to balance the needs of adult visitors with those of its younger guests. Grown-ups will enjoy the nightlife here, not to mention Cirque du Soleil's adult-oriented show *Zumanity*, but there's plenty for the young 'uns. The **Coney Island Emporium** (*see p125*) is nirvana for kids and wanna-be-kids-again, a mix of old-fashioned midway games, high-tech interactive videos and virtual-reality rollercoasters. The hotel's real rollercoaster, the **Manhattan Express** (*see p125*), twists, turns and rolls around the property. The pool and spa are, alas, real letdowns: a replica of the famous Vertical Club would have been fitting. Or, perhaps, the Central Park Reservoir.

Accommodation

NYNY's rooms are concealed behind (but not in) an assortment of towers and skyscrapers. The rooms are done fairly nicely, in art deco-styled woods with black accents, and are maintained to a high standard. Although they're pretty small, they're bargains in comparison to some of their Strip competitors, especially during the week. Check when you make your booking that the Manhattan Express doesn't rumble by your window, or you'll be continually disturbed by the squeals of riders.

Eating & drinking

The restaurants aren't a match for those in the city on which they're modelled, but if they lack subtlety (and they do), they're at least a vibrant bunch. The smartest by far is **Gallagher's Steakhouse**, a Big Apple import; there's also competent Italian at **Il Fornaio**, reasonable Mexican at **Gonzalez y Gonzalez** and serviceable Chinese at **Chin-Chin**. **Nine Fine Irishmen** is a rather hokey but locally popular Irish pub, while the sports-themed **ESPN Zone** (*see p179*) is located by the sports book and gets rammed on game days. A food court fashioned after Greenwich Village (cobblestone streets, a subway station, apartment buildings) contains burgers, pizzas and fried fish, though – disappointingly – no knishes. However, the best eating option is the most straightforward: **America** (*see p153*), a 24-hour coffeeshop that delivers average-to-excellent renditions of dishes from all over the 50 states.

Entertainment

NYNY's leading show is Cirque du Soleil's **Zumanity** (*see p226*), an intriguing but only partly successful attempt at mixing Cirque's ever-dazzling acrobatics with the sexiness of the Strip-standard adult revue. After Rita Rudner moved to Harrah's, the casino decided to replace her with a roster of temporary engagements, though it's rumoured that the space may be turned into a nightclub. The other entertainments are all participatory: duelling piano players lead boozy singalongathons all night, every night at the **Bar at Times Square** (*see p178*), while **Coyote Ugly** (*see p179*) is a loud, lairy nightclub modelled on the film (which was, in turn, modelled on a New York City bar) of the same name. The **Big Apple Bar** (*see p187*), inspired by the supper clubs of the '30s, is a tad more sophisticated.

Gambling

The capacious casino is modelled on Central Park, without the muggers but with twice the crowds.

Casino action at **New York New York**.

Minimums for blackjack (practically all six-deck shoes) and craps are $10; it's $5 for roulette. The range of slots is one of the best on the Strip. Dim sum hors-d'oeuvres are served in the Asian-styled Dragon Pit, with saké, plum wine, Asian beer and teas.

Amenities *Bars (6). Business centre. Concierge. Disabled-adapted rooms. Gym. High-speed internet (ADSL $11.99). No-smoking floors. Pool (outdoor). Restaurants (8). Room service. Spa.* **Games** *Blackjack ($5-$5,000); Caribbean stud; casino war; craps (3x, 4x, 5x; from $5); Let it Ride; mini baccarat ($10-$5,000); pai gow poker; roulette (double zero); three-card poker. Gambling lessons (craps 11am daily).*

Planet Hollywood

3667 Las Vegas Boulevard South, between E Harmon Avenue & E Flamingo Road, Las Vegas, NV 89109 (reservations 1-877 333 9474/front desk & casino 785 5555/www.planethollywoodresort.com). Bus Deuce, 202/self-parking & valet parking E Harmon Avenue. **Rooms** *2,600.* **Rates** *$69-$499 double.* **Map** *p336 A7* ⑯

The Aladdin rubbed its magic lamp for the last time in spring 2007 and out popped Planet Hollywood, a rather hipper casino version of the restaurant chain. Amenities at the new arrival include the **Planet Hollywood Spa by Mandara** (*see p208*), which promises to ready guests for their 15 minutes of fame; the adjacent **Miracle Mile Shops** (*see p192*), a

The curse of the lamp

'The story of Aladdin and his lamp is full of the magic and mystery of the Middle East. The history of the Aladdin Hotel & Casino… reveals more than a little intrigue of its own.'

Writer Don Steele began his recap of the Aladdin's hard-luck history back in 1992, backing up his thesis with three decades of evidence. But then, as if he'd learned nothing from his own words, Steele abruptly concluded his essay with a burst of optimism about how a young, successful executive named Joseph Burt would cause the hotel 'to realise its substantial potential'. A year later, the Aladdin's genie was snuffed out in a motorcycle accident. Jinx, anyone?

It all began so optimistically in February 1963 when Edwin Lowe, president of Tally-Ho Inns and inventor of Yahtzee, rolled the dice on the Strip as home for one of his Tudor-style resorts. It was one thing to put such understated architecture on the Strip, but his bright idea not to offer gambling was another matter. The 450-room Tally-Ho – 'a complete flop,' wrote Steele – was out of business by October. It reopened as the King's Crown in 1964 but failed to land a gaming licence, which meant a second death sentence.

Gaming pioneer Milton Prell bought the property in 1966, adding a 500-seat theatre, a gourmet room, the 'finest par-3 golf course west of the Mississippi' and the largest casino in Nevada. He named it the Aladdin; on April Fool's Day, traffic was backed up along the Strip for what was, by all accounts, a grand opening. But after a year, his ledger showed more liabilities than assets; a further year down the line, a stroke forced him to sell. After he sold, Prell's former 'jewel in the desert' would spend the next two decades tangled up with bad company, plagued by allegations of mismanagement during a $60-million expansion in the 1970s.

In the 1980s, TV legend Johnny Carson made a bid to buy the Aladdin. When the deal fell through, Wayne Newton picked it up. But he didn't get along with his partner, and soon after a new theme was unveiled for the Aladdin: chapter 11 bankruptcy. Ginji Yasuda, a rich Japanese playboy made a heroic effort in 1987, spending $30 million to remodel the casino. Two years later, he was bankrupt; four months after that, he was dead from cancer.

The Burt drama was the old Aladdin's last gasp. In 1998, it was imploded to make room for the new $1.3-billion Aladdin, which opened in August 2000… and filed for bankruptcy 13 months later. Maybe it was bad luck that 9/11 happened just as the mega-resort had survived a fragile first year, but most experts point to a flawed concept and execution: even finding the entrance was a problem.

The good news for **Planet Hollywood** (*see p85*), which has taken over and renovated the property, is that the old problems seem to have had more to do with poor decision-making than luck. The bad news is that history is against them.

galleria of familiar shops (Urban Outfitters, H&M) and eateries (Trader Vic's, Hawaiian Tropic Zone); and a modernised theatre. At the unveiling, owner Robert Earl was joined by Bruce Willis and Carmen Electra. But if the new Planet Hollywood plans to compete for the hipsters that flock to the Palms or the Hard Rock, it's going to have to appeal to Willis's kids rather than Willis himself. *Photo p91.*

Accommodation
The 2,600 movie-themed rooms and suites are done out in what is called 'Hollywood Hip' decor: contemporary shades of rich chocolate and royal purple, Googie-esque carpet and techie amenities such as high-definition plasma TVs. Guests can earn and redeem Starpoints at more than 750 Westin, Sheraton, W, St Regis and Luxury Collection hotels.

Eating & drinking
The new and improved dining scene features the obligatory slew of celebrity restaurateurs, including **Alfredo of Rome**, famous for creating the original fettuccine Alfredo; the Japanese-Californian fusion cuisine of **Koi**, already a haven for Hollywood's A-list; **Yolos**, a Mexican eatery complete with margarita fountain; and the Glazier family's **Strip House**, a sexy steakhouse that's anything but traditional. Smaller bites are served at the **Earl of Sandwich**, **Pink's** (*see p156*) for their famous hot dogs, and **Planet Dailies**, a high-energy coffeeshop. Polynesian-themed **Trader Vic's** and David Burke's **Hawaiian Tropic Zone** have joined beach-themed burger joint **Cheeseburger at the Oasis** in the Miracle Mile Shops. And the **Spice Market Buffet** is still one of the best in town, serving a variety of ethnic dishes (including many vegetarian options).

Entertainment
The only building left from the original Aladdin, the renamed **Planet Hollywood Theatre for the Performing Arts** (*see p252*) features a well-coiffed European illusionist by the name of Hans Klok in *The Beauty of Magic*, though touring acts will also perform here. On the mezzanine level, **Stomp Out Loud** (*see p233*) shakes things up in a new $28-million theatre. Correspondents from TV's *Extra* interview celebrities from their new Vegas headquarters, the **Extra Lounge**. Privé and the **Living Room**, imports from South Beach, add a little sizzle.

Gambling
The years-long transition from the Aladdin into Planet Hollywood has reconfigured the casino endlessly, and further changes may be on the way. Well-heeled players frequent the high-limit pit on the second floor: the salon features 30 high-limit tables including blackjack, roulette and baccarat and 100 high-denomination slot machines.

Amenities *Bars (3). Business centre. Concierge. Disabled-adapted rooms. Gym. High-speed internet (wireless $11.99). No-smoking floors. Pool (outdoor). Restaurants (7). Room service. Spa. TV: pay movies.* **Games** *Baccarat ($100-$15,000); Big Six; blackjack ($5-$3,000); Caribbean stud; casino war; craps (3x,*

4x, 5x; from $5); keno; Let it Ride; mini baccarat ($25-$5,000); pai gow poker; poker (10 tables); roulette (single zero & double zero). Gambling lessons (baccarat, blackjack, craps, poker & roulette 10am Mon-Fri).

Treasure Island
3300 Las Vegas Boulevard South, at Spring Mountain Road, Las Vegas, NV 89109 (reservations 1-800 288 7206/front desk & casino 894 7111/ www.treasureisland.com). Bus Deuce, 105, 203/self-parking or valet parking Las Vegas Boulevard South or Spring Mountain Road. **Rooms** 2,885. **Rates** $79-$999 double. **Credit** AmEx, DC, Disc, MC, V. **Map** p335 & p336 A6 🔞

An object lesson in what happens when you slavishly follow focus groups rather than your own commercial instincts. Treasure Island has struggled with an identity crisis in recent years – We're *Pirates of the Caribbean*! No, we're Robinson Crusoe! We're for families! No, adults! – and hasn't yet managed to make the transition from kid-friendly operation to more lucrative adult playground. Much of the campy pirate paraphernalia that lingered around the casino, leftovers from its original incarnation as a family resort, has been buried. But the general aesthetic doesn't quite match the fine assortment of adult-oriented shows, nightclubs and restaurants that the hotel has brought in to try and reposition itself in the market. It's not exactly helped by its signature event: the pyrotechnic pirate battle in the lagoon out front, which has dropped the kid-friendly content, employed some scantily clad women and rebranded itself **Sirens of TI**. It might be the most embarrassing and undignified spectacle in North America.

Still, though the hotel amounts to less than the sum of its parts, those parts are interesting and inviting enough to make Treasure Island an appealing option. The new line-up of restaurants is worlds better than what came before, as is the nightlife. For those who think not of gimlets but of golf when they hear the word 'club', the hotel offers access to the exclusive **Shadow Creek** course, a perk reserved for guests of MGM Mirage resorts. The **Wet Spa** is disappointing, but the pool is a good one, surprisingly unheralded in the city. And though Treasure Island has little shopping to speak of on its own property, a pedestrian bridge provides easy access to the adjacent **Fashion Show Mall** (*see p193*).

Accommodation
The 2,885 rooms in TI's 36-storey Y-shaped tower are good enough for the price, decorated in appealing shades and without any undue ornamentation. Many have decent views of the Mirage volcano and the Sirens show below. The 220 suites are spacious, with living rooms, wet bars, two baths, jacuzzis and impressive TVs; they're a good deal if you feel like splashing out but not breaking the bank.

Eating & drinking
There's northern Italian fare at **Francesco's** and hunks of meat at the **Steakhouse**, two essentially by-rote Strip eateries that offer special packages

Monte Carlo. *See p85.*

combining dinner with tickets for Cirque du Soleil's *Mystère*, and snacks from **Starbucks**, **Ben & Jerry's** and **Krispy Kreme**. However, there are also plenty more charismatic options on site; indeed, the hotel's ongoing reinvention has been at its most successful when applied to its restaurants. The highlight is indisputably the **Social House** (*see p162*), a sleek, chic sushi bar located above Tangerine and operated by the all-conquering Pure group. Richard Sandoval's buzzing Mexican spot **Isla** (*see p164*), which offers a similar *Mystère* deal to the Steakhouse and Francesco's, and the surprisingly interesting menu at the 24-hour **Coffee Shop** merits investigation. Other options include the obligatory buffet, a shiny offshoot of LA's **Canter's Deli** (*see p163*), and the slightly tacky **Kahunaville**.

Entertainment

Though the captivating pitch and tumble of Cirque du Soleil's **Mystère** (*see p232*) is still good G-rated fun, the rest of TI's offerings run to more lascivious tastes. Along with Sirens of TI, the hotel has jumped on the burlesque bandwagon with **Tangerine**, where would-be exotic dancers do a tame bump and grind to live music and shimmy down to decorative undies at 9.30pm and 10.30pm (Thur-Sat only). The martini crowd shakes things up at **Mist** (*see p180*), the small, clubby lounge brought to you by the folks behind the Bellagio's Light, Caramel and Fix.

Gambling

In the ever-crowded casino, you'll find all the usual games, as well as a race and sports book, but you're the one who's likely to be on the down side. As at the Mirage, table limits are high and six-deck shoes are the rule, but you can still find a few video poker machines with good payback percentages.

Amenities *Bars (5). Business centre. Concierge. Disabled-adapted rooms. Gym. High-speed internet (ADSL & wireless $11.99). No-smoking floors. Pool (outdoor). Restaurants (11). Room service. Spa.*
Games *Baccarat ($100-$15,000); blackjack ($5-$15,000); Caribbean stud; casino war; craps (3x, 4x, 5x; from $5); keno; Let it Ride; mini baccarat ($25-$10,000); pai gow poker; pai gow tiles; poker (8 tables); roulette (double zero); Spanish 21; three-card poker.*

Budget

Bill's Gamblin' Hall & Saloon

3595 Las Vegas Boulevard South, at E Flamingo Road, Las Vegas, NV 89109 (reservations 1-866 245 5745/front desk & casino 737 2100/www. billslasvegas.com). Bus Deuce, 202/self-parking & valet parking Las Vegas Boulevard South. **Rooms** 200. **Rates** $59-$199 double. **Credit** AmEx, DC, Disc, MC, V. **Map** p336 A7 ⓲

It's anyone's guess what'll happen to this formerly likeable little operation. Previously the Barbary Coast, a cosy slice of fin-de-siècle San Francisco with a prime mid-Strip location, the property was bought by Harrah's and renamed in 2007 for the firm's founder Bill Harrah. In short order, the property lost its two main selling points: Michael's and Drai's, two gourmet restaurants that lifted the place above its rivals. The casino itself remains atmospheric, done out with stained-glass and chandeliers, but the resort's future looks decidedly uncertain.

Accommodation

You'll be pleasantly surprised by the Victorian wallpaper and paintings, etched mirrors and white lace curtains in the 200 guestrooms, some of which have four-poster brass beds, minibars and whirlpools.

Eating & drinking

Well-regarded eaterie Michael's moved in 2007 to the South Point (*see p115*), and has been replaced by the **Steakhouse at Bill's**. **Drai's** restaurant has also gone, but the nightclub remains.

Entertainment

Pete Vallee as Big Elvis – you won't believe quite how big – plays in Bill's Lounge.

Gambling

This little Strip casino doesn't look like much, but it packs a decent punch: the casino often has lower minimums than its enormous neighbours.

Amenities *Bars (2). Disabled-adapted rooms. High-speed internet (wireless $10.99). No-smoking rooms. Restaurants (3). Room service. TV: pay movies.* **Games** *Blackjack ($5-$1,000); Caribbean stud; casino war; craps (3x, 4x, 5x; from $5); keno; pai gow poker; roulette (double zero); three-card poker. Gambling lessons (craps 10.30am daily).*

Casino Royale

3411 Las Vegas Boulevard South, between Sands Avenue & E Flamingo Road, Las Vegas, NV 89109 (reservations 1-800 854 7666/front desk & casino 737 3500/www.casinoroyalehotel.com). Bus Deuce, 105, 202, 203/self-parking Las Vegas Boulevard South/no valet parking. **Rooms** 152. **Rates** $49-$179 double. **Credit** AmEx, DC, Disc, MC, V. **Map** p335 & p336 A6 ⓱

Virtually the forgotten resort on the Strip, this independently operated, 152-room casino has nothing to do with the James Bond movie of the same name. Rather, it's a truly basic little casino-hotel that survives despite being surrounded by the city's major players. Favoured by budget travellers after cheap minimums and even cheaper drinks, it's a cheery place without much charisma but with plenty of value.

Accommodation

As you might expect from the cut-price room rates, the rooms here aren't anything special: they're basically motel-standard, though the mid-Strip location is ideal as a base from which to explore the city.

Eating & drinking

The **Outback Steakhouse** and **Denny's** are the closest things to signature restaurants here. The most notable feature of the bar is the dollar beers it offers around the clock.

Entertainment

You'll have to make your own here.

Gambling

There's not much to say about this place, though the minimums are low and it's the only casino on the Strip to offer 100x odds for craps, reducing the house edge to a mere 0.02%.

Amenities *Bars (1). Disabled-adapted rooms. No-smoking floors. Pool (outdoor). Restaurants (2).* **Games** *Blackjack ($5-$1,000); Caribbean stud; craps (100x; from $3); keno; roulette (double zero); Spanish 21.*

Circus Circus

2880 Las Vegas Boulevard South, between Desert Inn Road & W Sahara Avenue, Las Vegas, NV 89109 (reservations 1-877 434 9175/front desk & casino 734 0410/www.circuscircus.com). Bus Deuce/self-parking S Industrial Road/valet parking Las Vegas Boulevard South or S Industrial Road. **Rooms** 3,773. **Rates** $39-$399 double. **Credit** AmEx, DC, Disc, MC, V. **Map** p335 B5 ⓴

After MGM Mirage purchased additional plots of land bordering Circus Circus in recent years, many in town muttered that it must be just a matter of time before Lucky the Laughing Clown is asked to fold up his Big Top and beat it. After all, he's been luring tourists into this garish casino for nearly 40 years, a lifetime by Vegas standards, and not much has changed. Sure, MGM Mirage could ask performers from Cirque du Soleil to perform on the stage above the casino, and the carnie-style midway could be transformed into a futuristic arcade. But then there's a risk that the place would end up unrecognisable from its famous turn in *Fear and Loathing in Las Vegas*, and who wants that? *Photo p92.*

Accommodation

After several expansions, there are now 3,773 spartan rooms, mainly decorated with soft-blue carpeting, pastel bedspreads and upholstery, and dark wood furniture. The West Tower is the newest (built in 1997); the cheapest (and oldest) rooms are in the motel-like Manor section. Ask for a south-facing room in the Skyrise Tower for the best view of the Strip. Other amenities include pools and the 399-space Circusland RV Park.

Eating & drinking

The **Steak House** (*see p157*) is a surprisingly high-quality dining room, while **Mexitalia Xpress** serves both Italian and Mexican. Little-known fact: when Comedy Central wanted Chef from the animated series *South Park* to have worked in a Vegas buffet, they chose the super-cheap, super-mediocre **Circus Buffet**, famous for feeding up to 10,000 hungry souls a day.

Entertainment

Circus Circus never had a showroom; it no longer even has the G-string clad pony girls, who used to ride plastic ponies on a ceiling-hung track, tossing balloons at the kiddies. But the midway and circus acts remain: acrobats, trapeze artists and magicians perform every half-hour (11am-midnight). The 23 rides and attractions at the **Adventuredome** (*see p132*) include Nickelodeon's Spongebob SquarePants 4-D thrill ride, a rollercoaster, a carousel and bumper cars.

Gambling

Connected by walkways and a monorail, each of the three casinos offers the same gaming options. The race book is located near the back of the resort, in the Skyways Tower area. A five-dollar bill is enough to get you started at most tables; it might take all day to find someone risking more than $10. You'll probably want to hide out in the casino; the rest of this place is a pre-pubescent madhouse.

Bars (3). Business centre. Disabled-
~~ns~~. Gym. No-smoking floors. Pool
~~restaurants~~ (8). Spa. **Games** Big Six;
blackjack ($3-$3,000); Caribbean stud; casino war;
craps (2x; from $3); keno; Let it Ride; pai gow poker;
poker (8 tables); roulette (double zero); three-card
poker. Gambling lessons (blackjack, craps, roulette
10.30am Mon-Fri).

Excalibur

3850 Las Vegas Boulevard South, at W Tropicana
Avenue, Las Vegas, NV 89109 (reservations 1-877
750 5464/front desk & casino 597 7777/www.
excalibur.com). Bus Deuce, 201/self-parking & valet
parking W Tropicana Avenue. **Rooms** 3,991. **Rates**
$41-$501 double. **Credit** AmEx, DC, Disc, MC, V.
Map p336 A8 ㉑

The jury's still out on whether or not this caricature
of a castle will become the next generation's Circus
Circus. MGM Mirage has been too busy transforming the pirate-themed Treasure Island and the
Polynesian-tilted Mirage into hipper versions of
their former selves, leaving Excalibur to fend for
itself. However, there have been a few changes of
note, in particular the addition of dining and entertainment options that eschew the family-friendly
theme: a biker bar, the silly Dick's Last Resort, and
the 'edgy' comedy of everyone's favourite fat guy,
Louie Anderson. Identity crisis, anyone?

Accommodation

Housed in two towers behind the castle façade, the
small rooms have none of the elegance of the hotel's
adjacent sister resorts, the Luxor and Mandalay
Bay. But a handful of spacious Parlor Suites have
guest bathrooms, dining and living areas; with
bold colours, dark wood furniture and wrought-iron
fixtures, they're nowhere near as drab as those at
Circus Circus.

Eating & drinking

Tops among the restaurants is **Sir Galahad's Pub
& Prime Rib House**, where you'll find generous
portions of prime rib and Yorkshire pudding. The
Steakhouse at Camelot serves decent cuts, while
Regale dishes out pastas. At biker-themed **Octane**,
flair bartenders serve up such cocktails as Blood,
Sweat & Gears and Tailpipe Wind; also new is
Dick's Last Resort, a playfully tacky watering
hole that serves massive cocktails and finger foods
by the bucket. There's also a children's menu at the
24-hour **Sherwood Forest Café** and an extensive
Round Table Buffet.

Entertainment

The medieval (and still child-friendly) orientation
extends into the night with the entertaining
Tournament of Kings (see p234), which features
jousting, pyrotechnics and a surprisingly decent
game-hen dinner. The **Fantasy Faire Midway**
keeps children busy with two Magic Motion
Machine film rides, medieval-themed midway
games and an arcade. Comic **Louie Anderson** and
hilarious male revue **Thunder from Down
Under** provide adult-oriented fare.

Gambling

Neon knights slay neon dragons in the casino, one
of the few in town where photography is allowed.
Visitors are surrounded by images of playing-card
kings and queens, but the table games are affordable for any commoner. Thousands of slots jam the
joint; video poker is scarcer. When you're done
throwing coins in machines, toss a few in the moat
for good luck: they'll be donated to local charities.

Amenities Bars (4). Disabled-adapted rooms.
Gym. High-speed internet (ADSL $10.95). No-
smoking floors. Pool (outdoor). Restaurants (7).
Spa. **Games** Blackjack ($5-$2,000); Caribbean stud;
casino war; craps (3x, 4x, 5x; from $5); keno; Let
it Ride; mini baccarat ($10-$2,000); pai gow poker;
poker (14 tables); roulette (double zero); Spanish
21; three-card poker. Gambling lessons (blackjack,
roulette 10.30am daily; poker 2pm daily).

Hooters

115 E Tropicana Avenue, between Las Vegas
Boulevard South & Koval Lane, Las Vegas, NV
89109 (reservations 1-866 584 6687/front desk &
casino 739 9000/www.hchvegas.com). Bus Deuce,
201/self-parking & valet parking E Tropicana
Avenue. **Rooms** 696. **Rates** $39-$399 double.
Credit AmEx, DC, Disc, MC, V. **Map** p336 B6 ㉒

How does the hotel version of Hooters differ from
the restaurants familiar across middle America?
Simple: instead of a handful of hot female service-
industry workers in skimpy orange outfits, here
there are dozens (200, if you're counting). At the bar,
at the blackjack table, by the pool... even at the
hotel's very own Hooters restaurant. If you (or
your spouse) don't appreciate this amenity, stay
somewhere else. Although it was only rebranded
as Hooters in 2006 (it was formerly the San Remo),
it's rumoured that it will soon be turned over to
another operator.

Accommodation

There are 696 rooms (including 17 suites); the standard ones are comfortable and take a beach-house
theme. The pool is paradisical and the spa is a full-
service operation with a workout room.

Eating & drinking

Cuisine here begins and ends with chicken wings, of
course, but in between are a couple of fun surprises.
Dan Marino (yes, the old Dolphins quarterback) has
a slightly upscale restaurant that features entrées not
included in his Nutrisystem diet plan. **Pete &
Shorty's** offers real Midwestern man cuisine (aka
bar food), and the **Dam Restaurant** is a 24-7 café.

Entertainment

Hooters recently dumped its martini bar and turned
it into a showroom for headliner **Bobby Slayton**,
the 'Pit Bull of Comedy'. There's also live music at
Nippers Pool Bar and the **Porch Dogs** club.

Gambling

Hooters has struggled since it opened, which either
explains or is a direct result of its tight casino (perhaps both). The blackjack has terrible rules: dealer

Planet Hollywood. *See p85.*

hits soft 17, you can only double on 10 and 11, and all games pay 6:5 for naturals. Most tables have $10 or $25 minimums and some, mostly the ones in the Hooters Girls Fun Pit, are dealt by you know who. (One of the blackjack dealers was crowned Miss Hooters International 2006.) Beware of some of the video poker schedules: they look typical, but some of the payouts are short. Craps isn't bad, with 3-5x odds and a field 12 paying triple. The players club returns a decent 1% for slot play and 0.5% for video poker, but only in comps: there's no cashback.

Amenities *Bars (4). Concierge. Disabled-adapted rooms. Gym. High-speed internet (ADSL $12.95). No-smoking floors. Pool (outdoor). Restaurants (3). Room service. Spa. TV: pay movies.* **Games** *Blackjack ($10-$2,000); craps (3x, 4x, 5x; from $10); keno; Let it Ride; pai gow poker; poker (3 tables); roulette (double zero); three-card poker.*

Riviera

2901 Las Vegas Boulevard South, between E Sahara Avenue & E Desert Inn Road, Las Vegas, NV 89109 (reservations 1-800 634 6753/front desk & casino 734 5110/www.rivierahotel.com). Bus Deuce, 108, 204/self-parking Riviera Boulevard or Paradise Road/valet parking Las Vegas Boulevard South. **Rooms** 2,100. **Rates** $49-$199 double. **Credit** AmEx, DC, Disc, MC, V. **Map** p335 B5 ㉙

When the Riviera opened in 1955, Liberace headlined in its showroom. Though the original king of bling is long gone, the entertainment offerings at the Riv a half-century later are just as camp. The first high-rise hotel on the Strip continues to thumb its nose at family-style entertainment, staying true to its roots as an adult playground. Other throwbacks include two lighted tennis courts, an old-school pool (surrounded by hotel towers for too much shade) and guestrooms that haven't been dramatically upgraded for years. Still, there remains a market for this sort of hotel: unrepentantly old-fashioned, basic and – key to the entire operation's continued viability – cheap.

Accommodation

There are five levels of 2,100 rooms, two of them suites. The standard rooms are all in the original tower, while the deluxe rooms (better views) and suites are in the two newer towers. The newer tower rooms are smallish but not cramped, and decorated with dark wood furniture. Half the rooms have views over the pool; the rest face the surrounding mountains. Don't expect much – well, anything, to be honest – in the way of luxury.

Eating & drinking

As at most middlebrow resorts, there are a couple of smarter restaurants and a handful of casual, low-end ones. At the top, there's **Ristorante Italiano** and **Kristofer's Steakhouse**, though the specials at **Kady's** coffeeshop are better bargains. Elsewhere, **Hound Doggies** tilts at a 1950s diner vibe, the **World's Fare Buffet** offers a range of international food, and the food court contains such staples as **Pizza Hut** and **KFC**.

Entertainment

Both of the two signature shows, Frank Marino's cross-dressing, lip-synching **Evening at La Cage** (*see p227*) and creaking topless fandango **Crazy Girls** (*see p225*), have been in residence five minutes short of forever. The **Riviera Comedy Club** (*see p234*) presents two shows nightly, with a new line-up every week, while the once-swinging **Le Bistro**

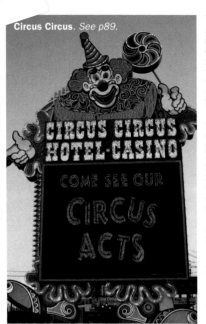
Circus Circus. See p89.

Lounge now runs a roster of shows that include Neil Diamond impersonator Jay White, comedy hypnotist Dr Scott Lewis and American Storm, a kind of cut-price Chippendales. The **SynCity** nightclub doesn't give the Palms any sleepless nights.

Gambling

The gaming area is an L-shaped expanse of red and mock gold with an elevated lounge and bar in the centre (your best bet for a meeting place that everyone can find). Minimums at the tables are not as low as the surroundings would suggest: $5-$10 blackjack in a $2 setting. The lowest limits and nickel slots are found in a part of the casino dubbed Nickel Town, a plausible nickname for the whole resort.

Amenities Bars (2). Business centre. Disabled-adapted rooms. Gym. High-speed internet (wireless $9.99). No-smoking floors. Pool (outdoor). Restaurants (4). Room service. Spa. TV: pay movies. Games Blackjack ($5-$2,000); Caribbean stud; craps (2x; from $5); keno; Let it Ride; mini baccarat ($25-$2,000); pai gow poker; poker (8 tables); roulette (double zero); Spanish 21; three-card poker. Gambling lessons (poker 2pm daily).

Sahara

2535 Las Vegas Boulevard South, at E Sahara Avenue, Las Vegas, NV 89109 (reservations 1-866 382 8884/front desk & casino 737 2111/www.sahara vegas.com). Bus Deuce, 108, 204/self-parking or valet parking Las Vegas Boulevard South or Paradise Road. **Rooms** *1,720.* **Rates** *$43-$259 double.* **Credit** *AmEx, DC, Disc, MC, V.* **Map** *p335 C4*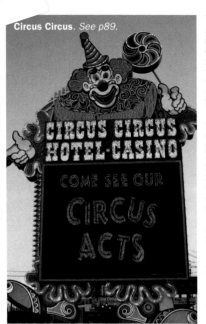

When the Sahara opened in 1952, its then-exotic African theme, from the famed camels perched outside on the Congo Showroom, seemed right at home on barren Las Vegas Boulevard. After a half-century of development, redevelopment and obliteration, the resort stands virtually alone at the north end of the Strip, an appropriate location for an operation that's far closer in spirit to the Stratosphere a few blocks north than to Wynn Las Vegas just south.

No longer exciting, the Sahara in 2007 is a somewhat faded property, ragged around the edges and soaked in a smoky fug. In some ways, though, its isolation has worked in its favour: with the Strip's headline-grabbers just out of walking distance for most visitors, guests tend to stay on site, playing in the basic casino, dining in the NASCAR Café (the hotel is hugely popular among petrolheads, especially during NASCAR weekend in March) and sticking around for a show or two.

However, hope is on the horizon. The Sahara was sold in March 2007 to younger LA developer Sam Nazarian, who was quick to state his desire to improve the property. Watch this space…

Accommodation

The 1,720 guestrooms range from standard through three different sizes of suite. They're usually among the cheapest on the Strip, and you get what you pay for. Still, it's a safe and secure operation.

Eating & drinking

The reborn classic **House of Lords** steakhouse, which does what you might expect, is the hotel's main eaterie, but there's also Mexican food at **Paco's Hideaway**, a 24-hour coffeeshop and a buffet. The car-themed **NASCAR Café** *(see p236)* is proof of the resort's mid-America appeal.

Entertainment

Old classics are delivered nightly in the Congo Room by the **Platters, Cornell Gunter's Coasters & Beary Hobbs' Drifters**, but original members are conspicuous by their absence; hell, the show doesn't even feature Hobbs, who died of cancer in 1996, and Gunter, murdered in 1990. Late-night entertainment comes courtesy of acerbic magician the **Amazing Johnathan** *(see p228)*. The **Casbar Lounge** is where Louis Prima made a splash in the 1950s; today's performers have less potential. You won't escape without seeing the **Las Vegas Cyber Speedway** *(see p132)*, an entertaining $15-million indoor racing-car simulation that offers the thrill of driving a high-performance motor without the risk. **Speed–The Ride** *(see p132)* is a rollercoaster that zips around the front entrance.

Gambling

Alas, the days of $1 blackjack at the Sahara have been lost in the sands of time. But you can still find single-deck, double-deck and shoe blackjack games with $5 minimums: among the Strip's lowest, though the single-decks pay 6:5 for naturals. Minimum crap bets are $5. Low-limit Texas hold 'em and seven-card stud games are spread daily in the card room.

Amenities *Bars (6). Business centre. Disabled-adapted rooms. High-speed internet (ADSL $11.99). No-smoking floors. Pool (outdoor). Restaurants (5). Room service. Spa. TV: pay movies.* **Games** *Blackjack ($5-$1,000); Caribbean stud; craps (5x; from $5); keno; Let it Ride; pai gow poker; poker (16 tables); roulette (double zero); Spanish 21; three-card poker. Gambling lessons (poker 10am Mon-Fri; craps 11.30am Mon-Fri; blackjack noon Mon-Fri).*

Stratosphere

2000 Las Vegas Boulevard South, at W St Louis Avenue, Las Vegas, NV 89104 (reservations 1-800 998 6937/front desk & casino 380 7777/www. stratospherehotel.com). Bus Deuce, 108/self-parking & valet parking Las Vegas Boulevard South. **Rooms** 2,444. **Rates** $35-$319 double. **Credit** AmEx, DC, Disc, MC, V. **Map** p335 C4 🌀

The Stratosphere strives to be a destination resort out of necessity: it's between the Strip and Fremont Street, essentially no-man's land. Its lure starts at the summit, with a variety of rides atop the highest free-standing observation tower in the US (1,149ft/107m). There are indoor and outdoor observation decks, a revolving restaurant, and thrill rides with names like **Insanity** (*see p132*). Down below are some 40 Tower Shops (not exactly the Fashion Show Mall), a remodelled casino and even a new nightclub. *Photo p94.*

Accommodation

Guestrooms in the tower would be interesting, but all the Stratosphere's sleeping quarters are in separate buildings below. Some are in the original Vegas World mid-rise; a more recent tower brought the total to 2,444 rooms and suites. There are an overwhelming 13 different types of room, from the smallish standard rooms to the massive Premier Suites. On the eighth floor, there's a big pool and recreation deck.

Eating & drinking

Eating options run from the pricey **Top of the World** (*see p166*), which rotates once every 90 minutes, to **McDonald's**. Among those in the middle are **Lucky's**, a 24-hour café, and **Roxy's**, which has a '50s diner motif and rock 'n' roll singing waiters.

Entertainment

As impersonator shows go, the Strat's **American Superstars** is pretty good. If you like semi-nudity in your Vegas shows, *Bite* offers it... and vampires. On the tower, there's an indoor/outdoor observation deck, plus a trio of terrifying rides (*see p132*). Nightlife is provided at **Polly Esther's** (*see p257*).

Gambling

The casino area is spacious and comfortable, if not particularly noteworthy. The layout approximates a series of circles, which looks good but seriously complicates any attempt to get directly from one end of the complex to the other. The emphasis is on liberal machines and table-game gimmicks which go some way to improve players' odds. The Stratosphere advertises a 98% return on more than 150 $1 dollar slots, a 100% return on

Meet the regulars North Strip

Folks from the North Strip wear sensible walking shoes because they don't trust taxis. A fanny pack is a must: it typically contains tissues, a roll of nickels and an emergency supply of Skittles. Their watches are plastic and digital; but, hey, they keep good time. North Strippers prefer economy lodging and can be heard saying things like, 'Who cares what the room looks like if you're only going to sleep in it?' For that is all they do: they haven't had sex since 1978. If a trip is too long to walk, they take a shuttle and don't tip the driver. That would just be a waste of good gambling money.

By day, North Strippers scour magazines for coupons or spend several hours at a high-pressure timeshare sales pitch for which they receive two free buffets and some steak knives. In the gift shop, they pick up T-shirts for the kids and vulgar towels for the neighbours, but not sodas: the hotels charge a mark-up. When gambling, they plant themselves in front of a nickel slot machine themed after their favourite TV show, then visit the promotions booth after an hour to see if they've earned any comps. Dinner is the hard-earned free buffet, and the steak knives come in handy on the tough brisket labelled as prime rib. Afterwards, they may hit the nickel slots for more action, or go up to the room to watch a few hours on the keno channel. Either way, they'll be asleep by nine to ensure they can get up early enough to hit the casino before all the complimentary doughnuts have run out.

some video poker machines and 10x odds on craps, as well as double-exposure blackjack and crapless craps (with a bunch of cockamamie rules that aren't player-friendly).

Amenities *Bars (7). Business centre. Concierge. Disabled-adapted rooms. Gym. High-speed internet (wireless in some rooms $9.95). No-smoking floors. Pools (outdoor). Restaurants (5). Room service. Spa. TV: pay movies.* **Games** *Big Six; blackjack ($5-$3,000); Caribbean stud; craps (10x; from $5); Let it Ride; mini baccarat ($5-$1,000); pai gow poker; poker (6 tables); roulette (single & double zero); three-card poker. Gambling lessons (roulette 10.30am daily; craps 11am daily).*

Tropicana

3801 Las Vegas Boulevard South, at E Tropicana Avenue, Las Vegas, NV 89109 (reservations 1-888 826 8767/front desk & casino 739 2222/www. tropicanalv.com). Bus Deuce, 201/self-parking & valet parking Las Vegas Boulevard South, E Tropicana Avenue or Reno Avenue. **Rooms** 1,878. **Rates** $45-$329 double. **Credit** AmEx, DC, Disc, MC, V. **Map** p336 A8 ㉖

The Tropicana was at the heart of the biggest bidding war in casino history when, in 2006, Columbia Sussex (owner of various Westin, Sheraton and Marriott hotels) paid $2.75 billion for the rights to redevelop the 50-year-old 'Tiffany of the Strip'. The Polynesian-themed hotel will soon undergo a multi-million-dollar, property-wide expansion, transforming it into the largest casino-resort in the city. Until then, the Trop is worth a look if you want a nice peek – between the hotel's two towers lie 5 acres of tropical landscaping with pools, lagoons, waterfalls and swim-up blackjack tables – without paying too much for it.

Accommodation

The original two-storey motor inn buildings surround the pool and are thus conveniently close to it; although they're the oldest at the resort, they can be comfortable if you get one with a balcony and pool view. The newer tower rooms are generally better, though they could do with a renovation.

Eating & drinking

Mizuno's, a Japanese-style *teppan* room and steakhouse where staff cook food (steaks, Gulf shrimp and Australian lobster) at your table, is one of the resort's best eateries. The colossal shrimp cocktail and prime rib at **Legends Steak & Seafood** is a throwback to the classic Vegas steakhouse. Other choices include **Tuscany** for pizza and pasta, and the obligatory, all-you-can-eat **Island Buffet**.

Entertainment

The Trop is home to the carefully old-fashioned feathers-and-sequins spectacular **Folies Bergere** (*see p231*): the longest-running production show in America, it opened here in 1959. It shares the Tiffany Theatre stage with **Xtreme Magic Starring Dirk Arthur**. There's also the **Comedy Stop** (*see p234*), which has a weekly rotation of stand-ups. But the biggest draw has to be **Bodies: the Exhibition**

(*see p124*), 21 meticulously dissected human bodies that put under the microscope what happens to the lungs and liver after one too many trips to Vegas.

Gambling

The swim-up blackjack bar is the Tropicana's one unique gaming pull. Otherwise, there's the usual variety of games, with a bit less video poker than other places and some of the slots showing their age. The casino is on the smallish side, and cramped, with a tiny, dingy sports book at the bottom of a stairway at the back, hidden as if the hotel were embarrassed by it. Which they should be.

Amenities *Bars (3). Business centre. Disabled-adapted rooms. Gym. High-speed internet (wireless in tower rooms $11.95). No-smoking floors. Pool (indoor/outdoor). Restaurants (5). Room service. Spa. TV: pay movies.* **Games** *Blackjack ($5-$3,000); Caribbean stud; craps (3x, 4x, 5x; from $5); keno; Let it Ride; pai gow poker; poker (6 tables); roulette (double zero); three-card poker. Gambling lessons (blackjack, craps, poker 10am Wed-Sat).*

Into the **Stratosphere**… See p93.

Non-casino hotels

Expensive

Four Seasons
3960 Las Vegas Boulevard South, at W Hacienda Drive, Las Vegas, NV 89119 (reservations 1-800 819 5053/front desk & casino 632 5000/www. fourseasons.com/lasvegas). Bus Deuce, 104, 105/ no self-parking/valet parking Las Vegas Boulevard South. **Rooms** 424. **Rates** $270-$610 double. **Map** p336 A9 ㉗
The first boutique hotel to open on the Strip remains its most popular. It has its own private driveway, entrance, lobby, valet and crack concierge staff, as well as an award-winning spa, landscaped gardens surrounding a secluded pool, restaurants and lounges. The twist is that the 424 rooms and suites are located in the Mandalay Bay resort, though they're accessed by private elevators. Guests may use Mandalay Bay's facilities, as well as those within Thehotel at Mandalay Bay (*see p95*).

The guestrooms are spacious and luxurious, especially the large marble bathrooms with sunken jacuzzis and L'Occitane products. Extra points are garnered for superior service: complimentary cocktails greet guests upon arrival, and repeat guests have room keys waiting for them at valet, while families will find rooms child-proofed and stocked with age-appropriate amenities (nappies for babies, Playstations for older children). Joggers get chilled water and towels after exercising. Dining options include **Charlie Palmer Steak** (*see p155*) and the popular **Verandah Café** (*see p157*), which features Italian-influenced American fare.
Amenities Bars (1). Business centre. Concierge. Disabled-adapted rooms. Gym. High-speed internet (wireless $10). No-smoking floors. Pool (outdoor). Restaurants (2). Room service. Spa. TV: DVD/ pay movies.

Thehotel at Mandalay Bay
3950 Las Vegas Boulevard South, at W Hacienda Avenue, Las Vegas, NV 89119 (reservations 1-877 632 7800/front desk & casino 632 7777/www. mandalaybay.com). Bus Deuce, 104, 105/self-parking & valet parking W Hacienda Avenue. **Rooms** 1,117. **Rates** $159-$1,799 suite. **Credit** AmEx, DC, Disc, MC, V. **Map** p336 A9 ㉘
The rather clumsy name of this property has reputedly caused cab drivers no end of confusion, to the point where a change has been rumoured. The hotel itself, though, needs no such alterations. Located around the back of Mandalay Bay (follow the signs carefully), Thehotel has filled a gap in the market that most major cities have plugged with a W Hotel, which is to say that it's chic without being too fashionable, and a big hit with hipsters in their late twenties while being careful not to exclude everyone else.

The rooms here are all suites, decorated in rich colours and furnished with chairs and beds that manage to be both stylish and extremely comfortable. Most suites have high-speed internet, a nod to the

Classic elegance at the **Four Seasons**.

business travellers who choose this hotel for its absence of gambling. The restaurants, shows and gaming at Mandalay Bay are a corridor away, but the handsome hotel lobby is slot-free. Atop the rooms tower is Alain Ducasse's ultra-posh restaurant **Mix** (*see p160*), and its attached lounge (*see p257*). The **Bathhouse** spa (*see p206*) is also excellent. The whole place doesn't feel like Vegas, which, for many guests, is part of the appeal. Recommended.
Amenities Bars (1). Business centre. Concierge. Disabled-adapted rooms. Gym. High-speed internet (ADSL $12). No-smoking floors. Pools (outdoor). Restaurants (2). Room service. Spa. TV: pay movies.

Trump International
3128 Las Vegas Boulevard South, between Spring Mountain & Desert Inn Roads, Las Vegas, NV 89109 (www.trumplv.com). Bus Deuce, 203. **Rooms** tbc. **Rates** tbc. **Credit** tbc. **Map** p335 A5 ㉙
A joint venture between The Donald and Phil Ruffin, the owner of next door's New Frontier, Trump's first Vegas property promises to be as posh as sister properties in New York and Florida. When Trump revealed his plans to build a condo-hotel tower here on *The Apprentice*, the condos were all reserved within three weeks. It was no surprise when, in a subsequent episode, he announced plans to build a second tower a little further down the line.

The 1,200-plus spacious condo guestrooms will feature floor-to-ceiling windows, spa tubs, plasma TVs and, of course, lots and lots of marble. The

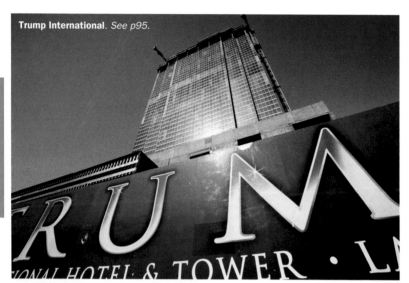

Trump International. *See p95.*

property is due to open in the first half of 2008; Jack Christie, VP of Sales and Marketing, promises that 'guests will have everything they need to live the Trump lifestyle in Las Vegas', including 24-hour concierge and security services, white-gloved doormen, and the finest in gourmet and casual dining. **Amenities** *tbc.*

Off-Strip

Hotel-casinos

Expensive

Hard Rock
4455 Paradise Road, at E Harmon Avenue, Las Vegas, NV 89109 (reservations 1-800 473 7625/front desk & casino 693 5000/www.hardrockhotel.com). Bus 108/self-parking Paradise Road/valet parking E Harmon Avenue. **Rooms** 647. **Rates** $99-$549 double. **Credit** AmEx, DC, Disc, MC, V. **Map** p336 C7

The exact point at which rock 'n' roll sold its soul is a mystery, but you can bet the Hard Rock took a healthy cut. The image of Sid Vicious adorns slot machines, Bob Dylan's lyrics line the elevators, and a notice reminds guests that smart dress is required, a rule that would bar more or less every one of the casino's icons. Still, despite its blazingly middle-American appropriation of rock imagery, the Hard Rock has been an unqualified success since its 1995 opening. The golf-shooting, Dockers-wearing baby-boomer brigade is here in force midweek, but on weekends, the hotel draws a crowd of boisterous fun-seekers, A-list glitterati and local hipsters.

The Palms may have stolen some of its thunder over the past few years, particularly on the nightlife front, but the Hard Rock remains a premier party place. The casino design (circular, with a bar in the middle) is a beauty, and means the place always feels buzzing even when it's half-empty. Out back, the pool scene's even hotter: sandy beaches, waterfalls and swim-up blackjack. Amenities include the RockSpa (hey, don't shoot the messenger), electric purple limos and SUVs for guests, some terrific restaurants and the coolest sundries boutique in town: selling everything from liquor to lube, it embodies the concept of the convenience store.

After taking over the hotel from founder Peter Morton in early 2007, the Morgans Hotel Group (formerly owned by Ian Schrager) announced an expansion of the property, which looks likely to include 600 additional rooms, 400 VIP suites, a new convention centre and a mini-mall. Work is scheduled to be completed by the end of 2009. *Photo p98.*

Accommodation
The casino itself may be like a zoo, but the upstairs guestrooms are remarkably peaceful and minimalist, with mod space-agey furnishings that are sort of *Jetsons* meets the I-Ching. And thanks largely to the fact that the Hard Rock was built very recently, they're also very spacious. Most rooms have been decorated with museum-quality photos of rock stars. Try to get digs overlooking the pool.

Eating & drinking
The Hard Rock really excels with its eating options: there are only five of them, but each one is well worth a visit. **Nobu** (*see p168*) offers the city's best sushi, while **AJ's Steakhouse** (*see p167*) gave a retro, twentysomething twist to the meat-beat formula long

before it was fashionable to do so. **Simon Kitchen & Bar** (*see p167*) dishes out high-concept, high-calibre American comfort food; the **Pink Taco** (*see p169*) specialises in gentrified Mexican cooking, while also boasting a kinetic early-evening bar scene; and **Mr Lucky's 24/7** (*see p167*) is the city's coolest coffeeshop. For people-watching, try the **Center Bar**, in the middle of the circular casino, and the **Viva Las Vegas Lounge** (*see p183*). In summer, head out to the pool bar, or to Sunday's raucous Rehab pool party.

Entertainment
When it opened a decade ago, the 3,000-capacity **Joint** (*see p250*) helped bust any lingering music industry stigma about playing Vegas, and it remains one of the strongest music venues in the city. There's more music, albeit of a rather lower grade, in the **Viva Las Vegas Lounge**. After-hours, the party continues in **Body English** (*see p256*), a fantastically fashionable nightclub full of fantastically fashionable women and the men who (would like to) love them. Avoid **Beacher's Madhouse**, a sporadically star-studded but ultimately dull variety show hosted each month by indefatigable self-publicist Jeff Beacher.

Gambling
A mid 1990s beast it may be, but this is still a hip and extremely popular gambling den. The casino remains small by Vegas standards: only 800 slots and video poker machines and 76 tables. The main floor is one big circle, with an outer hardwood walkway and an elevated bar in the centre. Dealers are encouraged to be friendly and enthusiastic; some will even give you a high-five if you hit a natural blackjack, a stunt that would give the pit boss a heart attack anywhere else.

Amenities *Bars (7). Concierge. Disabled-adapted rooms. Gym. High-speed internet (wireless $11.95). No-smoking rooms. Pool (outdoor). Restaurants (5). Room service. Spa. TV: pay movies.* **Games** *Baccarat ($100-$3,000); blackjack ($10-$5,000); Caribbean stud; craps (3x, 4x, 5x; from $5); Let it Ride; mini baccarat ($5-$2,000); pai gow poker; roulette (double zero); three-card poker.*

Moderate

Las Vegas Hilton
3000 Paradise Road, between E Sahara Avenue & E Desert Inn Road, Las Vegas, NV 89109 (reservations 1-888 732 7117/front desk & casino 732 5111/www.lvhilton.com). Bus 108, 204, 213/ self-parking Paradise Road or Joe W Brown Drive/valet parking Paradise Road. **Rooms** *3,000.* **Rates** *$59-$319 double.* **Credit** *AmEx, DC, Disc, MC, V.* **Map** *p335 C5* ❸❶
Given that it has the biggest stake in Vegas's convention business, it's no surprise that the Hilton is as self-sufficient as resorts come. There are 3,000 rooms, a smörgåsbord of fine restaurants and an endless list of amenities – a full-service spa, a rec deck with tennis courts, wedding facilities

(at the only place where Elvis himself got married), a *Star Trek* theme park…

Accommodation
Just east of the Strip, the Hilton is perfect for those who want to be close to, but not in the middle of, the bustle. (The on-site monorail station can connect you to that in a hurry.) The seven room 'levels' each have their own decor, more than just increasingly plush renditions of the standard look. Park Avenue, for instance, is classic Manhattan style, while Classic goes for 1920s Hollywood. Some standard rooms are dark and claustrophobic. In addition to the standard ('deluxe') room, there are six 'levels' of suites.

Eating & drinking
Teppanyaki chain **Benihana** has an impressive 'Japanese village' setting, though the food is costly. Three other Asian spots (**Garden of the Dragon**, **Teru Sushi**, **888 Noodle Bar**) join **Andiamo** (Italian), the **Hilton Steakhouse** and the *Star Trek*-themed **Quark's Bar & Restaurant** (*see p183*).

Entertainment
Dating back to Elvis and his 837 straight sold-out performances in the 1970s, the Hilton has a long-standing reputation for its headliners. The current king is **Barry Manilow**, whose regular engagement is called *Music & Passion* (*see p230*). The Shimmer Cabaret is anchored by **Menopause: the Musical** (*see p231*) and a music-and-dance show called *Sunset Strip*. **Star Trek: the Experience** (*see p135*) features two intergalactic adventures.

Gambling
Aside from the kitschy Space Quest Casino, which has $5 tables and sci-fi slots that offer the singular experience of starting the game by passing your hand though a laser beam, this is a high-roller haven, where class divisions are more conspicuous than at most casinos and minimums go through the roof when there's a big convention in town. The baccarat pit and high-limit tables are detached from the main gaming area, and the Platinum Plus slot machines, $5 and up per pull, have their own space. High limits dominate the main floor: the $100 tables are jumping year-round. Managers will only bring out a single-zero roulette wheel if you agree to bet $25-plus per spin. Sports bettors still flock to the 400-seat Super Book, where explanations on how to bet on various sports are posted up to help novices.

Amenities *Bars (6). Business centre. Disabled-adapted rooms. Gym. High-speed internet (ADSL $10, wireless in café). No-smoking floors. Pool (outdoor). Restaurants (15). Room service. Spa. TV: pay movies.* **Games** *Baccarat ($100-$15,000); Big Six; blackjack ($10-$10,000); Caribbean stud; casino war; craps (3x, 4x, 5x; from $5); keno; Let it Ride; mini baccarat ($25-$5,000); pai gow poker; poker (1 table); roulette (double zero; single zero on request); three-card poker. Gambling lessons (craps 10.30am & 4pm Mon-Fri; blackjack 2pm Mon-Fri).*

Hipsters hang happily with conventioneers at the **Hard Rock**. *See p96.*

Palms

4321 W Flamingo Road, at S Valley View Boulevard, Las Vegas, NV 89103 (reservations 1-866 942 7770/ front desk & casino 942 7777/www.palms.com). Bus 201/self-parking W Flamingo Road, S Arville Street or S Valley View Boulevard/valet parking W Flamingo Road. **Rooms** 798. **Rates** $89-$359 double. **Credit** AmEx, DC, Disc, MC, V. **Map** p333 X3 ⓧ

Ever since MTV's *Real World* took over a floor of the Palms, owner George Maloof has shown a Midas touch for keeping up with everybody from twentysomething hipsters to blue-rinse daytime gamblers. At night, the Palms attracts a Who's Who of Hollywood players and sports stars with nightclubs, a new concert hall, chic restaurants, a tattoo parlour, 'bachelor suites' replete with dancer poles and some rooms with giant beds (Maloof and his brother own the Sacramento Kings basketball team). But the magic also works on locals, with a movie theatre, a food court, a slots-driven casino and, most of all, quality service. And still the expansion goes on: Palms Place, a condominium hotel and spa (and the 'final' installment in the hotel's $650-million expansion), will connect to the hotel and all of its amenities via a moving walkway called the SkyTube. *Photo p100.*

Accommodation

The rooms at the Palms aren't giant, but many compensate by having great views – and you get to curl up on the same beds as those you would find at the luxury Four Seasons. Two floors of Fantasy Suites include a Hugh Hefner Sky Villa with balcony pool; the Hardwood Suite, a vast playpen with a jacuzzi and a half-court basketball court; the Kingpin Suite, with a pool table and a bowling lane; and an Erotic Suite, with a circular, 8ft rotating bed with mirrored ceiling. The 'What happens in Vegas' line has surely been uttered more here than anywhere else.

Eating & drinking

Up in the penthouse of the original tower is **Alizé** (*see p170*), André Rochat's third French restaurant. Downstairs, there's **Little Buddha** (*see p170*), where you can dine on Asian dishes with a French twist or nosh with the beautiful people at the sushi bar. From Chicago comes **N9ne** (*see p169*), a steakhouse, champagne/caviar bar and celebrity hangout; the folks behind it also run **Nove** (*see p171*), an extravagant hotspot decked out in crystal chandeliers, purple leather and crocodile skins. **Garduño's** offers tasty Tex-Mex and the **Sunrise Café** is a serviceable 24-hour diner that's not as hip as it should be; there's also a buffet and food court.

Entertainment

The first **Playboy Club** to open in 25 years arrived in the Palms' Fantasy Tower in 2006. The first venue in town to combine gaming and lounging, Hef's haunt brought even more cachet to the Palms by injecting it with added sex appeal. Above it is **Moon**, a nightclub with a retractable roof.

Elsewhere, **Pearl** (*see p251*), an intimate concert hall, gives the House of Blues and the Joint serious competition. The three-storey **Rain** (*see p258*) shines as a proper nightclub; high above it all (and with an equally lofty attitude) is the white-on-white **Ghostbar** (*see p183*), kind of LA East. When the weather heats up, so does **Skin**, a twice-weekly pool party complete with cavorting 'mermaids'.

Don't look down

Casting your eyes to the floor in a casino can be a dizzying experience. Typically underfoot is a continuous sea of repeating, seemingly haphazard geometric shapes done up in the most nauseating of colours. The common perception among Vegas visitors is that these patterns are meant to camouflage the worst of splatters, from spilled cosmopolitans to the visceral product of actual nausea.

Take the seemingly apocryphal but apparently true tale of a shooting that occurred in one of the Strip casinos a few years back. Despite bloody injuries sustained by both a patron (who perished) and a security guard (who survived), the casino floor was up and running once more within a couple of hours. In all likelihood, the casino took advantage of the thousand or so yards of cheap 'attic stock' most properties maintain for such emergency operations. Then again, it's possible that no one even noticed among the swirly circles and hot magentas.

Not all hotels in Vegas go for bizarre and aesthetically displeasing carpets shipped in from Third World countries. Indeed, casinos no longer feel obligated to match their carpets to a repeated theme or colour scheme, or to convey an air of festivity through fibres. Modern design firms now try and inject artistic vision into their client's grander, more cultured carpet concepts: the stars and confetti of yore are slowly being replaced with mandalas, and the standard black backgrounds dotted with glowing golds are giving way to hand-woven carpets with custom colours.

According to designer Terrien Hale of Ulster Carpet Mills' Las Vegas design studio, today's sophisticated clients demand far more from their carpets than crazy patterns and the ability to conceal disgusting things. 'On average, it now takes three months from initial concept to actual installation,' says Hale, 'but depending on the complexity of the project, it could take more.' Typically, a designer interprets a client's concept and injects a percentage of her own hand into the design before shipping it out for production.

In Hale's case, her designs are created at company-operated looms in Ireland, where the 90 per cent wool/ten per cent nylon carpets are treated with a special polypropylene backing before being shipped back to Las Vegas. They're designed for durability and absorption, but also as a new sort of canvas for the manic and/or depressed feet of Las Vegas visitors.

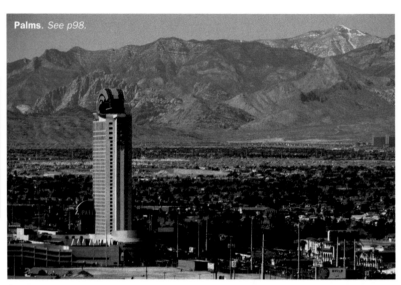

Palms. *See p98.*

Gambling

Underpinned by a classy hardwood floor, the casino includes 2,400 slots, 55 table games (many with $10 minimums), and a race and sports book. A survey conducted just after the casino opened found the slots to be the loosest in Las Vegas; judging from the video poker, this relative generosity lives on.

Amenities *Bars (6). Business centre. Concierge. Disabled-adapted rooms. Gym. High-speed internet (ADSL/wireless $11.99). No-smoking floors. Pool (outdoor). Restaurants (9). Room service. Spa. TV: DVD/pay movies.* **Games** *Baccarat ($100-$10,000); blackjack ($10-$5,000); Caribbean stud; casino war; craps (3x, 4x, 5x; from $5); Let it Ride; mini baccarat ($10-$5,000); pai gow poker; poker (10 tables); roulette (double zero); three-card poker. Gambling lessons (poker noon-Mon-Fri).*

Rio

3700 W Flamingo Road, at S Valley View Boulevard, Las Vegas, NV 89103 (reservations 1-866 746 7671/ front desk & casino 777 7777/www.harrahs.com). Bus 201/self-parking & valet parking W Flamingo Road, S Valley View Boulevard or Viking Street. **Rooms** 2,563. **Rates** $90-$480 suite. **Credit** AmEx, DC, Disc, MC, V. **Map** p333 X3 ❸

The Rio is another identity crisis in progress. In a bid to appeal to a younger audience, the all-suites Rio hired Prince to play here in 2006 and 2007, while Pure Management Group brought in hipster bowling lounge **Lucky Strike Lanes**. But some things remain unchanged: **Masquerade Show in the Sky** a free parade with musicians and dancers, is still staged seven times daily. It's part of the hyperactive **Masquerade Village**, which features two storeys of dining, a variety of drinking (from Irish

pub to wine cellar), dancing, shopping and shows. Other amenities include four waterfall-filled pools complete with sandy beach and volleyball courts, three wedding chapels and a floor of honeymoon suites, the top-of-the-line Michael's Salon, a spa, and access to the Rio Secco golf course, a half-hour away.

Accommodation

The comfortable mini-suites feature floor-to-ceiling windows, big (32in/81cm) televisions and fridges. The full suites, measuring 1,600sq ft (150sq m), come with better sound systems and wet bars.

Eating & drinking

The range of options here is wide and appealing: the **All-American Bar & Grille**, the award-winning Indian **Gaylord's** (*see p170*), wildly popular chain **Hamada of Japan**, solid Italian at **Antonio's**, **Buzio's** for seafood and **Bamboleo** for Mexican. The **Carnival World Buffet** (*see p177*) is a long-time favourite. Newest is the Italy-by-way-of-Philly **Café Martorano**, from East Coast restaurateur Steve Martorano, which goes nightclub afterhours.

Entertainment

The postmodern comedic magic of **Penn & Teller** (*see p229*) is the rock of the Rio, holding the fort in the Samba Theatre; the entrenched **Chippendales** (*see p225*) do exactly what you'd expect. For something different, try the interactive comedy theatre of **Tony 'n' Tina's Wedding** (*see p233*).

The nightlife has improved, mostly thanks to Prince's **Club 3121** and **Cafe Martorano**. Elsewhere, the **tI-Bar** combines natural earth elements (rock, water, light) with natural Vegas elements (dancing bartendresses in flesh-coloured costumes). The **Flirt Lounge** fits its billing as 'the haven for women to gather after seeing the Chippendales'. The formerly fashionable **VooDoo Lounge** offers ghastly decor, ordinary service and – the key – great views. **Lucky Strike**, a ten-lane hipster-heavy bowling alley contains a full-service restaurant and bar, retro decor and throbbing music.

Gambling

The casino is huge, sprawling for two blocks, and the predominant colours are green ($25) and black ($100): at weekends, it's hard to find $10-minimum blackjack. Smaller-stakes gamblers should aim for the lower-limit tables in the outlying areas of the casino; or better yet, walk across the street to the Gold Coast. Poker is offered – the Rio is home to the **World Series of Poker** (*see p215*) – but it's a tough room filled with locals. A shuttle bus runs between the Rio and the Strip (9am-1am daily).

Amenities Bars (10). Business centre. Concierge. Disabled-adapted rooms. Gym. High-speed internet (ADSL $12.95, wireless in convention area). No-smoking floors. Pool (outdoor). Restaurants (13). Room service. Spa. TV: pay movies. **Games** *Baccarat ($100-$15,000); Big Six; blackjack ($15-$10,000); Caribbean stud; casino war; craps (3x, 4x, 5x; from $5); keno; Let it Ride; mini baccarat ($25-$10,000); pai gow poker; pai gow tiles; poker (8 tables); roulette (double zero).*

Westin Casuarina

160 E Flamingo Road, at Koval Lane, Las Vegas, NV 89109 (reservations 1-800 937 8461/front desk & casino 836 5900/www.starwoodhotels.com). Bus Deuce, 202/self-parking & valet parking E Flamingo Road. **Rooms** 826. **Rates** $112-$299 double. **Credit** AmEx, DC, Disc, MC, V. **Map** p336 B7 ③④

The first Westin-branded hotel in Las Vegas is a low-key resort, which is just how the majority of its guests like it. There is a small casino here, and even (though you'll need to look to find it) a cosy little showroom, but the Casuarina is aimed less at holidaymakers and more at the kind of business traveller who wants to get some work done but also wants the bright lights of the Strip within easy reach. There's a good deal of meeting space, and rooms contain all the amenities a laptop-toting workaholic could want. But it's also a comfortable place to stop a while: the service is solid, the pool area is relaxing, and the **Hibiscus** spa has 15 treatment rooms and a full-service salon.

Accommodation

The rooms here are everything you'd expect from a Westin property, which is to say that they're comfortable, handsome (in a discreet way), immaculately maintained and well equipped for the business traveller. The 'Heavenly Beds' live up to their names.

Eating & drinking

Suede, the hotel's sole restaurant, offers comfort food 24-7; there's also a **Starbucks** on site.

Entertainment

There is a showroom here, but no single show seems to stick around for very long.

Gambling

The gambling here feels like an afterthought, with 300 machines and ten table games. However, it is one of the few non-smoking casino areas in the city.

Amenities Bars (1). Business centre. Concierge. Disabled-adapted rooms. Gym. High-speed internet (ADSL $9.95). No-smoking floors. Pool (outdoor). Restaurants (2). Room service. Spa. TV: pay movies. **Gambling** *Blackjack ($5-$500); craps (2x; from $5); roulette (double zero).*

Non-casino hotels

Expensive

Platinum

211 E Flamingo Road, at Koval Lane, Las Vegas, NV 89169 (reservations 1-877 211 9211/front desk 893 0824/www.platinumlasvegas.com). Bus 201/ no self-parking/valet parking E Flamingo Road. **Rooms** 255. **Credit** AmEx, DC, Disc, MC, V. **Map** p336 B7 ③⑤

The second condo-hotel to open in Las Vegas (the first was the Residences at the MGM Grand), this highly impressive property sits within a five-minute walk of the Strip. It's close enough for convenience, but the location also allows it to retain a welcome sense of distance. Free of both gambling and smoking, the Platinum is a refuge from the madness mere metres away: perfect for the residents who snapped up many of its 255 suites and now live here part-time, but also great for visitors keen on retaining their sanity while all around them are losing theirs. It's a very well-run operation, free of bustle but retaining a certain urban style in its restaurant (*see p167*), becalmed ground-floor bar and fabulously appointed spa. And the suites themselves are both capacious (the bathrooms in some suites are bigger than guestrooms at a couple of hotels in town) and handsome, done out with high-spec amenities and very comfortable beds. The cannily designed indoor-outdoor pool on the fifth floor is another nice touch in a property that's quietly full of them. *Photos p103.* *Amenities Bars (1). Disabled-adapted rooms. Gym. High-speed internet ($12.99). No-smoking rooms. Pool (indoor/outdoor). Restaurants (1). Room service. Spa. TV: pay movies.*

Renaissance

3400 Paradise Road, between E Desert Inn Road & E Twain Avenue, Las Vegas, NV 89109 (reservations 1-800 750 0980/front desk 733 6533/ www.renaissancelasvegas.com). Bus 108, 213/self-parking & valet parking Paradise Road. **Rooms** 548. **Rates** $119-$419 double. **Credit** AmEx, DC, Disc, MC, V. **Map** p335 & p336 C6 ③⑥

This 15-storey, 550-room Marriott hotel south of the Las Vegas Convention Center seems all business, with a list of amenities that includes the highest-tech wireless internet service (WiMAX), ergonomic desk chairs and even 'Exhibitor Suites'. The hotel has a sophisticated executive level with a lounge, a pool area, spa service, comfy beds with high-end linens

and piles of pillows, and flat-screen televisions in every room. There's no mention of a nightclub or casino for good reason: the Renaissance is the city's largest non-gaming property. Still, there is one type of sin on site: **Envy**, a Richard Chamberlain steak-house that serves a variety of rich comfort foods from a Kobe filet mignon to truffle mac and cheese, with 1,500 bottles of wine. Escaping work is easy, with a monorail station nearby and the Strip a block away.
Amenities *Bars (1). Concierge. Disabled-adapted rooms. Gym. High-speed internet (ADSL $12.95, wireless in lobby). No-smoking hotel. Pool (outdoor). Restaurants (1). Room service. Spa. TV: pay movies.*

Moderate

Alexis Resort & Villas

375 E Harmon Avenue, between Koval Lane & Paradise Road, Las Vegas, NV 89109 (reservations 1-800 582 2228/front desk 796 3300/www.alexis park.com). Bus 108, 213/self-parking E Harmon Avenue. **Rooms** 495. **Rates** $79-$299 suite. **Credit** AmEx, DC, Disc, MC, V. **Map** p336 C8 ⑰
Built as an apartment complex and later transformed into an all-suites hotel (where local teenagers booked suites on prom night, until the resort wised up and began requiring guests to be 21), the gaming-free, Mediterranean-style Alexis is a surprisingly sedate little operation. The two-storey buildings, nestled along winding pathways, house 500 well-appointed suites, ranging in size from 450sq ft to 1,275sq ft (42sq m to 120sq m) and offering a host of unexpected accoutrements (gas fireplaces, large bathrooms and, in some cases, upstairs lofts). But the main selling point? It's right by the **Hard Rock** (*see p96*).

Amenities *Bars (1). Business centre. Disabled-adapted rooms. Gym. High-speed internet (ADSL $5). No-smoking rooms. Pools (outdoor). Restaurants (1). Room service. Spa. TV: pay movies.*

Artisan

1501 W Sahara Avenue, at Highland Drive, Las Vegas, NV 89102 (reservations 1-800 554 4092/ front desk 214 4000/www.theartisanhotel.com). Bus 204/self-parking W Sahara Avenue/no valet parking. **Rooms** 64. **Rates** $119-$179 double. **Credit** AmEx, MC, V. **Map** p335 B4 ㊳
This boutique hotel, housed rather unexpectedly in a former Travelodge in the shadow of I-15, shares a trait with most Strip resorts: it has a theme. The old-world European decor is inspired by art and artists; paintings, a mix of pieces by local artists and reproductions of iconic works by the likes of Rembrandt and Van Gogh, cover virtually every inch of wall space in the public areas, and even decorate the ceilings. The theme continues in the **Artisan Lounge** (*see p183*), a late-night hotspot frequented by local hipsters, and in the hotel's dining room. The 64 individually decorated guestrooms and suites are priced a little highly for their location, but they're likeable enough and a good option if you fancy steering clear of the Strip. A spa is scheduled to open in 2007.
Amenities *Bars (1). Business centre. Concierge. Disabled-adapted rooms. Gym. High-speed internet (wireless free). No-smoking floors. Pools (outdoor). Restaurants (1). Room service. Spa. TV: pay movies.*

Carriage House

105 E Harmon Avenue, between Las Vegas Boulevard South & Koval Lane, Las Vegas, NV 89109 (reservations 1-800 221 2301 ext 65/front desk 798 1020/www.carriagehouselasvegas.com).

Artisan.

Platinum. See p101.

Bus Deuce, 201, 202/self-parking E Harmon Avenue or Audrie Street/no valet parking. **Rooms** 155. **Rates** $99-$145 double. **Credit** AmEx, DC, Disc, MC, V. **Map** p336 B8 ③⑨

Located next door to Grand Chateau, a new time-share resort owned and operated by Marriott, the Carriage House is often overlooked by visitors. However, the moderately priced rooms are great value for the location, the best of any hotel not actually on Las Vegas Boulevard South. The rooms and suites are kept in decent shape; even the smallest ones have kitchenettes. Outside, there's a tennis court, a heated pool and a simple sun deck.

Amenities *Business centre. Concierge. Disabled-adapted rooms. High-speed internet (ADSL free). No-smoking floors. Pool (outdoor). TV: DVD/pay movies.*

Comfort Inn

4350 Paradise Road, between E Flamingo Road & E Harmon Avenue, Las Vegas, NV 89109 (reservations 1-877 424 2000/www.choicehotels.com). Bus 108/self-parking Paradise Road/no valet parking. **Rooms** 199. **Rates** $79-$109. **Credit** AmEx, DC, Disc, MC, V. **Map** p336 C7 ④⓪

In truth, this outpost of the ubiquitous national chain isn't anything special. However, it's a useful standby in the event that the rest of the town is booked solid or running at often ridiculously high weekend prices: the rates here never seem to change by more than ten bucks a night, regardless of the time of year or the time of week. The hotel offers a similar range of amenities to those delivered by

Comfort Inns in the South-west: an outdoor pool, a very basic breakfast, and an assortment of kitchen utilities (microwave, coffeemaker) that no one ever seems to use. Still, it's kept in fair condition, and the location is terrific for hipsters: it's opposite the **Hard Rock** (*see p96*) and close to the **Double Down Saloon** (*see p181*).

Amenities *Disabled-adapted rooms. Gym. High-speed internet (ADSL free). No-smoking floors. Pool (outdoor). TV: pay movies.*

Courtyard by Marriott

3275 Paradise Road, at E Desert Inn Road, Las Vegas, NV 89109 (reservations 1-800 661 1064/ front desk 791 3600/www.marriott.com). Bus 108, 213/self-parking Paradise Road/no valet parking. **Rooms** 149. **Rates** $139-$269 double. **Credit** AmEx, DC, Disc, MC, V. **Map** p335 C5 ④①

While Las Vegas's status as the world's most ridiculous resort grabs the headlines, it's worth stressing that the city is also the convention capital of the US, welcoming millions of business travellers each year alongside all the leisure traffic. This outpost of Marriott's Courtyard chain is tilted squarely at those here for work purposes, and particularly at those who've flown in to attend an event at the Las Vegas Convention Center right opposite the property. All rooms have work spaces and free high-speed internet access, and decor that won't offer any distractions from the job at hand. It's one of several such chain-tied business hotels within walking distance of the LVCC; others include the immediately adjacent Residence Inn (3225 Paradise Road, 1-702 796 9300, www.marriott.com) and a tidy, well-equipped branch of the popular Embassy Suites hotel group (3600 Paradise Road, 1-702 893 8000, www.embassysuites.com).

Amenities *Bars (1). Business centre. Disabled-adapted rooms. Gym. High-speed internet (ADSL plus wireless in lobby $9.95). No-smoking floors. Pools (outdoor). Restaurants (1). TV: pay movies.*

Budget

Aruba Hotel
1208 Las Vegas Boulevard South, at E Charleston Boulevard, Las Vegas, NV 89104 (reservations 1-866 383 3150/front desk 383 3100/www.arubalas vegas.com). Deuce, 206/self-parking Las Vegas Boulevard South/no valet parking. **Rooms** 94. **Rates** $49-$99 double. **Credit** AmEx, MC, V. **Map** p335 C3 ⓸

The slightly shady stretch of Las Vegas Boulevard South between the Stratosphere and Charleston Boulevard is lined with old motels. Many of them are pretty sketchy places, as you'd expect given the signs out front advertising hourly rates and free adult movies, but a few stand out from the crowd. The Holiday Motel (2205 Las Vegas Boulevard South) is a pretty scruffy place, but its animated vintage neon sign is one of the most handsome in town. And up the road, the venerable Aruba at least makes an effort to elevate itself above its surroundings. This is still a pretty basic and thin-walled motel, sure, and the location isn't perfect. But a recent refurbishment has spruced it up a lot, with the management tilting at a vintage Vegas vibe, and the regular events in the Thunderbird Lounge (swing night on Fridays, occasional bands on Saturdays) are a nice touch.

Amenities *Bars (1). Disabled-adapted rooms. Gym. No-smoking rooms. Pool (outdoor). Restaurants (1). Room service. Spa. TV.*

Budget Suites
3655 W Tropicana Avenue, between S Valley View Boulevard & I-15, Las Vegas, NV 89103 (reservations 1-888 281 0480/front desk 739 1000/www.budgetsuites.com). Bus 201/self-parking Paradise Road/no valet parking. **Rooms** 480. **Rates** $199-$299/wk suite. **Credit** AmEx, MC, V. **Map** p333 A8 ⓸

Budget Suites are perfect for visitors planning on staying in Las Vegas for an extended period who require some self-catering facilities. The daily rates are nothing special, but a one-bed apartment can be rented for around $250 a week, with further discounts for monthly rentals. Each secure 220- to 300-unit complex is made up of basic mini-suites, each with their own kitchen and bathroom. Maid service is available, but you can save on the expense by bringing your own linen and towels. There are four locations dotted around Las Vegas, but this is the closest to the Strip.

Amenities *Disabled-adapted rooms. Pool (outdoor).*

Sin City Hostel
1208 Las Vegas Boulevard South, at E Charleston Boulevard, Las Vegas, NV 89104 (reservations & front desk 868 0222/www.sincityhostel.com). Deuce, 206/self-parking Las Vegas Boulevard South/no valet parking. **Rooms** 7. **Rates** $19.50-$39. **Credit** AmEx, MC, V. **Map** p335 C3 ⓸

The lack of youth hostels in Vegas is easily explained by the fact that you can get a room in a Downtown casino for $30 or so. Still, despite its location in the Naked City, the Sin City Hostel has built a nice reputation. The dorms are relatively cosy, and there are also semi-private doubles. Amenities include a free laundry, a high-speed internet terminal and a jacuzzi pool. Guests must produce a student ID or proof of international travel at check-in.

Amenities *Disabled-adapted rooms. No-smoking rooms.*

Downtown

In 1906, people were gambling in what is now Downtown. Sawdust joints, casinos with wooden boardwalks and floors, attracted railroad workers, ranchers and the like. For classic Vegas, you should head here, where old neon turns night into day and casinos offer fewer sideshows to distract from gambling. The house rules at the casinos are often more liberal than on the Strip and minimum bets tend to be lower. Still, poor attitudes on the casino floors, a result of poorer management, leaves Downtown gambling a sad shadow of its former self.

Hotel-casinos

Moderate

Golden Nugget
129 E Fremont Street, at S Casino Center Boulevard, Las Vegas, NV 89101 (reservations 1-800 846 5336/front desk & casino 385 7111/www.goldennugget.com). Bus Deuce & all DTC-bound buses/self-parking E 1st Street/valet parking S Casino Center Boulevard. **Rooms** 1,907. **Rates** $79-$189 double. **Credit** AmEx, DC, Disc, MC, V. **Map** p334 C1 ⓸

After two years in the hands of young duo Tim Poster and Tom Breitling, the venerable Nugget was taken over in 2005 by Landry's Restaurants. Many Downtown observers feared that the Texas-based restaurant chain would drain the place of its character, but a $100-million programme of renovations has actually pepped up the place no end. Following the improvements, the Nugget has consolidated its position as the best casino on Fremont Street.

The refurbishments have been dramatic, and almost entirely for the better. The casino floor now feels almost grand, complete with a new poker room and the city's most handsome sports book. A slew of new restaurants have revitalised what had

Swimming with sharks (well, nearly) in the pool at the **Golden Nugget**.

become a fairly tired catering programme. And then there's the fabulous pool area, complete with private cabanas, its own lounge (the Dive Bar, tee hee) and water slides running through a central shark tank. Well, why not?

Accommodation
The rooms here are not as swanky as some would have you believe; the recent renovations under Landry's were almost entirely limited to the property's public areas. Still, the lodgings here are still pretty decent, and better than those found at any other Downtown property. The three hotel towers contain a total of 1,907 rooms, topped by a number of plush suites (including some spread over two levels). The suites atop the spa tower are in a more modern style, the ones atop the original tower positively old Vegas opulence. Wireless internet access is an added bonus.

Eating & drinking
The arrival of Landry's resulted in a massive overhaul of the eating and drinking options at the Nugget; visitors returning to the casino after a few years away will scarcely recognise it. The key addition is a branch of **Vic & Anthony's** (*see p171*), with lighter fare offered at **Lillie's Noodle House** and the Italian-slanted **Grotto**. The **Carson Street Café** has been overhauled, but continues to serve a straightforward range of casual American classics, and the buffet rightly retains its reputation as the neighbourhood's finest. But perhaps the most dramatic addition is **Rush Lounge** (*see p184*), a nightclubby lounge that's worlds away from anything offered by its Fremont Street competitors.

Entertainment
The Nugget's new 600-seater deserves a rather more thrilling show than *Simply Ballroom*, its current incumbent. Guest headliners add a little variety.

Gambling
The Nugget's elegant marble lobby may seem out of place on Fremont Street, and the high minimums (mostly $10 for craps and blackjack) in the nicely renovated casino are are unusual for Downtown. There's a segregated pit for players with larger bankrolls who want to play baccarat and blackjack without the hoi polloi; it's the only high-limit pit Downtown. However, there are also good selections of slot and video poker machines from low to high denominations. The sports book was relocated to where the buffet used to be; it's now full-scale.

Amenities *Bars (4). Business centre. Concierge. Disabled-adapted rooms. Gym. High-speed internet (ADSL $11.99). No-smoking floors. Pools (outdoor). Restaurants (5). Room service. Spa. TV: pay movies.* **Games** *Blackjack ($5-$2,500); Caribbean stud; casino war; craps (3x, 4x, 5x; from $5); keno; Let it Ride; mini baccarat ($5-$2,500); pai gow poker; poker (9 tables); roulette (double-zero); Spanish 21; three-card poker. Gambling lessons (blackjack, craps, poker, roulette 10am daily).*

Main Street Station
200 N Main Street, at E Stewart Avenue, Las Vegas, NV 89101 (reservations 1-800 713 8933/front desk & casino 387 1896/www.mainstreetcasino.com). Bus Deuce & all DTC-bound buses/self-parking & valet parking N Main Street. **Rooms** *430.* **Rates** *$40-$110 double.* **Credit** *AmEx, DC, Disc, MC, V.* **Map** *p334 C1* **46**

Main Street Station is the nicest Downtown casino not called the Golden Nugget. Themed as a fin-de-siècle delight (check out the gaslamps that front the property), the casino is filled with antiques of all kinds, not all of them Victorian. Teddy Roosevelt's Pullman car is here, now a chic smoking lounge; a carved oak fireplace from Prestwick Castle in Scotland and a set of doors from an old London bank are also on display; and chunks of the Berlin Wall sit in the men's room. Accessible yet smart, upscale (for Downtown) yet fun, this isn't the most charismatic property, but it's likeable all the same.

Accommodation
The 430 guestrooms are comfortable, if rather basic.

Eating & drinking
The choice might be small, but it's all good stuff. Its name a nod to a railway theme that's delineated in fairly tasteful fashion, the **Pullman Grille** deals in surf and turf favourites. It's fine, but the **Triple 7 Brew Pub** (*see p185*) remains a better bet, the well-above-average burgers and sandwiches acting as perfect stomach-lining for the very decent beers brewed on site. Many locals swear by the **Garden Court Buffet**: the room is beautiful, the selections are excellent and the prices ($10.99 for dinner) are most definitely right.

Entertainment
Nothing, really.

Gambling
Main Street offers a good selection of slots and video poker, three-card poker and low limits at the tables; $5 single- and double-deck blackjack dominates and the crap tables offer 20x odds. An illuminated sign over the roulette area depicts a single-zero wheel, but the wheel itself contains two zeros.

Amenities *Bars (1). Disabled-adapted rooms. No-smoking rooms. Restaurants (3). Room service.* **Games** *Blackjack ($5-$1,000); craps (20x; from $5); keno; Let it Ride; pai gow poker (with a progressive); roulette (double zero); three-card poker.*

Budget

Binion's
128 E Fremont Street, at N Casino Center Boulevard, Las Vegas, NV 89101 (reservations 1-800 937 6537/ front desk & casino 382 1600/www.binions.com). Bus Deuce & all DTC-bound buses/self-parking N Casino Center Boulevard, E Ogden Avenue or E Stewart Avenue/valet parking N Casino Center Boulevard or Ogden Avenue. **Rooms** 366. **Rates** $39-$79 double. **Credit** AmEx, DC, Disc, MC, V. **Map** p334 D1 ⑰

Opened by Benny Binion as Binion's Horseshoe in 1951, this Fremont Street relic competes with the Flamingo and Caesars Palace for the title of the most iconic hotel-casino in Vegas history. Certainly, it's been one of the most influential. Binion, a fabulous character and a fairly unpleasant man, was arguably more responsible than any other individual for the tone of 21st-century gambling in the city; it was

Binion who abolished table limits for the first time, and Binion who effectively established the World Series of Poker here in the early 1970s.

So much for the past. After the Horseshoe stumbled into financial disrepair under the auspices of Binion's daughter Becky Behnen, the property fell into corporate hands (first Harrah's, then MTR Gaming) and it's not been the same since. The Horseshoe name has been lost to history, while the World Series of Poker has decamped to the Harrah's-owned Rio. A recent refurbishment of the casino has sapped all atmosphere from the space, leaving this historic property as just another Downtown grind joint. Shame.

Accommodation
Eighty of the rooms are from the original casino; the other 286 were added when the hotel acquired the Mint. The vast majority of them could use some fairly serious regeneration.

Entertainment
The main entertainment here comes courtesy of a mechanical bull, two words that could also be usefully employed when describing the recent remodelling of the casino.

Eating & drinking
Binion's Original Coffee Shop is still pretty decent, and there are excellent views from the 24th-floor **Binion's Ranch Steakhouse**, but there's otherwise not much here.

Gambling
When the Binions owned Binion's, you found savvy, renegade dealers, some of the best in town. But dramatic modifications have occurred since the change in ownership. Only four crap tables remain from what was once the centre of the dice universe. The blackjack pits have also shrunk, replaced by some newfangled poker derivatives that would've rendered Benny Binion apoplectic. Still, the video poker is only half bad; and the poker room is one of the largest in town. The race book occupies a former lounge in the West Horseshoe; the sports book is in a separate part of the casino.

Amenities *Bars (2). Disabled-adapted rooms. No-smoking rooms. Restaurants (3).* **Games** *Blackjack ($5-$3,000); craps (3x, 4x, 5x; from $5); keno; Let it Ride; mini baccarat ($5-$3,000); poker (35 tables); roulette (double zero); three-card poker. Gambling lessons (poker 11am daily).*

El Cortez
600 E Fremont Street, at N 6th Street, Las Vegas, NV 89101 (reservations 1-800 634 6703/front desk & casino 385 5200/www.elcortezhotelcasino.com). Bus Deuce & all DTC-bound buses/self-parking E Ogden Avenue/valet parking N 6th Street. **Rooms** 300. **Rates** $33-$110 double. **Credit** AmEx, DC, Disc, MC, V. **Map** p334 D2 ㊽

When its owners boast about the 'new El Cortez', don't get nervous. Yes, they've pumped $20 million into the old place, replacing smoke-saturated carpeting, widening the casino aisles, installing new table games, adding a wine cellar, revamping the valet entrance and remodelling the rooms. But the historic building's Spanish-style architecture is still intact, and so is another relic: Jackie Gaughan, who bought the property way back in 1963, still walks the floors daily, single-handedly keeping the spirit of post-war Downtown alive. Gaughan's mission statement – 'Give the customer a good deal and he'll come back' – is nice to hear in the age of resorts run by corporations. And they do come back, for low-stakes slots in the city's oldest operating casino, cheap rooms, bargain meals and nine-buck haircuts in the barbers.

Accommodation
The rooms are spartan to say the least (what do you expect for 30 bucks?), but those in the main hotel have been freshened up a little, and remodelling is under way on the 100 rooms across the street in the Ogden House portion of the property. The 'suites' are just slightly larger rooms.

Entertainment
You make your own fun here, though there are at least a number of new style bars just across the road.

Eating & drinking
If you fancy yourself as a character from *Fear and Loathing in Las Vegas*, you're in luck. The circular booths and kelly-green/hot-pink decor at **Roberta's** scream Tarantino; the porterhouse steak special here is a local favourite. **Careful Kitty's**, a 24-hour coffeeshop, provides both local colour and myriad late-night specials.

Gambling
The El Cortez is the place to go if you're short on cash and high on hope: there are plenty of penny and nickel video poker machines, and some of the few remaining $3 blackjack tables in town. Crap minimums go as low as $3, but 10x odds are continuous. Roulette often has a 25¢ minimum; like the 40¢ keno, it's good for cheap entertainment. The casino hosts

a twice-yearly social security number lottery: if your nine-digit number is drawn, you win $50,000.

Amenities *Bars (3). Disabled-adapted rooms. No-smoking rooms. Restaurants (2).* **Games** *Blackjack ($3-$500); craps (10x; from $3); keno; Let it Ride; mini baccarat ($5-$1,000); poker (2 tables); roulette (double zero). Gambling lessons (blackjack, craps 8.15am Tue, Fri).*

Fitzgeralds
301 E Fremont Street, at S 3rd Street, Las Vegas, NV 89101 (reservations 1-800 274 5825/front desk & casino 388 2400/www.fitzgeraldslasvegas.com). Bus Deuce & all DTC-bound buses/self-parking S 3rd Street/valet parking S 4th Street. **Rooms** *638.* **Rates** *$50-$179 double.* **Credit** *AmEx, DC, Disc, MC, V.* **Map** *p334 D1* ⑲
Luck might be a lady elsewhere in Vegas, but here she's a giant leprechaun, mounted on the roof and spilling a pot o' gold. The Irish theme aside, this is standard Downtown fare, though it does have some amusing lounge acts and an outdoor pool.

Accommodation
There are 638 guestrooms (including 14 suites) in the 34-storey hotel. There have been some modest attempts to modernise the property, including a new business centre.

Eating & drinking
Don B's Steakhouse is a recent upgrade from the old Limerick, but the menu isn't that different. If you're unsure, get food you can see first at **Molly's Buffet**. Plan C: Fitzgerald's proudly offers the only **McDonald's** on Fremont Street.

Entertainment
The Fitz shows signs of life in its lounge, featuring acts such as the **Spirit of the King Band** (an Elvis tribute) and impersonator **Larry G Jones**, billed somewhat optimistically as 'the Man of 1,002 Voices'.

Going to extremes Rooms

The cheapest rooms in town are Downtown. At the **El Cortez** (*see p106*), you can get a room for a mere $30; if you're prepared to really slum it at the **Western** (*see p111*), you may pay even less.

If your tastes are a little more upscale, try the **Las Vegas Hilton**'s Verona Villa (*see p97*), At 15,400 square feet (1,430 square metres), it's reportedly the largest hotel suite in the world. But is it worth the reputed $17,500 a night? The four-bedroom Garden Villa at the Mansion inside the **MGM Grand** (*see p81*) is smaller at 9,000 square feet (850 square metres), but it has an indoor pool and, at $15,000 a night, it's a little cheaper.

The three-bedroom Penthouse Suite on the 11th floor of the **Hard Rock** (*see p96*) has a bowling alley and a hot tub big enough for six. It's typically held for HR's biggest players, but you can rent it for a mere $50,000 per night. But the most extravagant deal is offered by the **Ritz-Carlton, Lake Las Vegas** (*see p118*). Taking in a two-night stay in the hotel's presidential suite, helicopter transport from the airport, 14 dozen roses, two private dinners, use of a luxury car, a shopping spree at Neiman Marcus, Cristal champagne, body treatments, a butler, monogrammed pillowcases and personalised bathrobes, it clocks in at a hefty $100,000.

Gambling

A typical Downtown grind joint spread over two levels, the Fitzgeralds casino has low minimums for all the table games, especially roulette ($2, with quarter wheel chips). The blackjack is mostly six-deck. If you look hard enough, you can find full-pay video poker in quarter denominations. Upstairs is a smaller gaming area outside the restaurants, and there's also a small outdoor deck off the bar, the only one of its kind Downtown.

Amenities *Bars (3). Business centre. Disabled-adapted rooms. No-smoking rooms. Pools (outdoor). Restaurants (4).* **Games** *Blackjack ($5-$500); Caribbean stud; craps (3x, 4x, 5x; from $3); Let it Ride; keno; pai gow poker; poker (6 tables); roulette (double zero); Spanish 21. Gambling lessons (craps times vary Fri, Sat).*

Four Queens

202 E Fremont Street, at S Casino Center Boulevard, Las Vegas, NV 89101 (reservations 1-800 634 6045/front desk & casino 385 4011/www.fourqueens.com). Bus Deuce & all DTC-bound buses/self-parking E Carson Avenue/valet parking S 3rd Street. **Rooms** 690. **Rates** $50-$120 double. **Credit** AmEx, DC, Disc, MC, V. **Map** p334 D1 ⑩

Fresh off a 40th anniversary, the Four Queens are still ladies in waiting; specifically, waiting for a genuine Fremont resurgence. But for visitors who like their gambling vacations cheap and to the point, this is a prime location for a taste of old-school Vegas.

Accommodation

The hotel's 690 guestrooms (including 45 suites) have been remodelled, but keep your hopes down. Still, the new flat-screen TVs are a nice touch.

Eating & drinking

The best of Downtown's bunch might be **Hugo's Cellar** (*see p171*), a romantic, quintessentially old-school restaurant: long-stem roses handed out at the door, salad cart, steak and lobster, and, of course, the flaming table-side cherries jubilee. **Magnolia's Veranda** is a standard Downtown 24-hour café (complete with the standard prime rib dinner), while the **Chicago Brewery** features microbrews, pizza and a cigar lounge. There's also a deli.

Entertainment

The Canyon Club, run by House of Blues expats, is a 600-capacity music venue that opened in 2007.

Gambling

Cramped and crowded, for some reason the Four Queens packs 'em in nightly. It's not that the gambling here is any stronger than next door or across the street, though the beers are better thanks to the presence of a brewpub. The roulette chips are dollars, with a $5 minimum. A $5 toke to the cocktail waitresses earns a huge smile and frequent service.

Amenities *Bars (3). Disabled-adapted rooms. No-smoking rooms. Restaurants (5).* **Games** *Blackjack ($5-$500); Caribbean stud; craps (5x; from $5); Let it Ride; keno; pai gow poker; roulette (double zero); Spanish 21.*

Fremont

200 E Fremont Street, at N Casino Center Boulevard, Las Vegas, NV 89101 (reservations 1-800 634 6182/front desk & casino 385 3232/www.fremontcasino.com). Bus Deuce & all DTC-bound buses/self-parking & valet parking N Casino Center Boulevard or E Ogden Avenue. **Rooms** 447. **Rates** $40-$150 double. **Credit** AmEx, DC, Disc, MC, V. **Map** p334 D1 ⑪

Most of the original charm has disappeared from the Fremont after a half-century, and a tropical island motif has moved in – along with a large Hawaiian clientele. The famous block-long neon sign still holds its own, except when outglared by the Fremont Street Experience that runs above it.

Accommodation

The hotel's 447 guestrooms (including 23 suites) are modern, and feature floral patterns in hues of emerald and burgundy.

Eating & drinking

The Fremont courts visitors from the Pacific Rim, hence the surprising **Second Street Grill**: an unexpectedly upscale and risk-taking fusion-focused dining room, it delights discerning visitors with mahi mahi and ono. The **Paradise Café** coffeeshop offers American and Chinese specialities in 'a rainforest setting', and **Lanai Express** is an Asian fast-food joint. There's also a **Tony Roma's**, reputedly the most successful in the nation. At night, the Paradise rolls out a buffet.

Entertainment

Nothing doing here.

Gambling

A nondescript grind joint in the middle of Grind Central, with nothing much to recommend it but also nothing much to criticise. There's usually a slot or slot-club promotion going on; if you're in the neighbourhood, enquire at the slot-club booth.

Amenities *Bars (4). No-smoking rooms. Restaurants (4).* **Games** *Blackjack ($5-$1,000); Caribbean stud; craps (2x; from $5); Let it Ride; keno; pai gow poker; roulette (double zero); Spanish 21; three-card poker.*

Golden Gate

1 E Fremont Street, at S Main Street, Las Vegas, NV 89101 (reservations 1-800 426 1906/front desk & casino 385 1906/www.goldengatecasino.net). Bus Deuce & all DTC-bound buses/self-parking & valet parking S Main Street. **Rooms** 106. **Rates** $45-$70 double. **Credit** AmEx, MC, V. **Map** p334 C1 ⑫

Being the oldest and smallest of anything aren't normally qualities about which a Vegas property brags, but the Golden Gate manages to pull it off. Having celebrated its 100th birthday in 2006 (it's been known as the Golden Gate only since 1955; it was opened as the Hotel Nevada), this 106-room property appears positively quaint alongside the flashy Golden Nugget, the enormous brash Plaza and the garish Fremont Street Experience. Owned by likeable local maverick Mark Brandenburg, who so far seems to have shown little inclination to drag his place into the modern world, the Golden Gate remains old Vegas at its most appealingly basic. *Photo p110*.

Accommodation
Many original 10ft-by-10ft bedrooms remain. Some have been updated with air-conditioning, but most are still characterfully old-fashioned, replete with mahogany doors, plaster walls and tiled bathroom floors. Aside from the addition of a relatively modern key-card system, there haven't been any major technological advances here since 1907, when the hotel announced that it had taken control of the first telephone in Nevada (boasting, of course, the number 1).

Eating & drinking
In 50 years, the 24-hour **San Francisco Deli** has served 25 million shrimp cocktails, tangy treats in tulip-shaped glasses that never fail to make the *Las Vegas Advisor*'s list of best bargains in the city. The **Bay City Diner** (*see p171*) offers a survey of American classics, dished out by waitresses seemingly borrowed from a Raymond Carver short story.

Entertainment
The piano player at the back of the casino is another fabulous nod to tradition. They're very good too.

Gambling
An old-time, no-frills, family-owned casino navigated by a multiitued of wheelchair-required small ramps. The carpet's worn, the tables and machines are packed like sardines, and the bosses brook no nonsense. From the far dice-table closest to the deli, you can make a dash for the famous 99¢ shrimp cocktail between rolls. The comps here are liberal: play $10 blackjack for an hour and ask for the coffeeshop for two.

Amenities Bars (1). No-smoking rooms. Restaurants (2). **Games** *Blackjack ($3-$300); Caribbean stud; craps (5x; from $3); pai gow poker; roulette (double zero).*

Plaza

1 N Main Street, at E Fremont Street, Las Vegas, NV 89101 (reservations 1-800 634 6575/front desk & casino 386 2110/www.plazahotelcasino.com). Bus Deuce & all DTC-bound buses/self-parking & valet parking S Main Street. **Rooms** 1,037. **Rates** $39-$149 double. **Credit** AmEx, DC, Disc, MC, V. **Map** p334 C1 ⑬

This iconic Downtown property opened as Jackie Gaughan's Plaza, but Jackie is long Gaughan (he now owns El Cortez) and the Plaza is currently owned by the Tamares Group (which also owns the Vegas Club, the Western and the Gold Spike; *see p111*).

Meet the regulars Downtown

Downtown, the patrons wear polyester hand-me-downs in clashing plaids. Like South Strippers, Downtowners wear Rolex watches, except theirs say 'Made in China' on the back and the second hands keep falling off. Rooms are graciously comped by a hotel as an apology for giving them legionnaires' disease last time they stayed.

Unlike North Strippers, Downtowners don't hunt for coupons; they come with an organiser full of them. They spend the day cashing matchplays, using free slot action and downing free cocktails. They've heard a rumour that people on the Strip pay money for liquor, but don't believe anyone could be so careless with their cash.

After completing a coupon run for a profit of $6.82, Downtowners gamble. Maybe they bet a few ponies or hit the crap table for a couple of hours, and then move to the pai gow table

because they're in the mood for something exotic. The drinks come so frequently that the guests know the cocktail waitresses' names, or at least they did earlier.

South Strippers, Downtowners enjoy cigars, provided they cost less than 50¢. Instead of saving them for after dinner, they smoke them before: the burning tobacco deadens the taste buds and makes the early-bird $6 prime rib taste more like $10.

After dinner, it's off to gamble. They read online that one hotel incorrectly programmed a Double Diamond slot to pay back 100.4%, so they grind away for a $3 profit before a slot technician hangs the 'Out of Order' sign on it. After pocketing the winnings, they put their feet up in the bingo hall but they'll stay awake until midnight: this is Vegas, baby, and the coffeeshop's steak-and-eggs specials don't start until then.

Golden Gate. *See p108.*

Even so, the Plaza retains a resolutely old Vegas feel, from the majestically over-the-top lighting beneath the shelter outside its main entrance to the unpalatably smoky casino floor and the resolutely down-market buffet. In truth, it's a fairly shambolic place that could really use a little TLC. Still, the prices are right, and the rooftop swimming pool is an appealing extra.

Accommodation
The Plaza can usually be relied upon to deliver some of Downtown's cheapest rooms. Once you've stayed in one of them, you'll understand why. All things considered, the basic lodgings here are in need of an upgrade.

Eating & drinking
While it retains a certain vintage Vegas charm and serves a creditable steak, the best things about the second-level **Center Stage** restaurant are the views straight down Fremont Street afforded from its window seats. The other eating options here are pretty much as you might expect: a round-the-clock diner, a super-cheap buffet (dinner is just $8.99) and a food court holding a handful of global chains.

Entertainment
The headline production here is *Shag with a Twist*, a surprisingly charming reanimation of 1960s culture aimed at those who enjoyed Broadway retro fave *Hairspray*. From 9pm to 1.30am, Thursdays to Sundays, the **Omaha Lounge** hosts the likes of shiny-shirted smooth jazz stylist **David van Such** and super-soft reggae quartet **Island Tyme**.

Gambling
The casino teems with 1,200 slot machines. In the pit, gamblers can play $1 craps or $5 blackjack. Seven-card stud, Texas hold 'em and Omaha hold 'em poker are played in the card room, where limits are low and the players are more gentlemanly than on the Strip. But if you really want to gamble on the cheap, the keno lounge is for you: the Plaza is the only place in the US that offers double keno (simultaneous action on two boards) with games starting at 40¢, a bargain, despite the rotten odds. The bingo room is on the third floor.

Amenities *Bars (5). Disabled-adapted rooms. Gym. No-smoking rooms. Pool (outdoor). Restaurants (4).* **Games** *Big Six; bingo; blackjack ($5-$500); craps (5x; from $5); keno; Let it Ride; mini baccarat ($5-$500); pai gow poker; poker (7 tables); roulette (double zero); three-card poker.*

Vegas Club
18 E Fremont Street, at N Main Street, Las Vegas, NV 89101 (reservations 1-800 634 6532/front desk & casino 385 1664/www.vegasclubcasino.net). Bus Deuce & all DTC-bound buses/self-parking & valet parking N Main Street. **Rooms** 410. **Rates** $64-$124 double. **Credit** AmEx, DC, Disc, MC, V. **Map** p334 C1

The future of this 410-room old stager on Fremont Street is uncertain after a pair of ownership changes in the last few years. Rumours have suggested that the Tamares Group, which quietly bought the venture from Barrick Gaming in 2005, may be planning to redevelop the Vegas Club as part of the ongoing Downtown revival. However, nothing has yet been confirmed, leaving the property formerly known as the Las Vegas Club to carry on in its long-established role as a good-value but feebly themed hotel-casino.

As well as the Vegas Club and the **Plaza** (*see above*), Tamares also owns a couple of other low-roller joints: these include the basic 110-room

Gold Spike (400 E Ogden Avenue, 1-877 467 7453, 384 8444, www.goldspikehotelcasino.com) and, west of Las Vegas Boulevard, the spartan **Western** (899 E Fremont Street, 1-800 634 6703, 384 4620, www.westernhotelcasino.com).

Accommodation
While Downtown drags itself kicking and screaming into the 21st century, the Vegas Club's motel-standard guestrooms remain firmly stranded in 1987. Still, while the decor isn't the height of fashion, the rooms aren't in bad condition, especially compared to those at a few of their more downmarket neighbours. The guestrooms in the North Tower are in the best shape, something usually reflected in the prices.

Eating & drinking
The **Great Moments** restaurant aims for a vintage Vegas vibe, and sometimes gets away with it. Two sports-themed joints offer snacks: the **Upper Deck** and the 24-hour **Seventh Inning Scoop**.

Entertainment
Nothing.

Gambling
The casino here is bigger than it first appears, stretching around the ground floor to the newer wing along Ogden Avenue. In line with the rest of the hotel, it's in pretty good shape following a recent clean-up, though there's not much in the way of atmosphere. The blackjack has good rules, if you know how to take advantage of them using a slightly altered basic strategy. Find a long-time dealer and ask him or her for a little advice.

Amenities Bars (2). Disabled-adapted rooms. No-smoking rooms. Restaurants (4). **Games** *Big Six; bingo; blackjack ($3-$500); craps (3x, 4x, 5x; from $5); keno; Let it Ride; pai gow poker; roulette (double zero); three-card poker.*

The Rest of the City

Expensive

Green Valley Ranch
2300 Paseo Verde Drive, at S Green Valley Parkway, Henderson, NV 89052 (reservations 1-866 782 9487/ front desk & casino 617 7777/www.greenvalley ranchresort.com). Bus 111/self-parking & valet parking S Green Valley Parkway or Paseo Verde Parkway. **Rooms** 490. **Rates** $129-$349 double. **Credit** AmEx, DC, Disc, MC, V.
The Green Valley Ranch was a gem right out of the box in 2001, and it hasn't stopped polishing itself since. In its third expansion, the former boutique-style resort with the Argentinian cattle baron motif has doubled its guestroom capacity, improved its gambling options, and added a 500-seat entertainment lounge. Amenities already in place before the

renovation included District, a main-street-style shopping mall (*see p193*), a great mix of restaurants and one of the hottest pool areas in town.

Accommodation
The rooms are done out with old world decor, supplemented by goose-down pillows and fluffy robes. The huge penthouse suite comes complete with a baby grand, a dining table for ten, his and hers baths, a full kitchen and innumerable plasma screens. There's a cutting-edge spa out back, part of the eight-acre Whiskey Beach area; rent a cabana and order bottle service at the private pool called the Pond.

Eating & drinking
The gaming area is lined with dining options, including a couple of Asian options (**China Spice** and **Sushi + Sake**), upscale Italian at **Il Fornaio**, Irish fusion pub grub at **Fado**, and a re-creation of vintage Vegas at **Hank's**, which boasts of 'fine steaks and martinis'. Still hungry? You need the **Feast Around the World Buffet**, a local favourite.

Entertainment
There are outdoor concerts at **Whiskey Beach** (*see p252*) in summer, some at the 2,000-seat Grand Events Center, and in the new **Ovation Lounge**, booking everything from Grand Funk Railroad to Big Bad Vooodoo Daddy. Every night, there's Vegas-club-style action at **Whiskey** (*see p260*), a high-flyin', star-attractin' club that insouciantly spills out to outdoor lounging in the beach area. Back inside, there's a new 500-seat entertainment lounge and a ten-screen cinema. Adjacent to the hotel is the **District** shopping mall, with roughly 50 shops and restaurants.

Gambling
The pit, which surrounds the Drop Bar, is a bit cramped, though the slot areas are more expansive. A recent renovation brought a new 22-table poker room and a state-of-the-art sports book. Mini baccarat starts at $10 a hand. The video poker has been consistently strong over the past few years.

Amenities Bars (12). Business centre. Disabled-adapted rooms. Gym. High-speed internet (ADSL $12.99). No-smoking rooms. Pools (outdoor). Restaurants (14). Room service. Spa. TV: pay movies. **Games** *Mini baccarat ($10-$1,000); blackjack ($5-$5,000); Caribbean stud; casino war; craps (3x, 4x, 5x; from $10); keno; pai gow poker; roulette (double zero); Spanish 21; three-card poker.*

JW Marriott Summerlin
221 N Rampart Boulevard, at Summerlin Parkway, Summerlin (reservations 1-888 236 2427/front desk & casino 869 7777/www.jwlasvegasresort.com). Bus 207/self-parking & valet parking N Rampart Boulevard. **Rooms** 555. **Rates** $194-$289 double. **Credit** AmEx, DC, Disc, MC, V.
This expansive Spanish-style spa and golf resort is not your typical Marriott. The resort sits on some 54 acres in the heart of Summerlin, and boasts spectacular views of the Red Rock Conservation Area and access to eight of the area's most sought-after golf courses. There's also a beautiful waterfall pool,

a splendid spa, a new full-service beauty salon, a fully equipped fitness centre, several restaurants and clubs, and a few shops. A complimentary shuttle provides access to the Strip.

Accommodation
Divvied between two towers, the resort's spacious rooms are more luxurious than anything you'd usually encounter at a Marriott. All rooms feature oversized raindrop showers and separate whirlpool baths.

Eating & drinking
Local celebrity chef Gustav Mauler has carved a neat niche for himself with the Italian trattoria **Spiedini**. **Shizen** offers sushi and teppanyaki, while a lively standing-room crowd enjoys bangers 'n' mash and top-shelf Irish whiskey at **JC Woolooughan's Irish Pub**. Fine-dining options include **Ceres**, which serves breakfast, lunch and dinner amid gorgeous views of the resort's waterfalls; the intimate **Carmel Room**, which features fine continental cuisine served with Mediterranean flair; and, in season, light fare poolside at the **Waterside Grille**.

Entertainment
There's Celtic folk and rock in JC Woolooughan's.

Gambling
The Marriott casino is among Vegas's most expansive and luxurious, with a stunning, palm-painted backlit dome over the pit. The table and slot chairs are extremely swish, helping to make this a hugely comfortable place. There's a story behind it all: the casino was originally designed to attract affluent visitors, but few took the $50 cab ride from the Strip and the place went bankrupt. The new owners hired a veteran management group that instead targeted affluent Summerlin locals with unexpectedly low minimums and decent slot-club benefits.

Amenities Bars (1). Business centre. Concierge. Disabled-adapted rooms. Gym. High-speed internet (ADSL $9.95). No-smoking floors. Pools (outdoor). Restaurants (3). Room service. Spa. TV: pay movies. Games Baccarat ($100-$5,000); blackjack ($5-$5,000); Caribbean stud; casino war; craps (3x, 4x, 5x; from $5); keno; mini baccarat ($5-$500); pai gow poker; roulette (double zero); Spanish 21; three-card poker.

Red Rock Resort

11011 W Charleston Boulevard, at I-215, Las Vegas, NV 89135 (reservations 1-866 767 7773/front desk & casino 797 7777/www.redrocklasvegas.com). Bus 206/self-parking & valet parking W Charleston Boulevard. Rooms 815. Rates $149-$599 double. Credit AmEx, DC, Disc, MC, V.

Like Green Valley Ranch, it's nestled in an affluent suburb. And like Green Valley Ranch, there's a Rande Gerber-owned nightclub on site. But the comparisons between Red Rock and its sibling end there. This billion-dollar operation pays homage to the classic resort architecture of the early 1950s and '60s as well as the natural landscape that surrounds it. The rusty red and tan exterior mimics the colours of the nearby mountain range, while floor-to-ceiling

glass walls afford splendid views. There's even an Adventure Spa that takes full advantage of the desert surroundings by offering horseback riding, guided hikes and mountain biking. For pure relaxation, the **Red Rock Spa** (*see p208*).

Gold-leaf ceilings, Swarovski-crystal chandeliers and crocodile leather wall panels are just a few of the more luxurious elements that set Red Rock apart from other neighbourhood casinos; indeed, the steakhouse, trendy nightclub and martini bar mirror the Strip's hipster aesthetic. The centrepiece is the palm tree-lined, circular Sandbar Pool complete with a 'beach' with 19 private cabanas, six wading pools and, best of all, blackjack. *Photo p114.*

Accommodation
The guestrooms are fashionably outfitted with modern furniture and accessories that don't sacrifice comfort for style. Slip into the plush robe and slippers, plug in your iPod and pour yourself a drink from the self-service martini bar. Try the villa suite, which features a private patio complete with its own bar, a ten-person whirlpool spa and views of the beach area.

Eating & drinking
The choice here is wide and appealing. **T-Bones Chophouse** is an elegant steakhouse with a great wine list, while the authentic Italian dishes of **Terra Rossa** (*see p174*) come courtesy of *Hell's Kitchen* winner Heather West. **Salt Lick BBQ** serves Texas-style 'cue; **Cabo Cantina** offers Baja-style Mexican; and **Tides Oyster Bar** dishes up creole-style po'boys and pan roasts. In the heart of the casino, you'll find the **Lucky Bar**, home to those red patent leather crocodile panels as well as an awe-inspiring crystal chandelier. The **Onyx Lounge** specialises in signature martinis, while the **Sand Bar** serves cool poolside libations.

Entertainment
Cherry (*see p256*), nightclub impresario Rande Gerber's latest foray into Vegas, reigns supreme as the off-Strip hotspot, while house band Zowie Bowie keeps the **Rocks Lounge** jumping with dance covers. In warm months, the **Sandbar** hosts poolside shows from the likes of Damien Marley. There's a 16-screen cineplex with private viewing boxes and a 72-lane bowling alley.

Gambling
The name of the game here is machines: there are more than 3,200 of them, split evenly between slots and video poker. Table minimums are reasonable. Look for the one-of-a-kind giant Wheel of Fortune Super Spin slot machine that seats several players around a big bubble (it's by the cinema entrance).

Amenities Bars (15). Business centre. Concierge. Disabled-adapted rooms. Gym. High-speed internet (ADSL $12.99). No-smoking rooms. Pool (outdoor). Restaurants (9). Spa. Games Baccarat ($100-$10,000); bingo; blackjack ($5-$5,000); Caribbean stud; casino war; craps (3x, 4x, 5x; from $5); keno; mini baccarat ($5-$10,000); pai gow poker; poker; roulette (double zero); Spanish 21; three-card poker.

Moderate

Orleans

*4500 W Tropicana Avenue, between S Decatur &
S Valley View Boulevards, Las Vegas, NV 89103
(reservations 1-800 675 3267/front desk & casino
365 7111/www.orleanscasino.com). Bus 103,
104, 201/self-parking & valet parking W Tropicana
Avenue, Cameron Street or S Arville Street.* **Rooms**
1,886. **Rates** $60-$175 double. **Credit** AmEx, Disc,
MC, V. **Map** p333 X3 ⑤⑤

The theme at the Orleans is more Disneyland than
French Quarter. Still, the locals don't seem to mind,
mostly because the Vegas-style action is very real.

Located very close to the Strip (and within a five-
minute walk of the Palms), the Orleans is one of the
few casinos at which locals and tourists happily mix
in every part of the operation. The rooms aren't especially exciting, but they're kept in good condition
and by no means offensively designed. In any case,
it's hard to grumble at these prices.

The 11 restaurants run the casino-dining gamut,
including steak and seafood (**Canal Street**), prime
rib (**Prime Rib Loft**), buffet (**French Market**),
Mexican (**Don Miguel's**) and the nearly ubiquitous
Irish pub (**Brendan's**). The sure eating bet here is
the grilled-to-order burger at **Terrible Mike's**.
Entertainment comes courtesy of the **Orleans**

Red Rock Resort.

Gold Coast. *See p116.*

Arena, home of hockey's Wranglers and arena football's Gladiators; the **Century Orleans 18** cinema (*see p242*); and the 70-lane bowling centre (*see p362*). You might occasionally find Bourbon Street-style jazz or modern rock in the 999-seat **Orleans Showroom**, though country and nostalgic rock are the norms.

But the gambling is the main draw for locals, with the casino offering lively, low-limit action. The poker room is one of the best in town, with 'bad-beat jackpots' (awarded to the player who loses with a very big hand) and regular tournaments. The blackjack is mostly double-deckers that pay 3:2 for naturals. **Amenities** *Bars (7). Business centre. Disabled-adapted rooms. Gym. High-speed internet (wireless $10.95). No-smoking floors. Pool (outdoor). Restaurants (11). Spa.* **Games** *Bingo; blackjack ($5-$2,000); Caribbean stud; craps (2x; from $5); keno; Let it Ride; mini baccarat ($5-$1,000); pai gow poker; poker; roulette (double zero); Spanish 21; three-card poker.*

Silverton

3333 Blue Diamond Road, at I-15, Las Vegas, NV 89139 (reservations 1-866 946 4373/front desk & casino 263 7777/www.silvertoncasino.com). Bus 117/self-parking & valet parking Dean Martin Drive. **Rooms** 300. **Rates** $69-$199 double. **Credit** AmEx, DC, Disc, MC, V.

Its location, just off I-15 several miles south of the Strip, doesn't flatter the Silverton. However, this is a surprisingly attractive property that, while by no means offering the Palms or Caesars much competition in the coolness or extravagance departments, is nonetheless smarter and more stylish than you might expect. The rooms are decent if somewhat expensive for the location, and the casino offers the usual array of table games and slots. Entertainment is by and large limited to shows from guitar bands that could politely be described as 'vintage'; hell, the hotel has even persuaded Hootie & the Blowfish to lend their name to the agreeably retro **Shady Grove Lounge**. Eating options are headlined by the **Twin Creeks** steakhouse, with the **Sundance Grill** offering round-the-clock American classics and **Seasons** providing all-you-can-eat buffet fare. Bonus: Just across I-15 is the Bootlegger (*see p174*). The casino is surprisingly expansive and upscale, with 1,400 slots and nearly 50 table games; the video poker has long been good enough to attract the pros. **Amenities** *Bars (5). Disabled-adapted rooms. Gym. High-speed internet (wireless $10). No-smoking floors. Pool (outdoor). Restaurants (5). Room service. TV: pay movies.* **Games** *Blackjack ($5-$2,000); craps (10x; from $5); keno; mini baccarat ($10-$3,000); pai gow poker; poker; roulette (double zero); three-card poker.*

South Point

9777 Las Vegas Boulevard South, at E Silverado Ranch Boulevard, Las Vegas, NV 89183 (reservations 1-866 791 7626/front desk & casino 796 7111/www.southpointcasino.com). Bus 117/self-parking E Silverado Ranch Boulevard/valet parking Las Vegas Boulevard South. **Rooms** 1,354. **Rates** $50-$180 double. **Credit** AmEx, Disc, MC, V.

After effectively selling the Coast casino chain to Boyd Gaming in 2004, Michael Gaughan (son of legendary local casino operator Jackie) began working for his former competitors, watching as they spent more than $500 million building the South Coast casino on an isolated site several miles south of the Strip. When, after a year, it failed to achieve lift-off, Gaughan jumped in and bought the resort, first changing its name and upgrading both its facilities and its image. It's an appealing place, its rooms decorated with attractive colours and without unnecessary ornamentation. Amenities include a 64-lane bowling alley, a 16-screen cinema and, right out of left field, a 4,400-seat equestrian arena. Dining is headlined by **Michael's**, recently relocated from Bill's Gamblin' Hall on the Strip (formerly, under Gaughan's ownership, the Barbary Coast); there's also an Italian eaterie (**Don Vito's**), a steakhouse (the **Silverado**), an oyster bar (**Big Sur**) and the obligatory buffet (the **Garden**). The big casino includes more than 2,400 machines (with decent video poker schedules) and 60 table games, along with a 300-seat indie race and sports book. A shuttle bus runs to and from the southern tip of the Strip. **Amenities** *Bars (10). Business centre. Disabled-adapted rooms. Gym. High-speed internet (wireless $10.99). No-smoking floors. Pools (outdoor). Restaurants (7). Room service. Spa. TV: pay movies.* **Games** *Bingo; blackjack ($5-$2,000); Caribbean stud; craps (2x; from $5); keno; mini baccarat ($5-$5,000); pai gow poker; poker; roulette (double zero); three-card poker.*

Budget

Arizona Charlie's

4575 Boulder Highway, at E Twain Avenue, Las Vegas, NV 89121 (reservations 1-888 236 9066/front desk & casino 951 9000/www.arizonacharlies boulder.com). Bus 107/self-parking & valet parking S Decatur Boulevard. **Rooms** 350. **Rates** $31-$125 double. **Credit** AmEx, DC, Disc, MC, V.

Arizona Charlie's is a no-frills, 258-room bunkhouse for serious players who need a place to drop. The theme is the Yukon gold rush, though you won't notice: the interior design is little more than a floor, a ceiling and rows of machines. One effort to keep up with the local competition was the replacement of the Yukon Grille with a link from the **Outback Steakhouse** chain. But the surest bet at Charlie's is still the **Sourdough Café**, where the steak-and-eggs special will set you back just $2.99. There's also a buffet. The **Naughty Ladies Saloon** plays host to a range of lounge acts. The blackjack games here are decent, with typical low minimums, as is some of the video poker. You can also find $2 craps at times, but often with only 2x odds. There's a strong selection of slots for nickel and quarter players. **Amenities** *Bars (3). Disabled-adapted rooms. No-smoking floors. Pool (outdoor). Restaurants (3). TV: pay movies.* **Games** *Bingo; blackjack ($5-$1,000); craps (2x, 5x; from $2); Caribbean stud; keno; Let it Ride; pai gow poker; roulette (double zero).*

Boulder Station

4111 Boulder Highway, at E Desert Inn Road, Las Vegas, NV 89121 (reservations 1-800 683 7777/ front desk & casino 432 7777/www.boulderstation. com). Bus 107, 213/self-parking & valet parking Boulder Highway. **Rooms** 300. **Rates** $49-$169 double. **Credit** AmEx, DC, Disc, MC, V.

This Victorian-styled Station casino on the Boulder Strip lures locals with solid entertainment in the **Railhead** (*see p252*) from a stable of B-list headliners (from Loverboy to Diane Schuur), family-friendly amenities such as an 11-screen movie theatre and a **Kids Quest** childcare centre (*see p239*) and some decent dining options: the **Feast Gourmet Buffet** is popular, and the **Broiler**'s Sunday champagne brunch is one of the best in Vegas (and only $19.99). The casino is typical for the Station chain, though the minimums in this part of town seem to run a little lower, with some $3 tables scattered about, 10x odds at craps, and 50¢ roulette chips. The newest machines seem to show up here first.

Amenities *Bars (5). Disabled-adapted rooms. High-speed internet (ADSL $9.99). No-smoking floors. Pools (outdoor). Restaurants (6). Room service.* **Games** *Bingo; blackjack ($3-$1,000); Caribbean stud; craps (10x; from $2); keno; Let it Ride; mini baccarat ($5-$1,000); pai gow poker; pai gow tiles; poker; roulette (double zero); three-card poker.*

Fiesta Rancho

2400 N Rancho Drive, at W Lake Mead Boulevard, Las Vegas, NV 89130 (reservations 1-888 899 7770/front desk & casino 631 7000/www.fiesta rancholasvegas.com). Bus 103, 106, 210, 211/self-parking N Rancho Drive, W Lake Mead Boulevard or Carey Avenue/valet parking W Lake Mead Boulevard. **Rooms** 100. **Rates** $30-$250 double. **Credit** AmEx, DC, Disc, MC, V.

The slot-club at the Fiesta Rancho is known for regular triple-point days and no-hassle food comps. There's also a 300-seat bingo room and a drive-up sports-betting window, where you don't even have to get out of the car to bet on an upcoming game. Recent additions include a new poker room, complementing video poker that was voted the best in the city by the *Review-Journal* in 2007.

Besides the gaming, it's the party-style atmosphere that draws visitors to the north-west part of the city. A variety of live acts play **Club Tequila**, where the emphasis is on Latin music; the obligatory Mexican food comes courtesy of **Garduno's** (with a ridiculous 300 flavours of margarita) and the **Blue Agave Steakhouse**. Escape the desert heat in the outdoor swimming pool or the NHL-size ice arena.

Amenities *Bars (4). Disabled-adapted rooms. High-speed internet (ADSL $9.99). No-smoking rooms. Pools (outdoor). Restaurants (4). Room service. Spa. TV: pay movies.* **Games** *Bingo; blackjack ($5-$1,000); casino war; Caribbean stud; craps (10x; from $2); keno; Let it Ride; pai gow poker; poker; roulette (double zero); three-card poker.*

Gold Coast

4000 W Flamingo Road, at S Valley View Boulevard, Las Vegas, NV 89103 (reservations 1-800 331 5334/front desk & casino 367 7111/www.goldcoast casino.com). Bus 201/self-parking & valet parking S Valley View Boulevard, W Flamingo Road or Wynn Road. **Rooms** 711. **Rates** $44-$124 double. **Credit** AmEx, DC, Disc, MC, V. **Map** p333 X3 ⑤⑥

Boyd Gaming took hold of Coast Casinos in 2006, renaming the Barbary Coast and leaving this spot as the oldest link in Michael Gaughan's chain. So far, it's relying on the same formula for success. Locals love the GC's machines and the players club, both of which usually take top honours in the *Las Vegas Review-Journal*'s 'Best of Vegas' survey. There's plenty of $5 blackjack, $5 pai gow and $1 roulette for low rollers, one of the city's bigger bingo rooms (eight sessions daily) plus a 70-lane bowling alley. The 711 rooms have been upgraded with the seemingly mandatory 32in LCD TVs. *Photos p113.*

For food, choose from the **Cortez Room**, a mid-priced steakhouse; **Arriva**, which serves bargain seafood and Italian cuisine; the all-Asian **Ping Pang Pong**; the **Monterey Room** coffeeshop; or the buffet, rated highly by locals. The one new addition is an oyster bar called **Captain Charlie's**.

Amenities *Bars (5). Business centre. Concierge. Disabled-adapted rooms. Gym. High-speed internet (ADSL $10.99). No-smoking floors. Pool (outdoor). Restaurants (6). Room service. TV: pay movies.* **Games** *Bingo; blackjack ($5-$2,000); Caribbean stud; craps (2x; from $2); keno; mini baccarat ($10-$1,000); pai gow poker; poker; roulette (double zero); Spanish 21; three-card poker.*

Palace Station

2411 W Sahara Avenue, at N Rancho Drive, Las Vegas, NV 89102 (reservations 1-800 634 3101/ front desk & casino 367 2411/www.palacestation. com). Bus 104, 204/self-parking & valet parking W Sahara Avenue, N Rancho Drive or Teddy Drive. **Rooms** 1,006. **Rates** $39-$299 double. **Credit** AmEx, DC, Disc, MC, V. **Map** p336 A4 ⑤⑦

The original Station casino has been a favourite of locals for more than 30 years, thanks largely to the popular gaming promotion. You'll find 1,800 slot and video poker machines here, along with 57 gaming tables, a 600-seat bingo room, a nine-table poker room, a keno lounge, and a race and sports book. The hotel draws its share of tourists too, due to its close proximity to the Strip and cheap rooms.

Several of the restaurants offer fine neighbourhood fare: the **Feast Gourmet Buffet**, steaks and seafood in the **Broiler**, and a food court. There's lounge music in **Sound Trax** and **Jack's**, an Irish pub; and the new **Cabo Bar** opens in 2007. The 1,000-plus rooms and suites range from economy courtyard rooms to deluxe tower rooms, due to be remodelled in 2007.

Amenities *Bars (4). Business centre. Disabled-adapted rooms. Gym. High-speed internet (ADSL $9.99). No-smoking rooms. Pool (outdoor). Restaurants (7). Room service. TV: pay movies.* **Games** *Baccarat ($10-$5,000); bingo; blackjack*

($5-$3,000); Caribbean stud; craps (3x, 4x, 5x, 10x; from $5); keno; Let it Ride; pai gow poker; pai gow tiles; poker; roulette (double zero).

Sam's Town

5111 Boulder Highway, at E Flamingo Road, Las Vegas, NV 89122 (reservations 1-800 897 8696/ front desk & casino 456 7777/www.samstownlv. com). Bus 107, 115, 202/self-parking & valet parking Boulder Highway, E Flamingo Road or Nellis Boulevard. **Rooms** 646. **Rates** $34-$250 double. **Credit** AmEx, DC, Disc, MC, V.

If you like Old West-style casinos, this is your place. Though gunfire is kept to a minimum, the theme is nonetheless prevalent, from the saloon-style bars to **Roxy's**, the rowdy dance hall. There's even a quality western store (**Sheplers**). Elsewhere, modern amenities include a 24-hour bowling centre, an 18-screen movie theatre and **Sam's Town Live!**, a 1,100-seat multi-use venue that stages a variety of country and pop concerts. In the middle of all this is Mystic Falls Park, a ten-storey atrium whose indoor nature walk (with trees and chirping birds) gets interrupted four times daily by the Sunset Stampede, a laser light and water show. Check out the TV sets over the tables in some of the pits, and bet up to 20x odds at the crap tables. There are thousands of video poker machines, though few, if any, are full-pay. **Amenities** Bars (6). Disabled-adapted rooms. High-speed internet (wireless $10). No-smoking rooms. Pool (outdoor). Restaurants (5). TV: pay movies. **Games** Bingo; blackjack ($5-$3,000); craps (20x; from $5); keno; Let it Ride; pai gow poker; poker; roulette (double zero).

Santa Fe Station

4949 N Rancho Drive, at US 95 (junction 90A), Las Vegas, NV 89130 (reservations 1-866 767 7771/ front desk & casino 658 4900/www.santafestationlas vegas.com). Bus 101, 102, 106, 219/self-parking & valet parking N Rancho Drive or Lone Mountain Road. **Rooms** 200. **Rates** $50-$190 double. **Credit** AmEx, DC, Disc, MC, V.

One of the earliest locals' casinos is evidently now the best: the Las Vegas Review-Journal said so in its 2006 'Best of Las Vegas' poll, crediting the property's classier look after a major remodel, the renovation of the 200 rooms, a new race and sports book, and the addition of the **Chrome** nightclub and a cineplex. Santa Fe staples include a 488-seat bingo room and a wide variety of slots, and a state-of-the-art bowling centre. Locals enjoy great Mexican fare at **Cabo**, where flair bartenders blend equally entertaining margaritas; other options include the endlessly popular **Feast Buffet** and unexpectedly impressive **Charcoal Room** for steak and seafood. Santa Fe also operates a **Kids Quest** childcare and entertainment centre (see p239).

The smallish casino has low-limit table games, though with no competition nearby, the rules are not altogether favourable. The video poker is typical for Station: there are a few 99% machines, but the rest lower. There is also a 450-seat bingo room, the aforementioned new sports book and a variety of slots.

Amenities Bars (8). Business centre. Disabled-adapted rooms. Gym. High-speed internet (ADSL $9.99). No-smoking rooms. Pool (outdoor). Restaurants (7). Room service. TV: pay movies. **Games** Blackjack ($5-$1,000); craps (10x; from $5); Let it Ride; pai gow poker; roulette (double zero); three-card poker.

Suncoast

9090 Alta Drive, at N Rampart Boulevard, Las Vegas, NV 89145 (reservations 1-877 677 7111/ front desk & casino 636 7111/www.suncoastcasino. com). Bus 207/self-parking & valet parking Alta Drive & Rampart Avenue. **Rooms** 427. **Rates** $50-$180 double. **Credit** AmEx, DC, Disc, MC, V.

This Coast casino shares the qualities of its siblings but with one major difference: it's in Summerlin, and thus surrounded by 81 holes of world-class golf, and an assortment of upper-scale shopping and dining options. Stay on site, though, and you'll find a large and player-friendly casino floor, with 50 table games, plenty of slots and some full-pay video poker, bingo, a race and sports book, and a progressive players club that plies regulars with comps.

Entertainment is focused on the 500-seat showroom, which stages the unlikely likes of Air Supply and the Smothers Brothers. There's also a 64-lane bowling alley plus, as is the case at many locals' joints, a 16-screen movie theatre. Foodwise, there's a standard buffet and a coffeeshop, but you'd be better off with the steaks, seafood and lamb at **Primo's**, or **Señor Miguel**'s tasty Mexican specialities. The **Kid's Tyme** childcare centre is open seven days a week; there's also a beauty salon and fitness centre. **Amenities** Bars (6). Disabled-adapted rooms. Gym. High-speed internet (wireless $11). No-smoking rooms. Pool (outdoor). Restaurants (7). Room service. TV: pay movies. **Games** Baccarat ($15-$2,500); bingo; blackjack ($5-$2,000); Caribbean stud; craps (2x; from $5); keno; Let it Ride; pai gow poker; poker; roulette (double zero); Spanish 21; three-card poker.

Sunset Station

1301 W Sunset Road, between N Stephanie Street & I-515, Henderson, NV 89014 (reservations 1-888 786 7389/front desk & casino 547 7777/www.sunset station.com). Bus 114/self-parking & valet parking Stephanie Street, W Sunset Road, Marks Street or Warm Springs Road. **Rooms** 457. **Rates** $59-$189 double. **Credit** AmEx, DC, Disc, MC, V.

Slot-clubbing locals keep every inch of the capacious Sunset Station casino buzzing. The usual table games, with $5-$10 minimums (and 10x odds at craps), are situated under a stained-glass ceiling. There are wide ranges of slots and video poker machines, though full-pay variety are few and far between.

Naturally, there are plenty of other ways in which to spend your money. A 13-screen **Regal Cinema** (see p242), a **Kids Quest** childcare centre (see p239) and a very with-it bowling centre all appease both adults and kids; grown-ups may prefer the new **Club Madrid**, where you'll find name acts in an intimate lounge. During swimming season, big-name entertainers (from Styx to Clint Black) perform at the 5,000-seat amphitheatre by the Mediterranean-style pool. But the restaurants are the steady draws, with cuisine that ranges from wings at **Hooters** to the smarter **Sonoma Cellar Steakhouse**. In between, there's the worth-the-wait **Feast Buffet**, plus the **Guadalajara Bar & Grille** and its sweet little tequila collection. And don't miss the gaudy **Gaudí Bar** in the centre of the action.

Amenities Bars (11). Disabled-adapted rooms. High-speed internet (ADSL $9.99). No-smoking rooms. Pool (outdoor). Restaurants (8). Room service. **Games** Bingo; blackjack ($5-$5,000); craps (10x; from $2); keno; Let it Ride; mini baccarat ($5-$1,000); pai gow poker; poker; roulette (double zero); three-card poker.

Texas Station

2101 Texas Star Lane, at N Rancho Drive, between W Lake Mead Boulevard & Vegas Drive, Las Vegas, NV 89032 (reservations 1-800 654 8888/front desk & casino 631 1000/www.texasstation.com). Bus 103, 106, 210, 211/self-parking N Rancho Drive/valet parking W Lake Mead Boulevard or N Rancho Drive. **Rooms** 200. **Rates** $40-$250 double. **Credit** AmEx, DC, Disc, MC, V. **Map** p333 X1 **58**

Bigger is better in this Lone Star-themed hotel, which features a 60-lane bowling centre, an 18-screen movie theatre, a 5,000sq ft (470sq m) arcade, and 2,300 very popular slot and video poker machines. In the poker room, the game of choice is, inevitably, Texas hold 'em. And where would Texas be without a steak-house? The award-winning **Austins** is a fine example of what a steakhouse should be: prime steaks dry-aged for 21 days, hand-cut on the premises and then marinated in Austins' secret sauce. Texas-style entertainment can be found in **Club Armadillo** and the 2,000-seat **Dallas Events Center** with the likes of Merle Haggard. Surprisingly, there are only 200 rooms, making the hotel side of this casino almost boutique. Texas also has a **Kids Quest** childcare and entertainment centre (see p239).

Amenities Bars (8). Disabled-adapted rooms. High-speed internet (ADSL $10.99). No-smoking rooms. Pool (outdoor). Restaurants (5). Room service. TV: pay movies. **Games** Bingo; blackjack ($5-$1,000); craps (10x; from $5); keno; Let it Ride; pai gow poker; poker; roulette (double zero); three-card poker.

Non-casino hotels

Expensive

Loews Lake Las Vegas

101 Montelago Boulevard, off Lake Las Vegas Parkway, Henderson, NV 89011 (reservations 1-800 235 6397/front desk 567 6000/www.loewshotels.com). No bus/self-parking & valet parking Lake Las Vegas Parkway. **Rooms** 493. **Rates** $144-$399. **Credit** AmEx, DC, Disc, MC, V.

Despite changing hands (it used to be a Hyatt), this Lake Las Vegas property still has a Moroccan theme and most of the same amenities. But Loews has upgraded the rooms, resurfacing the pools and giving the hotel a nice facelift. Most dramatically, the small casino has gone, converted into a venue for weddings, meetings and, yes, ballroom dancing (every Saturday).

As for food, **Marssa** has taken over from Japengo but still serves Pacific Rim cuisine and sushi prepared by master chef Osamu Fujita. **Café Tajine** serves breakfast, lunch and dinner in a bright, laid-back atmosphere. The **Arabesque Lounge** has beautiful views of the lake and mountains; for outdoor dining, try the **SandsaBar Grill**.

Along with hiking, biking and birdwatching, the major sports are on a 320-acre private man-made lake (sailing, canoeing, kayaking, windsurfing and fishing), and three golf courses. There's a well-groomed white-sand beach as well as a sports area with a small putting green, basketball, volleyball and tennis.

Amenities Bars (2). Business centre. Concierge. Disabled-adapted rooms. Gym. High-speed internet (wireless $9.95). No-smoking floors. Pools (outdoor). Restaurants (5). Room service. Spa. TV: pay movies.

Ritz-Carlton, Lake Las Vegas

1610 Lake Las Vegas Parkway, off E Lake Mead Parkway, Henderson, NV 89011 (reservations 1-800 241 3333/front desk 567 4700/www.ritzcarlton.com). No bus/self-parking & valet parking Lake Las Vegas Parkway. **Rooms** 349. **Rates** $179-$1,500. **Credit** AmEx, DC, Disc, MC, V.

Carefully isolated within the Lake Las Vegas community, roughly 20 miles south-east of the Strip, the Ritz-Carlton is one of the most luxurious resorts in the Vegas metropolitan area, in no small part because it doesn't really feel much like Las Vegas. Key to this, of course, is the lack of an in-house casino: gamblers can wander next door to the Casino Montelago (939 8888, www.casinomontelago.com), but the Ritz-Carlton remains unsullied by the incessant blinking lights and tinkling melodies that characterise most major resorts in the region.

The hotel itself offers all the luxury you'd expect to find in a Ritz-Carlton property. The rooms themselves are handsome without being needlessly flashy, kitted out with plush beds and chairs, fabulously generous bathrooms and most conceivable amenities (minibars, high-speed internet access and so on). The lobby bar, **Firenze**, delivers worthwhile cocktails, decent sandwiches and, on weekend afternoons at 1pm, a Florentine-style high tea. The real culinary action is downstairs in the renowned **Medici**, which serves a winning range of Mediterranean-influenced American dishes for breakfast, brunch (Sundays only), lunch and dinner.

The luxury extends to the hotel's capacious spa, rightly regarded as one of the city's best. Nearby amenities include the Falls and Reflection Bay golf courses, which essentially adjoin the hotel, and Montelago Village, a sort of upscale Italianate theme park dotted with expensive boutique shops, restaurants and bars.

Amenities Bars (1). Business centre. Concierge. Disabled-adapted rooms. Gym. High-speed internet (wireless; included in $25 resort fee). No-smoking floors. Pools (outdoor). Restaurants (2). Room service. Spa. TV: pay movies.

Sightseeing

Features

Liberace Museum. *See p149.*

Introduction

Just like the sign says…

Has any major tourist-driven city been built on less than Las Vegas? As will be apparent as you descend into McCarran Airport, Sin City now sprawls out for miles in every direction, edging ever closer to the mountains that ring the valley in which it lies. But despite this expansion, many visitors nonetheless spend the duration of their stay on a single, solitary street: Las Vegas Boulevard South, aka the Strip, the most absurd, immense and overwhelming road in North America.

Sightseeing here is unlike sightseeing in any other city, because Las Vegas is effectively its own main attraction. There are only a few museums here, and fewer family-friendly entertainments. The parks are mostly

unremarkable and the natural beauty is just out of town (*see pp276-304*). Tour companies are conspicuous by their absence; and so, at least off the Strip, are pedestrians. Sure, people head to the city with a few specific aims: to gamble and party, to see a show and hit a nightclub. But most visitors to Las Vegas are here simply to see and experience the sheer sensory overload and the inimitable ridiculousness of the city itself, and of the Strip in particular.

For full details of the city's hotel-casino resorts, *see pp65-118*. Our **Casinos & Hotels** section covers every major casino in Vegas, detailing everything from its entertainment to its eating options, its guestrooms to its golf courses. These Sightseeing chapters should be taken as a brief primer to the city. Follow the cross-references to find full reviews of galleries, nightclubs and restaurants that are mentioned only in passing here.

The one mistake made by many visitors is not leaving the Strip; understandable, given the hypnotic, wow-inducing glitz of the place. But there is a whole city beyond it, relatively low on sights and arts but with plenty of restaurants, bars and points of local interest worthy of your attention. Try to get out and see a couple.

ORIENTATION

The Las Vegas Valley is split into quarters by two freeways that cross each other: I-15, coursing north–south through the centre of town on its way from Salt Lake City to LA, and US 95 (aka I-515), a north–south freeway that makes an east–west jink across the city. On a map, these roads approximate a twisted pinwheel shape, with a pivot just north-west of Downtown.

In street numbering terms, Ground Zero is at the junction of Fremont and Main Streets in Downtown. From the Plaza at 1 S Main Street, numbers increase as you travel in any direction. Main Street ends at its intersection with Las Vegas Boulevard South (by the Stratosphere); street addresses either east or west of the Main Street/Las Vegas Boulevard artery are tagged accordingly with 'E' or 'W'. North/south street delineations are based on an imaginary line from the eastern end of Charleston Boulevard, along Fremont Street in Downtown as far as Main Street, and then on to US 95 to the west.

Metropolitan Las Vegas is made up of four jurisdictions: Las Vegas, North Las Vegas, Henderson and unincorporated Clark County. Within and overlapping these jurisdictions are a number of areas and neighbourhoods, only some of which have widely recognised names. The Sightseeing section of this guidebook has been divided into five chapters: **The Strip** (see pp123-133), the nickname for the stretch of Las Vegas Boulevard South between Russell Road in the south and Sahara Avenue in the north; **Off-Strip** (see pp134-136), loosely covering the streets immediately surrounding the Strip; **Downtown** (see pp137-143), centred around the junction of Fremont Street and Las Vegas Boulevard; and **The Rest of the City** (see pp144-150), covering everywhere else.

Trips & tours

Drive-Yourself Tours

565 8761/www.drive-yourselftours.com. **Credit** AmEx, Disc, MC, V.

A nice idea, this, if slightly outmoded. For $14.95, you get a 90-minute cassette and map, with which you can direct yourself around Las Vegas, Mount

Charleston and Red Rock Canyon, among other areas. The catch: most rental cars now come only with CD players…

Gray Line Tours

1-800 634 6579/www.graylinelasvegas.com. **Credit** AmEx, Disc, MC, V.

Gray Line offers a handful of Vegas-based bus tours, including an evening city tour (6hrs, $40), plus trips out to the Grand Canyon (10hrs, $155), and a half-day jag to Lake Mead and the Hoover Dam (7hrs, $75). Discounts are often available by booking in advance online.

Sundance Helicopters

1-800 653 1881/736 0606/www.helicoptour.com. **Credit** AmEx, Disc, MC, V.

If you care to disregard the concerns of Las Vegas locals and Grand Canyon environmentalists, then Sundance is Nevada's best regarded helicopter tour operator. City tours run from $85, with trips to the Grand Canyon (the company offers quite a variety) starting at around $375. Other by-air options include Grand Canyon Airlines and Papillon Grand Canyon Helicopters (for both, see p291).

Things to do

Leave the Strip

And take in one of the city's three main off-kilter attractions: the **Atomic Testing Museum** (see p135), the **Liberace Museum** (see p149) or the **Neon Museum** (see p141 **Lighting up the past**).

See a show

There's not quite the proverbial something for everyone, but it's not far off. For a full list of the town's entertainments, complete with reviews, see pp224-235.

Take a ride

Speed: the Ride at the Sahara and the Stratosphere's **Insanity: the Ride** (for both, see p142) will both bring your stomach closer to your mouth than you would ordinarily appreciate.

Try your luck

The only people who ever got rich from gambling are the casinos, but that doesn't stop most visitors from trying to buck a century-old trend. For a guide, see pp41-62.

Walk the walk

It's longer than it looks (choose your shoes with care), but every visitor should stroll the length of the Strip at least once, to get the measure of its absurdity. See pp123-133.

Sightseeing

OUR CLIMATE NEEDS
A HELPING HAND TODAY

Be a smart traveller. Help to offset your carbon emissions from your trip by pledging Carbon Trees with Trees for Cities.

All the Carbon Trees that you donate through Trees for Cities are genuinely planted as additional trees in our projects.

Trees for Cities is an independent charity working with local communities on tree planting projects.

www.treesforcities.org   Tel 020 7587 1320

Trees for Cities
Charity registration number 1032154

The Strip

Greetings from the most preposterous four-mile stretch in America.

When he built the tropical-themed, volcano-fronted Mirage in 1989, Steve Wynn lit the fuse on a renaissance that would see Las Vegas Boulevard virtually rebuilt within 15 years. The city awoke from a long dormancy – the years when it was popular with those slightly embarrassing friends of your parents – and began to deal in high-volume density.

At first, families were the target. As Wynn followed the volcano-fuelled Mirage with the pirate ships of Treasure Island, populist attractions began to spring up all along the Strip, effectively the stretch of Las Vegas Boulevard South between the 'Welcome' sign and Sahara Avenue. Hotels were fashioned after pyramids, castles and even a Disney-esque version of New York. In 1998, Wynn steered the race in another direction, defining a new era of quality with the Bellagio. High-end travellers

who previously had cared little about either gambling or rollercoasters discovered a city that now offered celebrity chefs and one-of-a-kind shows. By the time Wynn finished Wynn Las Vegas in 2005, resorts such as Mandalay Bay, the Venetian and Caesars Palace had already added boutique environs or were getting ready to do so, further upping the upmarket ante.

On the eve of the city's centennial in 2005, a new phase dawned. The Strip was now hip, beckoning twentysomethings who couldn't care less about Wayne Newton or prime-rib buffets with an explosion of all-night dance clubs and swanky lounges. The latest wave of construction is reshaping the skyline with high-rise condos and mixed-use properties that will be virtual cities of their own. Will Trump towers and glitzy high-rises erase the neon legend of the old Vegas? Watch this space.

Russell Road to Tropicana Avenue

Map p336 A9-A8

As the tiny, neon-lit motor courts of the 1950s and '60s near Russell Road continue to perish under the wrecking ball, only the classic **Welcome to Fabulous Las Vegas** sign

Roar power: the **Lion Habitat** at the MGM Grand. *See p125.*

Luxor.

reminds visitors of the old California highway that once beckoned hot, thirsty drivers to get out of the heat. First-timers still brave the traffic to get a snap under this iconic landmark; you can purchase a miniature version, complete with flashing lights, at various gift shops along Las Vegas Boulevard. Facing the sign, the old Howard Hughes air terminal is behind you to the east (right), while the **Panevino** restaurant (*see p161*) lies beyond the runways on Sunset Road, offering gorgeous views of the Strip and aircraft in transit. At your back, 300 miles away, is Los Angeles; in front of you lies the Strip, Las Vegas's raison d'être.

To the east is the **Little Church of the West** wedding chapel (*see p274*). Dating to 1942, it's the oldest building on the Strip, though with the caveat that it's been moved several times, most recently from the front lawn of the old Hacienda casino (imploded in 1996) to its current site. Across the Boulevard is the **Bali Hai Golf Club** (*see p264*), one of only two golf courses on the Strip (the other is the guests-only facility at Wynn Las Vegas).

Just north, where the Hacienda once stood, is the South Seas-themed **Mandalay Bay** (*see p71*), effectively the beginning of the 21st-century Strip. The hotel's **Shark Reef** aquarium (*see right*) is the best of the many animal-focused attractions in the city, but the resort is also home to a broad range of excellent eateries, the folk-art decorated **House of Blues** (*see p250*), retro burlesque joint **Forty Deuce** (*see p257*), the **Mandalay Place**

mini-mall (*see p192*) and two other hotels, the tranquil **Four Seasons** and the chic **Thehotel at Mandalay Bay** (for both, *see p95*).

Next to Mandalay Bay is the unmistakable onyx pyramid of the **Luxor** (*see p80*), lights racing up its angles and exploding in a dramatic sky-bound beacon. Inside is an **IMAX Theatre** (*see p242*), a games arcade and an impressive re-creation of Tutankhamun's burial chamber (*see right*). Just north of the Luxor lies the intersection of the Strip and Tropicana Avenue, home to more hotel rooms than you'll find in the whole of San Francisco. All around, crowds spill on to street corners and squeeze through pedestrian overpasses.

On the south-east corner of this ever-crazed junction are the white towers of the **Tropicana** (*see p94*): it was built in 1957 and looks its age (new owners are making plans to play catch-up), but the **Folies Bergère** (*see p231*) offers the old-Vegas showgirl revue that's fast fading into history. An exhibition devoted to the *Titanic* proved popular enough to earn permanent residency. If it sounds a bit soft, head for **Bodies** (*see right*), which offers a peek at the human anatomy beneath the skin.

Across Tropicana to the north is the forever-expanding **MGM Grand** (*see p81*). The signature lion guarding the entrance is the nation's largest bronze sculpture; there are more felines inside the resort, lurking in the **Lion Habitat** (*see right*), the **Crazy Horse Paris** cabaret (*see p225*) and sprawling nightclub **Studio 54** (*see p258*).

Opposite the MGM Grand (and connected by an overhead skywalk) is the gloriously preposterous **New York New York** (*see p84*). Overhead runs the **Manhattan Express** rollercoaster (*see below*); inside, kids will enjoy the **Coney Island Emporium** (*see below*), while adults sweat at Cirque du Soleil's sexy **Zumanity** (*see p226*). Across a walkway to the south, completing the circle of casinos, looms the medieval-themed **Excalibur** (*see p90*). It's still family-friendly but, in perhaps the most blatant symbol of the Strip's recent drift, replaced its puppet show with a motorcycle-themed bar called Chrome.

Bodies

Tropicana *3801 Las Vegas Boulevard South, at E Tropicana Avenue (739 2222/www.tropicanalv.com).* Bus Deuce, 201. **Open** 10am-11pm daily (last entry 10pm). **Admission** $26. **Credit** AmEx, Disc, MC, V. **Hotel** p94. **Map** p336 A8.
In the unlikely event that you've ever fancied dropping the best part of $30 in order to peek underneath the skin of dead strangers, this is the show for you. Having donated their remains to science, around 20 altruistic souls have been dissected, preserved and put on display for the edification of visitors to the Trop. All things considered, the merchandise is in surprisingly good taste.

Coney Island Emporium

New York New York *3790 Las Vegas Boulevard South, at W Tropicana Avenue (740 6414/ www.nynyhotelcasino.com).* Bus Deuce, 201. **Open** 9am-midnight Mon-Thur, Sun; 9am-1am Fri, Sat. **Admission** free. **Hotel** p84. **Map** p336 A8.
This arcade and family amusement centre attempts to recreate the atmosphere of the original Coney Island with more than 200 video and midway games, Bumper Cabs, a prize counter and lots of sticky candyfloss (but, sadly, no freak show).

In Search of the Obelisk

Luxor *3900 Las Vegas Boulevard South, at W Hacienda Avenue (262 4000/www.luxor.com).* Bus Deuce, 104, 105. **Open** 10am-11pm daily. **Admission** $9.99. **Credit** AmEx, DC, Disc, MC, V. **Hotel** p80. **Map** p336 A9.
This motion-simulator survivor of the Strip's family era takes the audience on a *Raiders of the Lost Ark*-style action adventure through the Luxor archaeological dig.

King Tut Museum

Luxor *3900 Las Vegas Boulevard South, at W Hacienda Avenue (262 4000/www.luxor.com).* Bus Deuce, 104, 105. **Open** 10am-11pm daily. **Admission** $9.99. **Credit** AmEx, DC, Disc, MC, V. **Hotel** p80. **Map** p336 A9.
This full-size re-creation of Tutankhamun's burial chamber and his golden throne and sarcophagus, apparently hand-crafted by Egyptian artisans from historically correct materials, is extremely kitschy but undeniably fun.

Lion Habitat

MGM Grand *3799 Las Vegas Boulevard South, at E Tropicana Avenue (891 7777/www.mgm grand.com).* Bus Deuce, 201. **Open** 11am-10pm daily. **Admission** free. **Hotel** p81. **Map** p336 A8.
Not to be outdone by the Mirage's tigers, the MGM has its own pride of 'display' lions. The habitat is pretty small, but the glass walls mean you can get a close-up view of cubs and adult lions. *Photo p123.*

Manhattan Express

New York New York *3790 Las Vegas Boulevard South, at W Tropicana Avenue (740 6969/ www.nynyhotelcasino.com).* Bus Deuce, 201. **Open** 11am-11pm Mon-Thur, Sun; 10am-midnight Fri, Sat. **Tickets** $12.50. *Re-rides $6. All-day Scream Pass $25.* **Hotel** p84. **Map** p336 A8.
Gotham never saw anything like it: a rollercoaster soaring around skyscrapers and Miss Liberty. The Express twists, loops and dives at breakneck speeds, and features the first ever 'heartline roll', which creates the sensation a pilot feels when going through a barrel roll in an aeroplane. Try hard to smile in the last section: this is where the photos are taken.

Shark Reef

Mandalay Bay *3950 Las Vegas Boulevard South, at W Hacienda Avenue (632 4555/www.mandalay bay.com).* Bus Deuce, 104, 105. **Open** 10am-11pm daily (last entry 10pm). **Admission** $15.95; $12.95 reductions; free under-4s. **Credit** AmEx, Disc, MC, V. **Hotel** p71. **Map** p336 A9.
A 'walk-through' aquarium, the AZA-accredited Shark Reef is filled with 100 species of underwater life, including rays, jellyfish, eels and, of course, 11 varieties of shark. A perfect complement to the South Seas-themed Mandalay Bay, the Shark Reef is an unexpected gem in a city lacking in the educational entertainment department.

Titanic: the Exhibition

Tropicana *3801 Las Vegas Boulevard South, at E Tropicana Avenue (739 2222/www.tropicanalv.com).* Bus Deuce, 201. **Open** 10am-11pm daily (last entry 10pm). **Admission** $22. **Credit** AmEx, Disc, MC, V. **Hotel** p94. **Map** p336 A8.
More than 3,000 bits and pieces recovered from the mother of all seafaring disasters are now on permanent display at the Tropicana in this diverting show, which also affords visitors the chance to experience a simulation of the kind of weather experienced by the poor unfortunates on the night in question.

Tropicana Avenue to Harmon Avenue

Map p336 A8

A pleasant pedestrian boardwalk that morphs into a replica Brooklyn Bridge leads north on the eastern side of New York New York as far as the **ESPN Zone** sports bar (*see p179*). As you stroll, note the classic 'Pepsi and Pete' sign

Sightseeing

on the wall of a replica brownstone building, challenging the Times Square-style giant neon Coke bottle on the **Showcase Mall** across the street. The mall houses the Strip's only cinema (the **UA Showcase 8**; *see p242*), **M&M's World** (*see below*), and a huge arcade with the world's tallest indoor climbing wall.

Further on, past the **Empire Ballroom** (*see p256*) and fronting the **Polo Towers** timeshare, sits the **Hawaiian Marketplace**. It's surprising that this shambolic jumble of shops, restaurants and a bird show has survived the wrecking ball, especially when you see what's going on across the road. The fountains and arches of the middle-market **Monte Carlo** (*see p84*) still draw the crowds, but it's the activity directly north of it that has observers excited.

Right now, the Las Vegas skyline is lined with cranes, as Strip casinos add new towers, and vacant lots are filled with condo towers. However, no one stretch defines the future of Vegas more dramatically than the vast plot of land between the Monte Carlo and the Bellagio on the west side of the Strip. The key development on the Strip – and, for that matter, in the city – is MGM Mirage's vast, ambitious hotel-casino-condo-retail-dining complex **CityCenter** (*see p28*), due to open in phases during 2009 and 2010. Directly north of it is the **Cosmopolitan**, a dazzlingly modern condo-hotel resort scheduled for completion in 2009. Together, these two developments will house 5,000 condo units and nearly 6,000 hotel rooms. Time will tell if demand matches supply.

GameWorks

Showcase Mall, 3785 Las Vegas Boulevard South, between E Tropicana & E Harmon Avenues (432 4263/www.gameworks.com). Bus Deuce, 201. **Open** 10am-midnight Mon-Thur, Sun; 10am-1am Fri, Sat. **Admission** free. **Credit** AmEx, Disc, MC, V. **Map** p336 A8.
If you'd rather shove quarters into a video game than a slot machine, this place is for you. This huge madhouse is a great place in which to try out the latest games: you can save money if you pay by the hour, though none of it's cheap. There are more than 250 games, a billiards lounge, two restaurants, a coffee bar and a 75ft (23m) indoor climbing wall.

M&M's World

Showcase Mall, 3785 Las Vegas Boulevard South, between E Tropicana & E Harmon Avenues (736 7611/www.m-ms.com). Bus Deuce, 201. **Open** 9am-11pm Mon-Thur, Sun; 9am-midnight Fri, Sat. **Admission** free. **Credit** MC, V. **Map** p336 A8.
This is a four-level chocolate-lover's paradise. Check out M&M Academy, an interactive entertainment attraction showing visitors how these chocolate candies earn their trademark. The attraction includes a 3-D movie, and 'graduates' get a diploma. Yes, it's a bit overmarketed. But at least it's free.

Map p336 A7

Planet Hollywood (*see p85*), which opened as the Aladdin in 2000, sits on the east side of the Strip at Harmon Avenue. The Aladdin was never one of the Strip's more popular casinos; the new owners hope that by getting rid of the ill-timed Baghdad motif, things will turn around, though history isn't on their side (*see p84* **The worst of luck**). Alas, you won't find the Terminator dealing cards: unlike at the Planet Hollywood restaurants, the movie bric-a-brac is confined to the guestrooms, and the neutrally decorated casino lacks a specific theme. The hotel connects to the **Miracle Mile** mall (formerly Desert Passage; *see p192*), itself subjected to a facelift in 2007.

To the north of Planet Hollywood is the spectacular (but small, in Vegas terms) **Paris Las Vegas** (*see p74*), complete with half-scale Eiffel Tower (*see right*), grand fountains and sidewalk café (**Mon Ami Gabi**; *see p160*). From here, it's a skip north to the original 'Four Corners', where the Strip meets Flamingo Road. On the south-west corner of the street, at **Bally's** (*see p77*), a video screen competes with the bizarre tunnel entrance. To its north sits **Bill's Gamblin' Hall & Saloon**, recently bought and renamed (it was the Barbary Coast until 2007; *see p88*) by Harrah's amid rumours that it's not long for this world. Either way, both Bally's and Bill's are overshadowed by their neighbours right across the Strip.

At the south-west corner of the Strip–Flamingo intersection is the **Bellagio** (*see p68*), the most renowned property in the city since it opened in October 1998. The fountains that dance upon the large replica of Lake Como are one of the best-loved attractions in Las Vegas (*see right*), but there's plenty of note inside: the **Gallery of Fine Art** (*see p243*), Cirque du Soleil's O (*see p232*) and the glass-domed **Conservatory & Botanical Gardens**, which lie beyond the lobby and are home to thousands of exotic plants and flowers.

With its striking blue-white lighting and huge fountains, the opulent and ever-expanding **Caesars Palace** (*see p68*) commands attention as the sole Strip casino to successfully mate the past with 21st-century Vegas. Little of Jay Sarno's Roman kitsch remains; the resort has successfully reinvented itself as an altogether more chic property. Just to the north of the main fountain is a small Brahma shrine, where visitors worship and leave offerings of fruit and flowers in exchange for good luck.

Near where Caesars meets the Mirage is the entrance to the Roman-themed **Forum Shops** (*see p191*), a vast atrium served by a spiral escalator and filled with luxury boutiques. The high-end shopping is conducted under an ever-changing 'sky' that's spelled by a Disney-like robot show. Animated statues come to life for a bizarre and very loud seven-minute revel with dancing water and laser lights.

Bellagio Fountains

Bellagio *3600 Las Vegas Boulevard South, at W Flamingo Road (693 7111/www.bellagio.com).* *Bus Deuce, 202.* **Shows** 3pm-midnight Mon-Fri (every 30mins 3-8pm; every 15mins 8pm-midnight); noon-midnight Sat, Sun (every 30mins noon-8pm; every 15mins 8pm-midnight). **Admission** free. **Hotel** p68. **Map** p336 A7.

The Bellagio's lake throws up entrancing fountain displays choreographed to music from Pavarotti to Sinatra (and, less appealingly, Lee Greenwood). The 1,200 water cannons, arranged in lines and circles, shoot water that dances and sways to the music, reaching as high as 240ft (73m). The best seats are in the Bellagio restaurants, but you get a good view from the pavements out front, and from the top of the Eiffel Tower at Paris Las Vegas.

Eiffel Tower Experience

Paris Las Vegas *3655 Las Vegas Boulevard South, at E Flamingo Road (946 7000/www.harrahs. com).* *Bus Deuce, 202.* **Open** 9.30am-12.30am daily. **Tickets** $9-$12; $7-$10 reductions; free under-5s. **Credit** AmEx, DC, Disc, MC, V. **Hotel** p74. **Map** p336 A7.

OK, so it's only half the size of the original, but the Vegas Eiffel Tower gives visitors a great view of the Strip and the surrounding mountains, something you won't find in Paris. Take a lift to the 46th-floor observation deck; go at dusk to watch the Strip suddenly light up as if someone's flicked a switch.

Flamingo Road to Spring Mountain Road

Map p336 A7-A6

Wedged against Bill's Gamblin' Hall & Saloon, the **Flamingo** (*see p78*) is one of the Strip's most storied properties, although nothing remains of Bugsy Siegel's 1941 original. In its place is a lush pool area and winding pathways that take you past penguins, Chilean flamingos, Mandarin ducks and koi fish swimming in ponds under three-storey-high waterfalls. If it weren't for the tennis courts, pool and spa, it could be a wildlife habitat, albeit the only one in the world with a plaque honouring a mobster.

This stretch of the Strip, covering Bill's Gamblin' Hall, the Flamingo, the low-priced, casino-only **O'Sheas** (No.3355, 697 2711), the faded **Imperial Palace** (*see p80*) and the altogether unremarkable **Harrah's** (*see p79*), is owned by Harrah's Entertainment, a mid-market corporation that's second only to MGM Mirage in terms of its influence on the city. It's been widely speculated that the firm will demolish the Imperial Palace and build a new

Sightseeing

Reel around the fountains at the **Bellagio**.

property that allows for an uninterrupted flow of gamblers along this stretch. While the Palace remains, the chief reason for non-guests to visit is the **Auto Collections** museum, behind the hotel on top of the parking garage (*see right*). And just past Harrah's, a 24-hour parade of hungry characters scoff food at Denny's inside the small and still independently owned **Casino Royale** (*see p89*), a worthwhile stop if you're slumming for Hunter S Thompson's Vegas.

Back across the street, north of Caesars is a block-long tropical paradise that begins with the **Mirage** (*see p73*), which in 1989 became the Strip's first modern mega-resort. When it opened, the Mirage introduced the first large-scale free spectacle to Las Vegas: a 54-foot (16-metre) volcano right on the Strip. The revamped volcano is small, lacks a cinder dome and looks more like a granite wall than Mount Etna. However, the brief spectacle (every 15 minutes, 7pm-midnight daily), spewing fire and a piña colada scent into the palm trees, waterfalls and lagoon, is worth a look.

Inside the resort, pygmy sharks swim in a large aquarium behind the registration desk. After looking tired for years, the Mirage got a much-needed shine in advance of **Love** (*see p231*), Cirque du Soleil's much-heralded

Beatles show. After the show, fans can huddle at the **Revolution** lounge (*see p180*) to decide if they liked it; if, that is, they don't fancy hitting any of the Light Group-operated hotspots elsewhere: in-the-moment nightclub **Jet** (*see p257*), and eateries **Stack** (*see p157*) and **Japonais** (*see p162*).

Just up from the Mirage sits **Treasure Island** (*see p87*), now marketing itself as TI in an attempt to shake off its family image. The resort fronts the Strip with a replica of an 18th-century sea village set on a lagoon, surrounded by cliffs, palm trees and nautical artefacts. The focus of attention, however, are the two fully rigged ships on which the **Sirens of TI** clash with a band of renegade pirates (every 90 minutes, 7-11.30pm daily). Formerly a family-friendly pantomime, the show received a crass revamp that tries to rebrand the property as a more adult resort. Regardless, it fills the pavement to capacity, as onlookers stare slack-jawed at the blazing cannons, toppling masts, exploding powder kegs and – key to the whole thing – heaving bosoms.

Opposite TI and the Mirage on the eastern side of the Strip, just north of Casino Royale, sits the **Venetian** (*see p75*), Sheldon Adelson's hugely successful reinterpretation of the city of canals. Attractions include super-fashionable

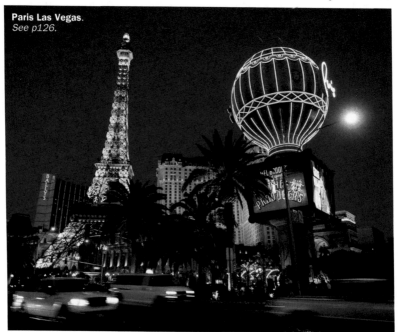

Paris Las Vegas.
See p126.

Sirens of TI.

restaurant-club **Tao** (*see p166*), **Madame Tussaud's** (*see below*), the highfalutin **Grand Canal Shoppes** (*see p191*) and **singing gondoliers** (*see below*), who drag embarrassed tourists along the resort's canals. Culture is provided by the **Guggenheim Hermitage Museum** (*see p244*); a larger museum space closed in 2003. Crowds are sure to show up in even greater numbers when the adjoining **Palazzo**, a related yet entirely separate 3,000-room resort, opens in 2008.

Gondola Rides

Venetian *Grand Canal Shoppes, 3355 Las Vegas Boulevard South, between Sands Avenue & E Flamingo Road (414 1000/www.venetian.com). Bus Deuce, 105, 203.* **Open** 10am-11pm Mon-Thur, Sun; 10am-midnight Fri, Sat. **Tickets** *Indoor ride* $15; $7.50 under-12s; $60 2-passenger gondola. *Outdoor ride* $12.50; $5 under-12s; $50 2-passenger gondola. **Credit** AmEx, DC, Disc, MC, V. **Hotel** p75. **Map** p335 & p336 A6.

Purchase your tickets at St Mark's Square, then take a ride along canals that weave through replica Venetian architecture. The wooden boats are authentic and the singing gondoliers are tuneful. However, despite the number of newly married couples that take the ride, the backdrop of gawking tourists will dampen any hopes of a romantic moment.

Imperial Palace Auto Collections

Imperial Palace *3535 Las Vegas Boulevard South, between Sands Avenue & E Flamingo Road (731 3311/www.imperialpalace.com). Bus Deuce, 105, 203.* **Open** 9.30am-9.30pm daily. **Admission** $6.95; $3.50 reductions. **Credit** AmEx, DC, Disc, MC, V. **Hotel** p80. **Map** p336 A6.

Tucked away in the parking garage are 200 rare and speciality cars (part of a rotating collection of 750, all for sale). Among them are Hitler's 1936 Mercedes, JFK's 1962 Lincoln, vehicles that once belonged to Al Capone, WC Fields and Howard Hughes, and a room full of Duesenbergs. This latter room was where former casino owner Ralph Engelstad held secretive 'Hitler birthday parties', before being fined by the Nevada Gaming Control Board for the activity.

Madame Tussaud's

Venetian *3355 Las Vegas Boulevard South, between Sands Avenue & E Flamingo Road (367 1847/www.venetian.com). Bus Deuce, 105, 203.* **Open** 10am-10pm daily. **Admission** $24; $14-$18 reductions; free under-6s. **Credit** AmEx, DC, Disc, MC, V. **Hotel** p75. **Map** p335 & p336 A6.

The first US incarnation of London's all-conquering attraction contains more than 100 wax celebs in various settings and rendered with various degrees of accuracy (Johnny Depp good, Shaquille O'Neal less impressive). The comparatively small attraction tones down the British history in favor of celebrity and pop culture 'encounters': a photo opportunity to don a wedding dress and 'marry' George Clooney, for example, or a chance to sing in front of Simon Cowell. Hokey but fun.

Secret Garden & Dolphin Habitat

Mirage *3400 Las Vegas Boulevard South, between Spring Mountain & W Flamingo Roads (791 7188/www.miragehabitat.com). Bus Deuce, 105, 202, 203.* **Open** *Summer* 11am-7pm Mon-Fri; 10am-7pm Sat, Sun. *Autumn-spring* 11am-5.30pm Mon-Fri; 10am-5.30pm Sat, Sun. **Admission** $15; $10 reductions; free under-3s. **Credit** AmEx, DC, Disc, MC, V. **Hotel** p73. **Map** p335 & p336 A6.

...arine mammals in the desert? Nothing's impossible in fabulous Las Vegas. Here, bottle-nosed dolphins frolic in a special habitat behind the Mirage. Adjacent to their home is the Secret Garden, a small but attractive zoo with Asian-themed architecture and some big-ticket animals: white tigers, white lions, Bengal tigers, an Indian elephant, a panther and a snow leopard.

Spring Mountain Road to Convention Center Drive

Map p335 B6-B5

For 15 years, the stretch of the Strip north of Spring Mountain Road was old Vegas through and through, a parade of forgotten resorts and empty plots of land. A few of the old casinos remain, but it's mostly all change around here, and has been since about 2005. In a nutshell, the difference between then and now is the difference between Sinatra's *Ocean's 11* and Clooney's *Ocean's Eleven*.

Naturally, Steve Wynn is at the centre of it all. It was Wynn who kickstarted the Vegas renaissance by building the Mirage in 1989. Then, 16 years later and just a couple of stone's throws from its front door, he opened the $2.7-billion **Wynn Las Vegas** (*see p76*), a hyperreal return to the 'intimacy' of old Las Vegas. Symbolically, the resort sits on land formerly occupied by the Desert Inn, a Vegas classic that bit the dust just a few years earlier.

In a reversal of the philosophy of streetside spectacle pioneered at the Mirage, Wynn Las Vegas is hidden from the Strip by a mountain. Behind it is a golf course, a lavish spa, top-end shops and even a Ferrari dealership; Wynn has never done things by halves. Right next to the resort, Wynn is currently building a second tower in a similar style to the first. However, Encore will stand apart as a separate resort when it opens in late 2008 or early 2009.

Directly across the road, the **Fashion Show Mall** (*see p193*) is further accelerating the redefinition of Vegas. The two 13-storey

Stealth mountain

The Mirage volcano, the Treasure Island pirate show and the Bellagio's dancing waters are the most popular free attractions on the Strip. All three were conceived by Steve Wynn, and were designed to lure passing visitors inside each resort. A decade later, though, Wynn reversed his previous policy of visibility. The volcano, the siren show and the fountains all front directly on to the Strip. But at Wynn Las Vegas (*see p76*), visitors have to go inside the casino to find the signature attraction.

From outside the resort, visitors can see a small hill covered in trees: nearly 500 of them, some 65 feet (20 metres) tall and 60 years old (transplanted from the old Desert Inn golf course). Mount Wynn, however, isn't immediately obvious, either from here or from inside the resort. To get the full effect, you'll need to take the spiral staircase down to the terraces at the SW Steakhouse or Daniel Boulud; there's also a small outdoor bar and a tiny free-viewing platform.

The mountain consists of four environments that provide the backdrop for the row of restaurants and bars, each with its own distinct alfresco view. Eight waterfalls descend into the three-acre Lake of Dreams and its 4,000-plus individually controlled and submerged LEDs. A freestanding 70-foot

(21-metre) wall serves as the projection screen for a free light-and-sound show that plays every half-hour starting at 9pm.

The mountain serves a second and perhaps equally important purpose. It blocks the lights and drowns out the sounds of the Strip, cocooning Wynn Las Vegas and providing the visual centrepiece for the whole property. Once, that is, you've figured out where to look.

towers would dominate the landscape were it not for the Cloud, a 479-foot (150-metre) metal oval suspended between them (*see p33* **What's that?**). The Cloud serves as an outdoor projection screen, but it also provides much-needed shade for the de facto piazza and four rare (for Vegas) restaurants featuring outdoor seating facing the Wynn, including **Ra Sushi**, serving rock 'n' roll Japanese food, and **Café Ba Ba Reeba** (*see p158*), dealing in tapas. In coincidental but purposeful synergy with Wynn Las Vegas, the Fashion Show is a theme-free shopping centre; before long, themed resorts will seem as dated as the old casinos did in 1989.

North of the Fashion Show sits what is, unexpectedly, the most expensive piece of land in Las Vegas. For decades, the south-west corner of the Strip and Desert Inn Road was home to the **New Frontier**, built in 1942 (as the Last Frontier) and one of the first resorts on what became the Strip. The resort trod water for years, as rumours came and went about owner Phil Ruffin's plans for redevelopment. But then, after mapping out his ambition to build a Montreux-themed resort on the site, Ruffin abruptly sold up to New York-based developers El Ad in May 2007. The firm hopes to raze the Frontier in late 2007 and built in its place a replica of New York's Plaza Hotel, which should make a rather more appropriate neighbour for the new **Trump International Hotel & Tower** just behind it. The price for the 36-acre site was $1.2 billion, or just over $33 million per acre. When this real estate bubble bursts, it's going to make one hell of a pop.

Across the Desert Inn Arterial, an east–west expressway that avoids both the Strip (by tunnelling under) and I-15 (by flying over), further changes are afoot. The plot of land on the western side of the street was home to the Stardust for nearly 50 years. Proving that nothing is sacred, the iconic resort was demolished in 2007 to make room for **Echelon Place**, a 90-acre, multi-hotel complex due to open in 2010. Developer Boyd Gaming has previously concentrated on the locals' market with off-Strip properties such as Sam's Town; Echelon Place represents a clear attempt to join MGM Mirage and Harrah's in the premier league of Vegas casino operators.

The opposite side of the Strip is an altogether more sedate sight. Development here has yet to really take hold, leaving the Catholic **Guardian Angel Cathedral** (336 Guardian Angel Way, 735 5241) to go about its business in relative peace. The themed stained-glass windows here are one of the few places where you can still see old Vegas icons such as the Landmark Hotel. Rumour has it that the church accepts casino chips in its collection plate.

Convention Center Drive to Sahara Avenue

Map p335 B5-C4

North of Convention Center Drive, the Strip quickly peters out into disrepair. A couple of scruffy strip malls sit adjacent to and opposite some creaking old casinos, though the most eye-catching features are the acres of empty lots and the clusters of construction work. The north Strip may be on the rise, but it's got a little way to travel before it reaches lift-off.

A fun little ode to the '70s stubbornly survives in the shape of **Peppermill's Fireside Lounge** (*see p180*), though the lounge recently ruined its cosy, Playboy-like atmosphere by bolting flat-panel TVs on every surface. The site next door was once home to the delightfully Googie-style La Concha Motel. But after innumerable plans for redevelopment fell by the wayside, the land is currently, stubbornly vacant, while the motel's old lobby has been moved Downtown by the Neon Museum (*see p141* **Lighting up the past**).

It's back to blazing neon at the 50-year-old **Riviera** (*see p91*), where the façade and sign very nearly constitute overkill even by Vegas standards. You can skip the actual show, but don't miss the life-sized bronze statues promoting the **Crazy Girls** (*see p225*) just in front of the casino; punters rub their butts for a boozy photo-op. However, the Riv seems to be marking time while it awaits extinction, a refuge for the cost-conscious traveller but easily skipped by those not staying there.

Lucky the Clown still leers cheerfully over the Strip from the front of **Circus Circus** (*see p89*) across the road, though the original family fun palace is now showing its age. The casino under the pink concrete big top stages free circus acts (11am-midnight daily) above the casino floor, while the **Horse-a-Round Bar** (*see p180*) was immortalised in Hunter S Thompson's *Fear and Loathing in Las Vegas*. The cramped space and shabby decor lessen the spectacle; it's an odd experience watching a spangly trapeze artist fly overhead. While mom and pop gamble away the rent, kids whoop it up at **Adventuredome**, a popular indoor amusement park (*see p132*).

North of here, there's much promise but, at least for now, little tangible excitement. Much of the land between here and Sahara Avenue was purchased by Circus Circus owners MGM Mirage in 2007, though no development plans have yet been announced for the largely vacant site. Across the road, construction is under way on a Las Vegas version of Miami's famous **Fountainbleu**. But until it's completed,

?009, visitors will have to get
mes at the **Sahara** (*see p92*),
camels on a fibre-optic sign
cious customers into a bright
porte cochere. Thrill-seekers flock to the virtual
racing at the **Las Vegas Cyber Speedway**
and to **Speed: the Ride** (for both, *see below*).

For many, the Strip begins and ends
right here at Sahara Avenue, although the
Stratosphere's looming tower has pushed the
unofficial boundary another half-mile north.

Adventuredome

Circus Circus *2880 Las Vegas Boulevard South,
between W Sahara Avenue & Desert Inn Road
(794 3939/www.adventuredome.com). Bus Deuce.*
Open 10am-6pm Mon-Thur; 10am-midnight Fri, Sat;
10am-8pm Sun. **Admission** *Unlimited rides $22.95;
$14.95 reductions; free toddlers. Individual rides
$4-$7.* **Credit** AmEx, DC, Disc, MC, V. **Hotel** p89.
Map p335 B5.

The five-acre park, climate-controlled under a pink
plastic dome, is a scene Fred Flintstone would love:
waterfalls, faux mountains and animated spitting
dinosaurs stuck in fake tar pits. The rides here are
good, though hardly white-knuckle; the best is the
double-loop, double-corkscrew rollercoaster ($5), but
it lasts a disappointingly brief 90 seconds. Tots will
like the bumper cars, Ferris wheel and other small
rides, as well as an obstacle course for creative
crawling. In October, the park transforms into the
pleasantly creepy FrightDome.

Speedworld

Sahara *2535 Las Vegas Boulevard South, at W
Sahara Avenue (737 2111/www.saharavegas.com).
Bus Deuce, 108, 204.* **Open** 11am-9pm Mon-Thur,
Sun; 11am-11pm Fri, Sat. **Admission** *$10 1 ride;
$18 2 rides. All-day joint ticket with Speed: the Ride
$21.95.* **Credit** AmEx, DC, Disc, MC, V. **Hotel** p92.
Map p335 C4.

This high-tech virtual reality racing simulator teams
effectively with the neighbouring NASCAR Café (*see
p236*): you should see this place on race weekends.
It's a fun schtick and frighteningly realistic; at these
prices, so it should be.

Speed: the Ride

Sahara *2535 Las Vegas Boulevard South, at W
Sahara Avenue (737 2111/www.saharavegas.com).
Bus Deuce, 108, 204.* **Open** 11am-9pm Mon-Thur,
Sun; 11am-11pm Fri, Sat. **Admission** *$10 all-day
pass. All-day joint ticket with Las Vegas Cyber
Speedway $21.95.* **Credit** AmEx, DC, Disc, MC, V.
Hotel p92. **Map** p335 C4.

Although it may look like one, Speed is not, according to the strict definition, a rollercoaster: it doesn't
have a lift hill, nor does it run by gravity. Instead,
it's driven by the force of magnetic impellers that
rush it from zero to soil-your-pants in three seconds.
Riders shoot out from the Sahara into a tunnel drop,
only to re-emerge directly into a vertical loop and up
a 23-storey tower at 70mph. And then they do it all
over again… backwards. Twice.

Stratosphere Area

Map p335 C4-C3

The lot at the south-western corner of Sahara
and the Strip is eye-catchingly vacant, while
the much-rumoured redevelopment of the
north-eastern plot has yet to occur. Diagonally
opposite the Sahara, **Bonanza Gifts** (*see p203*)
holds the fort at the intersection's north-western
corner; claiming to be the world's largest gift
shop, it sells a vast array of souvenirs, in a
pleasantly kitschy time-travel to the Route 66
era. Just west is the rising pricey condo tower
of Allure overlooking the Strip, and the classic
Golden Steer Steak House (*see p169*).

Standing outside Bonanza, you'll be able
to hear screams. Glance north, and you'll see
why. At the top of the **Stratosphere** (*see p93*),
the tallest building in Nevada, is a trio of thrill
rides: the **Big Shot**, which propels passengers
vertically; **X Scream**, which dangles them over
the edge of the tower; and **Insanity: the Ride**,
an inverted centrifuge that spins over the edge
of the observation deck at a 70-degree angle. It's
enough to make anyone scream… including Bob
Stupak, the Stratosphere's former owner, who
suffered a series of financial and construction
setbacks when trying to complete the tower.

The Stratosphere sits where Main Street and
Paradise Road cross Las Vegas Boulevard and
turn into each other by way of St Louis Avenue.
Approaching it from the south are a string of
downmarket motels, though the old **Holiday
House Motel** (No.2211, 732 2468) is notable
for its animated neon sign and Palm Springs-
like motor court design. At the intersection
with Oakey Boulevard is the **White Cross
Drugstore**; in it is Tiffany's, one of the few
drugstore food counters left in town.

Big Shot, X Scream & Insanity: the Ride

Stratosphere *2000 Las Vegas Boulevard South, at
St Louis Avenue (380 7777/www.stratospherehotel.
com). Bus Deuce, 108.* **Open** 10am-1am Mon-Thur,
Sun; 10am-2am Fri, Sat. **Tickets** *$8 each. All 3 rides
$24.95. All-day pass $29.95.* **Credit** AmEx, DC, Disc,
MC, V. **Hotel** p93. **Map** p335 C4.

If you're afraid of heights, stay away from the 1,150ft
(350m) Stratosphere Tower. And even if you don't
suffer from vertigo, you might want to steer clear of
the resort's thrill rides. The Big Shot will rocket you
160ft (49m) up the tower's spindle under a force of
four Gs; at the top, you'll experience a moment of
weightlessness before free-falling back to the launch
pad. X Scream will propel you headfirst 27ft over
the edge of the Tower and then leave you there to
dangle. And during Insanity, an arm will extend 64ft
(20m) over the edge of the tower and spin you around
at a terrifying rate. Best save dinner for later.

Get around

In an effort to eliminate – or at least reduce – the Strip's gridlock of rental cars, Hummers and limos, the city offers two competing systems of public transport. Part of the city's public transit network, the **Deuce** is a fleet of pimped-out double-decker buses that troll the Strip, dropping passengers in front of hotel-casinos, timeshares and restaurants. The **Las Vegas Monorail**, meanwhile, travels on an overhead concrete platform east of the Strip, with seven stops at the back of hotels and at the Convention Center; it's privately owned and operated by the Las Vegas Monorail Company. Each has its pros and cons; the following table may help you choose which option best suits your travel needs.

Las Vegas Monorail.

THE DEUCE	THE MONORAIL
The buses are double-deckers with cool paint jobs and nice seats.	The monorails are even cooler: they aren't buses.
It's cheap at $2 a ride or $5 for an all-day pass.	It's pricey at $5 a ride or $15 for an all-day pass.
It covers the entire Strip and also goes all the way to Downtown.	It goes only from the MGM Grand to the Sahara.
The buses run 24 hours a day, seven days a week, and they let folks ride even if they're drunk.	The trains run 7am-2am on weekdays, and 7am-3am on weekends. In other words, they stop when you most need someone else to drive.
Drunks throw up on it.	The trains are virtually vomit-free.
The stops are frequent and right on the Strip.	The stops are infrequent and never on the Strip.
It's so convenient that anyone can ride, including the obese, the smelly and the obnoxious. And they will sit next to you.	It's so inconvenient that only the fittest can walk to its stops, but they may be a bit sweaty by the time they sit down.
The leisurely pace of Strip traffic is great for sightseeing, novel-writing and beard-growing.	The high speed of the monorail makes up for the quarter-hour it took you to walk to and from its stops.
Has yet to lose a wheel while running.	Has lost a wheel while running.
Is more popular and more widely used than anyone expected.	Is currently a financial failure. When faced with falling popularity, it raised its fares, only to see ridership drop further. At the current rate, it should be down to one passenger by 2012, who pays $7 million per ride.

Off-Strip

Guess what? More casinos…

Atomic Testing Museum.

East of the Strip

You wouldn't expect to confuse **Paradise Road** for the Strip. Lined with an erratic hodge-podge of posh hotels and scruffy apartment blocks, convention facilities and adult clubs, strip malls and, er, more strip malls, Paradise is a low-key thoroughfare. However, as the Las Vegas Convention Center draws ever-increasing numbers of conventioneers and the Strip attracts even more tourists, so the traffic along it gets fiercer. Paradise Road now resembles Las Vegas Boulevard in one crucial regard: if you're foolish enough to try driving down it in rush hour, you'll be waiting a while.

Running parallel to the Strip, Paradise Road has been the site of major development since 1969, when the Landmark and International casinos opened south of Sahara Avenue. The Landmark was erased a while ago (see *Mars Attacks!* to witness its real-life destruction), while the International was renamed the **Las Vegas Hilton** (*see p97*) in 1971, the same year that it starred as the Whyte House in *Diamonds Are Forever*. The Hilton's showroom staged Elvis Presley's record-breaking run of 837 sell-outs in the 1970s; prosaically, it now hosts nightly concerts by Barry Manilow. The hotel is also home to the unstoppable **Star Trek: the Experience** (*see right*); directly behind it is the exclusive **Las Vegas Country Club**.

Sprawling out from the south end of the Hilton and across Desert Inn Road, the **Las Vegas Convention Center** (*see p309*) has been more responsible than any one hotel for

the extraordinary growth in visitor numbers over the last decade. Seven million travellers arrive in the city for conventions each year, and many of them pass through this immense site to do business. The assortment of uncharismatic chain hotels nearby stand testament to its influence. At the intersection with Desert Inn Road, **Envy** (*see p167*) serves hungry conventioneers; across the street is a shuttle to whisk patrons to the Wynn Las Vegas resort.

Further south, the road widens and the traffic eases. At Twain Avenue begins a collection of eateries known as 'restaurant row'. However, the stretch of Paradise between Flamingo and Tropicana holds more points of interest. On the eastern side of the road lies a succession of strip malls that house a slew of excellent restaurants (try **Origin India**; *see p168*), dive bars (such as the **Double Down Saloon**; *see p181*) and gay hangouts (in the **Fruit Loop**; *see pp246-249*). East of all these businesses sits the campus of UNLV, which more or less backs on to Paradise Road. And on the western side of Paradise, at the junction with Harmon Avenue, is the **Hard Rock** hotel-casino (*see p96*), crammed with memorabilia, suntanned hipsters and cash-happy baby boomers. Despite competition from Palms, the Hard Rock is holding its own as a favoured resort for the young and restless.

South of Tropicana sits the vast **McCarran International Airport** (*see p306*), which seems to grow bigger and busier by the week. East on Tropicana is the **Atomic Testing Museum**, located on the Desert Research

Institute campus. And to the west of Paradise, between Flamingo and Tropicana, sit a maze of small streets and empty lots, awaiting the inevitable redevelopment but content for now to serve as a rat run for the savvy drivers smart enough to avoid both Paradise and the Strip.

Atomic Testing Museum

755 E Flamingo Road, between Swenson Street & Paradise Road (794 5151/www.atomictesting museum.org). Bus 202. **Open** *9am-5pm Mon-Sat; 1-5pm Sun.* **Admission** *$12; $9 reductions; free under-6s.* **Credit** *AmEx, Disc, MC, V.* **Map** *p333 Y3.*
From the city that once trotted out atomic pin-up girls in mushroom-cloud swimsuits for cheesy publicity stills comes a one-of-a-kind insight into the Nevada Test Site, the US's principal on-continent nuclear weapons testing facility from 1951 to 1992. The story it tells is fascinating: how nuclear power came to represent the future in the USA, how it came to be something approaching a tourist attraction in this most carefully blasé of states, and – most crucially, and in layman's terms – how it actually works.

The headline exhibit is the motion-simulator that endeavours to give visitors a taste of what it must have been like to sit in on one of the several hundred tests carried out at the site between 1951 and 1992. But the real keys to the museum's success are the clarity with which it tells its tale (chronologically, through a succession of themed rooms), and the eye-popping quality of the exhibits (some kitsch, some terrifying). The last two or three rooms essentially comprise an advertorial for nuclear power, which doesn't sit well after what's gone before. But this is still comfortably the most interesting and enlightening museum in the city.

Flyaway

200 Convention Center Drive, between Las Vegas Boulevard South & Paradise Road (1-877 545 8093/ 731 4768/www.flyawayindoorskydiving.com). Bus Deuce, 108. **Open** *10am-6pm Mon-Thur, Sun; 10am-9pm Fri, Sat.* **Rates** *$70.* **Credit** *AmEx, Disc, MC, V.* **Map** *p335 B5.*
Skydiving without an airplane? Well, sort of: you can free-fall in one of only three skydiving simulators in the world, an indoor 21ft vertical wind tunnel that generates air speeds of up to 130mph. After an hour of instruction, you get 15 minutes of flying time shared with five others.

Star Trek: the Experience

Las Vegas Hilton *3000 Paradise Road, between E Sahara Avenue & E Desert Inn Road (732 5111/ www.startrekexp.com). Bus 108, 204, 213.* **Open** *Attraction noon-8pm daily. Shops 11am-10pm Mon-Thur, Sun; 10am-11pm Fri, Sat.* **Admission** *$42.99.* **Credit** *AmEx, DC, Disc, MC, V.* **Hotel** *p97.* **Map** *p335 C5.*
Promising to boldly go where no Vegas attraction has gone before, this perpetually popular piece of inter-galactic hokum offers two different immersive 'experiences'. Although your trip includes a 'beaming' to the bridge of the *Starship Enterprise* and a ride in a

virtual shuttle, most of your time is spent looking at costumes, props and weaponry from every Trek incarnation. Ferengi and Klingons roam the site, happy to pose for photos and chat you up about their last trip through the Gamma Quadrant. There's also the Space Quest Casino, which uses dozens of monitors disguised as portholes to create the illusion that you're orbiting Earth. If you're not keen on throwing cash into 24th-century slot machines, at least step into Quark's Bar & Restaurant (*see p183*). You may not be surprised to learn that the management found room to squeeze in a couple of souvenir shops.

West of the Strip

The area between busy Las Vegas Boulevard and unremarkable Valley View Boulevard is bisected by I-15, which carves a rift into a section of land that didn't offer much resistance to it. Wedged next to it and running parallel, Frank Sinatra Drive offers quicker, back-door access to many Strip hotels. Continuing north, Industrial Road itself is just as speedy, but is otherwise notable only for the parade of strip clubs that lines its western edge.

Overpasses at Tropicana, Flamingo or Sahara take drivers across I-15 to Valley View Boulevard (which, incidentally, isn't continuous between Tropicana Boulevard and Flamingo Road). If you're heading this way from the Strip, Flamingo is the road to take: it's lined with a quartet of very different hotel-casinos, each with something to offer the visitor.

On the northern side of Flamingo sits the **Rio** (*see p100*), still touting its tropical theme with its tired but free Masquerade Show in the Sky; staged seven times daily, it's a kind of floating Mardi Gras parade, but without the topless girls or free tequila. Just past the Rio are the **Gold Coast** (*see p116*) and the **Orleans** (*see p113*), a pair of locals' casinos with bowling alleys, movie theatres and other attractions.

More likely, though, you'll end up at the **Palms** (*see p98*), the closest competitor to the Hard Rock in terms of attracting the beautiful people. The nightlife here is energising, with nightclubs such as **Moon** (*see p257*) competing with the **Pearl** music venue (*see p251*) and a whole slew of restaurants for the attentions of visitors. The nightclub-esque **Brenden Las Vegas 14** (*see p240*), one of the top cinemas in town, complements the fun; it even has a disco ball spinning in the lobby.

Beyond the Rio, the Gold Coast and the Palms, Valley View Boulevard continues north through a semi-residential, semi-industrial district. An easterly turn at Sahara leads past small strip malls ad infinitum until the train-themed casino **Palace Station** (*see p116*) just before I-15.

Sightseeing

The vanishing

Sightseeing

Will Self once compared the constant, inevitable and yet barely tangible regeneration of urban landscapes to an intruder entering one's house in the middle of the night and moving all the furniture by a couple of inches. You know something's changed, but you can't quite tell what, or how, or even when.

In Las Vegas, things are different: progress happens instantaneously yet takes forever. Structures are erased without ceremony or sentiment, the swing of a wrecking ball bouncing from building to building like a dice cascading backwards from the wall of a craps table. And then begins the inexorably tedious yet painfully visible process of regenerating the space. What takes five minutes to destroy can take five years to rebuild, by which time everyone has lost interest.

The streets surrounding the Strip are filled with casualties that time hasn't managed to erase. The Bourbon Street casino (formerly at 120 E Flamingo Road) was levelled by Harrah's in 2006, but its sidewalk remains lined with stars that together comprise a chips-cheap jazz walk of fame. South of the Strip and closed since 2006, the crumbling Klondike (5191 Las Vegas Boulevard South) is the first casino most visitors see as they drive north from the airport into the city. And then there are the high-profile casualties on the Strip itself: the Stardust, erased in 2007; the Algiers, a memory since 2004; even the El Rancho, built in 1941 as the first resort on what became the Strip but closed since 1960.

The one thing that these casinos have in common is that the land they once occupied remains empty. Their demise was brought about by real estate moguls with the grandest of plans fot their lots. Eight-figure sums were spent, but on nothing more than a crash, a bang and an 'And finally' item on the nightly news. After all, they eventually figured, why build on the land if we can make as much cash by leaving it empty?

Harrah's has been slow to announce plans for the Bourbon Street's plum site. For a change, though, there's still something in its way. The land surrounding the scruffy, unassuming **Stage Door** casino at the corner of Flamingo Road and Audrie Street, across from the Bourbon Street lot, is empty; the single-storey building is in the shadow both of its skyscraping neighbours and the monorail that runs above it. But the owners have bucked a citywide trend and refused to sell to Harrah's, who own the vacant lots around it.

Inside, the Stage Door is like any blue-collar local bar late in the evening. Outside, the world wanders by, looking on with amusement at this mutinous holdout. The owners would make far more by selling up than they are by staying open, but pride is keeping them rooted to the spot. Usually used to advertise some putatively terrific gambling schedule or food special, the building's frontage now reads, with insouciant defiance, 'WE HAVE 23 YEARS LEFT ON OUR LEASE'. The furniture, for now, remains unmoved.

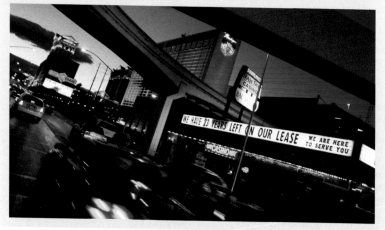

Downtown

Where it all began.

Giant cranes and land-movers are as ubiquitous in Las Vegas as bright lights and dim odds of winning. The city, or at least the montage swatch of colour and flash seen ad nauseam in popular media, needs to foster a steady flow of development and redevelopment in order to retain its magic. Las Vegas Boulevard, itself a perpetual reinvention, can appear a different landscape between two successive shoots by film crews hoping to capture its uniqueness.

North of the Strip, Downtown Las Vegas is another world. Sure, there's been a splash of paint here and an outrageously uninteresting electronic canopy there, but Downtown hasn't changed much in spirit for as long as anyone can remember. After years in the shadow of the Strip, it's slowly and painfully been becoming the graveyard of dreams, a place where plans for revitalisation were long articulated but never realised. Cheerleaders waited years for *something* to happen, only to see their hopes fleeing further with each passing year.

Imagine the local surprise, then, when a 21st-century Downtown began to sprout in 2006. Giant cranes and land-movers arrived, bringing steel beams, glass panes and concrete. With them came speculators armed with small-scale business plans and modest amounts of capital, who soon began seeing uncharacteristically swift fruition of their notions. Whatever next?

ONE HUNDRED YEARS OF HISTORY

Regardless of where its borders now lie, Las Vegas began at what is now the core of Downtown. In May 1905, settlers and speculators gathered in front of a wooden railroad platform, land now occupied by the Plaza hotel, in order to bid on the 1,200 lots that constituted the original town site. In the 1930s and '40s, hotels and casinos dotted Fremont Street, the area's main commercial drag for decades. But the rise of the Strip saw trade drain from Downtown, where there was no space for expansion. In time, the area grew dowdy.

The construction of the Fremont Street Experience in 1995, which turned a five-block section of the road into a pedestrian-friendly gambling mall and covered it with a flashy canopy that screens light and sound shows, succeeded in luring some tourists back to Glitter Gulch. Despite the later addition of some painstakingly restored vintage neon signs, some locals complained that it destroyed much of Fremont Street's character. But the march of progress is irresistible; not as irresistible as it is on the Strip, granted, but still inevitable.

In implosion-friendly Las Vegas, where experiments are sometimes shelved before their natural expiration date, don't be too upset or surprised if today's guidebook treasure is tomorrow's empty lot. Even so, there's never been a better time to discover Downtown, an amorphous amalgamation of things gone right and wrong. By turns sleazy and chic, downcast and upmarket, desperate and enthusiastic, it's a section of town in which constant and concerted efforts to make something incredible have failed only in specificity. Something wonderful *is* emerging, just not quite as originally intended.

GETTING THERE

If you're using public transport, you can reach Downtown from the Strip by catching the double-deckered Deuce bus. If you're driving, head north on I-15 and then east on US 93/95, taking the Casino Center exit (the faster route); alternatively, drive north on the Strip and 4th Street (the more interesting route). The parking garages off Fremont Street are all safe places to park, though you may need to get your parking ticket validated inside one of the casinos or other local businesses to get free parking.

Fremont Street

Once the centre of Las Vegas and then a scruffy shadow of its former self, **Fremont Street** has been officially tabbed as the focus of efforts to save Downtown. The old casinos remain, lining the stretch of Fremont west of Las Vegas Boulevard much as they have done for decades. But as proved by the 2007 arrival of the Las Vegas Grand Prix, an open-wheel race around the streets of Downtown, things are changing around here.

Fremont Street.

The Fremont Street Experience

Many tourists think that Downtown begins and ends under the electronic canopy that covers Fremont Street between Las Vegas Boulevard and Main Street. It doesn't, but on the grounds both of safety and of convenience, this stretch is the best starting and finishing point for an exploration of the area.

Inaugurated in 1995 and modified several times since, the five-block **Fremont Street Experience** was Downtown's attempt to drag a formerly desolate road into the 21st century. It's been a qualified success, but it's never quite drawn the crowds it was intended to muster. Sure, tourists come to this pedestrianised mall and in great numbers, especially for the special free weekend events (concerts, car shows and the like). Still, the demographic hasn't changed much in decades; this remains a blue-collar corner of Vegas's sprawling network of resorts.

The pedestrianised mall is dominated by a huge LED-studded canopy that flows 90 feet (27 metres) above it, flickering into action on the hour each night with intermittently entertaining sound and light shows. More interesting is **Vegas Vic**, the 75-foot (23-metre) neon cowboy who's been waving to visitors since 1951; sadly, he no longer calls out 'Howdy, pod'ner!' from a hidden speaker. Across the street, Vic's female counterpart Vegas Vicky kicks up her heels over the recently renovated **Girls of Glitter Gulch** strip club, a long-standing embarrassment to a city desperate to make seedy Downtown into a respectable destination. A strip club ringed by casinos beneath a vintage neon sign that itself sits under a vainglorious 21st-century bibelot; it is at this corner that Downtown's attractions and distractions congeal into one.

At night, the FSE is littered with crazy-eyed desperados, too-tanked hoochies and wide-mouthed tourists craning their necks to see every pixel of the jet fighter images soaring above them to some-or-other patriotic song. Keep your eyes at eye level: the street is a vital gathering spot for the keen people-watcher. Vitality seeps from the schlock-and-kitsch compendium of street performers and retail kiosks: see the souvenir beads flow from the giant mermaids, the speed-painting airbrush artist, the deep-fried Twinkies. And don't miss – how could you? – the only two-time winner of the International Liberace Pianist Competition, tickling the ivories into a frenzied rendition of 'Chariots of Fire' on a piano mounted upon a giant flatbed truck in the middle of the street. But for all the flash and filigree, the casinos remain the main draw: partly for the gambling rules, more generous here than on the Strip, but mostly due to the low accommodation prices.

Once upon a time, the former Binion's Horseshoe was the Wild West home of outlaw gaming, the World Series of Poker and true no-frills, no-nonsense gambling. Scandal and debt gave rise to a sequence of ownership shuffles that resulted in it losing its family ownership, its name (it's now just **Binion's**; *see p106*) and its magic. Across the street, the **Golden Nugget** (*see p104*) has changed hands a few times in recent years, but with a more attractive outcome. After a renovation brought swanky lounges, upscale restaurants and, most eye-catchingly, shark tanks in the swanky new pool, the Nugget continues to bring a little glamour back to far-from-fancy Fremont.

Happily unchanged down the years is the **Golden Gate** (*see p108*), the city's oldest hotel. Built in 1906 as the Hotel Nevada, the Golden Gate was known for decades as the Sal Sagev (try reading it backwards). In a nod to the past, the hotel's Bay City Diner still serves a 99¢ shrimp cocktail in a classic tulip glass, and may be the only property in town where the smiling casino owner can be seen enjoying a cup of chicken soup in the booth next to yours.

Further nods to old Vegas can be found with the throwback elegance and overwrought decor of Hugo's Cellar at the **Four Queens** (*see p108*), and with the utterly basic interior of the **Fremont** (*see p108*), the archetypal Downtown grind joint. However, they're both topped by the **Plaza** (*see p109*), sitting at the end of Fremont like the old man at the head of the table but trying harder than any Downtown property to reinvent itself as hip. *Shag With a Twist*, the hotel's new signature show, is a musical murder mystery set at a Tupperware party in the 1960s. It's touted in press materials as cool and campy; based in a hotel adjacent to the Greyhound bus depot, how could it be anything but?

Around Neonopolis

At the opposite end of the Fremont Street Experience to the Plaza, closer to Las Vegas Boulevard, the attractions are a little patchier. On the north side sits **Neonopolis**, a three-storey mall that's a melancholy reminder of previous efforts to regenerate the area. A mere two tenants remain open: **Jillians**, an outpost of the Dallas-based restaurant chain that offers billiards, bowling and a sports bar, and a first-run cineplex (*see p242*). The whole enterprise is seemingly begging for the wrecking ball.

In the open-air courtyard, the central elevator tower of Neonopolis is adorned with a dozen restored neon signs from around the US. They're a nice counterpoint to the open-air **Neon Museum**, a small but growing collection of classic Vegas signs that have been restored

Sightseeing

and placed on poles between Neonopolis and the FSE parking garage. For more on the signs, *see p141* **Lighting up the past**.

Several such signs can be found on N 3rd Street between Fremont and Ogden Streets, a stretch that both complements and anticipates the changes further east (*see below*). The western side of 3rd has been taken over by a slew of new businesses that pay homage of sorts to old Downtown: witness the steakhouse swank of **Triple George** (*see p171*), the cultured **Sidebar** (*see p184*) and the often-raucous **Hogs & Heifers** (*see p184*). And back across from the Neonopolis on Fremont are **Hennesseys**, **Mickie Finnz** (*see p171*) and **Brass**, three new spots that are trying to draw a mix of tourists and locals with upscale bar food, local bands and gambling.

Downtown is home to a number of public artworks in the City of 100 Murals series, commissioned to celebrate the city's centennial in 2005. Most have some sort of gaming theme, but one abstract stand-out are the five-panelled light sculptures located by the elevators of the Fremont Street parking garage. Designed by Las Vegas artists Mary Warner and Rayann Figler, it refashioned the discarded bulbs of the FSE when it converted to LED technology.

East of Las Vegas Boulevard

Across Las Vegas Boulevard, Fremont Street is an almost unrecognisably different place. This stretch is protected not by a vast, LED-studded canopy but by shady security staff, protecting the interests of their employers by keeping the drunks, drug dealers and down-and-outs away. The **El Cortez** (*see p106*) and **Western** (*see p110*) supplement the seamy feel with a portion of Vegas charm at its most reliably basic.

Things, though, are changing, thanks to the city's official plan to install an 'entertainment overlay'. The Fremont East Entertainment District, it's putatively called, a soon-to-flourish (hopefully) string of bars and restaurants that will have to make it on charm and liquor alone: gambling will be conspicuous by its absence, as Vegas aims to construct an urban core that bears comparison with the likes of San Diego. Local authorities have widened the streets, shuffled the urban blight down the way and given decent tax incentives to new businesses.

A few pioneering daddios have taken the bait already. The Vegas version of the tiny but mighty **Beauty Bar**, first to arrive in 2004, was followed in 2007 by the swanky **Downtown Cocktail Room** and the more pubby **Griffin** (for all, *see p184*). These bars, now supplemented by tasty fast-food joints such as **Kabob Korner** (*see p172*), look set

to be joined by coffeehouses, stores and perhaps even a music venue. In time, the overlay may pay off for those who have invested so much in reinvigorating the famous Glitter Gulch of yore. For now, though, it's the up-and-coming part of town, and local hipsters are already dreading the day when the tourists discover it.

Further down Fremont Street, shabby old Downtown returns, a wonderworld of decrepitude and danger. Walking around here after dark isn't advisable, but if you lock your car doors, it makes a great night drive. The road is lined with vintage neon motel signs, giving a glimpse of the era when east Fremont resembled the Strip. The 1960s-mod **City Center Motel** stands at the corner of Fremont and 7th Streets; further down Fremont are **Fergusons Motel** (between 10th & 11th Streets) and the kitschy red-and-yellow-trimmed motor court of the **Gables** (at 13th Street). En route, stop by the vintage **Atomic Liquors** (*see p183*) for a beer in an authentically edgy atmosphere.

North to Washington Avenue

Parallel to Fremont Street a couple of blocks north, Stewart Avenue is where Downtown winds down. The corner with Las Vegas Boulevard is currently home to **City Hall**, which offers an interesting art gallery and near-constant sightings of the happiest mayor/movie star/gin spokesman in the world: Oscar B Goodman, who will gladly autograph your Martini olives if you ask nicely. Also on Stewart is Squires Park, the site of sporadic free concerts, and the original federal courthouse building, which formerly housed a post office. The interesting example of neo-classical architecture was sheathed in white in early 2007, as renovation work began on converting it into a cultural centre.

To the north along Las Vegas Boulevard sit more remnants of the city's past. Beyond the **Neon Boneyard** (*see p141* **Lighting up the past**) are a series of low-key attractions that have been designated, slightly optimistically, as the Cultural Corridor: the **City of Las Vegas Galleries** in the Reed Whipple Cultural Center (*see pp243-244*), the **Las Vegas Natural History Museum** and the **Lied Discovery Children's Museum** (for both, *see p142*).

Just to the east is **Cashman Field**, where the Las Vegas 51s, the Los Angeles Dodgers' AAA team, play baseball through the heat of summer (*see p261*). Also in the general area is the fascinating **Old Las Vegas Mormon Fort Historic Park** (*see p142*). And those into old architecture should check the Biltmore Bungalows, which aren't all bungalows at all. Located a block west of Las Vegas Boulevard on Bonanza Road, they were built to house all the

Lighting up the past

If there's one piece of the past that lovers of Las Vegas miss above all others, it's the old-time signs. Just listen to Alan Hess, author of *Viva Las Vegas: After-Hours Architecture*, wax nostalgic about one of his favourites: the 15-storey, 40,000-bulb Aladdin sign from the 1960s. 'It was a full-blown fantasia, a dreamy mirage made real. The artistry that requires – to put that much steel and neon up in the desert sky and make it convincing, otherworldly, floating – is tremendous. It represented the ultimate achievement of that era of Las Vegas design. And it's an art that has not been recaptured in recent years.'

Discarding the past is itself a key part of Vegas history. The giant movie set known as the Strip constantly moves on to the next big idea without so much as a glance behind it. These days, though, the town's two-million-strong permanent community of non-tourists carries enough influence to preserve some of the neon left in the wake of the economic machine. The main voice of this movement is a non-profit project called the **Neon Museum,** set up 'to collect, preserve, study and exhibit neon signs and associated artefacts to inspire educational and cultural enrichment'.

One of the museum's first achievements was to refurbish the genie's lamp that once crowned the old Aladdin sign and install it at the corner of Fremont Street and Las Vegas

Boulevard in 1996, 40 years after its original debut. Since then, the collection has expanded apace, and now includes everything from 1940s pieces to the recently decommissioned Stardust sign. Piece by piece, each sign is moved from its location to the Neon Boneyard on Las Vegas Boulevard, where it undergoes just enough work to spruce it up without washing away its patina.

There are 11 old signs dotting Downtown, in so-called 'outdoor galleries' on or just off Fremont Street. The old Hacienda horseman is riding high again, and the long-defunct Nevada Hotel continues to help light up the night, alongside smaller signs devoted to the Aladdin casino, the Flame Restaurant, the Chief Hotel Court and the Anderson Dairy. The museum has also put several signs on display at the Old Las Vegas Mormon Fort Historic Park (*see p142*), including the shapely Arabic 'A' from the Sahara.

The best, though, is yet to come. In 2009, the Neon Boneyard is scheduled to be converted into a full-scale museum, a three-acre park full of historic Vegas signage. The landmark lobby from the old La Concha hotel, one of the city's great Googie structures, has been rescued and moved up the boulevard to serve as the visitor centre, gallery and gift shop for the museum. Keep track of progress by visiting www.neonmuseum.org.

Old Las Vegas Mormon Fort Historic Park, the oldest structure in Nevada.

civilian workers stationed in Las Vegas to aid in the war effort, and remain a great representation of a mid-century, master-planned community.

Las Vegas Natural History Museum
900 Las Vegas Boulevard North, at E Washington Avenue (384 3466/www.lvnhm.org). Bus 113, 208. **Open** 9am-4pm daily. **Admission** $7; $3-$6 reductions; free under-2s. **Credit** AmEx, Disc, MC, V. **Map** p334 E1.
This small, enthusiastically run museum doesn't offer much in the way of bells and whistles. The Marine Life Room features small sharks in a large tank, the Wild Nevada Room has exhibits on the flora and fauna of Nevada and the Young Scientist Center has some interactive displays. However, the big draw is five roaring, robotic dinosaurs, among them a vast T-rex. Combine a visit with a trip to the nearby Lied Discovery Children's Museum.

Lied Discovery Children's Museum
Las Vegas Library, 833 Las Vegas Boulevard North, between W Washington Avenue & Bonanza Road (382 5437/www.ldcm.org). Bus 113, 208. **Open** *Summer* 10am-5pm Mon-Sat; noon-5pm Sun. *Autumn-spring* 9am-4pm Tue-Fri; 10am-5pm Sat; noon-5pm Sun. **Admission** $8; $7 reductions. **Credit** AmEx, Disc, MC, V. **Map** p334 D1.
A stimulating museum similar to (though much smaller than) the Exploratorium in San Francisco, the Lied features dozens of scientific exhibits that involve the viewer as a part of the demonstration. Don't be put off by the name: this is the sort of place that many adults would visit by themselves if they thought they could. Creative exhibits include a tin can telephone, which should entertain the kids for hours. Rumour has it that the museum will soon be moving to a new location, leaving behind the public library that surrounds it. Check before making a special trip.

Old Las Vegas Mormon Fort Historic Park
500 E Washington Avenue, at Las Vegas Boulevard North (486 3511/www.parks.nv.gov/olvmf.htm). Bus 113, 208. **Open** 8am-4.30pm Mon-Sat. **Admission** $3; $2 reductions; free under-6s. **No credit cards. Map** p333 Y2.
Built by a group of Mormon missionaries in 1855 and then left to become part of the Las Vegas Ranch, this is Vegas's pioneer settlement site, the oldest Euro-American structure in the state and an example of what Vegas was like before the railroad arrived. Though only remnants of the original structure remain, restoration and reconstruction have brought the compound back to life, and guides are on hand to answer any questions you may have.

South to Oakey Boulevard

Las Vegas Boulevard grows less pleasant the further south of Fremont you travel, but the stroll does at least begin with several points of interest. The **Lloyd George Federal Courthouse** is a handsome steel-and-glass building that hosts occasional cultural events during lunchtimes and less official protests on the streets outside. Across the street is the under-renovation Fifth Street School, due to house an arts and design campus.

Nearby on Lewis Avenue stand two very singular attractions: **André's** (*see p172*), the best French restaurant in Nevada, and the **Poets Bridge**, done out with a curious water feature, a sidewalk engraved with quotes from 20 Nevadan poets. The bridge's main feature is a brass plaque on which is inscribed 'The Long Shot'; written by New York writer (and former Las Vegas resident) Gregory Crosby, it's perhaps the best poem ever written about Las Vegas.

There's ancient history around these parts; though in Las Vegas, that means the 1930s at the earliest. Although most of residential Las Vegas is unimaginatively cast in the same faux-Mediterranean stucco, the area bounded by 6th Street, Bridger Avenue, 9th Street and Oakey Boulevard is a rare example of architectural diversity and small-town comfort: well-kept single-storey homes with large yards and wide driveways are typical. The list of 1940s and '50s buildings in the area is headed by the **Las Vegas Academy of International Studies & Performing Arts** (*see p267*), the only piece of 1930s art deco architecture in the city.

On S 7th Street just before Charleston Boulevard sits a cluster of attractive, early 20th-century bungalows with plaster walls and wooden floors; it's now known as 'Lawyer's Row', after the punk attorneys who've taken over the locale. South of Charleston, meanwhile, is the **John S Park Neighbourhood**. Filled with 1940s bungalows and swankier dwellings from the '50s and '60s, it was the city's first official Historic District. Self-guided tours created by the City Historical Preservation Division are available from City Hall.

Back on Las Vegas Boulevard, the scene soon degenerates, the street lined with shady-looking storefronts and vintage motels that do most of their business either by the hour or by the month. Among the various buildings offering quickie marriages, the angels-on-crack painted ceiling of the 24-hour drive-thru **Little White Wedding Chapel** (*see p274*) is worth a look. For the most part, the street isn't as dangerous as it looks, but nor is it an especially salubrious or attractive part of town.

Things spruce up a little just before Oakey Boulevard, near the point at which Main Street meets Las Vegas Boulevard. Chow on an omelette with a side of trout at **Tiffany's**, a classic 24-hour counter service joint inside the White Cross Drugstore (and one of the main settings for Drew Barrymore vehicle *Lucky You*; 1700 Las Vegas Boulevard South); follow it with the city's greatest dessert at **Luv-It Frozen Custard** (*see p166*); and wash it all down with a beer at **Dino's** (*see p181*).

When you're sufficiently lubricated, two nearby adult businesses are waiting to take the dollars you didn't donate to Dino's video poker machines: the relatively smart **Olympic Garden** (*see p222*) and the more down-at-heel **Talk of the Town** (1238 Las Vegas Boulevard South), home of the ten-dollar lap dance. The latter sits opposite the **Aruba Hotel** (*see p104*), where the vast **Thunderbird Lounge** (*see p184*) hosts everything from swing dance lessons to alternative theatre.

The Arts District & around

Walk south of Fremont Street along Main Street, and the pickings are slimmer than on Las Vegas Boulevard. Pricey modern imbiberie the **Ice House** (*see p184*) sits steps away from old-fashioned eaterie **El Sombrero** (*see p172*); the low-end thrifting at **Opportunity Village** (921 S Main Street, at E Hoover Avenue, 383 1082) is within a stone's throw of the high-end retro duds offered at the **Attic** (*see p199*) and the card-playing, chip-tossing paraphernalia of the **Gamblers General Store** (*see p203*).

When you reach Charleston Boulevard, you'll be on the edge of the **Arts District**, loosely bordered by Charleston, Las Vegas Boulevard, Wyoming Avenue and the railroad. The focal point of the area is the **Arts Factory** (*see p243*), a block-long, two-storey 1940s building filled with an ever-changing line-up of galleries (such as **Dust** and **G-C Arts**; *see p244*), studios and other creative businesses. But the district also holds an array of shops (among them the **Funk House**; *see p208*) and bars (including the **Art Bar**; *see p183*), all of which bring culture and edge to a once-downtrodden part of town. The Arts District is at its best on **First Friday** (*see p216*), a monthly block party when the streets come alive with festive cheer.

East along Charleston are a number of other new Downtown landmarks. At the corner of Charleston and Grand Central Parkway stands the **Holsum Lofts**, a longtime commercial bakery that's lately been regenerated into a little cultural centre of sorts with a decent grill (*see p171*), galleries, artists' studios and shops such as **Las Vegas Paper Doll** (*see p204*).

North up Grand Central, the open-air **Las Vegas Premium Outlets** (*see p194*) yields cut-price goodies from the likes of Kenneth Cole and Banana Republic. And nearby stand two landmark buildings: the ever-expanding **World Market Center** (*see p211* **Take a seat**), a hulking slab on the horizon, and the **Clark County Government Amphitheatre** (*see p33* **What's that?**), which hosts First Friday concerts. Nearby is where **Union Park** will eventually reshape Downtown, with a performing arts centre, medical campus, condos, retail operations and other enterprises.

The Rest of the City

Glimpses of old Vegas; eyefuls of the glistening new elite communities.

Las Vegas Spring Preserve: where Old West explorers parked their horses. *See p146.*

Like Los Angeles, off-Strip Las Vegas is a sprawling, unwalkable suburb made up of still-mushrooming residential developments, with the institutions and infrastructures that any large city requires scattered within their midsts. New estates spring up seemingly overnight, barely keeping pace with the 8,000 people who migrate to Clark County every month. Its interest lies not in great beauty or a wealth of visitor attractions (it has neither), but as a reassuringly benign refuge from neon overload. Yet despite Vegas's well-earned reputation as a town devoid of coherent town planning, you will find glimpses of a rich history, pockets of character and a defiant civic identity.

When you set out, keep in mind that this is not just your average sprawling, unwalkable suburb: it can be downright hostile to pedestrians. The bus system is reliable and will get you to most places of note, but a car is necessary to explore the city properly. Leave plenty of time for delays caused by the new construction work. But fear not: it's hard to get lost in a flat city that's built on a grid network and that has, at its centre, the tallest observation tower west of the Mississippi.

The neighbourhoods in this chapter are arranged clockwise, starting in the south-west corner of town and finishing in the south-east.

South-west Las Vegas

Much of south-west Las Vegas is unremarkable in that, like much of the town, it consists largely of middle-class suburban homes surrounded by strip malls. Past the **Orleans** (*see p113*), a locals' joint, Tropicana Avenue and its adjoining streets offer little more than bland private tract homes and apartment blocks. Further west, halfway to the mountains, are the ultra-posh and guardedly private residential developments of **Spanish Trail** and **Spanish Hills**, home to many of Las Vegas's notable figures. Go north at Rainbow and you'll head through **Spring Valley**, one of the older Vegas locales. Taking the new beltway (I-215) south unveils an area of town that until recently was, like the north-west before it, scattered with ranch homes on large lots. Now, it's covered by ever more indistinct sprawl, including new yuppie enclave **Southern Highlands**.

North-west Las Vegas

Sahara Avenue

Like the majority of Las Vegas's east–west streets, Sahara Avenue yields little of interest to the travelling motorist. Chains dominate the landscape; there are few better examples than the four-cornered **Sahara-Decatur Pavilions** at the junction of Sahara and... well, you know. National chains make up most of the tenants, though there's fine Persian food at independent eaterie **Habib's** (No.4750, 870 0860). Continuing on, you'll pass countless car dealerships and chain eateries before reaching Rainbow Boulevard, surrounded by residential properties and heavy commercial development.

Further west, past the excellent **Rosemary's Restaurant** (*see p173*), is Durango Drive. This is the beginning of the Lakes neighbourhood, where the waterside homes afford residents the chance to go boating and fishing. Lake East Drive features a walking trail that twists through the surrounding parks, eventually dumping you out at Twain Avenue.

Sahara's western reaches are home to the beautiful **Sahara West Library** (*see p312*) and the adjoining **Las Vegas Art Museum** (*see p245*). The cinema at neighbouring **Village Square** (*see p242*) is known for the indie film selections it regularly screens, though blockbusters take up most of the space. At the far-western end of Sahara Avenue, nestled at the base of the mountains, lies the **Red Rock Country Club** (2466 Grassy Spring Place, 360 3100), a desert golf community that gives new meaning to the word 'exclusive'.

Charleston Boulevard

Flat, wide and seemingly endless, Charleston cuts a broad swathe through the city, extending westwards right out to the foothills of the mountain from which it takes its name. It's more residential than Sahara, though not much more attractive. Still, there are occasional diversions, including, close to the Strip, the Charleston Heights Arts Center, home to one of the **City of Las Vegas Galleries** (*see pp243-244*).

Along the way, Charleston defines the southern edge of **Summerlin**. The planned community incorporates homes ($100,000 condos to multi-million-dollar mansions), parks, schools and businesses to create a regular prefab life; the infrastructure is magnificent, but the *Truman Show* effect is disconcerting. European visitors won't have trouble navigating the numerous roundabouts, but the wayward local motorists, unaccustomed to such complexity, seem to have a little more trouble.

At Rampart Boulevard, development has transformed what were once empty acres into a commercial area. The **Boca Park Fashion Village**, an upscale 'lifestyle centre' of shops (Ligne Roset, Talulah G) and restaurants (Kona Grill, Melting Pot), sits close to **Rampart Commons**, home to the likes of Banana Republic and Pottery Barn. A skip north are two resorts: the so-so **Suncoast** (*see p117*) and the smarter **JW Marriott Summerlin** (*see p111*), surrounded by the green, manicured fairways of several major golf courses.

Further west, across from the **Summerlin Town Center** mall at Charleston's intersection with Town Center Drive, sits the **Red Rock** resort (*see p112*), the first billion-dollar off-Strip casino-hotel. If you head still further west across the Beltway, you'll enter open country, and the gorgeous canyon from which the casino takes its name (*see pp281-282*). Just past it, you'll find an agreeable taste of the Wild West at **Bonnie Springs Old Nevada** (*see p282*), an honest-to-goodness mining town back in the 1800s. Don't miss the general store, if only for the fun of spotting the 'Made in China' stickers on the bottom of nearly every souvenir.

Rancho Drive

Bordered by Oakey and Charleston Boulevards, Rancho Drive and I-15, the **Scotch 80s** offers a different taste of old Vegas. Mayor Oscar Goodman is among those who live within this swanky neighbourhood of large-lot homes built mostly in the 1950s and '60s, an 80-acre enclave just a dice roll from Downtown. The quiet labyrinth of tree-lined streets hides ranch-style estates and one-acre home sites, along with surprisingly lush gardens: underground water meant the area was once almost swampy. To the south of here are the **Glen Heather Estates**, smallish homes with a modernist bent; west lie the 1950s-vintage **McNeil Estates**, where young professionals are joining more established residents in a bid to restore the charming ranch-style homes.

If you continue north, you'll reach the corner of Rancho and Alta Drives. Just north is **Rancho Circle**: perhaps the city's most exclusive old district, it's home to Bob Stupak and Phyllis McGuire. Slightly west of here, loosely bordered by US 95, Valley View Boulevard and Alta Drive, is the historic 180-acre **Las Vegas Springs Preserve**, recently reopened as a visitor attraction (*see p146*). And east of Rancho Drive at Tonopah Drive is **Binion Ranch**, the home of the legendary gambling family who launched – and, until recently, owned – Binion's. Family patriarch Benny Binion once lived in this long-boarded-up block-and-timber ranch house;

Sightseeing

as recently as the 1990s, horses and cattle were still kept on the property.

The primarily African American area of West Las Vegas spreads north-east from Bonanza Road, home to the long-closed **Moulin Rouge** (900 W Bonanza Road). In the bad old days, when Vegas was called 'the Mississippi of the West', hotels forced African American entertainers to flee the Strip after showtime. Performers such as Nat King Cole and Sammy Davis Jr sought refuge at the Moulin Rouge and generated a legendary stint of after-hours shows. In 1960, five years after the Moulin Rouge opened, casino bosses signed an agreement here that ended the city's racial segregation. However, plans to revive the casino ground to a halt when it was gutted by a suspicious fire in 2003.

To the west of Rancho Drive sits **Lorenzi Park**, home of the **Nevada State Museum & Historical Society** (*see below*). Further north leads you past the **Southern Nevada Zoological Park** (*see below*); a turn west at Vegas Drive passes the palatial home of master illusionists Siegfried & Roy. It's on the north side; look for the white adobe walls and the wrought-iron gate bearing the initials S and R. Tiger Woods wannabes can try out their skills at the **Las Vegas Golf Club** (*see p264*) across the road; budding Schumachers might prefer the **Las Vegas Mini Gran Prix** (*see p238*).

Rancho Drive continues in a north-westerly direction past the **Texas Station** (*see p118*), **Fiesta Rancho** (*see p116*) and **Santa Fe Station** (*see p117*) casinos en route to the outdoor attractions of **Floyd Lamb State Park** and **Mount Charleston** (*see pp282-283*). Five years ago, much of this area was empty desert. Today, though, stucco has engulfed everything and shows no sign of abating.

Las Vegas Springs Preserve

333 S Valley View Boulevard, at Meadows Lane (822.8344/www.springspreserve.org). Bus 104, 207. **Open** *Summer* 10am-10pm daily. *Winter* 10am-6pm daily. **Admission** $18.95; $10.95 reductions; free under-5s. **Map** p333 X1.

Also known as Big Spring, this is where legendary Old West explorers Kit Carson and John Fremont parked their horses in the mid 1800s. Huge cottonwoods and natural scrub fill the area, surrounding an early 19th-century well house. The land has survived both fire and the threat of being paved over in the name of freeway expansion; it was restored as the Central Park of Las Vegas for the city's centennial in 2005 and opened to the public two years later as the Las Vegas Springs Preserve, a huge site given over to botanical gardens, nature trails and a number of museum exhibits. All in all, a very laudable endeavour. For more, *see p239* **The greenest show in town**. *Photos p144*.

Nevada State Museum & Historical Society

Lorenzi Park, 700 Twin Lakes Drive, at Washington Avenue (486 5205). Bus 106, 208. **Open** 9am-5pm daily. **Admission** $4; $3 reductions; free under-17s. **No credit cards. Map** p333 X1.

The Nevada State Museum has permanent exhibits on the natural and anthropological history of the region, from ancient Paiute Indians to 19th-century pioneers, and the men and women of the Nellis Gunnery School in World War II. The standout exhibit tells the story of Bugsy Siegel's Flamingo, complete with interactive recordings of Bugsy (played by an actor) threatening business partners. There are plans to move the museum to the Las Vegas Springs Preserve in 2008; call ahead to check.

Southern Nevada Zoological Park

1775 N Rancho Drive, between Vegas Drive & Lake Mead Boulevard (648 5955/www.lasvegaszoo.org). Bus 106. **Open** 9am-5pm daily. **Admission** $7; $5 reductions; free under-2s. **Credit** AmEx, Disc, MC, V. **Map** p333 X1.

It'll never be confused with the similar operations in the Bronx or San Diego, but Vegas's zoological park contains an interesting collection of reptiles and birds indigenous to the state of Nevada, as well as a variety of endangered cats and the last family of Barbary apes in the US. The park also has a coati exhibit, botanical displays of endangered palms and rare bamboos, plus a children's petting zoo.

North Las Vegas

A working-class city that grew from the Nellis Air Force Base to the north-east, the officially incorporated city of North Las Vegas has experienced a limited renaissance of late, a result of the growth in the valley as a whole. African American, Asian and Hispanic residents have moved in as Anglos have moved out, turning the area into a melting pot of ethnicities; new homes and shops have sprung up to fill land north of Craig Road (between Rancho Drive and I-15) in a pricey new development known informally as the **Golden Triangle**. The shiny new locale seems somewhat removed from its surroundings, but that's the price of progress.

Largely untouched by redevelopment, the older sections of North Las Vegas carry more urban flavour than does Las Vegas itself. To reach it, turn off either US 95 or Rancho Drive and head west along Craig Road, then turn north back towards Downtown along Las Vegas Boulevard North. En route, you'll pass **Jerry's Nugget** casino (No.1821, 399 3000), numerous ethnic eateries, the historic public **Forest Lawn Cemetery** and the **Las Vegas Paiute Indian Reservation** (1 Paiute Drive, 386 3926), which represents the original ten acres deeded to the Paiute by Helen Stewart back in the 1900s.

Play the silver ball

For the most part, a pinball machine is just a pinball machine. To some folks, though, it's a kinetic monument to a simpler time when mindless entertainment didn't necessarily involve sex, hyper-violence or the pixelated undead, a perfectly designed blend of challenge, workmanship and skill. In Tim Arnold's world, it's all these things and more besides. How else to explain his **Pinball Hall of Fame** (for listings, *see p148*), a functioning museum of sorts where more than 100 operational pinball machines spanning seven decades are on show? The Pinball Hall of Fame (or PHoF, as it is awkwardly described on its MySpace page) is a true mecca in a city of replicated ones.

Over the years, Arnold has assembled a vast array of machines from Gottlieb, Bally, Williams and other oddball manufacturers, from gear-and-magnet models to modern digital wonders. Descriptions of each machine's attributed and historic values have been attached to them, most handwritten on index cards. And then, best of all, Arnold invites all-comers to play his machines. All you need is quarters; and if you don't have them, he can change your bills into them.

Arnold has re-cast some of these machines so visitors can best appreciate their inherent beauty. Take, for example, his painstaking public refurbishment of a 1978 Bally machine devoted to the band Kiss. Paying attention to the smallest detail (excepting, perhaps, an actual drop of Ace Frehley's blood in the back glass), Arnold is like an Italian restoration specialist working on the Sistine Chapel. But while both share a certain reverence in their respective circles, only at the PHoF can you both touch the art and shake it around.

In possession of all 384 Gottlieb pinball machines, Arnold claims to have the only complete set of one manufacturer in the world. Sadly, not all of them are on display, thanks to lack of cash, staff and, right now, visitors. When asked to name his favourite machine, he deadpans, 'the one with the box full of coins.' It's a straight response from somebody who owned his first pinball machine at age 14 but who always seemed more interested in the collecting and tinkering than the playing. 'It's all I've ever done. It's all I know,' says the man who refers to himself as the simple ringmaster of this peculiar and beautiful show. 'Someone's got to wear the top hat.'

Planetarium

Community College of Southern Nevada, 3200 E Cheyenne Avenue, between Las Vegas Boulevard North & Van Der Meer Street (651 4759/www.ccsn. edu/planetarium). Bus 110. **Shows** 6pm, 7.30pm Fri; 3.30pm, 7.30pm Sat. **Admission** $4; $2.50 reductions. **Credit** AmEx, Disc, MC, V.

The small cinema has a 360° screen. After the day's last performance, you can also scan the sky through the planetarium's telescopes (weather permitting).

East Las Vegas

Once characterised by ugly quick-build housing tracts and trailer parks, East Las Vegas has been unable to avoid the incursion of new development. Still, the once-posh **Commercial Center** (953 E Sahara Avenue, between S 6th Street & S Maryland Parkway) has resisted change. One of the city's older malls, it's a

Liberace Museum. *See p148.*

scruffy spot that's home to the city's best ethnic restaurant (**Lotus of Siam**; *see p169*), various gay bars (*see pp246-49*) and, incongruously, a trio of swingers' clubs (*see p223*). South on Maryland is the smarter (and swinger-free) **Boulevard Mall** (*see p193*); behind it is the modernist **Paradise Palms**, another old 'hood at the earliest stages of revival. Further down Maryland is the University District (*see below*).

The casinos at Fremont Street's western extremity grab the headlines, and with good reason. But the road has a life further east, well away from the bright lights Downtown. What it doesn't have is much tangible and engaging history, at least not since the **Green Shack** bit the dust. In continuous operation from the 1920s until 1999, the restaurant evoked decades of memories: construction workers building the Hoover Dam (*see p18*) stopped here, as did politicos and gangsters. But despite protests from preservationists, the building was demolished in 2005 to make way for a banqueting hall that's yet to be built.

South of Sahara, Fremont becomes the **Boulder Highway**, along which sit several locals' casinos. Catch a movie at **Boulder Station** (*see p116*); if you're here in December, don't miss the Christmas lights at **Sam's Town** (*see p117*). A turn east down Tropicana Avenue (or an interstate ride from town) takes you to the **Acacia Demonstration Gardens** (50 Casa Del Fuego Street, 267 4000, www.snwa.com), where you can explore gardens and wetlands dedicated to animal habitats. West along Tropicana, at the north-east corner with Pecos Avenue, is the **Pinball Hall of Fame**.

At the far eastern end of the valley is Frenchman's Mountain, commonly known as **Sunrise Mountain**. Here, in the 1960s and '70s, the independently minded rich who had declined spots in the Scotch 80s built modern desert homes with pools and panoramic views of the city. Following their lead, most new housing development in this area has been focused in this part of town.

Pinball Hall of Fame
3330 E Tropicana Avenue, at N Pecos Avenue (no phone/www.pinballmuseum.org). Bus 202. **Open** 11am-11pm daily. **No credit cards.** *See p147* **Play the silver ball.**

The University District

Bounded roughly by Flamingo Road, Paradise Road, Tropicana Avenue and Eastern Avenue, the University District is an enclave of normality and casual sophistication a mere skip from the Strip. Most businesses of note are on Maryland Parkway, with the rest of the area given over to apartments.

The University of Las Vegas, aka **UNLV** (4505 S Maryland Parkway, 895 3011), runs along S Maryland Parkway, where the stunning **Lied Library** (*see p312*) and a beautiful **desert garden** compete for visitors' attention. The university also has many walking paths and trees, a tranquil refuge from the summer sun. The **UNLV Barrick Museum** (*see p149*) and the **Donna Beam Fine Arts Gallery** (*see p244*), both on campus, stage shows by student and professional artists; the former also houses a permanent natural history exhibition.

Local businesses reflect the presence of the university, which is to say that prices are keen. **Paymon's Mediterranean Café & Market** (*see p176*), a local lunch favourite, is adjoined at the corner of Maryland and Flamingo by the **Hookah Lounge** (*see p186*), a Bedouin-styled cocktail bar. Across the way is the used-clothing superstore **Buffalo Exchange** (*see p199*); further up Maryland are two shopping centres filled with pizza joints, coffee-houses such as the **Coffee Bean & Tea Leaf** (which offers free Wi-Fi; No.4550, 944 5029), bars including

the **Freakin' Frog** (*see p186*), the new
University Theatre (*see p254*), and even a
tattoo studios: the **Pussykat Tattoo Parlor**
(*see p208*) is one of the best in town. And
standing alone on nearby Tropicana is the
Liberace Museum (*see below*), as if you could
have mistaken the neon piano-topped, giant
keyboard-wrapped ark for anything else.

Liberace Museum

*Liberace Plaza, 1775 E Tropicana Avenue, at
Spencer Street (798 5595/www.liberace.org). Bus
201.* **Open** 10am-5pm Tue-Sat; noon-4pm Sun.
Admission $12.50; $8.50 reductions; free under-10s.
Credit AmEx, MC, V. **Map** p333 Y3.
Unless you have a pathological aversion to camp,
don't miss this place, a testament to Las Vegas's
indefatigable dedication to the ersatz. On display are
Mr Showmanship's rhinestones, stage jewellery
(including a piano-shaped ring set with 260 diamonds), sequinned jackets, hot pants and a genuine
mirrored Rolls-Royce. More than a dozen of his finest
antique pianos are also on show; on selected afternoons, Wes Winters' extraordinary tribute offers a
taste of the deeply sinister pianist and entertainer.
As Las Vegas rediscovers what it once meant to be
'Vegas, baby!', this shrine to excess and bad taste is
a kitschy storehouse of the city's heritage.

UNLV Barrick Museum

*4505 S Maryland Parkway, at E Tropicana Avenue
(895 3381/www.unlv.edu). Bus 109, 201.* **Open** 8am-
4.45pm Mon-Fri; 10am-2pm Sat. **Admission** free.
No credit cards. Map p333 Y3.
Technically UNLV's natural history museum, the
Barrick has fine permanent displays on ancient and
modern Vegas, including a wonderful collection of
folk-art masks. It's also one of the city's finest exhibition spaces: a number of excellent shows have
graced its front rooms, drawing from UNLV's art
faculty and regional sources. It's a must for any
gallery crawl; call for details of current shows.

Green Valley & Henderson

The history of Henderson and Green Valley is a
tale of two cities within two cities. Henderson
itself was founded in 1941 as a company town
for workers at the then-new Basic Magnesium
Plant. North-west of Henderson across US 95,
Green Valley is technically a part of the city of
Henderson, but contains the vast majority of its
visitor attractions. If you've time, a few hours
spent down here makes an engaging diversion,
especially if you're en route to **Boulder City**
and the **Hoover Dam** (*see p18*).

Henderson

Thanks to its origins, Henderson garnered
a reputation as an industrial city, one that it
retains to some extent. The city has kept its

original downtown, centred on Water Street.
It's currently undergoing a revitalisation
spearheaded by the city government, which is
making an active effort to bring galleries and
pedestrian-friendly shops; the purchase of land
by loft developers is a sign that the area may soon
soar skywards. The **City of Lights Gallery**
(No.26, 260 0300, www.citylightsart.com), is
attempting to lead the way in the creation of
the arts district; it's something of a moot point
whether the **Ron Lee Gallery** (7665
Commercial Way, 434 1700, www.ronlee.com),
'the world's largest collection of limited-edition
clown sculptures', would make the cut.
Elsewhere, less sophisticated pockets of
original tract houses, mobile home parks and
low-rent apartments survive, and are unkindly
referred to as 'Hendertucky'. Even so, the area's
not without appeal. Manufacturing continues at
Ethel M Chocolates (*see below*), which offers
tours to the public. And not far from here, the
Clark County Heritage Museum (*see below*)
is also worth a look.

Clark County Heritage Museum

*1830 S Boulder Highway, between Horizon Drive
& Wagon Wheel Avenue (455 7955/www.co.clark.
nv.us). Bus 107.* **Open** 9am-4.30pm daily.
Admission $1.50; $1 reductions; free under-3s.
Credit MC, V.
Long before Las Vegas was a resort mecca, it was
just another western railroad town. Here you'll find
an assortment of exhibits relating to southern
Nevada's past: a recreated city street featuring historic area homes with period furnishings, a 'timeline'
mural and a 1918 Union Pacific steam engine.

Ethel M Chocolates

*2 Cactus Garden Drive, at Sunset Way & Mountain
Vista Street (458 8864/www.ethelm.com). Bus 217.*
Open 8.30am-7pm daily. **Admission** free.
Chocolate producer Ethel M offers self-guided factory tours complete with samples. To offset any feel-
ings of overindulgence, it also has an environ-
mentally aware cactus garden and a fascinating 'living machine', showing how plants can recycle waste-
water. Here during the holidays? Check out the
gardens, bedecked in millions of lights (*see p219*).

Green Valley

Green Valley was established in the late 1970s
as the valley's first master-planned community.
Its design, and its eventual success, proved
massively influential across the whole region;
developments such as Summerlin wouldn't
have happened without it.
The presence of homes in all price ranges
has drawn all kinds of people: ethnic eateries,
creative businesses and cultural events thrive
here, creating a sense of community synergy
of which others in the metropolis are envious.

Take the Biosphere at Vanderburg Elementary School, for example, a large rainforest habitat complete with a waterfall, plants, fish and even free-roaming lizards. The $1.2 million cost of building it was covered by private donations and proceeds from campus fundraisers.

The high-tone **Green Valley Ranch** (*see p111*) is the subdivision's best accomplishment, its bars, day spa and comfortable casino all drawing visitors and locals. In summer, the resort's outdoor pool area, which flaunts bocce courts and a design by Michael Czyz, hosts shows at its amphitheatre.

Virtually next door is the **District**, an open-air esplanade of upscale restaurants and shops; among the latter is the **Flea Bags Barkery & Bowtique** (2225 Village Walk Drive, 702 914 8805), selling gourmet pet biscuits (named after favourite customers) and Juicy Couture pet carriers. Across from here is the **Henderson Pavilion**, an outdoor performing arts facility that hosts an annual Shakespeare in the Park event and the **Vegas Valley Book Festival** (*see p218*). And south on Green Valley Parkway is **Anthem**, an over-the-top country club set-up that introduces the absurdist notion of gated communities within gated communities.

In the older section of Green Valley, the **Green Valley Town Center** offers for a perfect example of the area's community focus. The north-east side of the mall and plaza, located at the corner of Sunset Road and Green Valley Parkway, is home to **Café Sensations** (456 7803), a mom-and-pop coffee-shop, pub and restaurant that serves meatloaf sandwiches and killer peanut butter cookies; just behind it is **Barley's** (458 2739), a microbrewery and casino. Further attractions lie on Sunset Road: to the east is **Sunset Station** (*see p117*), a neighbourhood casino with a fabulous,

Gaudi-inspired bar, while a spin westbound will lead you past the **Ambiance Bistro** (*see p173*), Wayne Newton's home (at the south-west corner of Russell Road) and the huge **Sunset Park** (at Eastern Avenue, 455 8200), which contains picnic sites, grills and games courts.

Lake Las Vegas

While Las Vegas grew, failed, grew, stagnated and grew again during the last century, the land that now holds Lake Las Vegas remained isolated and undeveloped. Eventually, it was settled not by Spanish traders, indomitable frontiersmen or stop-at-nothing prospectors, but by 'Ronald F Boeddeker, President and Chairman of Transcontinental Properties, Inc, [who] envisioned a body of cool water surrounded by an unparalleled Mediterranean resort destination showcasing mountains, homes, golf courses, hotels, gaming, restaurants and boutiques' (the quote is from the official Lake Las Vegas website). Under the supervision of Mr Boeddeker, construction began here 20 years ago. It hasn't stopped since.

Lake Las Vegas is now a resort community with hotels, homes and golf courses surrounding a vast man-made lake that empties into Lake Mead. Set in a desert environment, the opulent homes start at $750,000, but the prices aren't any deterrent: evidence of further construction is everywhere in a corner of the city that's part luxury resort, part building site. The **Ritz-Carlton** (*see p118*) offers the Strip's Four Seasons serious competition in the ultra-luxe, casino-free lodgings sector; adjoining it is the **MonteLago Village**, a twee lakeside spot with tiny boutiques, restaurants and a wine bar. In the summer, bring a blanket and watch as musicians take to the marina.

Lakeside **MonteLago Village**, a little piece of Disneyfied Italy in Nevada.

Eat, Drink, Shop

Features

Downtown Cocktail Room. *See p184.*

Restaurants & Buffets

Celebrity chefs next to all-you-can-eat buffets? Only in Vegas…

Nowhere in Las Vegas is the power of cash more evident than in its array of restaurants. For years, food here was designed purely to provide stomach-lining for drinkers and fuel for gamblers. The sole aim of catering crews was to get diners in and out of their restaurants as quickly as possible, sending them back to the gambling tables where the real profits were to be made. The choice of cuisine didn't extend far beyond all-you-can-eat buffets, 24-hour coffeeshops and, for the rich visitor, swanky steakhouses.

How times change. Since the arrival in 1992 of Wolfgang Puck, the first star chef to open a restaurant in the city, Las Vegas's dining scene has been turned on its head. The range and variety of restaurants in the casinos is broader than ever, catering to more or less every taste and budget. The casino moguls have spent millions luring the world's best chefs to the city, forking over even more cash on spectacular interior design and fresh ingredients, flown in from around the country every day of the year. The buffets and all-night eateries remain, but many of them have been upgraded and are virtually unrecognisable from days of yore.

Despite all the welcome improvements, things aren't perfect. Many of the star chefs who've lent the weight of their names and/or reputations to restaurants in the city don't cook here, though that doesn't stop them from setting extremely high prices. There's still plenty of mediocrity: overpriced steakhouses, inauthentic Chinese eateries, dreary breakfast bars and the like. And a few of the town's high-end, big-name restaurants coast along on autopilot after an initial marketing blitz, when reputations are made and trends are set. But many others sustain a high standard. Indeed, the smart restaurateurs are aware that even in a resort town such as this, word-of-mouth is a powerful tool, especially now internet messageboards mean that everyone can be a critic.

Away from the Strip, things are less consistent but often impressive. Carnivores are well served by a fine array of steakhouses and barbecue joints; a handful of excellent low-key, high-value Asian restaurants sit tucked away in unlikely strip-mall locations; and there's even a plethora of Middle Eastern eateries. Follow the recommendations in this chapter, and you can't go far wrong.

PRACTICALITIES

The ebb and flow of visitors through Las Vegas is so unpredictable that making reservations, while not always necessary, is nonetheless recommended for all major Strip restaurants, especially those at the higher end of the scale. Weekends are busy, but many eateries do a brisk trade during the week thanks to the influx of conventioneers. Aside from some special Sunday feeds (such as the **Sterling Brunch** at Bally's; *see p177*), casino buffets don't accept reservations; prepare to queue at busy times. Away from the Strip, you'd do well to book for Friday and Saturday nights.

Vegas is a pretty casual town, and only a few restaurants enforce a dress code that moves much beyond an insistence on shoes and a shirt. You should be all right if you employ common sense: you can get away with almost any uniform at the **Burger Bar** (*see p155*), but men would do well to wear a jacket when dining at **Picasso** (*see p161*). If in doubt, it's always advisable to ask staff when you make your reservation.

The best Restaurants

For a brilliant breakfast
Bouchon (*see p158*), Hash House a-Go Go (*see p173*) or Sunday brunch at the Verandah Café (*see p157*).

For a lovely lunch
Corsa Cucina (*see p161*), NM Café (*see p156*) or 'Wichcraft (*see p157*).

For a sneaky snack
Luv-It Frozen Custard (*see p166*) or Pink's (*see p156*).

For a divine dinner
Craftsteak (*see p155*), Joël Robuchon (*see p160*) or Rosemary's Restaurant (*see p173*).

For a midnight meal
America (*see p153*), Bay City Diner (*see p171*) or Mr Lucky's 24/7 (*see p167*).

Eat, Drink, Shop

Japonais. *See p162.*

Restaurants

The Strip

American & steakhouses

America

New York New York *3790 Las Vegas Boulevard South, at W Tropicana Avenue (740 6451/www. nynyhotelcasino.com). Bus Deuce, 201.* **Open** 24hrs daily. **Main courses** $12-$24. **Credit** AmEx, DC, Disc, MC, V. **Hotel** p84. **Map** p336 A8 ❶

Like the casino in which it's housed, America is terrific fun. In both, a simple concept is executed with wonderfully playful enthusiasm. The all-purpose menu offers innumerable dishes from across the country, many of them inspired by a particular corner of the US: chicken quesadillas by way of Albuquerque, for example, or Philadelphia cheese steaks. It's not really about the authenticity, mind; this is just good, solid cooking served with an exclamation mark, a wide smile and a heartfelt 'have a nice day!'

❶ Purple numbers given in this chapter correspond to the location of each restaurant on the street maps. *See pp333-336.*

Aureole

Mandalay Bay *3950 Las Vegas Boulevard South, at W Hacienda Avenue (632 7401/www.charlie palmersteak.com). Bus Deuce, 104, 105.* **Open** 6-10.30pm daily. **Set menu** $69-$85. **Credit** AmEx, Disc, MC, V. **Hotel** p71. **Map** p336 A9 ❷

Vegas is full of dramatic restaurants, but where else can you dine within sight of a four-storey, 4,500-bottle wine tower, up and down which float harnessed wine angels, fetching your choice on demand? The food, orchestrated by Charlie Palmer and overseen by Vincent Pouessel, is also a delight, with seasonal American dishes including caramelised Sonoma duck and fennel steamed Alaskan salmon. Megan Romano's ethereal sweets make breaking your diet well worthwhile. *Photo p163.*

Boa Steakhouse

Caesars Palace (Forum Shops) *3570 Las Vegas Boulevard South, at W Flamingo Road (733 7373/ www.boasteak.com). Bus Deuce, 202.* **Open** noon-10pm Mon-Thur; noon-11.30pm Fri, Sat; noon-10pm Sun. **Main courses** $27-$45. **Credit** AmEx, Disc, MC, V. **Hotel** p68. **Map** p336 A7 ❸

The austere, clinical design is contemporary and a long way from the gentlemen's-club standard fittings that decorate more traditional steak-houses, but then the menu at Boa (an LA import) goes beyond surf 'n' turf cliché. The classics are rendered well here, though there's plenty of fun to be had on a list of appetisers that might include such novelties as truffle nachos and goat's cheese baklava. Prices are high.

Bradley Ogden

Caesars Palace *3570 Las Vegas Boulevard South, at W Flamingo Road (731 7410/www.harrahs.com).* *Bus Deuce, 202.* **Open** 5-11pm daily. **Main courses** $37-$175. **Credit** AmEx, DC, Disc, MC, V. **Hotel** p68. **Map** p336 A7 ④

Ogden has cultivated relationships with regional suppliers and boutique growers across the US, with everything from Utah salt to Oregon seafood purchased direct from specialist providers. The result is an American cuisine that doesn't come cheap, but if melt-in-the-mouth rack of Colorado lamb or slow-roasted Muscovy duck with purple artichokes and rhubarb ring your bell, consider this an essential stop. The best bit? Ogden sticks around to cook it.

Burger Bar

Mandalay Bay *3950 Las Vegas Boulevard South, at W Hacienda Avenue (632 9364/www.mandalay bay.com). Bus Deuce, 104, 105.* **Open** 10.30am-11pm Mon-Thur, Sun; 10am-3am Fri, Sat. **Main courses** $8-$60. **Credit** AmEx, DC, Disc, MC, V. **Hotel** p71. **Map** p336 A9 ⑤

Cast images of McBurgers out of your mind: the burgers at this chic yet amenable spot are fresh, meaty and deeply delicious, especially once you've garnished them with your choice of toppings. (Veggie options are available.) Ironically, it took a Frenchman to reinvent this most American of meals: it's the brainchild of Hubert Keller, the chef behind Fleur de Lys (*see p160*).

Charlie Palmer Steak

Four Seasons *3960 Las Vegas Boulevard South, at W Hacienda Drive (632 5120/www.charliepalmer steak.com). Bus Deuce, 104, 105.* **Open** 5.30-10.30pm daily. *Lounge* 5pm-midnight daily. **Main courses** $24-$42. **Credit** AmEx, DC, Disc, MC, V. **Hotel** p95. **Map** p336 A9 ⑥

Every upscale steakhouse chain in America has an outpost in Vegas. However, Charlie Palmer (who, alongside Megan Romano, is also at the helm of Mandalay Bay's Aureole; *see p153*) stays a cut above the rest by offering ever-changing variations on the staple steak-spuds-seafood fare, thanks to resident chef de cuisine Stephen Blandino. There are classic cuts to please even the most jaded of palates, plus Romano's fantastic desserts.

Craftsteak

MGM Grand *3799 Las Vegas Boulevard South, at E Tropicana Avenue (891 7800/www.craftrestaurant. com). Bus Deuce, 201.* **Open** 5.30-10pm Mon, Sun; 5-10pm Tue-Thur; 5-10.30pm Fri, Sat. **Main courses** $26-$110. **Set menu** $90. **Credit** AmEx, DC, Disc, MC, V. **Hotel** p81. **Map** p336 A8 ⑦

The selection of meats (grass-fed veal, lamb shank, filet mignon, braised short ribs) is impressive, but the sides and the quiet invention shown in the kitchen both elevate Tom Colicchio's Craftsteak from more run-of-the-mill casino steakhouses. Ingredients come from small family farms and other below-the-radar sources, and you can tell. It's all served in a cultured atmosphere, if a slightly noisy one.

Fix

Bellagio *3600 Las Vegas Boulevard South, at W Flamingo Road (693 8400/www.bellagio.com). Bus Deuce, 202.* **Open** 5pm-midnight Mon-Thur, Sun; 5pm-2am Fri, Sat. **Main courses** $30-$60. **Credit** AmEx, DC, Disc, MC, V. **Hotel** p68. **Map** p336 A7 ⑧

The idea at Fix, the first of the three sexy Light Group eateries in town, is to bring you the 'scene and the cuisine': rather than sequestering its cast of primped diners, it opens its classy, undulating interior design to the casino so everyone can smell the wood-fired surf 'n' turf. We suggest a lounge seat, a pomegranate martini, and salmon and caviar forks.

Mesa Grill

Caesars Palace *3570 Las Vegas Boulevard South, at W Flamingo Road (731 7410/www.mesagrill.com). Bus Deuce, 202.* **Open** 11am-3pm, 5-11pm Mon-Fri; 10.30am-3pm, 5-11pm Sat, Sun. **Main courses** *Brunch* $13-$24. *Lunch* $15-$24. *Dinner* $23-$45. **Credit** AmEx, DC, Disc, MC, V. **Hotel** p68. **Map** p336 A7 ⑨

Rather like Bobby Flay, the celebrity chef behind this popular restaurant, the Mesa Grill is a little on the brash side. The room itself is dazzling in all the best ways, a flourish-packed riot of colour and energy. But the nuevo-American food, like Flay, could do with a little more subtlety. The likes of pork tenderloin with sweet potato tamale and crushed pecan butter are fine, but they read better than they sound and don't justify their high price tags.

The popular **Strip Steak**. *See p157.*

Eat, Drink, Shop

NM Café

Neiman Marcus, Fashion Show Mall, 3200 Las Vegas Boulevard South, at Spring Mountain Road (697 7340/www.neimanmarcus.com). Bus Deuce, 105, 203. **Open** 11am-6pm Mon-Sat; noon-6pm Sun. **Main courses** $9-$18. **Credit** AmEx, Disc, MC, V. **Map** p335 & p336 A6 ❿

Next door to Neiman Marcus's ultra-chic Mariposa (*see p160*) sits its trendier sibling, more Juicy Couture than Chanel. Perch at the sleek bar nibbling on classic Middle Eastern fare from the meze sampler or sip cosmos on the shaded patio. Fashionistas flock here to see and be seen, but also to try exec chef Jason Horwitz's shrimp chermoula and greek salad, and NM's famous chocolate chip cookies.

Nobhill

MGM Grand *3799 Las Vegas Boulevard South, at E Tropicana Avenue (693 7223/www.michaelmina.net). Bus Deuce, 201.* **Open** 5.30-10pm Mon-Thur, Sun; 5.30-10.30pm Fri, Sat. **Main courses** $29-$62. **Credit** AmEx, DC, Disc, MC, V. **Hotel** p81. **Map** p336 A8 ⓫

A classy San Franciscan treat on the Strip, Michael Mina's Nobhill serves such Bay Area classics as chicken tetrazzini, lobster pot pie and North Beach cioppino. Just as popular are his contemporary creations, particularly Niman Ranch rack of lamb. Cosy up in a bar booth made for two, throw back a few Cable Cars, slather sourdough bread in cheese fondue and polish off a tarte tatin for dessert.

Olives

Bellagio *3600 Las Vegas Boulevard South, at W Flamingo Road (693 8181/www.toddenglish.com). Bus Deuce, 202.* **Open** 11am-2.30pm, 5-10.30pm Mon-Thur; 11am-10.30pm Fri-Sun. **Main courses** *Lunch* $15-$22. *Dinner* $20-$38. **Credit** AmEx, DC, Disc, MC, V. **Hotel** p68. **Map** p336 A7 ⓬

A revamp by Jeffrey Beers has breathed new life into Todd English's 'casual' Las Vegas establishment overlooking the Bellagio's lake. Boston-based English (the original Olives is in Charlestown, MA) keeps his 'interpretive Mediterranean' cuisine alive and well with such innovations as white clam pizza and butternut squash tortellini.

Pink's

Planet Hollywood *3667 Las Vegas Boulevard South, between E Harmon Avenue & E Flamingo Road (785 5555/www.pinkshollywood.com). Bus Deuce, 202.* **Open** 8am-5pm daily. **Main courses** $6-$7. **Credit** AmEx, DC, Disc, MC, V. **Hotel** p85. **Map** p336 A7 ⓭

You're unlikely to catch the great and the good of Hollywood here, as you might if you spend enough time hanging around by the 70-year-old LA original. However, if you're in the mood for a diet-busting dog topped with all manner of greasy gloop, there's really nowhere else in town for such superior junk food.

Postrio

Venetian *3555 Las Vegas Boulevard South, between Sands Avenue & E Flamingo Road (796 1110/www.wolfgangpuck.com). Bus Deuce, 105, 203.*

Verandah Café.

Open 11.30am-10pm daily. **Main courses** *Lunch* $9-$28. *Dinner* $9-$50. **Credit** AmEx, DC, Disc, MC, V. **Hotel** p75. **Map** p335 & p336 R6 ⓮

The most intimate – and, some say, best – restaurant in Wolfgang Puck's Vegas collection, Postrio blends San Francisco and Venice to achieve a romantic atmosphere. Food fuses Mediterranean and Asian influences; seasonal specials include pan-roasted Vermont farm quail with sweet potato gnocchi, and Peking-style roasted duck with warm sesame crêpes. The desserts are a must: try the warm chocolate tart with crumbled toffee ice-cream and fresh raspberries.

Prime

Bellagio *3600 Las Vegas Boulevard South, at W Flamingo Road (693 7223/www.bellagio.com). Bus Deuce, 202.* **Open** 5-10pm daily. **Main courses** $25-$48. **Credit** AmEx, DC, Disc, MC, V. **Hotel** p68. **Map** p336 A7 ⓯

Prime indeed. In fact, one could go further: first class, superior and pre-eminent pretty much sum up Jean-Georges Vongerichten's steakhouse, where the striking setting comes with a perfect view of the Bellagio's fountains. There's magic on the plate, too: steaks are the highlights, but don't overlook the free-range chicken, seared ahi tuna, wood-grilled veal chop and a selection of 11 sauces and seven mustards.

Spago

Caesars Palace (Forum Shops) *3500 Las Vegas Boulevard South, at W Flamingo Road (369 6300/ www.wolfgangpuck.com). Bus Deuce, 202.* **Open** *Café* 11am-11pm Mon-Thur, Sun; 11am-midnight Fri,

Sat. *Restaurant* 5.30-10pm daily. **Main courses**
Lunch $8-$33. *Dinner* $14-$68. **Credit** AmEx, DC,
Disc, MC, V. **Hotel** p68. **Map** p336 A7 ⑯
The eaterie that reinvented Vegas dining in 1992,
Spago has managed to stay smart with the tourists
and power-lunchers by regularly reinventing itself,
most recently with the addition of art by Vegas success stories David Ryan and Tim Bavington.
Options in the formal dining room include seasonal
specialities (lobster, truffles) and organic vegetarian offerings; in the indoor patio café, there are signature salads, pizzas and sandwiches.

Stack

Mirage *3400 Las Vegas Boulevard South, between
Spring Mountain & W Flamingo Roads (792 7801/
www.mirage.com). Bus Deuce, 105, 202, 203.*
Open 5-11pm Mon-Thur, Sun; 5pm-midnight Fri,
Sat. **Main courses** $17-$44. **Credit** AmEx, DC,
Disc, MC, V. **Hotel** p73. **Map** p335 & p336 A6 ⑰
The name refers to the design by the Graft Lab of
Berlin, in which the mahogany walls have a canyon-
like appearance. It will lure you in; the American-
style cuisine (giant steaks, Kobe burgers, whipped
potatoes and comfort desserts such as modern-day
cookies and milk) will make you glad you stayed.

Steak House

Circus Circus *2880 Las Vegas Boulevard South,
between W Sahara Avenue & Desert Inn Road
(794 3767/www.circuscircus.com). Bus Deuce.*
Open 5-10pm Mon-Fri, Sun; 5-11pm Sat. **Main
courses** $28-$38. **Credit** AmEx, DC, Disc, MC, V.
Hotel p89. **Map** p335 B5 ⑱
The casino in which it's housed neuters some of the
sophistication, but this is still an excellent choice if
you've a yen for a large lump of cow. The steaks here
are aged for 21 days and then mesquite-grilled; even
more so than usual, order rare or miss out on some
of the flavour. What's more, the prices are well below
those of other beef emporia along the Strip. A Vegas
legend of sorts.

Strip Steak

Mandalay Bay *3950 Las Vegas Boulevard South,
at W Hacienda Avenue (632 7414/www.michael
mina.net). Bus Deuce, 104, 105.* **Open** 5.30-10.30pm
daily. **Main courses** $28-$85. **Credit** AmEx, Disc,
MC, V. **Hotel** p71. **Map** p336 A9 ⑲
Star chef Michael Mina's first steakhouse is also his
first slight misstep. It's not that the food is bad,
because it isn't. But at prices this extreme ($50 for a
10oz filet mignon, eight bucks for a side of baked
potato), it really needs to be dazzling, and it's rarely
quite that good. The slow-poached prime rib is the
best bet, but that said, do try and save room for the
supreme desserts. The open-plan restaurant area can
get pretty loud when it's busy, which is reasonably
often. *Photo p155.*

Tableau

Wynn Las Vegas *3131 Las Vegas Boulevard
South, between E Desert Inn Road & Sands Avenue
(770 3463/www.wynnlasvegas.com). Bus Deuce, 203.*

Open 8am-10.15am, 11.30am-2.15pm, 5.30-10pm
Mon-Fri; 8am-2.30pm, 5.30-10pm Sat, Sun. **Main
courses** *Breakfast & brunch* $11-$25. *Lunch* $19-
$25. *Dinner* $38-$49. **Credit** AmEx, DC, Disc, MC,
V. **Hotel** p76. **Map** p335 & p336 B6 ⑳
Mark LoRusso cut his teeth working for increasingly
visible chef Michael Mina; you can tell, and in a very,
very good way. While Mina reigns more or less
supreme towards the south of the Strip, LoRusso's
cultured take on American cuisine is among the best
restaurants at this end of the boulevard, his kitchen
displaying a real lightness of touch when dealing
with variations on classic themes such as rack of
lamb. A real gem of a restaurant.

Verandah Café

Four Seasons *3960 Las Vegas Boulevard South,
at W Hacienda Drive (632 5121/www.fourseasons.
com). Bus Deuce, 104, 105.* **Open** 6.30am-10pm
Mon-Fri; 7am-10pm Sat, Sun. **Main courses**
Breakfast $16-$23. *Lunch* $18-$25. *Dinner* $16-$34.
Credit AmEx, Disc, MC, V. **Hotel** p95. **Map**
p336 A9 ㉑
Outfitted in everything from suits to tennis shorts,
rock stars, real estate magnates and other riff-raff
find this comfortable California country club-styled
spot irresistible. The under promoted yet popular
Sunday brunch is an all-you-can-savour taste treat,
putting other buffets to shame at a price that says it
should. A large poolside dining area (request when
booking) spirits you away to Santa Barbara for belli-
nis and blintzes.

'Wichcraft

MGM Grand *3799 Las Vegas Boulevard South,
at E Tropicana Avenue (891 3166/www.craft
restaurant.com). Bus Deuce, 201.* **Open** 10am-6pm
Mon-Thur, Sun; 10am-8pm Fri, Sat. **Main courses**
$6-$9. **Credit** AmEx, DC, Disc, MC, V. **Hotel** p81.
Map p336 A8 ㉒
Tom Colicchio's overexcited little sibling to
Craftsteak (*see p155*) peps up the previously dreary
world of American sandwich culture; visitors used
to Subway-standard sammiches will be dazzled.
Generally speaking, the more appetising the description, the nicer the sandwich, so skip the so-so roast
turkey in favour of the more exotic varieties. There's
plenty for vegetarians, a novelty in such a meat-
oriented town. Breakfast is served all day.

Wolfgang Puck Bar & Grill

MGM Grand *3799 Las Vegas Boulevard South,
at E Tropicana Avenue (891 3000/www.wolfgang
puck.com). Bus Deuce, 201.* **Open** 11.30am-11pm
Mon-Thur; 11.30am-11.30pm Fri; 10am-11.30pm
Sat; 10am-11pm Sun. **Main courses** $17-$28.
Credit AmEx, DC, Disc, MC, V. **Hotel** p81.
Map p336 A8 ㉓
Styled on a California beach bungalow, and a very
modish one at that, this Puck outpost offers a contemporary take on Californian cuisine. Signature
dishes include truffled potato chips with blue cheese,
duck bratwurst and Puck pizzas; all of it is very edible indeed, and perfectly suited to a lazy lunch.

Eat, Drink, Shop

Chinese

Fin

Mirage *3400 Las Vegas Boulevard South, between Spring Mountain & W Flamingo Roads (791 7337/ www.mirage.com). Bus Deuce, 105, 202, 203.* **Open** 11am-2pm, 5-11pm daily. **Main courses** *Lunch* $13-$22. *Dinner* $14-$295. **Credit** AmEx, DC, Disc, MC, V. **Hotel** p73. **Map** p335 & p336 A6 **㉔**

The menu isn't anything out of the ordinary; certainly, there's nothing on here to frighten the horses. But Chi Choi's renditions of Chinese classics, some slightly adapted for the modern world, are nonetheless very good, and the space in which they're served is sublime and cultured. There are options suitable for most wallets.

Pearl

MGM Grand *3799 Las Vegas Boulevard South, at E Tropicana Avenue (693 7223/www.mgmgrand. com). Bus Deuce, 201.* **Open** 5.30-10pm daily. **Main courses** $16-$48. **Credit** AmEx, DC, Disc, MC, V. **Hotel** p81. **Map** p336 A8 **㉕**

A quiet, time-honoured winner on the Strip's upscale restaurant scene, Pearl offers a fresh take on classic Chinese cuisine from Canton and Shanghai provinces with dishes that rotate to reflect the changing of the seasons. There are also plenty of memorable touches off the menu, including an exotic-tea cart and an elegant contemporary room designed by Tony Chi.

Wing Lei

Wynn Las Vegas *3131 Las Vegas Boulevard South, between E Desert Inn Road & Sands Avenue (770 3388/www.wynnlasvegas.com). Bus Deuce, 203.* **Open** 5.30-10.30pm daily. **Main courses** $26-$88. **Set menus** $78-$128. **Credit** AmEx, DC, Disc, MC, V. **Hotel** p76. **Map** p335 & p336 B6 **㉖**

As if naming your casino after yourself wasn't outlandish enough, Steve Wynn has also lent his identity to this super-smart restaurant: Wing translates as 'Wynn' in Chinese. Happily, the mogul's vanity doesn't extend to taking charge of the kitchen: chef Richard Chen looks after that side of the operation, dispensing cultured Chinese food in a predictably luxurious environment.

French & Mediterranean

Alex

Wynn Las Vegas *3131 Las Vegas Boulevard South, between E Desert Inn Road & Sands Avenue (770 3463/www.wynnlasvegas.com). Bus Deuce, 203.* **Open** 6-10pm Tue-Sun. **Set menu** $145. *Tasting menus* $195-$325. **Credit** AmEx, DC, Disc, MC, V. **Hotel** p76. **Map** p335 & p336 B6 **㉗**

While running oft-overlooked Renoir at the Mirage, Alessandro Stratta earned a reputation among many locals as the city's finest chef. At Alex, he's getting the chance to prove it to the world. With a sweeping staircase inspired by the film *Hello, Dolly!* this is the most elegant restaurant in the Strip's most elegant casino; there are even individual stools for ladies' purses, so they don't have to touch the floor. And Stratta's seasonal dishes, inspired by the flavours of the French Riviera, are as good as it gets.

L'Atelier de Joël Robuchon

MGM Grand *3799 Las Vegas Boulevard South, at E Tropicana Avenue (693 7223/www.mgmgrand.com). Bus Deuce, 201.* **Open** 5-10.30pm Mon-Thur, Sun; 5-11pm Fri, Sat. **Main courses** $14-$54. **Credit** AmEx, DC, Disc, MC, V. **Hotel** p81. **Map** p336 A8 **㉓**

This workshop-style dining room, right next door to Robuchon's signature restaurant (*see p160*), features a few tables and a counter at which you can sit and watch some of the world's best dishes (simpler and cheaper than at the other place) being prepared. Try a side order of the gorgeous *pommes purées* or push the boat out and go for the discovery tasting; it's worth the $150 price tag.

Bouchon

Venetian *3555 Las Vegas Boulevard South, between Sands Avenue & E Flamingo Road (414 6200/www.frenchlaundry.com). Bus Deuce, 105, 203.* **Open** 7-10.30am, 5-11pm Mon-Fri; 8am-2pm, 5-11pm Sat, Sun. *Oyster bar* 3-11pm daily. **Main courses** *Breakfast* $8-$22. *Lunch & dinner* $17-$33. **Credit** AmEx, Disc, MC, V. **Hotel** p75. **Map** p335 & p336 B6 **㉙**

Inside this bistro and oyster bar, much-garlanded Thomas Keller serves authentic French country fare modelled after the cuisine served in the original *bouchons* of Lyon. Indoors or on poolside seating in the gardens, indulge in Bouchon French toast for breakfast, served bread-pudding style with warm layers of brioche, custard and fresh fruit with maple syrup; or, for dinner, try the *truite aux amandes*, pan-roasted trout with almonds, brown butter and green beans.

Café Ba Ba Reeba

Fashion Show Mall, 3200 Las Vegas Boulevard South, at W Spring Mountain Road (258 1211/ www.cafebabareeba.com). Bus Deuce, 105, 203. **Open** 11.30am-11pm Mon-Thur, Sun; 11.30am-midnight Fri, Sat. **Main courses** $5-$33. **Credit** AmEx, DC, Disc, MC, V. **Map** p335 & p336 A6 **㉚**

The spunky menu, featuring tapas and paella, suggests that this might not be the quietest spot on the Strip. So it proves. It's run by the people behind Mon Ami Gabi (*see p160*); the Spanish theming here is similarly inauthentic but just as enjoyable. Great Spanish restaurants are hard to find in the US. This isn't one, but it's good enough, and the sangria is excellent. The restaurant's north-side patio is home to the self-explanatory Stripburger.

Le Cirque

Bellagio *3600 Las Vegas Boulevard South, at W Flamingo Road (693 7223/www.bellagio.com). Bus Deuce, 203.* **Open** 5.30-10pm daily. **Set menus** $105-$145. **Credit** AmEx, DC, Disc, MC, V. **Hotel** p68. **Map** p336 A7 **㉛**

This Vegas version of the New York institution is overseen by Mario Maccioni, who grew up playing and working in his father Sirio's original. Chefs come and go at Le Cirque; some of the best in the world have passed through the kitchens of its various locations. But the unparalleled French cuisine and world-class service never change, and this incarnation has one attribute that none of the three New York locations could ever boast: views of the Bellagio's elegant Lake Como.

Daniel Boulud
Wynn Las Vegas *3131 Las Vegas Boulevard South, between E Desert Inn Road & Sands Avenue (770 3463/www.wynnlasvegas.com). Bus Deuce, 203.*

Open 5.30-10.30pm daily. **Main courses** $26-$44. **Credit** AmEx, DC, Disc, MC, V. **Hotel** p76. **Map** p335 & p336 B6 🙄

New York superstar Boulud received a special exemption from Steve Wynn's edict that every head chef in his hotel must work there full-time. But his absence isn't evident in this perfectly executed brasserie, which gives diners a chance to sample his less formal fare (burgers, raw bar selections, sweetbread schnitzel). The casually cultured dining room has an incredible view of the hotel's man-made waterfall and surrealist light show.

Going to extremes Food

The most venerable and beloved snack in Las Vegas is the shrimp cocktail at the **Golden Gate** (*see p108*). For 99¢, you get six ounces of firm, white, cold-water shrimpies in a tulip glass with cocktail sauce, lemon and crackers. But for the meal deal of the millennium, try the steak-dinner special at **Ellis Island** (4178 Koval Lane, at E Flamingo Street, 733 8901, www.ellisislandcasino. com), where $4.95 buys you a ten-ounce filet-cut (thick, cooked to order) top sirloin, salad, a potato, green beans and rolls.

At the other end of the wallet, a dozen steak specials can buy you a single burger at Mandalay Bay's **Burger Bar** (*see p155*). Not just any burger, mind: this one is made with Kobe beef, truffles and foie gras.

For the same $60, sit down to the **Sterling Brunch** at Bally's (*see p177*), with caviar, lox, leg of lamb, duck, ostrich, rabbit and good champagne. Alternatively, try a 42-ounce porterhouse – USDA Prime, dry-aged and cooked only rare – at **Charlie Palmer Steak** (*see p155*), a snip at $110.

Moving up the scale, the 16-course tasting menu at **Joël Robuchon** (*see p160*) costs $360; wine's not included. Plan on spending $1,250 on dinner for two. And if that's not flashy enough, try the FleurBurger 5000 at Mandalay Bay's **Fleur de Lys** (*see p160*). The burger itself (Kobe, with truffles and goose pâté) is 'only' $75, but the bottle of Château Petrus 1990 to accompany it will set you back an extraordinary five grand.

Shrimp cocktail at the **Golden Gate**.

Eat, Drink, Shop

Eiffel Tower Restaurant

Paris Las Vegas *3655 Las Vegas Boulevard South, at E Flamingo Road (948 6937/www.eiffel towerrestaurant.com). Bus Deuce, 202.* **Open** 11am-3pm, 5-10pm Mon-Thur, Sun; 11am-3pm, 5-10.30pm Fri, Sat. **Main courses** $30-$50. **Credit** AmEx, DC, Disc, MC, V. **Hotel** p74. **Map** p336 A7 ③

The food – lamb, foie gras, steaks, which is to say high-class French dishes with subtle twists – doesn't live up to the location, but then how could it? Eleven floors above the Strip in the Eiffel Tower (with great views of the Bellagio's fountains) and designed with a beautifully modern sophistication, it's a stunner. The prices reflect this state of affairs, but then this is more about occasion than cuisine.

Fleur de Lys

Mandalay Bay *3950 Las Vegas Boulevard South, at W Hacienda Avenue (632 9400/www.mandalay bay.com). Bus Deuce, 104, 105.* **Open** 5.30-10pm Mon-Thur, Sun; 5.30-10.30pm Fri, Sat. **Set menus** $79-$99. **Credit** AmEx, DC, Disc, MC, V. **Hotel** p71. **Map** p336 A9 ③

Fleur de Lys features 30ft walls of cultured stone, a floral sculpture containing more than 3,000 fresh-cut roses, semi-private cabana tables and, in the wine loft, a private dining area. There are DJs in the lounge, but the USP remains Hubert Keller's contemporary French cuisine. For the last word in indulgence, the Fleurburger, a Kobe burger served with truffles and foie gras, and accompanied by a bottle of 1990 Château Petrus, costs a cool $5,000.

Joël Robuchon

MGM Grand *3799 Las Vegas Boulevard South, at E Tropicana Avenue (693 7223/www.mgmgrand.com). Bus Deuce, 201.* **Open** 5.30-10pm Mon-Thur, Sun; 5.30-10.30pm Fri, Sat. **Main courses** $25-$155. **Set menus** $225 6 courses; $360 16 courses. **Credit** AmEx, DC, Disc, MC, V. **Hotel** p81. **Map** p336 A8 ③

The only US fine dining restaurant by the so-called 'Chef of the Century' has a lot to live up to. But what goes on in the kitchen, from Robuchon's famous *pommes purées* to dishes such as *la semoule de blé dur* (confit of lamb with Mediterranean couscous), is even more spectacular than the five-room space, which feels like a 1930s Parisian mansion. It comes at a price, of course. But once you're here, you might as well splash out on the exquisite tasting menus.

Mariposa

Neiman Marcus, Fashion Show Mall, 3200 Las Vegas Boulevard South, at Spring Mountain Road (697 7330/www.neimanmarcus.com). Bus Deuce, 105, 203. **Open** 11.30am-3pm Mon-Sat. **Main courses** $9-$23. **Credit** AmEx, DC, MC, V. **Map** p335 & p336 A6 ③

Only a few tottering stiletto steps from the temples to haute couture on the second floor of Neiman Marcus, David Glass's equally fashionable temple to haute cuisine mixes American classics with Asian, nouveau continental and Mediterranean flavours. Think truffle asiago mac and cheese, black angus burger with melted gorgonzola, caramelised onions

The ultimate indulgence at **Fleur de Lys**.

and Belgian fries, or miso-glazed ahi tuna burger. Request a seat by the floor-to-ceiling windows, and you'll enjoy unobstructed views of the Strip.

Mix

Thehotel at Mandalay Bay *3950 Las Vegas Boulevard South, at W Hacienda Avenue (632 9500/www.mandalaybay.com). Bus Deuce, 104, 105.* **Open** 6-10.30pm daily. **Main courses** $35-$55. **Credit** AmEx, DC, Disc, MC, V. **Hotel** p95. **Map** p336 A9 ③

The food isn't cheap, but it appears that culinary legend Alain Ducasse might not be taking his Vegas eaterie as seriously as his more expensive restaurants in other cities. Both service and preparation seem rushed as the staff turn out more meals than perhaps they can manage. It's hard to fault the view from the 43rd floor, but you'll get the same view, and more bang for your buck, in the lounge next door (*see p257*).

Mon Ami Gabi

Paris Las Vegas *3655 Las Vegas Boulevard South, at E Flamingo Road (944 4224/www.mon amigabi.com). Bus Deuce, 202.* **Open** 11.30am-11pm Mon-Thur, Sun; 11.30am-midnight Fri, Sat. **Main courses** $12-$32. **Credit** AmEx, Disc, MC, V. **Hotel** p74. **Map** p336 A7 ③

Chicago-based Lettuce Entertain You Enterprises (ouch!) is responsible for, among others, the Eiffel Tower Restaurant (*see above*) and this spot on the ground floor. While the Eiffel is decidedly upscale, Mon Ami Gabi wears its French theming more casually. As such, it's enjoyable; and if the food some-times fails to live up to its reputation, it's a people-watching paradise, especially from the alfresco bit.

Pâtisserie Jean-Philippe
Bellagio *3600 Las Vegas Boulevard South, at W Flamingo Road (693 8788/www.bellagio.com). Bus Deuce, 202.* **Open** 7am-11pm Mon-Thur, Sun; 7am-midnight Fri, Sat. **Pastries** $3.50-$6. **Credit** AmEx, DC, Disc, V. **Hotel** p68. **Map** p336 A7 ㊴
The cascading chocolate fountain stops passers-by in their tracks, but it's pastry chef Jean-Philippe Maury's biscotti, truffles, macaroons, jellies and jams that lure them inside. This European-style pâtisserie sells an impressive range of sweet and savoury lux-uries for people on the go (limited seating is avail-able), plus exotic teas and coffees. Don't miss the Nutella brioche filled with caramelised hazelnuts.

Picasso
Bellagio *3600 Las Vegas Boulevard South, at W Flamingo Road (693 8105/www.bellagio.com). Bus Deuce, 202.* **Open** 6-9.30pm Mon, Wed-Sun. **Set menu** $95-$105. **Credit** AmEx, DC, Disc, MC, V. **Hotel** p68. **Map** p336 A7 ㊵
When your room is lined with $20 million of Picasso paintings, you have to work pretty hard to make an impression. No matter: Julian Serrano usually manages it. Unlike a lot of celebrity chefs with high-profile restaurants in Vegas, Serrano actually cooks at Picasso, building two crisp, daisy-fresh and wonderfully uncomplicated French-slanted menus nightly. Service is a treat and the wine list is stellar.

Pinot Brasserie
Venetian *3555 Las Vegas Boulevard South, between Sands Avenue & E Flamingo Road (414 8888/www.venetian.com). Bus Deuce, 105, 203.* **Open** 7-10am Mon-Fri; 11.30am-3pm, 5.30-10pm daily. **Main courses** *Lunch* $14-$17. *Dinner* $21-$37. **Credit** AmEx, DC, Disc, MC, V. **Hotel** p75. **Map** p335 & p336 B6 ㊶
Joachim Splichal gives his French cuisine a lighter touch, with pastas, seafood, steak and wild game. The homey decor is *très rustique*, with copper pots, leather club chairs and paintings depicting wildlife frolicking in the French countryside. The bistro also has a large rotisserie and oyster bar.

Restaurant Guy Savoy
Caesars Palace *3570 Las Vegas Boulevard South, at W Flamingo Road (731 7410/www.harrahs.com). Bus Deuce, 202.* **Open** 5-11pm Wed-Sun. **Set menus** $190 4 courses; $290 10 courses. **Credit** AmEx, DC, Disc, MC, V. **Hotel** p68. **Map** p336 A7 ㊷
Managed by Guy's son Franck Savoy, with Adam Sobel presiding over the kitchen, this is among the most expensive dining rooms in Vegas. However, it's worth every penny, providing a level of culinary sophistication rarely glimpsed here. Highlights include artichoke and black truffle soup served with toasted mushroom brioche, and a guinea hen cooked inside a pig's bladder to preserve the moisture. If you have the cash, try the ten-course *menu prestige*.

Italian

Corsa Cucina
Wynn Las Vegas *3131 Las Vegas Boulevard South, between E Desert Inn Road & Sands Avenue (770 3463/www.wynnlasvegas.com). Bus Deuce, 203.* **Open** 5-10.30pm Mon, Tue; 11.45am-2.30pm, 5-10.30pm Wed-Sun. **Main courses** *Lunch* $17-$24. *Dinner* $24-$46. **Credit** AmEx, DC, Disc, MC, V. **Hotel** p76. **Map** p335 & p336 B6 ㊸
Chef Steven Kalt takes everyday Italian cuisine and infuses it with novel gourmet touches in this recently remodelled spot. The results will please din-ers in the market for something traditional or exper-imental. Try the cannelloni, made with sheep's milk ricotta, spinach and a sauce of butter, walnuts and aged pecorino romano. And the tomato and moz-zarella appetiser – a modern spin on the classic cap-rese salad with chopped tomato tartare, basil and balsamic vinegar, beautifully arranged in the shape of a rose – is not to be missed.

Fiamma
MGM Grand *3799 Las Vegas Boulevard South, at E Tropicana Avenue (891 7800/www.mgmgrand.com). Bus Deuce, 201.* **Open** 5.30-10.30pm Mon-Thur, Sun; 5.30-11pm Fri, Sat. **Main courses** $21-$39. **Credit** AmEx, DC, Disc, MC, V. **Hotel** p81. **Map** p336 A8 ㊹
Stephen Hanson remodelled the once-proud Olio into this beautiful if oversized trattoria, a sister to his Fiamma Osteria in New York's Soho. A favourite for its cosy, trendy bar scene, Fiamma also dishes up Italian faves, such as lobster gnocchi and short rib raviolini, as well as a few chophouse-style steak, seafood and poultry dishes. Save room for the crochette dessert, three ridiculously delicious fried doughnuts.

Panevino
246 Via Antonia Avenue, at S Gillespie Street (222 2400/www.panevinolasvegas.com). Bus Deuce. **Open** 11am-3pm, 5-10pm Mon-Fri; 5-10pm Sat, Sun. **Main courses** *Lunch* $11-$30. *Dinner* $15-$45. **Credit** AmEx, DC, MC, V. **Map** p333 X4 ㊺
The number one reason to eat at Panevino is the panoramic view, offered through architecturally enhanced windows that run the length of the restau-rant and frame the action at McCarran International Airport. The food, though, comes a close second: the menu has plenty of interesting offerings, including risottos, pastas, pizzas and seafood.

Rao's
Caesars Palace *3570 Las Vegas Boulevard South, at W Flamingo Road (731 7410/www.harrahs.com). Bus Deuce, 202.* **Open** 11am-3pm, 5-11pm daily. **Main courses** *Lunch* $14-$25. *Dinner* $18-$31. **Credit** AmEx, DC, Disc, MC, V. **Hotel** p68. **Map** p336 A7 ㊻
The original Rao's has been operating in New York City for over 110 years, and is known as one of the toughest reservations in the Big Apple. The Caesars Palace spinoff is a lot easier to access, although

Contemporary design at **Social House**.

you'll still need to book ahead. And the food is worth the wait, classic Italian recipes that have been fine-tuned by the same family for more than a century. The house speciality is lemon chicken, but everything on the menu is sure to please.

Sensi

Bellagio *3600 Las Vegas Boulevard South, at W Flamingo Road (693 7223/www.bellagio.com). Bus Deuce, 202.* **Open** 11am-2.30pm, 5-10pm daily. **Main courses** *Lunch* $14-$22. *Dinner* $22-$42. **Credit** AmEx, DC, Disc, MC, V. **Hotel** p68. **Map** p336 A7 **⑰**
Japanese firm Super Potato designed this culinary theatre to complement Martin Heierling's world cuisine, a combination of Italian and Asian influences, grilled dishes and seafood classics. Four glass-enclosed kitchens in the middle of the room provide an interactive stage: watch curries plunge into a red-hot tandoori oven on the Asian stage; spot focaccias with vacherin cheese and black truffles slipped into a wood-fire oven in the Italian corner; and see blue point oysters shucked in the raw section.

Trevi

Caesars Palace (Forum Shops) *3500 Las Vegas Boulevard South, at W Flamingo Road (735 4663/www.trevi-italian.com). Bus Deuce, 202.* **Open** 11am-11pm Mon-Thur, Sun; 11am-midnight Fri, Sat. **Main courses** $13-$30. **Credit** AmEx, DC, Disc, MC, V. **Hotel** p68. **Map** p336 A7 **⑱**
For the most part, Caesars and the adjacent Forum Shops wear their theming fairly lightly. One notable

exception is this Italian eaterie, named for the fountain and located right by its Vegas reworking. It's a replacement for long-serving Bertolini's, and previous visitors may not notice a great deal of difference in its menu of Italian comfort food. But this is still a reliable option; and next to its competitors in the Forum Shops, it's pretty fairly priced.

Valentino

Venetian *3555 Las Vegas Boulevard South, between Sands Avenue & E Flamingo Road (414 3000/www.valentinorestaurantgroup.com). Bus Deuce, 105, 203.* **Open** 5.30-10.30pm daily. **Main courses** $34-$42. **Credit** AmEx, DC, Disc, MC, V. **Hotel** p75. **Map** p335 & p336 B6 **⑲**
Piero Selvaggio's take on Italian cuisine, delivered by executive chef Luciano Pellegrini, is authentic in almost every regard but the prices, which are a good deal higher than they need to be. Still, this is the Venetian; and in any case, the food here is pretty impressive, delivered in a room that stays the right side of a line separating handsome from gauche.

Japanese

Japonais

Mirage *3400 Las Vegas Boulevard South, between Spring Mountain & W Flamingo Roads (792 7979/www.mirage.com). Bus Deuce, 105, 202, 203.* **Open** 5-10.30pm Mon-Wed, Sun; 5-11pm Thur-Sat. **Main courses** $14-$65. **Credit** AmEx, DC, Disc, MC, V. **Hotel** p73. **Map** p335 & p336 A6 **㊿**
Jun Ichikawa offers only the most traditional styles of sushi, shunning fusion cuisine and American-style rolls. Meanwhile, French-trained Gene Kato offers a large selection of entrees and hot appetisers. *Robata* (Japanese charcoal grill) is a speciality. The lounge is located under the Mirage's domed atrium, with a 110ft (34m) glowing red firewall alongside a multi-level main dining room. *Photo p153.*

Shibuya

MGM Grand *3799 Las Vegas Boulevard South, at E Tropicana Avenue (891 7800/www.mgmgrand.com). Bus Deuce, 201.* **Open** 5.30-9.30pm Mon-Thur, Sun; 5.30-10pm Fri, Sat. **Main courses** $22-$54. *Teppanyaki* $42-$105. **Credit** AmEx, DC, Disc, MC, V. **Hotel** p81. **Map** p336 A8 **㉛**
Shibuya is really three beautiful restaurants in one: a 50ft (15m) marble sushi bar; a collection of traditional *teppanyaki* (table cooking) grills under hot pink stainless steel canopies; and a pair of modern rooms where guests can indulge in chef Stephane Chevet's French spin on modern Japanese cuisine. Guests in any section are free to order from the various menus, and everything is easily shared.

Social House

Treasure Island *3300 Las Vegas Boulevard South, at Spring Mountain Road (894 7777/www.socialhouselv.com). Bus Deuce, 105, 203.* **Open** 5pm-2am Mon-Thur, Sun; 5pm-3.30am Fri, Sat. **Main courses** $25-$55. **Credit** AmEx, DC, Disc, MC, V. **Hotel** p87. **Map** p335 & p336 A6 **㉜**

Chef Joseph Elevado staked his claim as a major food force on the Strip when Social House opened in mid 2006. The food is great, with sushi a speciality, and the atmosphere is also a treat. Trendsetting New York design company AvroKO have created an elegant and intriguing multi-room, multi-level set-up, joined at the hip to Tangerine (*see p88*). Living up to its name, Social House ingeniously converts itself into a stylish nightclub after dinner; the tables even lower themselves to coffee table level – perfect for cocktails.

Sushi Roku

Caesars Palace (Forum Shops) *3700 Las Vegas Boulevard South, at W Flamingo Road (733 7373/ www.sushiroku.com). Bus Deuce, 202.* **Open** noon-10pm Mon-Thur, Sun; noon-11.30pm Fri, Sat. **Main courses** $22-$49. **Credit** AmEx, DC, Disc, MC, V. **Hotel** p68. **Map** p336 A7 ⑤③

As if Las Vegas wasn't enough like LA, in slinks this Santa Monica/Hollywood hotspot, all dressed up and ready for some celebrity action. Boasting similar prices to Nobu (*see p168*) but less of the cachet, Sushi Roku proves that getting super-fresh fish in the desert isn't cheap. Fanatics are split on whether it's worth the price tag, but anyone worth their $300 jeans knows that the Strip views and loungey bar scene are draws equal to the sensational sashimi.

Jewish

Canter's Deli

Treasure Island *3300 Las Vegas Boulevard South, at Spring Mountain Road (894 7111/www.treasure island.com). Bus Deuce, 105, 203.* **Open** 10.30am-11pm daily. **Main courses** $6-$17. **Credit** AmEx, DC, Disc, MC, V. **Hotel** p87. **Map** p335 & p336 A6 ⑤④

Drink up

Not that long ago, Las Vegas's reputation for wine could be summed up in one imaginary but by no means implausible conversation.

Waiter: 'Red or white?'
Diner: 'Yes.'

While there are still some restaurants in which that conversation continues to take place, the wine in many restaurants is much better, much more expensive and much more likely to complement that Kobe beef steak. And it will be expertly selected and uncorked at the table by somebody whose sole responsibility is to select and uncork wines.

Every restaurant worth its salt in Vegas these days has a sommelier, if not a full-on director of wine. It's hardly surprising, given the number of vintages on offer. **Alizé** at the Palms (*see p170*) has a 65-page wine menu; **Alex** at Wynn Las Vegas (*see p158*) has more than 200 bottles of Burgundy alone; and wine director William Sherer at **Aureole** (*see p153*) has filled a wine tower that's so high (four storeys) and mighty (55,000 bottles) that it has a computer tablet for a menu and 'wine angels' who rop up in search of your choice. Indeed, the demand for master sommeliers is such that two of the best have been employed by a strip joint: Steven Geddes, former wine director of Aureole, runs the two upscale kitchens at the **Men's Club** (*see p221*), while Darius Allyn manages the 11,000-bottle wine collection and champagne room.

For all the changes, which began with the improvement of the town's dining in the early 1990s, Las Vegas wealth actually stems more from the beer-drinking legions of visitors from middle America. So why the demand for sommeliers? Jaime Smith, a former wine director at MGM Grand who now works at Las Vegas mega-distributor Southern Wine & Spirits, has a theory. 'As opposed to large metro areas where, generally speaking, the public is in tune with wine and seeking it out, here people come to turn their brains off. They need someone to help them decide.'

William Sherer at **Aureole**. See p153.

Eat, Drink, Shop

New York-style cheesecake served in a famous LA restaurant? Welcome, of course, to Las Vegas. The original Canter's Deli is a glorious old shambles, its 75-year-old Naugahyde fittings lit by too-bright fluorescence and overseen by Jewish dears who've seen it all before. By comparison, the Vegas outpost lacks charm, but the sandwiches and soups hold their own.

Carnegie Deli

Mirage *3400 Las Vegas Boulevard South, between Spring Mountain & W Flamingo Roads (866 339 4566/www.carnegiedeli.com). Bus Deuce, 105, 202, 203.* **Open** *7am-2am daily.* **Main courses** *$14-$21.* **Credit** AmEx, DC, Disc, MC, V. **Hotel** p73. **Map** p335 & p336 A6 ⑤⑤
Las Vegas has long delighted in bringing the world to its doorstep and reconstituting it for a theme-park crowd, a trend that reached its absolute apogee with the arrival of this Manhattan institution. Gone are the wisecracking staff and gigantic sandwiches; in their place are polite servers and surprisingly expensive (yet still sizeable) meals. It's not bad, but anyone who's been to the original may feel let down.

Latin American

Border Grill

Mandalay Bay *3950 Las Vegas Boulevard South, at W Hacienda Avenue (632 7403/www.bordergrill. com). Bus Deuce, 104, 105.* **Open** *11.30am-10.30pm daily.* **Main courses** *$10-$30.* **Credit** AmEx, DC, Disc, MC, V. **Hotel** p71. **Map** p336 A9 ⑤⑥
Imported from Santa Monica, this Angeleno take on Mexican food is not especially authentic, but works a treat regardless. Mary Sue Milliken and Susan Feniger, frontwomen of popular show *Too Hot Tamales*, have given some classic dishes a twist (the quesadillas are a great call), but also look to their home state for inspiration: witness the deep-fried snapper, served over refried beans. Lively stuff.

Diego

MGM Grand *3799 Las Vegas Boulevard South, at E Tropicana Avenue (891 7800/www.mgmgrand.com). Bus Deuce, 201.* **Open** *5.30-10pm Mon-Thur, Sun; 2-10pm Fri, Sat.* **Main courses** *$17-$40.* **Credit** AmEx, DC, Disc, MC, V. **Hotel** p81. **Map** p336 A8 ⑤⑦
The experience at MGM's lively *cocina* starts as soon as you see the bold colours and backlit tequila-bottle tower. Traditional Mexican recipes are exemplified and often modernised; Oaxacan *carne asada* (mesquite-grilled chilli-marinated beef), Yucatan-style braised pork, cactus and tequila salsa, and so on. A tasting menu offers more unique bites, such as braised pit-style goat and table-made shrimp cocktail.

Isla

Treasure Island *3300 Las Vegas Boulevard South, at Spring Mountain Road (894 7349/www.treasure island.com). Bus Deuce, 105, 203.* **Open** *4-10.45pm Mon, Thur, Sun; 4-9.15pm Tue; 4-11.45pm Wed, Fri, Sat.* **Main courses** *$9-$18.* **Credit** AmEx, DC, Disc, MC, V. **Hotel** p87. **Map** p335 & p336 A6 ⑤⑧
Treasure Island's rebranding from family resort to adult pleasure palace hasn't been wholly successful, but the dining is certainly a vast improvement. The reinvention has been led by Richard Sandoval's Isla, which really adds a spark to some of the old Mexican favourites (burritos, chicken mole) while also bringing a slightly Californian angle to some less familiar dishes. They offer an enourmous variety of different tequilas and will be happy to recommend the perfect cocktail to accompany your dinner or dessert choices.

Pampas

Planet Hollywood *3667 Las Vegas Boulevard South, between E Harmon Avenue & E Flamingo Road (737 4748/www.aladdincasino.com). Bus Deuce, 202.* **Open** *11.30am-10pm daily.* **Set menus** *Lunch $19. Dinner $37.* **Credit** AmEx, DC, Disc, MC, V. **Hotel** p85. **Map** p336 A7 ⑤⑨
This Brazilian *churrascaria rodizio* restaurant is an all-you-can-eat establishment where various barbecued meats are paraded from table to table on large skewers, and sliced right there and then for hungry diners. Not an ideal venue for vegetarians, perhaps, but carnivores will be licking their lips with delight at the very idea.

Seafood

Aquaknox

Venetian *3555 Las Vegas Boulevard South, between Sands Avenue & E Flamingo Road (414 3772/www.aquaknox.net). Bus Deuce, 105, 203.* **Open** *5-11pm Mon-Thur, Sun; 5-11.30pm Fri, Sat.* **Main courses** *$28-$65.* **Credit** AmEx, DC, Disc, MC, V. **Hotel** p75. **Map** p335 & p336 B6 ⑥⓪
The prevalence of so many excellent seafood restaurants in this desert resort town remains baffling to outsiders, and understandably so, but Aquaknox stands as solid proof that with a little expense and a good deal of effort, it's possible to conjure up excellent fish out of next to nothing. Served in a sleek room that nods constantly to the cuisine's watery theme, Tom Moloney's food lets its fresh ingredients do the work; good idea.

Bartolotta Ristorante di Mare

Wynn Las Vegas *3131 Las Vegas Boulevard South, between E Desert Inn Road & Sands Avenue (770 7000/www.wynnlasvegas.com). Bus Deuce, 203.* **Open** *5.30-10.30pm daily.* **Main courses** *$35-$100.* **Credit** AmEx, DC, Disc, MC, V. **Hotel** p76. **Map** p335 & p336 B6 ⑥①
If you're lucky, you'll land a table with a view of the water outside at this posh, but by no means flashy, eaterie within the Wynn resort, all the better to get you in the right frame of mind for Paul Bartolotta's cultured take on the Mediterranean seafood tradition. (That said, the menu also features pastas and a few meat options.) The expensive prices mean it's probably one best saved for those really special occasions.

No Crybabies

Otto's Malt Shop. *See p167.*

Joe's Seafood, Prime Steak & Stone Crab

Caesars Palace (Forum Shops) *3500 Las Vegas Boulevard South, at W Flamingo Road (792 9222/www.icon.com/joes). Bus Deuce, 202.* **Open** 11.30am-10pm Mon-Thur, Sun; 11.30am-11pm Fri, Sat. **Main courses** $18-$50. **Credit** AmEx, DC, Disc, MC, V. **Hotel** p68. **Map** p336 A7 ⑥②

When it opened a few years back, Joe's (affiliated with the legendary Miami restaurant) impressed many with its fresh-daily seafood, bone-in steaks and gracious service. Since then, more pricey seafood and steak joints of higher pedigree have elevated local expectation. Still, Joe's represents rare value in the field of upscale Vegas dining, and is one of the gems of the Forum Shops expansion.

Michael Mina

Bellagio *3600 Las Vegas Boulevard South, at W Flamingo Road (693 7223/www.michaelmina. net). Bus Deuce, 202.* **Open** 5.30-10pm daily. **Main courses** $38-$85. **Set menus** $85-$105. **Credit** AmEx, DC, Disc, MC, V. **Hotel** p68. **Map** p336 A7 ⑥③

Michael Mina's flagship restaurant in Vegas may have changed its name (it was formerly Aqua), but it still delivers what is, next to Mina's SeaBlue restaurant (*see right*), the best seafood anywhere on the Strip. His caviar parfait is legendary, but the

ever-changing menu also features such deep-sea delights as savoury black mussel soufflé and a miso-glazed Chilean sea bass.

RM

Mandalay Bay *3950 Las Vegas Boulevard South, at W Hacienda Avenue (632 9300/www.mandalay bay.com). Bus Deuce, 104, 105.* **Open** 5.30-10.30pm daily. **Main courses** $22-$70. **Credit** AmEx, Disc, MC, V. **Hotel** p71. **Map** p336 A9 ⑥④

Rick Moonen moved to Vegas from New York to ensure that everything at his restaurant lives up to his initials. As a result, the room is cosily contemporary, the service is classic and the seafood is out of this world. For about half the price, you can sample Moonen's cooking bistro-style downstairs at the R Bar Café, which features a raw menu.

SeaBlue

MGM Grand *3799 Las Vegas Boulevard South, at E Tropicana Avenue (891 7800/www.michaelmina.net). Bus Deuce, 201.* **Open** 5.30-10pm Mon-Thur, Sun; 5.30-10.30pm Fri, Sat. **Main courses** $27-$75. **Credit** AmEx, DC, Disc, MC, V. **Hotel** p81. **Map** p336 A8 ⑥⑤

Following on from Nobhill at the MGM Grand (*see p156*) and his eponymous seafooder at Bellagio (*see left*), Michael Mina's third Las Vegas venture is intimate and well designed, but aren't they all? Fish entrées grilled over wood and/or baked in clay are tasty, but what makes this place stand out is its big raw bar. Even the gimmicky lobster corndog appetiser is worth a bite.

Thai, Vietnamese & Pan-Asian

Noodles

Bellagio *3600 Las Vegas Boulevard South, at W Flamingo Road (693 7111/www.bellagio.com). Bus Deuce, 202.* **Open** 11am-2am Mon-Thur; 11am-3am Fri-Sun. **Main courses** $12-$30. **Credit** AmEx, DC, Disc, MC, V. **Hotel** p68. **Map** p336 A7 ⑥⑥

Once a gem showcasing the subtle, modern elegance of Tony Chi's pan-Asian dishes, Noodles has somewhat declined in recent years. Still, you'll still enjoy the urban diner feel, the late hours, and the selection of dim sum (lunch), Hong Kong barbecue and, of course, the hot and chilled noodle dishes from across Asia. Reliable, at the very least.

Red 8

Wynn Las Vegas *3131 Las Vegas Boulevard South, between E Desert Inn Road & Sands Avenue (770 3463/www.wynnlasvegas.com). Bus Deuce, 203.* **Open** 11am-11pm Mon-Thur, Sun; 11am-1am Fri, Sat. **Main courses** $10-$88. **Credit** AmEx, DC, Disc, MC, V. **Hotel** p76. **Map** p335 & p336 B6 ⑥⑦

Many of the restaurants at Wynn set the sky as their limit when pricing their dishes, but this pleasingly simple Asian bistro keeps things so affordable that even the riff-raff can eat here. Stick with the noodle dishes and you won't be disappointed.

Eat, Drink, Shop

Ultra-stylish dining with authentically spicy dishes at **Origin India**. *See p168.*

Tao

Venetian *3555 Las Vegas Boulevard South, between Sands Avenue & E Flamingo Road (388 8338/www.taolasvegas.com). Bus Deuce, 105, 203.* **Open** *5pm-midnight Mon-Thur, Sun; 5pm-1am Fri, Sat.* **Main courses** $20-$88. **Credit** AmEx, DC, Disc, MC, V. **Hotel** p75. **Map** p335 & p336 B6 ⊕
This ever-fashionable NYC import is best known these days as a nightclub and lounge (*see p258*) that attracts the beautiful people and microcelebs with money to burn. However, the pan-Asian food is also pretty good, especially when twinned with one of the club's speciality drinks.

Stratosphere Area

American & steakhouses

Luv-It Frozen Custard

505 E Oakey Boulevard, at Las Vegas Boulevard South (384 6452/www.luvitfrozencustard.com). Bus Deuce. **Open** *1-10pm Tue-Thur; 1-11pm Fri, Sat.* **Main courses** $3-$6. **No credit cards.** **Map** p335 C3 ⊕
This little shack doesn't look like much, but it dispenses the most moreishly delicious desserts in the city. Frozen custard looks like ice-cream and even tastes a bit like ice-cream, but it's richer and smoother than anything either Ben or Jerry could conjure. Now run by Greg Tiedemann, whose grandparents opened the business in 1973, Luv-It offers four flavours a day, served in cups, sundaes and shakes. A Western sundae's a good start, but you can't go wrong with any of it.

Top of the World

Stratosphere *2000 Las Vegas Boulevard South, at W St Louis Avenue (380 7711/www.topoftheworldlv.com). Bus Deuce, 108.* **Open** *11am-3pm, 5.30-10.30pm Mon-Thur, Sun; 11am-3pm, 5.30-11pm Fri, Sat.* **Main courses** *Lunch* $10-$15. *Dinner* $33-$60. **Credit** AmEx, DC, Disc, MC, V. **Hotel** p93. **Map** p335 C4 ⊕
The views are the main selling point of this restaurant at the top of the Stratosphere, and with good reason: they're spectacular, especially on a clear night. However, the food is better than it needs to be, a brisk, cultured mix of American and French-influenced classics. Prices are almost as high as the restaurant itself; you can just stop by for a drink if the food is out of budgetary range.

Latin American

Florida Café

Howard Johnson *1401 S Las Vegas Boulevard South, at W Charleston Boulevard (385 3013/www.floridacubancafe.com). Bus Deuce, 206.* **Open** *8am-10pm Mon-Thur; 7am-11pm Fri-Sun.* **Main courses** $8-$17. **Credit** AmEx, MC, V. **Map** p335 C3 ⊕
A rather scruffy-looking motel at the wrong end of Las Vegas Boulevard provides the unlikely setting for the most popular Cuban restaurant in Las Vegas. This isn't subtle food, by any means, and nor is it especially healthy. But don't let that stop you – as comfort cooking goes, it's just exotic enough to stand out from the pack. Try a Cuban sandwich if you're not absolutely ravenous.

Thai, Vietnamese & Pan-Asian

Thai BBQ
*1424 S 3rd Street, at Las Vegas Boulevard South
(383 1128). Bus Deuce.* **Open** 11am-10pm daily.
Main courses $7-$18. **Credit** AmEx, DC, Disc,
MC, V. **Map** p335 C3 �72
Despite its gritty locale, Thai BBQ remains one of
the best Thai eateries in town. The friendly and helpful service makes choosing from the large menu of
Thai specialities simple; the hearty portions of such
classics as pad Thai are worth the trip. Highlights
include papaya salad, excellent satay, and rich and
spicy beef noodle soup.

East of the Strip

American & steakhouses

AJ's Steakhouse
Hard Rock *4455 Paradise Road, at E Harmon
Avenue (693 5500/www.hardrockhotel.com).
Bus 108.* **Open** 6-11pm Tue-Sat. **Main courses**
$19-$37. **Credit** AmEx, DC, Disc, MC, V. **Hotel** p96.
Map p336 C7 ⓣ78
The vibe outside AJ's upholstered door may be Hard
Rock, but it's a Rat Pack state of mind within.
Named after the father of Hard Rock founder Peter
Morton, AJ's is a flashback to old Vegas. Powerful
martinis at the bar, a pianist crooning standards and
some of the finest cuts of meat in town are just a few
reasons that so many stars make it a regular haunt.

Brewed Awakenings
*2305 E Sahara Avenue, at S Eastern Avenue (457
7050). Bus 110, 204.* **Open** 6.30am-4pm Mon-Fri;
7am-2pm Sat. **Main courses** $5-$7. **Credit** AmEx,
DC, Disc, MC, V. **Map** p333 Z2 ⓣ74
Take out the casino buffets, the stuff-yourself-silly
diners and the ubiquitous Starbucks, and there
aren't many spots in Las Vegas in which to enjoy a
light breakfast and a meditative coffee. This is one
of the few. The menu here is pretty short: oatmeals
and sandwiches, coffees and teas. But it's all pretty
decent stuff, and the environment is blissfully quiet.

Envy
Renaissance *3400 Paradise Road, between E
Desert Inn Road & E Twain Avenue (784 5716/
www.envysteakhouse.com). Bus 108, 213.* **Open**
6.30am-2pm; 5-10.30pm daily. **Main courses**
Breakfast $11-$19. *Lunch* $12-$18. *Dinner* $28-$56.
Credit AmEx, DC, Disc, MC, V. **Hotel** p101.
Map p335 C6 ⓣ75
Plenty of big deals are hammered out at this modern steakhouse during convention season. House
specialities include American Kobe (or more properly, Wagyu) beef, and a bone-in filet served with
foie gras and preserved cherry sauce; lobster arrives
with a decadent vanilla-infused butter. Wash everything down with one of the 1,500 bottles of wine
housed in a candlelit, walk-in cellar and wine wall.

Mr Lucky's 24/7
Hard Rock *4455 Paradise Road, at E Harmon
Avenue (693 5592/www.hardrockhotel.com).
Bus 108.* **Open** 24hrs daily. **Main courses** $9-$19.
Credit AmEx, DC, Disc, MC, V. **Hotel** p96.
Map p336 C7 ⓣ76
The prices have gone up a little, the servings seem
to be smaller, and the previously hush-hush $7.77
steak-and-shrimp special is now advertised on a cue
card placed on every table. However, the Hard
Rock's mid '90s reinvention of the classic diner oth-
erwise rolls on unchanged, dishing out burgers,
sandwiches and breakfast classics (try the huevos
rancheros) to a disparate pre- and post-party crowd.
Great people-watching too.

Otto's Malt Shop
*4440 S Maryland Parkway, at E Harmon Avenue
(796 6886/www.ottosmaltshop.com). Bus 109.*
Open 11am-8pm Mon-Fri; noon-5pm Sat. **Main
courses** $5-$7. **Credit** DC, MC, V. **Map** p333 ⓣ77
Housed in one of Maryland Parkway's scruffiest
strip malls, this jaunty little hangout is done out with
a rather curious mix of sci-fi memorabilia and
bargain-basement diner furniture. However, you're
really here for the food: alongside the eponymous,
unmissable malts, Otto Miller and Ruthie Colgrove
together dish up the best burgers in the city,
serving their crowd of collegiate regulars with a
smile. *Photo p165.*

Platinum Restaurant
Platinum *211 E Flamingo Road, at Koval Lane
(365 2525/www.platinumhotel.com). Bus 202.*
Open 6am-3pm, 5-10pm daily. **Main courses**
Breakfast $10-$19. *Lunch* $12-$50. *Dinner* $19-$49.
Credit AmEx, DC, Disc, MC, V. **Hotel** p101.
Map p336 B7 ⓣ78
Chef Brenton Hammer is Las Vegas's foremost
devotee of the new molecular gastronomy school,
whereby chefs rely on cutting-edge science to create
novel dishes. His specialties include lamb served
with a glass of 'rosemary air', and sorbet coated with
Pop Rocks. But don't be intimidated. The food may
sound weird and look silly, but Hammer relies on
the finest ingredients. Breakfast and lunch are more
traditional, but still on the playful side.

Simon Kitchen & Bar
Hard Rock *4455 Paradise Road, at E Harmon
Avenue (693 4440/www.hardrockhotel.com). Bus
108.* **Open** 6-10.30pm Mon-Fri; 6-11pm Sat, Sun.
Main courses $22-$44. **Credit** AmEx, DC, Disc,
MC, V. **Hotel** p96. **Map** p336 C7 ⓣ79
With the sale of the Hard Rock, rumours persist that
Simon, arguably the city's first scene eatery, might
be short on life. But for now, the scene is very much
alive and kicking. When he's in town, Kerry Simon
acts the consummate host, while groovy music
provides the backdrop to top-shelf retro comfort
food (massive shrimp cocktail, meatloaf, giant bowls
of cotton candy). No matter if your album hasn't hit
platinum: the hosts do a great job of making
everyone a star.

French & Mediterranean

Firefly

3900 Paradise Road, between E Flamingo Road & Sands Avenue (369 3971/www.fireflylv.com). Bus 108. **Open** *11.30am-2am Mon-Thur; 11.30am-3am Fri; 5pm-3am Sat; 5pm-2am Sun.* **Main courses** *$11-$20. Tapas $3-$10.* **Credit** AmEx, Disc, MC, V. **Map** p336 C6 ⑩

This popular tapas bar is populated by a parade of pretty locals almost every night of the week. Music (downtempo to Latin house) competes with sangria-fuelled chatter, as small plates – scrumptious bacon-wrapped dates, mushroom tarts, shrimp ceviche – emerge from the busy kitchen. The loungey scene and reasonable prices conspire to let you spend as little or as much as you'd like.

Pamplemousse

400 E Sahara Avenue, at Paradise Road (733 2066/ www.pamplemousserestaurant.com). Bus 108, 204. **Open** *5.30-10.30pm Tue-Sun.* **Main courses** *$18-$29.* **Credit** AmEx, DC, MC, V. **Map** p335 C4. ⑪

Along with André's (*see p172*) and the Bootlegger (*see p174*), Georges La Forge's eaterie is one of a very few non-casino old Vegas classics, having served country-style French fare to such regulars as Wayne Newton and Robin Leach for years. The menu-less tradition continues today: the staff recite the choices, so be sure to pay attention. Dishes include fettuccini a la Georges, reportedly invented when Frank Sinatra asked La Forge to create him a dish he'd never forget.

German

Hofbrauhaus

4510 Paradise Road, at E Harmon Avenue (853 2337/www.hofbrauhauslasvegas.com). Bus 108. **Open** *11am-11pm Mon-Thur, Sun; 11am-midnight Fri, Sat.* **Main courses** *Lunch $9-$15. Dinner $15-$25.* **Credit** AmEx, DC, Disc, MC, V. **Map** p336 C8 ⑫

Planting this near-identical replica of the famous Munich beerhall across from the Hard Rock was a great idea, but the results are hot and cold. To wit: pretzel girls, hot; the rest of the menu, not. Still, while the authentic German grub is mostly bland, the beer makes up for it. Unlike the Munich original, the *biergarten* (beer garden) has a roof, making it feel like little more than a glorified cafeteria.

Indian

Gandhi

4080 Paradise Road, at E Flamingo Road (734 0094/www.gandhicuisine.com). Bus 108, 202. **Open** *11am-2.30pm, 5-10.30pm daily.* **Main courses** *Lunch buffet $11. Dinner $10-$23.* **Credit** AmEx, Disc, MC, V. **Map** 336 C7 ⑬

Good Northern Indian and Southern Indian cuisine, including a fine selection of vegetarian dishes,

are combined at this longtime local favourite. The all-you-can-eat lunch buffet is nice and spicy, and stars such dishes as chicken pakora, keema naan (stuffed bread with minced lamb) and chicken tikka masala for next to nothing.

Origin India

4480 Paradise Road, at E Harmon Avenue (734 6342/www.originindiarestaurant.com). Bus 108. **Open** *11.30am-11.30pm daily.* **Main courses** *$10-$23.* **Credit** AmEx, DC, Disc, MC, V. **Map** p336 C7 ⑭

Having reigned unchallenged for years, Gandhi has some genuine competition for the title of Vegas's best Indian eaterie, and less than a half-mile down the street. The lowlit swank of Origin India differentiates it from its competition, but the pleasingly spicy food is also a class apart, with classics such as *saag gosht* (lamb with spinach) and a creamy chicken *makhani* rendered in technicolour brilliance. *Photo p166.*

Japanese

Nobu

Hard Rock *4455 Paradise Road, at E Harmon Avenue (693 5090/www.hardrockhotel.com). Bus 108.* **Open** *6-11pm daily.* **Main courses** *$11-$80.* **Credit** AmEx, DC, Disc, MC, V. **Hotel** p96. **Map** p336 C7 ⑮

Plenty of imitators have emerged in recent years, trying to replicate chef Nobu Matsuhisa's Japanese fusion cuisine and ultra-hip room. But Nobu remains the original, one reason why it will probably never lose its credibility or its appeal. Big prices and little slices follow the leads of its New York and London brethren. If you can, indulge in the chef's Omakase tasting menu.

Togoshi Ramen

855 E Twain Avenue, at Swenson Street (737 7003). Bus 203. **Open** *11.30am-9.30pm daily.* **Main courses** *$6-$12.* **Credit** MC, V. **Map** p333 Y3 ⑯

If the only ramen you've tried is the bulk, packaged, grocery-store ramen with powdered flavouring, hike here and try the real stuff. Known for its Japanese comfort-food fare, such as tonkatsu, gyoza and curry rice, this place specialises in much more than noodle soup. The menus are in English, but the specials are listed on the walls in Japanese and appeal to the true Japanese palate. Food is inexpensive.

Latin American

Esmerelda's

1000 E Charleston Boulevard, between E Charleston Boulevard & S Maryland Parkway (388 1404). Bus 109, 206. **Open** *11am-9pm daily.* **Main courses** *$6-$15.* **Credit** AmEx, MC, V. **Map** p333 D3 ⑰

There are a few Mexican dishes on the menu, a nod to the origins of its clientele. But the real reason to visit this unprepossessing storefront eaterie is for its range of calmer but still hearty Salvadorean specialities. Chow down on a *pupusa* or two, a flat corn tortilla stuffed variously with cheese or any number of different meats. Subtlety isn't a strong point of the kitchen here, but you'll leave replete.

Pink Taco

Hard Rock *4455 Paradise Road, at E Harmon Avenue (693 5000/www.hardrockhotel.com). Bus 108.* **Open** 11am-10pm Mon-Thur, Sun; 11am-midnight Fri, Sat. **Main courses** $8-$14. **Credit** AmEx, DC, Disc, MC, V. **Hotel** p96. **Map** p336 C7 ⑥⑧
Only the Hard Rock could get away with giving a restaurant such a jaw-droppingly euphemistic name. Happily, though, this Mexican eaterie transcends its rather smutty moniker. The menu doesn't hold any surprises, at least not if you stick to the favourites (burritos, enchiladas). Join the buzzing bar scene between 4pm and 7pm during the week for two for one beers and margaritas, plus half-price appetisers.

Thai, Vietnamese & Pan-Asian

Komol

Commercial Center, 953 E Sahara Avenue, between S 6th Street & S Maryland Parkway (731 6542/www. komolrestaurant.com). Bus 109, 204. **Open** 11am-10pm Mon-Sat; noon-10pm Sun. **Main courses** $8-$18. **Credit** AmEx, DC, Disc, MC, V. **Map** p333 Y2 ⑥⑨
Despite its location in the run-down Commercial Center, where it competes with the nationally renowned Lotus of Siam and a pair of nationally infamous sex clubs, Komol remains hugely popular

N9ne.

for its authentic rendering of Thai cuisine, a vast vegetarian menu, plus 1950s Americana such as egg foo yung, all at bargain prices. Specify the degree of heat you'd like, and the kitchen will try to comply.

Lotus of Siam

Commercial Center, 953 E Sahara Avenue, between S 6th Street & S Maryland Parkway (735 3033/www.lotusofsiamlv.com). Bus 109, 204. **Open** 11.30am-2pm Mon-Fri; 5.30-9pm daily. **Main courses** Lunch buffet $8. Dinner $8-$29. **Credit** AmEx, Disc, MC, V. **Map** p333 Y2 ⑨⓪
The knowledgeable folks at *Gourmet* magazine have rated this the best Thai restaurant in the US. We might not go quite that far, but Lotus of Siam is certainly a rare and unexpected treat in an unprepossessing strip mall otherwise dominated by gay bars and swingers' clubs. Saipin Chutima puts her specialities on the easy-to-read menu, and isn't afraid to make her food spicy. However, many diners opt for the excellent and super-cheap lunch buffet.

American & steakhouses

Golden Steer Steak House

308 W Sahara Avenue, between Las Vegas Boulevard South & S Industrial Road (384 4470/www.goldensteerlv.com). Bus 204. **Open** 5-11pm daily. **Main courses** $25-$85. **Credit** AmEx, Disc, MC, V. **Map** p335 B4 ⑨①
The enormous (and, yes, golden) steer that signposts this old-school steak place on Sahara Avenue also advertises its decor. Discreet it certainly is not: think updated bordello crossed with an Old West saloon and you're almost there. But the steaks are classic: large, juicy and perfectly grilled, albeit served at prices that could stun a cow at 20 paces. Sinatra and Dino both ate here; four-plus decades later, it remains vintage Vegas at its most unreconstructed.

N9ne

Palms *4321 W Flamingo Road, at S Valley View Boulevard (933 9900/www.n9nesteaks.com). Bus 201.* **Open** 5.30-10pm Mon-Thur, Sun; 5.30-11pm Fri, Sat. **Main courses** $25-$150. **Credit** AmEx, DC, Disc, MC, V. **Hotel** p98. **Map** p333 X3 ⑨②
Superb steak and seafood? Absolutely. A quiet spot for a date? Absolutely not. A busy bar scene, a DJ, busy lighting and acoustics seemingly designed to force diners to yell make N9ne, feel like a nightclub – and it's all intentional. The appetisers and sides are well-executed complements to the mains, and the flaming S'mores dessert is a show unto itself. A Saturday booking requires an A-list name or months of planning.

Omelet House

2160 W Charleston Boulevard, at S Rancho Drive (384 6868/www.omelethouse.net). Bus 206. **Open** 7am-3pm daily. **Main courses** $5-$9. **Credit** MC, V. **Map** p335 A3 ⑨③

Eat, Drink, Shop

Nove offers spectacular views and stylish interiors – at a price.

Omelettes aren't just the speciality at this basic, unassuming little diner: they're more or less the only thing on the menu. Sure, they make 'em in around 60 varieties, but eggs is eggs is eggs, and the kitchen here does 'em as well as anyone. Making plans for a subsequent dinner is unnecessary: each omelette is made with a preposterous six eggs, and will have you napping at the table until the heartburn wakes you up.

French

Alizé

Palms *4321 W Flamingo Road, at S Valley View Boulevard (951 7000/www.alizelv.com). Bus 201.* **Open** 5.30-10pm daily. **Main courses** $30-$50. **Credit** AmEx, DC, Disc, MC, V. **Hotel** p98. **Map** p333 X3 ❷❹

Up on the 56th floor, venerated local André Rochat (of longstanding Downtown restaurant André's; *see p172*) has hired chef Mark Purdy to maintain his classics and deliver some fresh takes on French cuisine. Many of the seasonal dishes – pan-seared Muscovy duck with peach and foie gras tarte tatin – taste as great as they sound. It comes at a price, but Rochat, who's been cooking foie gras in Vegas since Dan Tana was around, is the business.

Little Buddha

Palms *4321 W Flamingo Road, at S Valley View Boulevard (942 7778/www.littlebuddhalas vegas.com). Bus 201.* **Open** 5.30-11pm Mon-Thur,

Sun; 5.30pm-midnight Fri, Sat. **Main courses** $16-$50. **Credit** AmEx, DC, Disc, MC, V. **Hotel** p98. **Map** p333 X3 ❷❺

Buddha Bar's sexy baby sister serves decent fusion food in a dramatic setting. For want of space, the now-larger sushi bar is in the back room, but you can still belly up to the main room bar to bark your sashimi order over the soundtrack. Come here for the lively scene, the sounds and the sushi, and be sure to look as fabulous as possible, but leave the Asian cooking to the restaurants a mile north at Chinatown Plaza, where similar fare can be had for a lot less money.

Indian

Gaylord

Rio *3700 W Flamingo Road, at S Valley View Boulevard (777 2277/www.gaylordlv.com). Bus 202.* **Open** 11.30am-2.30pm, 5-11pm daily. **Main courses** $14-$28. **Credit** AmEx, DC, Disc, MC, V. **Hotel** p100. **Map** p333 X3 ❷❻

The best in-casino Indian restaurant in Las Vegas is also, the last time we checked, the only in-casino Indian restaurant in Las Vegas. Still, that's not to underplay the quality of the cooking at Gaylord, which remains higher than you might expect. Although the food does seem to have been toned down for an American audience, and prices are high, it retains a reassuring hint of authenticity. The decor is pleasing, and service is both friendly and efficient.

Italian

Nove

Palms *4321 W Flamingo Road, at S Valley View Boulevard (942 6800/www.n9negroup.com). Bus 201.* **Open** 5-11pm daily. **Main courses** $20-$60. **Credit** AmEx, Disc, MC, V. **Hotel** p98. **Map** p333 X3 ⑰

This expensive sister to N9ne (*see p169*) sits atop the Palms' new super-luxury Fantasy Tower and boasts one of the best views in town, along with beautiful modern decor. The steaks are mediocre and the service is steeped with attitude. But for all that, the only complaint you'll hear about the Nove spaghetti, prepared with lobster, shrimp, crab, scallops, calamari and basil, will relate to its $42 price tag.

Downtown

American & steakhouses

Bay City Diner

Golden Gate *1 E Fremont Street, at S Main Street (385 1906/www.goldengatecasino.net). Bus Deuce & all DTC-bound buses.* **Open** 24hrs Mon, Fri-Sun; 6am-2am Tue-Thur. **Main courses** $5-$15. **Credit** AmEx, DC, Disc, MC, V. **Hotel** p108. **Map** p334 C1 ⑱

Like the casino in which it's housed, this is an icon of old Vegas. There's nothing fussy or upscale about the Bay City Diner: it's just a small room serving basic food for 20 hours a day. But it oozes history, from the grainy decor via the predictable menu to the ageing, no-nonsense waitresses. Anyone interested in the city's past should eat here at least once.

Grill on Charleston

241 W Charleston Boulevard, between Las Vegas Boulevard South & I-15 (380 1110/www.lvgrill.com). Bus 206. **Open** 11am-2pm, 5pm-10pm daily. **Main courses** *Lunch* $8-$16. *Dinner* $12-$35. **Credit** AmEx, Disc, MC, V. **Map** p335 A3 ⑲

This little spot in the Holsum Lofts started out American, but new management brought an Italian slant to the menu in mid 2007. They're off to a good start with fuss-free Italian classics (*caprese*, fresh-baked pizza), plus imported wines and beers.

Hugo's Cellar

Four Queens *202 E Fremont Street, at S Casino Center Boulevard (385 4011/www.fourqueens.com). Bus Deuce & all DTC-bound buses.* **Open** 5-10pm daily. **Main courses** $38-$60. **Credit** AmEx, Disc, MC, V. **Hotel** p108. **Map** p334 D1 ⑩⓪

One of Vegas's original fine dining establishments. Hugo's old traditions are still good ones: pampering wait staff, a tableside visit from the famous salad cart, a solid wine list and a rose for the lady. The menu is vintage Vegas gourmet rather than fusion; heavy on the meat and seafood (steak and lobster are the stars), and just what you'd expect for dessert (cherries jubilee, bananas Foster).

Mickie Finnz Fish House

425 E Fremont Street, at Las Vegas Boulevard South (382 4204). Bus Deuce & all DTC-bound buses. **Open** 11am-2am daily. **Main courses** $6-$17. **Credit** AmEx, MC, V. **Map** p334 D1 ⑩①

Part of a Fremont Street triple threat since 2007 (alongside Irish pub Hennesseys and upscale Brass), this vaguely tiki spot is perfect for the laid-back Downtown crowd. Don't let the name trick you into thinking seafood is the main menu staple: although the grilled fish tacos really are delicious, the menu also offers a large selection of bar food and snakes (nachos, burgers, pizzas) intended to lay a good foundation for the drinking later on. Music at weekends (from local bands) veers from the unfortunate to the unexpectedly good.

Potato Valley Café

801 Las Vegas Boulevard South, at E Charleston Boulevard (363 7821/www.potatolasvegas.com). Bus Deuce, 206. **Open** 8am-4pm Mon-Fri. **Main courses** $4-$8. **Credit** AmEx, Disc, MC, V. **Map** p334 C3 ⑩②

The first western outpost for this urban business lunch mini-chain (the other two are in Annapolis, MD, and Washington, DC) features oven-roasted potatoes as a main course. When topped with everything from Cuban chicken to broccoli and blue cheese, they work a treat, albeit a very carb-heavy one. Less calorific options include a decent selection of sandwiches and salads.

Triple George

201 N 3rd Street, at E Ogden Avenue (384 2761/ www.triplegeorgegrill.com). Bus Deuce & all DTC-bound buses. **Open** 11am-4pm Mon; 11am-10pm Tue-Thur; 11am-11pm Fri; 4-11pm Sat. **Main courses** *Lunch* $9-$27. *Dinner* $17-$34. **Credit** AmEx, MC, V. **Map** p334 D1 ⑩③

A lunch haven for business suits but an evening haunt for more casually clad Downtowners, this subtly chic art deco room was conceived as a San Francisco-style chophouse, with a central wooden bar surrounded by several private dining enclosures. The steaks, seafood and chops are good, but it's the Louis salads and own-made soups that are the real highlight here. A valiant, upmarket addition to the area. *Photo p172.*

Vic & Anthony's

Golden Nugget *129 E Fremont Street, at S Casino Center Boulevard (386 8399/www.goldennugget. com). Bus Deuce & all DTC-bound buses.* **Open** 5-11pm daily. **Main courses** $22-$85. **Credit** AmEx, DC, Disc, MC, V. **Hotel** p104. **Map** p334 C1 ⑩④

Modelling itself as a classic Vegas steakhouse, with a live Maine lobster tank, masculine decor and attentive service, Vic & Anthony's manages to make a meal in a new restaurant feel like a step back in time. Start off the experience with a strong cocktail and a tray of fresh Blue Point oysters, then move on to mains of various seafood dishes, grain-fed beef or lamb and veal chops. A smart start to a vintage Vegas weekender.

Eat, Drink, Shop

French & Mediterranean

André's

*401 S 6th Street, at E Lewis Avenue (385 5016/
www.andresfrenchrest.com). Bus Deuce or 206.*
Open 6-11pm Mon-Sat. **Main courses** $28-$65.
Credit AmEx, DC, MC, V. **Map** p334 D2
Check out the expense-account crowd at this
Downtown institution, with patio dining that's
oh-so-New York. Chef and owner André Rochat
(also of Alizé; *see p170*), a local legend of sorts,
serves French haute cuisine accompanied by a
world-class wine cellar (though with few bargains).
The Monte Carlo branch even has a plush cigar and
cognac lounge.

Italian

Chicago Joe's

*820 S 4th Street, between E Gass & Hoover
Avenues (382 5637/www.chicagojoesrestaurant.
com). Bus Deuce, 206.* **Open** 11am-10pm Tue-Fri;
5-10pm Sat. **Main courses** $10-$39. **Credit** AmEx,
DC, Disc, MC, V. **Map** p334 C2
The kind of no-frills, fair-prices locals' favourite that
everyone loves, CJ's – located in a tiny 1932 brick
house – has lasted 30 years, thanks to its solid southern Italian cooking and regional specialities (Chicago
spicy lobster), and its homey, authentic but quirky
setting. Joe's is far removed from the $50 pasta joints
on the Strip, and that's the whole point.

Tinoco's Bistro

*103 E Charleston Boulevard, at S Main Street
(464 5008). Bus 206.* **Open** 11am-3pm, 5-10pm
Mon-Sat. **Main courses** *Lunch* $12-$18. *Dinner*
$17-$25.* **Credit** AmEx, DC, Disc, MC, V.
Map p335 C2
The arty industrial space was recently expanded to
meet demand (especially at lunch), and the menu
was slightly revamped, but chef Enrique Tinoco's
urban bistro remains an Arts District gem. Delicious
continental fare features (crab-stuffed shrimp on
risotto, veal picatta, and more) and the own-made
soups are a must.

Latin American & Southwestern

Doña Maria's

*910 Las Vegas Boulevard South, at E Charleston
Boulevard (382 6538). Bus Deuce, 206.* **Open** 8am-
10pm daily. **Main courses** *Lunch* $8-$12. *Dinner*
$12-$15.* **Credit** AmEx, DC, Disc, MC, V.
Map p334 C3
The prices are good and the location is central, but
Doña Maria's is very popular with the city's large
Mexican community for one reason above all others:
the loud and occasionally boisterous place offers
some of Vegas's best Mexican food. The tamales
(spicy chopped meat and ground corn, served in a
corn husk) are the real draw, but the tortas (sandwiches) and fiery salsas help keep the place busy.

Triple George. *See p171.*

El Sombrero

*807 S Main Street, at E Gass Avenue (382 9234).
Bus Deuce.* **Open** 11am-4pm Mon-Thur; 11am-
8.30pm Fri, Sat. **Main courses** $7-$13. **Credit**
AmEx, MC, V. **Map** p334 C2
The oldest continuously operating non-casino
eaterie in the city approaches its 60th birthday
much as it neared its 50th: with a shrug. Curiously,
gloriously oblivious to the last two decades of Strip
development, this small hut continues to dispense
unflashy but hearty Mexican peasant food to its
patrons, many of whom have been coming here for
years. Definitely a better bet than its rival Casa Don
Juan just down the street.

Middle Eastern

Kabob Korner

*507 E Fremont Street, at Las Vegas Boulevard
South (384 7722/www.kabobkornerlv.com). Bus
Deuce & all DTC-bound buses.* **Open** 10am-11pm
daily. **Main courses** $7-$9. **Credit** AmEx, DC,
Disc, MC, V. **Map** 334 D2
A tidy, tiny and unassuming urban storefront bang
in the middle of fast-rising Fremont Street, Kabob
Korner is a family-run and relatively inexpensive
boite. It serves a broad menu with something for
everyone; burgers, subs and pitta sandwiches, as
well as Halal-certified selections (try the tikka and
kebab dishes). This stretch of Fremont Street is fast
filling with increasingly fashionable bars, but this
agreeably basic enterprise remains its best eating
option at present.

Eat, Drink, Shop

The rest of the city

American & steakhouses

Big Mama's Rib Shack
2230 W Bonanza Road, at N Rancho Drive, North Las Vegas (597 1616/www.bigmamasribs.com). Bus 106. **Open** 11am-9pm Mon-Thur; 11am-10pm Fri, Sat; noon-8pm Sun. **Main courses** $3-$18. **Credit** AmEx, Disc, MC, V. **Map** p333 X1 ⓫
Other restaurants in town have their fans, but, at least for our money, this spartan place on a slightly sketchy stretch of Bonanza Road is the best barbecue joint in Las Vegas. Eat here two or three times a week, and you'll figure out why Mama got to be Big: this stuff is rich, hefty and irresistible.

Hash House a-Go Go
6800 W Sahara Avenue, at S Rainbow Boulevard (804 4646/www.hashhouseagogo.com). Bus 101, 204. **Open** 7.30am-2.30pm, 5-9.30pm Mon-Thur; 7.30am-2.30pm, 5-10pm Fri, Sat; 7.30am-2.30pm Sun. **Main courses** $10-$27. **Credit** AmEx, Disc, MC, V.
'Twisted farm food', advertises the menu, an altogether less appetising prospect than the excellent comfort cooking that's actually served at this capacious roadhouse. The dinners (chicken and biscuits, meat loaf) are great if pricey, and the lunches (sandwiches, burgers as big as your head) also impress. But to see the Hash House at its best, come for the phenomenal breakfasts and weekend brunches, which'll fill even the emptiest of stomachs.

M&M's Soul Food
3923 W Charleston Boulevard, at S Valley View Boulevard, West Las Vegas (453 7685/www.mmsoul foodcafe.com). Bus 104, 206. **Open** 7am-8pm daily. **Main courses** $12-$20. **Credit** AmEx, Disc, MC, V.
Speaking of comfort food, it doesn't get much heartier than the soul food dished up here. It's a pretty basic room; indeed, it feels a tad dreary after dark. But the food is fabulous, chicken, short ribs and other goodies dished up a variety of ways with an array of moreish sides (try the yams and the macaroni cheese). Get there in good time, mind: it closes early.

Table 34
600 E Warm Springs Road, between Bermuda & Paradise Roads, South-east Las Vegas (263 0034). Bus 217. **Open** 11am-3pm Mon-Fri; 5-9.30pm Tue-Sat. **Main courses** $14-$28. **Credit** AmEx, MC, V.
The comfortably modern decor serves as a palate cleanser for Puckish pizza (chef Wes Kendrick is a Wolfgang protégé), home-made soups and New American entrées such as braised pot roast, and mac and cheese with smoked ham and English peas, all surprisingly affordable.

Vintner Grill
10100 W Charleston Boulevard, at Hualapai Way, Summerlin (214 5590/www.vglasvegas.com). Bus 206. **Open** 11am-10pm Mon-Thur, Sun; 11am-11pm Fri, Sat. **Main courses** $17-$34. **Credit** AmEx, DC, Disc, MC, V.
The Corrigan family elevates the neighbourhood dining experience with this well-hidden New American bistro. With a dramatic interior design reminiscent of old Hollywood and a large patio area segmented into cosy dining nooks, Vintner almost overnight became the hottest table for well-heeled Summerlin folks. Could it be the Mediterranean-influenced menu (lamb osso bucco, wood-fired pizza)? The comfortable lounge? The sexy crowd?

Chinese

Shanghai Noon
3943 Spring Mountain Road, at S Valley View Boulevard, West Las Vegas (257 1628). Bus 104, 203. **Open** 11am-11pm daily. **Main courses** $7-$14. **Credit** MC, V. **Map** p333 X3 ⓬
The best Chinese food in Vegas? Perhaps, but unless you have the stomach for adventure, you'll be relegated to raving about the incredible noodles. This immensely popular hole-in-the-wall cockily struts out one gorgeous, low-priced plate after another of exotic, otherworldly sounding delights (seafood, hot pots; all translated on the specials menu) to giddy patrons who know their way around.

French & Mediterranean

Ambiance Bistro
3980 E Sunset Road, at Annie Oakley Drive, Henderson (454 3020/www.ambiancelasvegas. com). Bus 212. **Open** 11am-9pm Mon-Thur; 10am-9pm Fri, Sat. **Main courses** $14-$20. **Credit** AmEx, Disc, MC, V.
Though more and more people are discovering this lovely French bistro/bakery, it remains the province of those in the know (or in Cirque du Soleil, members of which frequent the place). Speaking French helps you get by, but staff will serve anyone with an appetite for proper pastries and French fare. For dinner, there's an upscale bistro menu.

Bonjour Bistro
9055 S Eastern Avenue, at E Pebble Road, Henderson (270 2102/wwwbonjourvegas.com). Bus 110. **Open** 5-10pm daily. **Main courses** $19-$25. **Credit** AmEx, MC, V.
Expat natives of Cannes operate this cheerful Green Valley bistro, where the service and the food more than justify the prices. A recent move has allowed for somewhat fancier decor, although the casual neighbourhood vibe remains. A well-chosen selection of wines complements a lengthy list of French Riviera traditions in appetisers (frogs' legs, onion soup), salads and entrées (seafood, steak au poivre).

Rosemary's Restaurant
8125 W Sahara Avenue, at S Cimmaron Road, West Las Vegas (869 2251/www.rosemarys restaurant.com). Bus 204. **Open** 11.30am-2.30pm, 5.30-10.30pm Mon-Fri; 5.30-10.30pm Sat, Sun. **Main courses** *Set lunch* $20. *Dinner* $25-$45. **Credit** AmEx, DC, Disc, MC, V.

Behind the strip-mall doors lies an alluring, comfortable room, and a kitchen that produces food on a par with more or less any restaurant on the Strip. The French-slanted, American-influenced menu lives up to its appetising descriptions: start with the carpaccio of beef and Maytag blue cheese, then try the pan-roasted sea scallops with parsnip potato purée, apple cider beurre blanc and crispy prosciutto. The wine list is among the best in town; the beer menu is a match for it.

Italian

Bleu Gourmet

8751 W Charleston Boulevard, between S Rampart Boulevard & S Durango Drive (363 2538/www.bleu gourmet.com). Bus 206. **Open** 10am-10pm daily. **Main courses** $13-$32. **Credit** AmEx, DC, Disc, MC, V.

Occupying the intersection of a Venn diagram consisting of a deli, a café, a wine bar and a bistro, this noble operation is all things to all people. Well, to some people, anyway: Bleu Gourmet never seems as busy as it deserves to be. However, it's worth the detour: the short, Italianate menu, available for eat-in or takeout, is cultured, and the wine and beer lists are both excellent. There's free Wi-Fi, too.

Bootlegger Bistro

7700 Las Vegas Boulevard South, at Blue Diamond Road, South of Strip (736 4939/www.bootlegger lasvegas.com). No bus. **Open** 24hrs daily. **Main courses** *Breakfast* $5-$13. *Lunch* $7-$13. *Dinner* $10-$31. **Credit** AmEx, Disc, MC, V.

This operation comes with a flamboyance that's two parts Italian, one part Las Vegan and three parts pure showbiz. There's a full menu here, Italian staples sold at prices several dollars too high. But the entertainment is the key: lounge acts with patter as old as the city itself. The fact that the owner is the Lieutenant Governor of Nevada, a lounge artist in her own right who'll happily do a turn when prompted, makes perfect sense. A 24-hour classic.

Casa di Amore

2850 E Tropicana Avenue, at S Eastern Avenue, East Las Vegas (433 4967/www.casadiamore.com). Bus 110, 201. **Open** 24hrs. **Main courses** *Lunch* $8-$10. *Dinner* $13-$24. **Credit** AmEx, Disc, MC, V. **Map** p 333 Z3 ⓭

The vibe in this cosy, clubby Amer-Italian spot is overwhelmingly '60s Vegas. The Rat Packmosphere and extended hours draw old-school Las Vegans around the clock for classic pizzas, authentic recipes (baked clams, chicken pasta soup) and seafood; however, it's at its busiest after-hours on weekends, when musicians entertain the crowds.

Gaetano's

10271 S Eastern Avenue, at Sienna Heights Drive, Henderson (361 1661). Bus 110. **Open** 5-10pm Mon-Thur; 5-10.30pm Fri, Sat; 5-9pm Sun. **Main courses** $12-$27. **Credit** AmEx, Disc, MC, V.

Henderson isn't known for its fine dining, but this *ristorante* holds its own among the Italian big boys thanks to mom-and-dad attention to detail. The charming Gaetano Palmeri and family are always there to ensure a good experience in this handsome dining room, where the tasty Northern Italian menu features the likes of gnocchi and osso buco.

Montesano's Deli & Restaurant

3441 W Sahara Avenue, between S Valley View Boulevard & S Rancho Drive, South-west Las Vegas (876 0348/www.montesanos.com). Bus 104, 204. **Open** 10am-9pm Mon-Sat. **Main courses** $7-$18. **Credit** AmEx, Disc, MC, V. **Map** p333 X2.

It might feel like a kitschy pop culture joint, but this long-time family-run establishment is an authentic slice of Brooklyn in Vegas that pre-dates *The Sopranos* by decades. In the deli/bakery, folks line up daily for fresh-baked bread, decadent desserts and tasty take-away. In the dining room, eggplant parmigiana and gnocchi with pink cream sauce compete with an extensive and original selection of pizzas. The tiramisu, cannoli and Italian cheesecakes are also superb.

Nora's Cuisine

6020 W Flamingo Road, at S Jones Boulevard, South-west Las Vegas (873 8990/www.noras cuisine.com). Bus 102, 202. **Open** 11am-2.30pm Mon-Fri; 4.30-10pm Mon-Thur; 4.30pm-midnight Fri, Sat. **Main courses** *Lunch* $5-$17. *Dinner* $8-$19. **Credit** AmEx, Disc, MC, V.

A classic family-run Italian restaurant, almost to the point of cliché. There are pizzas and there are mains, but the smart diner orders chicken Mount Etna, a cheese-topped chicken breast served over fried angel hair that's an absolute blast. Whatever you order, you won't need a starter: the bread is moreish and the portions are enormous. For variety, visit Nora's Wine Bar & Osteria (*see p187*).

Terra Rosa

Red Rock *11011 W Charleston Boulevard, at I-215, West Las Vegas (797 7576/www.redrock lasvegas.com). Bus 206.* **Open** noon-10pm Mon-Thur, Sun; noon-11pm Fri, Sat. **Main courses** $16-$46. **Credit** AmEx, DC, Disc, MC, V. **Hotel** p112.

Red Rock's signature Italian restaurant is too nice a room to suffer the indignity of shorts and T-shirts, and yet it does. A Tuscan menu (with some Italian-American choices) treats guests to own-made pasta, fresh fish specialities and the ubiquitous wood-fired pizza. Want something lighter? Dress well, snag a seat at the tiny bar and take a wine flight (from the 1,500-bottle wine room) with an antipasto appetiser.

Japanese

Sapporo

9719 W Flamingo Avenue, at I-215, West Las Vegas (216 3080/www.sapporestaurants.com). Bus 202. **Open** 4-11pm daily. **Main courses** $9-$16. **Credit** AmEx, DC, Disc, MC, V.

Rosemary's Restaurant offers an American take on classic French cuisine. *See p173.*

This suburban Las Vegas outpost of a Scottsdale favourite was reworked in 2007 to capitalise on the popularity of its indoor/outdoor lounge. The food is secondary to the socialising, but it's still very good. Most of the drink-and-diners are supping sushi, but a decent Pacific Rim menu and *teppanyaki* tables are available if you tire of the trendy bar scene.

Latin American

Agave
10820 W Charleston Boulevard, between I-215 & S Town Center Drive, Summerlin (214 3500/www.agave lasvegas.com). Bus 206. **Open** 24hrs daily. **Main courses** $11-$26. **Credit** AmEx, DC, Disc, MC, V.
This 24-hour cantina has emerged from its honeymooon period as a gathering place more than a restaurant. The menu reflects the adventurous decor, which offers a central Mexico vibe via imported Guadalajaran fixtures. Dishes such as goat tacos and a chile relleno stuffed with rock shrimp complement the numerous tequilas. The secluded patio is a wonderful spot to while away a happy hour.

Lindo Michoacan
2655 E Desert Inn Road, between S Eastern Avenue & S Pecos Road, East Las Vegas (735 6828/www. lindomichoacan.com). Bus 110, 213. **Open** 11am-10pm Mon-Thur; 10am-midnight Fri; 8am-midnight Sat; 8am-11pm Sun. **Main courses** *Lunch* $5-$7. *Dinner* $6-$17. **Credit** AmEx, DC, Disc, MC, V. **Map** p333 Z3 **115**

Las Vegas's favourite neighbourhood Mexican, Lindo is housed in a colourful, bigger-than-it-looks building out on Desert Inn, and is busy at virtually all times of day. The lunch specials are good value, but dinner is more enjoyable, with the menu of standards brought to life by an atmosphere that's never less than lively. The same family runs Bonito Michoacan on the west side (3715 S Decatur Boulevard, 1-702 257 6810) and Viva Michoacan in Henderson (2061 Sunset Road, 1-702 492 9888). *Photo p176.*

Zaba's Mexican Grill
3318 E Flamingo Road, at S Pecos Road, East Las Vegas (435 9222/www.zabas.com). Bus 111, 202. **Open** 10.30am-10pm Mon-Sat; 11am-8pm Sun. **Main courses** $5-$8. **Credit** AmEx, Disc, MC, V. **Map** p333 Z3 **116**
¡Aye-aye-aye! Part of the ever-growing trend of burrito and taco chains, Zaba's is as fresh as salsa fresca, with tender grilled meats and delectable guacamole. The decor is stark but the selections are miles away from fast food, despite the speed with which they're prepared. *¡Muy delicioso!*

Middle Eastern

Hedary's
7365 W Sahara Avenue, at S Buffalo Drive, West Las Vegas (873 9041/www.hedarys.com). Bus 204. **Open** 11am-3pm Mon-Sat; 5-10pm Mon-Thur; 5-11pm Fri, Sat. **Main courses** *Lunch* $9-$17. *Dinner* $13-$22. **Credit** AmEx, DC, Disc, MC, V.

Eat, Drink, Shop

¡Ay, caramba! Lively family-run Mexican joint **Lindo Michoacan**. *See p175.*

This comfortable outpost of the Lebanese Hedary family's Texas original offers fabulous, fresh renditions of falafel, houmous, tabouleh and kibbeh, plus plenty of speciality items (ftayir, mqaniq, lamb kebabs). For vegetarians, the tasting meze offers a never ending supply of incredibly good small plates.

Paymon's Mediterranean Café & Market
4147 S Maryland Parkway, at E Flamingo Road, University District (731 6030/www.paymons.com). Bus 108, 202. **Open** *Café* 11am-1am Mon-Thur; 11am-3am Fri, Sat; 11am-5pm Sun. *Market* 9am-8pm Mon-Fri; 10am-5pm Sat. **Main courses** $7-$15. **Credit** AmEx, DC, MC, V. **Map** p333 Y3 ⓲
Long before the idea caught on, Paymon Raouf was serving the kind of ethnic food that the college crowd adores. Even now, when so many Middle Eastern restaurants have opened up in Vegas, the Med – decent for dinner but best for lunch – still wins out, simply because its kebabs and salads are better than anyone else's. Next door's Hookah Lounge (*see p186*) makes an unlikely but effective companion.

Thai, Vietnamese & Pan-Asian

Satay Malaysian Grille
3755 Spring Mountain Road, at S Valley View Boulevard (362 2828/www.sataygrille.com). Bus 104, 203. **Open** 11am-11pm Mon-Thur, Sun; 11am-3am Fri, Sat. **Main courses** $8-$20. **Credit** AmEx, MC, V. **Map** p333 X3 ⓳

The chic, low-lit interior of this eaterie looks expensive, and the presence of an upscale cocktail menu raises fears that perhaps the owners have concentrated on style over substance. Happily, this is not the case. The food has few such ambitions, and remains firmly and pleasingly grounded in Malaysian tradition. The kitchen's rendition of nasi goreng is unflashy and thoroughly appetising, but the menu yields plenty of variety if you're in the mood for being adventurous.

Buffets

The idea of the buffet started in the 1940s at the original El Rancho. Looking to keep customers in his casino after the show, Beldon Katleman dreamed up the Midnight Chuckwagon Buffet, promising 'all you can eat for a dollar'. His idea of treating guests to a feast for a small price was soon copied and expanded by other hotels: why not offer it all day round?

Casino buffets typically serve breakfast, lunch and dinner, with many also offering an extended brunch at weekends. At most resorts, buffets cost $8-$15 for breakfast, $10-$17 for lunch and $15-$25 for dinner. Prices are lower in the locals' casinos away from the Strip; kids often eat for less (generally half-price). But whatever the price and time, all buffets work in the same way: you pay your money at the start and then stuff yourself silly from a range of at least 50 food selections, featuring everything from salads to cakes.

However, a few rules do apply to all buffets. Eat as much as you want while you're there, but don't take anything away with you. Health codes oblige you to take a new plate every time you return; leave your plates and a small tip on the table, to be picked up by the staff. And to avoid queuing, arrive early for breakfast, late for lunch and early for dinner.

In addition to the buffets detailed below, other hotel buffets are notable, whether by dint of size (the buffet at **Circus Circus** (see p89) serves up to 10,000 diners a day), price (**Palace Station** (see p116) is among the best of the cheaper options) or quality of food (the **Mirage** (see p73), **Main Street Station** (see p105) and **Caesars Palace** (see p68) all offer decent spreads). Locals' casinos such as the **Suncoast** (see p117) and **Sunset Station** (see p117) offer ordinary food at ridiculously cheap prices. And for the best-kept buffet secret in town, visit the **Verandah Café** (see p157) for weekend brunch.

Bay Side Buffet

Mandalay Bay *3950 Las Vegas Boulevard South, at W Hacienda Avenue (632 7777/www.mandalay bay.com). Bus Deuce, 104, 105.* **Buffets** *Breakfast 7-11am daily. Lunch 11am-2.45pm daily. Dinner 2.45-10pm daily.* **Prices** $9.25-$12.75 breakfast; $11.50-$15.50 lunch; $19.75-$22.75 brunch/dinner. **Credit** AmEx, DC, Disc, MC, V. **Hotel** p71. **Map** p336 A9 ⑪⑨
Flexing its marketing muscle in the direction of the sophisticated, moneyed traveller, Mandalay Bay has chosen not to make a big deal about its good quality buffet. A pity: while the selection isn't anything remarkable, it's very well executed and is decent value to boot.

Big Kitchen Buffet/Sterling Brunch

Bally's *3645 Las Vegas Boulevard South, at E Flamingo Road (967 4111/www.harrahs.com). Bus Deuce, 202.* **Buffets** *Big Kitchen Buffet: Brunch 7am-4pm daily. Dinner 4-10pm daily. Sterling Brunch: 9.30am-2.30pm Sun.* **Prices** *Big Kitchen Buffet* $12.95 brunch; $18.95 dinner. *Sterling Brunch* $58. **Credit** AmEx, Disc, MC, V. **Hotel** p77. **Map** p336 A7 ⑫⓪
The daily Big Kitchen Buffet at Bally's is one of the town's best. However, Sunday's swanky Sterling Brunch, which is held in a separate space, really takes the biscuit …and the caviar, the lobster, the beef tenderloin and the champagne cocktail. Skip church and indulge yourself.

Buffet at Bellagio

Bellagio *3600 Las Vegas Boulevard South, at W Flamingo Road (693 7111/www.bellagio.com). Bus Deuce, 202.* **Buffets** *Breakfast 8-10.30am Mon-Fri. Brunch 8am-3.30pm Sat, Sun. Lunch 11am-3.30pm*

daily. *Dinner 4-10pm Mon-Thur, Sun; 4-11pm Fri, Sat.* **Prices** $13.95 breakfast; $21.95 brunch; $17.95 lunch; $25.95-$33.95 dinner. **Credit** AmEx, Disc, MC, V. **Hotel** p68. **Map** p336 A7 ⑫①
The Buffet at Bellagio is much like the rest of the hotel: smart yet approachable, stylish yet undemonstrative, expensive yet probably just about worth it. Usual buffet fare gets upgraded with extras such as venison, steamed clams and crab legs.

Carnival World Buffet

Rio *3700 W Flamingo Road, at S Valley View Boulevard, West of Strip (777 7777/www.harrahs .com). Bus 202.* **Buffets** Carnival World Buffet: *Breakfast 7-11am Mon-Fri; 7.30-10.30am Sat, Sun. Brunch 10.30am-3.30pm Sat, Sun. Lunch 11am-3.30pm Mon-Fri. Dinner 3.30-10pm daily.* Village Seafood Buffet: *Dinner 4-10pm Mon-Thur, Sun; 4-11pm Fri, Sat.* **Prices** *Carnival World Buffet* $13.99 breakfast; $23.99 brunch; $16.99 lunch; $23.99 dinner. *Village Seafood Buffet* $34.99. **Credit** AmEx, Disc, MC, V. **Hotel** p100. **Map** p333 X3 ⑫②
A favourite among locals, the pioneering Carnival World Buffet journeys the planet for its food. It's an idea that several other casinos have since copied, but no one has yet topped the Rio's inter-continental spreads, which take in everything from lasagne to Peking duck. The separate Seafood Buffet offers sushi, oysters and lobster, as well as a surprising range of meat dishes.

Golden Nugget Buffet

Golden Nugget *129 E Fremont Street, at S Casino Center Boulevard, Downtown (385 7111/www.golden nugget.com). Bus Deuce & all DTC-bound buses.* **Buffets** *Breakfast 7-10.30am Mon-Fri. Brunch 8am-3.30pm Sat, Sun. Lunch 10.30am-3.30pm Mon-Fri. Dinner 3.30-10pm daily.* **Prices** $8.99 breakfast; $15.99-$16.99 brunch; $9.99 lunch; $16.99-$19.99 dinner. **Credit** AmEx, Disc, MC, V. **Hotel** p104. **Map** p334 C1 ⑫③
Revamped and relocated within the all-new Golden Nugget, Downtown's smartest buffet more than delivers the goods that its reputation demands of it. The new room isn't as cosy, but the quality of the food more than compensates. The offerings are near the top of the Vegas food chain, especially the carvery and the excellent desserts.

Le Village Buffet

Paris Las Vegas *3655 Las Vegas Boulevard South, at E Flamingo Road (946 7000/www.harrahs. com). Bus Deuce, 202.* **Buffets** *Breakfast 7-11am daily. Brunch 11am-3.30pm Sat, Sun. Lunch 11.30am-3.30pm Mon-Fri. Dinner 3.30-10pm daily.* **Prices** $12.95 breakfast; $24.95 brunch; $17.95 lunch; $24.95 dinner. **Credit** AmEx, DC, Disc, MC, V. **Hotel** p74. **Map** p336 A7 ⑫④
The one French-themed casino in town really should offer a good buffet, and so it goes. The 400-seat Le Village Buffet has stations representing five French provinces and dishes up a variety of surprisingly fine foods (it's especially good for meat-lovers). But go easy on starters and mains, so as to save room for the fresh pastries and desserts.

Bars & Lounges

The world's most weird and wonderful watering holes.

You're sporting a furry ushanka to ward off the sub-zero temperatures. You're sipping banana-flavoured vodka. You're staring at a giant bronze head of Lenin. You're in the 'vodka locker' (read: freezer) of **Red Square**, a bar that, by taking its theme to the zenith of ridiculousness, is perfectly, archetypally Vegas.

The hallucinatory creativity that built a neon oasis in the desert has also been employed in the construction of the city's bars. The resorts are dotted with the kind of piano bars, meat markets and casual lounges you might expect to find. However, you can also sink beers with swimming mermaids, down martinis on a revolving carousel, and piss on the Berlin Wall. Should these gimmicks fail to inculcate a sense of wonder, a bacon martini may do the trick.

Wherever you prefer to take your libations, one thing you won't hear very often is the phrase 'last call'. Liquor flows as freely at five in the morning as it does at five in the evening: most of the bars in town, including at least one in every casino, are open 24 hours a day, though it should be noted that you're just as likely to be refused service here as in other cities.

Although there are a few exceptions, among them the **Artisan** and the **Downtown Cocktail Room**, the bartops at most off-Strip, non-casino hangouts are lined with video poker machines. Indeed, many such bars are kept afloat as much by gambling revenue as by alcohol sales. If you're gambling, drinks are usually free with a minimal deposit (usually $10

to $20) into your nearest machine; always ensure that the bartender knows you're playing.

In early 2007, the wild west became a little more straight-laced when smoking was banned in bars that serve food. By the summer, some bars were strictly enforcing the new diktat, even closing their kitchens to ensure that they stayed within the law. Others exploited a loophole by inviting customers to order food from outside establishments (pizza delivery, for example). And still others turned a blind eye, aware that if the ban is broken, it's the customer rather than the bar owner who's in for punishment. Keep that in mind before lighting up.

In addition to the bars listed below, small music venues such as the **Bunkhouse Saloon** also function as bars; *see pp252-254*. A number of restaurants also boast busy bars, among them **Aureole** (*see p153*). And keep an eye out for the likeable, western-themed **Roadrunner** mini-chain (http://roadrunnerlasvegas.com).

THE LAW

You have to be 21 to consume or buy alcohol in Nevada. If you look less than 40, you'll regularly be required to produce photo ID, such as a driver's licence or passport. Las Vegas's drink-driving laws are as harsh and uncompromising as in any major US city, and the cops don't let too many woozy fish swim by. So leave the car behind: you can easily walk back and forth between bars on the Strip and Fremont Street, and a taxi ride to and from most of the more distant joints will be cheap. Cabs are plentiful around the Strip; elsewhere, the bartender will be happy to call one for you.

The best Bars

For old Vegas absurdity
Horse-a-Round Bar. See p180.

For new Vegas sophistication
Downtown Cocktail Room. See p184.

For making your day, punk
Double Down Saloon. See p183.

For joining in on the chorus
Bar at Times Square. See p178.

For the benefit of Mr Kite
Revolution. See p180.

The Strip

Bar at Times Square
New York New York *3790 Las Vegas Boulevard South, at W Tropicana Avenue (236 0374/www. nynyhotelcasino.com). Bus Deuce, 201.* **Open** 10am-2am Mon-Wed; 10am-3am Thur, Sun; 10am-4am Fri, Sat. **Credit** AmEx, Disc, MC, V. **Hotel** p84. **Map** p336 A8 ❶
Bellowing voices pour from this packed bar, where duelling pianos provide the upbeat entertainment.

❶ Pink numbers given in this chapter correspond to the location of each bar on the street maps. See pp333-336.

Centrifuge.

Sure, there's beer behind the emotion, but there's also a lot of genuine fun being had. The musicians can and will play anything if you've got the money to tip 'em. The best of the city's piano bars.

Caramel

Bellagio *3600 Las Vegas Boulevard South, at W Flamingo Road (693 8300/www.caramelbar.com). Bus Deuce, 202.* **Open** 5pm-4am daily. **Credit** AmEx, Disc, MC, V. **Hotel** p68. **Map** p336 A7 ❷
With opaque marble tables, one-way windows on to the casino floor and a sophisticated, ultra-modern atmosphere, Caramel seems less like a lounge than a private club. And that, naturally, comes at a price: $15 speciality martinis are the norm. As the night wears on and the crowds thicken, the swanky couches are reserved for parties willing to pony up about $300 or more for bottle service.

Centrifuge

MGM Grand *3799 Las Vegas Boulevard South, at E Tropicana Avenue (891 7777/www.mgm grand.com). Bus Deuce, 201.* **Open** 4pm-2am daily. **Credit** AmEx, DC, Disc, MC, V. **Hotel** p81. **Map** p336 A8 ❸
Having dramatically remade its range of restaurants in recent years, the MGM is now turning its attention to its bars. Along with Rouge, this 2007 addition is the most eye-catching, a circular bar near the front of the casino with TV screens, dancing girls and excellent cocktails. It's more expensive than it should be, but worth a look nonetheless.

Coyote Ugly

New York New York *3790 Las Vegas Boulevard South, at W Tropicana Avenue (740 6969/www. coyoteuglysaloon.com/vegas). Bus Deuce, 201.* **Open** 6pm-4am daily. **Credit** AmEx, Disc, MC, V. **Map** p336 A8 ❹
Belly-baring servers stomp to choreographed dances in this saloon, based on the New York bar that was the subject of a ghastly movie. The schtick goes that the girls invite boozed-up revellers to join them up on the bar, while simultaneously hurling insults at the crowd below. To add injury to insults, there's nowhere to sit, and it takes a lot of expensive liquor to make you forget the $10 cover charge (after 9pm).

ESPN Zone

New York New York *3790 Las Vegas Boulevard South, at W Tropicana Avenue (933 3776/www.espn zone.com/lasvegas). Bus Deuce, 201.* **Open** 11am-11pm Mon-Thur, Sun; 11am-midnight Fri, Sat. **Credit** AmEx, Disc, MC, V. **Hotel** p84. **Map** p336 A8 ❺
Each table at this restaurant/bar/funitorium has its own TV, and that's in addition to the two 16ft monitors, 12 flat screens and various headline tickers letting drinkers know what they've missed. The smell of testosterone is almost overwhelming.

Fix

Bellagio *3600 Las Vegas Boulevard South, at W Flamingo Road (693 8400/www.fixlasvegas.com). Bus Deuce, 202.* **Open** 5pm-midnight Mon-Thur, Sun; 5pm-2am Fri, Sat. **Credit** AmEx, Disc, MC, V. **Hotel** p68. **Map** p336 A7 ❻

This upscale bar and restaurant is known for its tasty appetisers and tantalising beverages, striking a careful balance between sleekness and comfort in both decor and menu. The waiting staff seem to have been selected from a genetic pool that counts hotness as the main determinant of survival.

Horse-a-Round Bar

Circus Circus *2880 Las Vegas Boulevard South, between W Sahara Avenue & Desert Inn Road (734 0410/www.circuscircus.com). Bus Deuce.* **Open** 4.30pm-midnight Fri, Sat. **Credit** AmEx, Disc, MC, V. **Hotel** p89. **Map** p335 B5 **7**

There are few more extraordinary places for a tipple in Las Vegas than this reopened merry-go-round bar, surrounded by screaming children, carousel horses, jugglers and deeply sinister clowns. Made famous by Hunter S Thompson in *Fear and Loathing in Las Vegas*, it remains an absolute must for seekers of the weird.

I Love this Bar & Grill

Harrah's *3475 Las Vegas Boulevard South, between Sands Avenue & E Flamingo Road (369 5000/www.harrahs.com). Bus Deuce, 105, 203.* **Open** 11.30am-11pm Mon-Thur; 11.30am-midnight Fri; 10am-midnight Sat; 10am-11pm Sun. **Credit** AmEx, Disc, MC, V. **Hotel** p79. **Map** p336 A6 **8**

Boot-scoot your way on down here for a cold domestic and some Southern-fried fun. Named after his hit single 'I Love this Bar', Toby Keith's place is tinged with country. But even those repelled by cowboy hats might find it's their kind of place, since it doesn't smash you over the ten-gallon hat with its theme.

Jimmy Buffet's Margaritaville

Flamingo *3555 Las Vegas Boulevard South, at E Flamingo Road (733 3302/www.margaritaville.com). Bus Deuce, 202.* **Open** 10.45am-2am Mon-Thur, Sun; 10.45am-3am Fri, Sat. **Credit** AmEx, DC, Disc, MC, V. **Hotel** p78. **Map** p336 A7 **9**

You've heard of Deadheads, right? Well, here you'll find their ornithological equivalent: Parrotheads, men dressed in khaki shorts and floral shirts with parrots perched on their heads, united in their devotion to the self-described 'gulf and western' music of Jimmy Buffet. The ambience is not for the faint of heart or the sophisticated of taste.

Mist

Treasure Island *3300 Las Vegas Boulevard South, at Spring Mountain Road (894 7330/www.mistbar.com). Bus Deuce, 105, 203.* **Open** 5pm-4am Mon-Fri; 10am-4pm Sat, Sun. **Credit** AmEx, Disc, MC, V. **Hotel** p87. **Map** p335 & p336 A6 **10**

Treasure Island's attempt to evoke the Bellagio's Caramel, Mist is a handsomely appointed but slightly soulless bar done out with dark colours and sleek, minimalist decor. Try the speciality Bugsy Siegel martini and then move right along; preferably before it hits 9pm, when you have to purchase a bottle to be allowed seating away from the bar.

Napoleon's

Paris Las Vegas *3655 Las Vegas Boulevard South, at E Flamingo Road (946 7000/www.harrahs.com). Bus Deuce, 202.* **Open** 4pm-2am Mon-Thur, Sun; 2pm-3am Fri, Sat. **Credit** AmEx, Disc, MC, V. **Hotel** p74. **Map** p336 A7 **11**

There are 100 varieties of champagne from which to choose at this longstanding hangout within the Paris resort. They're a better choice than the rather over-inventive cocktails, and certainly more authentic than the obligatory duelling pianists, who work their way through Parisian classics such as, er, 'Goodbye Yellow Brick Road' and 'Living on a Prayer'.

Parasol Up/Parasol Down

Wynn Las Vegas *3131 Las Vegas Boulevard South, between E Desert Inn Road & Sands Avenue (770 7000/www.wynnlasvegas.com). Bus Deuce, 203.* **Open** *Parasol Up* 24hrs daily. *Parasol Down* 9am-1am daily. **Credit** AmEx, DC, MC, V. **Hotel** p76. **Map** p335 & p336 B6 **12**

Whether you're up or down, there's a Parasol cocktail for you. These two pricey, Euro-chi-chi hangouts overlooking the waterfall, itself projected with images and colours, have more charm than standard casino bars, and are full of the sort of beautiful, wealthy people that like to hang out at this most chichi of resorts.

Peppermill's Fireside Lounge

2985 Las Vegas Boulevard South, at Convention Center Drive (735 7635). Bus Deuce, 203. **Open** 24hrs daily. **Credit** AmEx, DC, Disc, MC, V. **Map** p335 B5 **13**

Known for the seats around the combination firepit-fountain and for the luxuriant dresses worn by the bosomy waitresses, this place is old Vegas at its best. Or, at least, it was, until they put flat-screen TVs on every available surface and ruined the vintage feel. Still, the drinks are impressive; try a Scorpion, which will arrive in a glass that's bigger than your head.

Red Square

Mandalay Bay *3950 Las Vegas Boulevard South, at W Hacienda Avenue (632 7407/www.mandalaybay.com). Bus Deuce, 104, 105.* **Open** 5pm-2am Mon-Thur, Sun; 5pm-3am Fri, Sat. **Credit** AmEx, Disc, MC, V. **Hotel** p71. **Map** p336 A9 **14**

The vodkas here are so good they made Lenin lose his head. Well, that's the only rational explanation for the enormous decapitated statue of the father of the Soviet Union over the entrance, though you can always ask the barman what happened to Vlad's missing body part (it's in the walk-in 'vodka locker' on ice). The food is fine and the drinks are strong.

Revolution

Mirage *3400 Las Vegas Boulevard South, between Spring Mountain & W Flamingo Roads (791 7111/www.thebeatlesrevolutionlounge.com). Bus Deuce, 105, 202, 203.* **Open** 6pm-4am daily. **Credit** AmEx, Disc, MC, V. **Hotel** p73. **Map** p335 & p336 A6 **15**

Eat, Drink, Shop

Evenings by the fire come with a difference at **Peppermill's Fireside Lounge**.

If you want to drink to a Beatles soundtrack, arrive early, before the group are ditched in favour of a more contemporary soundtrack. That aside, the Fab Four theme of this spot is generally carried out pretty well, with subtle and not-so-subtle nods to classic songs (crystals hanging from the ceiling, portholes behind the bar). Interactive tabletops, like giant Etch-a-Sketches, are a highlight. For a more low-key spot, try the Abbey Road Bar just in front of Revolution.

Rockhouse
Imperial Palace *3535 Las Vegas Boulevard South, between Sands Avenue & E Flamingo Road (735 0977/www.imperialpalace.com). Bus Deuce, 105, 203.* **Hotel** p80. **Map** p336 A6 ⑯
The new Rockhouse is like an adolescent searching for his identity before realising that it's easier to find large-breasted women. Other attractions include a mechanical bull, go-go dancers, bottle service, multiple American flags, a stage, and a whole lot of people standing around, not quite sure what to do with themselves. If in doubt, ogle.

Shadow Bar
Caesars Palace *3570 Las Vegas Boulevard South, at W Flamingo Road (731 7110/www.harrahs.com). Bus Deuce, 202.* **Open** 4pm-2am Mon-Thur; 2pm-3am Fri, Sat; 2pm-2am Sun. **Credit** AmEx, DC, Disc, MC, V. **Hotel** p68. **Map** p336 A7 ⑰
Question: how do you get naked women to shake, writhe and strut their stuff without showing any flesh? Answer: shadow play. This saucy spot continues Las Vegas's hesitating shimmy towards bringing strip clubs to the Strip without having any

stripping. The ladies concerned, silhouetted on screens, play up what comes naturally (or, possibly, surgically), while expensive drinks add a haughty note. The dress code is smart-casual.

V Bar
Venetian *3555 Las Vegas Boulevard South, between Sands Avenue & E Flamingo Road (414 3200/www.venetian.com). Bus Deuce, 105, 203.* **Open** 5pm-3am Mon-Wed, Sun; 5pm-4am Thur-Sat. **Credit** AmEx, DC, Disc, MC, V. **Hotel** p75. **Map** p335 & p336 B6 ⑱
Brought to you by the creators of the Big Apple's Lotus and LA's Sunset Room, V Bar is as basic, simple and understated as its name. The young, attractive and affluent clientele who patronise the place put on a show for lesser mortals peeking in through small slits in the wall-length frosted glass windows. Dress smart-casual unless you want to join them on the outside.

Off-Strip

East of the Strip

Double Down Saloon
Paradise Plaza, 4640 Paradise Road, between E Harmon & E Tropicana Avenues (791 5775/ www.doubledownsaloon.com). Bus 108. **Open** 24hrs daily. **No credit cards. Map** p336 C8 ⑲
No head for drink? Then hand over $20 for puke insurance: if you barf, staff'll clean up. Otherwise, you're on your own at this darkly chaotic bar; 'The Happiest Place on Earth', they bill it, and with good

Eat, Drink, Shop

It's all in the mix

Throughout its history, Las Vegas has taken other people's ideas and twisted them into something altogether different. Alcoholically speaking, this tendency has borne fruit in many of the city's bars, which are constantly regenerating their cocktail menus to include an array of only-in-Vegas beverages. If you want to drink a Green Geisha, you'll have to go to **Chinois** at the Forum Shops (see p191). There's only one heavenly Cucumber Lavender mojito in town, and it's at **Parasol Up** (see p180). And while the combination of Sauza tequila, cilantro, cucumber and tabasco known as an Amante Picante is the perfect accompaniment to a Cuban cigar, it's served only at **Casa Fuente** (see p205).

The cocktail revival in Vegas began when Steve Wynn hired Tony Abou-Ganim, the best cocktail guy in the business, to help him open the Bellagio in 1998. Abou-Ganim worked with chefs to create cocktail lists while also teaching bartenders about spirits: how to mix them, how to serve them and how to tell their stories. A year later, Nevada's top liquor distributor, Southern Wine & Spirits, brought to town champion mixer Francesco Lafranconi, who raised the bar with his cocktails (visit Wynn Las Vegas and Casa Fuente for evidence) while also launching the one-of-a-kind Academy of Spirits & Fine Service.

These days, you're behind the times if you don't rotate your cocktail menu seasonally, draw ingredients fresh from organic farms or employ at least one master mixologist who's trying to outdo the guy at the next resort. Fancy, house-invented drinks are the rage up and down the Strip. However, the Bellagio is still *the* place to soak up the cocktail zeitgeist. Drew Levinson, who oversees the resort's 140 bartenders and their 30,000 daily pours, has even derived what he loosely calls the 'Bellagio Crawl', an informal tour of some of the city's best signature beverages.

The quick version starts with a sampling of the Levinson-designed cocktail menu at **Sensi** (see p162), where you can try a seasonal 'salad in a glass' martini called the Caprese (tomato water and vodka muddled with basil) and a treat called a Regalo. Translating from the original Italian as 'gift', it contains Bacardi orange rum, orangecello, Alize red passion liqueur, orange juice, lime

Sensi's signature Regalo.

and passion fruit. Over at the **Petrossian** bar, try a fresh Bella Peach, the resort's new bestseller, or a Bellagio Breeze, invented and served by much-decorated bartender Darren West. Other stops should include the **Fontana Bar** (see p188) for Sean Bigley's Pom Pom (raspberry and Belvedere Pomarancza) and **Michael Mina**'s restaurant (see p165) for one of Abou-Ganim's Cable Cars.

From here, those with cash to splash should head to **Club Prive** for anything on the Lucky 8 cocktail menu. They do mean lucky: this one-of-a-kind menu, served only in the high rollers' lounge, features such rare treats as Hardy Rosebud cognac, which living legend bartender Ray Srp mixes with 150-year-old Grand Marnier in a drink he calls the Whale. How much it costs probably depends on how much you're gambling, but the Rosebud alone goes for $325 a shot. Nobody said the new Vegas was cheap.

reason. The music is loud, whether from the impeccably punkish jukebox or the regular bands (see p252), and the vibe is welcoming. Specialities include Ass Juice ($3 each, three for $11) and bacon martinis (no one's ever had two). Beers are a better bet.

Quark's Bar & Restaurant

Las Vegas Hilton *3000 Paradise Road, between E Sahara Avenue & E Desert Inn Road (697 8725/ www.startrekexp.com). Bus 108, 204, 213.* **Open** 11.30am-11pm daily. **Credit** AmEx, Disc, MC, V. **Hotel** p97. **Map** p336 C5 ⑳

We won't speak for the quality of the food at this establishment, which is named after the alien-run watering hole of *Deep Space Nine*. However, you can accompany your Harry Mudd martini or rum-based, dry-iced Warp Core Breach with Glop on a Stick (that's a corn dog to you) or the Holy Rings of Betazed (onion rings), while Feringis and Klingons walk around in character and poke fun at the humans.

Viva Las Vegas Lounge

Hard Rock *4455 Paradise Road, at E Harmon Avenue (693 5000/www.hardrockhotel.com). Bus 108.* **Open** 24hrs daily. **Credit** AmEx, DC, Disc, MC, V. **Hotel** p96. **Map** p336 C7 ㉑

Known as the 'side bar' owing to its location on the edge of the bustling Hard Rock casino floor, Viva Las Vegas is lively through the week but really jumps on Friday and Saturday nights, when young singles pack the place. The drinks are dear, but the quality of the people-watching makes it worth the cash. Surprisingly, there's no live music.

West of the Strip

Artisan Lounge

Artisan *1501 W Sahara Avenue, at Highland Drive (214 4000/www.theartisanhotel.com). Bus 204.* **Open** 24hrs daily. **Credit** AmEx, MC, V. **Hotel** p102. **Map** p335 B4 ㉒

Gold-framed prints and paintings cover the walls and ceiling here, almost to the point of absurdity; there are even empty frames suspended in the air, and statues interspersed with shelves full of books. Somehow, it all works. A unique amalgam of lodge, bar and gallery, the Artisan is arty Vegas's living room away from home. Thanks to the lack of gambling, it's also one of the quietest lounges in town.

Ghostbar

Palms *4321 W Flamingo Road, at S Valley View Boulevard (942 6832/www.palms.com). Bus 201.* **Open** 8pm-4am daily. **Cover** $10 Mon-Thur; $25 Fri-Sun. **Credit** AmEx, Disc, MC, DC, V. **Hotel** p98. **Map** p333 X3 ㉓

Suspended 51 floors above the city (check the see-through patio looking all the way to the ground), decked out in blues and space-age silvers, Ghostbar is a dramatic spot. Enter via the private elevator (and prepare to pay the private cover charge of $10-$20), and try and get here before the glamorous masses: it starts to get busy from 11pm.

Little Buddha

Palms *4321 W Flamingo Road, at S Valley View Boulevard (942 7778/www.littlebuddhalasvegas.com). Bus 201.* **Open** 5.30-11pm Mon-Thur, Sun; 5.30pm-midnight Fri, Sat. **Credit** AmEx, DC, Disc, MC, V. **Hotel** p98. **Map** p333 X3 ㉔

This restaurant and bar, a smaller version of Paris's famed Buddha Bar (it's operated by the same people), has a low-key and sophisticated air, as smooth and relaxing as the popular ambient DJ compilations created in its name. The bar area is small and crowded, but it's still worth a look for the Asian decor, the drinks and the sushi.

Lucky Strike

Rio *3700 W Flamingo Road, at S Valley View Boulevard (777 7999/www.luckystrikelv.com). Bus 201.* **Open** 11am-3am daily. **Credit** AmEx, DC, MC, V. **Hotel** p100. **Map** p333 X3 ㉕

By removing the glaring lights, reflective lanes and dirty foot smell, and adding loud music, buxom waitresses and higher prices, Lucky Strike have effectively eradicated the blue-collar cafeteria image of bowling. The bar and food menus are creative and tasty, with cotton-candy martinis, sliders, and mac and cheese bites. Even league play is a desirable prospect: at the time of writing, the winning team were due to be rewarded with a trip to the Bahamas.

Downtown

Art Bar

1511 S Main Street, at Utah Avenue (437 2787). Bus Deuce, 206. **Open** 2pm-6am daily. **Credit** AmEx, Disc, MC, V. **Map** p335 C3 ㉖

Cheap drinks and an offbeat style (there's an entire room of velvet Elvi) have helped the Art Bar become the most successful Downtown bar to open in recent years. Owned by wacky but loveable Elvis impersonator Jesse Garon, it's packed every weekend with artists, punks, average Joes, vagrants and the occasional suspiciously driven intellectual, sipping scotch and taking advantage of the free Wi-Fi.

Atomic Liquors

917 E Fremont Street, at S 9th Street (384 7371). Bus Deuce & all DTC-bound buses. **Open** 7am-11pm daily. **No credit cards.** **Map** p334 D2 ㉗

Founded in 1935 and located at the sketchy end of Fremont, this is a gem, from its cut-to-the-chase sign – 'Liquor' in huge white neon – to the cast of crims, bums and chancers who sup here. If you're looking for trouble, you came to the right place. However, although even the bartenders suggest that it's not the place for unaccompanied ladies, most of the barflies are harmless enough.

Beauty Bar

517 E Fremont Street, at Las Vegas Boulevard South (598 1965/www.beautybar.com). Bus Deuce & all DTC-bound buses. **Open** 9pm-2am Mon, Tue, Sun; 5pm-2am Wed, Thur; 5pm-4am Fri; 9pm-4am Sat. **Credit** AmEx, MC, V. **Map** p334 D2 ㉘

Eat, Drink, Shop

The New York version of this chain made famous the 'martinis and manicures' concept featured on *Sex and the City*; a shame, then, that cosmetology laws forbid full manicures here. The '50s decor was salvaged from the Capri Salon of Beauty in Trenton, NJ, with lighting from the old Algiers hotel in Vegas; it's matched by delightful themed cocktails, such as the Platinum Blonde, the Prell and the Red Head. Bands and DJs entertain more or less nightly.

Dino's
1516 Las Vegas Boulevard South, at W Utah Avenue (382 3894/www.dinoslv.com). Bus Deuce, 206. **Open** 24hrs daily. **No credit cards. Map** p335 C3 ❷
The sign on the side, advertising this as 'The last neighborhood bar in Las Vegas', is hyperbole. Still, this local dive offers an upbeat mix of hipsters, freaks, drunks and, on the karaoke nights hosted by Elton John doppelgänger Danny G (Thur-Sat; *see p253* **Stars in your eyes**), off-key crooners and wannabes. Bar regulars compete to join the Drunk of the Month Club.

Downtown Cocktail Room
111 Las Vegas Boulevard South, at E Fremont Street (300 6268/www.downtownlv.net). Bus Deuce & all DTC-bound buses. **Open** 4pm-2am Mon-Thur; 7pm-2am Fri-Sun. **Credit** AmEx, Disc, MC, V. **Map** p334 D2 ❸
Despite its name, this chic, upscale bar will make you forget you're in Downtown; or, at least, Downtown Las Vegas. Perhaps the most casually dramatic addition to the area, done out in deep, sexy reds and sheer curtains you can close for added nook privacy, this understated lounge will put you in the mood to leave with a date even if you didn't come in with one. DJs entertain nightly, though the music is generally pitched at conversation-friendly levels.

Griffin
511 E Fremont Street, at Las Vegas Boulevard South (382 0577). Bus Deuce & all DTC-bound buses. **Open** 5pm-4am Mon-Sat; 9pm-4am Sun. **Credit** AmEx, Disc, MC, V. **Map** p334 D2 ❸
Though it's at street level, this putatively Brit-styled joint on Fremont Street is the place to go medieval. Windowless with an eerie but romantic glow fed by candlelight and fireplaces, the new but old-feeling Griffin doubles as an after-work beer pub and a late night indie-rockin' haunt. Tattooed hotties pull Stellas while a dollar stirs T-Rex and the Smiths from the juke.

Hogs & Heifers
201 N 3rd Street, at E Ogden Avenue (676 1457/www.hogsandheifers.com). Bus Deuce & all DTC-bound buses. **Open** 1pm-4am daily. **No credit cards. Map** p334 D1 ❸
'Is that the sound you make when he takes you from behind?' yells a classy maven in boots from her roost on top of the bar. To some onlookers, Hogs & Heifers isn't pretty or fun; still, those onlookers seem to fall in the minority. The schtick here is similar to Coyote Ugly, but less choreographed and

more raunchy. Arrive on your Harley or bring along some red for your neck if you're fixin' to fit right in.

Huntridge Tavern
1116 E Charleston Boulevard, at S Maryland Parkway (384 7377). Bus 109, 206. **Open** 24hrs daily. **No credit cards. Map** p334 D3 ❸
For decades, this hangout has been everything a dive bar should be: low-estate without being seedy, intriguing without being dangerous, careworn without being ugly. Presumably, the fiftysomethings who warm the stools do go home to their families every once in a while. Still, with brews this cheap, you couldn't blame them if they just stayed put.

Ice House Lounge
650 S Main Street, at E Bonneville Avenue (315 2570). Bus Deuce, 105. **Open** 10am-2am daily. **Credit** AmEx, Disc, MC, V. **Map** p334 C2 ❸
To locals hoping for a Downtown renaissance, the Ice House (built by the site of the city's original ice house) seemed like a mirage: a $5-million freestanding art deco-style building across the way from a weekly-rental motel and a porn shop. It hasn't quite worked out that way, and the place never really hums outside of happy hour. Still, it remains something of a looker, and a good place to take in a game on the big-screen TVs.

Rush Lounge
Golden Nugget *129 E Fremont Street, at S Casino Center Boulevard (385 7111/www.goldennugget. com). Bus Deuce & all DTC-bound buses.* **Open** noon-4am daily. **Credit** AmEx, Disc, MC, V. **Hotel** p104. **Map** p334 C1 ❸
Before 2007, 'contemporary' wasn't an adjective that applied to the Golden Nugget casino. However, it's just about the most accurate description for its upscale new Rush Lounge, swathed in sexy reds, browns and horizontal stripes. A rare find among Downtown casinos, not least because it prefers table games to video poker.

Sidebar
201 N 3rd Street, at E Ogden Avenue (384 2761/www.sidebarlv.com). Bus Deuce & all DTC-bound buses. **Open** 5pm-midnight Mon-Thur; 5pm-2am Fri, Sat. **Credit** AmEx, Disc, MC, V. **Map** p334 D1 ❸
Shake up vintage Vegas appeal with 21st-century style and you have Sidebar, a louche spot attached to the Triple George steakhouse (*see p171*). Martinis are the speciality, drunk to a soundtrack provided by a piano player and with picture windows looking out to 3rd Street in the foreground. An ideal place to while away a few hours, perhaps discussing the difference between gentrification and revitalisation in America's downtowns.

Thunderbird Lounge
Aruba *1215 Las Vegas Boulevard South, at Park Paseo (383 3100/www.arubalasvegas.com). Bus Deuce, 206.* **Open** 4pm-8am Mon-Thur, Sun; 24hrs Fri, Sat. **Credit** AmEx, MC, V. **Hotel** p104. **Map** p335 C3 ❸

Style and sophistication at the **Downtown Cocktail Room**.

Eat, Drink, Shop

With a dark wood bar and an occasionally dingy ambience, this recently revived haunt is old Vegas through and through. There's a darker feel here than at, say, the Peppermill (*see p180*), mostly down to the hotel's location surrounded by quickie chapels, bail bondsmen and hourly-rate motels. Bands play from time to time.

Triple 7 Brew Pub

Main Street Station *200 N Main Street, at E Stewart Avenue (387 1896/www.mainstreetcasino. com). Bus Deuce & all DTC-bound buses.* **Open** 11am-7am daily. **Credit** AmEx, DC, Disc, MC, V. **Hotel** p105. **Map** p334 C1 ㉝

The Triple 7 serves fair beer and above-par bar food, and has an unbeatable $1-a-drink happy hour. But the real reason to visit this microbrewery is to gawk at the multi-million-dollar collection of antiques and collectibles, which even extends to the restroom: gentlemen are able to express their opinion on communism by relieving themselves on a portion of the Berlin Wall.

The rest of the city

Brendan's Irish Pub

Orleans *4500 W Tropicana Avenue, between S Decatur & S Valley View Boulevards, West Las Vegas (365 7111/www.orleanscasino.com). Bus 103, 104, 201.* **Open** 5pm-1am Mon-Thur; 10am-2am Fri-Sun. **Credit** AmEx, Disc, MC, V. **Hotel** p113.

The scene is fairly generic for an Irish pub with sports bar leanings. But while the setting is a little bland, the entertainment on weekends spices things up, with everything from Irish bands to Zydeco troupes on the agenda. The bands' daffy groupies are sometimes even more of a lark than the music.

Champagnes Café

3557 S Maryland Parkway, between E Desert Inn Road & E Twain Avenue, East Las Vegas (737 1699/ www.champagnescafe.net). Bus 109, 213. **Open** 24hrs daily. **No credit cards. Map** p333 Y3 ㉟

With velvety flock wallpaper, Frank and Dino on the jukebox, and a shrine (a Martini, a coffee cup and a cigarette) dedicated to former manager Marty, this vintage bar is a Dom Perignon '53 among Vegas saloons. Hipsters, barflies and discerning locals head here at all hours for cheap drinks; many find it understandably hard to leave.

Crown & Anchor Pub

1350 E Tropicana Avenue, at S Maryland Parkway, University District (739 8676/www.crownand anchorlv.com). Bus 109, 201. **Open** 24hrs daily. **Credit** AmEx, Disc, MC, V. **Map** p333 Y3 ㊵

The British-themed Crown & Anchor manages the feat, difficult in this town, of being a freestanding, independent pub, separate from a casino or a strip mall. Collegiate types and football-shirted expats head here to down pints of Boddingtons, tuck into fish 'n' chips and bash away hopefully at Thursday's quiz night. It gets packed during football matches.

Davy's Locker

1149 E Desert Inn Road, at S Maryland Parkway Avenue, East Las Vegas (458 6343). Bus 109, 213. **Open** 24hrs daily. **No credit cards. Map** p333 Y3 ㊶

Sadly, the interior of this longstanding fixture can't match the sign out front, a truly evocative old glory that's surely destined for the Neon Museum if the bar ever closes. After more than four decades, though, it seems pretty firmly ensconsed, a calm, slightly divey little wellspring of cheap drinks and melancholy on a forlorn stretch of Desert Inn Road.

Dispensary Lounge

2451 E Tropicana Avenue, at S Eastern Avenue, East Las Vegas (458 6343). Bus 110, 201. **Open** 24hrs daily. **Credit** MC, V. **Map** p333 Z3 ❷

You can look at the waterwheel, you can listen to the waterwheel, but you certainly can't touch it. Sort of like the waitresses. The Dispensary is a throwback to old Vegas, complete with shag carpets, fake plants and leotard-clad serving staff who become more boisterous and less balanced as the night wears on (well, you try wearing high heels on a shag carpet). A dark, quiet answer to a bright and frenetic city.

Drop Bar

Green Valley Ranch *2300 Paseo Verde Drive, at S Green Valley Parkway, Henderson (221 6560/www. greenvalleyranchresort.com). Bus 111.* **Open** 24hrs daily. **Credit** AmEx, Disc, MC, V. **Hotel** p111.

It's easy to be tricked into feeling that you're not old enough to be lounging with a glass of pinot noir on the frightfully white bar stools and leather couches at Drop. By contrasting the whites with deep, dark floors and walls, the designers have achieved a seriously sexy look, with sheer curtains providing separation from the lively casino. A luxurious place to celebrate a win or to lick your wounds.

Freakin' Frog

4700 S Maryland Parkway, at E Tropicana Avenue, University District (597 9702/www.freakinfrog.com). Bus 109, 201. **Open** 11am-3am daily. **Credit** AmEx, Disc, MC, V. **Map** p333 Y3 ❸

Despite its irritatin' name, the Frog is a locals' favourite, and not just because of the 400-strong beer selection. Located across the road from UNLV, this is about as close as Vegas gets to a college bar. Order some fried mac and cheese triangles or a corn dog to accompany your discussion of Peruvian beer versus, say, Colt 45 (both of which are stocked). There's a whiskey bar upstairs.

Hookah Lounge

Paymon's Mediterranean Café & Market, 4147 S Maryland Parkway, at E Flamingo Road, University District (731 6030/www.hookahlounge.com). Bus 109, 202. **Open** 5pm-1am Mon-Thur; 5pm-3am Fri, Sat. **Credit** AmEx, Disc, MC, V. **Map** p333 Y3 ❹

In this dark and ornate haven, a stark contrast to the adjoining Mediterranean Café (*see p176*), you'll be served at low tables by a hookah jockey, who dispenses cocktails and water pipe. Flavours range from the flowery to fruity, but we recommend something nutty and traditional, like Turkish pistachio. Take a couple of puffs and then pass it on. There's food and herbal smoke before 9pm; afterwards, the kitchen closes and the real tobaccco is brought out.

Freakin' Frog.

Hootie & the Blowfish's Shady Grove Lounge

Silverton *3333 Blue Diamond Road, at I-15, South Las Vegas (263 7777/www.silvertoncasino.com). Bus 117.* **Open** 24hrs daily. **Credit** AmEx, Disc, MC, V. **Hotel** p115.

Turns out that Hootie didn't disappear at all: he simply went where all past-their-primers end up. With decor that includes an Airstream trailer equipped with two mini bowling lanes, the Shady Grove is a curious place, but in a good, raising-the-brows kind of way. The Hootie references and memorabilia are noticeable enough to grab fans and subtle enough not to distract the rest of us.

Lucky Bar

Red Rock Resort *11011 W Charleston Boulevard, at I-215, West Las Vegas (797 7576/www.redrock lasvegas.com). Bus 206.* **Open** 24hrs daily. **Credit** AmEx, DC, Disc, MC, V. **Hotel** p112.

Summerlin's sister to the Drop Bar is an impressive, round and deep-red room well-hung with expensive crystal and furnished with flat screens, comfortable banquettes and rotating Austin-Powers love seats. The drinks are mixed well, and it only gets crazy on weekend nights., making this a nice escape.

Mermaid Bar & Lounge

Silverton *3333 Blue Diamond Road, at I-15, South Las Vegas (263 7777/www.silvertoncasino.com). Bus 117.* **Open** 11am-3am Mon-Thur, Sun; 24hrs Fri, Sat. **Credit** AmEx, Disc, MC, V. **Hotel** p115.

While you're sitting and sipping your Shark Attack and gazing into the 117,000-gallon aquarium, it might occur to you to wonder: where are the mermaids? Don't fret: they, and their companion mermen, will be along in a while, diving in on the hour in the evenings (except Tue) and performing underwater versions of *Swan Lake*. Cheap drinks and jellyfish tanks add to the eccentric appeal.

Nora's Wine Bar & Osteria

1031 S Rampart Boulevard, at W Charleston Boulevard, Summerlin (940 6672/www.noras winebar.com). Bus 206. **Open** 11am-10pm Mon-Thur, Sun; 11am-11pm Fri, Sat. **Credit** AmEx, Disc, MC, V.

Imagine giant wine dispensers holding 48 different vintages, all operated by the customer by simply inserting a card. The novelty! The freedom! The hangover potential! This, folks, is the Enomatic, which co-stars with wonderful cuisine at this lively venture. Choose from 1oz, 3oz or 6oz servings, or select one of 350 bottles, then soak it up with bruschetta or pizza from the wood-burning oven.

Lounges

Many visitors to Vegas leave town arguing that a number of the big shows staged in Strip casinos really aren't strong enough to merit an admission charge. But as long as people are willing to pay $50 to see a Neil Diamond impersonator or drop $25 to hear an impressionist, the casinos will be more than happy to take the money and run.

Conversely, few visitors make the case that the resorts should start charging for the free entertainment offered in their lounges. Traditionally, Vegas lounges have been reserved for acts on their way up or down the showbiz ladder: Louis Prima revived his career in the Sahara's Casbah Lounge, and others have made their name by playing Vegas lounges for little more than a tip and a wink. These days, though, the musicians who provide a soundtrack to the increasingly drunken gambling are of a rather lower grade.

There's a limit on the number of classic rock covers any sane person can stomach, and many visitors will have a similarly low tolerance for the too-smooth jazzers and *American Idol* wannabes who try just that little bit too hard to catch the eyes and ears of passing punters. Even so, pleasant musical surprises aren't as rare as you might expect, and even the worst rendition of 'Don't Stop Believing' can get the head nodding and the nostalgia flowing after liberal vodka infusion.

The Strip

Big Apple Bar

New York New York *3790 Las Vegas Boulevard South, at W Tropicana Avenue (740 6969/www. nynyhotelcasino.com). Bus Deuce, 201.* **Open** 24hrs daily. **Credit** AmEx, Disc, MC, V. **Hotel** p84. **Map** p336 A8 ⑮

Eat, Drink, Shop

Going to extremes Drink

Drinking on the cheap is easy in Vegas. Gamblers always drink for free, though tipping your waitress will result in more frequent service. And even if you're not gambling, you can usually find one-dollar draft or bottled beers at Strip venues such as **Casino Royale** (*see p89*) and Slots-a-Fun (2890 Las Vegas Boulevard South, 734 0410), and similarly cheap drinks along Fremont Street.

Further from the Strip, the happy hour at **Firefly** (3-6pm Mon-Fri; *see p168*) allows for half-price cocktails, meaning martinis are four bucks and mojitos are a mere $3.25. Nearby, the bar at **Pink Taco** (*see p169*) offers two-for-one deals on margaritas and beers during happy hour (4-7pm Mon-Fri). And from here, nip across to the **Divebar** (4-8pm Mon-Fri; *see p253*) for two-buck domestics and three-dollar import beers.

Such bargains are old Vegas through and through. New Vegas, though, demands luxury, and luxury demands expense. Start at **N9ne**

(*see p169*) with an 'ultimate margarita', made from Herradura Seleccion Suprema tequila and priced at $69. Then, head to **Aureole** (*see p153*) for a shot of Hardy Perfection cognac from a Lalique crystal bottle, yours for $350. But for the price of three Hardys, you could sample Chivas Regal 50-Year Salute, from one of 255 bottles produced from Queen Elizabeth II's coronation cask and released to celebrate her Golden Jubilee in 2002. Offered at the Bellagio's **Prime** restaurant (*see p156*), a single measure goes for $1,050.

Picasso (*see p161*), the gourmet room at Bellagio, was declared the eighth most expensive restaurant in the United States in a 2005 survey, mostly because of its wine list. A bottle of 1945 Chateau Mouton Rothschild retails for $16,888, with a 1947 Cheval Blanc going for $15,610. And at $13,500, the 1961 Chateau Petrus Classic makes the five-grand bottles at **Fleur de Lys** (*see p160*) look like bargains.

Reminiscent of a '40s supper club, this art deco-esque lounge in New York New York features a heady drinks menu and suitably reminiscent live music nightly from 8pm to 3am. If you can make it here, you'll make it – bam! bam! – anywhere.

Le Cabaret

Paris Las Vegas *3655 Las Vegas Boulevard South, at E Flamingo Road (946 7000/www.harrahs. com). Bus Deuce, 202.* **Open** 2pm-3am daily. **Credit** AmEx, Disc, MC, V. **Hotel** p74. **Map** p336 A7 **⑯**
Le Cabaret has more character than most antiseptic casino lounges. With its faux shady trees and sparkling lights, you'll almost feel like you're doin' the 'Neutron Dance' in gay Paree. Or, at least, you will after the eighth drink of the evening.

Carnaval Court

Harrah's *3475 Las Vegas Boulevard South, between Sands Avenue & E Flamingo Road (369 5000/www. harrahs.com). Bus Deuce, 105, 203.* **Open** noon-1am Mon-Thur, Sun; noon-2am Fri, Sat. **Credit** AmEx, Disc, MC, V. **Hotel** p79. **Map** p336 A6 **⑰**
At this outlandish outdoor bar, the show-off entertainment is just as prevalent among the bartenders as the musicians: it's not uncommon to see a barkeep pouring shots into the upturned mouths of waiting patrons, like baby birds begging to be fed. For a Vegas kitsch sensation, check out entertainer Cook E Jarr, who performs here on Fridays and Saturdays from 6pm to 8pm.

Celebration Lounge

Tropicana *3801 Las Vegas Boulevard South, at E Tropicana Avenue (739 2222/www.tropicanalv.com). Bus Deuce, 201.* **Open** 24hrs daily. **Credit** AmEx, DC, Disc, MC, V. **Map** p336 A8 **⑱**
House band TKO's 'hip' billing on the hotel's website is a trifle optimistic, but they get the loungers out of their seats from Tuesdays through Saturdays from 8pm until late. If you think you can do better, the hotel's Tropics Lounge hosts regular karaoke.

Coral Reef Lounge

Mandalay Bay *3950 Las Vegas Boulevard South, at W Hacienda Avenue (632 7777/www.mandalay bay.com). Bus Deuce, 104, 105.* **Open** 9.30pm-2am daily. **Credit** AmEx, DC, MC, V. **Hotel** p71. **Map** p336 A9 **⑲**
Dance bands play at Mandalay Bay's largest music lounge and sushi bar, beyond restaurant row, and draw energetic crowds nightly. A mellower vibe can be found in the Island or the Orchid Lounge.

Fontana Bar

Bellagio *3600 Las Vegas Boulevard South, at W Flamingo Road (1-800 963 9634/693 7722/www. bellagio.com). Bus Deuce, 202.* **Open** 5pm-1am Mon-Thur, Sun; 5pm-2am Fri, Sat. **Credit** AmEx, Disc, MC, V. **Hotel** p68. **Map** p336 A7 **㊿**
The sophistication to which this lounge aspires is sometimes compromised by the function-band fluff who currently perform in it. Still, the views are great and the drinks are good; if the noise is too ghastly, adjourn to the balcony to watch the fountains.

Indigo Lounge

Bally's *3645 Las Vegas Boulevard South, at E Flamingo Road (739 4111/www.harrahs.com). Bus Deuce, 202.* **Open** 3pm-3am Mon-Thur, Sun; 3pm-4am Fri, Sat. **Credit** AmEx, Disc, MC, V. **Hotel** p77. **Map** p336 A7 **�密**
Right next to the Bally's/Paris Las Vegas walkway, this casual, enjoyable lounge features a scattering of pop, dance, Motown and R&B acts.

The rest of the city

Armadillo Lounge

Texas Station *2101 Texas Star Lane, at N Rancho Drive, between Lake Mead Boulevard & Vegas Drive, North Las Vegas (1-800 654 8888/ 631 1000/www.texasstation.com). Bus 103, 106, 210, 211.* **Open** 9pm-1am Fri, Sat. **No credit cards**. **Hotel** p118.
Go for the giant, mirrored armadillo disco ball, stay for the entertainment. On Fridays and Saturdays, this red-tin-roofed lounge hosts Lefty Lucy, who play country music mixed with rock from 9.30pm until 1.30am. On Sunday afternoons, sample a little swing music with Jerry Tiffe and his band.

Bourbon Street Cabaret

Orleans *4500 W Tropicana Avenue, between S Decatur & S Valley View Boulevards, West of Strip (365 7111/www.orleanscasino.com). Bus 103, 104, 201.* **Open** 6pm-3am Tue-Sun. **Credit** AmEx, DC, Disc, MC, V. **Hotel** p113. **Map** p333 X4 **㉲**
Local bands play a mix of rock, pop, Latin and disco in this small lounge six nights a week. It's styled like a French Quarter courtyard and adorned with wrought-iron decorations, with grand pianos suspended overhead. There's usually a two-drink minimum in effect.

Chrome

Santa Fe Station *4949 N Rancho Drive, at US 95 (junction 90A), North Las Vegas (658 4900/www. santafe.stationcasinos.com). Bus 101, 102, 106, 219.* **Open** hrs vary. **Credit** AmEx, Disc, MC, V. **Hotel** p117.
If 1980s music is your guilty pleasure, get over to this sleek club/showroom, where the Purple Reign tribute band play on Friday and Saturday nights for rather less money than it'll cost you to see Prince at the Rio. Wednesdays draw national touring blues performers, who always go great with bourbon.

Rock's Lounge

Red Rock Resort *11011 W Charleston Boulevard, at I-215, West Las Vegas (797 7777/www.redrock lasvegas.com). Bus 206.* **Open** hrs vary. **Credit** AmEx, Disc, MC, V. **Hotel** p112.
Fake smoke pours out of the lounge of this swanky neighbourhood casino, a thick haze that either beckons or repels you from cheese-o-rama. Zowie Bowie is the mainstay; though the bronzed blonde couple is neither Zowie nor Bowie, they belt out Top 40 hits, get their Scottsdale, AZ-inspired groove on and manage to get people dancing for hours.

Shops & Services

Our advice? Bring a spare suitcase…

Taking in a Broadway show? Check. Dining at a star-studded restaurant? Check. Rolling the dice or doubling down? Check. But… buying a pair of Manolos? *Really?*

It's true. Though few predicted it 15 years ago, the way in which tourists now enjoy Vegas has changed dramatically since the **Forum Shops** opened at Caesars Palace in 1992. According to the Las Vegas Convention & Visitors Authority, more than half of the city's 40 million visitors spend time shopping. The key is in the old something-for-everyone cliché: there's Nike Golf for the weekend duffer, Louis Vuitton for the label hound, and the Gap for just about everybody else.

Change has been rapid and dramatic. The 2004 opening of the cool, urban **Mandalay Place** was followed by dramatic renovations and expansion at the **Fashion Show Mall**, the christening of a new wing at the Forum Shops, the unveiling of the **Wynn Esplanade**'s selection of super-smart stores, and the 2007 remodelling (and renaming) of the **Miracle Mile Shops**. And that's just on the Strip: the **Las Vegas Premium Outlets** in Downtown has been a huge success, while the conversion of a landmark bakery into the **Holsum Design Center** has brought small local businesses into focus. The presence of **World Market Center** (*see p211* **Take a seat**), a vast complex of wholesale furnishings showrooms, is further proof that Las Vegas is fast becoming one of the west coast's commercial powerhouses.

Further changes are on the way. The Shops at Palazzo, the Venetian's new sibling, will be home to **Barneys**, Las Vegas's first branch of the department store favoured by New York's funky fashion elite. Further south on Las Vegas Boulevard, the new **Town Square** mall will contain 150 new stores, 12 restaurants and a cineplex. And the aforementioned Las Vegas Premium Outlets are set to expand, increasing their store count to 150.

If all this sounds too serious, rest assured that good taste hasn't completely taken over Vegas. You'll still be able to find all the kitschy knick-knacks you could possibly want in the town's many souvenir stores. Certainly, **Bonanza Gifts**, which declares itself the 'World's Largest Gift Store', isn't getting any smaller…

SERVICE WITH A SMILE?

It may come as a surprise, but service is not always a strong point here. Attendants can veer from wonderfully helpful to downright rude in seconds; it might seem rather odd in a city so completely based on pleasuring its visitors, until you work out that this is just about the only major service industry in town where the professionals stand no chance of being tipped handsomely for their work.

A 7.75 per cent sales tax will be added to your purchases at the till.

General

The best Shops

For a bit of everything
Forum Shops. *See p191.*

For stupendous sneaks
Epic Shoos. *See p201.*

For the folks back home
Gamblers General Store. *See p203.*

For local literature
Reading Room. *See p194.*

For an indelible souvenir
Pussykat Tattoo Parlor. *See p208.*

Department stores

The following stores stock a broad range of products, from fashion to homewares. In addition, the numerous branches of **Target** (www.target.com) in Vegas offer trendy designer labels (Isaac Mizrahi, Liz Lange, Mossimo) at discount prices. And be sure to look out for **Barneys**: New York's most fashionable export is set to open a branch in the Venetian's new Shops at Palazzo in late 2007 or early 2008.

Dillard's

Fashion Show Mall, 3200 Las Vegas Boulevard South, at Spring Mountain Road (733 2008/www. dillards.com). Bus Deuce, 105, 203. **Open** 10am-9pm Mon-Sat; 11am-6pm Sun. **Credit** AmEx, DC, Disc, MC, V. **Map** p336 & p336 B6.

Where to shop

THE STRIP

Most shoppers remain confined to the Strip, and not without good reason: the majority of the town's more interesting and popular malls are found on it.

DOWNTOWN

Fremont Street is pathetically devoid of decent shops. However, the Arts District is crammed with vintage stores and galleries; the Holsum Design Center offers an array of gift shops; and the Las Vegas Premium Outlets is great for bargains. The new mixed-use buildings (Juhl, Soho Lofts, Newport Lofts) also have street level retail due to open in 2008.

THE REST OF THE CITY

Along Maryland Parkway, you'll find a few vintage clothing stores that appeal to UNLV students. Otherwise, take your pick from any of the plentiful malls. The best of Las Vegas's independent retailers are in strip malls or stand-alone buildings all around the city. It really does pay to travel.

The American west's equivalent of Marks and Spencer has excellent beauty aisles, a good selection of women's shoes, and a great range of men's suits at decent prices. By the same token, there's not much to quicken the pulse.
Other locations throughout the city.

Macy's

Fashion Show Mall, 3200 Las Vegas Boulevard South, at Spring Mountain Road (737 8708/www. macys.com). Bus Deuce, 105, 203. **Open** 10am-9pm Mon-Sat; 10am-8pm Sun. **Credit** AmEx, Disc, MC, V. **Map** p335 & p336 B6.
The king of department stores, Macy's offers a variety of quality merchandise at competitive prices. Clothing, strong on both men's and women's lines, ranges from classic (Ralph Lauren) to hip (Ben Sherman) to utilitarian. The homewares-only branch on Spring Mountain Road has frequent sales.
Other locations throughout the city.

Neiman Marcus

Fashion Show Mall, 3200 Las Vegas Boulevard South, at Spring Mountain Road (731 3636/www. neimanmarcus.com). Bus Deuce, 105, 203. **Open** 10am-8pm Mon-Fri; 10am-7pm Sun. **Credit** AmEx, MC, V. **Map** p335 & p336 B6.
The world's best designers are on display at this upmarket department store, among them the catwalk-friendly likes of Prada, Manolo Blahnik, Escada, Missoni and Chanel. It also has a good range of accessories, make-up, lingerie and perfumes, and a fantastic housewares selection. It's nicknamed 'Needless Mark-Up' for a reason, but there are discounted goods down at the Fashion Outlets of Las Vegas in Primm (874 2100; *see p193*).

Nordstrom

Fashion Show Mall, 3200 Las Vegas Boulevard South, at Spring Mountain Road (862 2525/ www.nordstrom.com). Bus Deuce, 105, 203. **Open** 10am-9pm Mon-Sat; 11am-6pm Sun. **Credit** AmEx, Disc, MC, V. **Map** p335 & p336 B6.
Those who swear by Nordstrom agree that it's a good place for style-conscious people of any age to find great stuff at reasonable prices and with excellent service. Both men's and women's shoe departments are worth a look. Harking back to the days when shopping used to be an 'experience', Nordy's even treats its customers to piano music and a fine café. Those of lesser means should try its Henderson outlet.
Other locations Nordstrom Rack, 9851 S Eastern Avenue, at E Silverado Ranch Boulevard, Henderson (948 2121).

Saks Fifth Avenue

Fashion Show Mall, 3200 Las Vegas Boulevard South, at Spring Mountain Road (733 8300/ www.saksfifthavenue.com). Bus Deuce, 105, 203. **Open** 10am-8pm Mon-Wed; 10am-9pm Thur, Fri; 10am-7pm Sat; noon-6pm Sun. **Credit** AmEx, DC, Disc, MC, V. **Map** p335 & p336 B6.
For those with discriminating taste and a heavyweight bank account, a trip to Saks is like a visit to church: you go once a week to pay homage and hear the word. The men's and women's apparel sections are especially strong (Marc Jacobs, Dolce & Gabbana, Hugo Boss). If you've got the taste but not the money, check out Off 5th, Saks's outlet store at the **Las Vegas Outlet Center** (263 7692; *see p193*).

Malls

Casino malls

Casino malls tend to attract the high-end brands and big-name chains, rather than any discount outlets. For designer labels, head to the **Wynn Esplanade** (Chanel, Gaultier, Manolo Blahnik), **Via Bellagio** (Prada, Gucci, Fendi) and the **Forum Shops** (Marc Jacobs, Pucci, Carolina Herrera). The latter also houses a number of high-street staples (Gap, Banana Republic), as does Planet Hollywood's **Miracle Mile Shops**.

Le Boulevard

Paris Las Vegas *3655 Las Vegas Boulevard South, at E Flamingo Road (946 7000/www.parislas vegas.com). Bus Deuce, 202.* **Open** 9am-11pm daily. **Hotel** p74. **Map** p336 A7.
Just about every shop in this small but divine mall (it's basically an extended hallway) comes with a strong but delightful French influence. **La Boutique** offers a well-edited collection of high-end accessories

from such French labels as Celine, Hermès and Cartier; **Les Enfants** has Madeline, Babar the Elephant and Eloise toys and dolls; and **Les Mémoires** sells sweet-smelling boudoir and bath gifts. **La Cave** has cheeses, pâtés and wine, while **Lenôtre** is known for its bread and pastries. There's even a 24-hour gift shop (**Le Journal**) where you can purchase everything from a Paris Las Vegas T-shirt to diet coke and cigarettes.

Forum Shops
Caesars Palace *3500 Las Vegas Boulevard South, at W Flamingo Road (1-877 427 7243/893 4800/ www.caesars.com). Bus Deuce, 202.* **Open** 10am-11pm Mon-Thur, Sun; 10am-midnight Fri, Sat. **Hotel** p68. **Map** p336 A7.
Sure, it might be trying too hard with the faux-Roman vibe (classical pillars, statues, huge fountains), but the Forum Shops rakes in a whopping $1,300 in sales per square foot each year, the nation's highest per-foot revenue. Far and away the best of the casino malls, the Forum Shops is a must for anyone with a shopping jones.

In the main mall, mid-range chains (**Banana Republic, Gap, Abercrombie & Fitch, Diesel, Kenneth Cole**) punctuate the serious designer line-up: **Dolce & Gabbana, Christian Lacroix, Robert Cavalli, Valentino** et al. Accessorise your outfit at **Chopard, David Yurman, Bulgari, De Beers, Harry Winston** or **Tiffany & Co**. But the real jewels are the refined shops that front directly on to the Strip. Spiral escalators and marble floors help create a swanky setting for tenants such as fashion powerhouses **Kate Spade, Marc**

Jacobs, Pucci, Thomas Pink and **Carolina Herrera**. Recent arrivals include **Judith Ripka, Miss Sixty** and **Ron Herman**. There are attractions at either end of the mall: statues come to life at one extremity, with Atlantis rising from the waves at the other.

Grand Canal Shoppes & Shops at Palazzo
Venetian *3377 Las Vegas Boulevard South, between Sands Avenue & E Flamingo Road (414 4500/www.grandcanalshoppes.com). Bus Deuce, 203, 213.* **Open** 10am-11pm Mon-Thur, Sun; 10am-midnight Fri, Sat. **Hotel** p75. **Map** p336 A6.
The Grand Canal Shoppes felt like a second-rate Forum Shops when it opened in 1999. In places, that's what it still resembles. The walkways are narrow and cramped, but the smaller space does at least give a reasonable impression of an intimate city streetscape. **Lladró, Movado, Jimmy Choo, St John Sport** and **Burberry** are among the best of the generally high-end retailers; there's pleasant 'patio' dining at **Postrio** (*see p156*) and a hyper-fashionable scene at **Tao** (*see p166 & p258*).

When the Palazzo, a sister resort to the Venetian, opens next door in late 2007 or early 2008, it'll bring with it the **Shops at the Palazzo**. The tight-lipped suits behind the development were slow to release information about its tenants. However, **Barneys** and **Barneys Co-op** will anchor the new wing of the Grand Canal Shoppes, which will also include 80 other new stores and restaurants when it opens at the beginning of 2008.

Forum Shops.

Eat, Drink, Shop

On the runway at the **Fashion Show Mall**.

Mandalay Place

Mandalay Bay *3950 Las Vegas Boulevard South, at W Hacienda Avenue (632 9333/www.mandalay bay.com). Bus Deuce, 104, 105.* **Open** 10am-11pm daily. **Hotel** p71. **Map** p336 A9.

What separates this smallish retail experience from other Strip malls is its vow to 'break the chains': it leases its stores only to companies otherwise absent from Vegas. It's a savvy move, and one that brought the city its first **Urban Outfitters** (which has since also opened in the Miracle Mile Shops); **Lik Design**, featuring beautiful palm wood furniture by Aussie designer Bruce Dowse; and the **Reading Room**, the city's best independent bookstore. The handful of great boutiques includes **Fornaria, Nora Blue, Elton's Men Store** and **Max&Co**; other highlights include the modern furniture, lighting and accessories at **Blankspace**, and **Lush Puppy**, which carries fashion-conscious accessories for cats and dogs. For nibbles, try the **Burger Bar** (*see p155*). The mall is located on a bridge that connects Mandalay Bay to the Luxor, and is accessible from either resort.

Miracle Mile Shops

Planet Hollywood *2667 Las Vegas Boulevard South, between E Harmon & E Flamingo Roads (1-888 800 8284/www.miraclemileshopslv.com). Bus Deuce, 202.* **Open** 10am-11pm Mon-Thur, Sun; 10am-midnight Fri, Sat. **Hotel** p85. **Map** p336 A7.

Formerly the Desert Passage, this 1.2-mile ring-mall recently underwent a multi-million-dollar makeover, transforming it from a Moroccan-style market into a contemporary urban centre. The Hollywood-style facelift added trendier, younger labels to attract the kind of hipsters usually found hanging at the Palms

or the Hard Rock, among them **Ben Sherman, H&M, Bettie Page Las Vegas, Metropark, Quiksilver, Marciano** and **Urban Outiftters**. Peckish? Grab a **Cheeseburger at the Oasis** or head to **Trader Vic's** for mai tais and chicken curry.

Via Bellagio

Bellagio *3600 Las Vegas Boulevard South, at W Flamingo Road (693 7111/www.bellagio.com). Bus Deuce, 202.* **Open** 10am-midnight daily. **Hotel** p68. **Map** p336 A7.

In line with its upmarket image, the Bellagio's small mall contains ten of the smartest designer names this side of Wynn Las Vegas. Longstanding tenants such as **Tiffany & Co, Prada, Gucci, Chanel, Dior, Giorgio Armani** and **Hermès** have been joined of late by the likes of **Fendi** and **Bottega Veneta**. If your wallet can't cope, at least pop in to enjoy the location: the venue is a shrine to materialism, with daylight streaming through the vaulted glass ceilings on to opulent walkways and tidy storefronts. The food is a cut above regular mall fodder too: try **Olives** (*see p156*), a Mediterranean bistro overlooking the lake.

Wynn Esplanade

Wynn Las Vegas *3131 Las Vegas Boulevard South, between E Desert Inn Road & Sands Avenue (770 7000/www.wynnlas vegas.com). Bus Deuce, 203.* **Open** 10am-11pm Mon-Thur, Sun; 10am-midnight Fri, Sat. **Hotel** p76. **Map** p335 & p336 B6.

Steve Wynn took **Oscar de la Renta** on a personal tour of a then under-construction Wynn Las Vegas, in an attempt to convince the couture tsar that it would be the finest resort in town. It worked. De la Renta located his signature shop inside the Wynn

Esplanade, as have **Jean-Paul Gaultier, Brioni, Manolo Blahnik** (the second signature store in the US) and **Jo Malone** perfumers, to name but a few. Peppered throughout the rest of the resort are other interesting spots, such as **Shoe In** (an assortment of designer shoes from Stuart Weitzman, Christian Louboutin and Giuseppe Zanotti), **Outfit** (ready-to-wear clothes from Zac Posen, Narciso Rodriguez and Martin Margiela) and **Wynn LVNV** (home accessories that include the Wynn's dreamy beds, Murano chandeliers and chocolates by Frédéric Robert). There's also the requisite collection of designer labels, among them **Chanel, Dior** and **Louis Vuitton**.

Non-casino malls

Even without its casino malls, Vegas caters efficiently and effectively for shoppers. The revamped **Fashion Show Mall** leads the way, with a host of chain and department stores, supplemented by the more prosaic **Boulevard Mall** and other less notable developments.

In addition, Las Vegas now has its very own 'lifestyle centres', open-air complexes that 'serve as multi-purpose leisure-time destinations' (according to the International Council of Shopping Centers). The best is the **District** out in Green Valley. Others include **Rampart Commons** (1055 S Rampart Boulevard, at W Charleston Boulevard, Summerlin), home to Nevada's first Pottery Barn, and the nearby **Boca Park Fashion Village** (8950 W Charleston Boulevard, at S Rampart Boulevard, Summerlin) and boutiques such as **Talulah G** (see p197).

Boulevard Mall

3528 S Maryland Parkway, at W Desert Inn Road, East Las Vegas (732 8949/www.boulevardmall.com). Bus 109, 213. **Open** 10am-9pm Mon-Sat; 11am-6pm Sun. **Map** p333 Y3.

A bastion of the Las Vegas shopping scene and the first mall of its type to open in the city: centrally located, reasonably priced and loaded with familiar favourites such as **Sears, Dillard's, Macy's** and **JC Penney**. When you're weighed down with bags and nearing collapse, head to the **Panorama Café's** food court for cheap international cuisine.

District

Green Valley Ranch *120 S Green Valley Parkway, between Paseo Verde Parkway & I-215, Henderson (564 8595/www.thedistrictatgvr.com). Bus 114.* **Open** 10am-9pm Mon-Sat; 11am-7pm Sun.

Highlights at the open-air District include **REI, Anthropologie** and **Francesca's Collection**, a sweet little accessories and gift shop. Eateries, among them **Lucille's Barbecue, Kennedy's** and **King's Fish House**, are an important part of the mix. The District recently crossed over Green Valley Parkway to include the city's second **Whole Foods Market** (see p202), its first **West Elm** and chic women's boutique **Chelsea**.

Fashion Show Mall

3200 Las Vegas Boulevard South, at Spring Mountain Road (369 0704/www.thefashionshow. com). Bus Deuce, 105, 203. **Open** 10am-9pm Mon-Sat; 11am-7pm Sun. **Map** p335 & p336 B6.

A $1-billion expansion of the Fashion Show Mall included the addition of the Cloud, an amazing image projection screen/sunshade that hovers over the front of the shopping centre and broadcasts to the Strip. However, it's the line-up of shops that's the real eye-catcher. The mall has nearly doubled in size; original tenants such as **Macy's, Neiman Marcus** and **Saks Fifth Avenue** have been joined by anchor tenants including **Bloomingdale's Home, Nordstrom** and speciality shops such as **Paul Frank, Apple, Puma, Teavana** and **Zara**. Other recent arrivals include a cheaper, more casual version of J.Crew called **Madewell**, and the metropolitan **Ruehl**, Abercrombie & Fitch's take on clothing for young professionals. The range of restaurants is also very fine: try **Ra Sushi, Café Ba Ba Reeba** (see p158) and **Capital Grille**.

Discount malls

For brand-name bargains, you can't beat a discount mall, where stores sell last season's stock at a fraction of its original price. Vegas boasts two of its own (see below), but there are more bargains south of the city: the **Fashion Outlets of Las Vegas** mall in Primm (32100 Las Vegas Boulevard South, Primm, 874 1400, www.fashionoutletlasvegas.com) houses over 100 stores, among them big-names such as **Old Navy** and **Gap** that don't have outlets in Vegas.

Swap meets, at which new and used goods are hawked at bargain rates, are also worth a look. Both the **Broadacres Open Air Swap Meet** (2934 Las Vegas Boulevard North, at N Pecos Road, North Las Vegas, 642 3777) and the **Fantastic Indoor Swap Meet** (1717 S Decatur Boulevard, at W Oakey Boulevard, South-west Las Vegas, 877 0087) are both open Friday to Sunday.

Las Vegas Outlet Center

7400 Las Vegas Boulevard South, at E Warm Springs Road, South of Strip (896 5599/www. premiumoutlets.com). Bus Deuce, 117. **Open** 10am-9pm Mon-Sat; 10am-8pm Sun.

Now owned by the same company as the newer Las Vegas Premium Outlets, this long-established outlet centre has decent bargains from **Calvin Klein, Off 5th** (the Saks Fifth Avenue discount outlet), **Nike, Adidas, Harry & David Coach** and **Bose**. The giant carousel should keep the kids content.

Las Vegas Premium Outlets

875 S Grand Central Parkway, at W Charleston Boulevard, Downtown (474 7500/www.lasvegas premiumoutlets.com). Bus 105, 106, 108, 207. **Open** 10am-9pm Mon-Sat; 10am-8pm Sun. **Map** p335 C2.

As the name suggests, this excellent outdoor outlet mall, which opened in late 2003, is geared to the higher end of the fashion market. Labels on site include **Armani**, **Dolce & Gabbana**, **Brooks Brothers**, **Lacoste**, **Theory** and **Ralph Lauren**, to name but a few. Twenty-five new shops and a new parking garage, all scheduled for autumn 2007, will up the ante still further.

Specialist

Books & magazines

There are branches of both the big book chains in Las Vegas. The nearest **Barnes & Noble** to the Strip is at 3860 S Maryland Parkway (at E Flamingo Road, 734 2900, www.barnesandnoble.com), while the closest **Borders** is at 2323 S Decatur Boulevard (at W Sahara Avenue, 258 0999, www.borders stores.com). However, the latter chain will be within far easier reach when it opens a branch at the new Town Square mall in late 2007.

General

Reading Room
Mandalay Bay (Mandalay Place) *3950 Las Vegas Boulevard South, at W Hacienda Avenue (632 9374). Bus Deuce, 104, 105.* **Open** 7am-11pm daily. **Credit** AmEx, Disc, MC, V. **Hotel** p71. **Map** p336 A9.
The first bookshop in a Vegas casino has become a favourite with Las Vegans: not only does it have a strong local interest selection, but it also stocks many well-regarded and obscure books from around the globe. The staff picks are always on the mark.

Specialist

Gamblers Book Club
630 S 11th Street, at E Bonneville Avenue, Downtown (382 7555/www.gamblersbook.com). Bus 105, 106, 108, 207. **Open** 9am-5pm Mon-Sat. **Credit** Disc, MC, V. **Map** p334 D3.
The Gamblers Book Club is supposedly the world's largest distributor of gambling books, be they coffee-table tomes, industry histories or tips on beating the system. If you don't just want to read, there are also cards, chips and gambling-related software for sale.

Used & Antiquarian

Dead Poet Books
937 S Rainbow Boulevard, between W Charleston Boulevard & Alta Drive, West Las Vegas (227 4070). Bus 101, 206. **Open** 10am-6pm daily. **Credit** AmEx, Disc, MC, V.

You'll find a charming hotchpotch of antiquarian books here on almost every topic; specialities include metaphysical cookbooks (yes, really), military histories and first editions.

Children

Fashion

Gap Kids and **BabyGap** can both be found in the Miracle Mile Shops (862 4042; *see p192*); check www.gap.com for other locations. **Las Vegas Premium Outlets** (*see p193*) also has a whole slew of children's stores, among them **OshKosh B'Gosh** (221 1400), **Strasburg Children** (676 1459), **Carter's** (386 3082) and **Stride Rite Keds Sperry** (388 2055).

Along Came a Spider
Fashion Show Mall, 3200 Las Vegas Boulevard South, at W Spring Mountain Road (735 2728). Bus Deuce, 105, 203. **Open** 10am-9pm Mon-Sat; 11am-6pm Sun. **Credit** AmEx, DC, Disc, MC, V. **Map** p336 B6.
At this upscale boutique, stage mums tussle over designer apparel by Juicy Couture, Diesel, Phat Farm and Flowers by Zoe for their budding 'Idol'. There's also a great selection of dress-up clothes.

Dagerman's Just For Kids
2370 S Rainbow Boulevard, at W Sahara Avenue, West Las Vegas (798 5437/www.dagermans.com). Bus 101, 204. **Open** 10am-6pm Mon-Sat; noon-5pm Sun. **Credit** AmEx, MC, V.
This family-owned boutique is one of the most popular children's stores in town. Alongside upscale clothes, it also sells strollers, toys, bedding and other accessories for infants.

Janie & Jack
Fashion Show Mall, 3200 Las Vegas Boulevard South, at Spring Mountain Road (892 9571/www. janieandjack.com). Bus Deuce, 105, 203. **Open** 10am-9pm Mon-Fri; 10am-8pm Sat; 11am-7pm Sun. **Credit** AmEx, Disc, MC, V. **Map** p336 B6.
This precious addition to the Gymboree family relies on a sugar-coated colour palette to dress up its sweet ensembles for babies and toddlers. Personalised baby gifts include embroidered fleece blankets.

Toys

Build-a-Bear Workshop
Planet Hollywood (Miracle Mile Shops) *3667 Las Vegas Boulevard South, between E Harmon Avenue & E Flamingo Road (836 0899/ www.buildabear.com). Bus Deuce.* **Open** 10am-11pm Mon-Thur, Sun; 10am-midnight Fri, Sat. **Credit** AmEx, Disc, MC, V. **Map** p336 A7.
An individual teddy bear makes a cute gift for the one you love, or indulge the kids by letting them pick out their own gift. Choose your bear's fur colour,

Best-sellers and obscure tomes in the **Reading Room** at Mandalay Place.

eye colour, costume (the range is huge) and stuffing type, and watch as it is assembled by teddy experts. A real treat for children and the young at heart. **Other locations** Fashion Show Mall (*see p193*; 388 2574).

FAO Schwarz
Caesars Palace (Forum Shops) *3500 Las Vegas Boulevard South, at W Flamingo Road (796 6500/ www.fao.com). Bus Deuce, 202.* **Open** 10am-11pm Mon-Thur, Sun; 10am-midnight Fri, Sat. **Credit** AmEx, DC, Disc, MC, V. **Hotel** p68. **Map** p336 A7.
For kids, FAO Schwarz is right up there with Willy Wonka's Chocolate Factory: three storeys of playthings make it one of the largest toy shops in the US. There's also a private room for serious collectors.

Five Little Monkeys
Mandalay Bay (Mandalay Place) *3950 Las Vegas Boulevard South, at W Hacienda Avenue (632 9382/www.5littlemonkeys.com). Bus Deuce, 104, 105.* **Open** 10am-11pm daily. **Credit** AmEx, Disc, MC, V.
The toys here are organised by theme (fairies, pirates, dinosaurs) and feature such brands as Calico Critters, Whoozit and Corolle dolls. There are also arts and crafts to distract the little ones during dinner.

Toys of Yesteryear
2028 E Charleston Boulevard, at S Eastern Avenue, East Las Vegas (598 4030). Bus 110, 206. **Open** 11am-3pm Tue-Sat. **Credit** AmEx, DC, Disc, MC, V. **Map** p333 Z2.
Forget the dice clocks and gambling chips: this tiny shop has old-fashioned toys and collectibles for adults as well as children, including Kewpie dolls, *Star Wars* figures, books and cast-metal toys.

Electronics & photography

General
Best Buy (3820 S Maryland Parkway, at E Flamingo Road, 732 8283, www.bestbuy.com) and **Circuit City** (3778 S Maryland Parkway, at E Flamingo Road, 731 0374, www.circuit city.com), national chains dealing in audio, visual and computing kit of every stripe, have stores throughout the city. For troubleshooting, Best Buy also offers a **Geek Squad** (1-800 433 5778), who are available 24 hours a day for any computer-related emergencies (in store or call-out).

For affordable, non-digital film processing, head to one of the myriad branches of chain drugstores **Walgreens** (*see p206*) or **Smith's** (*see p202*). **Ritz Camera** (Sahara Pavilion, 2580 S Decatur Boulevard, at W Sahara Avenue, South-west Las Vegas, 889 1998), part of the Wolf Camera group, will also develop film.

Fry's Electronics
6845 Las Vegas Boulevard South, at I-215, South of Strip (932 1400/www.outpost.com). Bus Deuce, 105. **Open** 8am-9pm Mon-Fri; 9am-9pm Sat; 9am-7pm Sun. **Credit** Disc, MC, V.
This San Jose-based retailer is best known for out-fitting Silicon Valley's dotcommers during the boom. This branch stays true to Fry's not-so-humble roots, but also caters to those who merely want high quality computing, audio and video equipment –

most of it at very competitive prices. Fry's will move across Las Vegas Boulevard when the Town Square mall opens in autumn 2007.

Sahara Camera Centre

2305 E Sahara Avenue, at S Eastern Avenue, East Las Vegas (457 3333). Bus 110, 204. **Open** 9am-6pm Mon-Fri; 10am-5pm Sat. **Credit** AmEx, Disc, MC, V. **Map** p333 Z2.

Claiming to be 'Nevada's largest full-service camera store', the Sahara Camera Centre pretty much has – and does – it all, with rentals and repairs, quality new and used equipment, knowledgeable staff and one-hour photo processing. Prices are fair.

Specialist

For hi-fi buffs, the Fashion Show Mall (*see p193*) houses branches of audio-visual high-flyer **Bang & Olufsen** (731 9200) and the **Apple Store** (650 9550). You'll find the latest Sony technology at **Sony Style** (697 5420) in the Forum Shops at Caesars.

Tweeter

Boca Park Shopping Center, 8950 W Charleston Boulevard, at S Fort Apache Road, Summerlin (940 0900/www.tweeter.com). Bus 206. **Open** 10am-8pm Mon-Fri; 10am-7pm Sat; noon-6pm Sun. **Credit** AmEx, Disc, MC, V.

Tweeter has created a totally interactive store that shows visitors what their world would be like if it were completely computerised: home theatre, lights, security and so on. It also sells stand-alone plasma screens, computers, satellite radios and the like.

Fashion

Las Vegas's wild and unexpected growth as a shopping mecca has benefited one industry above all others: fashion. Every major chain is represented here, and a good many designer labels have also shown up to claim their stake. Some savvy European shoppers now come to Las Vegas instead of New York for a chance to restock their wardrobes at US prices. However, the city does still lack its own fashion scene: there aren't really many local designers working here, just plenty of very well-dressed Las Vegans.

There's a lot more to shopping in Vegas than the stores mentioned below, and the vast malls can make for an overwhelming experience. To get the most out of your limited shopping time, check out the malls' websites for a little pre-trip browsing and planning.

Designer

Most international design houses have stores in Vegas, which are to be found in the casino malls. **Via Bellagio** (*see p192*) offers **Prada**

(866 6886) and **Giorgio Armani** (893 8327), while the **Wynn Esplanade** (*see p192*) features **Jean Paul Gaultier** (770 3490), **Oscar de La Renta** (770 3487), **Brioni** (770 3440) and **Dior Homme** (770 3496). Across at the **Grand Canal Shoppes** (*see p191*), you'll find British brand **Burberry** (735 2600).

Dolce & Gabbana (892 0880) and rarely seen imports such as **Christian Lacroix** (731 0990) and classic London shirtmaker **Thomas Pink** (731 0263) reside at the **Forum Shops** (*see p191*), which also offers menswear from the likes of **Brooks Brothers** (369 0705), **Ralph Lauren** (650 5656) and **Roberto Cavalli** (893 0369). And **Mandalay Place** (*see p192*) also has a few stores that you won't find elsewhere, most notably Italian boutiques **Fornarina** (215 9300) and **Max&Co** (795 1015).

C Level

Boca Park Fashion Village, 750 S Rampart Boulevard, at W Charleston Boulevard, Summerlin (933 6867/www.clevel-lv.com). Bus 206. **Open** 11am-7pm Mon-Sat; 11am-6pm Sun. **Credit** AmEx, Disc, MC, V.

Budding socialites visit this two-storey loft space to keep up with owner Edith Castillo's well-edited, ever-changing collection of established and emerging designer labels (for men and women), including Heather Hawkins, Eugenia Kim and Rachel Pally.

Chelsea Boutique

Green Valley Ranch (District) *120 S Green Valley Parkway, between Paseo Verde Parkway & I-215, Henderson (270 7924). Bus 114.* **Open** 10am-9pm Mon-Sat; 11am-7pm Sun. **Credit** AmEx, Disc, MC, V. **Hotel** p111.

Owners Rebecca and Christa Becker (no relation) modelled their suburban version of a metropolitan boutique after NYC's trendy Chelsea neighbourhood. They even paid homage to the architecture by designing their space to look like a real brownstone, the perfect backdrop for feminine, flirty designs by Susana Monaco, Tracey Reese and Mint.

Indra Grae

6085 S Fort Apache Road, between W Russell & W Sunset Roads, West Las Vegas (636 9700). No bus. **Open** 10am-7pm Mon-Sat; noon-6pm Sun. **Credit** AmEx, MC, V.

Taking its cue from fashion capitals around the country (New York, LA, San Francisco), this shop stocks trendy labels with an eye for detail, including Charlotte Ronson, Rebecca Beeson and Free People. There's also a fabulous selection of affordable jewellery and handbags.

Intermix

Caesars Palace (Forum Shops) *3500 Las Vegas Boulevard South, at W Flamingo Road (731 1922/www.intermixonline.com). Bus Deuce, 202.* **Open** 10am-11pm Mon-Wed, Sun; 10am-midnight Thur-Sat. **Credit** AmEx, Disc, MC, V. **Hotel** p68. **Map** p336 A7.

The Keledjian brothers stock a mix of European and American designer womenswear in this growing chain of eclectic boutiques. Rather than buy an entire outfit, they prefer to help customers mix and match pieces (hence the name) from different collections by designers such as Chloé, Stella McCartney, Matthew Williamson and Missoni.

Ice Accessories

Caesars Palace (Forum Shops) *3500 Las Vegas Boulevard South, at W Flamingo Road (696 9700). Bus Deuce, 202.* **Open** 10am-11pm Mon-Thur, Sun; 10am-midnight Fri, Sat. **Credit** AmEx, Disc, MC, V. **Hotel** p68. **Map** p336 A7.
Beaded evening bags, dazzling costume jewellery and funky hair accessories from such designers as Konstantin, Isabelle Fiore and LuLu Guinness. There's also a selection of chic home accessories.

John Varvatos

Caesars Palace (Forum Shops) *3500 Las Vegas Boulevard South, at W Flamingo Road (939 0922/ www.johnvarvatos.com). Bus Deuce, 202.* **Open** 10am-11pm Mon-Thur, Sun; 10am-midnight Fri, Sat. **Credit** AmEx, DC, Disc, MC, V. **Hotel** p68. **Map** p336 A7.
This men's lifestyle collection has been going since 2000, finding bad-boy credibility by using the likes of Chris Cornell, Iggy Pop and Velvet Revolver to front its ad campaigns. Shop here for eclectic tailored suits, funky sportswear, accessories and great boots.

Mojitos Resort Wear

Wynn Las Vegas (Esplanade) *3131 Las Vegas Boulevard South, between E Desert Inn Road & Sands Avenue (770 3545/www.wynnlasvegas.com).*

Bus Deuce, 203. **Open** 9am-10pm Mon-Thur, Sun; 9am-11pm Fri, Sat. **Credit** AmEx, Disc, MC, V. **Hotel** p76. **Map** p335 & p336 B6.
This high-end boutique caters to vacationing jetsetters with designer labels for men, women and kids.

Scoop

Caesars Palace (Forum Shops) *3500 Las Vegas Boulevard South, at W Flamingo Road (734 0026/www.scoopnyc.com). Bus Deuce, 202.* **Open** 10am-11pm Mon-Thur, Sun; 10am-midnight Fri, Sat. **Credit** AmEx, DC, Disc, MC, V. **Hotel** p68. **Map** p336 A7.
This NY-based boutique chain has been hugely successful with its 'ultimate closet' concept, allowing hip shoppers (men, women and children) to find everything they need under one roof. Prices vary, with clothes, accessories and shoes from the likes of James Perse, Marc Jacobs and Lolita Jaca.

Still

Fashion Show Mall, 3200 Las Vegas Boulevard South, at W Spring Mountain Road (696 1209/ www.shopstill.com). Bus Deuce, 105, 203, 213. **Open** 10am-9pm Mon-Sat; 11am-7pm Sun. **Credit** AmEx, DC, Disc, MC, V. **Map** p336 B6.
Todd Burden has struck the fashion motherlode with this urban hipster boutique that sells super clothing by metro-magnets such as Rich & Skinny, Hysteric Glamour and Vivienne Westwood.

Talulah G

Fashion Show Mall, 3200 Las Vegas Boulevard South, at Spring Mountain Road (737 6000/www. talulahg.com). Bus Deuce, 105, 203. **Open** 10am-9pm Mon-Sat; 11am-7pm Sun. **Credit** AmEx, Disc, MC, V. **Map** p336 B6.

Eat, Drink, Shop

Pony up!

One unexpected benefit of the ten-day **National Finals Rodeo** (NFR; *see p219*), held in the city each December, is that it gives the city's mainstream retailers a well-deserved cowboy-booted kick in the ass. If you're looking to refurnish your ranch, saddle your hoss or outfit your nearest and dearest cowboy or cowgirl, bring your biggest pick-up truck and prepare to fill 'er up at one of three separate fairs, selling everything from housewares to jeans, linens to leather goods. There are even experts on hand who can steam your stetson and bend it to your liking.

The North Hall at the Las Vegas Convention Center (*see p309*) houses the **Original Cowboy Christmas**, the NFR's only officially sanctioned western shopping experience. Fans can find licensed goods from the NFR among the 400 vendors, as well as fashion shows and autograph signings. And in recent

years, a few savvy souls have started new gift shows as competition for the Original Cowboy Christmas: the Sands Expo hosts the **Country Western Gift Expo** during the NFR, while Mandalay Bay offers the **Cowboy Marketplace**.

Good news: the renegade salesmen bring more stuff to town. Bad news: a lot of times, it's the same stuff. Although the booths at each site change every year, shoppers looking for big brands (Lee, Levi Strauss, Tony Lama et al) will likely find them at all three sites. Smaller businesses, meanwhile, tend to shop at the same wholesale outlets, and so they end up with the same or similar items. However, if you look real close, you'll find a few stalls selling top-notch antique and vintage goods, as well as some talented craftsmen and artisans hawking their own one-of-a-kind creations.

Owner Meital Grantz is a New York expat with a fantastic eye. Her strong selection includes pieces by Sonia Rykiel, Matthew Williamson, Havaianas and Citizens of Humanity, and her obvious success in Las Vegas has led to a branch in Newport Beach's Fashion Island.

Other locations Boca Park Fashion Village, 750 S Rampart Boulevard, at W Charleston Boulevard, Summerlin (932 7000); Red Rock Resort, 11011 West Charleston Boulevard, at I-15, Summerlin (797 7848).

General

Miracle Mile (*see p192*) has a good range of trendy stores for those on a budget, among them **Urban Outfitters** (733 0058), **H&M** (coming soon) and **Ben Sherman** (688 4227), while the **Grand Canal Shoppes** (*see p191*) include branches of **Kenneth Cole** (836 1916) and **Ann Taylor** (731 0655).

However, as is often the case, the **Forum Shops** (*see p191*) comes out on top by a long way. Stores here include the pick of the US chains, among them **Abercrombie & Fitch** (731 0712) and perennial favourite **Banana Republic** (650 5623), alongside chic accessible designer labels such as **DKNY** (650 9670).

The **Fashion Show Mall** (*see p193*) mixes upscale with casual in a similar way to the Forum Shops, and with almost as much success. Among those present are surf shack **Quiksilver** (734 1313) and femme favourite **Betsey Johnson** (735 3338), plus the trendier likes of **Lucky Brand** (369 4116), **Diesel** (696 1055) and the youthful brand **Paul Frank** (369 2010). Don't forget the town's discount malls (*see p193*): you'll find over 150 different labels at the **Las Vegas Premium Outlets**, among them **Tommy Hilfiger** (383 8660), **Calvin Klein** (366 9898) and **Timberland** (386 3045).

Francesca's Collections

Green Valley Ranch (District) *120 S Green Valley Parkway, between Paseo Verde Parkway & I-215, Henderson (435 3288/www.francescas.net). Bus 114.* **Open** 10am-9pm Mon-Sat; 11am-7pm Sun. **Credit** AmEx, MC, V. **Hotel** p111.
Stocked with a treasure trove of trendy street fashions, girly baubles, glittering hair accessories and playful gifts, Francesca's is the perfect place to pick up that last-minute gift for the girls back home, at very affordable prices.

Jacqueline Jarrot

Planet Hollywood (Miracle Mile Shops) *3667 Las Vegas Boulevard South, between E Harmon Avenue & E Flamingo Road (731 3200/www. jacquelinejarrot.com). Bus Deuce.* **Open** 10am-11pm Mon-Thur, Sun; 10am-midnight Fri, Sat. **Credit** AmEx, Disc, MC, V. **Hotel** p85. **Map** p336 A7.

Paul Frank.

Probably the best place in town for casual accessories, from sunglasses to handbags to toe rings, this shop offers wares by over 300 trendy designers.

Lacoste

Caesars Palace (Forum Shops) *3500 Las Vegas Boulevard, at W Flamingo Road (791 7616/www. lacoste-usa.com). Bus Deuce, 202.* **Open** 10am-11pm Mon-Thur, Sun; 10am-midnight Fri, Sat. **Credit** AmEx, Disc, MC, V. **Hotel** p68. **Map** p336 A7.
The polo shirt reated by French tennis champion René Lacoste in the 1930s, bears the crocodile logo which comes from his nickname. There are cheaper goodies in the firm's shop at Las Vegas Premium Outlets.
Other locations Fashion Show Mall (*see p193*; 796 6676).

Suite 160

9350 W Sahara Avenue, at S Fort Apache Road, West Las Vegas (562 6136). Bus 204, 213. **Open** 10am-7pm Mon-Sat; 1-6pm Sun. **Credit** AmEx, Disc, MC, V.
The street chic brainchild of former skateboarder Jeffrey Brown. Look for old-school favourites from plus new urban lines by (among others) Elwood.

Ted Baker

Caesars Palace (Forum Shops) *3500 Las Vegas Boulevard South, at W Flamingo Road (369 4755/ www.tedbaker.co.uk). Bus Deuce, 202.* **Open** 10am-11pm Mon-Thur, Sun; 10am-midnight Fri, Sat. **Credit** AmEx, Disc, MC, V. **Hotel** p68. **Map** p336 A7.

This London-based label – there is no 'Ted Baker' per se – stocks well-cut, tidy but fun apparel for men and women. Their collection of shirts, suits and traditional (but quirky) gentlemen's accessories particularly stand out.

Used & vintage

Attic
1018 S Main Street, at E Charleston Boulevard, Downtown (388 4088/www.atticvintage.com). Bus 105, 106, 108, 207. **Credit** AmEx, DC, Disc, MC, V. **Map** p335 C3.
Its claim to be the largest vintage store in the world is as silly as the $1 admission charge (refundable on purchase, but that's not the point). Despite this, and its high prices, the Attic is still the best vintage store in Vegas. The ground floor has homewares and custom-made clothing; shoes and accessories are upstairs.

Buffalo Exchange
4110 S Maryland Parkway, at E Flamingo Road, University District (791 3960/www.buffaloexchange. com). Bus 109, 202. **Open** 10am-8pm Mon-Sat; 11am-7pm Sun. **Credit** MC, V. **Map** p333 Y3.
This countrywide vintage chain is more popular than ever, especially with students at nearby UNLV. Its prices range from budget to middling; the clothing is mainly second-hand or from shop clearances. There are plans for remodelling and expansion.

D'Loe's House of Style
220 E Charleston Boulevard, at S 3rd Street, Downtown (382 5688/www.houseofstylethenandnow. com). Bus Deuce, 105, 106, 108, 204. **Open** noon-6.30pm Tue-Sat. **Credit** AmEx, Disc, MC, V. **Map** p334 C3.
Mario D'Loe cut his teeth as a costume designer for Vegas shows before filling this store with finds from the 1960s and '70s. A few blocks away is Valentino's Zoot Suit Connection (906 S 6th Street, at E Charleston Boulevard, 383 9555), which offers similar vintage fare with the emphasis on eveningwear.

Fashion accessories & services

Clothing hire

Al Phillips (*see right*) rents men's formalwear. For details on weddings in Vegas, *see p270*.

David's Bridal
2600 W Sahara Avenue, at S Rancho Drive, West of Strip (367 4779/www.davidsbridal.com). Bus 106, 204. **Open** 11am-9pm Mon-Fri; 10am-6pm Sat; noon-6pm Sun. **Credit** AmEx, Disc, MC, V.
Off-the-rack gowns at reasonable prices in a variety of styles are this store's speciality. There are also tons of accessories, including frocks for the bridal party and dyeable shoes.

I&A Formalwear
3345 S Decatur Boulevard, between W Desert Inn & Spring Mountain Roads, West Las Vegas (364 5777/www.iaformalwear.com). Bus 103, 213. **Open** 9am-6pm Mon-Fri; 9am-5pm Sat. **Credit** MC, V.
The biggest range of designer-name tuxedos (Cardin, de la Renta, Dior) in Las Vegas. Tuxedo rentals start at $77 and gowns from $149.

Williams Costume Company
1226 S 3rd Street, at W Colorado Avenue, Downtown (384 1384). Bus Deuce, 105, 108, 206. **Open** 10am-5pm Mon-Sat. **Credit** AmEx, Disc, MC, V. **Map** p335 C3.
The only place in town that carries sufficient ancient Egyptian, Renaissance gentry and Elvis costumes to dress the bride, groom and all the guests in your chosen theme. Nightly rental is $50 to $100, plus deposit.

Cleaning & repairs

Al Phillips (www.alphillips-thecleaner.com) has locations all over Vegas, the most central is at 4130 Koval Lane (at E Flamingo Road, 733 1043). All branches provide dry-cleaning, laundry and repairs, and rent men's formalwear.

Cora's Coin Laundry
1097 E Tropicana Avenue, at S Maryland Parkway, University District (736 6181). Bus 109, 201. **Open** 8am-8pm daily. **No credit cards**. **Map** p333 Y3.
Just two miles off the Strip, Cora's is popular with UNLV folk, offering self-service or drop-off laundry, dry-cleaning and – of course – video poker.

Shoe Lab
3900 Paradise Road, between Sands Avenue & E Flamingo Road, East of Strip (791 2004/www.shoe lab.org). Bus 108. **Open** 8am-6pm Mon-Fri; 9am-4pm Sat. **Credit** AmEx, DC, Disc, MC, V. **Map** p333 C5.
The Shoe Lab can work miracles on any broken shoe or damaged handbag. It also sells leather care accessories such as polish, brushes and shoe trees.

Jewellery

Hit the jackpot? Vegas is the place to flash your cash on blinging baubles. Blow your winnings, or simply max out the credit cards at **Via Bellagio** (*see p192*) by picking up a **Tiffany & Co** tiara (697 5400) or indulge your loved one with a string of diamonds by **Fred Leighton** (693 7050). Trip the light fantastic with understated luxury at **Harry Winston** (933 7370) or invest in a future family heirloom from **Cartier** (733 6652), both to be found at the **Forum Shops** (*see p191*). Smaller spenders might prefer the pirate's treasures of **Jewelers of Las Vegas** (2400 Western Avenue, at W Sahara Avenue, West of Strip, 382 7411, www.thejewelers.com). Some of the shops listed under **Luggage** (*see p200*) also carry jewellery and fashion accessories.

Eat, Drink, Shop

Rocks rock at **Chrome Hearts**.

Chrome Hearts

Caesars Palace (Forum Shops) *3500 Las Vegas Boulevard South, at W Flamingo Road (893 9949/ www.chromehearts.com). Bus Deuce, 202.* **Open** 10am-11pm Mon-Thur, Sun; 10am-midnight Fri, Sat. **Credit** AmEx, DC, Disc, MC, V. **Hotel** p68. **Map** p336 A7.
Free your inner rock wild side at this fine silver and leather shop. Its signature handcrafted silver jewellery is adorned with skulls, crossbones, crucifixes and flames, but the store also sells some of the softest and most stylish leather jackets, trousers and coats money can buy.

Lingerie & underwear

Agent Provocateur

Caesars Palace (Forum Shops) *3500 Las Vegas Boulevard South, at W Flamingo Road (696 7174/ www.agentprovocateur.com). Bus Deuce, 202.* **Open** 10am-11pm Mon-Thur, Sun; 10am-midnight Fri, Sat. **Credit** AmEx, MC, V. **Hotel** p68. **Map** p336 A7.
The smarties behind Agent Provocateur know that there's something rather empowering about wearing fine lingerie, whether or not you share it. Look for some of the most titillating and trashy yet tasteful creations currently on the market.

Bare Essentials Fantasy Fashions

4029 W Sahara Avenue, at S Valley View Boulevard, West of Strip (247 4711/www.bareessentialsvegas. com). Bus 104, 204. **Open** 10am-7pm Mon-Sat; noon-5pm Sun. **Credit** AmEx, Disc, MC, V. **Map** p333 X2.

Whatever your fantasy (or gender), Bare Essentials will do you right. The camp-as-cowboys owners are correct in their claim that they make women feel at ease, but there are also men's essentials, costumes and 'accessories'.

Love Jones

Hard Rock *4455 Paradise Road, at Harmon Avenue, East of Strip (693 5007/www.lovejones. com). Bus 108.* **Open** 10am-11pm Mon-Thur, Sun; 10am-1am Fri, Sat. **Credit** AmEx, DC, Disc, MC, V. **Hotel** p96. **Map** p336 C7.
Fur-lined handcuffs, paddles, silk stockings, garter belts and lingerie from the likes of Honey Dew and Christie's make this a mentionable unmentionables boutique. It also sells a few flavoured lotions, potions and toys (but nothing electric). Hotel guests have access to 24-hour room service.

Luggage

Bloomingdale's Home (*see p209*) and **Macy's** (*see p190*) also stock a variety of travel bags and luggage in the lower price ranges.

Bags, Belts & Baubles

Wynn Esplanade *3131 Las Vegas Boulevard South, between E Desert Inn Road & Sands Avenue (770 3555/www.wynnlasvegas.com). Bus Deuce, 203.* **Open** 9am-11pm Mon-Thur; 9am-midnight Fri, Sat. **Credit** AmEx, Disc, MC, V. **Hotel** p76. **Map** p335 & p336 B6.
Leather goods, handbags, jewellery, sunglasses and other accessories by the likes of Bottega Veneta, Nancy Gonzalez and Adrienne Landau are displayed like miniature works of art in this well-designed shop. It's the perfect accompaniment to Outfit, the chic women's clothing store at Wynn.

Corsa Collections

Caesars Palace (Forum Shops) *3500 Las Vegas Boulevard South, at W Flamingo Road (733 9442). Bus Deuce, 202.* **Open** 10am-11pm Mon-Thur, Sun; 10am-midnight Fri, Sat. **Credit** AmEx, DC, Disc, MC, V. **Hotel** p68. **Map** p336 A7.
Handbags are this store's speciality. The designer collection includes bags by Marc Jacobs, Michael Kors, Longchamp, Furla, as well as luggage from Tumi, Kipling and Swiss Army.

Shoes

There are plenty of brand-name shoe stores scattered around the Strip, whether your taste is for slingbacks or sneakers. The selection at the **Grand Canal Shoppes** (*see p191*) is led by super-chic **Jimmy Choo** (733 1802) and the more casual **Rockport** (735 5082), while the **Fashion Show Mall** (*see p193*) has smart-casual Brit-import **Clarks** (732 1801), sports label **Puma** (892 9988) and the all-conquering **Skechers** (969 9905). Over at the **Forum Shops** (*see p191*), you'll find Italian designer

Salvatore Ferragamo (933 9333), the very Californian footwear of **Donald J Pliner** (796 0900) and **Niketown** (650 8888).

Designer Shoe Warehouse

2100 N Rainbow Boulevard, at W Lake Mead Boulevard, West Las Vegas (636 2060/www. dswshoe.com). Bus 101, 210. **Open** 9am-9pm Mon-Sat; 10am-7pm Sun. **Credit** AmEx, DC, Disc, MC, V.
The finest selection of discounted designer cobbling in town with footwear stacked from floor to ceiling. While the shoes may be not be this season's latest design, they're still fabulous. Accessories are available in the form of handbags and scarves.
Other locations Sun Mark Plaza, 671 Marks Street, at W Sunset Road, Henderson (547 0620).

Epic Shoos

1209 S Main Street, at W Charleston Boulevard, Downtown (388 4343/www.epicshoos.com). Bus 206. **Open** 11am-7pm Tue-Sat; noon-6pm Sun. **Credit** AmEx, DC, Disc, MC, V. **Map** p335 C3.
Todd Burden, owner of hipster clothing boutique Still (*see p197*), opened this minimalist sneaker shop in autumn 2006, specialising in the freshest brands (BBC, Creative Recreation) and old-school favourites (Nike, Reebok). Drop by on First Fridays (*see p216*) for new-release parties.

New Rock Boots

804 Las Vegas Boulevard South, at E Gass Avenue, Downtown (614 9464). Bus Deuce. **Open** 11am-8pm Mon-Sat. **Credit** AmEx, DC, Disc, MC, V. **Map** p334 C3.

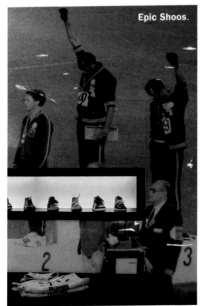

Epic Shoos.

Cross John Fluevog's edgy style with the Doc Martens aesthetic, stir in the 1970s rock 'n' roll style of Kiss, and lo: New Rock Boots. Decorative touches such as buckles, straps, flames and skulls make the boots popular with punks, goths and bikers, but there's also a wide selection of stilettos.

Shoe In

Wynn Las Vegas *3131 Las Vegas Boulevard South, between E Desert Inn Road & Sands Avenue (770 3460/www.wynnlasvegas.com). Bus Deuce, 203, 213.* **Open** 10am-11pm Mon-Thur, Sun; 10am-midnight Fri, Sat. **Credit** AmEx, Disc, MC, V. **Hotel** p76. **Map** p335 & p336 B6.
Shoe In specialises in fine footwear (boots, stilettos, Mary Janes, flip-flops) by well-know designers such as Christian Louboutin, Emma Hope and Stuart Weitzman. It's the best selection of unique shoes outside a department store in the city.

Food & drink

Bakeries

Cupcakery

9680 S Eastern Avenue, at E Silverado Ranch Boulevard, Henderson (207 2253/www.thecupcakery. com). Bus 110. **Open** 8am-6pm Mon-Fri; 10am-6pm Sat; noon-6pm Sun. **Credit** AmEx, MC, V.
Tickle Me Pink, Boston Dream, Kir Royale... the fanciful little cakes taste as good as they sound. They can even print a digital photo on the top.

Lenôtre

Paris Las Vegas (Le Boulevard) *3655 Las Vegas Boulevard South, at E Flamingo Road (946 4341). Bus Deuce, 202.* **Open** 6.30am-11pm daily. **Credit** AmEx, DC, Disc, MC, V. **Hotel** p74. **Map** p336 A7.
Lenôtre is loaded to the gunwales with the most luscious eclairs, pains au chocolat, cookies and croissants. You have to order cafeteria-style, but the premises are bright and spacious, and there's plenty to feast your eyes on while you wait.

Nothing Bundt Cake

9711 S Eastern Avenue, at E Silverado Ranch Boulevard, Henderson (314 0520/www.nothing bundtcakes.com). Bus 110. **Open** 9am-6pm Mon-Fri; 9am-4pm Sat. **Credit** AmEx, MC, V.
The chocolate-chocolate-chip is a crowd-pleaser, but the carrot Bundt cake (it's a corruption of German Bund cake) is the real show-stopper. Other flavours include lemon, pineapple-upside-down, spice and plain chocolate.
Other locations 8512 W Sahara Avenue, at S Durango Drive, West Las Vegas (871 6301).

Drinks

Las Vegas has the usual liquor stores, plus several options for wine buffs. **Bleu Gourmet** also has a superb selection of wines, *see p174*.

Eat, Drink, Shop

55° Wine + Design

Mandalay Bay (Mandalay Place) *3930 Las Vegas Boulevard South, at W Hacienda Avenue (632 9373/www.55degreeslasvegas.com). Bus Deuce, 104, 105.* **Open** 10am-11pm daily. **Credit** AmEx, DC, Disc, MC, V. **Map** p336 A9.

Brought to you by the people behind the four-storey wine tower at Aureole (*see p153*), 55° offers a comprehensive wine selection, a tasting bar and interactive PCs enabling customers to select wines.

Lee's Discount Liquor

3480 E Flamingo Road, at S Pecos Road, East Las Vegas (458 5700). Bus 111, 202. **Open** 9am-10pm Mon-Thur; 9am-11pm Fri, Sat; 9am-9pm Sun. **Credit** AmEx, Disc, MC, V. **Map** p333 Z3.

Old favourites, hard-to-find European wines and dirt-cheap prices make Lee's the best liquor store in town. There's a surprisingly good range of beers from around the planet, and a few ciders as well. **Other locations** throughout the city.

Marché Bacchus

2620 Regatta Drive, at Mariner Way, West Las Vegas (804 8008/www.marchebacchus.com). Bus 210. **Open** 10am-10pm Mon-Sat; 10am-3pm Sun. **Credit** AmEx, MC, V.

This fabulous little French store sells fine wines, champagnes, pâtés, cheeses, some sandwiches and salads, and tasting kits. There are also monthly wine-tasting sessions, and outdoor seating on a terrace by the lake where you can enjoy an à la carte Sunday brunch (10am-4pm).

Valley Cheese & Wine

1770 W Horizon Ridge Parkway, at Arroyo Grande, Henderson (341 8191/www.valleycheeseandwine. com). Bus 114. **Open** 10am-8pm Mon-Sat; 11am-5pm Sun. **Credit** AmEx, MC, V.

This gourmet wine and cheese shop supplies Las Vegas with artisanal and handcrafted wine, beer, speciality food and cheeses. Owner Bob Howald will be happy to help select wines to match your food.

General

There isn't a major supermarket on the Strip, but all the main chains have branches within easy reach. Just east of the Strip, the branches of Safeway-owned **Vons** (1131 E Tropicana Avenue, at S Maryland Parkway, 798 8697, www.vons.com) and **Smith's** (2540 S Maryland Parkway, at E Sahara Avenue, 735 8928, www.smithsfoodanddrug.com) are both open 24 hours daily. In Downtown, try **Albertsons** (1760 E Charleston Boulevard, at S Bruce Street, Downtown, 366 1550, www.albertsons.com), open 6am to midnight daily.

British Foods

3375 S Decatur Boulevard, at W Desert Inn Road, South-west Las Vegas (579 7777/www.britishgrocers. com). Bus 103, 213. **Open** 10am-6pm daily. **Credit** AmEx, Disc, MC, V.

Vosges Haut-Chocolat.

British Food offers Las Vegas's 40,000 resident expats a taste of home: HP sauce, Heinz baked beans, proper marmalade, teas and so on.

Trader Joe's

2101 S Decatur Boulevard, at W Sahara Avenue, West Las Vegas (367 0227/www.traderjoes. com). Bus 103, 204. **Open** 9am-9pm daily. **Credit** AmEx, Disc, MC, V.

An old-style grocery store with a twist: all products are tested to ensure that they are 'the best' (it claims). You can find gluten-, sodium- and GM-free produce as well as chocolate cookies and party foods. **Other locations** throughout the city.

Whole Foods

8855 W Charleston Boulevard, at S Fort Apache Road, Summerlin (254 8655/www.wholefoodsmarket. com). Bus 206. **Open** 7am-10pm daily. **Credit** AmEx, Disc, MC, V.

The produce and meat sections at the world's leading natural and organic grocer are great, but don't miss the seafood case, the deli (for wonderful cheeses and breads) and the impressive prepared foods. **Other locations** 100 S Green Valley Parkway, at Paseo Verde Parkway, Henderson (361 8183).

Specialist

Chocaholics in Vegas shouldn't miss the **Ethel M Chocolates** factory in Henderson (*see p149*), but in central Vegas there are only really three options. The most distinctive is Chicago-based chocolatier **Vosges Haut-Chocolat** (at the

Forum Shops; 836 9866), which offers some glorious truffle concoctions. Otherwise, Belgian confectioner **Godiva** is at the Forum Shops, Miracle Mile, the Grand Canal Shoppes and the Fashion Show Mall, while Swiss chocolatier **Teuscher** is at Miracle Mile (866 6624).

Gee's Oriental Market

4109 W Sahara Avenue, at S Arville Street, West Las Vegas (362 5287). Bus 104, 204. **Open** 8am-8pm Mon-Sat; 9am-5pm Sun. **Credit** Disc, MC, V.
The best place for Chinese, Thai, Vietnamese and Filipino groceries, with first-rate fresh produce and seafood. Should you have developed a craving, this is the only place in Las Vegas that sells the delicacy *meang da na* (a cockroach-like insect).

International Marketplace

5000 S Decatur Boulevard, at W Tropicana Avenue, West Las Vegas (889 2888). Bus 103, 201. **Open** 9am-6pm Mon-Sat. **Credit** AmEx, Disc, MC, V.
This huge building is basically a warehouse containing every kind of imported edible goodie and gadget, with prices on the better side of cheap.

Siena Deli

2250 E Tropicana Avenue, at S Eastern Avenue, East Las Vegas (736 8424). Bus 110, 201. **Open** 8am-6pm Mon-Sat. **Credit** AmEx, Disc, MC, V. **Map** p333 Z3.
Siena's Italian owner continues to bring the best of Italian cuisine to Vegas. Prices can be steep (119-year-old balsamic vinegar at $149.95!) but the quality is beyond doubt. Siena also stocks Italian cookware.

Rainbow's End Natural Foods

1100 E Sahara Avenue, at S Maryland Parkway, East Las Vegas (737 1338/www.rainbowsendlas vegas.com). Bus 109, 204. **Open** 9am-8pm Mon-Fri; 10am-8pm Sat; 11am-5pm Sun. **Credit** AmEx, Disc, MC, V. **Map** p333 Y2.
The closest place to the Strip to buy good quality fresh fruit also offers a broad range of herbs, vitamins and bodycare items.

Wild Oats Natural Marketplace

7250 W Lake Mead Boulevard, between N Buffalo Drive & N Rainbow Boulevard, Summerlin (942 1500/www.wildoats.com). Bus 210. **Open** 7am-10pm daily. **Credit** AmEx, Disc, MC, V.
Prices are a bit steep, but Wild Oats' stock of organic produce, health foods, natural bodycare products, homeopathic medicines and macrobiotic supplies is exemplary. The café offers juices and healthy snacks.
Other locations 517 N Stephanie Street, at W Sunset Road, Henderson (458 9427).

Gifts & souvenirs

Las Vegas souvenirs

As the cash-spending hordes schlep through the malls buying stuff you can pick up in any US city, savvy shoppers go off the beaten track for local souvenirs with more charisma. If you're after something specific to Las Vegas, the Strip is dotted with tatty shops selling everything from snow domes (it's the desert, folks!) to dice clocks, and more gambling mementos than you could shake a croupier's rake at. For unique works of art, try **Dale Chihuly**'s gallery at Via Bellagio, or the **Entertainment Galleries**.

Bonanza Gifts

2460 Las Vegas Boulevard South, at W Sahara Avenue (385 7359/www.worldslargestgiftshop.com). Bus Deuce, 204. **Open** 8am-midnight daily. **Credit** AmEx, Disc, MC, V. **Map** p335 C4.
Bonanza's huge sign declares it to be the 'world's largest gift store'; certainly, it's hard to imagine one much bigger. The store sells everything from postcards to place mats, Elvis shot glasses to dice clocks, playing cards to earrings. Harkening back to the days of Route 66 gift shops, there's also plenty of American Indian turquoise and silver jewellery.

Chihuly Store

Bellagio (Via Bellagio) *3600 Las Vegas Boulevard South, at W Flamingo Road (693 7995/ www.portlandpress). Bus Deuce, 202.* **Open** 10am-midnight daily. **Credit** AmEx, DC, Disc, MC, V. **Hotel** p68. **Map** p336 A7.
It's fitting that glass sculptor Dale Chihuly should open his first signature gallery inside the Bellagio: his largest sculpture, with more than 2,000 pieces of glass, hangs from the ceiling of the hotel lobby. While mainly focusing on affordable Chihuly glass editions, which sell like hot cakes, the store also has some more elaborate (and expensive) pieces.

Entertainment Galleries

Venetian (Grand Canal Shoppes) *3355 Las Vegas Boulevard South, at Sands Avenue (866 6813/www.s2art.com). Bus Deuce, 105, 203, 213.* **Open** 10am-11pm Mon-Thur, Sun; 10am-midnight Fri, Sat. **Credit** AmEx, DC, Disc, MC, V. **Hotel** p75. **Map** p336 A6.
This amazing lithograph shop specialises in limited editions of Hollywood movie posters and classic French posters, which it produces on 130-year-old printing presses in the Downtown Arts District (at the S² Art Group Atelier).
Other locations Jack Gallery, Mandalay Place (*see p192*; 632 4770); Jack Gallery, Fashion Show Mall (*see p193*; 731 0074).

Gamblers General Store

800 S Main Street, at E Gass Avenue, Downtown (382 9903/www.gamblersgeneralstore.com). Bus Deuce, 105, 106, 108. **Open** 9am-6pm daily. **Credit** AmEx, Disc, MC, V. **Map** p334 C2.
This well-stocked shop is packed with gift ideas for that special gambler in your life. There's something to suit all budgets, from a single casino chip costing a couple of coins to vintage video poker machines. Along with the collectibles are pretty much everything you need to play any of the casino games, including a library of 'how to' gaming books.

Las Vegas Paper Doll

*231 W Charleston Boulevard, at Grand Central
Parkway, Downtown (385 7892/www.lvpaperdoll.
com). Bus 206.* **Open** *10am-6pm Mon-Sat.* **Credit**
AmEx, MC, V. **Map** *p335 C3.*

Owner Anne Kellogg's passion for paper is evident
in this beautiful stationery and gift boutique inside
the historic Holsum bread building. Someone's birthday? Here's where to find the card, the gift and the
paper in which to wrap it. The eclectic stock of
magnets, books, cards, jewellery and baby goods are
the direct result of Kellogg's keen eye for design.

Rainbow Feather Dyeing Company

*1036 S Main Street, at E Charleston Boulevard,
Downtown (598 0988/www.rainbowfeatherco.com).
Bus Deuce, 105, 106, 108.* **Open** *9am-4pm Mon-Fri;
9am-1pm Sat.* **Credit** *MC, V.* **Map** *p335 C2.*

Master feather-crafter Bill Girard sells big, beautiful, colourful and handmade boas to everyone from
showgirls to Cirque du Soleil at his unassuming
store in the emerging Arts District.

Serge's Showgirl Wigs

*Commercial Center, 953 E Sahara Avenue, between
S 6th Street & S Maryland Parkway, East of Strip
(732 1015/www.showgirlwigs.com). Bus 109, 204.*
Open *10am-5.30pm Mon-Sat.* **Credit** *AmEx, Disc,
MC, V.* **Map** *p333 Y2.*

In Las Vegas, wigs never went out of fashion.
Serge's is the world's largest wig retailer, offering
thousands of natural and synthetic hairpieces
in hundreds of styles and colours.

Sex & erotica

The best of the adult bookstores, the **Rancho
Adult Entertainment Center** (4820 N Rancho
Drive, at W Lone Mountain Drive, North-west
Las Vegas, 645 6104), is open 24-7. Its staff are
friendly and they welcome female shoppers.

Adult Superstore

*3850 W Tropicana Avenue, at S Valley View
Boulevard, West of Strip (798 0144). Bus 104,
201.* **Open** *24hrs daily.* **Credit** *AmEx, Disc,
MC, V.* **Map** *p333 X3.*

There are four branches of this locals' favourite, but
this is the biggest of them. The magazine and video
sections are devoted to every fetish and fantasy
that's legal in Nevada, and there's an unequalled
selection of toys, fetish gear and sexy food items.
Other locations throughout the city.

Love Boutique

*3275 Industrial Road, at Spring Mountain Road,
West of Strip (731 5655/www.dejavu.com). Bus 105,
203.* **Open** *10am-4am daily.* **Credit** *Disc, MC, V.*
Map *p336 A6.*

Located next to the Déjà Vu (*see p223*), Love sells
an extensive collection of lingerie and novelty gift
items. Kick off a bachelor/bachelorette party here.
Other locations throughout the city.

Paradise Electro Stimulations

*1509 W Oakey Boulevard, at S Western Avenue,
Stratosphere Area (474 2991/www.peselectro.com).*

Las Vegas Paper Doll.

Bus Deuce, 105, 108. **Open** 10am-6pm Mon-Thur; 10am-7pm Fri; noon-6pm Sat. **Credit** AmEx, DC, Disc, MC, V. **Map** p335 B3.
'The Studio' is known for its electric muscle-stimulation devices: dildos, plugs and sheaths, all composed of crystal-clear plastic and attachable to an electrical impulse control unit that stimulates the user from the inside out, 'harmonising with the body's own electrical impulses'. If you say so.

Tobacconists

Casa Fuente
Caesars Palace (Forum Shops) *3500 Las Vegas Boulevard South, at W Flamingo Road (731 5051). Bus Deuce, 202.* **Open** 10am-11pm Mon-Thur, Sun; 10am-midnight Fri, Sat. **Credit** AmEx, Disc, MC, V. **Hotel** p68. **Map** p336 A7.
The first store from the Arturo Fuente brand is halfway between a shop and a cigar bar. The vast walk-in humidor holds cigars from around the world; also on sale is a ton of accessories.

Havana Cigar Bar
3900 Paradise Road, between E Flamingo Road & Sands Avenue, East of Strip (892 9555/www. havanasmoke.com). Bus 108. **Open** 9am-2am Mon-Thur; 9am-1am Fri; 2pm-1am Sat; 2-10pm Sun. **Credit** AmEx, Disc, MC, V. **Map** p336 C7.
Aficionados swear this cigar and wine bar is the best place in town to some take some time out, sit down and enjoy the pleasure of a fine cigar and a good glass of wine. Its range of accessories is as strong as that of its cigars.

Las Vegas Cigar Co
3750 Las Vegas Boulevard South, between E Tropicana & E Harmon Avenues (262 6100/www. lvcigar.com). Bus Deuce. **Open** 8am-10pm daily. **Credit** AmEx, DC, Disc, MC, V. **Map** p336 A8.
The LVCC's 12 established varieties of cigar are hand-rolled daily, in-house, using Cuban-seed tobacco imported from Ecuador and Dominican Republic.

Health & beauty

Complementary medicine

Body Works Massage Therapy
5025 S Eastern Avenue, between E Tropicana & E Hacienda Avenues, East Las Vegas (736 8887). Bus 110, 201. **Open** by appt. **Credit** AmEx, Disc, MC, V. **Map** p333 Z4.
For more than ten years, Body Works' masseurs and masseuses have been kneading, prodding and pounding, with treatments including Swedish deep tissue and Chinese mix, as well as muds and salts.

T&T Ginseng
Chinatown Mall, 4115 Spring Mountain Road, between S Arville Street & Wynn Road, West Las Vegas (368 3898). Bus 104, 203, 213. **Open** 10am-8.30pm daily. **Credit** AmEx, Disc, MC, V.

At this fascinating store and Chinese herbal pharmacy, diagnosis and treatment are handled with ancient wisdom and extreme care. An oriental medical doctor and herbalist are on duty every day.

Worton's Palmistry Studios
4644 W Charleston Boulevard, at S Decatur Boulevard, West Las Vegas (386 0121). Bus 206. **Open** by appt. **No credit cards.**
The first licensed psychic in Las Vegas, Worton's has been offering professional palmistry and astrology readings since 1958.

Hairdressers & barbers

ARCS: a Robert Cromeans Salon
Mandalay Bay (Mandalay Place) *3950 Las Vegas Boulevard South, at W Hacienda Avenue (632 6130/www.robertcromeans.com). Bus Deuce, 104, 105.* **Open** 9am-7pm Mon-Fri; 8am-8pm Sat; 10am-6pm Sun. **Credit** AmEx, Disc, MC, V. **Hotel** p71. **Map** p336 A9.
The prices at crazy coiffeur Cromean's trendy Paul Mitchell salon are about the same as his California salons: in other words, eye-watering.

Globe Salon
Westland Fair Center, 1121 S Decatur Boulevard, at W Charleston Boulevard, West Las Vegas (938 4247/www.globesalon.com). Bus 103, 206. **Open** 11am-4pm Tue; 11am-7pm Wed, Thur; 9am-4pm Fri; 9am-5pm Sat. **Credit** AmEx, MC, V.
This award-winning Bumble+Bumble network hair and skin care salon is run by Vegas native and 'Hairstylist to the Hip' Staci Linklater, who oversees a talented team of professionals in a mod-style space just west of the Strip. There's a branch coming to Downtown in 2008.

Truefitt & Hill
Caesars Palace (Forum Shops) *3500 Las Vegas Boulevard South, at W Flamingo Road (735 7428/ www.truefittandhill.com). Bus Deuce, 202.* **Open** *Store* 9am-11pm daily. *Barber* 9am-8pm daily. **Credit** AmEx, Disc, MC, V. **Hotel** p68. **Map** p336 A7.
Gents have been getting cropped and shaved at Truefitt & Hill in London since 1805, and in Las Vegas since 2004. The look of the store (mahogany woods, navy accents) reflects the company's rich history, as do the classic cuts. Other services include straight-razor shaves, manicures and shoe shines.

Opticians

Frame Fixer (*3961 W Charleston Boulevard, at S Valley View Boulevard, West Las Vegas, 735 7879*) does fast, friendly and gentle repairs.

Lunettes
Fashion Show Mall, 3200 Las Vegas Boulevard South, at Spring Mountain Road (733 7624). Bus Deuce, 105, 203. **Open** 10am-9pm Mon-Sat; 11am-7pm Sun. **Credit** AmEx, DC, Disc, MC, V. **Map** p335 & p336 B6.

Shades are a must in a city that sees an average of 320 days of sun per year. Lunettes sells products by designers including Gucci, Oliver Peoples, Cartier and Kia Yomoto. Also in the Fashion Show Mall, Sunshades (731 3598) has a similarly strong selection, including sportier shades from Oakley and fancier specs from Kate Spade.

Nu Vision Cyclery/Sport Optics

8447 W Lake Mead Boulevard, at N Rampart Boulevard, Summerlin (228 1333/www.nuvision cyclery.com). Bus 210. **Open** 10am-6pm Mon-Fri. **Credit** MC, V.

Mike Hileman, a licensed optician and avid cyclist, runs this one-stop shop where sportspeople can find cool prescription eyewear that stays on the head, no matter how rough the play. Hileman sells and services Oakley Rx, Adidas, Rudy Project and Dragon Optical, and also stocks sports goggles for swimming and skiing.

Oculus

Caesars Palace (Appian Way Shops) *3570 Las Vegas Boulevard South, at W Flamingo Road (731 4850/www.oculusltd.com). Bus Deuce, 202.* **Open** 10am-8pm Mon-Thur, Sun; 10am-9pm Fri, Sat. **Credit** AmEx, Disc, MC, V. **Hotel** p68. **Map** p336 A7.

This outpost of Dr Ed Malik's stylish Eyes & Optics boutique offers an excellent selection of frames from designers such as Oliver Peoples and Alain Mikli, plus eye examinations, spectacle repairs and sunglasses. The optician is also available for prescription emergencies.

Pharmacies

You'll find drugstores all over the city. There's a 24-hour branch of **Walgreens** (www.walgreens.com) near the MGM Grand on the Strip (3765 Las Vegas Boulevard South, 739 9645). There's another 24-7 branch Downtown (495 E Fremont Street, at S 5th Street, 385 1284), though the pharmacy is open limited hours (9am-7pm Mon-Fri; 9am-6pm Sat; 10am-6pm Sun).

Shops

The major department stores (*see pp189-190*) stock all the big-name brands. Canadian giant **MAC** has a store (369 8770) in the Forum Shops.

Aveda

Planet Hollywood (Miracle Mile Shops) *3667 Las Vegas Boulevard South, between E Harmon Avenue & E Flamingo Road (732 3290/ www.aveda.com). Bus Deuce.* **Open** 10am-11pm Mon-Thur, Sun; 10am-midnight Fri, Sat.

Divine-smelling, all-natural hair care, skin care and beauty products. The signature lip balm is a must. **Other locations** Fashion Show Mall (*see p193*; 733 6660); Aveda Institute, 4856 S Eastern Avenue, at E Tropicana Avenue, East Las Vegas (459 2900).

Fresh

Caesars Palace (Forum Shops) *3500 Las Vegas Boulevard South, at W Flamingo Road (631 5000/ www.fresh.com). Bus Deuce, 202.* **Open** 10am-11pm Mon-Thur, Sun; 10am-midnight Fri, Sat. **Credit** AmEx, MC, V. **Hotel** p68. **Map** p336 A7.

Clean gets tasty with Fresh bath products, made with sugar, milk, soya and even saké. The line also includes some great perfumes and basic cosmetics in natural-looking hues for all skin tones.

Kiehl's

Caesars Palace (Forum Shops) *3500 Las Vegas Boulevard South, at W Flamingo Road (784 0025/ www.kiehls.com). Bus Deuce, 202.* **Open** 10am-11pm Mon-Thur, Sun; 10am-midnight Fri, Sat. **Credit** AmEx, MC, V. **Hotel** p68. **Map** p336 A7.

The simplicity of the skin- and hair-care products sold at Kiehl's is part of their appeal, as is its commitment never to test on animals. It sells lotions and potions for all skin and hair types, created with the entire family in mind.

Sephora

Venetian (Grand Canal Shoppes) *3377 Las Vegas Boulevard South, between Sands Avenue & E Flamingo Road (735 3896/www.sephora.com). Bus Deuce, 105, 203.* **Open** 10am-11pm Mon-Thur, Sun; 10am-midnight Fri, Sat. **Credit** AmEx, Disc, MC, V. **Hotel** p75. **Map** p335 & p336 B6.

The most comprehensive cosmetics emporium in town contains stock from Dior and Yves Saint Laurent, hip offerings from Smashbox, Nars, Paul & Joe, and an impressive and good-value own-brand range. Test out the goods in the application areas or let a pro get to work on you.

Other locations Miracle Mile (*see p192*; 737 0550).

Spas & salons

The odds are that you didn't travel to Las Vegas to consult a nutritionist, improve your sleeping habits or (shudder) detox. There's only one thing that most visitors want from a spa in Sin City: pleasure. Many casinos have spas these days, those listed below are among the best in the city. For men's treatments, *see right; It's a man's world.*

Bathhouse

Thehotel at Mandalay Bay *3950 Las Vegas Boulevard South, at W Hacienda Avenue (1-877 632 9636/632 9636/www.mandalaybay.com). Bus Deuce, 104, 105.* **Open** 6am-8.30pm daily. **Daily pass** *Hotel guests* $30. *Visitors* $35. *All* free with spa services over $50. **Hotel** p95. **Map** p336 A9.

The first clue that the Bathhouse differs from other Vegas spas is revealed the moment you step into the long, suede-lined hallway and are greeted graciously by staff clad in slick, space-age uniforms before a backdrop of textured slate, frosted glass, cool running water and hints of shocking chartreuse. Indulge in an Asian tea bath (chai or green) capped off by the bamboo sugar scrub. Not a rubber ducky in sight.

It's a man's world

Look carefully and you'll find it between the chakra balancing and the prenatal body massage. The 'Man Zone': two pages of offerings just for guys at Caesars' Qua Spa. Two among a dozen pages of girly pampering.

Men are still not getting equal treatment from the spa industry. Most menus are like those at Qua, and some have even fewer male-oriented offerings. It's partly the fault of the men themselves. For one thing, there are more fabulous man-things to do in Vegas than exfoliate. And for another, after that whole massage-table incident in *The Godfather*, who can blame the gents for being a little standoffish?

But guys are slowly getting closer, one hydrotherapy at a time, and spas do seem more willing to meet men in the middle with a little masculinity. So, as a nudge towards holistic vacationing (or, at least, an alternative hangover cure to bloody marys), here are five of the more manly treatments being offered in Sin City...

Arabian Knights Facial & Body Treatment

Qua Spa at Caesars Palace (see p208); $260.
Strange but apparently true: coffee has 'skin-healing properties'. Staff put ground Arabica and Dead Sea salts on your body to 'slough away dead cells'. And then? 'After your coffee application, you will receive a purifying and relaxing facial.' We'll take a venti!

Mana'ia Escape

Bathhouse at Thehotel at Mandalay Bay (see left); $325.
If you want to be metrosexual and spend a half-day in the spa, this package ('beautiful man' in Hawaiian) is for you: a body buff, a eucalyptus wrap, a 'gentleman's facial' and a hot stone massage.

A Man for Four Seasons

Spa at Four Seasons (632 5000); $485.
A package 'for the man who appreciates the finer things in life'. Apparently, this means 'a gentlemen's facial followed by a therapeutic massage and champagne mud wrap'. Sorry: no beer substitutes.

Executive Men's Back Treatment

Spa Bellagio at Bellagio (693 7472); $90.
A facial for your back! The therapy consists of 'a deep pore enzyme cleansing, exfoliation and extractions along with a repair ampoule massage and specialty mask suited for your specific needs'. Hair waxing not included.

Icelandic Fire & Ice Experience

Grand Spa at MGM Grand (891 3077); $280.
'Derived from Iceland, this treatment is based on elements that are harvested from geo-thermal pools and the sea.' Manly! The treatment consists of a salt scrub, body wrap with sea kelp and spruce oil, and the grand finale: a friction foot massage. Well, what kind of happy ending did you expect?

Bathhouse at Thehotel at Mandalay Bay.

Planet Hollywood Spa by Mandara

Planet Hollywood *3667 Las Vegas Boulevard South, between E Harmon & E Flamingo Roads (785 5772/www.mandaraspa.com).* **Bus** Deuce, 202. **Open** 6am-7pm daily. **Daily pass** $25. **Hotel** p85. **Map** p336 A7.

With its variety of resurfacing facials, miracle lip and eye therapies and scalp massages, the new Planet Hollywood spa will have you ready for your 15 minutes of fame. If you really want to be pampered like an A-lister, book the signature Mandara massage, a blend of Japanese shiatsu, Hawaiian Lomi Lomi, Swedish and Balinese massage techniques performed by two experienced therapists. Lights, camera, relax.

Qua Baths & Spa

Caesars Palace *3570 Las Vegas Boulevard South, at W Flamingo Road (731 7776/www.quabathsand spa.com).* **Bus** Deuce, 202. **Open** 6am-8pm daily. **Daily pass** $35; free with spa services over $75. **Hotel** p68. **Map** p336 A7.

Housed in the Augustus Tower, Caesars' luxurious spa is themed after Roman baths. Within tubs of mineral-rich waters, a Laconium sauna (inspired by ancient Roman steam baths) and an arctic ice room (heated floors and benches under falling snow), therapists practise ritualistic therapies. Take Qua's Mystic Journey and enjoy a bamboo body exfoliation, a lotus flower and water lily wrap and an essential oil facial and scalp massage. When in Rome…

Red Rock Spa

Red Rock *221 N Rampart Boulevard, at Summerlin Parkway, West Las Vegas (798 7878/ www.redrocklasvegas.com).* **Bus** 206. **Open** 6am-8pm daily. **Daily pass** *Hotel guests* free. *Visitors* $35; free with spa services. **Hotel** p112.

This modern retreat is frequented by local socialites as much for its proximity to their homes as for its sleek aesthetic. Situated next to the lush pool, the treatment suites appear to float on water. After a hike, order a Champagne Pedicure and Caviar Creams: this champagne cocktail for you and your feet includes 80 minutes of deep exfoliation, soothing masques, moisturising caviar lotion, menthol foot balm massage plus, of course, a glass of champagne. Cheers!

Spa at Wynn

Wynn Las Vegas *3131 Las Vegas Boulevard South, between E Desert Inn Road & Sands Avenue (770 3900/www.wynnlasvegas.com).* **Bus** Deuce, 203, 213. **Open** 9am-7pm daily. **Daily pass** $25; free with salon services over $75. **Hotel** px76. **Map** p335 B6.

Reserve one of the 45 treatment rooms inside this Asian-inspired retreat and indulge in a bamboo lemongrass body scrub, a saké body treatment or a shiatsu massage. The Good Luck Ritual is based on feng shui, with a 50-minute heated Thai herb massage, a moisturising hand and foot massage, and a wild lime botanical scalp treatment. Hotel guests may use the lavish spa facilities without booking a salon session; non-guests can only use the spa by booking a salon treatment (Mon-Thur only).

Tattoos & piercings

Hart & Huntington Tattoo Company

Palms *4321 W Flamingo Road, at S Valley View Boulevard, West of Strip (942 7777/http://hartand huntingtontattoo.com).* **Bus** 201. **Open** 11am-2am Mon-Fri; 10am-2am Sat, Sun. **Credit** AmEx, Disc, MC, V. **Hotel** p98. **Map** p333 X3.

Motocross legend Carey Hart and club promoter John Huntington (the man behind the original Pimp 'n' Ho Costume Ball) have set up this hip tattoo parlour inside the Palms, and promptly landed their own TV show, 'Inked.' Huntington has since sold the shop to Hart, but the patrons hardly seem to care. Guests can book a slot at the same time as they make their hotel reservations.

Pussykat Tattoo Parlor

4972 S Maryland Parkway, at E Tropicana Avenue, University District (597 1549). **Bus** 109, 201. **Open** hrs vary. **Credit** AmEx, Disc, MC, V. **Map** p333 Y3.

Owner/artist Dirk Vermin is a Vegas native and local legend who has dedicated his life to bettering the local subculture. His tattoo work is well known among aficionados; you will need to book ahead to see Vermin himself.

House & home

Antiques

Charleston Antique Mall

307 W Charleston Boulevard, at S Western Avenue, Downtown (228 4783). **Bus** Deuce, 104, 105, 108, 206. **Open** 10am-5pm Mon-Sat; 11am-5pm Sun. **Credit** AmEx, DC, Disc, MC, V. **Map** p335 B3.

Formerly part of the Red Rooster Antique Mall, the old 7-Up bottling company has been restocked and renovated with 35 vendors. If you like the look of that tiki bar, snap it up: the good stuff goes fast.

Funk House

1228 S Casino Center Boulevard, at E Colorado Avenue, Downtown (678 6278/www.thefunkhouse lasvegas.com). **Bus** Deuce, 104, 105, 108, 206. **Open** 10am-5pm Mon-Sat. **Credit** AmEx, MC, V. **Map** p335 C3.

Cindy Funkhouser's ever-growing collection is especially strong in late 1950s and early '60s pieces, and there's a wide variety of glass, jewellery and toys. One of the best antiques stores in town, the Funk House is also ground zero for First Friday (*see p216*).

Gypsy Caravan Antique Village

1302 S 3rd Street, at W Colorado Avenue, Downtown (868 3302). **Bus** Deuce, 104, 105, 108, 206. **Open** 10am-5pm Tue-Sat. **Credit** AmEx, Disc, MC, V. **Map** p335 C3.

This colourful antiques avenue comprises several historic bungalows. There are particularly strong selections of Victorian light fixtures, furnishings and typewriters. Be sure to investigate the courtyard and its medley of patio furnishings.

Pussykat Tattoo Parlor.

Eat, Drink, Shop

Main Street Antiques
500 S Main Street, at Bonneville Avenue, Downtown (382 1882). Bus Deuce, 104, 105, 108. **Open** 9am-6pm daily. **Credit** AmEx, Disc, MC, V. **Map** p335 B3.
Two stories of vendors sell vintage merchandise, including unique Vegas-style antiques such as glass-encased showgirl costumes.

Modify
8 E Charleston Boulevard, at S Main Street, Downtown (384 6555/www.modifylv.com). Bus Deuce, 104, 105, 108, 206. **Open** 1-7pm Wed-Sat. **Credit** MC, V. **Map** p335 C3.
This mid-century modern boutique specialises in Danish modern and space age lighting, rugs, pottery, textiles, books and custom pillows from vintage fabrics. Hipster brands Diesel and Urban Outfitters kitted out their stores with this stuff.

Red Rooster Antique Mall
1109 S Western Avenue, at W Charleston Boulevard, Downtown (382 5253). Bus Deuce, 104, 105, 108, 206. **Open** 10am-6pm Mon-Sat; 11am-5pm Sun. **Credit** AmEx, Disc, MC, V. **Map** p335 B3.
A labyrinth of cluttered rooms and individually run stalls, with racks of dusty magazines holding shelf space next to $100 antique bottles. There's fabulous casino memorabilia: ashtrays, chips and postcards.

General

Among the best homewares stores in town is **Unicahome** (7540 Dean Martin Drive, 616 9280, www.unicahome.com; *photo p210*), which stocks everything from books to flatpack furniture by the likes of Tom Dixon. The store is moving during 2007; call to check location.

Blank Space
Mandalay Bay (Mandalay Place) *3950 Las Vegas Boulevard South, at W Hacienda Avenue (632 9399). Bus Deuce, 104, 105.* **Open** 10am-11pm daily. **Credit** AmEx, Disc, MC, V. **Hotel** p71. **Map** p336 A9.
The only modern home accessories store on the Strip, this well-curated shop stocks furniture and home accessories from Vitra Design, Cassina, Kartell, Mooi and Jonathan Adler.

Bloomingdale's Home
Fashion Show Mall, 3200 Las Vegas Boulevard South, at Spring Mountain Road (784 5400/ www.bloomingdales.com). Bus Deuce, 105, 203. **Open** 10am-8pm Mon-Wed; 10am-10pm Thur-Sat; 11am-7pm Sun. **Credit** AmEx, DC, Disc, MC, V. **Map** p335 & p336 B6.
The only Bloomingdale's in Vegas (and the Nation's first Bloomingdale's Home) is a furnishings store carrying bath and bedding (DKNY, Michael Kors, Natori), cookware and bakeware (All-Clad, Cuisinart, Calphalon), home decor (Nambe, Waterford, Kosta Boda) and luggage (Tumi, Victorinox).

Durette Studios
1007 S Main Street, at W Charleston Boulevard, Downtown (368 2601/www.durettecanditodesign. com). Bus Deuce, 206. **Open** 9am-5pm Mon-Fri; by appt Sat. **Credit** AmEx, MC, V.

Unicahome. *See p209.*

Durette Candito's Arts District studio is Nevada's most prestigious supplier of decorative hardware, lighting and home accessories, many of which are exclusive, handcrafted imports from some of the best clans of craftsmen around the world. Her architectural and interior design skills also can't be beaten.

Lik Design

Mandalay Bay (Mandalay Place) *3950 Las Vegas Boulevard South, at W Hacienda Avenue (736 5227). Bus Deuce, 104, 105.* **Open** 10am-11pm daily. **Credit** AmEx, DC, Disc, MC, V. **Hotel** p71. **Map** p336 A9.

In addition to his photography gallery, Peter Lik presents Pacific Green furniture by Aussie designer Bruce Dowse. The one-of-a-kind furniture collection is built of palm wood from unwanted coconut palms, and is therefore eco-friendly.

Lynn Peri Collection

Holsum Design Center, 241 W Charleston Boulevard, at Grand Central Parkway, Downtown (366 9171). Bus 206. **Open** 11am-5pm Tue-Sat. **Credit** AmEx, MC, V.

Jerry Hall and James Drewry showcase art glass by Barbara and Larry Domsky, art furniture by Leslie Rowland and Italian fine art etchings in this gallery-style retail shop.

Music & entertainment

Blockbuster is everywhere; to find a branch, use the store locator at www.blockbuster.com. Alternatively, try the lower-key **Hollywood**

Video (www.hollywoodvideo.com). Some mainstream new-release CDs are sold at massive discounts at **Best Buy** (*see p195*).

Zia Record Exchange

4225 S Eastern Avenue, at Flamingo Road, East of Strip (735 4942/www.ziarecords.com). Bus 110, 202. **Open** 10am-midnight daily. **Credit** AmEx, Disc, MC, V.

This Arizona transplant, now comfortably the rest music store in town, buys and sells music and movies, trading with recording companies as well as the man off the street. It even deals in vinyl.

Sport & fitness

The two best general sports stores are chains. Both **Big 5** (2797 S Maryland Parkway, at E Sahara Avenue, 734 6664, www.big5sporting goods.com) and **Sports Authority** (2620 S Decatur Boulevard, at W Sahara Avenue, 368 3335, www.sportsauthority.com) sell a wide range of clothing and equipment from multiple locations around the city. Fashion sportswear is also well represented: the Forum Shops is home to a **Niketown** (650 8888), while the Showcase Mall has America's first **Adidas Sports Performance Store** (262 1373).

Bass Pro Shops Outdoor World

8200 S Industrial Road, at Blue Diamond Road, Silverton (730 5200/www.basspro.com). Bus 117. **Open** 9am-10pm Mon-Sat; 9am-7pm Sun. **Credit** AmEx, Disc, MC, V.

With a firing range, a gunsmith, an archery range and a custom tie shop (for anglers), this massive store is a lesson in retail as entertainment. The displays include a host of animal trophies from around the world: a stuffed giraffe, a pride of lions and Nevada's own state animal, the bighorn sheep.

Desert Rock Sports

8221 W Charleston Boulevard, between S Buffalo & S Durango Drives, West Las Vegas (254 1143/ www.desertrocksportslv.com). Bus 206. **Open** 9am-7pm daily. **Credit** AmEx, Disc, MC, V.
Desert Rock carries super-cool climbing, hiking, camping and backpacking gear for the outdoor enthusiast, as well as stuff for children and dogs. You can rent equipment at next door's Powerhouse Rock Climbing Centre (254 5604). *Photo p221.*

McGhie's

4035 S Fort Apache Road, at W Flamingo Road, South-west Las Vegas (252 8077/www.mc ghies.com). Bus 204. **Open** 10am-7pm Mon-Fri; 10am-6pm Sat; 10am-5pm Sun. **Credit** AmEx, Disc, MC, V.
In business for 40 years, McGhie's embraced the snowboarding craze in the early 1990s, and later added mountain biking to its ski (both water and snow) goods. Rentals, plus advice on the area's better recreation areas, are also available.

Pro Cyclery

7034 W Charleston Boulevard, at Antelope Way, West Las Vegas (228 9460/www.procyclery.com). Bus 206. **Open** 10am-7pm Mon-Fri; 10am-5pm Sat. **Credit** AmEx, Disc, MC, V.

Take a seat

Las Vegas is on the cusp of becoming an international centre for an industry entirely unrelated to gambling; and, for that matter, to any of the other hedonistic pursuits for which the city is so notorious. The two blockish buildings on the skyline east of Downtown, imaginatively named Building A and Building B, are just the beginnings of the **World Market Centre** (WMC), a cluster of wholesale furniture showrooms that developers claim will be the 'most comprehensive trade show complex in the world'.

With acres of land ripe for development, plus an abundance of hotel rooms and amenities to service it, Las Vegas has seized the opportunity to enhance its non-gaming economy. Conventions and trade shows head here year-round, the biggest using facilities at the Las Vegas Convention Center. However, the World Market Center is a departure: its facilities are custom-built for the needs of the furniture designers who come each January and June for the Las Vegas Market event.

The iconic but austere-looking buildings are the work of Bellagio and Fremont Street Experience architect Jon Jerde, who designed the site to resemble a series of Italian piazzas surrounding a central courtyard. Housing 230 showrooms, Building A proved such a success upon opening in 2005 that plans were soon made to extend the area of the original WMC design to a staggering 12million square feet (1.1million square metres). With Building B completed in 2007 and Building C on schedule for July '08, the developers now intend to open one new building a year until 2013, plus a series of raised skywalks linking each structure.

The World Market Centre hasn't just changed the physical landscape of Las Vegas: it's delivered a huge boost to the city's economy, with the creation of 35,000 new jobs. It also feeds the tourism sector, attracting up to 110,000 buyers and retailers from all over the world for every trade fair that it hosts. But most importantly, it's also brought the promise of economic diversification to a region that has henceforth relied on the frivolous businesses of gambling and partying for its daily bread.

This long-term fixture on the Vegas cycling scene is a great source of gear for both hire and purchase. Experienced cyclists and novices are all made to feel welcome.

REI
Green Valley Ranch (District) *2220 Village Walk Drive, at S Green Valley Parkway, Henderson (896 7111/www.rei.com). Bus 111.* **Open** 10am-9pm Mon-Sat; 11am-6pm Sun. **Credit** AmEx, Disc, MC, V. **Hotel** p111.

In 1938, 20 mountain climbing enthusiasts formed a co-operative so they could purchase some of the better gear available in Europe. Recreation Equipment Inc now has over two million members worldwide, and 70 store locations. This shop is great for backpacking, biking, mountain climbing and kayaking gear.

Subskates
9151 W Sahara Avenue, at Fort Apache Road, Summerlin (258 3635). Bus 101, 208. **Open** 11am-6.30pm Mon-Sat; noon-5pm Sun. **Credit** AmEx, Disc, MC, V.

Anyone in Las Vegas with a fondness for balancing on a board heads here to buy their gear. The stock includes everything from boards to bearings, plus all the accessories you're likely to need. Other essential gear includes clothes and shoes from the likes of Fallen and Etnies.

Other locations 9151 W Sahara Avenue, at S Fort Apache Road, Summerlin (233 3842).

Tickets

Ticketmaster (474 4000, www.ticketmaster. com) sells tickets for many events, although the booking fees can be high. They may be slightly lower at Ticketmaster desks in **Macy's** (*see p190*) and branches of **Smith's** (*see p202*).

Toys & games

See p194.

Travellers' needs

For **airlines**, *see p306*; for **car hire firms**, *see p308*. If you're in need of extra suitcases to hold all that excess shopping, your best bets on the Strip are **Bloomingdale's Home** (*see p209*) and **Macy's** (*see p190*), though prices are more reasonable at **Target** (*see p189*).

You can rent mobile phones on a weekly or daily basis from **Roberts Rent-a-Phone** (1-800 964 2468, www.roberts-rent-a-phone.com), which delivers to any US address within 24 hours. However, it may be cheaper simply to buy a phone from a store such as **Best Buy** (*see p195*). For more on phones, *see p315*.

If your laptop fails, try the Best Buy Geek Squad (*see p195*), available 24 hours a day. Mac users should try the **Apple Store** (*see p196*).

Find all the gear you'll need for serious climbing at **Desert Rock Sports**. *See p211.*

Arts & Entertainment

Features

Playboy Club. *See p257.*

Festivals & Events

Las Vegas's chock-full calendar proves there's always something to celebrate.

Las Vegas has a habit of attracting the kind of parties that don't happen anywhere else. As the spiritual home of gambling, it's obvious that the city should host the **World Series of Poker**, while a town that revels in the nickname Sin City is a natural location for the **Fetish & Fantasy Halloween Ball**. Still, that doesn't explain the presence of **Pet-a-Palooza**, several rodeo competitions, and innumerable events dominated by vintage cars, bikes and scooters.

Where no price is listed, entrance is free. For information on temporary attractions in town, check the *Las Vegas Weekly* or *CityLife* (see p313). For details of convention dates, *see p309*.

Spring

NASCAR Nextel Cup

Las Vegas Motor Speedway, 7000 N Las Vegas Boulevard, at Speedway Boulevard, North Las Vegas (information 644 4444/tickets 1-800 644 4444/www. lvms.com). No bus. **Tickets** $40-$150. **Date** early Mar.
One of the biggest auto racing weekends of the year, the Vegas leg of NASCAR's Nextel Cup sees thousands of enthusiasts descend upon the city. Visitors should book accommodation well in advance. For details of other events at the Las Vegas Motor Speedway, *see p261*.

Monster Jam World Finals

Sam Boyd Stadium, 7000 E Russell Road, at Boulder Highway, South-east Las Vegas (739 3267/www. monsterjamonline.com). Bus 107, 201A. **Tickets** $30-$40. **Date** mid Mar.
Bring your inner 13-year-old with this feast of automotive carnage, featuring an array of giant trucks with enormous wheels; the 2007 champion, Batman the Monster Truck, was basically a hulked-out Batmobile. The pit party is also worth a look.

St Patrick's Day

Around Las Vegas. **Date** 17 Mar.
Vegas more than makes up for its lack of Irish heritage on St Patrick's Day. There's a parade in downtown Henderson and a three-day party at New York New York's Nine Fine Irishmen bar, which sprawls on to the casino's mini-Brooklyn Bridge. Elsewhere, Hennesseys on the Fremont Street Experience celebrates with music, drink and 'Irish nachos'.

▶ For **film festivals**, *see p242*.
▶ For **gay & lesbian events**, *see p247*.
▶ For **sporting events**, *see pp261-263*.

Extreme Thing Festival

Desert Breeze Skate Park, 8275 W Spring Mountain Road, at S Durango Drive, South-west Las Vegas (474 4000/www.extremething.com). Bus 203. **Tickets** $17-$20. **Date** late Mar.
Extreme sports, such as skateboarding, BMX and wrestling championships. Extreme body modification, chiefly piercing and tattoos. And extreme music: punk, lots of it. Expect teenage aggression by the bucketload.

Pet-a-Palooza

Location varies (www.mix941.fm). **Date** late Mar.
Rock bands share the stage with animal performers at this pet-friendly festival. The fairgrounds are lined with booths hosted by animal rescue and non-profit organisations, and there are pet-oriented vendors hawking their wares.

Viva Las Vegas

Gold Coast *4000 W Flamingo Road, at S Valley View Boulevard, West of Strip (1-562 496 4287/ www.vivalasvegas.net). Bus 104, 202.* **Tickets** $75-$125. **Hotel** p116. **Map** p333 X3. **Date** Easter wknd.
In order to dance to old-school rockabilly bands from all over the world, check out the burlesque competition and shop for the perfect '50s cocktail dress at the swap meet, you'll have to buy a pricey ticket. However, the breathtaking hot rod car show atop the Gold Coast's parking garage is open to all. Dress in Sailor Jerry tattoos and Brylcreem to blend in.

Las Vegas Grand Prix

Downtown (www.vegasgrandprix.com). **Date** Apr.
Champ Car racing arrived in Vegas in 2007, with autos whizzing around the streets of Downtown. The three days of open-wheel racing were popular enough to ensure the event will return.

Mardi Gras Celebration

Fremont Street, at Las Vegas Boulevard South, Downtown (www.vegasexperience.com). Bus Deuce and all DTC-bound buses. **Map** p334 D2. **Date** early Apr.
The only reason Mardi Gras is New Orleans' festival is because Las Vegas didn't think of it first. That doesn't stop the Fremont Street Experience from hosting its own version slightly later in the year.

Pure Aloha Festival

Cannery *2121 E Craig Road, at Collinson Avenue, North Las Vegas (604 9438/www.vizzun.com). Bus 115.* **Admission** $5; $2 reductions. **Date** mid Apr.
Immerse yourself in two days of Polynesian food, music, art and dance. The city's community of transplanted Hawaiians help make the festival rich in traditional and contemporary interpretations of aloha.

Clark County Fair & Rodeo

*Clark County Fairgrounds, on I-15, Logandale
(1-888 876 3247/www.ccfair.com). No bus.*
Admission *Fair* $5. *Rodeo* $9. *Season pass* $18.
Free under-5s. **Date** mid Apr.
For a taste of hometown South-western life sans glitter, drive a little way north for all kinds of ropin', ridin', country music and carnival fun.

UNLVino

Paris Las Vegas *3655 Las Vegas Boulevard
South, at E Flamingo Road (946 7000/www.unl
vino.com). Bus Deuce, 202.* **Tickets** $75-$100.
Hotel p74. **Map** p336 A7. **Date** mid Apr.
More than 100 international wine-growers participate in this fundraiser for UNLV. There are auctions of wine-themed art and vintage crates, but the real treat is chatting with the growers and sampling the wines. Designated drivers are thoughtfully provided.

Epicurean Affair

Location varies (878 2313/www.nvrestaurants.com).
Tickets $125-$150. **Date** late Apr-late May.
Local restaurants unveil their latest attempts to outdo each other in this industry festival of culinary hedonism. Expect a full-blown onslaught of the senses from exotic food, drink and spectacle.

Cinco de Mayo

*Lorenzi Park, 3333 W Washington Avenue, at
N Rancho Drive, North-west Las Vegas (229 1087).
Bus 106, 208.* **Map** p333 X1. **Date** wknd
closest to 5 May.
The city's Mexican community comes together in a show of pride with all-day dancing, mariachi bands, fireworks and traditional cuisine.

Dark Skies Arts Festivals

Near Primm (http://darkskies.vegasartists.com).
Tickets $40-$125. **Date** mid May.
A kind of pocket-sized Burning Man, this festival of art and culture blazes for three days in the desert. The tribal event describes itself as radically inclusive: no spectators, only participants. Expect themed camps, decorated cars and things set (artistically) on fire. A second event takes place later in the year.

Helldorado Days

*Various locations (229 6776/www.elks
helldorado.com).* **Date** mid May.
Instituted in 1935 to attract tourists to the area after the completion of the Hoover Dam, this revived celebration of Las Vegas's beginnings plays up the city's western roots while also including golf and poker tournaments, trap shooting contests, art auctions, trail rides and a Downtown parade.

Vegas Cruise

*Fremont Street, at Las Vegas Boulevard South,
Downtown (www.vegasexperience.com). Bus Deuce
& all DTC-bound buses.* **Map** p334 D2. **Date** late
May/early June.
This three-day classic car event sees enthusiasts showing off gleaming vintage vehicles on Fremont Street. Onlookers may be blinded by all the chrome.

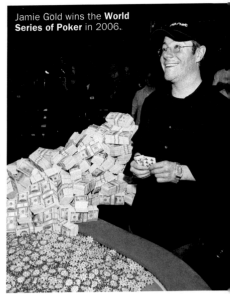

Jamie Gold wins the **World Series of Poker** in 2006.

Summer

World Series of Poker

Rio *3700 W Flamingo Road, at S Valley View
Boulevard, West of Strip (777 7777/www.harrahs.
com). Bus 202.* **Hotel** p100. **Map** p333 X3.
Date June-July.
It's a matter of conjecture whether the popularity of poker fuelled the popularity of this two-week tournament or vice versa. Either way, the WSOP continues to expand each year, to the point where the main event in 2006 saw nearly 9,000 competitors and a cool $12 million awarded to winner Jamie Gold.

Red White & Boom

*Desert Breeze Park, Spring Mountain Road, at S
Durango Drive, South-west Las Vegas (455 8838/www.
redwhiteboom.com). Bus 203.* **Tickets** $17.50-$22
1 day; $30 2 days; free under-12s. **Date** 4 July wknd.

The best Festivals

For roaring engines
NASCAR Nextel Cup. *See p214.*

For soaring aircraft
Las Vegas Balloon Classic. *See p218.*

For boring drunks
New Year's Eve. *See p219.*

With a fireworks display second only to the Strip's, a monstrous carnival, plus a passel of national rock acts, this two-day, vaguely patriotic party really is fun for the whole family, jaded teens included.

Las Vegas Harvest Festival

Cashman Center, 850 Las Vegas Boulevard North, at E Washington Avenue, Downtown (1-415 447 3205/www.harvestfestival.com). **Admission** $8; free under-12s. **Map** p333 Y1. **Date** mid Aug.

Hundreds of artisans from across the country bring their hand-blown glass, silver jewellery and jars of chutney to this fair.

Star Trek Las Vegas Convention

Las Vegas Hilton *3000 Paradise Road, between E Sahara Avenue & E Desert Inn Road, East of Strip (732 5111/www.creationent.com). Bus 108, 204, 213.* **Tickets** $314. **Credit** AmEx, Disc, MC, V. **Hotel** p97. **Map** p335 C5. **Date** mid Aug.

The annual convention for hardcore Trekkies is hosted at – where else? – the Star Trek Experience at the Hilton (*see p135*). Sci-fi celebrities and obscure memorabilia make it a holy pilgrimage for some, though non-fans will be unphased.

Autumn

Greek Food Festival

St John the Baptist Greek Orthodox Church, 5300 S El Camino Road, at E Hacienda Road, South-west Las Vegas (221 8245/www.vegasgreekorthodox.com). No bus. **Admission** $5-$10. **Date** early Sept.

This 35-year-old institution is one of Las Vegas's few true ethnic festivals. Enjoy four days of folk dancing, retsina and *souvlaki* with a boisterous crowd.

First Friday

One of the city's most popular festivals is its most regular. Held from 6pm to 10pm on the first Friday of every month in the Downtown Arts District, anchored on the streets immediately surrounding the Funk House (*see p208*), **First Friday** (www.firstfriday-lasvegas.org) is essentially a massive block party with an artistic bent. Local galleries and shops stay open late into the night; bands and DJs play on the specially erected stages; and there's tons of great street food and drinks on offer. After the event winds down around 10pm, there are after-parties at **Dino's** (*see p184*), where a local band plays a two-hour set before Danny G takes over with a karaoke night, and the **Beauty Bar** (*see p183*), which hosts a fantastic funky soul night called the Get Back.

Black & White Party

Palms *4321 W Flamingo Road, at S Valley View Boulevard, West of Strip (382 2326/http://afanlv.org). Bus 201.* **Tickets** $40. **Hotel** p98. **Map** p333 X3. **Date** mid Sept.

Affordable but still satisfyingly posh, the city's main AIDS fundraiser brings the community together with black-and-white costumes, food from the best chefs in town, and risqué amusements such as a spanking booth.

SuperRun

Downtown Henderson (643 0000/www.superrun.com). **Date** mid Sept.

The area's largest classic car show takes over downtown Henderson for three days with hundreds of classic vehicles of all kinds, from fully-built custom hot rods to a well-preserved hearse used when the Mob ran Vegas.

Las Vegas BikeFest

Fremont Street, at Las Vegas Boulevard South, Downtown (1-866 245 3378/450 7662/www.lasvegasbikefest.com). Bus Deuce & all DTC-bound buses. **Tickets** $35-$40. **Map** p334 D2. **Date** late Sept/early Oct.

Even non-bikers can enjoy the classic Harleys, demo rides and 'Artistry in Iron' master builder championships at this get-together for the black-leather set.

Grand Slam for Children

MGM Grand *3799 Las Vegas Boulevard South, at E Tropicana Avenue (information 227 5700/tickets 474 4000/www.agassifoundation.org). Bus Deuce, 201.* **Tickets** Concert $50-$90. **Hotel** p81. **Map** p336 A8. **Date** early Oct.

Andre Agassi hosts an exclusive gala auction and dinner to benefit his children's foundation each year, bursting with the country's great and good. The concert that follows, at the MGM's Garden Arena, is always given by an A-list performer.

San Gennaro Feast

Location varies (286 4944/www.sangennarofeast.net). **Admission** $7. **Date** Sept.

This Italian-American festival is mostly about the food, but it also includes carnival rides and a traditional procession.

Age of Chivalry Renaissance Fair

Sunset Park, E Sunset Road & S Eastern Avenue, East Las Vegas (455 8200/tickets 474 4000/www.lvrenfair.com). Bus 110, 212. **Admission** *1 day* $10; $5 reductions. *3 days* $25; $10 reductions; free under-5s. **Date** mid Oct.

Chivalrous battles, costumed maidens and other displays of questionable historical accuracy. We can recommend the roast turkey leg.

Professional Bull Riders Tour

Thomas & Mack Center, 4505 S Maryland Parkway, at E Tropicana Avenue, University District (information 1-719 471 3008/tickets 474 4000/www.pbrnow.com). Bus 109, 201. **Tickets** $30-$60. **Date** mid Oct.

Back to the future

Dr Lonnie Hammergren's home is a grand old place, three connected houses that form a 12,500-square-foot (1,150-square-metre) mansion with ten bedrooms and nine bathrooms. However, it's what sits inside and outside the house that's really notable. A retired neurosurgeon, Hammargren was Nevada lieutenant governor from 1994 to 1998. These days, though, he's best known for his enormous collection of... well, stuff. By accident and design, Hammargren has accumulated a huge, dazzling collection of Nevada-related memorabilia.

Peering into the Hammergren's backyard, you can see everything from a montage of ungulate antlers to the actual railcar in which Howard Hughes came to Las Vegas. Indeed, transportation is a recurring theme in the collection: the yard contains a submarine, an experimental plane, a train engine (straight out of an old mining operation) and an authentic space capsule used for training Apollo astronauts. When the Stratosphere's High Roller 'coaster was removed in 2006, guess where a large portion of it ended up?

Other unusual items include a missile silo, the doors to the first Clark County jail, the hand and torch from a scale model of the Statue of Liberty, and Liberace's last dressing room. The front façade of the buildings is a replica of a Mayan Mexican governor's palace. Hammergren has also haunted all the casinos that have closed in the past 30 years and rounded up signs, bars, decorations and other junk to add to his collection. Also indoors are an observatory and a planetarium, a 19th-century western saloon, a dinosaur from a 1930s movie and miles of train tracks (with working trains).

The collection can be viewed on **Nevada Day** (31 October) when Hammergren and long-suffering wife Sandy hold an open house, which draws crowds of up to 20,000. But if you just want to drive past for a quick peek, they're at 4318 Ridgecrest Drive. Head east on Flamingo Road from the Strip for about four miles, then turn right on S Sandhill Road. The collection in the backyard is visible from Sandhill; go round the front, turn right on Rosecrest Circle, then left on to Ridgecrest.

Vespas and Lambrettas galore at the **High Rollers Scooter Weekend**.

It isn't as prestigious as the National Finals Rodeo (*see right*), but this competition provides a more affordable chance to rub shoulders with the world's finest bull riders and their fans and see some of the action up close.

Rockabilly Rod Reunion

Las Vegas Motor Speedway, 7000 N Las Vegas Boulevard, at Speedway Boulevard, North Las Vegas (632 8213/www.rockabillyrodreunion.com). No bus. **Admission** $15; $6 reductions; free under-5s. **Date** mid Oct.
More than a hot rod car show and automotive swap meet, the Rocakbilly Rod Reunion mixes vintage dragsters, rockabilly bands, DJs and burlesque acts. Don't miss the burnout contest from hell.

Las Vegas Balloon Classic

Silver Bowl Park, 6800 E Russell Road, at Boulder Highway, South-east Las Vegas (452 8066). Bus 217. **Date** 3rd wknd in Oct.
Hot-air balloons fill the sky for this weekend of flying competitions. The Saturday sundown 'balloon glow' demonstration is a must-see. Crafts and vendors help make it a great event for kids.

Halloween

Around Las Vegas. **Date** 31 Oct.
Nearly every nightclub and bar hosts a fancy-dress party for Hallowe'en, many overflowing with grown-ups playing naughty dress-up. The Fetish & Fantasy Ball, held in 2007 at the Alexis Park hotel (*see p102*), reigns supreme for debauchery, dazzling costumes and Vegas-calibre spectacle. For something a bit less risqué, hit the Beaux Arts Ball at Studio 54 (*see p258*): it features some of the best entertainers on the Strip and an over-the-top costume contest, with all proceeds going to AIDS charity Golden Rainbow.

Vegas Valley Book Festival

Various locations (895 1878/www.vegasvalleybook fest.org). **Tickets** free-$10. **Date** early Nov.
Local authors, historians and poets get a chance to shine in this three-day celebration of bibliophilia that brings local literary heros and such names as Chuck Palahniuk to town for readings, signings dabates and panel discussions.

Motor Trend International Auto Show

Las Vegas Convention Center, 3150 Paradise Road, at Convention Center Drive, East of Strip (892 0711/ www.motortrendautoshows.com/lasvegas). Bus 108, 213. **Admission** $8; $4 7-12s. **Map** p335 C5. **Date** late Nov.
A chance to see all the shiniest new models and prototypes from the world's automobile manufacturers before anyone else, though sadly you can't drive them away. Free parking is available at the Convention Center's Silver Lot 3.

Winter

Christmas

Around Las Vegas. **Date** Dec.
The most spectacular festive event in the region is the annual **Light the Night** display in the cactus garden at Ethel M Chocolates in Henderson (*see p149*). The space is dotted with millions of lights, while carol-singers reel off all the festive favourites. Be sure to get yourself into the factory before 7pm for free chocolate samples.

Other events around the city bring good cheer in similar ways during December. A drive-through trail entitled **A Gift of Lights** winds through the whole of Sunset Park (E Sunset Road, at S Eastern Avenue, East Las Vegas), with some proceeds going to charities. The **Magical Forest** at Opportunity Village (6300 W Oakey Boulevard, between S Jones Boulevard & S Torrey Pines Drive) contains a castle, giant candy canes, a forest of decorated trees and two million lights. And numerous seacraft sail around Lake Mead as part of the **Parade of Lights**.

National Finals Rodeo

Thomas & Mack Center, 4505 S Maryland Parkway, at E Tropicana Avenue, University District (information 895 3900/1-888 6737 6336/ www.nfr-rodeo.com). Bus 109, 201. **Tickets** $70-$1,100. **Map** p333 Y3. **Date** early Dec.
Cowboys and girls set Vegas ablaze for nine days as part of this massive event. Tickets are distributed by lottery a year beforehand, but you can watch proceedings on TV at the Gold Coast (*see p116*). Buy western duds from the Cowboy Christmas Gift Show (*see p197*), then party at Sam's Town (*see p117*).

New Las Vegas Marathon & Half-Marathon

Around the city (731 1052/www.lvmarathon.com). **Date** early Dec.
The run starts and ends at Mandalay Bay (*see p71*), which then hosts an all-day post-marathon festival. If you want to run, register online: the earlier you do so, the cheaper the fee.

New Year's Eve

Around Las Vegas. **Date** 31 Dec.
Las Vegas Boulevard and Fremont Street become absolutely rammed on New Year's Eve, a night filled with parties, one-hit celebrities, air displays, fireworks and general chaos. Room rates soar; to be honest, the whole thing is probably best avoided.

An American Trilogy

Cannery, 2121 E Craig Road, at Las Vegas Boulevard North, North Las Vegas (1-866 999 4899/507 5700/www.cannerycasinos.com). Bus 113. **Tickets** prices vary. **Credit** AmEx, Disc, MC, V. **Date** mid Jan.
This annual celebration of the King welcomes hosts of Elvis-lovers around 16 Jan, his birthday. The buffet serves his beloved fried banana and peanut butter sandwiches.

Chinese New Year.

African American History Month

West Las Vegas Library, 951 W Lake Mead Boulevard, at Concord Street, West Las Vegas (507 3980/www.lvccld.org). Bus 210, 214. **Date** Feb.
The West Las Vegas Library houses a permanent collection of artefacts, photographs and documents relating to African American history in the West. During February, its theatre hosts a celebration of African American community and culture in the region, with spoken word, dance, theatre and music.

High Rollers Scooter Weekend

Around the city (www.lvscooterrally.com). **Date** mid Feb.
Rockers on motorbikes steer clear: this weekend of mod rock and showing off is for sharp-looking multi-mirrored scooters and the aficionados who love them.

Chinese New Year Celebration & Asian Food Festival

Las Vegas Chinatown Plaza, 4255 Spring Mountain Road, between S Valley View Boulevard & S Decatur Boulevard, South-west Las Vegas (221 8448/www. lvchinatown.com). Bus 104, 203. **Admission** $3; $1 reductions; free under 5s. **No credit cards**. **Date** 25 Feb.
The Chinese New Year celebrations in Vegas are actually pan-Asian; they also celebrate Japanese, Tahitian and Thai culture. Expect traditional lion and dragon dances and a feast of eastern delicacies.

Arts & Entertainment

Adult Entertainment

Lust remains a firm favourite as Sin City lives up to its nickname with pride.

The past 15 years have been a rollercoaster ride for Sin City. As Las Vegas has changed from a far-flung hedonistic escape to a world-class tourism destination, the growing pains have sometimes been traumatic. First came the ill-fated attempt to ditch the sin and catch the family market. Topless showgirls started to conceal the surgeon's skill, and pushchairs became de rigueur on the Strip. Then, when the absurdity of Vegas apeing Disneyland sank in, the *Swingers*-inspired New Rat Pack tried to recapture the bacchanalian spirit of the city in its heyday. Upscale strip clubs offered elaborate interiors, and risqué showroom revues were again the norm. In other words, sin was in.

Now, as the city faces down the end of its first decade as a 21st-century city, modern Las Vegas has emerged as a mostly respectable destination. Sex hasn't been stripped from Vegas; indeed, there are more adult clubs and shows than ever. But the mainstreaming of US adult entertainment has forced it to share centre stage, as Las Vegas now caters efficiently to all of the seven deadly sins. Even the 'what happens in Vegas, stays in Vegas' ad campaign played off this fact: were the girls really just shopping and eating last weekend, or was something more naughty going down? After all, every vice, from drinking to dirty dancing, is available 24-7, with no breaks for penance.

One result of the local population growth has been an increase in the breadth of adult entertainment. While the industry still caters mostly to the straight male libido, there are now several places at which women can grasp at men's G-strings. **Sapphire**'s Playgirl Lounge stages *Men: the Show*, while the **Olympic Garden** hosts the Men of Olympus five nights a week. It's a trend that has moved into the casinos, with the likes of *American Storm* at the Riviera and the *Chippendales* at the Rio. While women have no problem getting attention (and lap dances) from female dancers at mainstream clubs, gay men still find themselves admiring the go-go boys at the city's gay clubs (*see p248*). The one recent exception is **Hot Rods**, a nude male strip joint for men (*see p249*).

Adult entertainment falls into three categories: casino clubs and revues; topless or nude clubs; and swingers' clubs. For adult shops, *see p204*. Whatever your pleasure, remember that prostitution is illegal in Clark County, in which Las Vegas sits. No matter what the ads, pamphlets or signs say, pay to play and you run the real risk of being busted, or worse.

Casino clubs & revues

A few years ago, rumours were rife that strip clubs would soon open in casinos. At the time, owning a topless strip club (with a limited gaming licence) appeared to be a cash generator second only to operating a full-blown casino.

The feverish speculation has cooled, but it's no secret that upscale adult clubs, many of them situated right off the Strip, are leeching cash from casinos. That's why many high-end gambling halls are skating the legal line by adding as much nudity as permissable in the form of topless pool areas, risqué performances and even old-school burlesque clubs.

Still, while joints such as **Ivan Kane's Forty Deuce** (*see p257*) and Tangerine at Treasure Island (*see p87*) entice patrons with the promise of theatrical burlesque, the stage shows, however impressive, are far too brief. Once the girls have gone, it's just another nightclub where the emphasis is on the bar tab.

In all, there are 11 adult-themed shows to be found in casino showrooms, ranging from the Riviera's long-running, campy *Crazy Girls* to the revamped *Crazy Horse Paris* at the MGM. Classic feathers-and-sequins shows *Folies Bergere* (at the Tropicana) and *Jubilee!* (at Bally's) are the last two of their kind on the Strip; more modern adult shows can take the tack of the lesbian-chic rock 'n' roll vampires of *Bite* at the Stratosphere, or the Cirque du Soleil cabaret *Zumanity* at New York New York. For all adult-oriented shows, *see pp225-226*.

The best Adult clubs

For dazzle
Minxx. See p222.

For diversity
Spearmint Rhino. See p222.

For dinner
Men's Club. See p221.

Arts & Entertainment

Zumanity.

Topless bars

Southern Nevada was once home to scores of tiny, smoky topless clubs, most little more than a dive bar with a small stage. For better or for worse, few of these seedy hangouts remain, but if do still fancy walking into a Bukowski short story, try the gloriously unpretentious **Larry's Villa** (2401 W Bonanza Road, at N Rancho Drive, 647 2713).

These days, most of these former dives have either upscaled with a plush refit or are aspiring to do so. Many are crowded at weekends, for sporting events and during conventions (also, not coincidentally, when the best and best-looking dancers make the roster). But a quiet midweek visit can be more fun, as you won't have to scramble for a seat. A continuous parade of strippers shimmies to DJ music, stripping down to a G-string, a pair of stilettos and, if you're lucky, a smile.

Topless dancers must be at least 21 years old and are more chatty than those in nude clubs. The clubs all have full bar service (some with bottle service and food) and are open to patrons aged 21 and over. Most are located in dark warehouse areas, so you're best catching a cab. Be sure to specify which club you want to visit: it's not unheard of for cabbies to be paid kickbacks by door staff for dropping tourists at particular venues. All admission prices are for visitors; locals who can show a Nevada ID usually pay less.

Cheetahs Topless Club

2112 Western Avenue, between W Wyoming & W Sahara Avenues, West of Strip (384 0074/www. cheetahsnv.com). Bus 105, 204. **Open** 24hrs daily. **Admission** $30 after 8pm. **Credit** AmEx, Disc, MC, V. **Map** p335 B4.

This remains Vegas's most relaxed topless bar, neither seedy nor pretentious. Large enough to have five stages yet as homey as a neighbourhood sports bar, Cheetahs has a reputation as a locals' hangout. It's packed during football season, when Monday Night Football parties offer $10 'touchdown dances'. Girls have less silicone than at other clubs; bouncers and bartenders are friendly enough.

Girls of Glitter Gulch

20 E Fremont Street, at N Main Street, Downtown (385 4774/www.glittergulchlv.com). Bus Deuce & all DTC-bound buses. **Open** 1pm-4am daily. **Admission** 2-drink min. **Credit** AmEx, Disc, MC, V. **Map** p333 C1.

Recently renovated to the shimmy of $3 million, this diminutive club is the only one in town located on a piece of prime real estate. The interior has been spiffied up nicely, and the proximity to Downtown's casinos is a boon. The small size makes it hard to blend in and enjoy a drink as the entertainers work the room for dances, but you could do worse.

Men's Club

3500 W Naples Drive (between W Flamingo Road & W Tropicana Avenue), between I-15 & S Valley View Boulevard, West of Strip (899 6367/www.mensclublv. com). Bus 104. **Open** 4pm-late Mon, Tue, Thur-Sun, 11.30am-late Wed. **Admission** $30. **Credit** AmEx, DC, Disc, MC, V. **Map** p333 X3.

Arts & Entertainment

Open since 2007, this is the most unusual strip club in town. At first, it feels like the house party of a wealthy libertine: the Euro-Gothic style, combined with plush finishes, beautiful people, diverse music and a 10,000-bottle wine cellar gives the place real class. The main room has a performance stage on two levels, while there are great restaurants upstairs and downstairs (*see p222* **Tastes of honey**). A welcome alternative to the mega-clubs.

Minxx

4636 Wynn Road, between W Harmon & W Tropicana Avenues, West of Strip (220 9416/www. minxx.net). Bus 104. **Open** 24hrs daily. **Admission** $30. **Credit** AmEx, MC, V. **Map** p333 X3.

All curvy lines, retro furniture and modern details, Minxx feels like a film set. And despite its 15,000sq ft (1,400sq m) size, the club offers the illusion of intimacy. There's but one large stage, surrounded by chairs and bottle-service VIP tables. You can belly up to the lighted bartop and still see the performers, but the real treat are the VIP rooms, which come complete with flat screens and personal audio systems.

Olympic Garden

1531 Las Vegas Boulevard South, at E Wyoming Avenue, Stratosphere Area (385 9361/www.ogvegas. com). Bus Deuce. **Open** 24hrs daily. **Admission** $20. **Credit** AmEx, Disc, MC, V. **Map** p335 C3.

Locals call the city's original upscale club 'the OG'; thanks to its location on Las Vegas Boulevard between Downtown and the Strip, it remains popular. Two storeys, multiple stages and dozens of often surgically enhanced hotties keep everyone happy. Upstairs, the Men of Olympus entertain female visitors (Wed-Sun). Handily, it's within walking distance of Luv-It (*see p166*) and the Arts District.

Sapphire

3025 S Industrial Road, at Stardust Road, West of Strip (796 6000/www.sapphirelasvegas.com). Bus 105. **Open** 24hrs daily. **Admission** $30. **Credit** AmEx, Disc, MC, V. **Map** p335 B5.

The largest adult club in the world features a pulsing main room that's almost too big, bottle service, 13 private (and pricey) skyboxes, and the Playgirl Lounge, offering male dancers at weekends. Swing shift (11pm onwards) generally sees the best dancers, though on a busy weekend it can be a madhouse.

Scores

3355 S Procyon Avenue, at W Desert Inn Road, West of Strip (367 4000/www.scoreslasvegas.com). Bus 104, 213. **Open** 24hrs daily. **Admission** $30. **Credit** AmEx, MC, V.

Howard Stern's favourite strip club chain came west to take over the former Jaguars joint, remodelling what was a beautiful but poorly designed club into a very comfortable space. The plush environmment remains, but the stages and seating have been vastly improved. The hourly erotic aerialist performances and the free happy hour buffet (5-6pm daily) are added attractions.

Spearmint Rhino

3340 Highland Drive, at W Desert Inn Road (access via Spring Mountain Road), West of Strip (796 3600/www.spearmintrhino.com). Bus 105. **Open** 24hrs daily. **Admission** $30. **Credit** AmEx, MC, V. **Map** p335 A5.

Something about this comfortable spot captivates the young and stylish, making it the choice for the nightclub-hopping crowd. It might be the diverse parade of entertainers – from bleached blondes to tattooed rockers – and their eclectic music choices that make it so fun. Popular with locals and couples, it's busy on nights when other clubs are sleepy.

Treasures

2801 Westwood Drive, at Highland Drive, West of Strip (257 3030/www.treasureslasvegas.com). Bus 105. **Open** 4pm-6am Mon-Thur, Sun; 4pm-9am Fri,

Tastes of honey

It would be easy to dismiss serving raw oysters in a strip club as a winking publicity stunt. After all, several clubs have enticed patrons with the promise of gourmet food, only for them to shift the marketing focus back to the dancers (Scores) or abandon the idea (Sapphire). Food at Vegas strip clubs, where it exists, is usually a bar-food buffet favoured by patrons trying to stave off drunken hunger. Until recently, the only consistently successful strip club kitchen was the Treasures Steakhouse, which supplements the club-wide appetiser menu with a dinner menu of American classics.

However, the 2007 opening of the **Men's Club** (*see p221*), and its two upscale restaurants, may change things. Downstairs in the Raw Bar, guests enjoy dozens of items from sushi to scallops, while upstairs, the Alchemy Kitchen menu includes seafood risotto, filet mignon with foie gras, and baked salmon, all of which can be paired with a selection from a 10,000-bottle cellar. The menu is overseen by former Aureole sommelier Steven Geddes and the wines by Darius Allyn; certainly, this doesn't look like a fly-by-night gimmick.

Even the timing makes sense. Alongside casinos, strip clubs are the only businesses exempt from new laws that prohibit smoking wherever food is served, making them one of the last bell-ringers of do-as-you-please old Vegas. Enjoy it while it lasts.

Get in on the action at **Spearmint Rhino**.

Sat. **Admission** $20-$30. **Credit** AmEx, Disc, MC, V. **Map** p335 A4.
With its two storeys, mansion-styled room and two primary stages, Treasures reads like an OTT version of Scores. In the large main room, dancers perform on poles unders special lighting and fog machines. With its pleasant service and upscale ambience, Treasures is Vegas's Playboy mansion.

Nude clubs

Nude clubs are similar to topless bars save for one important difference: the full-nudity licence prohibits alcohol, and so the clubs (except for the Palomino) are open to anyone over 18. Without the cash cow of alcohol sales, the environments are much less plush and attract less affluent patrons. It's easy to be a star guest by tipping well and smiling. As the focus is elsewhere, there's less silicone and more emphasis on pole tricks and personality.

Déjà Vu Showgirls
3247 Industrial Road, between Stardust Road & W Sahara Avenue, West of Strip (894 4167/www. dejavu.com). Bus 105, 204. **Open** 11am-6am Mon-Sat; 6pm-4am Sun. **Admission** $20. **Credit** MC, V. **Map** p336 A5.
Dancers at Déjà Vu have an honest-to-goodness personality that's hard to find in the land of silicone sameness. Look out for theme nights, from oil wrestling to shower parties, and the neighbouring Déjà Vu Adult Emporium. Dress: no tank tops.

Little Darlings
1514 Western Avenue, at W Wyoming Avenue, Stratosphere Area (366 1141/www.showgirl.com). Bus 105. **Open** 11am-6am Mon-Sat; 6am-4am Sun. **Admission** $15. **Credit** MC, V. **Map** p335 B3.
Stark lighting, annoying DJs and plastic soda cups are indicative of the tarted-up recreation hall feel at this Déjà Vu-run club. Many of the dancers look like they just stepped out of the indie rock bar down the block. Amateur nights can get pretty sexy and private dances can be wild, but the performers aren't chatty. Dress: no tank tops.

Palomino Club
1848 Las Vegas Boulevard North, at E Owens Avenue, North Las Vegas (642 2984). Bus 113. **Open** 4pm-5am daily. **Admission** $30. **No credit cards**. **Map** p333 Y1.
The granddaddy of Vegas clubs is ragged, but merits its reputation as the city's most atmospheric nude club: it's the only one with a liquor licence. Upstairs, an egalitarian roster of dancers works a small stage, while downstairs (open weekends and busy seasons) 'feature dancers' (porn actresses, centrefolds) take to the catwalk. Changes in North Las Vegas may soon spell the end of adult entertainment here, so get your drink and your nudity while you can.

Swingers' clubs

The euphemistically named 'couples scene' in Las Vegas is finally getting comfortable with itself. Swingers' clubs don't offer gambling or alcohol (you can bring your own), but they often have pool tables, dancefloors and stripper poles. You pay an entrance fee (or 'donation'), which is usually $40-$50 for each single male, less for couples, and next to nothing for single women.
Notable for its ethnic eateries and gay bars, the down-at-heel Commercial Center (953 E Sahara Avenue) also contains three swingers' clubs: **Red Rooster 3** (732 2587, www.red rooster-3.com), the **Fantasy Social Club** (893 3977, www.fantasysocialclub.com) and the wildly popular **Green Door** (732 4656, www.greendoorlasvegas.com). The former two are open from early evening until 5am, with the Green Door opening at 1pm and staying open until 7am on weekends; prime time is 10pm-1am. The **Red Rooster** in old Henderson (451 6661, www.vegasredrooster.com), unaffiliated to the Red Rooster 3, attracts a more mature, old-school 'lifestyle' crowd.
Aside from these fixed-location swingers' clubs, a few groups organise off-premises parties, which are essentially elite, PG-rated social mixers in nightclubs and bars, and private, pre-screened 'mansion parties', where almost anything goes. Among them are **Red Twilight** (www.redtwilight.com) and **MoodSwing** (www.moodswingparty.com).

Arts & Entertainment

Casino Entertainment

It's showtime...

During the late 1990s and early 21st century, Las Vegas entertainment was turned on its head. The tired old revues that had defined the city for years were ushered out of the door, replaced by big-budget, high-concept pieces of populist performance art delivered by **Cirque du Soleil** (of whom more in a moment). A generation of tired comics and hoarse singers was replaced by still-popular stand-ups and musicians who remained on speaking terms with the charts. And the grinning showgirls were gradually pensioned off, put out to pasture in favour of dancers prepared to show a little more than their feathers.

After such a dramatic shift in priorities, Las Vegas has lately been content simply to consolidate. Indeed, when it comes to entertainment, the city remains an impersonator rather than an innovator. The Broadway and West End shows that arrive here are tried and tested (**Mamma Mia!**, **Spamalot**), while the musical headliners are big names who won't frighten your parents (**Barry Manilow**, **Bette Midler**). And after Cirque du Soleil's first show **Mystère** broke box office records, every casino on the Strip wanted one just like it. As a result, there are no fewer than five Cirque productions in town, with at least two more on the way. Heaven only knows what Sinatra and Elvis would make of it all... especially since the latter is set to 'star' in a Cirque production of his own.

INFORMATION AND TICKETS

Although most of the shows listed in this section are expected to run for the shelf-life of this guide, others open and close all the time. For the most up-to-date information, check 'Neon' in Friday's *Las Vegas Review-Journal*, free magazines such as *What's On*, the town's two alternative weeklies and www.vegas.com. In any given week, there are also a few big-name acts working short engagements in the city, either filling in for vacationing headliners or working in auditoria that only deal with temporary bookings (such as the **Hollywood Theatre** at the MGM Grand).

You're always best off buying tickets at the hotel-casino's own box office, either in person, by phone or online. If you get stuck, try **Ticketmaster** (*see p212*), but prepare to pay over the odds. If you book by phone or online, pick up the tickets at the 'will call' window. Try and book as far ahead as possible for the big shows. However, even if the show has sold out, it's worth calling the box office, especially midweek, to check for cancellations. You can also find half-price tickets to some shows at **Tickets Tonight** (1-888 484 9264, www.tickets2nite.com) in the Showcase Mall (*see p126*); the booth opens at noon daily.

Shows are expensive in Las Vegas. The cheapest tickets for most big shows go for upwards of $50, and the best seats are routinely priced at three-figure sums. Some quoted prices include tax, others don't; many shows include a drink in their prices. However, there are bargains. Many shows offer discounts with coupons on flyers or in magazines. If you're a heavy gambler, you might even get comped into a show in the casino in which you've been playing.

Tickets for many shows allocate the theatregoer specific seats. If you have tickets for a show that offers only 'general admission' (unnumbered) seating, which is relatively rare these days, arrive early if you want a good

Penn & Teller, little and large. *See p229*.

Arts & Entertainment

spot. If you're not satisfied with your seat's location, try discreetly tipping the maître d' $10 or $20. Some shows, especially those with a degree of nudity, come with age restrictions; always check if you have kids in tow. For music venues, *see pp250-254*; for nightclubs, *see pp255-260*.

Resident shows

Las Vegas's first stage productions were known as 'floor shows'. When Sophie Tucker performed at the El Rancho and Jimmy Durante played the Flamingo in the 1940s and '50s, they were preceded by a line of girls, a comic or a magician, and a speciality act (a juggler, say).

Entertainment in the city changed radically when the Stardust premièred *Lido de Paris* in 1958. The fabulous spectacle played to packed houses and set the template for productions such as **Folies Bergere** and **Jubilee!**; both remain, dated yet enjoyable examples of what visitors to Las Vegas in the 1960s would have enjoyed in the city's showrooms.

There are still plenty of production shows on display, though they've moved on a little bit since the town's tits-and-feathers heyday. **Cirque du Soleil** now has no fewer than five shows here, all built especially for Vegas, but many other big-budget shows have been tried and tested elsewhere before being picked up by the casino moguls. **Mamma Mia!**, **Spamalot**, **The Producers** and **Phantom** all made millions on Broadway or in London's West End before shipping out to the desert, while the likes of **Stomp** and **Menopause: the Musical** have played all over the world.

Elsewhere, magicians still draw the crowds: even with Siegfried & Roy gone, there's still plenty of choice. Other options include celebrity impersonator shows, in which lookalikes sing live or lip-synch in imitation of pop-culture heroes and heroines, and adult revues, featuring a parade of hardbodies taking it off for crowds of women and (more often) men. And many casinos carry on the time-honoured tradition of booking star headliners, with full-timers such as **Toni Braxton** and **Rita Rudner** joined by semi-resident performers such as **Elton John** and regular guests such as **Jay Leno**.

Adult revues

Chippendales

Rio *3700 W Flamingo Road, at S Valley View Boulevard, West of Strip (1-888 746 7784/777 7776/www.harrahs.com).* Bus 202. **Shows** 8pm Mon, Tue, Thur, Sun; 8pm, 10.30pm Fri, Sat. **Tickets** $47.25-$58.25. No under-18s. **Credit** AmEx, DC, Disc, MC, V. **Hotel** p100. **Map** p333 X3.

Shows
The best

For the Beatles on trapezes
Love. *See p231.*

For Broadway in Vegas
The Producers. *See p232.*

For big names in a small space
Hollywood Theatre. *See p234.*

For afternoon magic
Mac King. *See p228.*

For late-evening laughs
George Wallace. *See p228.*

But if you only have time for one show...
O. *See p232.*

Ladies, why let the guys have all the fun in Vegas when these chiselled male specimens can gyrate for your pleasure? Equal parts theatricality and sensuality, this time-tested father of all male revues makes for the perfect bachelorette, birthday or divorce party setting. The performers won't let you just sit back and passively take it all in; arriving drunk and uninhibited ensures a much better time.

Crazy Girls
Riviera *2901 Las Vegas Boulevard South, between E Sahara Avenue & E Desert Inn Road (1-877 892 7469/794 9433/www.rivierahotel.com).* Bus Deuce, 108, 204. **Shows** 9.30pm Mon, Wed-Sun. **Tickets** $49-$75. No under-18s. **Credit** AmEx, DC, Disc, MC, V. **Hotel** p91. **Map** p335 B5.

'Girls! Girls! Crazy girls!' goes the infernally catchy theme song. Well, crazy they ain't, and, if local legend is to be believed, the butts displayed in bronze outside the Riviera by way of advertisement aren't all female. Regardless, this low-budget titfest, which celebrated its 20th birthday in September 2007, is a giggle: about as arousing as a kick in the teeth, granted, but lovers of Vegas camp will be in heaven.

Crazy Horse Paris
MGM Grand *3799 Las Vegas Boulevard South, at E Tropicana Avenue (1-877 880 0880/891 7777/ www.mgmgrand.com/entertainment).* Bus Deuce, 201. **Shows** 8pm, 10.30pm Mon, Wed-Sun. **Tickets** $64.90. No under-18s. **Credit** AmEx, DC, Disc, MC, V. **Hotel** p81. **Map** p336 A8.

Formerly known as La Femme but revamped in 2007, Crazy Horse Paris claims to 'reinvent the female form as art', a boast that somehow doesn't go unfounded. Lighting effects and film, ballet and cabaret, canvasses and zodiac signs: all add up to a show with lashings of international flair. Its dozen stars have performed with the original Crazy Horse

Arts & Entertainment

Elvis hasn't left the building

After Elvis Presley's death, Las Vegas was swamped by impersonators who would perform on any stage, jump from aeroplanes and throw out the first pitch at ballgames. According to people who keep these sorts of statistics, there were more Elvises (Elvi?) in Nevada than in Tennessee. Once, at a show called *Memories of the King*, we found ourselves sitting next to another Elvis who, after the performance, was going backstage to meet the star and thenceforth to meet other Elvises at an Elvis karaoke night.

Three decades after Presley went way down for the last time, he's conspicuous by his absence in Vegas. The Elvis-a-Rama museum on Industrial Road closed its doors in 2006, and most Elvis impersonators have left town. Maybe it's because the new, slicker Vegas has little use for old-fashioned rock 'n' roll. But still, although the King is no longer omnipresent, he's by no means gone: just ask Jesse Garon, Elvis-impersonating owner of the **Art Bar** (*see p183*). He's usually sans jumpsuit, but you'll have no trouble recognising those sideburns.

Pete Vallee is the biggest Elvis impersonator in Las Vegas. Literally. Revelling in the self-explanatory stage name of **Big Elvis**, the obese singer performs sweat-soaked shows more or less daily in the lounge at Bill's Gambling Hall & Saloon (*see p88*). Pretending to be neither the young nor the old Presley, Vallee is more like the Ghost of Elvis Future, assuming the King had continued to wolf down fried banana sandwiches at the same rate for the last 30 years.

The city's flashiest Elvis is **Trent Carlini,** star of *The Musical History of the King* at the Sahara. Carlini fashions himself after the younger, thinner Elvis, but with a generous amount of Vegas-style rhinestones. The show covers the music from Presley's rockabilly beginnings in the 1950s to the comeback songs of the late '60s. Unlike the Pelvis, Carlini remains a middleweight.

True Elvis fans can live out the ultimate fantasy and have the King consecrate their marriage. Te **Viva Las Vegas** and **Graceland** wedding chapels (*see pp270-274*) both offer Elvis packages that include low-key performances, *Blue Hawaii* themes and, sometimes, commemorative T-shirts. Remember: the more you pay, the younger and thinner your Elvis will be. You'll also have to pay extra for one who actually performs the ceremony, and doesn't just show up with a boombox to belt out a couple of songs. Rates are reasonable and will probably remain so until 2009, when MGM Mirage and Cirque du Soleil launch a big new show based on the songs of the King who never quite lost his crown.

---

dance troupe in Paris, a phenomenon dating back to 1951. Who says Vegas has no sense of history?

Fantasy

Luxor *3900 Las Vegas Boulevard South, at W Hacienda Avenue (1-800 557 7428/262 4400/ www.luxor.com). Bus Deuce, 104, 105.* **Shows** 10.30pm Mon, Wed, Fri, Sun; 8pm, 10.30pm Tue; 11pm Sat. **Tickets** $53-$64. No under-18s. **Credit** AmEx, DC, Disc, MC, V. **Hotel** p80. **Map** p336 A9.
Choreographed by Chris Judd and Tiger Martina, Fantasy stages and interprets an array of top-shelf seduction scenarios. Charismatic host Sean Cooper keeps energy and anticipation running high with his comedic impersonations, singing and dancing, but you may find that you've seen this all before, and less rigidly, in your dreams.

Fashionistas

Empire Ballroom, 3765 Las Vegas Boulevard South, between E Tropicana & Harmon Avenues (836 0833/www.fashionintheshow.com). Bus Deuce. **Shows** 9pm Mon, Tue, Thur-Sun. **Tickets** $54.95-$87.95. Over 21s only. **Credit** AmEx, Disc, MC, V. **Map** p336 A7.

An adult revue for the artsy set. Under the supervision of adult-film magnate John 'Buttman' Stagliano, envelope-pushing costumes, visceral multimedia imagery and music by the likes of Tool meld even more than the show's own notions of gender identity in this story involving a love triangle, high fashion and a hearty helping of S&M.

Zumanity

New York-New York *3790 Las Vegas Boulevard South, at W Tropicana Avenue (1-866 606 7111/ 740 0815/www.zumanity.com). Bus Deuce, 201.* **Shows** 7.30pm, 10.30pm Wed-Sun. **Tickets** $75.90-$141.90. No under-18s. **Credit** AmEx, DC, Disc, MC, V. **Hotel** p84. **Map** p336 A8.
The idea of asking Cirque du Soleil to compile its own adult revue was an unexpected one. In parts, it pulls it off, most notably the more comic stretches and the two-women-in-a-fishtank section towards the start of the show. A little too often it seems unsure whether it's better off trying to dazzle or arouse the audience, but those on the love seats (or, as the box office coyly calls them, 'duo sofas') seem to go upstairs happy enough.

Celebrity impersonators

An Evening at La Cage

Riviera *2901 Las Vegas Boulevard South, between E Sahara Avenue & E Desert Inn Road (1-877 892 7469/794 9433/www.rivierahotel.com). Bus Deuce, 108, 204.* **Shows** 7.30pm Mon, Wed-Sun. **Tickets** $71-$82. Ages 13-18 with adult. **Credit** AmEx, DC, Disc, MC, V. **Hotel** p91. **Map** p335 B5.
It may look from the stalls as though 95% of the ticket price has gone on the succession of increasingly preposterous frocks that Marlboro-voiced Vegas legend and host Frank Marino dons during the course of this drag revue. What remains has been used to enlist a number of dolled-up queens who are lip-synching to J-Lo, Madonna and (a scarily convincing) Celine Dion. It's entertaining enough, but it's nothing you won't find at FreeZone (*see p248*).

Danny Gans

Mirage *3400 Las Vegas Boulevard South, between Spring Mountain & W Flamingo Roads (1-800 963 9634/796 9999/www.themirage.com). Bus Deuce, 105, 202, 203.* **Shows** 8pm Tue, Wed, Fri, Sat. **Tickets** $100. No under-5s. **Credit** AmEx, DC, Disc, MC, V. **Hotel** p73. **Map** p335 & p336 A6.
Any old impersonator can pull off a credible Elvis or Bill Clinton. But only actor/comedian/singer Danny Gans, who celebrated his 11th anniversary as a Strip headliner by extending his contract through to 2009, promises a vocal bank of more than 200 characters. Family-friendly and always packed, his show has something for everyone – including locals, who love his act as much as tourists.

Gordie Brown

Venetian *3555 Las Vegas Boulevard South, between Sands Avenue & E Flamingo Road (1-800 258 3626/www.blueman.com). Bus Deuce, 105, 203.* **Shows** 8pm Mon, Wed, Thur, Sun; 7pm, 10pm Tue, Fri, Sat. **Tickets** $76.50-$126. No under-5s. **Credit** AmEx, DC, Disc, MC, V. **Hotel** p75. **Map** p335 & p336 B6.
De Niro, Eastwood and Nicholson; Dylan, Pavarotti and Armstrong… Only a very few high-profile entertainers escape the attentions of this energetic singer/comic/actor/impressionist, a former political cartoonist from Canada who made his Vegas name up at the Golden Nugget before heading south in 2006. Some have accused Brown of trying too hard, of sacrificing himself to his characters, but it's a likeable enough show.

Legends in Concert

Imperial Palace *3535 Las Vegas Boulevard South, between Sands Avenue & E Flamingo Road (1-888 777 7664/794 3261/www.imperialpalace.com). Bus Deuce, 105, 203.* **Shows** 7.30pm, 10pm Mon-Sat. **Tickets** $49.95-$59.95; $34.95-$44.95 ages 2-12. **Credit** AmEx, Disc, MC, V. **Hotel** p80. **Map** p336 A6.
Sorry you missed Elvis? Came here on a weekend when Tom Jones isn't performing at the MGM? Wish Barbra Streisand didn't charge $500 a ticket? Worry not: they're all here in this long-running tribute show. Unlike other shows of this type, these performers – backed by a fine band and surrounded by showgirls – actually sing, usually doing several numbers or a medley of top hits.

The Tribute to Frank, Sammy, Joey & Dean

Greek Isles *305 Convention Center Drive, between Las Vegas Boulevard South & Paradise Road, East of Strip (1-800 634 6787/737 5540/798 5606/www.greekislesvegas.com). Bus Deuce 112.* **Shows** 8.15pm Mon-Thur, Sat, Sun. **Tickets** $62-$79. **Credit** AmEx, Disc, MC, V. **Map** p335 B5.
The set-up's a bit artificial, to say the least: God (Buddy Hackett, in a marvellous voiceover cameo) sends back the fantastic four (with a 'Happy Birthday'-singing Marilyn tagging along) for one night in Vegas, where they recreate their Sands act. But complete with a nine-piece band, and all the off-colour jokes and locker-room razzing you remember, the show's a humdinger.

Comedians

Carrot Top

Luxor *3900 Las Vegas Boulevard South, at W Hacienda Avenue (1-888 777 0188/262 4400/www.luxor.com). Bus Deuce, 104, 105.* **Shows** 8pm Mon, Wed-Fri, Sun; 7pm, 9pm Sat. **Tickets** $58.45-$69.45. No under-18s. **Credit** AmEx, DC, Disc, MC, V. **Hotel** p80. **Map** p336 A9.
Once you get past the 'zany prop comic' stigma, it's easy to see why Carrot Top's popularity has endured. The flame-maned, newly bulked-up comedian otherwise known as Scott Thompson invents visual puns by the truckload. Lightning-quick, Top combines subtle political, social and cultural commentary with music, video and – yes – those infamous props for a family-friendly comedic concoction like no other in town.

Gordie Brown.

George Wallace

Flamingo *3555 Las Vegas Boulevard South, at E Flamingo Road (1-800 221 7299/733 3333/www. harrahs.com). Bus Deuce, 202.* **Shows** 10pm Tue-Sat. **Tickets** $76.75-$93.30. No under-5s. **Credit** AmEx, Disc, MC, V. **Hotel** p78. **Map** p336 A7.

George Wallace's evenly-paced, conversational style of social criticism makes audiences think as well as laugh. Named one of Comedy Central's 100 greatest stand-ups of all time, Wallace veers between, 'Yo' mama' jokes, comic bewilderment at the English language and crowd interaction; and you never know who (Jerry Seinfeld, Chris Tucker) might show up. Don't be surprised to find him mingling on the casino floor after the show.

Rita Rudner

Harrah's *3475 Las Vegas Boulevard South, between Sands Avenue & E Flamingo Road (1-800 392 9002/369 5111/www.harrahs.com). Bus Deuce, 105, 203.* **Shows** 8pm Mon-Thur, Sat; 9pm Fri. **Tickets** $54.90-$99. No under-7s. **Credit** AmEx, Disc, MC, V. **Hotel** p79. **Map** p336 A6.

In the mood for comedy that's not too blue-blooded, blue-collar or just plain blue? The former chorus girl's observational material is witty without being wanton, classy instead of crass. You'll be hard-pressed to find anyone with better bits on relationships, family and shopping, nor will you find a more earnest, likeable performer on the Strip. After five years at New York New York, she's now at Harrah's.

Magicians

Amazing Johnathan

Sahara *2535 Las Vegas Boulevard South, at E Sahara Avenue (1-800 634 6787/737 2515/www. saharavegas.com). Bus Deuce, 108, 204.* **Shows** 10pm Mon, Tue, Fri-Sun. **Tickets** $57.40-$68.40. Ages 12-18 with adult. **Credit** AmEx, Disc, MC, V. **Hotel** p92. **Map** p335 C4.

Tagged as 'the Freddy Krueger of comedy', John Szeles delivers an adult-oriented show that relies heavily on audience participation, sight gags, explosive language and outrageous effects; not to mention the 'aid' of his goofily loveable sidekick, Psychic Tanya. The Amazing Johnathan doesn't toe the line when it comes to good taste: he makes it disappear in a plume of smoke.

Lance Burton

Monte Carlo *3770 Las Vegas Boulevard South, between W Harmon & W Tropicana Avenues (1-877 386 8224/730 7160/www.lanceburton.com). Bus Deuce, 201.* **Shows** 7pm, 10pm Tue, Sat; 7pm Wed-Fri. **Tickets** $69.50-$75.55. **Credit** AmEx, DC, Disc, MC, V. **Hotel** p84. **Map** p336 A8.

Blessed with all the personal dynamism of a ventriloquist's dummy – his interaction with the audience is still mesmerically awkward, despite the fact that he's been performing professionally for upwards of two decades – Burton relies purely on his magic to keep the audience wrapped around his finger. He just about manages it, too, pulling doves from napkins, coins from ears and geese – geese! – from all over the place. One for all the family.

Mac King

Harrah's *3475 Las Vegas Boulevard South, between Sands Avenue & E Flamingo Road (1-800 392 9002/369 5111/www.harrahs.com). Bus Deuce, 105, 203.* **Shows** 1pm, 3pm Tue-Sat. **Tickets** $27.95. No under-5s. **Credit** AmEx, Disc, MC, V. **Hotel** p79. **Map** p336 A6.

One of the real gems of Vegas's family entertainment roster is also one of its cheapest shows. Sure, there are no big bangs or grand illusions here: the

Steve Wyrick jets into Planet Hollywood for six shows a week. *See p230.*

Coming soon?

In their day, Celine Dion and Elton John were superstars who sold millions of records and played the world's biggest arenas. Now in the relative twilight of their careers, they're among a number of performers who are cashing in on their former fame and glory before finally becoming tomorrow's punchline.

But who's next? Which fading star will try to keep his or her lustre a little longer with a stint on the Strip? Rumours abound that Britney Spears and Michael Jackson are coming to town, but we think the following acts might beat them to it...

Morrissey

Never has despair looked so dazzling as in the former Smiths frontman's high-energy spectacle at Mandalay Bay. The singer's tales of angst and misery will be the centrepiece of a show that also features 20 befeathered showgirls, an animatronic dragon, two white tigers and a tank of dolphins. Budget travellers should investigate the 'Meat is Murder' dinner-and-show package that includes a sumptuous vegetarian buffet.

Fiona Apple

The Blue Man Group's psychedelic show will only be the second weirdest in town when this wan poet-singer brings her toe-tapping musical *When the Pawn Hits the Conflicts He Thinks Like a King What He Knows Throws The Blows When He Goes to the Fight and He'll Win the Whole Thing 'Fore He Enters the Ring* to the Danny Gans Theater at the Mirage. During each show, Apple will curl up in the foetal position in a corner of her stage and howls, 'Nobody understands me! I hate you all!' while state-of-the-art lasers and fog machines create illusions of happiness and true love.

Hulk!

The implicitly homoerotic spectacle of pro wrestling collides with the explicitly homoerotic drama of Broadway when Hulk Hogan opens his new revue at the Wynn. The show will spotlight the city's only competition-quality weightlifting, as well as greased men and women flying off turnbuckles. In the touching finale, the Hulkster salutes grandparents and piledrivers with an Edith Piaf medley.

The Stars of American Idol

To be honest, it might take a few years before this one hits the Strip. When it does, though, the flashy singers of the hit TV show will be everywhere. One will take your bags to your room, while another serves your drinks at the buffet. Justin Guarini will make an excellent valet, and rumour has it that Taylor Hicks mixes a mean mai tai.

The Wiggles: Midnight Fantasy

What happens in Vegas stays in Vegas. That's why you won't want to tell your kids about the Luxor's erotic late-night revue with Sam, Jeff, Murray and Anthony, along with Tammi, Barbi, Toni and Candi as pole-grinding, dry-humping pirates and dinosaurs. Shaking your sillies out never looked so sexy.

budget extends to a pack of cards, some rope, a box of Fig Newtons and a silly suit. But King's warm manner, gentle humour and casually dazzling tricks keep the audience hooked, even now that King has moved to a bigger showroom. Look out for discount coupons in the local magazines, but even if you don't find 'em, this is well worth full price. A highly likeable afternoon.

Penn & Teller

Rio *3700 W Flamingo Road, at S Valley View Boulevard, West of Strip (1-888 746 7784/777 7776/www.harrahs.com). Bus 202.* **Shows** 9pm Mon-Thur, Sat, Sun. **Tickets** $85.80-$96.80.

No under-5s. **Credit** AmEx, DC, Disc, MC, V. **Hotel** p100. **Map** p333 X3.

Burly man-mountain Penn Jillette and the mute, mono-monikered Teller are the Reservoir Dogs to most other magicians' Ocean's Eleven: edgy, angry, and always seemingly on the verge of going off. They've become scourges of the Magic Circle by showing the audience how tricks are done, but they deserve equal credit for the pzazz with which they pull off the illusions they don't explain. The closing bullet routine is the only one that falls flat, but the rest of the evening is very entertaining. Bonus: stick around afterwards for the inevitable autograph signings, and you may hear Teller speak. *Photo p224.*

Blue Man Group. Some people just feel the cold a little more than others.

Steve Wyrick: Real Magic

Planet Hollywood (Miracle Mile) *3667 Las Vegas Boulevard South, between E Harmon & E Flamingo Roads (777 7794/www.miraclemileshopslv. com). Bus Deuce, 202.* **Shows** 7pm, 9pm Mon-Thur, Sat, Sun. **Tickets** $73-$95. **Credit** AmEx, Disc, MC, V. **Hotel** p85. **Map** p336 A7.

For fast-paced, no-frills magic performed in an intimate setting, *Steve Wyrick: Real Magic* can't be beat; lock up your jets and motorcycles. When it comes to both magic and nightlife, Wyrick believes bigger is better: witness his new $34-million entertainment complex, comprising the Steve Wyrick Theater, the Magiq Shoppe retail store and a club/ultralounge punningly named Triq. *Photo p230.*

Musical headliners

Barry Manilow: Music & Passion

Las Vegas Hilton *3000 Paradise Road, between E Sahara Avenue & E Desert Inn Road, East of Strip (1-800 222 5361/702 5111/www.lvhilton.com). Bus 108, 204, 213.* **Shows** 8pm Wed-Sat. **Tickets** $110-$253. **Credit** AmEx, DC, Disc, MC, V. **Hotel** p97. **Map** p335 C5.

The Hilton is so convinced that *Music & Passion* will always be in fashion that in 2007, it immortalised Manilow on a gigantic building wrap, the largest of its kind in town. What's not to love? With classy back-up singers, a descending catwalk and a set list of favourites that takes in 'Mandy', 'Can't Smile Without You' and 'Copacabana', the man who writes the songs that make the whole world sing also gets the audience on its feet.

Bette Midler

Caesars Palace *3570 Las Vegas Boulevard South, at W Flamingo Road (1-877 723 8836/866 1400/ www.harrahs.com). Bus Deuce, 202.* **Shows** 7.30pm Mon-Wed, Fri, Sat. **Tickets** $95-$250. **Credit** AmEx, DC, Disc, MC, V. **Hotel** p68. **Map** p336 A7.

Her show having grossed more than $500 million in its five-year run, Celine Dion will be leaving sizeable shoes to fill when she ends her Caesars Palace run at the end of 2007. From February 2008, the divine Miss M will be attempting to match her. With Midler in place for 100 shows a year and Elton John (*see below*) playing a further 50, Caesars looks likely to enlist a third headliner to plug the gaps; check the website for details.

Elton John

Caesars Palace *3570 Las Vegas Boulevard South, at W Flamingo Road (1-888 435 8665/866 1400/ www.harrahs.com). Bus Deuce, 202.* **Shows** 7.30pm, days vary. **Tickets** $100-$250. **Credit** AmEx, DC, Disc, MC, V. **Hotel** p68. **Map** p336 A7.

The Queen of England eschews his patchier recent material for a whirlwind of greatest hits, opening a 100-minute show with 'Bennie and the Jets' and playing everything you'd hope to find in an Elton John set list. David LaChapelle's outlandish films and increasingly ridiculous set decoration celebrate Elton's past; the veteran performer is sensible enough not to dwell on his less engaging present, making this blockbuster well worth a look if you're in town for one of its 50 annual shows.

Toni Braxton Revealed

Flamingo *3555 Las Vegas Boulevard South, at E Flamingo Road (1-800 221 7299/733 3333/ www.harrahs.com). Bus Deuce, 202.* **Shows** 7.30pm Tue-Sat. **Tickets** $79.75-$123.75. No under-5s. **Credit** AmEx, Disc, MC, V. **Hotel** p78. **Map** p336 A7.

With six Grammys and 40 million sales under her tiny belt, Braxton is the latest bona fide pop star to set up here. The former Broadway performer struts and sparkles (check out the million-dollar, diamond-studded microphone) her way through soulful R&B hits such as 'Unbreak My Heart', 'Breathe Again' and 'Love Shoulda Brought You Home'. Still, her financial and emotional histories make it a bit hard to swallow the on-top-of-the-world persona.

Production shows

Blue Man Group

Venetian *3555 Las Vegas Boulevard South, between Sands Avenue & E Flamingo Road (1-800 258 3626/www.blueman.com). Bus Deuce, 105, 203.*

Shows 8pm Mon, Wed, Thur, Sun; 7pm, 10pm
Tue, Fri, Sat. **Tickets** $76.50-$126. No under-5s.
Credit AmEx, DC, Disc, MC, V. **Hotel** p75.
Map p335 & p336 B6.
It's no surprise that Blue Man Group is such an
international phenomenon: their witty, rhythmic and
colourful appeal is universal, and very carefully
pitched at all ages. In this industrial-themed theatre
at the Venetian, the three blue baldies cull comedy
from multimedia high jinks, a festival environment
from audience reactions, and music from just about
everything they can get their hands on. Few performers express so much while saying so little.

Folies Bergère

Tropicana *3801 Las Vegas Boulevard South, at
E Tropicana Avenue (1-800 829 9034/739 2411/
www.tropicanalv.com). Bus Deuce, 201.* **Shows**
7.30pm, 10pm Mon, Wed, Thur, Sat; 8.30pm Tue,
Fri. **Tickets** $68.90-$78.90. No under-16s for late
show. **Credit** AmEx, DC, Disc, MC, V. **Hotel** p94.
Map p336 A8.
This elaborate spartan feathers-and-sequins show, a
by-the-decades homage to women's attitudes and
fashion (including the obligatory can-can), opened
in 1959 and is looking its age. But it's still packed
with gorgeous showgirls – in bikinis for the early
show from Monday to Thursday, topless for the late
show and all weekend – and merits investigation
simply for its status as one of the last remaining
shows of its type in Vegas.

Jubilee!

Bally's *3645 Las Vegas Boulevard South, at
E Flamingo Road (1-877 374 7469/967 4567/
www.harrahs.com). Bus Deuce, 202.* **Shows** 7.30pm,
10.30pm Mon-Thur, Sat, Sun. **Tickets** $65.77-$82.
No under-18s. **Credit** AmEx, DC, Disc, MC, V.
Hotel p77. **Map** p336 A7.
Jubilee!'s staging of the sinking of the *Titanic* and
Samson's destruction of the Philistines in the temple are beyond lame. But the production numbers in
this long-running spectacle, which feature endless
parades of beauties wearing nothing more than out-
landishly coloured feathers, headdresses and rhinestones, make it one of a kind.

Kà

MGM Grand *3799 Las Vegas Boulevard South,
at E Tropicana Avenue (1-877 880 0880/891 7777/
www.mgmgrand.com). Bus Deuce, 201.* **Shows** 7pm,
9.30pm Tue-Sat. **Tickets** $75.90-$165, half price for
5-11s. No under-5s. **Credit** AmEx, DC, Disc, MC, V.
Hotel p81. **Map** p336 A8.
Having pushed the boat out for *O* (literally, in a couple of scenes), Cirque du Soleil had to work hard to
top it in this multi-million-dollar extravaganza. *Kà*
differs from other Vegas-based Cirque shows in
that it has a plot (about twins struggling to reunite).
The story gets a bit lost in an array of ever more
breathtaking routines; yet for all the excess, the most
touching moment in the piece is a section involving
hand-shadows. It's undeniably very impressive, but
O and *Love* are better.

Love

Mirage *3400 Las Vegas Boulevard South, between
Spring Mountain & W Flamingo Roads (1-800
963 9634/796 9999/www.themirage.com). Bus
Deuce, 105, 202, 203.* **Shows** 7pm, 10pm Mon,
Thur-Sun. **Tickets** $75.90-$165. No under-5s.
Credit AmEx, DC, Disc, MC, V. **Hotel** p73.
Map p335 & p336 A6.
This could have been horrific, a parade of paperback
writers coming together in Sgt Pepper's yellow submarine to help Jude get back, or something. Sure,
Cirque du Soleil's Beatles show is a little too literal
with the lyrics in places, but from its spectacular
opening until its cheesy climax, *Love* is mostly great
fun, packed with Cirque's trademark acrobatics and
punctuated with playful humour. Oh, and the
music's never sounded better. *Photo p232.*

Menopause: the Musical

Las Vegas Hilton *3000 Paradise Road, between
E Sahara Avenue & E Desert Inn Road, East of
Strip (1-800 222 5361/www.lvhilton.com). Bus 108,
204, 213.* **Shows** 7pm Mon-Fri; 4pm, 7pm Sat, Sun.
Tickets $59.46. No under-14s. **Credit** AmEx, DC,
Disc, MC, V. **Hotel** p97. **Map** p335 C5.
The *Menopause* juggernaut finds a home in a city
known for its own frequent hot flushes. Set in the
lingerie department of Bloomingdale's, *Menopause*
unites not only its four stars but women everywhere
tackling 'the change', head-on through dialogue and
two dozen pop parodies. Women under 40 and men
of all ages should stay as far away as possible.

Mamma Mia!

Mandalay Bay *3950 Las Vegas Boulevard South,
at W Hacienda Avenue (1-877 632 7400/474 4000/
www.mandalaybay.com). Bus Deuce, 104, 105.*
Shows 7.30pm Mon-Thur, Sun; 6pm, 10pm Sat.
Tickets $49.50-$110. No under-5s. **Credit** AmEx,
DC, Disc, MC, V. **Hotel** p71. **Map** p336 A9.

Jubilee!.

Arts & Entertainment

While the story – a young woman trying to find her father on the eve of her wedding – plays a little too earnestly for the featherweight songs, fans of 1970s group Abba will have a heap of fun seeing how and where their favourite tunes – among them 'Take a Chance on Me' and 'Gimme! Gimme! Gimme!' – pop up in this West End smash hit. Hang in there: they'll get to 'Dancing Queen' eventually. The show is scheduled to close in mid 2008.

Mystère

Treasure Island *3300 Las Vegas Boulevard South, at Spring Mountain Road (1-800 392 1999/796 9999/www.treasureisland.com). Bus Deuce, 105, 203.* **Shows** 7pm, 9.30pm Mon-Wed, Sat; 4.30pm, 7pm Sun. **Tickets** $66-$104.50. **Credit** AmEx, DC, Disc, MC, V. **Hotel** p87. **Map** p335 & p336 A6.

The first Cirque du Soleil show to reach Vegas, *Mystère* holds up very well next to the more spectacular and expensive siblings that have joined it. The reason? It doesn't take itself too seriously, and plays for slapsticky laughs (get there 20 minutes early) as much as it does for astonishment (taiko drumming, bunraku puppetry, dazzling did-you-see-that gymnastic exhibitions). The design is showing its age a little, but otherwise, this long-runner is in rude health.

O

Bellagio *3600 Las Vegas Boulevard South, at W Flamingo Road (1-888 488 7111/796 9999/ www.bellagio.com). Bus Deuce, 202.* **Shows** 7.30pm, 10.30pm Wed-Sun. **Tickets** $102.85-$165. No under-5s. **Credit** AmEx, DC, Disc, MC, V. **Hotel** p68. **Map** p336 A7.

It's been surpassed in the extravagance stakes by *Kà* (*see p231*), but this is still the best Cirque du Soleil production in town, and maybe the best show on the Strip. *O* – a pun on *eau*, French for water – is a spectacle of Fellini-esque tableaux coupled with acrobatic feats performed by 70-plus swimmers, divers, aerialists, contortionists and clowns in, on, above and around a pool/stage containing 1.5 million gallons of water. None of which goes any way towards describing just how beautiful it all is.

Phantom

Venetian *3555 Las Vegas Boulevard South, between Sands Avenue & E Flamingo Road (1-800 258 3626/414 1000/www.venetian.com). Bus Deuce, 105, 203.* **Shows** 7pm Mon, Tue, Thur-Sat; 10pm Tue, Sat; 5pm, 8pm Sun. **Tickets** $82-$157. No under-6s. **Credit** AmEx, DC, Disc, MC, V. **Hotel** p75. **Map** p335 & p336 B6.

One of the most beloved musicals of all time is now one of Vegas's most seductive shows. Housed in a theatre designed to evoke the show's own Paris Opera House, the abbreviated, snazzed-up *Phantom* claims to challenge the dramatic superiority of the original Lloyd Webber production. In truth, there's really nothing new to see here, but the production remains thrilling all the same.

The Producers

Paris Las Vegas *3655 Las Vegas Boulevard South, at E Flamingo Road (1-877 762 5746/ www.harrahs.com). Bus Deuce, 202.* **Shows** 8pm Mon, Tue, Thur, Fri, Sun; 2pm, 8pm Sat. **Tickets** $69-$143.50. No under-6s. **Credit** AmEx, DC, Disc, MC, V. **Hotel** p74. **Map** p336 A7.

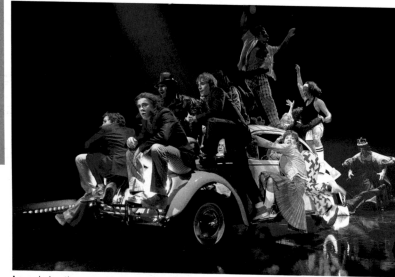

Love: baby, they can drive your car. *See p231.*

Tournament of Kings. See p234.

The most honoured musical in Broadway history heads from the Great White Way to Eiffel Way. Mel Brooks's tale about a scheming producer and a starry-eyed accountant hoping to make a mint from a surefire flop called *Springtime for Hitler* boasts the most outrageous plotlines, costumes and accents in town, not to mention the hottest tickets. But whittled down to a tourist-friendly hour and a half, it sacrifices the original's heart and humour.

Le Rêve

Wynn Las Vegas *3131 Las Vegas Boulevard South, between E Desert Inn Road & Sands Avenue (1-888 320 7110/770 9966/www.wynnlasvegas.com).* Bus Deuce, 203. **Shows** 7pm, 9.30pm Mon, Thur, Sun; 8.30pm Fri; 8pm, 10.30pm Sat. **Tickets** $102.95-$162.95. **Credit** AmEx, DC, Disc, MC, V. **Hotel** p76. **Map** p335 & p336 B6.
Named after mogul Steve Wynn's favourite Picasso painting ('the dream' in French), this big-budget spectacular features diving, acrobatics and amazing choreography, all performed in an aqua-theater with intimate, in-the-round seating. With out-of-the-box aesthetics and an independent vision (courtesy of several very public overhauls), it's pretty to watch, but it fades from memory as fast as a dream itself.

Spamalot

Wynn Las Vegas *3131 Las Vegas Boulevard South, between E Desert Inn Road & Sands Avenue (1-888 320 7110/770 9966/www.wynnlasvegas.com).* Bus Deuce, 203. **Shows** 8pm Mon, Wed, Sun; 7pm, 10pm Tue, Fri, Sat. **Tickets** $52.95-$102.95. **Credit** AmEx, DC, Disc, MC, V. **Hotel** p76. **Map** p335 & p336 B6.
Boys meet Grail. Boys lose Grail. Boys are taunted by French knights, aided by a showboating Lady of the Lake and terrorised by one very perturbed rabbit in this stage adaptation of *Monty Python and the*

Holy Grail. Crammed with nonsensical British humour, Vegas in-jokes and audience interaction, Spamalot delivers more laughs than any other show in town. Non-fans may scratch their heads, but Python devotees won't be able to bag their very own gift-shop coconut halves, ingeniously 'imported' to the gift shop 'by African swallows', fast enough.

Stomp Out Loud

Planet Hollywood *3667 Las Vegas Boulevard South, between E Harmon & E Flamingo Roads (1-866 919 7472/785 5555/www.planethollywood resort.com).* Bus Deuce, 202. **Shows** 8pm Mon, Tue, Thur-Sun. **Tickets** $50-$110. **Credit** AmEx, Disc, MC, V. **Hotel** p85. **Map** p336 A7.
At up to $110 a ticket, those must be some expensive trashcan lids, brooms and cigarette lighters that Stomp's cast spend 90 minutes tapping and bashing with such exuberance. The Stomp formula hasn't changed much since the troupe burst to attention on the Edinburgh Fringe more than 15 years ago, but it has been slightly refined for this often deafening show. They're one-trick ponies, but it's a good trick.

Tony 'n' Tina's Wedding

Rio *3700 W Flamingo Road, at S Valley View Boulevard, West of Strip (1-888 746 7784/777 7776/www.playrio.com).* Bus 202. **Shows** 7pm daily. **Tickets** $90.15-$140.50. **Credit** AmEx, DC, Disc, MC, V. **Hotel** p100. **Map** p333 X3.
In this inventive, interactive show, ticket-holders become wedding guests taking in the nuptials and reception of an Italian-American couple coping with eccentric families, a pregnant maid of honour, a drunk priest and more. The set-up is jolly enough to make you want to brush up on your singing and dance moves (think 'YMCA'). But once dinner is served (an Italian buffet, natch), you'll want to high-tail it like a groom on the business end of a shotgun.

Arts & Entertainment

Tournament of Kings

Excalibur *3850 Las Vegas Boulevard South, at W Tropicana Avenue (1-800 933 1334/597 7600/ www.excalibur.com). Bus Deuce, 201.* **Shows** 6pm, 8.30pm daily. **Tickets** $61.24. **Credit** AmEx, DC, Disc, MC, V. **Hotel** p90. **Map** p336 A8.

The phrase 'dinner and a show' takes on new meaning here. Kids and those with time-period fetishes will dig the jousting knights, dancing maidens and galloping horses, as King Arthur and company recreate a bygone era with fine-tuned costumes, dialogue and mannerisms. One meal sans utensils is cool and all, but you may prefer to dive knife-and-fork-first into any number of casino buffets. *Photo p233.*

V: the Ultimate Variety Show

Planet Hollywood (Miracle Mile) *3667 Las Vegas Boulevard South, between E Harmon & E Flamingo Roads (892 7790/www.vtheshow.com). Bus Deuce, 202.* **Shows** 7.30pm, 9pm daily. **Tickets** $64-$74; half price 2-12s. **Credit** AmEx, Disc, MC, V. **Hotel** p85. **Map** p336 A7.

V strives to feature the best of the best in variety acts: comedy, magic, music, juggling, acrobatics, daredevil stunts and the King Charles Troupe, which nearly treads Harlem Globetrotters territory through the little-known art of unicycle basketball. It's fast-paced and family-friendly, though the action can get a little schizoid at times.

Comedy clubs

Comics are as much a Vegas staple as magicians, showgirls and second-mortgage-inducing blackjack losses. In addition to marquee funnymen such as **Steven Wright** and **Jerry Seinfeld**, who make regular pilgrimages to Vegas's biggest showrooms, and acts such as **Rita Rudner** and **George Wallace** (*see p228*), who have nightly residencies here, the city boasts a number of pretty good comedy clubs. Shows typically run for about 80 minutes and feature two or three stand-ups plus an MC.

Comedy Stop

Tropicana *3801 Las Vegas Boulevard South, at E Tropicana Avenue (1-800 829-9034/739 2714/www. comedystop.com). Bus Deuce, 201.* **Shows** 8pm, 10.30pm daily. **Tickets** (incl 1 drink) $19.95. **Credit** AmEx, DC, Disc, MC, V. **Hotel** p94. **Map** p336 A8.

This 300-capacity fixture on the Las Vegas comedy circuit features 'three comics and a mic' in two separate shows every night of the week. Performers tend to be in residence for a week at a time, and there's surprisingly little repetition of acts.

Improv

Harrah's *3475 Las Vegas Boulevard South, between Sands Avenue & E Flamingo Road (369 5223/ www.harrahs.com). Bus Deuce, 105, 203.* **Shows** 8.30pm, 10.30pm Tue-Sat. **Tickets** $27.95. No under-21s. **Credit** AmEx, DC, Disc, MC, V. **Hotel** p79. **Map** p336 A6.

After more than 40 years in the funny business, the jokes here at the Improv are still pretty fresh. The comedy isn't improv at all – it's actually straightforward stand-up, delivered by a weekly-changing roster of three comics.

Lounge

Palms *4321 W Flamingo Road, at S Valley View Boulevard, West of Strip (474 4000/www.palms.com). Bus 104, 202.* **Shows** 8pm, 10.30pm last Sat of mth. **Tickets** $44. No under-21s. **Credit** AmEx, DC, Disc, MC, V. **Hotel** p92. **Map** p333 X3.

This normally dark lounge lights up one Saturday a month with Playboy Comedy, studded with relatively well-known comics you may recognise from Comedy Central, HBO or other TV shows.

Riviera Comedy Club

Riviera *2901 Las Vegas Boulevard South, between E Sahara Avenue & E Desert Inn Road (794 9433/ www.rivierahotel.com). Bus Deuce, 108, 204.* **Shows** 8.30pm, 10.30pm daily. **Tickets** $19.95. **Credit** AmEx, DC, Disc, MC, V. **Hotel** p91. **Map** p335 B5.

The Riv's comedy club does pretty much what you might expect, booking three (or sometimes four) solid acts for two shows nightly in a fairly dreary room. As at the Trop, the line-ups change weekly.

Second City

Flamingo *3555 Las Vegas Boulevard South, at E Flamingo Road (1-800 221 7299/733 3333/ www.harrahs.com). Bus Deuce, 202.* **Shows** 8pm Mon, Tue, Fri; 8pm, 10pm Thur, Sat, Sun. **Tickets** $39.95. **Credit** AmEx, DC, Disc, MC, V. **Hotel** p79. **Map** p336 A7.

The razor-witted Chicago troupe ditches the stand-up/headliner format in favour of comedy sketches and improv games that riff on topical events and all sorts of Vegas wackiness.

Showrooms

Many hotel-casinos have smallish showrooms that host touring productions, concerts and other special events. Prices vary by performer and location: tickets for big-name acts at Strip venues (David Copperfield at the MGM, say) will set you back around $100, while past-their-prime hitmakers can often be seen for a mere $20 or so.

The best showroom on the Strip is the **Hollywood Theatre** at the **MGM Grand** (*see p81*), a cosy, 740-seat room that regularly hosts Tom Jones, Howie Mandel and the aforementioned David Copperfield among a roster of regular guests. There are also strong selections of name-brand entertainment at theatres within several locals' casinos, chiefly the 800-seater **Orleans** (*see p113*), the larger **Sam's Town** (*see p117*) and the more intimate **Suncoast** (*see p117*). For larger venues that host big-name bands and other one-night stands, *see pp250-252*.

They say the neon lights are bright

After four years of starring in *The Producers* on Broadway and in London, Brad Oscar thought he knew the moments that drew the biggest laughs. But when the show launched at Paris Las Vegas in February 2007, Oscar, who plays producer Max Bialystock, was puzzled. The usual guffaws, chuckles and bursts of applause just weren't happening.

The reason, Oscar figured out, was simple inexperience. 'Quite a few of these people have never been to a Broadway musical – this is completely new to them. We worry they're too quiet.' But once they relax, he adds, 'They're on their feet cheering by the end.'

Not all Broadway imports have been as adept at winning over Las Vegas. For $125 a ticket, audiences expect a spectacle on a par with Cirque du Soleil, and some Broadway shows just don't measure up. Steve Wynn spent $40 million on a custom-built theatre for witty satire *Avenue Q* at Wynn Las Vegas. But while the original continues to flourish on the Great White Way, the Strip version went dark just nine months after its debut.

One curiosity of theatregoing in Las Vegas is that most of the productions are cut-down versions of the originals, shortened to satisfy the attention spans of fidgety tourists and the impatience of cash-hungry casino proprietors. This penchant for truncating shows dates back to the 1950s, when the entertainment was always a side order and never the main event. But as the city has changed, so have its theatre audiences. More visitors are coming for the shopping, the dining and – yes – the entertainment. Witness the success of Mandalay Bay's full-length production of *Mamma Mia!*, which will have run for five years by the time it closes in 2008.

Wynn's expensive lesson didn't deter him from trying again. In spring 2007, Monty Python's *Spamalot* opened at Wynn Las Vegas, greeted by strong advance sales and enthusiastic reviews. At the same time, it was joined by *The Producers* and *Phantom*, the Venetian's $80-million production of Andrew Lloyd Webber's *Phantom of the Opera*. The show cleaves the running time down to 90 minutes, but one Lloyd Webber devotee admitted she barely noticed the missing musical numbers, even wondering if perhaps the original wasn't a tad on the long side.

The early success of *The Producers* and *Spamalot* suggests Vegas audiences are now ready to embrace musical theatre on a Broadway scale. Oscar certainly hopes so. 'I know the audiences love it; there's no reason these shows can't play here and thrive.' Even so, no producer has yet made plans to bring more dramatic fare to town. The closest serious drama has come to the Strip was a stock presentation of *Hamlet* at the Clark County Government Center's amphitheatre. The audience gave the performers a standing ovation, perhaps because the heavily edited production clocked in at a mere 90 minutes.

Arts & Entertainment

The Producers.

Children

Who said Sin City was just for grown-ups?

The rebranding of TI says a lot about the target audience for 21st-century Las Vegas. The resort spent a lot of money sexing up its wholesome past as the family-friendly Treasure Island; in the process, it got rid of the free pirate show, a must-see back in the family-oriented days of the '90s. Oh, there's still a show, and it's still free, but the stars are now the scantily clad, silicone-enhanced Sirens of TI. Like most Las Vegas attractions today, kids might enjoy the show, but it's not designed with their enjoyment in mind.

That said, where there's a gap in the market, someone in Las Vegas will be only too happy to fill it, which is why there are still plenty of child-friendly amusements in the city. Video arcades and rollercoasters line the Strip; and even without Siegfried & Roy, animals remain perhaps the ultimate all-ages crowd-pleaser. Most of the major shopping malls offer an array of amusements alongside the stores. And in the showrooms, the old staples – magicians, impersonators and variety acts – still thrive. With Cirque du Soleil alone now offering five different shows (one of which, *Zumanity*, is unsuitable for kids), there's no shortage of entertainment options.

There's also plenty of choice if you want to take in a movie or go bowling, especially if you're prepared to leave the Strip. Las Vegas has more bowling lanes per capita than any place on earth, and they all seem to have the latest high-tech stuff and gimmicks (cosmic bowling, anyone?). Even the upscale Red Rock Casino has a 72-lane centre. And for something completely different, try the **Las Vegas Springs Preserve** (*see p146 and p239* **The greenest show in town**), a 180-acre eco-park and the town's newest attraction.

THE LAW

State law forbids under-21s from lingering on casino floors. Children are allowed to pass through casino areas when accompanied by an adult, but they cannot stay by any of the gaming tables or machines. If they do, a security guard is likely to ask them – politely, but firmly – to leave the casino. Parents are not permitted to bet when they have youngsters in tow.

A Clark County curfew dictates that unaccompanied under-18s are not allowed on the Strip after 9pm on weekends and holidays. Off the Strip, the curfew is 10pm, or midnight

on Fridays and Saturdays and during school holidays. Teenagers have the roughest time because, until they're 21, they can't go into bars, nor most clubs and showrooms.

Where to stay

Many hotel-casinos on the Strip have an arcade and/or a cinema to help keep kids entertained. That said, some resorts are more family-friendly than others: the best of the bunch are **Circus Circus** (*see p89*), **Excalibur** (*see p90*), the **Luxor** (*see p80*) and **Mandalay Bay** (*see p71*), all of which are owned by MGM Mirage. The **Monte Carlo** (*see p84*) is a good, lower-priced option, while **New York New York** (*see p84*) gets a gold star for its efforts to keep the kids happy. The gambling-free **Four Seasons Las Vegas** (*see p95*) doesn't offer flashy entertainments, but the service is child-friendly, and the hotel is attached to the attraction-filled Mandalay Bay.

Off the Strip, the **Stratosphere** (*see p93*) and **Palms** (*see p98*) have good childcare facilities, as do a number of the locals' casinos, particularly **Boulder Station** (*see p116*), **Santa Fe Station** (*see p117*), **Sunset Station** (*see p117*) and **Texas Station** (*see p118*). Out at the **Loews Lake Las Vegas**, great family amenities include water activities, a sports court and a special kids' programme. For more on the city's accommodation, *see pp65-118*.

Eating & drinking

As in most towns, the best family restaurants are heavily themed and often quite loud. The **Rainforest Café** in the MGM Grand (*see p81*; 891 8580, www.rainforestcafe.com, open 8am-11pm Mon-Thur & Sun, 8am-midnight Fri & Sat) is filled with fake foliage, life-size robotic animals and large aquariums with (real) fish. There's even the odd 'thunderstorm'. Sports fans will enjoy the **ESPN Zone** at New York New York (*see p179*), with fun food and a cool arcade, and the **NASCAR Café** at the Sahara (*see p92*; 734 7223, www.nascarcafelasvegas.com, open 11am-11pm Mon-Thur & Sun, 11am-midnight Fri & Sat). But the most fun of all is the *Star Trek*-themed **Quark's Bar & Restaurant** (*see p183*) at the Las Vegas Hilton.

Arts & Entertainment

The thrills are on a grand scale at **Adventuredome**.

Sightseeing

Animal & water attractions

The off-Strip **Southern Nevada Zoological Park** (*see p146*) is too far out for many visitors. However, if you combined the numerous animal habitats along the Strip, you'd have a pretty good menagerie, albeit one that's rather old-fashioned and not very politically correct.

Siegfried & Roy may not perform any more, but the duo's **Secret Garden** is still open for business at the Mirage (*see p129*). Check out the lions, the tigers and the playful Asian elephant, before adjourning to the **Dolphin Habitat**. There are more big cats over at the MGM Grand's slight but satisfying **Lion Habitat** (*see p125*). Even if the lions are asleep, they'll probably be lying on top of a glass tunnel through which you can walk for a closer look. Wait at both spots to see the animals being fed and handled by the staff. But the best animal attraction is Mandalay Bay's **Shark Reef** (*see p125*): it features more than 75 species of fish and reptiles. At the touch pool, kids can get their hands wet touching sharks, rays and horseshoe crabs.

Over at the Mystic Falls park at **Sam's Town** (*see p117*), a four-times-daily laser and water show, **Sunset Stampede**, tells the story of the western pioneer experience.

Arcades & rides

Most major casinos have games arcades. Some consist of little more than a room with a dozen old video games, but others boast superlative arcades and even fairground attractions. Those at both the **Excalibur** (on the Fantasy Faire level; *see p90*) and **Circus Circus** (where the games surround a central ring with circus acts; *see p89*) are decent, but the best are the **Coney Island Emporium** (*see p125*) at New York New York, the **Games of the Gods** arcade at the Luxor (*see p80*) and, especially, the non-casino **GameWorks** (*see p126*) in the Showcase Mall.

Of the clutch of theme parks in the city, the indoor **Adventuredome** (*see p132*) at Circus Circus rules the roost, yet it's never so busy that you'll spend the bulk of your time in queues. The Canyon Blaster is a short but furious double-loop, double-corkscrew rollercoaster; other exciting rides include the head-rushing Inverter and the Rim Runner water flume (yes, you will get wet). There are half a dozen low-intensity rides for the little ones, plus carnival games, miniature golf and the Xtreme Zone, where you can test your mettle with rock climbing and bungee jumping.

Other rides in town range from the ridiculous to the heart-stoppingly thrilling. Arguably the most harrowing is the **Manhattan Express** rollercoaster (*see p125*), which twists and loops through New York New York. However, the Sahara's **Speed: the Ride** (*see p132*) is not far

The best Kids' stuff

For earth
Las Vegas Springs Preserve. See p239.

For wind
Rides at the Stratosphere. See p238.

For fire
The volcano at the Mirage. See p73.

Arts & Entertainment

Sunset Stampede. See p237.

behind in terms of thrills. The rollercoaster is accessible via the NASCAR Café, which itself offers a ride of sorts in the shape of the **Cyber Speedway** race simulator. Further north is the Stratosphere, which hosts three monstrous thrill rides some 1,000 feet (300 metres) above the Strip: **X Scream**, the **Big Shot** and **Insanity: the Ride** (for all, *see p132*).

The **Forum Shops** (*see p191*) at Caesars Palace have free animatronic shows in the mall and two IMAX rides. Sci-fi-loving teens may prefer the motion simulator at **Star Trek: the Experience** (*see p135*) at the Las Vegas Hilton, which gives riders a view of the action around their simulated shuttlecraft. Off the Strip, the **Las Vegas Mini Gran Prix** (1401 N Rainbow Boulevard, at US 95, 259 7000, www.lvmgp.com) features an indoor arcade, a miniature rollercoaster and four go-karting tracks, where the size and speed of the vehicles match the increasing age and skill of the young drivers. Height and weather restrictions apply for many thrill rides in Las Vegas.

Educational attractions

Aside from the **Las Vegas Springs Preserve** (*see p146 and p239* **The greenest show in town**), the **Lied Discovery Children's Museum** and, across the street, the **Las Vegas Natural History Museum** (for both, *see p142*) are tilted at kids.

Parks

Sunset Park (E Sunset Road & S Eastern Avenue), **Lorenzi Park** (W Washington Avenue & N Rancho Drive) and **Floyd Lamb**

State Park (Tule Springs Road, off US 95 north of Las Vegas) are a trio of large, grassy parks with lakes and volleyball courts; Sunset and Lorenzi Parks also have tennis facilities. For details on all parks, call 455 8200.

Arts & entertainment

Aside from the stand-alone **UA Showcase 8** movie theatre on the Strip, many off-Strip casinos have in-house cinemas, with those at the **Orleans** and the **Palms** closest to the Strip. Many of the Station casinos have movie theatres; **Sam's Town**, another locals' casino, counts an 18-screen multiplex among its selling points. The **IMAX Theatre** at the Luxor screens family-oriented flicks, some educational. For all, *see pp240-242*.

Most shows on the Strip are adult-oriented, whether in terms of explicit content or complex themes; tickets for those that are suitable for children, such as Cirque du Soleil's fabulous **Mystère**, exotic **O** and Beatles-themed **Love** (for all, *see pp231-232*), can cost more than $100. However, there are some bargains: magicians **Lance Burton** and **Mac King** (for both, *see p228*) both produce good, child-pleasing shows, with King's show conveniently staged in the afternoons.

Directory

Babysitting & children's supplies

Several agencies in Las Vegas offer licensed babysitters who have been cleared through the sheriff's department and by the FBI. Every hotel worth its salt can arrange babysitting services;

Arts & Entertainment

many even offer on-site babysitters. Many hotels can also arrange the delivery of children's supplies (strollers, cots, car seats, even video games); if yours can't, try **Baby's Away** (1-800 560 9141, 458 1019, www.babysaway.com).

Nurseries & activity centres

Although few of the large Strip resorts have nurseries, many of the town's neighbourhood hotel-casinos do run some kind of childcare centre. Most such operations require written consent from the parents and may ask you to leave valid ID; they may also insist that the child is potty trained and no longer in nappies. Most centres have a three-hour time limit; only the person who drops off the children can collect them. You don't have to be an overnight guest at the hotel, but you do have to remain on the premises while your child is in the nursery.

In addition to **Kids Quest** (*see below*), the **Kids Tyme** facilities at the Orleans (*see p113*) and the Suncoast (*see p117*) have licensed supervisors to entertain kids with movies, toys and crafts. Each has a five-hour limit.

Kids Quest
Boulder Station *4111 Boulder Highway, at E Desert Inn Road, East Las Vegas (1-800 683 7777/ 432 7777/www.kidsquest.com). Bus 107, 213.* **Open** *Summer* 9am-midnight Mon-Thur; 9am-1am Fri-Sun. *Winter* 9am-11pm Mon-Thur, Sun; 9am-1am Fri, Sat. **Rates** $6-$8/hr. **Credit** Disc, MC, V. **Hotel** p116.
Kids Quest has all manner of attractions, including a Barbie area, a big cliff and jungle area (very popular, these) and, of course, computer games. Kids aged from six weeks to 12 years can be dropped off for up to three and a half hours, but parents must remain on site. There are also Kids Quests at Santa Fe, Sunset and Texas Stations (*see p118*), as well as at the Palms (*see p98*) and the Red Rock (*see p112*).

Trips out of town

Don't miss the assortment of natural and man-made attractions just outside town. **Hoover Dam, Valley of Fire State Park, Red Rock Canyon** and **Bonnie Springs/Old Nevada** are all great for exploring with children (for all, *see pp278-283*). Further afield, children love the Desperado rollercoaster and other rides at Buffalo Bill's resort in **Primm**.

The greenest show in town

Down on the Strip, there are resorts devoted to New York City, Venice and Paris, to Italian luxury and Egyptian history, to the circus, to Hollywood and even to medieval England. However, a few miles north-west, Las Vegas's newest attraction boasts a rather different theme to any of its high-profile neighbours. How do geology, green issues and desert history grab you?

The $250-million, 180-acre **Las Vegas Springs Preserve** (for listings, *see p146*) attempts to educate visitors about how best to live on this troubled planet. As you park under a canopy topped by photovoltaic cells (capturing solar energy) and walk down a serpentine path that's shaded by an undulating roof of corrugated steel (representing flowing water), you'll start to realise that this is no typical Vegas attraction. However, it's far from the earnest, desert-dry enterprise you might expect. The creators promise that all its educational medicine will go down with a nice big spoonful of sugar.

The many cool presentations include a flash-flood experience: in a cave-like room, you'll stand on a rock above a gully as a rainstorm causes a raging torrent around you. Your kids can also pretend to be 1930s dam workers,

riding perilously high on a pulley cart (thanks to a large-scale diorama). Outside, there's a life-size Anasazi pit house (the ancients knew a thing or two about sustainable homebuilding), a Pullman train car, a lizard pit and a bat cave.

Down a path is the Desert Living Center, an incarnation of the concept of 'green' living. One of its core exhibits, Inside Out, shows visitors the sustainable secrets of several buildings, from a cut-out showing straw-bale wall insulation to roofing rigged for catching rainwater. Across the way, the Sustainability Gallery offers an array of interactive exhibits and demonstrations of recycling, conservation and alternative energy. While Dad finds out how a Toyota Prius runs so efficiently, the kids can crawl on a rubber compost pile.

Other attractions include the Botanical Gardens; a children's playground, with a mini-amphitheatre surrounded by concrete terrain featuring peepholes, crawl spaces and a giant snake; and trails that take you through Las Vegas at its most natural desert state. Perhaps the kids will appreciate the constructive irony that, in the land of glitz and excess, sustainability is the central theme of the attraction. Or perhaps they'll just enjoy a fun day out.

Arts & Entertainment

Film

Hollywood East comes of age.

With Las Vegas slowly but surely attaining the status of an honorary suburb of LA, it was only a matter of time before the city immersed itself completely in the glitzy twin worlds of film and fame. In the past, Vegas occasionally served as a location for movies, many of them iconic. But in the last decade, with its popularity speedily soaring among the Hollywood jet set, the city has found itself creeping into more and more feature films and TV shows, its profile rising even faster than the condo towers on Las Vegas Boulevard.

For moviemakers, then, Vegas now is more attractive than it has ever been. But for moviegoers, it's a different story. It's not hard to find the big-ticket Hollywood blockbusters in one of the city's enormous cineplexes, most of which are housed in off-Strip casinos. But of these, only Cinemark's **Century Suncoast 16** has shown any commitment to non-mainstream fare, leaving the non-casino-tied **Regal Village Square 18** as Vegas's independent/foreign cinema mecca.

That said, inroads are being made. The city's cinematic calendar is pepped up by a variety of movie-related events, from one-night marathons to the eleven-day **CineVegas Film Festival** (*see p242*). And the folks behind CineVegas are also responsible for the Screening Series at the **Galaxy Neonopolis 14**, which runs pre-DVD indie and global releases that would otherwise never make it to town.

INFORMATION AND TICKETS

The *Las Vegas Review-Journal's* Friday 'Neon' supplement, *CityLife* and *Las Vegas Weekly* all provide cinema schedule information. By phone, try **MovieFone** (222 3456); knowing your zip code beforehand will help you select the closest

cineplex. Online, head to http://lasvegas. mrmovietimes.com for details of what's on and when or where it's showing.

Tickets can be bought in person from the cinema's box office, or by phone and online through **Fandango** (1-800 326 3264, www.fandango.com).

Movie theatres

Nearly 20 movie houses populate the Vegas Valley, a sure sign of the area's rapid population growth. Those listed here are among the most notable and/or accessible.

Those after a break from the Hollywood norm have a handful of options in addition to those detailed below. The **Winchester Cultural Center** (3130 S McLeod Drive, East Las Vegas, 455 7340, www.co.clark.nv.us) and the **Charleston Heights Arts Center Theater** (800 S Brush Street, North-west Las Vegas, 229 6383, www.artslasvegas.org) both showcase left-of-centre cinema with themed monthly series throughout the year. Meanwhile, the **Clark County Library** (*see p312*) serves as Las Vegas's de facto revival movie house.

Brenden Las Vegas 14

Palms *4321 W Flamingo Road, at S Valley View Boulevard, West of Strip (507 4849/www.brenden theatres.com). Bus 201.* **Admission** *Regular screens* $9.75; $6.25-$8.75 *reductions;* $7.25 *before 6pm.* IMAX $11.50; $8.50 *reductions, and before 6pm.* **Hotel** p98. **Map** p333 X3.

Countless consumer awards and regular high-profile premières pay tribute to the Brenden Palms' central role in the Vegas moviegoing experience. With the exception of June's CineVegas Film Festival (*see p242*), blockbusters dominate, with one major feature usually configured for the sole IMAX screen.

Century Orleans 18

Orleans *4500 W Tropicana Avenue, between S Decatur & S Valley View Boulevards, West of Strip (227 3456/www.cinemark.com). Bus 103, 104, 201.* **Admission** $9.50-$9.75; $6 *reductions;* $6.75 *before 6pm.* **Hotel** p113.

This 18-screener at the Orleans ushered Las Vegas into the cineplex era with such amenities as stadium seating and THX-equipped auditoria. Although it isn't as chic as its chief competitor, the nearby Brenden Las Vegas 14 at the Palms (*see above*), it's remained one of the valley's most beloved movie theatres. Every so often, the roster includes a major studio-sanctioned art flick.

The best Cinemas

For quality
Brenden Las Vegas 14. *See above.*

For convenience
UA Showcase 8. *See p242.*

For excitement
CineVegas. *See p242* **Festivals**.

Screen tests

Using Las Vegas as a backdrop for film productions is a risky manoeuvre, owing to the city's proclivity for upstaging nearly every actor who tries to stand in front of it. Practically everyone knows what the town looks like, not to mention what kind of story to expect when a movie opens, as so many have, with an aerial shot of the Strip. Perhaps because of Las Vegas's star quality, the city's grand mythos is slowly being whittled down to a handful of visual clichés: lines of showgirls mid-kick, slot machines

disgorging fountains of coins, disembodied hands sweeping cards off blackjack tables.

Made in 1960, **Ocean's 11** defined Vegas as metonymic of a particular cultural epoch. Its five Rat Packers are practically golden as they hustle their way through a five-casino heist without breaking a sweat or creasing their single-breasted suits. The effect that the film had on every heist movie that followed is indisputable, but it also started a long and fruitful cinematic streak for Vegas.

Some Sin City films, such as Elvis Presley's **Viva Las Vegas** (1963) were vehicles for performers. Others placed unlikely characters in the Vegas mix, such as Sean Connery's ageing Bond in **Diamonds Are Forever** (1971). The latter, a lesser chapter in Connery's Bond tenure but one of the best Vegas films, played fast and loose with Howard Hughes (named 'Willard Whyte' for the film) while also presenting the town in a glamorous light that hasn't dimmed in the three decades since.

Martin Scorsese's **Casino** (1995) manages to perfectly evoke the same period in Vegas's history. It's a fictionalised account of the life of Frank 'Lefty' Rosenthal (Sam 'Ace' Rothstein in the film), one of the most colourful Vegas figures alleged to have been involved in organised crime. Rosenthal's attorney, a man who also represented Tony 'The Ant' Spilotro and Meyer Lansky, was asked by Scorsese to reprise his role for the film. The attorney, one Oscar Goodman, readily agreed; five years on, he became mayor Goodman, which he remains today.

Las Vegas's most famous cinematic wipeout is Paul Verhoeven's deathless **Showgirls** (1995). Filmed in part at Cheetahs (*see*

p221), though the interiors were shot at the San Diego branch of the club, the movie is the anti-*Ocean's 11*; if the Sinatra film is Vegas in a sharp suit, *Showgirls* is the city in a filthy raincoat. Yet even the Vegas of *Showgirls* has a strange cinematic appeal; the film has developed a cult following in recent times.

Other movies have approached Vegas in more general terms. Tim Burton managed to get some spectacular footage in **Mars Attacks!** (1996), including the real-life destruction of the saucer-topped Landmark Hotel. **Honeymoon in Vegas** (1992), while only mildly funny, did offer viewers the Flying Elvis troupe, performing a heroic parachute drop in front of Bally's. Three years later, star Nicolas Cage returned to the city in **Leaving Las Vegas** and, playing failed screenwriter Ben Sanderson, proceeded to drink himself to death. Doug Liman's **Swingers** (1996) almost single-handedly revived swing music and Vegas culture; even people who haven't seen the movie have been known to utter its rallying cry: 'Vegas, baby. Vegas!' And in 1998, Terry Gilliam's funny, fever-dream interpretation of Hunter S Thompson's **Fear and Loathing in Las Vegas** had its own kind of swing, the kind one gets after chasing Elvis-sized fistfuls of painkillers with a swig of rum.

But perhaps most significant was Steven Soderbergh's 2001 re-creation of **Ocean's Eleven**. Opening with thrilling aerial shots of the city and closing with a dialogue-free sequence set against the Bellagio fountains, the film expresses the romance that Las Vegas effuses on its best days. You truly believe that somehow you could win your way into the kind of life you've seen in the movies.

Century Suncoast 16

Suncoast *9090 Alta Drive, at N Rampart Boulevard, North-west Las Vegas (341 5555/www. cinemark.com). Bus 207.* **Admission** $9.50-$9.75; $6 reductions; $6.75 before 6pm. **Hotel** p117.

The 16-screen theatre at the Suncoast is a popular choice among Summerlin residents, while Vegas cineastes willing to make the trek also enjoy the CineArts series, which includes anywhere from one to three independent and foreign films.

Cinemark also runs a number of other movie theatres in the city, all based in casinos and all specialising in mainstream fare. Among them are the **Century 18 Sam's Town** (547 7469; for location, *see p117*), the **Century Stadium 16 Rancho Santa Fe** (395 0222; *see p117*) and the **Century 16 South Point** (896 6323; *see p115*).

Galaxy Neonopolis 14

Neonopolis, 450 E Fremont Street, at Las Vegas Boulevard South, Downtown (383 9600/www.galaxy theatres.com). Bus Deuce & all Downtown buses. **Admission** $8.50; $5-$5.50 reductions; $5.50 before 6pm. **Map** p334 D1.

Galaxy's Downtown outpost is part of the erstwhile Neonopolis entertainment centre, making it a perfect choice for avoiding crowds. Hipsters looking to kill some time before the area's bars start filling up can catch one of the CineVegas Screening Series' two weekly features. Parking (and validation) are available underneath the Neonopolis mall.

Regal Cinemas

Boulder Station 11 *4111 Boulder Highway, at E Desert Inn Road, East Las Vegas. Bus 107, 213.* **Hotel** p116.

Colonnade 14 *8880 S Eastern Avenue, at E Pebble Road, Green Valley. Bus 110.*

Green Valley Ranch 10 *2300 Paseo Verde Drive, at S Green Valley Parkway, Henderson. Bus 111.* **Hotel** p111.

Red Rock Resort 16 *11011 W Charleston Boulevard, at I-215, West Las Vegas. Bus 206.* **Hotel** p112.

Sunset Station 13 *1301 W Sunset Road, between N Stephanie Street & I-515, Henderson. Bus 114.* **Hotel** p117.

Texas Station 18 *2101 Texas Star Lane, at N Rancho Drive, between Lake Mead Boulevard & Vegas Drive, North Las Vegas. Bus 103, 106, 210, 211.* **Hotel** p118.

Village Square 18 *9400 W Sahara Avenue, at S Fort Apache Road, North-west Las Vegas. Bus 204.* **All venues** *221 2283/www.regmovies.com.* **Admission** $9.75-$10; $6.25-$9 reductions; $7.25 matinee. Additional fees for 3D shows.

The Regal cineplexes are among the busiest in town: partly due to their locations in the popular Station Casinos, but also thanks to the variety of programming. The best by far is the cinephile-favoured Village Square 18-screener, which shows as many as five non-mainstream films (plus concert simulcasts) at any given time. The Red Rock location is the city's newest.

Festivals Film

Founded in the late 1990s by Danny and Robin Greenspun of the local Greenspun media dynasty, the **CineVegas Film Festival** (www.cinevegas.com) is Sin City's own little Sundance. With the help of Dennis Hopper, now enlisted as chairman of the board, programming director (and longtime Sundance staffer) Trevor Groth brings together a mix of upcoming features, decades-old obscurities and underground fare, including some locally made movies. The festival lasts roughly ten days each June at the Palms' **Brenden Las Vegas 14** (*see p240*) cineplex.

UA Showcase 8

Showcase Mall, 3785 Las Vegas Boulevard South, at W Tropicana Avenue (221 2283/www.regmovies. com). Bus Deuce, 201. **Admission** $9.75-$10; $6.25-$9 reductions; $7 matinees. **Map** p336 A8.

You can catch the latest blockbuster at the only movie theatre on the Strip, but don't expect lots of locals, any great luxury or cutting-edge cinema technology at this ageing cineplex just north of the MGM Grand. Parking in the Showcase garage is free with validation; if, that is, you can get past the parking lot that is Las Vegas Boulevard.

West Wind Las Vegas Drive-In

4150 W Carey Avenue, at N Rancho Drive, North-west Las Vegas (646 3565). **Admission** $6 per person; $4 Tue. **No credit cards.**

This 50-year-old institution has survived several changes in ownership and the increasing popularity of indoor multiplexes, leaving it as Vegas's only remaining drive-in. It's ideal for traditionalists and cheapskates who favour bringing their own drinks and snacks, though lights emanating from the surrounding sprawl have affected visibility. Six screens offer double features of current releases; sound is available through your FM radio.

IMAX cinema

Luxor IMAX Theatre

Luxor *3900 Las Vegas Boulevard South, at W Hacienda Avenue (1-800 557 7428/262 4629/ www.luxor.com). Bus Deuce, 104, 105.* **Admission** $11.99. **Hotel** p80. **Map** p336 A9.

Documentary-style and family-friendly features play all day at Luxor's towering seven-storey theatre, most of them screened in 3D (wraparound goggles are provided). Tickets can only be purchased in person at least 15 minutes before showtime from the Pharaoh's Pavilion box office. There's also an IMAX screen at the Brenden Las Vegas 14 (*see p240*).

Galleries

Art in Sin City: where highbrow and kitsch converge.

Let's face it: the majority of Las Vegas-bound travellers did not choose the city for its plethora of cultural attractions. Yet the self-proclaimed entertainment capital of the world does have a lively visual arts scene, concentrated for the most part in the Arts District towards the southern edge of Downtown.

The most prominent hub of activity in the Arts District is the **Arts Factory**, a collection of studios and gallery spaces at the intersection of Charleston and Casino Center Boulevards. The **Holsum Lofts** (at Charleston Boulevard and Grand Central Parkway) is home to shops and galleries; due south, the **Commerce Street Studios** (at Commerce Street and Wyoming Avenue) holds 11 studio spaces, while **Dust** and **G-C Arts** (both on Main Street) still have the corner on the city's market for critically acclaimed contemporary art. One focus of the Arts District's cultural activity is **First Friday** (see p216), a monthly event that draws thousands of revellers – locals, mainly – to the area. A street festival atmosphere prevails, and the shops and galleries stay open late.

Beyond First Fridays, Las Vegas offers the a handful of artistic experiences that you won't find in any other metropolis. Take, for example, the **Neon Boneyard**, a three-acre dirt lot in which massive, defunct neon signs spend their limbo, awaiting resurrection as refurbished artefacts of the city's bygone years. Or visit one of the art museums inside casinos, the **Guggenheim-Hermitage** at the Venetian and the **Bellagio Gallery of Fine Art**, and experience a true culture clash: clanging slot machines one minute and an urbane exhibition of master works of art the next. It's a real dichotomy of sensory immersion.

Indeed, fine art is a serious part of hotel design in contemporary Las Vegas, a trend that has supplanted the 1990s era of fancifully themed hotels. Witness the blue-chip decor of **Thehotel at Mandalay Bay** (see p95), including a massive Arturo Herrera painting behind the front desk, or the serious modern collection that spruces up the **Red Rock** (see p112), with works by the likes of Takashi Murakami and Robert Indiana on permanent display at the resort.

Galleries & art museums

In addition to the galleries listed below, space inside the **Funk House** antiques shop (see p208) is also dedicated to art by local artists. And don't forget the **Neon Boneyard**, open for tours by appointment (see p141 **Lighting up the past**).

Archinofsky Gallery
1551 S Commerce Street, between W Utah & W Wyoming Avenues, Downtown (no phone/ www.archinofsky.com). Bus Deuce, 105, 108, 206. **Open** 6-10pm First Friday; noon-3pm Sat; by appt. **Map** p335 C3.
Located inside the Commerce Street Studios, Archinofsky showcases worthwhile exhibits of photography, as well as the occasional sculptural installation by emerging US artists. It's a must-visit on First Fridays, when art enthusiasts might also venture a gander at the other funky establishments (grittier galleries, a tattoo parlour) in the building.

Bellagio Gallery of Fine Art
Bellagio *3600 Las Vegas Boulevard South, at W Flamingo Road (693 7871/www.bgfa.biz). Bus Deuce, 202.* **Open** 10am-6pm Mon-Thur, Sun; 10am-9pm Fri, Sat. **Admission** $15; $12 reductions. **Credit** AmEx, DC, Disc, MC, V. **Hotel** p68. **Map** p336 A7.
The longest-standing gallery on the Strip stages a strong selection of shows; they're here on a temporary basis, but the last three shows have been in residence for a year apiece. Following a wildly popular and surprisingly meaty Monet exhibit leased from the Museum of Fine Arts, Boston, another Impressionism show and an exhibition of Ansel Adams photographs, the gallery launched a show devoted to Picasso's ceramics, due to run until early 2008.

City of Las Vegas Galleries
Bridge Gallery *2nd Floor, City Hall, 400 E Stewart Avenue, at Las Vegas Boulevard South (229 6383). Bus Deuce & all DTC-bound buses.* **Map** p334 D1.

Don't miss Galleries

For affordable art
Trifecta Gallery. *See p245.*

For a stimulating art lecture
Las Vegas Art Museum. *See p245.*

For emerging artists
Donna Beam Fine Art Gallery. *See p244.*

Arts & Entertainment

Trifecta Gallery.

Charleston Heights Art Center *800 S Brush Street, between W Charleston Boulevard & Evergreen Avenue, North-west Las Vegas (229 6383). Bus 206.*
Reed Whipple Cultural Center *821 Las Vegas Boulevard North, at E Washington Avenue, North Las Vegas (229 6211). Bus 113.* **Map** *p334 D1.*
West Las Vegas Art Center *947 W Lake Mead Boulevard, between I-15 & N Martin Luther King Boulevard, West Las Vegas (229 4800).*
All *www.artslasvegas.org.* **Open** *Bridge Gallery* 8am-5pm Mon-Fri. *Others* 11am-9pm Tue-Fri; 10am-6pm Sat, Sun.

The City of Las Vegas puts a great deal of thought into the shows it exhibits in its municipal galleries. All four spaces offer satisfying exhibits by serious artists from across the US, many of whom demonstrate a decidedly academic bent. The West Las Vegas Art Center stages shows by and for the largely African American community in the neighbourhood. Artists without local representation who show at Reed Whipple will sometimes sell work at a big discount owing to the space's non-profit status.

Donna Beam Fine Art Gallery

Alta Ham Fine Arts Building, UNLV, 4505 S Maryland Parkway, between E Flamingo Road & E Tropicana Avenue, University District (895 3893/ http://finearts.unlv.edu/galleries). Bus 109, 201. **Open** 9am-5pm Mon-Fri; 10am-2pm Sat. **Map** *p333 Y3.*

A bit tricky to find, this gallery is best visited on a weekday, when you're sure to run into an art student who can point you towards it. During the academic year (Sept-May), it hosts work by students and faculty of UNLV's fine art programme, along with the occasional travelling exhibit.

Dust

1221 S Main Street, at E California Street, Downtown (880 3878/www.dustgallery.com). Bus Deuce, 105, 108, 206. **Open** noon-5pm Wed-Sat. **Map** *p335 C3.*

When Dust opened a few years back, it breathed real life into Downtown's art scene. Today, together with the neighbouring G-C Arts (*see below*), it provides the area's heartbeat. Rotating every six weeks, shows include everything from design abstraction to figural painting, from artists in New York, Los Angeles and Las Vegas. It's all good.

G-C Arts

1217 S Main Street, at E California Street, Downtown (452 2200/www.gcarts-lv.com). Bus Deuce, 105, 108, 206. **Open** 10am-6pm Tue-Sat. **Map** *p335 C3.*

The town's first blue-chip gallery, G-C is where serious collectors go for original and limited edition works by Ruscha and Rauschenberg, as well as fine art objets by Koons et al. Director Michele Quinn has a New York pedigree, and it shows.

Guggenheim-Hermitage Museum

Venetian *3555 Las Vegas Boulevard South, between Sands Avenue & E Flamingo Road (414 2440/www.guggenheimlasvegas.org). Bus Deuce,*

105, 203. **Open** 8.30am-7.30pm daily. **Admission** $19.50; $9.50-$15 reductions; free under-6s. **Credit** AmEx, Disc, MC, V. **Hotel** p75. **Map** p335 & p336 B6.

Designed by Rem Koolhaas, this is a joint project between the Guggenheim in New York and the Hermitage Museum of St Petersburg. Shows, which draw on both institutions' collections as well as that of Vienna's Kunsthistorisches Museum, have previously included 'The Pursuit of Pleasure': designed for Sin City, it featured paintings depicting celebration, flirtation and gaming.

Las Vegas Art Museum

Sahara West Library, 9600 W Sahara Avenue, between S Fort Apache Road & Grand Canyon Drive, West Las Vegas (360 8000/www.lasvegasart museum.org). Bus 204, 213. **Open** 10am-5pm Tue-Sat; 1-5pm Sun. **Admission** $6; $3-$5 reductions; free under-12s. **Credit** AmEx, Disc, MC, V.

Under new leadership and currently on the lookout for a space closer to the centre of town, the Las Vegas Art Museum aims to become one of the most important venues for the exhibition of contemporary art in the American west. Shows staged here since noted American art critic and curator Libby Lumpkin took over as director include major prints by Roy Lichtenstein, an overview of California minimalism, and an exhibition of the working models of architect Frank Gehry.

Lynn Peri Collection

Holsum Lofts, 231 W Charleston Boulevard, at Grand Central Parkway, Downtown (366 9171). Bus 206. **Open** 11am-5pm Tue-Sat. **Map** p335 C3.

This gallery showcases some artwork and a variety of appealing examples of functional design objects perfect for imaginative home decorating. It's one of the stand-outs in the Holsum Lofts, a renovated bread bakery now home to a variety of gift stores and gallery spaces (*see p143*).

S² Art Group Atelier

1 E Charleston Boulevard, at S Main Street, Downtown (868 7880/www.s2art.com). Bus Deuce, 105, 108, 206. **Open** 9am-5pm Mon-Fri. **Map** p335 C3.

S² reproduces fine art lithographs and sells them at various venues, among them the three Jack Gallery locations at Mandalay Bay, the Venetian and the Fashion Show Mall. The 19th-century French and German presses turn out reproductions of posters by Mucha and Toulouse-Lautrec, vintage film ads and other old favourites, as well as contemporary works. Visitors can watch the presses while touring the large selection of prints.

Trifecta Gallery

Arts Factory, 103 E Charleston Boulevard, between S Main Street & Casino Center Boulevard, Downtown (366 7001/www.trifectagallery.com). Bus Deuce, 105, 108, 206. **Open** noon-4pm Wed-Fri; noon-2pm Sat; or by appt. **Map** p335 C3.

Tiny Trifecta is the labour of love of Las Vegas artist Marty Walsh, whose masterful, nostalgic paintings memorialise mid-century modern appliances and other artefacts. She also has an ingenious curatorial eye, and alternates showings of her own work with pieces by talented emerging painters. With shows that regularly sell out, Trifecta is the place for serious art collectors on a budget.

You hum it, I'll paint it

As Las Vegas continues to develop the kind of sophisticated art scene one would expect to find in a metropolitan area of nearly two million people, several locally based artists are making names for themselves, and the city, elsewhere around the world. Chief among them is **Tim Bavington**, arguably the town's most ascendant art star of the moment.

Born in London but transplanted to the US in his teens, Bavington's career began to bloom when he fell under the tutelage of prominent art critic and curator Dave Hickey at UNLV in the late 1990s. Since then, his work has struck a chord – literally and figuratively – with art enthusiasts who share his affinity for rock 'n' roll. Bavington has landed on a visual riff that allows him to translate popular rock tunes into paintings, with notes assigned a hue and a width.

The resultant brilliantly coloured stripe paintings have been compared to Gene Davis and others, but are arguably much more fun.

Although Bavington lives in a mid-century modern house in Downtown and works out of a spacious studio in the industrial district just west of the Strip, he rarely shows in Las Vegas. G-C Arts had a show in 2006; one painting hangs along a restaurant-and-retail corridor at Wynn Las Vegas, with another at Spago (*see p156*) in the Forum Shops; and the increasingly sophisticated Las Vegas Art Museum recently acquired a Bavington for its permanent collection. But after sold-out gallery shows in Los Angeles, New York, London and Paris, and the acquisition of one of his works by the Museum of Modern Art in New York, Bavington has as good a chance as any top contemporary artist today of becoming a household name.

Arts & Entertainment

Gay & Lesbian

Las Vegas, getting more fabulous by the minute.

You'd be forgiven for thinking that the original Sin City would be a natural playground for gays. After all, what other city in America can claim such a judgement-free, libertarian attitude, especially when it comes to late-night revelry? However, for years, the opposite has been the case. It's hard to say who has squandered the potential of Las Vegas's LGBT community more: the city itself or its own homosexual populace.

However, the scene has been coming out with a vengeance, and visitors have been the main beneficiaries. Showrooms now lean heavily on Broadway spectacles, and hotels such as **New York New York** (*see p84*) and **Paris Las Vegas** (*see p74*) have lately been marketing themselves to the international gay community. The Strip is also now home to **Krave**, the town's first gay megaclub.

The local scene is also starting to look up, if gradually. The majority of gay venues reside in two dominant LGBT hubs where tourists and locals mingle freely: the so-called **Fruit Loop**, the streets around the intersection of Paradise Road and E Harmon Avenue, and **Commercial Center**, up on Sahara Avenue. Gay bars dot the valley, from old stagers such as **Snick's Place** to newcomers like **Piranha**. **Hot Rods**, the city's first gay-oriented strip club, opened in 2007 for the enjoyment of both the boys and (less so) the girls. And the city's springtime **Pride** event (*see p247* **Festivals**) has grown enough to take over Downtown for a weekend.

LESBIAN LAS VEGAS

There aren't any lesbian bars in Vegas, and women make up a very small constituent of the city's gay nightlife. However, gay bars are devoting an increasing number of nights

Get Booked. *See p249*

to female-tilted events. **FreeZone** (*see p248*), the town's unofficial lesbian hangout, throws the popular Lick Her Bust party every Tuesday; **8½** (*see p248*) welcomes the ladies to Orchid on Wednesdays; and **Krave** (*see p248*) holds the LA-originated GirlBar event every Saturday in its lounge. Alternatively, **Betty's Outrageous Adventures** (991 9929, www.bettysout.com) is a social group that brings lesbians together for everything from movie nights to camping trips. Most events are all-inclusive, though some are women-only.

Eating & drinking

Restaurants & cafés

Suede Restaurant & Lounge

4640 S Paradise Road, between E Harmon & E Tropicana Avenues, East of Strip (791 3463/ www.suedelasvegas.com). Bus 108, 201. **Open** 5pm-2am Wed-Sun. **Main courses** $8-$17. **Credit** MC, V. **Map** p336 C8.

The best Gay venues

For dirty dancers
Hot Rods. See p249.

For queens of the desert
Las Vegas Lounge. See p247.

For brokeback mountaineers
Charlie's Las Vegas. See p247.

Formerly Sasha's, Suede is a Fruit Loop fixture and its only gay dining establishment. The menu is frequently updated, as are the entertainers. Drag shows (except Sun), karaoke, trivia contests, dance music and drink specials round out the experience.

Bars

As well as the gay bars below, a few places self-identify as 'alternative', essentially proclaiming themselves as gay-friendly operations.

Backdoor Lounge

1415 E Charleston Boulevard, at S 15th Street, Downtown (385 2018). Bus 206. **Open** 24hrs daily. **Admission** $5 Fri, Sat. **Credit** MC, V. **Map** p334 E3.
The Backdoor caters to Latino guys and their admirers. It's like any other Vegas bar during the week, but plays things up for the weekend with dance parties, drag shows and beauty contests.

Badlands Saloon

Commercial Center, 953 E Sahara Avenue, between S 6th Street & S Maryland Parkway, East of Strip (792 9262). Bus 109, 204. **Open** 24hrs daily. **No credit cards. Map** p333 Y2.
The smaller of the city's two western gay bars, Badlands is an intimate space patronised in the main by men over 30 and Commercial Center loyalists. A game of pool will set you back a mere quarter, making it the cheapest in Vegas (if not the state).

Buffalo

Paradise Plaza, 4640 S Paradise Road, between E Harmon & E Tropicana Avenues, East of Strip (733 8355). Bus 108, 201. **Open** 24hrs daily. **No credit cards. Map** p336 C8.
The true Fruit Loop alternative, Buffalo is the destination for leather and bear enthusiasts, though they don't always represent the majority of the bar's patrons. There's no diva posturing or twinky snobbery here, just cheap drinks and chatty customers.

Charlie's Las Vegas

5012 Arville Street, at W Tropicana Avenue, South-west Las Vegas (876 1844/www.charlieslasvegas.com). Bus 103, 201, 202. **Open** 24hrs daily. **No credit cards.**
Gay country fans and followers of the Nevada Gay Rodeo Association head to this western-themed bar with a large space for both line-dancing and socialising. The place attracts both men and women, especially on Sundays for the $5 beer bust (4-7pm) and Miss Kitty's ever popular drag show (9pm).

Escape Lounge

4213 W Sahara Avenue, between S Decatur & S Valley View Boulevards, West of Strip (364 1167/www.escapeloungelv.com). Bus 103, 104, 204. **Open** 24hrs daily. **Credit** AmEx, MC, V.
Escape is the closest thing to a gay sports bar in Vegas. Expect Disco and Top 40 tunes to be playing over the game; even if you're not a sports buff, Escape has one of the warmest vibes in the local scene.

Festivals Gay

As the Las Vegas gay community expands, so too do May's **Pride** festivities. What began in 1983 with around 100 revellers has become a fully fledged ten-day extravaganza attended by some 10,000 people. A series of small pageants, picnics and parties leads up to a Downtown parade, held on the second Friday of May. The following day, a family-friendly, all-day festival at the Clark County Amphitheatre welcomes local and national entertainers. For more, call 615 9429 or see www.lasvegaspride.org.

Las Vegas Eagle

3430 E Tropicana Avenue, at S Pecos Road, East Las Vegas (458 8662). Bus 111, 201. **Open** 24hrs daily. **Credit** AmEx, DC, Disc, MC, V. **Map** p334 Z3.
The Eagle is a favourite among older men and the Levi's/leather crowd, but the demographic expands for the Wednesday and Friday underwear parties, where those looking to drink for free must hand over their trousers at the door.

Las Vegas Lounge

900 E Karen Avenue, between Paradise Road & S Maryland Parkway, East of Strip (737 9350). Bus 108, 109, 204. **Open** 24hrs daily. **No credit cards. Map** p333 Y3.
Everyone on the Vegas scene has a story about how they went into the seemingly nondescript Las Vegas Lounge and suddenly realised that they were at a tranny bar. You'll find all the colours of the homo rainbow here; transsexual and cross-dressing go-go dancers perform more or less nightly.

Ramrod

900 E Karen Avenue, between Paradise Road & S Maryland Parkway, East of Strip (735 0885/www.ramrodlv.com). Bus 108, 109, 204. **Open** 11am-3am daily. **Credit** AmEx, Disc, MC, V. **Map** p333 Y3.
Previously Cobalt and, before that, the Rainbow Lounge, Ramrod has distinguished itself from previous incarnations with an upgraded dancefloor and daily drinks specials. A modest space for modest people, it usually stays open later on weekends.

Snick's Place

1402 S 3rd Street, between E Charleston & E Oakey Boulevards, Stratosphere Area (385 9298/www.snicksplace.com). Bus Deuce, 206. **Open** 24hrs daily. **No credit cards. Map** p335 C3.
Ask longtime gay Vegans where they first began meeting other similarly inclined men, and they'll probably mention Snick's, the oldest LGBT watering hole in town. Sure, it's seen better days, but it still boasts a loyal following.

Arts & Entertainment

Spotlight

Commercial Center, 957 E Sahara Avenue,
between S 6th Street & S Maryland Parkway,
East of Strip (696 0202/www.spotlightlv.com).
Bus 109, 204. **Open** 24hrs daily. **No credit cards.**
Map p333 Y2.

Commercial Center's most beloved neighbourhood bar, Spotlight is favoured for its down-to-earth guys, regular liquor busts and free-pizza nights. A firm favourite among the leather crowd.

Nightclubs

Although casino-housed clubs don't generally bother with LGBT promotions, you'll find gay revellers in most of the popular joints. For more, *see pp255-260.*

Flex Lounge

4347 W Charleston Boulevard, at S Arville Street,
West Las Vegas (385 3539/www.flexlasvegas.com).
Bus 103, 104, 206. **Open** 24hrs daily. **Admission**
$5 Sat after midnight. **Credit** AmEx, MC, V.

This enduring venue attracts a very diverse crowd within the gay community. The drag/stripper revue on Fridays and the hip hop party on Saturdays are the most popular events, but there's something going on here most nights.

FreeZone

610 E Naples Drive, at Paradise Road, East of Strip
(794 2300/www.freezonelasvegas.com). Bus 108,
213. **Open** 24hrs daily. *Food served* 6pm-2am Mon-Wed; 6pm-3am Thur-Sat. **No credit cards.** **Map**
p336 C8.

If the line at Piranha is too long or the drinks at Gipsy are too pricey, FreeZone is the next best Fruit Loop option. Thursday's boys-night party remains a draw; weekends are reserved for the Queens of Las Vegas, the city's longest-running drag show. Lick Her Bust on Tuesdays is a ladies' affair, but you'll find the lesbian community well represented on any night.

Gipsy

4605 Paradise Road, between E Harmon & E
Tropicana Avenues, East of Strip (731 1919/www.
gipsylv.net). Bus 108, 201. **Open** from 10pm daily.
Admission free; $7 Sun nights; $5 Mon nights.
No credit cards. Map p336 C8.

Until the arrival of Krave and Piranha, Gipsy had long reigned as the most popular gay nightspot in town. It still draws with its diva house soundtracks, female impersonator shows and no-cover weekends, but crowds are smaller than they once were.

GoodTimes

Suite 1, Liberace Plaza, 1775 E Tropicana Avenue,
at Spencer Street, University District (736 9494/
www.goodtimeslv.com). Bus 201. **Open** 24hrs daily.
No credit cards. Map p333 Y3.

GoodTimes has always been renowned for its youth-oriented Monday-night liquor bust. But competition from Piranha motivated management to abolish the cover and adopt a $1 well and draft beer promotion. Attendance is smaller during the rest of the week.

Krave

3663 Las Vegas Boulevard South, at E Harmon
Avenue (836 0830/www.kravelasvegas.com). Bus
Deuce, 201, 202. **Open** 11pm Tue-Sun. **Admission**
free locals (except Tue); $5-$20 non-locals. **Credit**
AmEx, Disc, MC, V. **Map** p336 A7.

Various enterprises have come and gone in this Strip space, but Krave has thrived as a true alternative club. Gay men constitute the venue's main clientele, though every demographic is made to feel welcome. There are Latin, hip hop, goth and lesbian promotions; Saturday's Everything You Desire, is the most popular night in the club, if not the entire gay scene.

Piranha & 8½

4633 Paradise Road, between E Harmon & E
Tropicana Avenues, East of Strip (791 0100/www.
piranhalasvegas.com). Bus 108, 213. **Open** from
9pm daily. **Admission** free locals; $10-$20 non-locals. **No credit cards. Map** p336 C8.

Strip scene

You'll find no shortage of people-watching opportunities in Las Vegas, but for gay men looking for like-minded types in town, it's not as easy as just prowling the casinos. True, separating the fannypackers from the Dolce & Gabbana set isn't difficult. But although there are numerous gay bars, clubs and spas elsewhere in town, looking for a gay scene on the Strip itself can be a challenge.

Those with cash to splash may want to try the casino spas. Gay men tend to favour **Nurture** at the Luxor (*see p80*), Mandalay Bay's **Spa Mandalay** (*see p71*) and the

Bathhouse (Thehotel at Mandalay Bay; *see p95*), but physical interaction is absolutely not encouraged; for that sort of scene, you'll need to go off-Strip to a non-casino spa.

It's hard to find many gay men in one place when the clubs are closed; the resort-hosted pool parties are oppressively heterosexual. However, gay men frequent the high-end malls such as the **Forum Shops** (*see p191*) and the **Fashion Show Mall** (*see p193*). Both centres feature a wide variety of gay-friendly fashion from the likes of Diesel; window-shopping isn't necessarily limited to the clothes.

Just an average night at **Krave**.

Done out with velvet curtains, a marble-topped bar and gigantic piranha aquariums, the $5-million Piranha dance hall and connecting 8½ lounge is gay Vegas's most beautiful nightlife palace. Go-go boys and girls are on display in Piranha, while guests take over the stage in 8½; the Skybox VIP rooms give welcome respite from the usual crowds. Cocktails can be expensive and low on booze, but it's easy to see why this complex has been a hit right out of the gate.

Shops

Desert Adult Books

4350 Las Vegas Boulevard North, at Craig Road, North Las Vegas (643 7982/www.mysexystore.com). Bus 113, 115. **Open** 24hrs daily. **Credit** AmEx, Disc, MC, V.

Open since 1972, this couple-friendly establishment is Nellis Air Force Base's de facto adult bookstore. Gay men shop and cruise the joint, which is stocked with the usual naughty wares and also boasts video booths of various sizes.

Get Booked

Paradise Plaza, 4640 Paradise Road, between E Harmon & E Tropicana Avenues, East of Strip (737 7780/www.getbooked.com). Bus 108. **Open** 10am-midnight Mon-Thur, Sun; 10am-2am Fri, Sat. **Credit** AmEx, Disc, MC, V. **Map** p336 C8.

This is the last remaining general gay retail shop in Las Vegas. It is located in the Fruit Loop and divides

its offerings between all the usual merchandise (T-shirts, books, greeting cards, CDs, gifts) and the naughty stuff (videos, DVDs, underwear, lubricants, adult magazines). *Photo p246.*

Cruising

The most popular non-nightclub cruising spots are virtual. Try **gay.com**, which usually has two and sometimes three chatrooms filled with randy surfers 'looking around', as the blushed parlance goes. Also popular are **manhunt.net** and **adam4adam.com**, which run (often explicit) user profiles for those in the city or visiting soon, while **cruisingforsex. com** surveys high-traffic peek-a-boo and public sex spots. Even **lasvegas.craigslist.com** has become a cruising HQ; you can post or search ads on pages devoted to men seeking men, casual encounter and erotic services.

In addition to the venues below, it's worth checking out the adult stores (*see above*) and the area around Commercial Center.

Apollo Health Spa

Commercial Center, 953 E Sahara Avenue, between S 6th Street & S Maryland Parkway, East Las Vegas (650 9191/www.apollospa.com). Bus 109, 204. **Open** 24hrs daily. **Admission** $10 day pass; $25 with a locker; $30 room. **Credit** MC, V. **Map** p333 Y2.

If hotel spas seem a little chaste, you can rely on this Greek-themed facility for a more bacchanalian experience. The closest thing to a local bathhouse, Apollo offers all the standard spa accoutrements (heated pool, sauna, steam room, two jacuzzis, workout equipment), plus a community video room, private booths with video feeds and an on-staff masseur.

Hawk's Gym

Commercial Center, 953 E Sahara Avenue, between S 6th Street & S Maryland Parkway, East of Strip (731 4295/www.hawksgymlv.com). Bus 109, 204. **Open** 24hrs daily. **Admission** $8. **No credit cards. Map** p333 Y2.

There is workout equipment here, of course. But with rooms such as the Cockpit and a blackout promo night (where, as the advertisement states, 'you almost have to feel your way around'), it's clear that Hawk's is no 24-Hour Fitness.

Hot Rods

3120 Sirius Lane, between S Valley View Boulevard & I-15, West of Strip (873 5046/www.hotrodsof vegas.com). Bus 104. **Open** 9pm-late Thur-Sun. **Admission** $20. **Credit** AmEx, Disc, MC, V. **Map** p333 X2.

Tucked within the warehouse district just west of I-15, Vegas's first and only gay adult cabaret features naked men (and women) performing on stage and providing dances in swanky private booths. The Queens of Las Vegas from FreeZone (*see p248*) are here every Thursday, which is also Amateur Night.

Music

Vegas's scene is diversifying, but mainstream acts still take centre stage.

Las Vegas's long time reputation as the last stop for any musical performer worth his or her salt is as far in the past as the Rat Pack's residency at the Sands. Sure, there's not much jazz, blues or classical music here. But when you combine the rock, pop, hip hop and country megastars appearing at major casino venues with the less refined gigs in bars and basements around town, it becomes clear that Sin City is gradually improving its musical image.

Big-name stars passing through town tend to perform at the often-sizeable concert halls and clubs inside the Strip's resorts. Smaller bands and local groups tend to perform in venues that are slightly more makeshift, either bars acting as part-time music clubs or fledgling theatres with few luxuries and hit-or-miss sound systems. Such a state of affairs is due in no small part to gambling regulations: venues with gambling machines are forbidden by law from charging admission, which means shows at the likes of the **Double Down Saloon** and the **Cooler Lounge** are free.

INFORMATION AND TICKETS

For information on what's on, pick up *Las Vegas Weekly* or *CityLife* (*see p.313*), or check online at www.vegas.com or www.yourlocalscene.com. Note that most small rock and jazz venues are restricted to patrons aged 21 and over; the main exceptions being the larger-scale casino venues, where age restrictions vary.

Tickets can generally be bought direct from venues and/or through **Ticketmaster** (474 4000; *see p212*), and prices vary wildly. Shows in bars rarely come with a cover of more than $10, and many are free (*see above*).

The best Venues

Top-drawer talent at top prices
MGM Grand Garden Arena. See p251.

The best of today at best prices
House of Blues. See right.

Up-and-comers for a steal
Art Bar. See p252.

However, tickets for shows at the bigger casino venues can run into three figures, with no price too high for some shows by big names at the **MGM Grand Garden Arena**.

Rock, pop & hip hop

Casino venues

Don't let the rather safe programme of music offered at the Colosseum in Caesars Palace put you off Vegas's grand casino venues. The **MGM Grand**, **Mandalay Bay**, the **Hard Rock** and now the **Palms** all house credible concert venues that showcase touring acts in most genres on an almost nightly basis.

Downtown, the best options are the recently renovated 400-seat **Golden Nugget Theatre Ballroom** (385 7111; *see p104*), home to occasional headliners playing everything from smooth jazz to alt-rock; and the new 600-seat **Canyon Club** at the Four Queens (*see p108*), which opened in 2007 and plans to host bands from Las Vegas and beyond. Also new for 2007 are **Ovation** at the Green Valley Ranch (*see p111*), with 500 seats, and **Fever**, a hybrid showroom-nightclub at South Point (*see p115*). The latter plans to offer Strip-style luxuries at a more reasonable cost, such as bottle service at a fraction of the on-Strip price.

House of Blues
Mandalay Bay *3950 Las Vegas Boulevard South, at W Hacienda Avenue (632 7600/www.mandalaybay.com). Bus Deuce, 104, 105.* **Tickets** $10-$70. **Credit** AmEx, Disc, MC, V. **Hotel** p71. **Map** p336 A9.
Though this is just one of several folk art-filled locations across the US, the House of Blues' exciting mix of up-and-coming and established artists makes it feel like a homegrown champion. The multi-level main floor is surrounded by three bars and tiered balcony seating. Kitschy cover bands play on weekend nights; it's Gospel Brunch on Sundays.

Joint
Hard Rock *4455 Paradise Road, at E Harmon Avenue, East of Strip (information 693 5000/tickets 474 4000/www.hardrockhotel.com). Bus 108.* **Tickets** $20-$250. **Credit** AmEx, DC, Disc, MC, V. **Hotel** p96. **Map** p336 C7.
Though it's lost some of its pulling power to other similar-sized locations in recent years, the Joint remains one of the strongest mid-sized rock venues

Every night is rockin' at the **Bunkhouse Saloon**. *See p252.*

in Las Vegas, playing host to acts as diverse as Marilyn Manson, No Doubt and Air. The main floor is a standing-room-only space; there's reserved table seating available on the balcony.

Mandalay Bay Beach

Mandalay Bay *3950 Las Vegas Boulevard South, at W Hacienda Avenue (information 632 7777/ tickets 474 4000/www.mandalaybay.com). Bus Deuce, 104, 105.* **Tickets** $10-$100. **Credit** AmEx, Disc, MC, V. **Hotel** p71. **Map** p336 A9.

Las Vegas's clement weather makes Mandalay Bay's man-made beach ideal for outdoor gigs, and its summer concert series draws in a variety of crowd-pleasing favourites, including Billy Idol, the B-52s and the Go-Gos. If standing in the sand (or water), watching the action up-close isn't your thing, shell out a few bucks more and enjoy the concert from Moorea Beach Club, an open-air lounge outfitted with its own pool, cabanas, bar, loungers and video screens displaying the performance from a safe (and dry) distance.

Mandalay Bay Events Center

Mandalay Bay *3950 Las Vegas Boulevard South, at W Hacienda Avenue (information 632 7777/ tickets 474 4000/www.mandalaybay.com). Bus Deuce, 104, 105.* **Tickets** $25-$200. **Credit** AmEx, Disc, MC, V. **Hotel** p71. **Map** p336 A9.

Though this massive arena isn't specifically a music venue per se (it also hosts expositions, boxing matches and awards ceremonies), it draws the biggest and the best international musical acts, from Aerosmith to Keith Urban via Luciano Pavarotti. Getting in and out of the Events Center (and, for that matter, the casino) becomes a logistical nightmare during big crowd-pullers, so plan accordingly.

MGM Grand Garden Arena

MGM Grand *3799 Las Vegas Boulevard South, at E Tropicana Avenue (information 891 7777/tickets 1-877 880 0880/www.mgmgrand.com). Bus Deuce, 201.* **Tickets** $30-$250. **Credit** AmEx, DC, Disc, MC, V. **Hotel** p81. **Map** p336 A8.

From Britney Spears and U2 to Alan Jackson and the Police, this massive arena showcases the world's rock and pop royalty, as well as occasional special events such as the Billboard Music Awards. There are different vehicle drop-off points at the venue, so be prepared for a possible ten-minute hike through the casino if you enter via the Strip.

Pearl

Palms *4321 W Flamingo Road, at S Valley View Boulevard, West of Strip (information 942 7777/ tickets 944 3200/www.palmspearl.com). Bus 201.* **Tickets** $25-$200. **Credit** AmEx, Disc, MC, V. **Hotel** p98. **Map** p333 X3.

Since opening, the Palms has appeared very keen to steal the Hard Rock's thunder: first with its boutique accommodation, then with its numerous rooftop clubs, and now with this music venue, which staged shows by Gwen Stefani, Tool and Fall Out Boy soon after opening. With a capacity ranging from 1,100 (seated) to 2,500 (standing), all within 120 unobstructed feet (35m) of the stage, the Pearl comes with an intimacy rarely found in a venue of this size.

Planet Hollywood Theatre for the Performing Arts

Planet Hollywood *3667 Las Vegas Boulevard South, at E Harmon Avenue (information 736 0111/ tickets 785 5000/www.planethollywoodresort. com). Bus Deuce.* **Tickets** $25-$150. **Credit** AmEx, Disc, MC, V. **Hotel** p85. **Map** p336 A7.

It was already one of the best-sounding concert halls in Vegas before a $25-million makeover in 2000, which explains why this gem was left standing even as the original Aladdin was razed. With any luck, the eclectic programming – everything from Nine Inch Nails to Jamie Foxx – will continue.

Railhead

Boulder Station *4111 Boulder Highway, at E Desert Inn Road, East Las Vegas (information 432 7777/tickets 547 5300/www.boulderstation.com). Bus 107, 213.* **Tickets** free-$65. **Credit** AmEx, Disc, MC, V. **Hotel** p116.

Don't let the suburban, local-casino location fool you: the intimate Railhead still rocks, albeit a little bit more slowly and quietly than some of its distant Strip cousins. Bands who play here tend to be at

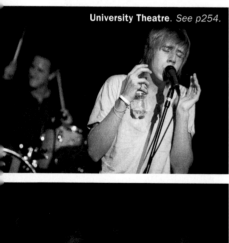

University Theatre. *See p254.*

the down-but-not-yet-out stage of their careers: Blue Oyster Cult, Soul Asylum and the Ohio Players have all recently headlined at the venue.

Whiskey Beach

Green Valley Ranch *2300 Paseo Verde Drive, at S Green Valley Parkway, Henderson (information 617 7777/tickets 547 5300/www.greenvalleyranchresort. com). Bus 111.* **Tickets** $25-$75. **Credit** AmEx, DC, Disc, MC, V. **Hotel** p111.

Located just outside upscale ultralounge Whiskey (*see p260*), this fabulous venue comes with immaculately sculpted pools, cosy cabanas and has hosted artists such as Seal, Kool & the Gang and Sean Paul, though some sightlines are miserable.

Non-casino venues

What with the emergence of the Killers and Panic! At The Disco, the uninitiated might be forgiven for assuming that the local music scene in Vegas is thriving. In truth, while it's not dead, it's never been particularly vibrant, relegated as it is to the back-rooms of bars and a continual revolving door of opening-and-closing all-ages venues.

However, the scene has had a resurgence of late, thanks mostly to a combination of Downtown revitalisation initiatives and hipster musical interests. The opening of the **Beauty Bar** (*see p183*), which stages frequent indie rock shows alongside its DJ nights and other special events, coincided with plans for the Fremont East Entertainment District, and the hangout has since been joined by other bars in the same neck of the woods. Indie rock bands have found a home in Downtown venues; chief among them is the **Art Bar** (*see p183*), which has hosted the likes of Of Montreal and Under the Influence of Giants on its tiny stage.

In addition to the venues listed below, a number of other spots offer regular music. Punk and alternative rock still rule the roost at the **Double Down Saloon** (*see p181*), while the **Ice House Lounge** (*see p184*) offers everything from drum 'n' bass DJs to goth acts, and **Dino's** (*see p184*) has live music every Friday night. Over by the university, the recently expanded **Freakin' Frog** (*see p186*) hosts jazz, experimental and rock bands almost nightly. And if you want to leave the flashing slot machines and bright lights behind you, **Matteo's Underground Lounge** (*see p279*) in Boulder City showcases rock and punk bands in quirky but cosy surroundings.

Bunkhouse Saloon

124 S 11th Street, at S Fremont Street, Downtown (384 4536/www.bunkhouselv.com). Bus 109, 207. **Open** 24hrs daily. *Shows* times vary. **Admission** free-$15. **Credit** MC, V. **Map** p334 E2.

This place is all about contrasts: though no longer a country bar, it has kept the animal heads and cowboy

Stars in your eyes

According to the wisdom of Vegasploitation films such as *Showgirls*, all you really need to make it in Las Vegas is a healthy admixture of treachery and NC-17 sex. Presumably, all sorts of characters find their way here with the clichéd dream of seeing their names in lights on the marquee next to the cutting-edge likes of Lola Falana and Susan Anton. But is it possible to do it straight? Can a tough-as-nails drifter with a heart of gold actually make the big time from the humble beginnings of... a karaoke night?

Las Vegas has over a hundred ongoing karaoke evenings, yet nary a real success story. No one, for example, has ever been 'discovered' at **Dino's** (*see p184*) doing much more than drinking unhealthy quantities of Miller Lite. However, its popular karaoke nights (Thursday to Sarurday), hosted by perennial master Danny G, are the place for people with issues to let their freak song fly.

These sing-it-yourself evenings at Dino's are peppered with 'only in Vegas' moments. One shining example occurred the night a frail octogenarian, his face weathered with the signs of a hard life, took to the stage and was spontaneously surrounded by a grinding group of bridesmaids who'd wandered in after a bachelorette party at the neighbouring Olympic Garden strip club. His number? Without a hint of irony, the Bee Gees' 'Stayin' Alive'.

Only slightly further up the evolutionary scale are the 'serious', Whitney-esque wannabe crooners at the no-schtick-please **Ellis Island** (4178 Koval Lane, at E Flamingo Road, 733 8901, www.ellisislandcasino. com). But the real prize is the Monday's celebrity karaoke at the **Bootlegger Bistro**

(*see p174*). A longtime hangout for the lounge-singer set and showroom ghosts of entertainment past, the Bootlegger allows the hoi polloi to mix it up with a steady stream of Vegas's professional artistes and antipasto. Where else can an average Joe start belting out his rendition of a Sheena Easton song, only to be joined on the stage by, you guessed it, Sheena Easton? (It happened.)

Sassy host Kelly Clinton has been known to refer karaoke standouts to showcase nights in smaller venues, making it possible, in theory, for your version of Patsy Cline's 'Crazy' to land you a job as a back-up singer for someone that no one outside the city has ever heard of. Oh, Las Vegas. We built this city on dreams; we built this city on rock and roll.

Arts & Entertainment

paraphernalia, but the place packs with hipsters in skinny pants throwing back Pabst Blue Ribbon every weekend. The Bunkhouse's stage showcases a variety of live music, ranging from blues and punk to indie rock and electronica, every night. *Photo p251.*

Cheyenne Saloon
3103 N Rancho Drive, at W Cheyenne Avenue, North-west Las Vegas (645 4139). Bus 106, 218. **Open** 24hrs daily. **Admission** free-$13. **Credit** AmEx, Disc, MC, V.
If you're looking for hard rock, you could do worse than to make the trip out here for some cheap beer and loud music. The stage is sizeable, the sound system is impressively robust, and the sunken dancefloor is an unexpected touch that makes this rough-edged strip mall dive a local favourite.

Cooler Lounge
1905 N Decatur Boulevard, at W Havelina Street, North-west Las Vegas (646 3009/www.coolerlounge. com). Bus 103, 210. **Open** 24hrs daily. **Admission** free. **No credit cards.**
For years, this cramped strip-mall dive bar has been drawing crowds for some of the best punk, metal and hard rock bands in the region and perhaps even the country. Notable names to have graced the tiny proto-stage include Michale Graves, TSOL, the Bad Samaritans, the Supersuckers and Dr Know.

Divebar
3035 E Tropicana Avenue, between S Eastern & S Pecos Avenues, East Las Vegas (435 7526/www.vegas divebar.com). Bus 201. **Open** 24hrs daily. **Admission** free. **Credit** AmEx, Disc, MC, V. **Map** p333 Z3.

It's questionable whether Divebar lives up (or down) to its name, but the popularity of this drinking hole-cum-music venue isn't in doubt. The space is divided into two rooms, one with pub tables and the other, divided by a cutaway wall, is home nightly to everything from open mic nights to garage rock bands. Above-average bar food is available 24-7.

New York Café

4080 Paradise Road, at E Flamingo Road, East of Strip (796 0589). Bus 108, 202. **Open** 24hrs daily. **Admission** free. **No credit cards. Map** p333 3Y.
Just a few blocks north of the Hard Rock (and completely unrelated to the New York New York casino), this dive bar hosts punk and hard rock bands in its lobby on a regular basis. It's a great place to see a free show, throw back some cold beers and chow down on a pizza.

University Theatre

4737 S Maryland Parkway, at W Tropicana Avenue, University District (information 262 9160/tickets Ticketmaster 474 4000). Bus 109, 201. **Open** hrs vary. **Admission** free. **Credit** *Ticketmaster* AmEx, Disc, MC, V. **Map** p333 Y3.
The first fully fitted concert hall to open in Vegas for some time, the 450-capacity University Theatre provides a smoke- and alcohol-free environment that packs in the kids for shows from touring alternative, punk and metal bands. It's an all-ages venue, though there's a bar next door for over-21s. *Photo p252.*

Jazz, blues & acoustic music

Given the fact that it's widely perceived to hold an overabundance of lounge acts, the jazz scene in Las Vegas is surprisingly slight. Most casino lounges have been overrun by pop cover bands; those that don't offer the kind of light jazz of which only Kenny G would be proud. Still, there are a few standard-bearers: in addition to the venues listed below, the **Bootlegger Bistro** (*see p174*) welcomes renowned jazz pianist Guy Mancuso on Wednesdays, while the **Italian American Club** (2333 E Sahara Avenue, at S Eastern Avenue, 457 3866) hosts the 18-piece Carl Lodico Ghost Band every Thursday.

It's a similar story for acoustic music, with many of the bigger nights in town slowly dying off. However, the **House of Blues** (*see p250*) fills some of the gaps with Unplugged Thursdays (weekly), featuring acoustic acts in its courtyard.

Garage-Ma-Hall

www.garagemahall.com. **Open** hrs vary. **No credit cards.**
Richard and Betty Stewart love acoustic music so much that up to ten times a year they turn their home into a music venue. Part of the Woodsongs Coffeehouse project (www.woodsongs.com), the Garage-Ma-Hall hosts singer-songwriters, folkies and other acoustic musicians. Check online for show invites and address information.

Pogo's Tavern

2103 N Decatur Boulevard, at W Lake Mead Boulevard, North-west Las Vegas (646 9735). Bus 103, 210. **Open** 9am-midnight daily. **Admission** free. **No credit cards.**
Las Vegas was robbed of a jazz legend when charismatic drummer and bandleader Irv Kluger died in 2006. Happily, though, keyboardist Dick Fazio has continued Kluger's old Friday sessions, leading an all-star line-up of old-timers through a couple of sets that bely both their collective age and the sterility of modern-day Vegas. The music starts around 8pm.

Sand Dollar Blues Lounge

3355 Spring Mountain Road, at Polaris Avenue, East Las Vegas (871 6651/www.sanddollarblues. com). Bus 107, 112. **Open** 24hrs daily. **Tickets** free-$30. **Credit** AmEx, Disc, MC, V.
After a spell when its survival was in the balance, this no-nonsense local favourite lives on as the best blues club in Vegas. It's a bit divey, with broken fixtures and weathered pool tables, but once the sun sets, it's transformed into a raucous explosion of blues.

Classical music

UNLV is key to classical music in Vegas. As well as providing a home for the **Las Vegas Philharmonic**, the university stages summer concerts associated with music director George Stelluto's annual **Las Vegas Music Festival** (www.lasvegasmusicfestival.org), which brings together new talent from the UNLV music department and top international musicians, and the **Charles Vanda Master Series** (895 2787, http://pac.nevada.edu), which hosts concerts by big names on a more or less monthly basis from autumn until spring.

Occasional performances by the **UNLV Symphony Orchestra** complete the classical music picture. And the university's music department is also home to a number of ensembles and bands that perform regularly on campus. For details, see http://music.unlv.edu.

Las Vegas Philharmonic

Artemus Ham Concert Hall, 4505 S Maryland Parkway, between E Flamingo Road & E Tropicana Avenue, University District (895 2787/www.lvphil. com). Bus 109, 201. **Tickets** $29-$73. **Credit** AmEx, Disc, MC, V. **Map** p333 Y3.
Since emerging in 1998, Las Vegas's resident orchestra gradually gained recognition under recently-retired music director Harold Weller; today, new director David Itkin and associate conductor Richard McGee continue the effort. Repertoire has remained largely highbrow, with new works occasionally commissioned from contemporary composers. Aside from the concerts at Ham Hall, the Phil also perform pop classics to family audiences in annual recitals timed to coincide with holidays such as Christmas and Independence Day.

Nightclubs

Everyone can party like a VIP in Vegas, at least if they've the cash to splash.

An expansive space with some unusual sounds: **Empire Ballroom**. *See p256.*

In terms of its quality, quantity and diversity, there are few cities in the US with a nightlife scene to rival that of Las Vegas. That said, an element of homogeneity has crept into the local scene of late, bringing the same music (MTV-cloned hip hop and poorly-mixed mash-ups), the same overpriced bottle service and the same long queues to venues all over town.

The success of the Light Group, which runs a half-dozen venues, and the Pure Management Group, which operates nearly a dozen spots, has resulted in many clubs run in very similar fashion. There are advantages: the firms command enough bargaining power to retain big-name residents (such as Pure's mash-up king DJ AM), and clubbers know they can expect certain standards of service. But at the same time, door policies, DJ programming and even venue design have become standardised.

If you're looking for less mainstream sounds, whether drum 'n' bass, trance or garage rock, a number of weekly promotions at local bars draw their own scenes. Most notable among them is the **Beauty Bar** (*see p183*), where you might find DJs spinning anything from indie rock to vintage soul. The **Red Room Saloon** (3101 W Sahara Avenue, West of Strip, 257 9663, www.vegasredroom.com) is also popular, especially for Edgar Reyes's progressive house Thursday-nighter Soul Kitchen. *See p260* **Hey Mr DJ** for more alternative nights.

INFORMATION AND TICKETS

For information on what's on, check *CityLife* or the *Las Vegas Weekly*. While some venues don't offer advance ticket sales, most of them allow

The best Clubs

For celeb-spotting
Pure. *See p258.*

For club kid flashbacks
Empire Ballroom. *See p256.*

For drinking with a view
Mix. *See p257.*

High spirits

Las Vegas's ascension as an upscale nightlife destination has brought with it the curse of VIP bottle service, first popular in Miami but now creeping into clubs all over the US. In order to reserve a table at many casino clubs, you'll need to buy an entire bottle of booze at a mark-up nearing 1,000 per cent: it's not uncommon to pay $300 (including mixers, excluding service) for a bottle of Grey Goose vodka. Many venues even run a two-bottle minimum.

There are 300 green-backed reasons why bottle service is a pretty unappealing trend. But if you're desperate to go to a particular venue and there are a number of people in your party (four to six is ideal), it's a surprisingly attractive way to approach the night ahead. (At least if you arrive promptly: lollygaggers have been known to have their 'reserved' table sold out from under them for more money.)

Paying the premium means no waiting in line, no snobby stares from the host and no cover for at least some of the party (all of them, if they're female). Men love VIP seating as a way to attract women; women love it as a way to escape men. And with cover charges running to $30 and poorly mixed martinis going for close to $20, it even makes financial sense. Sort of.

patrons to reserve a table in advance if they're willing to fork out for bottle service (*see left* **High spirits**). It's also a good idea to speak to your hotel concierge before settling on a venue: they may be able to offer guest-list privileges to clubs affiliated to the hotel.

Men: your power is in your wallets, not in your numbers. Large groups of guys are rarely admitted to clubs; conversely, women still get preferential treatment, often not even having to pay the cover charge. Admission prices listed below are for visitors, and can vary depending on the night; locals with Nevada ID usually pay less. And if you're under 21, forget it: the bouncers here are expert at checking IDs.

Nightclubs

Body English

Hard Rock *4455 Paradise Road, at E Harmon Avenue, East of Strip (693 4000/www.body english.com). Bus 108.* **Open** 10.30pm-4am Fri-Sun. **Admission** $30 men; $20 women. **Credit** AmEx, DC, Disc, MC, V. **Hotel** p96. **Map** p336 C7.
Body English resembles something like a mod, Brit-rock star's bachelor pad on overdrive, rich colours accented by crystal chandeliers. The most popular evening tends to be locals' night on Sunday, a good opportunity to avoid the tourist scene. If you grease a VIP host or make friends with the right person, you can check out the VIP parlour, an intimate, private space with its own DJ, booths and bar.

Cherry

Red Rock Resort *11011 W Charleston Boulevard, at I-215, West Las Vegas (797 7180/www.midnight oilbars.com). Bus 206.* **Open** 10pm-late Thur-Sat. **Admission** $20 men; free-$10 women. **Credit** AmEx, DC, Disc, MC, V. **Hotel** p112.
Rande Gerber's first full-on Vegas club (he also created ultralounge Whiskey; *see p260*) is a polished spot, smaller than those on the Strip. The red-toned, wood-and-steel interior creates a warm, intimate environment, and opens out to a gorgeous pool. Even the restrooms are a delight, with holographic projections, voyeuristic mirrors and, mouth-shaped urinals. Expect a slightly older, well-heeled locals' crowd.

Empire Ballroom

3765 Las Vegas Boulevard South, between E Harmon & E Tropicana Avenues (737 7376/www.empire ballroom.com). Bus Deuce, 201. **Open** hrs vary. **Admission** free-$20. **Credit** AmEx, Disc, MC, V. **Map** p320 A8.
Formerly the home of pioneering dance den Club Utopia, this big space (with a great patio) remains the only independent nightclub on the Strip. The club's independent-spirited tradition continues with after-hours promotion Late Night Empire (from 3am, Thur-Sat nights), which delivers the kind of house music that's rarely heard in Vegas. It also serves as a part-time music venue, hosting acts as varied as the Killers and Lady Sovereign. *Photo p255.*

Godspeed

Mandalay Bay *3950 Las Vegas Boulevard South, at W Hacienda Avenue (632 7777/www.hob.com). Bus Deuce, 104, 105.* **Open** 11pm-5am Mon. **Admission** $30. **Credit** AmEx, DC, Disc, MC, V. **Hotel** p71. **Map** p336 A9.

The House of Blues' exclusive Foundation Room atop Mandalay Bay opens its doors to non-members on Mondays. Resident and guest DJs provide a sexy house soundtrack, which, when combined with the lush Asian-inspired decor and breathtaking city views, creates an indulgent jet-set atmosphere.

Ivan Kane's Forty Deuce

Mandalay Bay *3950 Las Vegas Boulevard South, at W Hacienda Avenue (632 9442/www.forty deuce.com). Bus Deuce, 104, 105.* **Open** 10.30pm-4am (sometimes until 5am) Mon, Thur-Sun. **Admission** $25. **Credit** AmEx, DC, Disc, MC, V. **Hotel** p71. **Map** p336 A9.

Burlesque-oriented clubs started re-emerging in Sin City a few years ago, but only Forty Deuce is founded entirely on the combination of stage-trained dancers and DJ-spun club sounds. Though smallish and lacking a sufficient dancefloor, this offshoot of an LA original is worth a visit. You can buy the dancers' costumes in the adjacent Champagne Suzy's boutique.

Jet

Mirage *3400 Las Vegas Boulevard South, between Spring Mountain & W Flamingo Roads (792 7900/ www.lightgroup.com). Bus Deuce, 105, 202, 203.* **Open** 10.30pm-4am Mon, Fri, Sat. **Admission** $30. **Credit** AmEx, DC, Disc, MC, V. **Hotel** p73. **Map** p335 & p336 A6.

As at sister club Light (*see below*), the main dancefloor at Jet is a sunken rectangle surrounded by VIP seating and two bars. Hip hop and mash-ups keep the dancefloor packed, and clubbers drink cocktails served by gorgeous staff. But the real reasons to visit are the two side rooms, one with the latest in house and the other pumping out rock and '80s dance music.

Light

Bellagio *3600 Las Vegas Boulevard South, at W Flamingo Road (693 8303/www.lightlv.com). Bus Deuce, 202.* **Open** 10.30pm-4am Thur-Sun. **Admission** $30. **Credit** AmEx, MC, V. **Hotel** p68. **Map** p336 A7.

Light set the pace for the modern Las Vegas nightclub, introducing bottle service, exclusive door policies and a return to upscale dress codes. Though it has dumbed down a little in both its music (ubiquitous hip hop, bad rock remixes) and dress code, some things never change: groups of men larger than six are not allowed, VIP booths are scarce and the dancefloor is packed. But hey, it's all part of the experience.

Lure

Wynn Las Vegas *3131 Las Vegas Boulevard South, between E Desert Inn Road & Sands Avenue (770 3350/www.wynnlasvegas.com). Bus Deuce, 203.* **Open** 9pm-late Tue-Sat. **Admission** free-$30. **Credit** AmEx, Disc, MC, V. **Hotel** p76. **Map** p335 & p336 B6.

Lure has never quite carved out a proper niche for itself, teetering between intimate, sexy cocktail lounge and low-key nightclub. Dimly lit in soothing blues and draped with delicate fabrics, it's a gorgeous space, often overlooked in the dizzying array of nightspot options in Sin City. A laid-back alternative to busier, more boisterous clubs elsewhere.

Mix

Thehotel at Mandalay Bay *3950 Las Vegas Boulevard South, at W Hacienda Avenue (632 7777/www.mandalaybay.com). Bus Deuce, 104, 105.* **Open** 5pm-2am Mon-Thur, Sun; 5pm-3am Fri, Sat. **Admission** $20-$25. **Credit** AmEx, DC, Disc, MC, V. **Hotel** p95. **Map** p336 A9.

Surrounded by 30ft windows, the lounge at Alain Ducasse's dynamic restaurant (*see p160*) atop Thehotel at Mandalay Bay attracts locals with its impressive panoramic views. Mix also comes with the overly clubby feel that's attached to so many of the city's other towering venues. Its intimate atmosphere is enhanced by house and lounge sounds, though there's no proper dancefloor.

Moon

Palms *4321 W Flamingo Road, at S Valley View Boulevard, West of Strip (942 6832/http://moon-las-vegas.n9negroup.com). Bus 201.* **Open** 8pm-4am daily. **Admission** *Mon-Thur* $10. *Fri-Sun* $25. **Credit** AmEx, DC, Disc, MC, V. **Hotel** p98. **Map** p333 X3.

In space, no one can hear you scream. However, they sure can see you dance, at least if they happen to be looking through Moon's retractable roof. The club's space-age design has a retro feel, but its location 53 floors up the Palms' Fantasy Tower offers incredible views from its two balconies and its bead-curtained, floor-to-ceiling windows. The music can be a bit schizophrenic, ranging from top 40 remixes to hip hop/rock mash-ups and occasional house nights. Most evenings, admission includes access to the Playboy Club via a direct escalator. *Photos p259*.

OPM

Caesars Palace (Forum Shops) *3570 Las Vegas Boulevard South, at W Flamingo Road (369 4998/www.o-pmlv.com). Bus Deuce, 202.* **Open** 10pm-late Wed-Sun. **Admission** $20-$30. **Credit** AmEx, Disc, MC, V. **Hotel** p68. **Map** p336 A7.

It took a while for OPM, located on the top floor of Wolfgang Puck's Chinois in the Forum Shops, to find its identity. However, it's now become the prime destination for the upscale, hip hop crowd in Las Vegas. DJs also spin reggae and R&B; the urban sounds and intimacy of the venue keep the blinging patrons grinding week after week.

Polly Esther's

Stratosphere *2000 Las Vegas Boulevard South, at W St Louis Avenue (889 1980/www.pollyesthers lv.com). Bus Deuce, 108.* **Open** 10pm-4am Wed-Sat. **Admission** free-$20. **Credit** AmEx, Disc, MC, V. **Hotel** p93. **Map** p335 C4.

Arts & Entertainment

Forget the complications of contemporary life: this national chain offers four themed rooms dedicated to the music and paraphernalia of the 1970s (most popular), '80s, '90s and 2000s. From the *Brady Bunch* shrine to the *Back to the Future* DeLorean car via the *Partridge Family* bus bar, it's all cheese. But sometimes, a break from reality (and good taste) makes you appreciate just how far we've come.

Pure

Caesars Palace *3570 Las Vegas Boulevard South, at W Flamingo Road (731 7873/www.purethe nightclub.com). Bus Deuce, 202.* **Open** 10pm-4am Tue, Fri-Sun. **Admission** $20-$30. **Credit** AmEx, DC, Disc, MC, V. **Hotel** p68. **Map** p336 A7.

Soon after opening in 2005, Pure became the hottest megaclub in Las Vegas, and remains so several years down the line. Its multiple levels, including a massive terrace overlooking the Strip, are always packed with patrons vying for a glimpse of the latest Hollywood celebs hosting parties in the labyrinthine venue. Attached is the Pussycat Dolls Lounge, in which its namesake burlesque troupe perform at regular intervals nightly.

Rain

Palms *4321 W Flamingo Road, at S Valley View Boulevard, West of Strip (942 6832/www.rainatthe palms.com). Bus 201.* **Open** 11pm-4am Fri, Sat. **Admission** $25. **Credit** AmEx, DC, Disc, MC, V. **Hotel** p98. **Map** p333 X3.

One of the last Vegas clubs built in an oversized, industrial style, Rain now looks a bit dated. However, it's still the best at what it does, with the non-stop dance music and eyebrow-searing pyrotechnics perhaps best heard and viewed from one of the private cabanas that overlook all the action from upstairs.

Risqué

Paris Las Vegas *3655 Las Vegas Boulevard South, at E Flamingo Road (967 4589/www.harrahs.com). Bus Deuce, 202.* **Open** 10pm-4am Thur-Sun. **Admission** free-$10. **Credit** AmEx, Disc, MC, V. **Hotel** p74. **Map** p336 A7.

Though it bills itself as an ultralounge, Risqué defies categorisation. It's less spacious than most nightclubs but more involving than a mere bar, with modern Asian decor complementing a space with private balconies overlooking the Strip, an intimate salon (with its own events), a proper dancefloor and occasional performances from burlesque-style dancers.

Rumjungle

Mandalay Bay *3950 Las Vegas Boulevard South, at W Hacienda Avenue (632 7408/www.mandalay bay.com). Bus Deuce, 104, 105.* **Open** 11pm Mon, Wed, Fri, Sat; 11pm-2am Tue, Thur, Sun. **Admission** $10-$30. **Credit** AmEx, Disc, MC, V. **Hotel** p71. **Map** p336 A9.

The fire-and-water theme at Rumjungle perfectly complements the music, which varies from hip hop to reggaeton to Latin dance (especially during promotions such as Wednesday's Rumba). It's particularly popular with the college-age set, but its semi-strict dress code keeps out the rubes, and it's now far less crowded since the once-legendary swank contingent dispersed to newer venues.

Studio 54

MGM Grand *3799 Las Vegas Boulevard South, at E Tropicana Avenue (891 1111/www.mgm grand.com). Bus Deuce, 201.* **Open** 10pm-5am Tue-Sat. **Admission** $10-$20. **Credit** AmEx, Disc, MC, V. **Hotel** p81. **Map** p336 A8.

This 21st-century revamp of the legendary New York disco recently had a renovation, adding a high-ceilinged entry-way with lounge seating, more VIP areas on the upper levels and a private lounge for the DJ and his or her hangers-on. It remains a favourite with locals and visitors, thanks to top-notch sound and lighting, a cool, industrial feel and some of the most innovative promotions in Vegas.

Tabú

MGM Grand *3799 Las Vegas Boulevard South, at E Tropicana Avenue (891 7183/www.mgmgrand.com). Bus Deuce, 201.* **Open** 10pm-3am Mon, Wed-Sun. **Admission** free-$20. **Credit** AmEx, Disc, MC, V. **Hotel** p81. **Map** p336 A8.

Lots of spaces in Las Vegas call themselves ultralounges, but Tabú was the first and probably remains the best. Despite its lack of dancefloor and overabundance of seating, DJs manage to keep people on their feet all night in the upscale, modern space; especially during Super Slide Sundays, when B-boys and -girls tear up the floor as if *Breakin' 3* were being filmed right there in the room.

Tangerine

Treasure Island *3300 Las Vegas Boulevard South, at Spring Mountain Road (894 7580/www.tangerine club.com). Bus Deuce, 105, 203.* **Open** 9pm-4am Wed-Sat. **Admission** free-$20. **Credit** AmEx, DC, Disc, MC, V. **Hotel** p87. **Map** p335 & p336 A6.

One of the first clubs in the city to hop on the burlesque bandwagon, Tangerine continues to draw the crowds. The ladies do their stuff at 9.30pm and 10.30pm (Thur-Sat only) before leaving the club to the DJs. Hang out on the patio and watch the Sirens of TI show if you're here early enough.

Tao

Venetian *3555 Las Vegas Boulevard South, between Sands Avenue & E Flamingo Road (388 8588/www.taolasvegas.com). Bus Deuce, 105, 203.* **Open** 10pm-4am Thur, Fri; 9.30pm-4am Sat. **Admission** $20-$30. **Credit** AmEx, DC, Disc, MC, V. **Hotel** p75. **Map** p335 & p336 B6.

This NYC import rivals Pure as the favourite party-spot of celebs visiting Vegas. And who can blame them? The Zen- and Buddhist-themed decor is intoxicating, and the multiple lounges and VIP areas lend an air of exclusivity to the venue. Other attractions include an adjacent gourmet Asian fusion restaurant (*see p166*), a cosy Strip-facing patio, a rooftop pool party (summer only), gorgeous bathing ladies (really) and some of the town's hottest house DJs, though the music is more mainstream at weekends.

Playboy Club. *See p257* **Moon**.

Triq

Planet Hollywood *3667 Las Vegas Boulevard South, between E Harmon & E Flamingo Roads (785 5555/www.planethollywoodresort.com).* Bus Deuce, 202. **Open** midnight-8am Fri, Sat. **Admission** $20-$30. **Credit** AmEx, Disc, MC, V. **Hotel** p85. **Map** p336 A7.

The trick here is that Triq is simply a lounge, albeit a well-appointed one, within the massive complex known as the Steve Wyrick Entertainment Complex. But the place comes to life late on Fridays and Saturdays, spreading across all levels of the facility: the stage of Wyrick's 500-seat theatre becomes a dancefloor, while pole-dancing go-go girls entertain VIP guests in the lounge. Music is a Strip-standard mix of hip hop, 1980s rock and mash-ups.

Tryst

Wynn Las Vegas *3131 Las Vegas Boulevard South, between E Desert Inn Road & Sands Avenue (770 3375/www.wynnlasvegas.com).* Bus Deuce, 203. **Open** 10pm-4.30am Thur-Sun. **Admission** $20-$30. **Credit** AmEx, DC, Disc, MC, V. **Hotel** p76. **Map** p335 & p336 B6.

Descend the stairs and follow a passage through a womb-like hallway into a dark, sensual space. The dancefloor extends outside to overlook a private lagoon and 94ft (29m) waterfall, with waterside bottle service and corset-wearing servers. The atmosphere is completed by the Library, a VIP area with bookshelf-lined walls and a stripper pole. A decadent nightlife experience for those who can afford it.

Whiskey

Green Valley Ranch *2300 Paseo Verde Drive, at S Green Valley Parkway, Henderson (617 7777/ www.greenvalleyranchresort.com).* Bus 111. **Open** 6pm-2am Mon-Thur, Sun; 6pm-4am Fri, Sat. **Admission** free. **Credit** AmEx, DC, Disc, MC, V. **Hotel** p111.

Rande Gerber's first foray into Vegas nightlife has evolved over the years from a lounge into something approaching a suburban nightclub. The amenities are headed by the adjacent Whiskey Beach: one of the most breathtaking pool areas in the desert and host to all manner of outdoor concerts, it also affords unexpectedly fantastic views of the Strip.

Hey Mr DJ

You'd think the so-called 'American Ibiza' would have spawned its own distinctive nightclub sound. However, if there's one glaring weakness in the Las Vegas nightclub scene, it's a lack of musical identity. Casino clubs have generally demanded that DJs play records with popular appeal, with the result that the local scene shakes its blinkered booty to whatever MTV is spoon-feeding the kids. Happily, there are a number of brave turntablists who eschew corporate-mandated playlists in favour of something a bit more original, though they're not usually found in the clubs with the longest lines.

If the town boasts a current superstar DJ, it's **Faarsheed**, one of the lone spinsters who gets away with playing progressive house in the Strip's big rooms. A frequent headliner at Jet and the Empire Ballroom, the San Francisco native is known for dropping tunes already championed on the international clubbing scene; he's not exactly a maverick, but he's here.

Robert Oleysyck made a name for himself a decade ago as the first resident DJ to bring trance (and other genres) to Las Vegas Boulevard. Most of the big-box venues shun DJs with his versatility: Oleysyck spins everything from breaks to rave-era classics. However, at speciality locales such as Revolution (*see p180*), his multi-genre mixology is a natural fit. **DJ Morningstar**, the sonically flexible resident jock at Krave (*see p248*), does something similar.

Adventurous clubbers are most likely to find a whiff of underground dance music in the big clubs' ancillary rooms. Led by Keith Evan, with help from the likes of Carlos Sanchez and Brian Minogue, the **House Society** collective has managed to bring its signature deep sound to nearly every dance space and club patio in town. Its success has paved the way for fellow house-heads such as the Light Group's **Eddie MacDonald**, freelancer **Edgar Reyes** and **Douglas Gibbs**, resident at the V Bar (*see p181*).

The **Bargain DJ Collective**, another band of disco brothers, shuffles its vinyl-only collections at venues all over town, among them the Double Down Saloon (*see p181*) and the Beauty Bar (*see p183*). The latter, a real hipster enclave, also offers Rawkerz resident **Johnny Rox** blaring rhythmic indie rock, **DJ Aurajin** throwing down left-of-centre rap/R&B and, as an after-party to First Friday (*see p216*), the **Get Back**, at which dedicated vinyl-only jocks such as **John Doe** spin rare groove and funk gems. In a town that's plagued by glorified wedding DJs, Doe and his cratedigging peers are welcome anomalies that give the local scene some much-needed credibility.

Sport & Fitness

Get active in the city where you can ski and water ski on the same day.

Far be it from us to detract from the enjoyment of betting on your team, a predictably popular pastime in this town, but getting your heart rate pumping from sideline enthusiasm doesn't count as exercise. Happily, the word 'sports' isn't always followed by the word 'book' in Las Vegas: there are plenty of opportunities in and around the city for watching and taking part in an array of games.

That said, Vegas remains the largest US city without either a major league team or a major league-quality sporting arena. It's not for want of trying, at least on the part of the city's mayor. Oscar Goodman appears determined to bring a major-league team to the city, and he doesn't seem fussy about which sport gets here first. In 2005, he wooed the Florida Marlins baseball team; the following year, in the wake of Hurricane Katrina, the suddenly homeless New Orleans Saints of the NFL seemed another possibility. And in 2007, Vegas even managed to host the NBA All-Star Game. But neither the Marlins nor the Saints made the leap, and NBA commissioner David Stern then announced that basketball wouldn't be returning to Sin City unless or until a major-league calibre area is built. For now, the only options for spectators not keen on auto racing are minor-league or college sports.

The choices are broader if you're keen to get active. Bowling, tennis, swimming, cycling, horse riding and a bizarre homegrown activity known as Skyzone (*see p265* **Jump to it**) are all popular options, and Vegas is packed with excellent health clubs and spas. And despite being in the middle of the desert, the city is dotted with world-class golf courses. Further out, **Red Rock Canyon** (*see pp281-282*) is great for hiking, cycling and rock climbing, and **Lake Mead** (*see pp279-281*) is great for fishing and even scuba diving. Indeed, one of the many peculiarities about Las Vegas is that you can go water skiing (on Lake Mead) and skiing (at Mount Charleston) on the same day and still be back in the hotel for dinner, at least if you're prepared to get up miserably early and don't mind returning home exhausted.

Outside the inferno-like summer months, the climate here is pleasant and sunny year-round. Be sure to drink plenty of water and load up on sunscreen. In summer, plan outdoor activities for early in the day to avoid the midday sun.

Spectator sports

Auto racing

With two paved ovals, a dirt course and a drag strip, the 1,500-acre **Las Vegas Motor Speedway** (7000 Las Vegas Boulevard North, 644 4444, www.lvms.com) reverberates with events throughout the year, among them the VW frenzy that is October's **Bugorama**. The biggest is the **NASCAR 400 Nextel Cup** race in March, which draws more than 150,000 fans to Las Vegas (and, irony of ironies, creates huge traffic jams to and from the event).

For the **Las Vegas Grand Prix**, *see p214*.

Baseball

The AAA affiliate of the Los Angeles Dodgers, the **Las Vegas 51s** (www.lv51.com) play 72 games between April and September at **Cashman Field** (850 Las Vegas Boulevard North, at Washington Avenue, Downtown, 386 7200) from April to September. Although the 51s are among the most consistently successful teams in the Pacific Coast League, the 12,000-seat stadium is generally about half-full, and tickets ($8-$13) are usually available on the gate. The ballpark opens in March with an exhibition game featuring major league stars.

Basketball

With coach Lon Kruger at the helm, UNLV's **Runnin' Rebels** (http://unlvrebels.cstv.com) made it all the way to the Sweet 16 of the NCAA tournament in 2007. There hasn't been this much excitement around the team since the

The best Sports

For settling in
Fishing at **Lake Mead**. *See p263.*

For swinging through
Bali Hai Golf Course. *See p264.*

For striking out
All-night **bowling**. *See p263.*

Arts & Entertainment

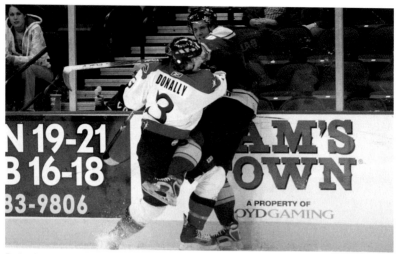

Body slammin': the **Las Vegas Wranglers** at the Orleans Arena.

days when towel-eating Jerry Tarkanian, aka Tark the Shark, led them to the NCAA title in 1990. Between November and March, games are played at the **Thomas & Mack Center** (E Tropicana Avenue & Swenson Street); call 739 3267 for tickets, which cost $15-$30.

The **Lady Rebels**, UNLV's women's basketball team ($9 a game), play at the **Cox Pavilion** (739 3267, http://unlvrebels.cstv.com), next door to the Thomas & Mack. The team has been posting as many wins as the men of late.

Boxing

With blood, sweat and spit, boxing draws the richest of the rich and the poorest of the poor, just like Vegas itself. The hotels used regularly for big bouts are **Mandalay Bay** (which also hosts numerous 'ultimate fighting' events; *see p71*), the **MGM Grand** (*see p81*) and **Caesars Palace** (*see p68*). Call each hotel or Ticketmaster (474 4000) ahead of the fight for tickets, which can cost several thousand dollars but nonetheless often sell out quickly.

Football

The **UNLV Rebels** college team plays under coach Mike Sanford at **Sam Boyd Stadium** (Boulder Highway & Russell Road, 739 3267, http://unlvrebels.cstv.com) between September and December. Tickets, on sale from July, cost $15-$30. Sam Boyd Stadium also hosts the **Las Vegas Bowl**, which features the best of the Mountain West Conference.

The indoor Arena Football League found a home here in 2002, with the arrival of the **Las Vegas Gladiators** (www.lvgladiators.com). Games are played at the **Orleans Arena** (4500 W Tropicana Avenue, at Arville Road, 284 7777, www.orleansarena.com) between March and June; tickets cost $15-$80.

Golf

In October, the PGA Tour rolls into town for the **Frys.com Open** (www.pgatour.com), at two courses: TPC at Summerlin and TPC at the Canyons (*see p264*). Daily tickets cost $15-$20, and are available on 242 3000. In 2007, the inaugural **World Series of Golf** tournament (www.worldseriesofgolf.com) was held in Primm, 45 minutes south of Las Vegas. The game manages to combine golf with, you guessed it, poker: players get to pass, bet or fold on each shot.

Ice hockey

The city's resident team, the **Las Vegas Wranglers** (471 7825, www.lasvegas wranglers.com), take to the ice between October and April at the 9,000-seat **Orleans Arena** (*see p113*). Competing in the West division of the National Conference, the team is a feeder club for the NHL's Calgary Flames. At $12.50-$36.75, tickets are worth their weight in body slams, ice brawls and speeding-puck action; the crowd's enthusiasm is even hotter than the temperatures outside.

Arts & Entertainment

Rodeo

Every December, the **National Finals Rodeo** (*see p219*) sweeps into town, packing the Thomas & Mack Center with riders who make riding a bucking bronco look as easy as sitting on a carousel horse. See www.nfrexperience. com for details of events. The relatively new **South Point Equestrian Center** (797 8005, www.southpointeventscenter.com) hosts events year-round, including the Western States Championship Ranch Rodeo.

In October, the best **professional bull riders in the world** come to the Thomas & Mack to compete in the **Built Ford Tough World Finals**. For tickets, call 1-877 632 7400 (first weekend) or 1-866 727 7469 (second weekend), or see www.pbrnow.com.

Tennis

Each February/March, the **Darling Tennis Center** (7901 W Washington Avenue, 229 2100, www.darlingtenniscenter.net) hosts the **Tennis Channel Open** (www.tennis channelopen.com), a high-profile, round-robin tournament. Lleyton Hewitt won in 2007.

Active sports

Auto racing

If you'd like to get out of the stands and into the car, contact the **Richard Petty Driving Experience** (1-800 237 3889, www.1800be petty.com) or the **Mario Andretti Racing School** (1-877 2637 3884, www.andrettiracing. com). Both offer the chance to sit in the passenger seat (around $150) or behind the wheel (roughly $400) of a speeding motor.

Bowling

A number of casinos have huge, 24-hour alleys, among them the **Suncoast** (64 lanes; *see p117*), **Sam's Town** (56 lanes; *see p117*) and the **Red Rock** (72 lanes with a VIP section; *see p112*). There are also alleys with slightly more limited hours at the **Gold Coast** (70 lanes; *see p116*), the **Orleans** (70 lanes; *see p113*) and **Santa Fe Station** (60 lanes; *see p117*). The newish **Strike Zone** at **Sunset Station** (72 lanes; *see p117*) is a little more modern, while the bowling and nightclub worlds collide at **Lucky Strike** at the **Rio** (10 lanes; *see p100*) with surprisingly delightful results. For all, call ahead before making a special trip: local bowling leagues take over entire alleys on selected nights, and some alleys are open only to over-21s at night.

Cycling

Looking around Vegas, you'd think that the only cyclists are Mormon missionaries. Don't be put off: although urban areas are incredibly auto-centric, there are thrilling cycle trails surrounding the city, even if you have to drive to get there.

McGhie's Ski Bike & Board (4035 S Fort Apache Road, between W Flamingo Road & W Saddle Avenue, 252 8077, www.mcghies bikes.com) rents out road and mountain bikes (from $35 a day), and can arrange group tours. McGhie's is the official bicycle tour operator for **Red Rock Casino Resort**, the closest resort to beautiful **Red Rock Canyon** and the most breathtaking biking spots in the area.

Other routes include the eight-mile off-road **Cottonwood Valley Loop** near Red Rock (head west on Highway 160 and look for a dirt road six miles past the junction with Highway 159) and the **River Mountain Peak**, a ten-mile trek between Las Vegas and Henderson (drive along I-93/95 to Equestrian Drive and turn east). There's also an unofficial mountain bike trail on the north-west corner of Tropicana Avenue and Decatur Boulevard. It's steep and challenging but well worn, running through one of the few undeveloped parcels of land in town.

Fishing

Lake Mead (*see pp279-281*) is stocked with half a million rainbow trout annually, and also contains black and striped bass; the upper Overton Arm of the lake is good for crappie, bluegill and catfish. **Lake Mohave** is also good for rainbow trout. In the city, check out **Lorenzi Park** (Rancho Drive & Washington Avenue), **Sunset Park** (Sunset Road & Eastern Avenue) or **Floyd Lamb State Park** (*see p283*).

To fish from any Nevada shore, you'll need a Nevada fishing licence ($18 for the first day, $7 for subsequent days); a special stamp is required for trout fishing. To fish from a boat on Lake Mead, you'll also need a stamp from Arizona, as the two states share jurisdiction of the lake. For details on all aspects of fishing in Nevada, contact the **Nevada Division of Wildlife** (486 5127, www.ndow.org), ask at a ranger station for the current hotspots or consult **Fish Incorporated** (565 8396, www.fishincorporated.com).

Golf

Las Vegas has about half the courses it needs to meet demand; call several weeks ahead and show up with a three-figure sum if you want to play on any of the best. **Las Vegas Preferred Tee-Times** (1-877 255 7277, www.lvptt.com)

can arrange reservations at a number of courses. Rates are cheaper in the heat of summer and later in the afternoon. Most courses are open from 7am to dusk; one exception is the par-three **Cloud Nine** course at Angel Park (254 4653, www.angelpark.com), where nine of the 12 holes are floodlit. Sharpen up your game at **Butch Harmon's School of Golf** at the Rio Secco Golf Club (777 2444, www.butchharmon.com).

Bali Hai Golf Club

5160 Las Vegas Boulevard South, at W Russell Road, South of Strip (450 8000/www.balihaigolf club.com). Bus Deuce, 104. **Green fees** *June-Aug* $175-$195; $125-$150 twilight. *Sept-May* $265-$325; $189-$229 twilight. **Credit** AmEx, DC, Disc, MC, V. **Map** p336 A9.
This challenging 7,002-yard, par-71 track, the only one on Las Vegas Boulevard, includes seven acres of water features, 2,500 palm trees, Augusta white sand and more than 100,000 tropical plants.

Craig Ranch Golf Course

628 W Craig Road, between N Martin Luther King Boulevard & Losee Road, North Las Vegas (642 9700). No bus. **Green fees** $19-$35; $5-$16 juniors. **Credit** V, MC.
Established in 1962, Las Vegas's first public course is a favourite with locals, thanks in part to the fabulously inexpensive prices.

Desert Pines Golf Club

3415 E Bonanza Road, at N Pecos Road, East Las Vegas (366 1616/www.golfdesertpines.com). Bus 111, 215. **Green fees** *June-Aug* $69-$79; $39-$49 twilight. *Sept-May* $99-$129; $69-$79 twilight. **Credit** AmEx, DC, Disc, MC, V. **Map** p333 Z1.
The public course at Desert Pines has been recognised as one of the premier upscale courses in the country by *Golf Digest*, with a tight, 6,810-yard, par-71 layout, tree-lined fairways and nine holes on water. The climate-controlled practice facility is the best in Las Vegas.

Las Vegas Golf Club

4300 W Washington Avenue, between N Decatur & N Valley View Boulevards, North Las Vegas (646 3003/www.americangolf.com). Bus 103, 208. **Green fees** $69-$89, $49-$69 twilight. **Credit** AmEx, Disc, MC, V.
This is the oldest course in the Valley, dating back to 1938. But with $5 million in improvements, you'd never know it. The 6,319-yard, par-72 public course is popular, and it's easy to see why. Book ahead.

Legacy Golf Club

130 Par Excellence Drive, at Green Valley Parkway, Henderson (897 2187/www.thelegacygc.com). Bus 114. **Green fees** *June-Sept* $75-$90; $55 twilight. *Oct-May* $100-$155; $75-$85 twilight. **Credit** AmEx, DC, Disc, MC, V.
This handsome, 7,233-yard, par-72 course is host each year to US Open qualifying, but is also a popular choice with the public.

Royal Links

5995 E Vegas Valley Drive, east of S Nellis Boulevard, East Las Vegas (450 8123/www.royal linksgolfclub.com). No bus. **Green fees** *June-Aug* $95-$155; $75-$85 twilight. *Sept-May* $175-$275; $125-$175 twilight. **Credit** AmEx, MC, V.
The Royal Links course is modelled on 11 different courses used for the Open championship; there's a replica of the Postage Stamp at Troon, and the Road Hole at St Andrew's. *Photo p266.*

TPC at the Canyons

9851 Canyon Run Drive, at Town Center Drive, Summerlin (256 2000/www.tpc.com). No bus. **Green fees** *June-Aug* $125-$150; $75 twilight. *Sept-May* $225-$275; $170-$190 twilight. **Credit** AmEx, DC, Disc, MC, V.
One of two courses to host the annual Frys.com Open (*see p262*), this 6,772-yard layout was co-designed by Bobby Weed and Ray Floyd.

Gyms & sports centres

Most major hotel-casinos have some sort of fitness facility on the premises.

Gold's Gym

Gold's Plaza, 3750 E Flamingo Road, at Sandhill Road, East Las Vegas (451 4222/www.goldsgym.com). Bus 111, 202. **Open** 24hrs daily. **Rates** $15/day; $35/wk. **Credit** AmEx, Disc, MC, V. **Map** p333 Z3.
Touted as a no-frills gym, Gold's offers all the aerobics classes, free weights, weight machines and CV equipment an exercise buff could handle.
Other locations throughout the city.

Las Vegas Athletic Club

2655 S Maryland Parkway, at Karen Avenue, East Las Vegas (734 5822/www.lvac.com). Bus 109, 204. **Open** 24hrs daily. **Rates** $15/day; $35/wk. **Credit** AmEx, DC, Disc, MC, V. **Map** p333 Y2.
All five Vegas branches have pools, saunas, jacuzzis, Nautilus, free weights and dozens of classes, plus childcare services. Most locations are open 24 hours.
Other locations: throughout the city.

24 Hour Fitness

2605 S Eastern Avenue, at E Sahara Avenue, East Las Vegas (641 2222/www.24hourfitness.com). Bus 110, 204. **Open** 24hrs daily. **Rates** $15/day. **Credit** AmEx, DC, Disc, MC, V. **Map** p333 Z2.
In addition to gym facilities, 24 Hour has a kids' club and rock climbing. Larger branches also have pools and basketball courts. A branch is due to open in late 2007 at the Molasky Building in Downtown.
Other locations: throughout the city.

Hiking

The **Sierra Club** (363 3267, www.sierra club.com), the granddaddy of environmental outfits, organises regular hikes around Red Rock Canyon, Mount Charleston and the Lake Mead area. All are open to non-members.

Horse riding

See p282.

Hunting & shooting

Call the **Nevada Division of Wildlife** (486 5127, www.ndow.org) for information on hunting dove, quail and waterfowl in the Lake Mead area, and details of seasonal hunting of deer, elk, antelope and bighorn sheep. A hunting licence for non-residents costs $142.

The **American Shooters Supply & Gun Club** (3440 Arville Street, between W Desert Inn & Spring Mountain Roads, 362 1223,

www.americanshooters.com) has the only 50-yard indoor range in Las Vegas. Meanwhile, the **Gun Store** (2900 E Tropicana Avenue, between McLeod & Harrison Drives, 454 1110, www.thegunstorelasvegas.com) offers more shooting options, from M16s to machine guns. Ladies shoot for free on Tuesday nights.

Pool & billiards

Cue Club

953 E Sahara Avenue, at S Maryland Parkway, East of Strip (735 2884/www.lvcueclub.com). Bus 109, 204. **Open** 24hrs daily. **Credit** AmEx, Disc, MC, V. **Map** p333 Y2.

Jump to it

The walls are padded. The floor too. The people just keep bouncing and bouncing and bouncing. But there are no straitjackets in sight, nor nurses with pill cups. So what gives?

Descriptions inevitably make it sound like an insane asylum, but **Skymania** (4915 Steptoe Street, at E Tropicana Avenue, 436 6887, www.skymaniafuncenters.com) is all in good fun. It's a room filled with a large grid of conjoined trampolines on which kids and adults bounce like popcorn to blaring music as they spring up and down, knees buckling and faces beaming with sweaty smiles.

This bouncy 'court' was created a few years ago for SkyZone, a team sport in which players soar through the air and attempt to put a ball into the goal hoop (sometimes following it through the goal in the process).

But the game's creators quickly decided that the court shouldn't be limited to SkyZone players, and opened the arena for all kinds of other bouncing activities. Some of them are organised, such as 3-D Dodgeball and SkyRobics (aerobics on the trampolines, which makes for an incredible workout). However, there are also hours set aside for open jumping and pizza parties; for the latter, get the digesting done before you start jumping.

It's doubtful that trampoline-jumping-while-passing-a-ball will ever achieve full Olympic status. Still, that's not really the point. The best part of Skymania is that it allows adults to rekindle with the joy of childhood bouncy castle parties. Trust Las Vegas to patent something so offbeat and over-the-top, yet also so alluring.

There's 15,000-square feet of ball-banging action at Vegas's largest pool hall. Located in the Commercial Center, it draws people from all walks of life to relax, drink and shoot stick.

Rafting & kayaking

See p283 **Rolling on the river**.

Rock climbing

If you don't fancy trekking to Red Rock Canyon (see pp281-282), you can practise at the **Nevada Climbing Center** (3065 E Patrick Lane, between S Eastern Avenue & S Pecos Road, 898 8192, www.nevadaclimbingcenter. com), **GameWorks** (see p126) and Circus Circus's **Adventuredome** (see p132).

Scuba & skin diving

See p280.

Snow sports

The mountains are closer (and snowier) than you think. Just 47 miles away, the **Las Vegas Ski & Snowboard Resort** (645 2754, snow conditions 593 9500, www.skilasvegas.com) at Lee Canyon on Mount Charleston (see p282) offers action for all abilities, and has a half-pipe and terrain park. In good years, the season runs from November to April, with the park open 10am-4pm.

A three-hour drive from Vegas on I-15 and SR 145 is the two-mountain, all-abilities **Brian Head Ski Resort** in Utah (435 677 2035, www.brianhead.com). Full-day lift passes are $40, or $47 during holidays.

Spas

See pp206-208.

Swimming

Almost every hotel and motel in Las Vegas has a pool, although most are leisure-oriented and not ideal for high-speed lap swimming. Open seasonally from early morning until twilight, the poshest hotel pools on the Strip include **Caesars Palace** (see p68), the vast **MGM Grand** (see p81), the **Rio** (with a beach for volleyball; see p100) and **Mandalay Bay** (see p71); many have sections given over to topless sunbathing. Downtown, the pool at the **Golden Nugget** (see p104) has an integrated shark tank. Most hotel pools are available only to guests at the resort (or, in some cases, at an affiliated property), but some of them reopen to all-comers for evening pool parties in summer; the Rehab pool party at the **Hard Rock** (see p96) on Sundays is always popular.

Tennis

It's becoming more difficult to find a tennis court on the Strip; unsurprising, given the price of land. However, some hotels still maintain courts; guests have priority, but they're open to the public. **Bally's** (see p77) has eight courts, twice as many as the **Flamingo** (see p78). You can also play at some sports centres and parks, such as **Sunset Park** (Sunset Road & Eastern Avenue, 455 8241, $3-$5/hr), and at the **Darling Tennis Center** (see p263; free-$5.50/hr).

Water-skiing

Behind the Hoover Dam, huge **Lake Mead** (see pp279-281) offers great water-skiing. **Tom's Water Sports** at Lake Mead Marina (558 0678, www.tomswatersports.com) rents equipment, and organises trips and lessons in water-skiing, tubing and wakeboarding.

Royal Links Gold Course. See p264.

Theatre & Dance

From blockbusters to body piercing, Las Vegas is full of drama.

Theatre in Las Vegas is dominated by the extended-engagement productions on the Strip: much larger than life, and always condensed for tourist audiences who are presumed not to be in the market for three hours of Brecht. You'll find little in the way of intricate storylines or even two-act structures in these bank-busting shows, but the levels of talent and professionalism can make for an engrossing spectacle. Two major Broadway hits, *Avenue Q* and *Hairspray*, bailed out early in 2006 after lacklustre sales, but Vegas-sized versions of *The Phantom of the Opera* (at the Venetian), *The Producers* (Paris Las Vegas) and Monty Python's *Spamalot* (Wynn Las Vegas) are hoping to cash in on the success of *Mamma Mia!*, Mandalay Bay's long-running favourite. For these and other casino-based shows, *see pp224-235*.

Off-Strip community theatre in Las Vegas lives very much in the shadow of these big-ticket blockbusters, but it's there if you know where to look. Companies such as the newish **Stagedoor Entertainment** and the well-established **Las Vegas Little Theatre** stage high-quality productions; the LVLT have both a 155-capacity main stage and the smaller Fischer Black Box at their disposal, and occasionally rent the latter to outside companies. For more alternative fare, look into the fringy, ambitious productions of **SEAT** and the high-energy **New American Theatre Project**. Both troupes have been piquing interest within the city's growing arts subculture, particularly in and around Downtown.

Tucked away within the sizeable **UNLV** campus is a thriving and forward-thinking theatre department. Major productions play in the 550-seat **Judy Bayley Theatre**; smaller shows are staged at the more intimate **Paul Harris Theatre** and the **Black Box**, which is also used for student projects and many of the more low-key productions put together by the **Nevada Conservatory Theatre**. Alongside the university's theatre programme, UNLV's Department of Dance is responsible for many of the more worthwhile dance performances, both from UNLV students and visiting troupes.

The city's library system contains three modern, comfortable spaces. The theatres at **Summerlin Library** and **West Las Vegas Library** both have proscenium stages and seat roughly 300; the auditorium at **Clark County Library** features a thrust stage and seats 400. Details of performances are at www.lvccld.org; for addresses and phone numbers of all libraries around the city, *see p312*.

INFORMATION & TICKETS

CityLife, the *Las Vegas Weekly* and the 'Neon' supplement in Friday's *Las Vegas Review Journal* all carry theatre listings. For advance tickets, which aren't always necessary, contact the theatres direct rather than an outside agent such as Ticketmaster.

Theatre companies

Las Vegas Academy
Theatre Department *315 S 7th Street, at Bridger Avenue, Downtown.*
Lowden Theater for the Performing Arts *entrance at S 9th Street & Clark Avenue, Downtown.* **Both** *information 799 7857/tickets 1-800 585 3737/ www.lvacademytheatre.org. Bus Deuce, 206.* **Tickets** $3-$20. **Credit** (phone or online only) AmEx, Disc, MC, V. **Map** p334 D2.
Las Vegas's oldest secondary school was nearly razed in the early 1990s, but instead found new life as a magnet school for performing arts and international studies. The LVA's new Lowden Theater for the Performing Arts is a state-of-the-art facility that hosts technically impressive shows in a variety of genres: the 2007 season included productions of *Miss Saigon* and *The Grapes of Wrath*. These kids are far better than they should be.

Las Vegas Little Theatre
Schiff City, 3920 Schiff Drive, at Spring Mountain Road & S Valley View Boulevard, South-west Las Vegas (362 7996/www.lvlt.org). Bus 104, 203. **Tickets** $10-$20; $9-$17 reductions. **Credit** (online only) AmEx, MC, V.

The best Theatre

For the past
Nevada Ballet Theatre. *See p269.*

For the present
SEAT. *See p268.*

For the future
Las Vegas Academy. *See above.*

Las Vegas's oldest community theatre company has settled well into its new space, with both the main stage and the Fischer Black Box regularly hosting sell-out productions. The companion Insomniac Project occasionally features less mainstream works; other fledgling companies sometimes rent the building for productions and workshops.

New American Theatre Project
360 9959/www.newamericantheatreproject.com. **Tickets** $15-$20.
Soon after its 2006 launch, the edgy, independent and energetic NATP succeeded in raising the community theatre bar by several notches, a hybrid big-time/small-time scene that's like nothing the city has experienced to date. Made up in part of performers moonlighting from their day jobs in *Le Rêve* and various Cirque du Soleil productions, the group often perform in the Las Vegas Little Theatre's Fischer Black Box (*see above*), but have also performed at the Aruba Hotel (*see p104*).

Rainbow Company
229 6553/www.nevada.edu/~treed/rainbow. **Tickets** $7; $3-$5 reductions.
Operated under the auspices of the Cultural Affairs department at City Hall, this youth theatre group stages about a half-dozen different family-friendly productions each year. Shows are staged at the Reed Whipple Cultural Center or the Charleston Heights Arts Center (for both, *see pp243-244*).

SEAT (Social Experimentation & Absurd Theatre)
Arts Factory, 103 E Charleston Boulevard, at S Casino Center Boulevard, Downtown (736 4313/ www.godsexandbowling.com/seat.html). Bus Deuce, 206. **Tickets** $10-$25. **Credit** MC, V. **Map** p335 C3.
The mixed-media experiments produced by SEAT are somewhat bizarre and occasionally a little controversial. However, they do hang together with surprising cohesion, and the company has garnered a reputation as one of the most jarring and hilariously imaginative in Las Vegas.

Stagedoor Entertainment
581 5008/www.stagedoorlv.com. **Tickets** $6-$18.
A newer company known chiefly for its often small-scale productions staged at the Fischer Black Box in the Las Vegas Little Theatre, Stagedoor does stage at least one full-size affair at the outdoor Super Summer Theatre venue. In 2007, it was *Ragtime*, the Tony-award winning musical based on EL Doctorow's novel of the same name.

Super Summer Theatre
Spring Mountain Ranch State Park, Red Rock Canyon (594 7529/www.supersummertheatre.com). No bus. **Tickets** $10-$15. **No credit cards.**
Complete with looming rock walls and flittering bats, this outdoor amphitheatre is an appealingly novel place to catch a production, not least because it's far cooler here in summer than it is in Vegas itself. The season runs from June to August (bring your bug spray and, yes, a sweater) and usually features three or four populist shows performed in rotation. Patrons rent chairs or spread out on blankets with picnic baskets; get there early for a good spot. Tickets are available from the UNLV ticket centre (*see below*).

UNLV Theatre Department
4505 S Maryland Parkway, between E Flamingo Road & E Tropicana Avenue, University District (895 2787/http://theatre.unlv.edu). Bus 109, 213. **Tickets** $5-$25. **Credit** AmEx, Disc, MC, V. **Map** p333 Y3.
Together with the Nevada Conservatory Theatre, a highly ambitious crew that includes seasoned pros from all over the world as collaborators in the

New American Theatre Project.

No pain, no gain

White tigers, disappearing aeroplanes, campy pop singers… Las Vegas certainly isn't short of entertainment options. But for visitors looking for something above and beyond the Strip-standard parlour tricks and showtunes, there's a more visceral option. Much more visceral.

While most people spend their lives generally avoiding discomfort, Andrew S and Kelvikta have turned direct interaction with sharp blades, skin-piercing skewers and broken glass into an art form with the truly fearsome **Swing Shift Side Show**. In a city known for its mysteries and illusions, their double act is the real deal, pushing their bodies to mental and physical extremes in the name of entertainment.

Andrew admits that he has been 'weird' since he was a young lad. However, about ten years ago, the Hawaii native started honing that weirdness to creative effect, developing the kind of freak-show skills that he continues to put to good use in his performances. 'I took everything that was controlling me and learned how to benefit from it,' he says.

Since the group's inception several years ago, Swing Shift Side Show has performed for all manner of curious audiences, from jaded indie rockers to corporate executives, tattoo conventions to college psychology classes. Sometimes accompanied by part-time collaborators Aaron Zilch, Lady Diablo and the deliciously named Jenn O Cide, the duo swallows swords, walks on glass, breathes on fire and accomplishes a number of other feats that you're unlikely to find elsewhere on the Strip. Gents: once you've

seen what thay can do with a guy's reproductive organs, no kick in the groin will ever hurt as much again.

Irony of ironies? By day, Andrew is a massage therapist, specialising in deep-tissue treatments. 'Half the week I hurt other people for a living,' he chuckles. 'The other half, I hurt myself.' You have been warned.
● *For details of forthcoming performances, see www.swingshiftsideshow.com.*

classroom and on stage, UNLV presents a large spread of productions during spring and autumn in the Judy Bayley Theatre. Great productions can also be found in the Paul Harris Theatre and in the Black Box, where the MFA playwriting programme workshops pieces by students and faculty. An annual series of student-penned one-act plays in spring and autumn typically yields some memorable stuff.

Dance companies

Nevada Ballet Theatre
243 2623/www.nevadaballet.com. **Tickets** $25-$60. Associated with UNLV, the Nevada Ballet Theatre remains Las Vegas's only fully professional ballet company, favouring classical works and other time-

tested pieces likely to entertain even complete neophytes. Most shows are held at UNLV's Judy Bayley Theatre (*see left*), though larger productions are staged at the nearby Artemus Ham Concert Hall, also on campus (*see p254*).

UNLV Dance Theatre
4505 S Maryland Parkway, between E Flamingo Road & E Tropicana Avenue, University District (895 2787/http://dance.unlv.edu). Bus 109, 213. **Tickets** free-$25. **Credit** AmEx, Disc, MC, V. **Map** p333 Y3. UNLV's dance programme features a mix of performances by faculty, students and guest artists. Classical ballet and modern works are both represented, with productions held at the Artemus Ham Concert Hall and the Judy Bayley Theatre.

Weddings

Las Vegas's other industry.

Nevada authorities never saw fit to enforce a waiting period on couples wanting to apply for a marriage licence. So when couples realised that they'd have to wait a whole three days for a marriage licence in California (thanks to the Gin Law, enacted in 1912 to dissuade drunken lovers from taking the plunge), whirlwind elopements to Vegas quickly became the fashion. The trend was begun by Hollywood celebrities such as Betty Grable and Rita Hayworth, but legions of ordinary couples soon followed. The lenient state laws continue to draw impatient sweethearts, keen to get spliced without a moment's delay: the world's top destination for star-crossed lovers, Las Vegas hosts around 120,000 weddings each year.

In the early days, weddings were performed in hotel rooms or, more often, by a justice of the peace at the county clerk's office. The first wedding chapel to provide a one-stop service centre was founded by the Reverend JD Foster in 1933. But the wedding business didn't really take off until the '40s, when diminutive white steeples started popping up like pointy mushrooms along Las Vegas Boulevard. The industry suffered from the general slump that befell the city in the 1970s, but it bounced back with the glittering '90s renaissance, as hotel-casinos began to provide increasingly luxurious alternatives to the independent chapels that still stand south of Downtown.

In the past, couples were attracted by two main attributes to a Vegas marriage: the casual modernity of an instant wedding, and the price. Today, though, the once-trendy thing-to-do has become a tradition of sorts, with a unique all-American romance of its own. And it's still pretty cheap. On the Strip, you can get married on a spacecraft, atop the Eiffel Tower and on a gondola. Or you could head north towards Downtown to one of the town's old-school independent chapels, where Elvis himself (sort of) could preside over the ceremony.

A basic package wedding at an independent Downtown chapel can cost as little as $50. However, this price excludes a number of crucial services ('donation' to the minister, tip for the limo driver, flowers, etc), all of which can result in a heftier bill than anticipated. Set charges tend to be rather higher at resort chapels, but the packages include more options and extras. Before making your decision, call

around; there'll be something to suit your budget. And whether your cultural touchstone for the experience is Joan Didion's comic essay 'Marrying Absurd' or the episode of *Friends* in which Ross and Rachel get spliced after getting drunk in their hotel room, the lavish and loopy or lavishly loopy Vegas wedding of your dreams can be yours.

HOW TO WED IN VEGAS

Before taking the plunge, both bride and groom will need a marriage licence. The happy couple should present themselves at the **Marriage Bureau** (201 Clark Avenue, at S Casino Center Boulevard, Downtown, 671 0600, www.co.clark.nv.us/clerk) with $55 in cash and valid photo ID; the office is open a hard-working 8am to midnight every day. To save time, download the marriage licence application form from the website and fill it out before you arrive. You'll need to be able to prove that you are who you say you are and that you're at least 18 years of age; US citizens will need their social security numbers, while foreigners should bring ID in English. If either of you have been married before, you'll need to give the date and time the marriage ended (whether through divorce, death or annulment), although you won't need to produce any certificates.

Once you've got a marriage licence, you'll need to hold the wedding ceremony within a year. It must be conducted in the state of Nevada by a licensed person, who will present you with a marriage certificate once the deed has been done. The quickest and cheapest option is to walk the two blocks from the bureau to the **Commissioner of Civil Marriage** (1st floor, 309 S 3rd Street, at Bridger Avenue, Downtown,

The best Weddings

For classic Vegas romance
Little Church of the West. *See p274.*

For modern Vegas opulence
Venetian. *See p272.*

For only-in-Vegas speed
A drive-through wedding. *See p273.*

Eternal flame: **Little Chapel of the Flowers**. *See p273.*

671 0600, open 8am-10pm daily). Bring a witness and you can finish the job for the bargain price of $50 (cash only; they don't give change). But with so many more charismatic chapels within walking or drive-through distance, it's best to look around.

You may not need a reservation at many of the city's freestanding chapels. However, it's always best to make one in advance in order to avoid queues or disappointment, especially at weekends or other busy times (Valentine's Day, for example). The whole procedure could all be over in no time at all, but some ceremonies are more time-consuming; it all depends on how much fuss you want to make (and how much you're willing to spend).

Although gay and lesbian couples aren't eligible for marriage licenses, there are options in the city, although a little advance planning is necessary. Many chapels, both stand-alone operations and casino-based facilities, offer 'commitment ceremonies' for same-sex couples. However, they generally won't call it a wedding, and other chapels simply don't stage lesbian and gay ceremonies at all. Always call ahead.

Non-US citizens will need certified copies of both the marriage licence and the marriage certificate for their union to be recognised at home. Both are available at nominal cost from the Marriage Bureau and the office of the Commissioner of Civil Marriage respectively, at the time or thereafter by post. Non-US citizens may also require an apostille in order that their marriage is recognised as legally binding in their home country. This is easily obtainable (for a small fee) from the Notary Division of the Secretary of State; further details are available on the Marriage Bureau's website.

Wedding chapels

Hotel-chapel weddings

Resort chapels are more formal than their Downtown counterparts; couples should plan on booking ahead.

Artisan

1501 W Sahara Avenue, at Highland Drive, West of Strip (1-800 554 4092 x112/214 4000/ www.theartisanhotel.com). Bus 204. **Credit** AmEx, DC, Disc, MC, V. **Hotel** p102. **Map** p335 A4.
Antiques and gilt-framed prints make the Artisan an elegant, funky and very un-Vegas spot for a wedding. The Gothic chapel is delightfully spooky, and the bar and the dining hall are perfect for a chic reception.

Bellagio

3600 Las Vegas Boulevard South, at W Flamingo Road (1-888 987 3344/693 7700/www.bellagio.com). Bus Deuce, 202. **Credit** AmEx, DC, Disc, MC, V. **Hotel** p68. **Map** p336 A7.
Whether you choose the grand South chapel or the intimate East chapel, Bellagio offers a Vegas take on old-fashioned European opulence. The Amore package starts at $1,500; the Casa Bella is a cool $15,000.

Excalibur

3850 Las Vegas Boulevard South, at W Tropicana Avenue (1-800 811 4320/597 7278/www.excalibur. com). Bus Deuce, 202. **Credit** AmEx, DC, Disc, MC, V. **Hotel** p90. **Map** p336 A8.
Get dressed up in ermine-trimmed Renaissance garb to marry the king or queen of your heart in the Excalibur's fairytale Canterbury Chapel.

Flamingo

3555 Las Vegas Boulevard South, at E Flamingo Road (1-800 933 7993/733 3111/www.harrahs.com). Bus Deuce, 202. **Credit** AmEx, DC, Disc, MC, V. **Hotel** p78 **Map** p336 A7.

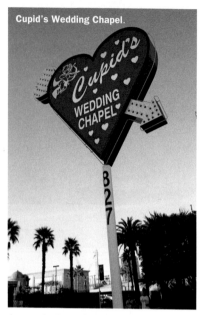

Cupid's Wedding Chapel.

Apparently, Bugsy Siegel's private suite was torn down to make room for the Flamingo Garden chapel, which remains one of the most elegant and old-school Strip-resort settings in which to marry.

Las Vegas Hilton

3000 Paradise Road, between E Sahara Avenue & E Desert Inn Road, East of Strip (1-866 945 5933/697 8750/www.lvhilton.com). Bus 108, 204, 213. **Credit** AmEx, DC, Disc, MC, V. **Hotel** p97. **Map** p335 C5.

The Hilton offers classic old-Vegas opulence, but you can also get married on the bridge of the *Enterprise* in the Star Trek Experience (*see p135*), with a Klingon as your witness and a reception in Quark's (*see p183*).

Paris Las Vegas

3655 Las Vegas Boulevard South, at E Flamingo Road (1-877 650 5021/946 7000/www.harrahs.com). Bus Deuce, 202. **Credit** AmEx, DC, Disc, MC, V. **Hotel** p74. **Map** p336 A7.

Whether you marry in the cavernous, 90-capacity chapel or choose a ceremony for 12 guests atop the Eiffel Tower, this is one way to say you got married in Paris and Las Vegas. For $69.99, bag yourself one of the resort's risqué wedding-cake toppers.

Rio

3700 W Flamingo Road, at S Valley View Boulevard, West of Strip (1-888 746 5625/777 7986/www. harrahs.com). Bus 202. **Credit** AmEx, DC, Disc, MC, V. **Hotel** p100. **Map** p333 X3.

Short of taking a helicopter or a hot-air balloon, the 50th-floor terrace at the Rio is the highest place to get wed in Vegas. Standard packages start at $150,

but it's better to build your own from the extensive list of options. Afterwards, head down to watch (of course!) *Tony 'n' Tina's Wedding* (*see p233*).

Venetian

3555 Las Vegas Boulevard South, between Sands Avenue & E Flamingo Road (1-866 548 1807/ 414 4280/www.venetianweddings.com). Bus Deuce, 105, 203. **Credit** AmEx, DC, Disc, MC, V. **Hotel** p75. **Map** p335 & p336 B6.

There's a traditional chapel here, but you can also say 'I do' on a gondola afloat a faux-canal in faux-Venice or on a footbridge under the blue faux-sky painted with faux-clouds. It's more charming than it sounds, though you'll pay for it: weddings range from $750 to $4,750.

Independent weddings

A Christian Pastor 2U

378 7000/641 9174/www.spiritofprophecy.org. **Credit** MC, V.

Pastor Rick and his family offer an evangelical Christian wedding service, which is something of a novelty in Vegas. The pastor is willing to travel to Cathedral Rock, Mount Charleston or elsewhere to conduct the ceremony.

Cupid's Wedding Chapel

827 Las Vegas Boulevard South, at Gass Avenue, Downtown (1-800 543 2933/598 4444/www.cupids wedding.com). Bus Deuce, 206. **Open** 10am-6pm Mon-Thur, Sun; 10am-1am Fri, Sat. **Credit** AmEx, Disc, MC, V. **Map** p334 C3.

This chapel's classic heart-shaped sign is one of the most striking beacons in the vicinity. Staff can be a little rude, but with packages starting at $179 (for the You Send Me wedding), who's complaining?

Graceland Wedding Chapel

619 Las Vegas Boulevard South, at Bonneville Avenue, Downtown (1-800 824 5732/382 0091/ www.gracelandchapel.com). Bus Deuce, 206. **Open** 9am-11pm daily. **Credit** AmEx, Disc, MC, V. **Map** p334 C2.

Rose bushes on the patio and a dove motif on the stained-glass windows complete the tidy air of this Elvistablishment, where options run from $199 to $799 (for the Famous Dueling Elvis package). The King will perform at any ceremony but he can only officiate at renewals.

Hitching Post Wedding Chapel

1737 Las Vegas Boulevard South, at E Oakey Boulevard, Stratosphere Area (1-888 540 5060/ 387 5080). Bus Deuce. **Open** 24hrs by appt. **Credit** AmEx, Disc, MC, V. **Map** p335 C4.

Billing itself as the oldest chapel in Las Vegas (a claim disputed by the Wee Kirk o' the Heather), the Hitching Post offers a wide range of packages. For $250, you can have Elvis witness your wedding; for $420, the King will walk the bride down the aisle. French, Polish, Russian and Spanish are spoken, though they appear to have difficulties with English.

A Hollywood Wedding

*2207 Las Vegas Boulevard South, between E
St Louis & E Sahara Avenues (1-800 704 0478/
731 0678/www.ahollywoodweddingchapel.com).*
Bus Deuce, 204. Open 10am-8pm Mon-Fri,
Sun; 10am-10pm Sat. **Credit** AmEx, MC, V.
Map p335 C4.
Deals at this spot just north of the Sahara range from
$99 to an all-inclusive top-end deal for $225. Add $100
and Elvis will sing and walk the bride down the aisle.

Las Vegas Wedding Specialists

*Suite A101, 4045 S Buffalo Drive, at W Flamingo
Road, West Las Vegas (1-888 638 4673/496 2613/
www.lasvegasweddingspecialists.com). Bus 202.*
Open by appt. **Credit** MC, V.

Multiple rooms (including a traditional chapel) and
costumes make this a good choice for a themed wedding, though they'll even come to your hotel room if
you're feeling really lazy. Saying 'I do' in a hot-air
balloon above the desert costs $675. Daphne will
provide religious ceremonies for same-sex couples.

Little Chapel of the Flowers

*1717 Las Vegas Boulevard South, at E Oakey
Boulevard (1-800 843 2410/735 4331/www.little
chapel.com).* **Bus Deuce. Open** 9am-9pm Mon-Thur;
9am-10pm Fri, Sat. **Credit** AmEx, Disc, MC, V.
Map p335 C4.
There are actually three chapels at this well-kept,
popular and very professional facility, along with
a florist and a photography studio. The chapel even

Driving me crazy

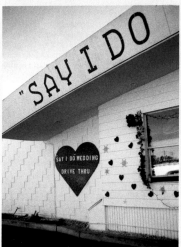

Two recently acquainted people stumble down
Las Vegas Boulevard with a yard of margarita
in one hand and ads for in-room strippers in
the other. Making out under the Eiffel Tower,
inspiration strikes. The pair decide, after
craps and blackjack and maybe another drink,
to go full-on Vegas (baby!) and get hitched.
A short ride to the Marriage Bureau ensues,
followed by the filling out of applications,
each party glancing over the other's shoulder
to learn their partner's surname.

Turning in their forms, they glance around
the tiny office and privately make bets as to
which of the other swaying couples will 'make
it'. The all-night clerk doesn't bother to check
a most-wanted list for bicoastal bigamist

killers stopping off from the desert leg of a
cross-country rampage and, instead, turns
the form into a licence.

So, where to go? How about the famous
Little Church of the West? Perhaps one of
the chapels whose signage inadvertently
advertises random celebrity couplings, such
as Joan Collins and Michael Jordan? Or maybe
they could get married by Elvis! Yes! But,
dammit, you have to book an Elvis in advance,
and time seems short. Then one of them
remembers you can get married in Vegas
without even leaving your car. You drive up,
roll down the window and greet an internet-
ordained minister leaning out to exchange
electroplated wedding bands for cash.

The ceremony, long on brevity and short on
belief structures, is pleasant but unlikely to
be remembered in its entirety. A few items
survive the haze: the wedding photo (the
happy couple show off their rings from the
front seats), a CD from an Arizona goth band
that they used in place of a wedding march
and a congratulatory gift pack from the chapel
containing, among other things, a heart-
shaped key ring and coupons for deodorant.

Las Vegas is beautiful in the morning, but
with daylight comes sobriety, and a reminder
that night is only night but daytime is Real
Life. The legally bound strangers emerge
from a Downtown motel, dry-mouthed and
slightly confused, and take a long look at
each other. Or a short one. Back in their
respective home towns, they initiate divorce
proceedings, surprised and disappointed
to learn that there isn't a drive-thru for that,
too, and, upon imparting their now-famous-
among-friends Vegas story, are often asked:
'So, did you get fries with that?'

offers couples the opportunity to broadcast weddings live on the internet, so the folks at home can share the joyful occasion. Prices start at $75; an additional $2,820 will buy you a wedding on the floor of the Grand Canyon, with helicopter flights included in the deal.

Little Church of the West

4617 Las Vegas Boulevard South, at W Russell Road (1-800 821 2452/739 7971/www.littlechurchofthe west.com). Bus Deuce. **Open** 10am-midnight daily. **Credit** AmEx, MC, V. **Map** p333 Y4.

Voted the city's best chapel for the last ten years by the *Las Vegas Review-Journal*, the quaint Little Church is in the National Registry of Historical Places. Celebs such as Zsa Zsa Gabor and Angelina Jolie have wed here; hopefully, your marriage will last a little longer.

Little White Wedding Chapel

1301 Las Vegas Boulevard South, at Park Paseo, Downtown (1-800 545 8111/382 5943/www.alittle whitechapel.com). Bus Deuce, 206. **Open** 8am-2am Mon-Thur, Sun; 24hrs Fri, Sat. **Credit** AmEx, Disc, MC, V. **Map** p335 C3.

It's not so little, actually: there are five chapels at this Vegas classic, where Frank Sinatra married Mia Farrow in 1966. The drive-through Tunnel of Love was designed for those with physical handicaps who perhaps found it difficult to leave their vehicles, but it's now popular with anyone after a quickie wedding in true only-in-Vegas style.

Mon Bel Ami

607 Las Vegas Boulevard South, at E Bonneville Avenue, Downtown (1-866 503 4400/388 4445/ www.monbelami.com). Bus Deuce, 206. **Open** 10am-10pm daily. **Credit** MC, V. **Map** p334 C2.

This well-landscaped and inviting chapel schedules its ceremonies a full hour apart. Hair and make-up artists, a manicurist and a massage therapist are among the services that can be arranged for couples. The Just for Two package starts at $99; the Ultimate costs $2,450 and includes the release of a white dove.

A Special Memory Wedding Chapel

800 S 4th Street, between E Bonneville Avenue & E Charleston Boulevard, Downtown (1-800 962 7798/384 2211/www.aspecialmemory.com). Bus Deuce, 206. **Open** 8am-10pm Mon-Thur, Sun; 8am-midnight Fri, Sat. **Credit** AmEx, DC, Disc, MC, V. **Map** p334 C2.

The original drive-through wedding costs just $25 plus gratuity. However, the inside of this three-chapel facility is bright and inviting; it even looks like a real church, albeit one with a lot of lights. Ceremonies cost anywhere from $199 to $1,899.

Sweethearts Wedding Chapel

1155 Las Vegas Boulevard South, between E Charleston & E Oakey Boulevards, Downtown (1-800 444 2932/385 7785/www.sweethearts chapel.com). Bus Deuce, 206. **Open** 10am-10pm daily. **Credit** Disc, MC, V. **Map** p335 C3.

This modest chapel seats 35 and has a bridal boutique on site. The $424 special includes a wedding gown, a headpiece, an underskirt, shoes and a tux. Items can also be selected on an 'à la carte' basis.

Vegas Adventure Wedding Chapel

1600 Las Vegas Boulevard South, at E Wyoming Avenue (1-888 463 1399/270 2522/www.vegas adventureweddings.com). Bus Deuce. **Open** 10am-8pm daily. **Credit** AmEx, Disc, MC, V. **Map** p335 C3.

This outfit essentially has two settings: traditional and extreme. You can get married in the chapel, where all weddings are scheduled at least an hour apart, or go for one of the helicopter-based options. The chapel is able to rent formalwear to guests.

Vegas Wedding Chapel

320 S 3rd Street, between E Bridger & E Lewis Avenues, Downtown (1-800 823 4095/933 3464/ www.702wedding.com). Bus Deuce & all DTC-bound buses. **Open** 9am-midnight daily. **Credit** AmEx, DC, Disc, MC, V. **Map** p334 C2.

This two-chapel venue is perfect for walk-ins: it's one of the closest to the Marriage Bureau. Packages start at $179, with the Tony, Tina's and Yours VIP package at $1,295; outdoor options include trips to Lake Mead and the Grand Canyon. Staff are able to broadcast weddings live on the internet.

Viva Las Vegas Chapel

1205 Las Vegas Boulevard South, at Park Paseo, Downtown (1-800 574 4450/384 0771/www.vivalas vegasweddings.com). Bus Deuce, 206. **Open** 9am-8pm Mon-Thur, Sun; 9am-10pm Fri, Sat. **Credit** AmEx, Disc, MC, V. **Map** p335 C3.

Known for its themed weddings, which range from sci-fi to western via the obligatory Elvis-slanted ceremony, Viva Las Vegas has more sets than some movie studios. Same-sex commitment ceremonies are treated with care.

Wee Kirk o' the Heather

231 Las Vegas Boulevard South, at Bridger Avenue, Downtown (1-800 843 5266/382 9830/www.wee kirk.com). Bus Deuce & all DTC-bound buses. **Open** 10am-8pm Mon-Thur, Sun; 9am-9pm Fri, Sat. **Credit** AmEx, Disc, MC, V. **Map** p334 D2.

This tiny chapel has been going since 1940 and is one of the oldest still in operation. Done out to resemble a toy version of a Scottish church, it's also one of the cutest. Prices range from $50 to $649.

Outdoor weddings

Many chapels can organise outdoor weddings, but how about exchanging vows at the top of a bungee tower before taking the plunge? For $400, **AJ Hackett** (385 4321) will take a video, pay the minister's fees and give you a helpful shove. For a more sedate experience, charter the 200-capacity **Desert Princess** paddlesteamer (www.lakemeadcruises.com) and get married on Lake Mead.

Trips Out of Town

Features

Grand Canyon. *See p284.*

Getting Started

Where to go when the money runs out.

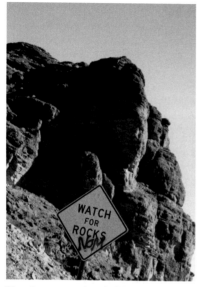

Though many test the principle when they come to Las Vegas, man cannot live on free cocktails and enormous buffets alone. After a while, iridescent sun will become more attractive than fluorescent striplights, and fresh air will appeal more than cranked-to-the-max air-conditioning; even if, as is the case in summer, the temperatures outside are well into three figures. Happily, the roads leading out of Las Vegas, from just north of Downtown and just south of the Strip, offer some terrific escape routes.

The options for day trips from Las Vegas are plentiful. Within 50 miles of the city, you'll find desert parks (**Red Rock Canyon**, **Valley of Fire**), boating and fishing (on **Lake Mead**), man-made marvels (**Hoover Dam**) and even somewhere to ski (**Mount Charleston**). Further afield lie more possibilities: to the north-west, the deserts of Nevada (and, eventually, the lights of **Reno**); to the east and north-east, the breathtaking national parks of Arizona and Utah (including the **Grand Canyon** and **Zion National Park**); and, to the west, the myriad glories of California, among them **Death Valley**.

GETTING AROUND

Though the **Greyhound** bus network (*see p306*) runs a service to many major towns and attractions, and though there are a number of companies offering tours to key sights such as the Grand Canyon (for details, *see p121*), by far the easiest and most comfortable way to travel from Las Vegas to the surrounding area is by car. The road connections from Vegas are good, with federal highways and interstates leading off at all points of the compass.

The main roads leaving the city are **I-15**, which runs south-west towards LA and north-east towards Salt Lake City, and **US 93** and **US 95**, which head, respectively, north into Nevada and south into Arizona and California. For details on renting a car, *see p308*.

THE DESERT

Lovers of the desert are drawn to the very starkness and nakedness that non-aficionados find so repellent. Compared to wetter, greener areas, deserts are easy to read: the 'bones' of mountains are laid bare before you, and the views are long and unobscured. And Las Vegas is one of the best places in the US from which to explore the country's dramatic desertscapes: it lies slap bang in the middle of one, the Mojave, and close to two others, the Great Basin and the Sonoran (also known as the Colorado Desert).

The standard definition of a desert is that it receives fewer than ten inches of precipitation a year and has high evaporation, but this is a pretty wide definition. Lack of cloud cover is important, because it causes heat to reradiate (go back into the sky) rapidly after it gets dark, hence the often high variation between daytime and night-time temperatures. All three deserts near Las Vegas share some characteristics, but they also exhibit great differences in landscape, vegetation and wildlife.

Covering the lower quarter of Nevada and part of southern California, the **Mojave Desert** is the smallest of the three types of desert. It includes the lowest absolute elevation and highest temperature recorded in the US (both in Death Valley, California), and receives almost no rain during an average year. However, not every year is average; when the rains do fall, the effects can be dramatic. The downpours that caused so much havoc in Death Valley during 2004 (*see p294*) also resulted in the most astonishing desert flowering in a generation:

in March 2005, parts of the park were briefly carpeted with flowers, and ancient dry lake beds were filled deep enough to support small boats.

Unless you venture far from Las Vegas, most of your driving will be in the Mojave Desert. You'll soon learn to recognise characteristic plants: the spidery creosote bush predominates, but its signature plant is the iconic, multi-armed Joshua tree, a yucca and a member of the lily family. Joshuas grow slowly and live up to 900 years, with an average height of 15 to 30 feet. In spring, the tips of the branches carry clusters of creamy flowers, which open for one night only and smell like mushrooms. After blossoming, the branch forks, eventually giving the Joshua its many-limbed form. The most extensive forests locally are found in the Mojave National Preserve (*see p293*).

The **Great Basin Desert**, which covers the northern three-quarters of Nevada and the western half of Utah, is the largest desert in the USA, extending over more than 158,000 square miles. It's described as a 'cold' desert, as more than half its precipitation occurs in winter in the form of snow, and its northern position and high base elevations mean it experiences lower average temperatures than areas to the south. It doesn't look much like a desert: silvery green sagebrush, Nevada's state plant, blankets vast areas, and many desert plants of popular imagination – such as large cacti, agaves and yuccas – are conspicuous by their absence. The transition between the Great Basin and the Mojave Deserts occurs north-west of Las Vegas, roughly between Beatty and Caliente.

The **Sonoran Desert** extends over part of southern California and the south-western quarter of Arizona. Like the Mojave, it's both lower and hotter than the Great Basin, and rain falls in both summer and winter. Unless you drive as far south as Joshua Tree National Park, you won't cross into the Sonoran.

The Colorado Plateau is a geological feature that includes south-eastern Utah and the north-eastern portion of Arizona.The colourful layers of sedimentary rock have been eroded into dramatic rock formations and stunning canyons, of which the Grand Canyon is the most magnificent.

DESERT SAFETY
Don't underestimate the dangers of travelling in the desert just because you'll be in an air-conditioned automobile: even the most modern cars can overheat and even break down under extreme conditions. If you're planning to drive any unpaved roads, check local conditions before you set out. Turn off air-conditioning on uphill stretches to lessen the chance of overheating the engine. Leave a window slightly open if you park the car for any length of time in the heat, and use a fold-up windscreen shade. Out of your vehicle, wear lots of sunscreen and light-coloured, body-covering clothing. Don't exert yourself in the midday sun. In or out of your car, carry plenty of water: you need to take on at least one gallon (four litres) a day.

Tourist information

Arizona Office of Tourism *1-866 275 5816/ 1-602 364 3700/www.arizonaguide.com.*
California Travel & Tourism Commission *1-800 862 2543/1-916 444 4429/ www.visitcalifornia.com.*
Nevada Commission on Tourism *1-800 638 2328/1-775 687 4322/www.travelnevada.com.*
Utah Travel Council *1-800 200 1160/1-801 538 1030/www.utah.com.*

Trip planning

Lake Mead National Recreation Area *293 8900/www.nps.gov/lame.*
Nevada Division of State Parks *Southern Nevada park information 486 5126/statewide office 1-775 684 2770/www.parks.nv.gov.*
US Forest Service *Humboldt-Toiyabe National Forest 1-775 331 6444/Spring Mountain National Recreation Area 515 5400/www.fs.fed.us/r4/htnf.*

Tours

See also p121.

Adventure Photo Tours
1-888 363 8687/889 8687/www.adventurephoto tours.com. **Credit** AmEx, Disc, MC, V.
Guided full- or half-day SUV trips to nearby spots such as Red Rock Canyon (4.5hrs, $89), Valley of Fire State Park (7hrs, $119) and Area 51 (8hrs, $195), as well as a variety of trips to the Grand Canyon.

Pink Jeep Tours
1-888 900 4480/895 6777/www.pinkjeep.com.
Credit AmEx, Disc, MC, V.
Trips to Red Rock (4hrs, $89), Valley of Fire (6hrs, $124) and a variety of other natural wonders around Vegas. In, yes, pink Jeeps.

The best Trips

For a short walk
Red Rock Canyon. *See p281.*

For a long drive
Reno. *See p298.*

For the big picture
Grand Canyon. *See p291.*

Trips Out of Town

Day Trips

Believe it or not, there's life beyond the neon.

Heading East

The Hoover Dam

The bare facts are staggering enough. It's 726 feet (221 metres) high. At its base, it's 660 feet (200 metres) thick; at its crest, it's 1,244 feet (379 metres) wide. It weighs 6.6 million tons. The building of it used enough concrete to pave a highway between San Francisco and New York. Its reservoir is 110 miles long and around 500 feet (150 metres) deep, and can hold enough water to cover the entire state of Nevada six inches deep. So far, so impressive. But then you actually catch sight of the Hoover Dam, and you can scarcely believe your eyes.

Without the Hoover Dam (née Boulder Dam, but renamed in 1947 for President Herbert Hoover, under whose administration the project was begun), much of the Southwest would not exist. The dam controls the Colorado River, providing electricity and water to nearly 20 million people in Nevada, California and Arizona, and makes it possible for cities and farmland to flourish in one of the driest, hottest and most inhospitable regions of the world.

In the early 20th century, the sheer power of the Colorado River made the building of the Hoover Dam both necessary and terrifying. Black Canyon was chosen as the location for the project, which was overseen by the Bureau of Reclamation and came with four main aims: flood prevention, silt control, water storage and electrical energy generation.

Building it was a mammoth task. First, the Colorado had to be temporarily diverted so the dam wall could be constructed. The concrete would have taken 100 years to set if left under normal conditions, so the cooling process was sped up by pumping ice-cold water through a network of pipes laid into each block of concrete. Next, vast pipes some 30 feet in diameter, known as penstocks, were lowered from an overhead cableway 800 feet (250 metres) above the canyon floor and squeezed into tunnels blasted out of the side walls. A vast army of 16,400 workers – remember, the project was built at the height of the Depression – laboured day and night for four years, finishing in February 1935... two years ahead of schedule.

The dam straddles the border between Arizona and Nevada. The skinny, perennially congested Highway 93 passes over the top, although the traffic will be eased in 2010 with the completion of the four-lane Hoover Dam Bypass a quarter-mile south of the dam.

The car park (parking $7) and the visitors' centre are on the Nevada side of the border. The latter is something of a necessary evil, through which the bulk of the 'Discovery' tour is conducted. Booking isn't required, but early arrival is recommended to beat both crowds and traffic. (The 'Hard Hat' tours, which took visitors closer to the action, were suspended post 9/11 and seem unlikely to resume.)

The tour ($11, $6-$9 reductions, free under-7s) is a mixed bag. The films are informative, but the constant waiting in line is frustrating and the way in which visitors are herded in and out of cinemas and galleries, while no fault of the knowledgeable, enthusiastic staff – it's to do with the hamfisted design of the centre itself – is an irritation. However, in between the movie and the exhibition, you'll get to see inside the dam, specifically a long hall that contains eight huge generators.

Back outside, note a few interesting features on or near the dam. Chief among them are two 30-foot sculptures, the Winged Figures of the Republic, flanking a flagpole above a terrazzo floor inlaid with a celestial map; it marks Franklin D Roosevelt's dedication of the dam in September 1935. The white mark on the shoreline indicates the flood level in 1983 when Lake Mead rose to within seven feet of the top. But while these are nice diversions, they won't be what you remember. That'll be the sheer size of the place, one of the greatest man-made constructions on the planet.

Getting there

To reach the Hoover Dam from Las Vegas, take US 93 south for 32 miles. You'll pass through Boulder City en route.

Tourist information

For information on tours, call 1-866 730 9097 or 494 2517, or see www.usbr.gov/lc/hooverdam. The **visitors' centre** is open 9am to 6pm daily; tours end at 5.15pm.

Hoover Dam.

Boulder City

Driving down Highway 93 from Vegas, you'll pass some small motels, and a few stalls selling Mexican pottery and other handicrafts. The occasional restaurant looms into view and then out of sight. Only slowly do you realise that something's missing. Built in 1931 to house the workers at the dam, Boulder City is the only town in Nevada where gambling is illegal.

Triangular in shape, Boulder City was the first 'model city' in the US, built according to progressive planning theories. The Bureau of Reclamation, government buildings and a park sit at the apex of the triangle, with the workers' houses radiating down from there. It was never intended to be a permanent settlement, it got a second wind during World War II and is now flourishing. There's more on the area at the **Boulder City/Hoover Dam Museum** (294 1988, www.bcmha.org, $1-$2) within the Boulder Dam Hotel, also home to a shop, a restaurant and the Chamber of Commerce.

Where to stay, eat & drink

Boulder City is small town Americana, and the best eating option in that vein is **Two Gals from Cal** (1632 Nevada Highway, 293 1793). **Milo's Best Cellars** (538 Nevada Highway, 293 9540, www.miloswinebar.com) in the old town offers outdoor seating, a lengthy wine list and a nice, lightish menu. Those who prefer the grain to the grape are directed to the newly opened **Boulder Dam Brewing Company** (453 Nevada Highway, 243 2739).

If the atmosphere appeals, stay at the historic **Boulder Dam Hotel** (turn right at Arizona Street; 293 3510, www.boulderdamhotel.com), a white and green building that counts Howard Hughes among its former guests. In the basement, **Matteo's Underground Lounge** (293 0098) stages regular shows by local bands.

Getting there

Boulder City is 25 miles south of Vegas (seven miles west of Hoover Dam) on US 93. To see the historic district, turn off at the business loop, which rejoins US 93 on the far side of the town.

Tourist information

In the Boulder Dam Hotel, the **Chamber of Commerce** (293 2034, www.boulder-city-chamber.com) has maps and local information.

Lake Mead

Around ten million visitors come to Lake Mead's 550 miles of shoreline each year to sail, fish, swim, water-ski, camp and generally enjoy watery pleasures in the desert. Wholly artificial, the lake was created when the Colorado was blocked by the Hoover Dam. It's an incongruous sight, a large blue splodge surrounded by barren mountains and canyon-tops.

The lake is the centrepiece of the huge **Lake Mead National Recreation Area**, which also includes Lake Mohave to the south (formed when the Colorado River was stemmed again in 1953 by the Davis Dam) and the desert east to

Trips Out of Town

the edge of Grand Canyon National Park (see p284) and north to Overton. There's a $5 permit fee per car (or $3 per person), which grants five days' access to the whole area.

Lakeside Scenic Drive (Highway 146) and Northshore Scenic Drive (Highway 167) skirt the western and northern sides of Lake Mead for nearly 60 miles. The route isn't very scenic, but it's the access road for five concession-operated marinas along the Nevada shoreline. All have small ranger stations, grocery stores and some form of restaurant; some also have swimming beaches (without lifeguards), picnic sites, motels, showers and gas stations. **Lake Mead Marina** on Boulder Beach (293 3484, www.riverlakes.com) and the **Las Vegas Boat Harbour** (565 9111, www.lasvegasboatharbour.com) are the largest, closest and busiest marinas; further north are the **Callville Bay Marina** (565 8958, www.callvillebay.com), the **Echo Bay Resort** (394 4000, www.echobay7c.com) and the **Overton Beach Resort** (394 4040, www.overtonbeachmarina.net).

The best way to explore the lake is by boat. There are numerous secluded coves, sandy beaches and narrow canyons accessible only by water, and the warm, clear lake is ideal for swimming: the water temperature averages 78°F (26°C) in spring, summer and autumn. You can hire a boat from the marinas; expect small fishing boats to cost around $20-$40 for two hours or $60-$120 per day, with large ski boats roughly three times the price. Alternatively, take a cruise on the *Desert Princess* paddlesteamer, run by **Lake Mead Cruises** (293 6180, www.lakemeadcruises.com).

Lake Mead offers some of the best year-round sport fishing in the country (see p263), but it's also one of the country's top freshwater scuba diving destinations. Visibility averages 30 feet and can reach double that in winter, better enabling divers to see the dramatic drop-offs, boat wrecks and even an underwater asphalt factory. The most popular location is **Scuba Park**, adjacent to Lake Mead Marina. You can rent equipment for around $35 a day from **American Cactus Divers** (3985 E Sunset Road, Henderson, 433 3483, www.americancactusdivers.com) or the **Blue Seas Scuba Center** (4661 Spring Mountain Road, South-west Las Vegas, 367 2822, www.blueseasscuba.com).

Where to stay, eat & drink

Try the eaterie on the water at the **Las Vegas Boat Harbor House Café** (565 9111) or the grander **Lake Mead Restaurant** at Echo Bay (394 4000). **Seven Crown Resorts** (1-800 752 9669, www.7crown.com) runs motels at **Echo Bay** (394 4000, rates $60-$115) and **Lake Mead Lodge** (293 2074, rates $85-$180). There are campgrounds (293 8491, rates $10) at all marinas bar Overton and Willow Beach. Close by is upscale **Lake Las Vegas** (see p150).

Lake Mead, more than a mere mirage in the heart – and the heat – of the desert.

Getting there

The visitors' center is 27 miles south of Vegas on Highway 93, at the junction with Lakeshore Scenic Drive (Highway 146). To reach Las Vegas Bay, Boulder Beach and Lake Mead marinas, bypassing the visitors' centre, take Boulder Highway south from Vegas and turn left at Lake Mead Drive (Highway 146), or take I-15/US 93 north to exit 45 in North Las Vegas and turn on to Lake Mead Boulevard east (Highway 147). Both routes join the shore road.

Tourist information

Consult the NPS website (www.nps.gov/lame). The **Alan Bible Visitor Center** (293 8990, 8.30am-4.30pm daily) on US 93 has maps and details on activities. There are also information stations at Overton Beach, Echo Bay, Callville Bay, Las Vegas Bay and Temple Bar.

Valley of Fire State Park

An hour north-east of Las Vegas lies a natural marvel that's every bit as spectacular as the resorts on the Strip. Bounded by the grey limestone Muddy Mountains to the south and west, Valley of Fire was the first state park in Nevada, and is still one of its most breathtaking.

The main attractions are the red sandstone formations, created from sand dunes deposited 135 to 150 million years ago and sculpted by wind and water into bizarre, anthropomorphic shapes: look for **Elephant Rock** and **Seven Sisters** along Highway 169, the east–west road through the park. A two-mile loop road runs past some of the most dramatic rock formations.

The park is easily explored in a day. Hiking is permitted, but there are few marked trails, and all are very short. Get advice on hiking and a trails map from the visitors' centre (*see below*). The road north from the centre offers a panoramic view of multicoloured sandstone at **Rainbow Vista** and ends at the White Domes picnic area. An easy trail from Rainbow Vista leads to spectacular rocks at **Fire Canyon**, from where you can see the spot where Captain Kirk met his doom in *Star Trek: Generations*.

Atlatl Rock on the scenic loop road has a number of petroglyphs, while others are visible on the short trail to **Mouse's Tank**, a natural water basin used in the 1890s as a hideout by a renegade Indian known as Mouse. Visit the **Lost City Museum** in Overton (397 2193, www.comnett.net/~kolson), eight miles north of the park, to learn about the Indian inhabitants, from the ancient Basketmaker people and the Puebloans (Anasazi) to the Paiute, whose descendants still live in southern Nevada.

Summer highs top 110°F (43°C); as such, the best times to visit are spring and autumn. If you're lucky, you may spy a desert tortoise (Nevada's state reptile) and you're sure to see antelope ground squirrels (aka chipmunks). Don't feed or pet them: they're suspected of carrying the fleas that transmit bubonic plague.

Getting there

Head north on I-15 for 33 miles to Highway 169: it's 17 miles to the park's western entrance. You can also enter the park from Lake Mead, off Northshore Scenic Drive (*see above*).

Tourist information

Advice on hiking and a trails map are available from the **visitors' centre** (397 2088, http://parks.nv.gov/vf.htm), which also has displays on the area's geology, ecology and human history. Signposted along Highway 169, it's open 8.30am-4.30pm daily. Park entrance is $6.

Heading West

Red Rock Canyon & around

A mere 20 miles from the gaming tables of Vegas is one of Nevada's most beautiful outdoor areas. The cool, deep-cut canyons of the Red Rock Canyon National Conservation Area make it a popular hiking spot year-round, while climbers come here from all over to enjoy some of the best rock climbing in the US.

Part of the Spring Mountains, Red Rock Canyon has as its centrepiece a nearly sheer escarpment of Aztec sandstone, the remnant of ancient sand dunes that covered the area 180 million years ago. Roughly 65 million years ago, the Keystone Thrust Fault pushed older grey limestone over younger sandstone, reversing the normal layering and resulting in today's dramatic landscape. The red and cream Calico Hills are more rounded, as they're not protected from erosion by a higher limestone layer.

Attracted by the water, Native Americans have used Red Rock Canyon since about 3500 BC: evidence remains in the form of rock art (etched petroglyphs and painted pictographs), as well as artefacts such as arrowheads and ceramics. More than 45 mammal species also inhabit the park, among them mountain lions, coyotes, kangaroo rats, mule deer and the near-mythical desert bighorn sheep, but you'll be lucky to spot any. The most visible animals are the non-native burros (donkeys), around 50 of which live around Red Rock Canyon.

Observe from a distance and never feed them (it's illegal and dangerous).

Stop first at the visitors' centre (clearly signed) for information and a map, before exploring the one-way, 13-mile scenic drive (also popular with cyclists; see p263) through the canyon. The road gives access to numerous hiking trails and three picnic sites. Some trails are not marked clearly and require some scrambling; best take a topo map (available at the visitors' centre) and a compass.

A good introduction to the Calico Hills at the start of the drive is the two-and-a-half-mile **Calico Tank** trail from Sandstone Quarry. Just above the tank is a fine view (smog permitting) of the valley and the Strip's casino monoliths. Other good short summer hikes include **Ice Box Canyon** and **Pine Creek Canyon**. For further details of the scores of other trails, pick up a copy of the BLM's trail leaflet. Guided hikes are led by park staff at the weekends and some weekdays, and by the Sierra Club (363 3267, www.sierraclub.org).

Red Rock is hugely popular with rock climbers. Stop at **Desert Rock Sports** (see p211) for gear and some practice on the indoor wall, before calling in at the visitors' centre. There's further detail in three guides: Joanne Urioste's *The Red Rocks of Southern Nevada* and *The Red Book Supplement* (both Verex Press, $21.95 & $19.95), and Todd Swain's *Rock Climbing: Red Rocks* (Falcon Press, $30). Alternatively, get to know the Old West like an old Westerner with **Cowboy Trail Rides** (387 2457, www.cowboytrailrides.com), which can saddle you up and take you on a tour of Red Rock. Rides are accompanied by a guide; first-timers are welcome, and booking is required.

If you'd prefer something less physical, head further west on Highway 159 to the green oasis of **Spring Mountain State Park**, at the base of the dramatic Wilson Cliffs. Admission to the park includes entrance to the New England-style ranch house, where the $6 day-use fee is payable (875 4141, http://parks.nv.gov/smr.htm, 10am-4pm daily). Stroll around the buildings in the fenced grounds and picnic on a grassy meadow. There are walking tours year-round, and open-air theatre and concerts in summer.

Bonnie Springs Old Nevada

1 Gun Fighter Lane, off Highway 159 (875 4191/ www.bonniesprings.com). No bus. **Open** *May-Oct* 10.30am-6pm daily. *Nov-Apr* 10.30am-5pm daily. **Admission** $20/car. **Credit** MC, V.

South on Highway 159 sits this mock Wild West town, with a melodrama and hanging staged daily (times vary by season). It's rather dilapidated but good fun; visitors can take a horse ride ($30), and there's also a free petting zoo, a restaurant and a motel (875 4400, rates $65-$145).

Getting there

To reach the visitors' centre, head west on Charleston Boulevard (Highway 159) for 20 miles. If you're staying near the southern end of the Strip, drive south on I-15, take Highway 160 (towards Pahrump), then turn right on to Highway 159, passing Bonnie Springs and Spring Mountain en route to Red Rock Canyon.

Tourist information

The **Red Rock Canyon visitors' centre** (515 5361, www.nv.blm.gov/redrockcanyon), offers information, maps and a chance to pay the $5-per-car fee. The centre is open daily from 8.30am to 4.30pm; however, the scenic drive itself is open longer hours (6am-8pm Apr-Sept; 6am-7pm Oct, Mar; 6am-5pm Nov-Feb).

Mount Charleston & around

It's true: you can jet-ski near Las Vegas in the morning and snow-ski in the afternoon. A mere 45 minutes north-west of the city lies the Spring Mountain Recreation Area, more commonly known as **Mount Charleston**. It's part of the massive Spring Mountain Range, dominated by Charleston Peak, the highest point in southern Nevada at 11,918 feet (3,633 metres). In the winter, you can ski and snowboard at Lee Canyon; in summer, hike the forested slopes, far cooler than the city. There are also picnic sites and several campgrounds in the area.

Watch the vegetation change as you climb into the mountains, moving from creosote, bursage and Joshua trees on the lower slopes to piñon and Utah juniper, through ponderosa pine and mountain mahogany, and finally to gnarled bristlecone pines where the tree-line peters out at 10,000 feet (3,000 metres). Due to the isolation of the range, around 30 species of flora and fauna are unique to this 'sky island'.

There are two roads into the area, both off US 95. Nearest to Las Vegas is Highway 157 (Kyle Canyon Road), which ascends prettily through winding canyons and wooded slopes to the **Mount Charleston Hotel** (see p283), a rustic-style lodge with a huge lobby warmed by an open fireplace. The road continues west for another few miles, past a small park office (872 5486, closed Mon & Tue in winter), terminating at **Mount Charleston Lodge** (see p283). Here, you'll find a 24-hour bar, restaurant, riding stables and some delightful log cabins.

From the Mount Charleston Hotel, Highway 158 (Deer Creek Highway) heads north to the junction with Highway 156 (Lee Canyon Road). Seven miles along Highway 158, the short Desert View Trail leads to a spectacular view of the valley and the mountains. At the junction with Highway 156, turn left for the ski area, usually open between November and April. The elevation here is 8,500 feet (2,600 metres), with three chairlifts leading up another 1,000 feet (300 metres) to 13 slopes. (For more on skiing in the area, *see p250*.) Drive back to US 95 on Highway 158 for a fine view of the desert below.

The US Forest Service prefers hikers to stick to designated trails, but there are numerous unmarked hikes around Mount Charleston (take a compass and a trail guidebook). The six-mile **Bristlecone Trail** provides worthwhile views of limestone cliffs and bristlecone pines; the short trail to **Mary Jane Falls** is both more strenuous and more rewarding, with hikers climbing 900 feet (270 metres) to a waterfall. The mother of all hikes, though, is the 18-mile round trip to **Mount Charleston Peak**, a difficult and demanding trail that's not clear of snow until as late as July. From the summit you can enjoy a stunning view of southern Nevada, eastern California and southern Utah. For all hikes, you'll need warm clothing and water.

On your way to Mount Charleston, stop off at **Floyd Lamb State Park**; it's the former site of Tule Springs Ranch, where prospective divorcees waited out their six-week residency requirement in the 1940s and '50s. Located 15 miles from the city (though now surrounded by sprawl), its lush lawns, shady cottonwoods and four lakes make it a popular picnicking and fishing spot. It's best to avoid weekends if you don't like crowds. However, during the week, it's a serene spot: not even the swankiest Strip hotels can match the peacocks that wander around the white ranch buildings. You can hire horses from the old stables ($20/hour). There's no camping, though: the park, for which admission costs $6 (486 5413, http://parks. nv.gov/fl.htm), is solely a day-use facility.

Further away is the **Desert National Wildlife Refuge** (646 3401, http://desert complex.fws.gov), established in 1936 to protect the desert bighorn sheep and its habitat. A gravel road leads to a self-service information centre, where you can pick up a leaflet on the refuge and stroll around the ponds of Corn Creek Springs. The western half of the refuge is used by the Nellis Air Force Range as a bombing area and is closed to the public, while the rest is a nature reserve, accessible by two unmaintained dirt roads: you'll need a high clearance or 4WD vehicle in order to gain access to them. Summer is the best time to spot the elusive bighorn sheep and the wildflowers are usually in bloom from March to May.

Where to stay, eat & drink

Accommodation and eating options on Mount Charleston are few and far between. The **Mount Charleston Hotel** (1-800 794 3456, 872 5500, www.mtcharlestonhotel.com) has a cavernous dining room and 57 rooms (rates $89-$400), though a better bet is the characterful **Mount Charleston Lodge** (1-800 955 1314, 872 5408, www.mtcharlestonlodge.com), where the cosy log cabins (rates $144-$214) come with desks and offer wonderful views down over the landscape. The restaurant serves solid American fare, and doubles as a bar in the evening. There are also several camping areas; midweek, you can often find a spot by driving in, though weekends book up early in season.

Getting there

Take US 95 north from Downtown for about 35 miles to reach Highway 157; Highway 156 is about 12 miles further on. In winter, you'll need snow chains on the mountain roads.

Rolling on the river

Lake Mead, the reservoir that sprawls off it, is unnatural; as, of course, is the Hoover Dam, which diverts water into it. Amid such man-made monsters so close to a city defined by artifice, it's easy to forget that the Colorado River itself is a living, breathing watercourse. But so it goes and so it flows, winding its way down through the Southwest towards the Gulf of California. You can join it for a while.

One of several firms that operates kayaking trips on the Colorado, **Desert Adventures** (510 4746, www.kayaklasvegas.com) offers visitors unique views of the Hoover Dam from

the water below. Sign up to DA's day-long kayaking tour and you'll set off from close to the dam's base; from here, you'll cruise eight miles downriver in the company of a guide, stopping for a packed lunch en route.

It can get windy down on the surface, but the dam and the width of the river both help mitigate against whitewater. It's perfect for the novice, not least because it's surprisingly easy to learn. The views are amazing and the exercise bracing. And after the awful traffic approaching the dam, all that open space will come as a glorious relief.

Arizona

Nature's awe-inspiring way of putting Las Vegas into perspective.

Of Arizona's two major towns, sprawling **Phoenix** has little to offer the visitor except sun and golf , while the more characterful **Tucson** is too far away to visit comfortably in a couple of days. It's no surprise, then, that most visitors to Arizona from Las Vegas head as directly west as the roads allow, towards one of the world's great natural wonders.

Note that Arizona observes Mountain Standard Time year-round, without daylight saving time in summer. This means that from the first Sunday in November until the second Sunday in March, Arizona is one hour ahead of Las Vegas, but is effectively in the same time zone for the remainder of the year.

Grand Canyon National Park

You'll have seen pictures, TV footage, maybe even an IMAX film on a larger-than-life-size screen. You'll have read about it, heard about it, talked about it. You may feel like you know it before you've ventured into it. And still nothing will prepare you for your first glimpse of the epic, breathtaking, unknowable Grand Canyon.

Grand Canyon National Park sprawls across a length of 277 miles, most of which is difficult to reach and rarely visited; just a tiny portion is accessible from the **South Rim**, where most visitors congregate. The canyon is misnamed: it's not just one rip in the earth, but a series of canyons surrounding the central gorge cut by the Colorado River, a staggering 5,000 feet (1,500 metres) from top to bottom. At an average elevation of 7,000 feet (2,150 metres), the South Rim isn't unbearably hot in summer, but temperatures a mile further down at the bottom can edge beyond 110°F (43°C). The best months to visit are April, May, September and October, avoiding the relatively rainy (and tourist-packed) summer months and the snowbound winters.

Entrance to the park costs $25 per car ($12 per person for pedestrians and cyclists), valid for seven days. Although it's possible to make a see-it-and-scram round trip in one long day, we recommend that you stay at least two nights, time to explore the village, spin around the rim drives, take in the various lookout points and venture into the canyon itself.

En route to the South Rim

Some 150 miles west of the South Rim, the Grand Canyon forms the northern boundary of the Hualapai Indian Reservation. Although it's not as spectacular as the South Rim, the western canyon is closer to Las Vegas and will give you a taste of the grandeur further east.

Roughly an hour south-east of Las Vegas, there's the option of a detour to a high-concept, high-budget attraction within the reservation. Opened in 2007, the **Grand Canyon Skywalk** (1-877 716 9378, 1-702 878 9378, www.grand canyonskywalk.com) is a freestanding glass bridge that extends directly over the canyon, giving visitors the opportunity to stand 4,000 feet (1,200 metres) above the earth and look down into it. So far so good, until you take into account the breathtaking $75 admission fee ($25 for the Skywalk, a further $50 to enter the reservation) and the fact that cameras aren't allowed on the damn thing.

If money is no object and you have a photographic memory, the Skywalk is accessible by taking a left off US 93 on to Pierce Ferry Road, 40 miles south of the Hoover Dam, and then turning right on to Diamond Bar Road 28 miles later. From here, it's a simple drive to the reservation's other attractions, such as rafting tours (1-928 769 2219), camping and helicopter rides. The tribal headquarters are a further south in **Peach Springs**, where the **Hualapai Lodge** (900 Route 66, Peach Springs, 1-928 769 2230) provides lodging and dining facilities along with permits for sightseeing, fishing and camping. For details, head to www.destinationgrandcanyon.com.

If you choose to pass on the Skywalk and continue along US 93, you'll hit **Kingman**. From here, you have a choice. If you're in a hurry, take speedy I-40 east. But if you've a little more time and a little more romance about your person, head along what is now the longest surviving portion of the iconic Route 66. Much of the 2,448-mile Mother Road, which originally linked Chicago with Santa Monica, has been bypassed or replaced by major highways, a victim of the motor travel whose population its construction predicted. But this portion survives, just about. In Kingman, swing by the **Route 66 Museum** (120 Andy Devine Drive, 1-928 753 9889, www.kingmantourism.org),

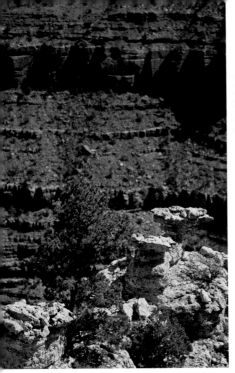

If you have sufficient patience to avoid driving straight to the rim, park your car and take a free shuttle bus to the **Canyon View Information Plaza**, where you'll find a visitors' centre and bookstore (open 8am-5pm daily). Pick up a variety of literature from here, offering comprehensive information on sights, transportation, facilities and activities, and ask the rangers for tips on hikes. Stroll to **Mather Point** for your first gob-smacking view of the canyon, before riding the shuttle bus from Information Plaza into Grand Canyon Village.

Grand Canyon Village

Travellers have been coming to gawp at the Grand Canyon since the 19th century, and Grand Canyon Village remains proud of its history. The village is dotted with historic buildings, many of them built by pioneering female architect Mary Colter for the Fred Harvey Travel Company.

Pick up a leaflet and take the self-guided walking tour around the village's historic district, starting at the **Santa Fe Railway Station** (1909), the terminus for the **Grand Canyon Railway** (*see p288*). Across the road on the canyon's edge is the luxurious **El Tovar Hotel**, a wooden structure in hunting-lodge style that cost a cool $250,000 to build in 1905. Next to it is the **Hopi House**, designed by Colter in 1904 as a showroom and salesroom for Indian handicrafts. Colter modelled the building on a terraced Hopi dwelling, using local stone and wood and employing Hopi builders. Nearby is **Verkamps**, completed in 1906 and one of the canyon's oldest continuously operating stores.

Walking west from the hotel along the Rim Trail, you'll pass the modern **Kachina** and **Thunderbird** lodges, and the pioneer-style, stone-and-log **Bright Angel Lodge**, designed by Colter in 1935. If you're here in winter, warm your hands at the fabulous 'geological' fireplace, the design of which mimics the layers of rock in the Grand Canyon. The hearth is made from stone from the bed of the Colorado River; at the top of the chimney breast sits a layer of Kaibab limestone.

Just beyond Bright Angel Lodge is the **Bucky O'Neill Suite**, which dates from the 1890s and is the oldest surviving building on the rim, and the **Lookout Studio** (Colter, 1914), which now houses a gift shop. Perched on the edge of the precipice, the studio was designed as an observation building from which visitors could view the canyon. Colter didn't want the building to detract from its surroundings, and created a stone structure that merges with the surrounding rock. From a distance, the structure is almost invisible.

before driving west through dusty **Hackberry**, the aforementioned Peach Springs and on to **Seligman**, where you can reconnect with I-40.

Continuing west along I-40 will bring you to the town of **Williams**, 60 miles south of the National Park. Some use the town as a staging post en route to the canyon, the entrance to which is 60 miles due north along Route 64 or along a picturesque, narrow-gauge steam railway (*see p288*). Others, though, prefer the larger **Flagstaff**, 35 miles east. Situated at the base of the **San Francisco Peaks**, the highest mountains in Arizona, this pleasant railroad and university town has motels, restaurants, cafés and a brewpub, as well as the **Lowell Observatory**, from which the planet Pluto was first spotted in 1930. For more, contact the Chamber of Commerce (101 E Route 66, 1-928 774 4505, www.flagstaffchamber.com).

The South Rim

The majority of the annual five million visitors to Grand Canyon National Park head for the **South Rim** and the restaurants, shops and sights of **Grand Canyon Village**, on the edge of the canyon lip. Inevitably, it's crowded, but it remains remarkably untouristy; or, in some cases, pleasantly retro-touristy. It's also closer to the Colorado River than the North Rim and affords much better views into the canyon.

The nearby **Kolb Studio** was built by pioneering photographers Ellsworth and Emery Kolb, who started snapping mule riders here in 1902. The lack of water on the rim meant the brothers were required to hike halfway down the canyon to their developing tent at Indian Gardens to process the photos, then clamber back to the top before the mules returned. (To this day, all water at the South Rim is pumped up from inside the canyon; look for the trans-canyon pipeline on the Bright Angel Trail.) The Kolbs were also the first to film a boat trip down the Colorado, in 1912. The studio houses a bookstore and gallery, and has displays on the brothers' work. Beyond here is the head of the Bright Angel Trail (*see p290*).

Along the South Rim

Two roads lead west and east from the village along the canyon rim, each providing very different views into the canyon. You can also walk along the edge of the rim on the 12-mile, pedestrian-only **Rim Trail**. The village section of the trail is paved; elsewhere it can get rocky.

The eight-mile **Hermit Road** is closed to private vehicles. Instead, visitors are encouraged to take the shuttle bus that departs from the western edge of the village to **Hermit's Rest**, built by Mary Colter as a refreshment stop in 1914. The building, now in use as a gift shop, is deliberately primitive in style, and was designed to blend with its natural surroundings (fortunately, a Swiss chalet design was rejected). From here, you can set off on the Hermit Trail into the canyon (*see p290*).

The shuttle bus stops at various observation points on its way west. Among them is the spectacular **Abyss**, where the Great Mohave Wall drops 3,000 feet (900 metres) to the Tonto Platform above the Colorado River. On its return, the bus stops only at Mohave Point and **Hopi Point**. If you're planning to watch the sunset, check the time of the last bus before you leave to avoid a long, dark walk back to the village.

Along the East Rim, **Desert View Drive** runs 25 miles in the opposite direction as far as the park's eastern entrance. On the way, the road passes several excellent lookout points, with access to the **South Kaibab** and **Grandview Trails** (*see pp290-291*). Near the end of the drive, there's an 800-year-old ruin of an Anasazi pueblo and the **Tusayan Museum**, which provides somewhat scanty information on the history and culture of the canyon's Native American inhabitants.

The drive finishes at **Desert View**, which offers the clearest views of the Colorado River. This is also the location of the **Watchtower**, a circular, 70-foot (21-metre) tower regarded as Colter's masterpiece. A remarkable re-creation of the ancient Indian towers Colter had seen at Mesa Verde and Canyon de Chelly, the ground-floor room is modelled after a kiva (or sacred ceremonial chamber), while the roof provides a panoramic view of the Grand Canyon, the Painted Desert and the San Francisco Peaks, 40 miles to the south. The centrepiece is the **Hopi Room**, decorated with vivid Hopi designs depicting various gods and legends.

To learn more about the geology, history and archaeology of the South Rim, join one of the National Park Service's ranger-guided walks or activities. Check the park's website or ask at the visitors' centre for a programme schedule.

Where to eat & drink

There are three restaurants, two self-service cafés and a takeaway snack bar in the Grand Canyon Village, all open daily. The splendid, dark wooden dining room with its large Indian murals at the **El Tovar Hotel** is very popular: you can take your chances at breakfast (6.30-11am) and lunch (11.30am-2pm), but must book for dinner (5-10pm; 1-928 638 2631 ext 6432); hotel guests take priority over non-guests.

Nearby are the less formal **Bright Angel Restaurant** (6.30am-10pm) and the **Arizona Room** steakhouse (4.30-10pm, also 11.30am-3pm during peak season). **Maswik Lodge** has a sports bar (5-11pm) and an inexpensive but rather institutional cafeteria (6am-10pm); there's a larger cafeteria at **Yavapai Lodge** (6.30am-8pm). Wherever you dine, have a drink in the lounge at the El Tovar (11am-11pm), decorated by the ubiquitous Colter. There are also snack bars at Hermit's Rest (9am-5pm) and Desert View (9am-4pm), and a deli at Market Plaza (8am-6pm).

Where to stay

There's plenty of accommodation in Grand Canyon Village, and demand is high: book as far ahead as you can (we're talking months, not weeks). That said, there are sometimes rooms available for walk-in visitors at Yavapai and Maswik Lodges, occasionally even in high season. Book through **Xanterra Parks & Resorts** (1-888 297 2757, 1-303 297 2757, www. grandcanyonlodges.com). Generally speaking, the more expensive rooms at the hotels and lodges listed below come with a canyon view.

Complete with a grand lobby adorned with stuffed animal heads, The **El Tovar Hotel** (double $142-$205), offers the most splendid lodging in the village. Try to get a room with a spacious private balcony overlooking the rim.

Trips Out of Town

Other options are the 1930s **Bright Angel Lodge** (double $52-$143) and the more modern, motel-style **Kachina** and **Thunderbird Lodges** (double $139-$152), also on the edge of the canyon. **Maswik Lodge** (double $77-$138) and **Yavapai Lodge** (double $97-$126) are located in a pine forest a short walk away.

There are also two campsites at the South Rim, run by the National Park Service. There are more than 300 pitches at the **Mather Campground**, but booking is recommended from March to mid November (1-877 444 6777, www.recreation.gov). Outside these times, campsites are available on a walk-up basis, and the standard $18 fee drops by $3. Roughly 25 miles east of Grand Canyon Village, **Desert View Campground** is open from mid May to mid October on a walk-up basis ($12).

A few miles south of Grand Canyon Village, just outside the park, is **Tusayan**. At the National Geographic Visitor Center, there's a supremely superfluous IMAX cinema and a rather more useful park fee pay-station, which will mean you don't have to queue on entry. Among the basic motels are the **Red Feather Lodge** (1-800 538 2345, 1-928 638 2414, www.redfeatherlodge.com), the **Best Western Squire Inn** (1-800 622 6966, 1-928 638 2681, www.grandcanyonsquire.com) and a **Holiday Inn Express** (1-888 473 2269, 1-928 638 3000, www.grandcanyon.hiexpress.com). A free shuttle-bus service runs between Tusayan and the village. There are also plenty of motels in Flagstaff and Williams.

For lodging options in the canyon, *see p291.*

Getting there

By air

Several companies offer scheduled flights from the Las Vegas area to Grand Canyon Airport at Tusayan. Among them are **Air Vegas** (1-800 940 2550, 1-702 433 1677, www.airvegas.com), which operates several flights a day from the airport at Boulder City; a return flight costs $159. For details of sightseeing flights over the Grand Canyon, *see p121.*

By bus

Bus service between Flagstaff, Williams and Grand Canyon Village is offered by **Open Road** (1-800 766 7117, 1-928 226 8060, www.openroadtours.com), which charges $27 one-way or $54 return between Flagstaff and the Grand Canyon. **Greyhound** (*see p306*) runs bus services from Las Vegas to Flagstaff (5.5hrs-6hrs; $50.50 single, $101 return).

By car

To reach the South Rim, head south-east on US 93 to I-40 east, then turn left (north) on to Highway 64 at Williams. It's 290 miles from Vegas and the journey takes about 5hrs. As an alternative, drive to Williams and board the Grand Canyon Railway (*see below*).

By rail

The **Grand Canyon Railway** (1-800 843 8724, 1-928 773 1976, www.thetrain.com) runs train services from the depot in Williams to the old **Santa Fe Station** in the heart of Grand Canyon Village. Trains leave Williams at 10am and depart from the Grand Canyon at 4pm except during busy periods, when two services are run in each direction (9am and 10.30am from Williams, 3pm and 4.30pm in the opposite direction). There are various 'classes' of service in an assortment of historic carriages, and characters in costume entertain passengers en route. The trip takes 2.25hrs; tickets, which exclude the park fee, cost $65-$170 ($30-$95 reductions).

Getting around

To encourage a more serene appreciation of nature, the park service has limited private-vehicle access in some areas and is expanding pedestrian and bicycle routes around the South Rim. The bus shuttles are a pleasant and workable alternative to private transport.

By bus

A free shuttle-bus service operates on three interconnecting services around the South Rim: the **Village Route**, serving Canyon View Information Plaza and the main village destinations; the **Hermit's Rest Route**, along the rim from the west side of the village to Hermit's Rest; and the **Kaibab Trail Route**, from Canyon View to Yaki Point. A route for visitors needing mobility assistance operates from Canyon View to Mather Point.

By car

Canyon View Information Plaza, Mather Point, Yaki Point Road and Hermit Road are not accessible to private vehicles.

By coach

Choose from various Xanterra-run sightseeing trips around the canyon rim, including the **Hermit's Rest Tour** ($18.25 per person), the **Desert View Tour** ($31.50), and popular 90min **Sunrise** and **Sunset Tours** ($14.50). For reservations, call 1-888 297 2757 or 1-303 297 2757; alternatively, visit the desks at Bright Angel, Maswik and Yavapai Lodges, or at Canyon View Information Plaza.

By taxi

A 24hr taxi service is available on 1-928 638 2822.

The North Rim

From the South Rim, you can see lightning forks hit the **North Rim** ten miles across the canyon. However, to reach it, you'll have to hike down to the bottom and back up again, drive 220 miles all the way around the canyon, or catch the daily shuttle bus.

The North Rim is 1,000 feet (300 metres) higher than the South Rim and is only open from mid May to mid October. It has fewer

facilities and, thus, fewer visitors than the South Rim, which is why many longtime visitors prefer it up here; the tranquil atmosphere can still evoke what it may have been like to visit the canyon in the early days. That said, you should book ahead for lodging, which is at a premium during busy seasons. Facilities include a visitors' centre, a grocery, a camping supplies shop and a post office.

Where to stay, eat & drink

Run by Xanterra, **Grand Canyon Lodge** (1-888 297 2757, 1-303 297 2757, same-day reservations 1-928 638 2611, www.grandcanyon northrim.com) is the only lodging inside the park at the North Rim. Cabins cost $97-$128; there's also a dining room and a campsite (1-800 365 2267, 1-877 444 6777, www.recreation.gov, $15-$20), for which booking is advisable. There are also lodging and eating facilities at **Kaibab Lodge** (1-928 638 2389, http://kaibab lodge.com, cabin $85-$155) and **Jacob Lake Inn** (1-928 643 7232, www.jacoblake.com, double/cabin $87-$142), respectively 18 and 45 miles north of the park.

Getting there

By bus

The only public transport to the North Rim is the **Trans Canyon Shuttle** bus service, which leaves the South Rim at 1.30pm daily and makes the return ride at 7am (May-Oct only). The journey takes about 4.5hrs and costs $65 ($120 round trip). Call 1-928 638 2820 for details.

By car

From Las Vegas, head north on I-15, then east on Hwy 9, Hwy 59 and US 89A to **Jacob Lake**. The park entrance is 30 miles south of Jacob Lake on Hwy 67; the rim is a further 14 miles. At a distance of 263 miles, the North Rim is nearer to Las Vegas than the South Rim, but the journey to it will take longer.

Exploring the canyon

Hiking in the canyon

However limited your time may be, try to hike at least part of the way into the canyon. As jaw-dropping as the views undoubtedly are from the rim, the gulf is almost too huge to allow a full appreciation of this unique environment. Really, you need to get closer: to soak up the stunning colours of the cliffs, to identify the different geological layers of rock, and to see the turbulent brown waters and hear the roar of the Colorado River. The basic rule of hiking into the canyon is that it takes twice as long to hike up as down; if you have three hours, turn around after an hour.

Although the upper trails teem with crowds, remember that you're not at a theme park. The extremes of terrain and climate are dangerous: always seek and heed advice from rangers, and ensure you're in decent physical shape and properly equipped. Note, too, that overnight hikes require a backcountry permit, which are issued on a strictly limited basis. Always try and apply for one in advance via the website; you can take your chances on the day and turn up at the Backcountry Information Center at 8am, but you may find yourself with a lengthy wait.

Hikers should note that mule riders have priority on the Bright Angel, South Kaibab and North Kaibab trails. Stop walking when the mules approach, and follow any instructions given by the rider leading the tour. For further details of mule rides, *see p291*.

Backcountry Information Center

Grand Canyon National Park, PO Box 129, Grand Canyon, AZ 86023 (1-928 638 7875 1-5pm Mon-Fri). Open Mid May-mid Oct, walk-in visitors 8am-noon, 1-5pm daily. Rates Permit $10, plus $5/night. **No credit cards**.

Apply here for a backcountry permit, required for all overnight camping trips except those that involve designated campgrounds. Applications open four months prior to the month in which you plan to hike; for example, applications for hiking trips in May are processed from January 1. Apply as early as possible.

Bright Angel Trail

Grand Canyon Village to Plateau Point. **Round trip** 19.2 miles. **Duration** 2 days.

This popular, maintained trail follows the line of a wide geological fault, which shifted the layering of the rock strata; as you descend, you'll notice that the layers on the left are much higher than those on the right. Water is usually available (May-Sept) at the resthouses 1.5 miles and three miles from the trail-head (the first also has toilet facilities). They're good day-hike destinations but can get crowded. Experienced hikers could head for the campground at Indian Gardens (4.5 miles); the tall cottonwoods here, planted in the early 1900s, can be seen from the rim. From Indian Gardens, continue to Plateau Point (6.1 miles) for a dramatic view into the river gorge.

Grandview Trail

Grandview Point to Horseshoe Mesa. **Round trip** 6.4 miles. **Duration** 1 day.

This unmaintained trail is steep and should only be attempted by experienced hikers. There's no water en route, but there are toilet facilities at Horseshoe Mesa, the site of an abandoned mining works.

Hermit Trail

Hermit's Rest to Colorado River. **Round trip** 18.4 miles. **Duration** 2-3 days.

This difficult trail passes Hermit Gorge, Santa Maria Spring and the Redwall Formation en route to the Colorado River and is recommended for experienced desert hikers only. A precipitous side trail leads for 1.5 miles to Dripping Springs. There is no drinking water on the trail; spring water must be treated.

North Kaibab Trail

North Rim to Colorado River Bridge. **Round trip** 29.2 miles. **Duration** 3-4 days.

The North Kaibab trail starts about 1.5 miles from Grand Canyon Lodge on the North Rim and begins with a beautiful but steep hike through the trees. The Supai Tunnel (1.8 miles) is an ideal day hike with a great view of the canyon, plus water and toilet facilities. There is little shade beyond this point. More experienced hikers might make it to Roaring Springs, but should not attempt to go further than this and back in one day. Beyond Roaring Springs, the trail continues to Phantom Ranch (13.8 miles) and the Colorado River Bridge (14.6 miles).

South Kaibab Trail

Yaki Point to Phantom Ranch. **Round trip** 12.6 miles. **Duration** 2 days.

This trail, which starts five miles east of Grand Canyon Village, is shorter but steeper than Bright Angel trail, dropping 5,000ft (1,500m) in six miles. The route follows a series of ridge lines, crossing the Colorado at the Kaibab Suspension Bridge on its way to Phantom Ranch. There is no campground or water en route; hike to the tree-dotted plateau of Cedar Ridge (1.5 miles) if you're short of time.

Mule rides

Mule rides into the canyon are operated by **Xanterra** (*see p287*), and booking is essential. The seven-hour **day trip** ($148 per person) takes you 3,200 feet (1,000 metres) down the Bright Angel Trail to Plateau Point. On the **two-day trip** ($401 one person, $709 two people, $321 each additional person), you'll go down the Bright Angel Trail and stay overnight in a cabin at Phantom Ranch (*see below*) before returning on the shorter South Kaibab Trail, allowing you to see the canyon from a different perspective. You can even defy saddle-soreness with a **three-day trip**, which includes two nights at Phantom Ranch ($566 one person, $946 two people, $406 each additional person). All rates include accommodation and food.

Plane & helicopter rides

Plane and helicopter rides over the rim are a major cause of air and noise pollution in the canyon, reducing visibility and disturbing the area's natural tranquillity. Rides are not available from within the park. However, if you must get a bird's-eye view, various outfits operate services out of Grand Canyon Airport in Tusayan. Plane rides start from around $90-$100; helicopter rides are more expensive. For flights departing from Las Vegas, *see p111*.

Air Grand Canyon *1-800 247 4726/1-928 638 2686/www.airgrandcanyon.com.*
Grand Canyon Airlines *1-866 235 9422/1-928 638 2359/www.grandcanyonairlines.com.*
Papillon Grand Canyon Helicopters *1-800 528 2418/1-928 638 2419/www.papillon.com.*

River rafting

Follow in the wake of one-armed explorer Major John Wesley Powell, who in 1869 became the first man to navigate the length of the Colorado River by boat, by taking a river trip through the rapids of the Grand Canyon. It's a major undertaking: you'll need at least eight days to travel the 277 miles downriver from Lees Ferry at the far eastern end of the Grand Canyon to Pearce Ferry on Lake Mead, and you'll have to book months in advance. A list of approved operators is on the NPS's Grand Canyon website; follow the links from 'Things to do'.

You can take a shorter trip by hiking in or out of the canyon. Firms such as **Canyoneers** (1-800 525 0924 outside Arizona, 1-928 526 0924 within Arizona, www.canyoneers.com) also offer shorter trips that start or finish at **Bright Angel Beach** near Phantom Ranch. Trips such as these entail less time on the river, and you'll also have to hike in or out of the canyon at the beginning or end of your trip.

For whitewater trips from **Diamond Creek** in Grand Canyon West, roughly a four-hour drive from the South Rim, *see p284*.

Staying in the canyon

Phantom Ranch, down at the bottom of the canyon, was designed by Mary Colter in 1922 and is a welcome oasis after the rigours of a strenuous hike. Hikers who stay here do not need backcountry permits, but will need to book months in advance: the dorms ($34 bed) are usually filled to capacity. Non-guests can eat here, but must book meals in advance ($17.50 breakfast, $10 packed lunch, $22-$36 dinner).

There are campsites at **Indian Gardens**, **Bright Angel** (next to Phantom Ranch) and **Cottonwood Springs** (May-Oct, accessible from the North Rim on the North Kaibab Trail). You'll need a backcountry permit to stay at any of them; *see p290*.

Tourist information

For general information, call the National Park Service on 1-928 638 7888. Alternatively, check the detail-packed if slightly convoluted website at www.nps.gov/grca, which has information on accommodation, hiking and backcountry permits, plus maps of the area.

Trips Out of Town

California

Get out of town and into the great wide open.

Rode the six hundred into **Death Valley**. *See p294.*

The relationship between Nevada and southern California has always been an uneasy one. Nevadans view their near-neighbours with wariness, while California natives look back with downright suspicion. And yet the traffic between the two states has never been greater.

The route between the two states takes the driver through pioneer country, traversed in the 19th century by migrants heading westwards, celebrated in the 20th century in Hollywood Westerns, and now offering 21st-century trippers a dramatic landscape. We cover LA in detail in *Time Out Los Angeles* (UK: £12.99; US: $19.95), but there are several desert attractions just across the Nevada–California border.

Parts of southern California are uninhabited and often scorching. Take suitable precautions when driving and hiking (*see pp276-277*).

Along I-15

You can throw the dice one last time at a pair of mini-gambling resorts along I-15, south of Las Vegas but before the border with California. **Jean**, the closest of the pair to Vegas, is soon to get a shot in the arm from MGM Mirage, which plans to build a planned mixed-use community on the site of the closed Nevada Landing casino. Until it does, the sole reasons to stop here are to throw a few dollars in the direction of the **Gold Strike** (1-800 634 1359, www.stopatjean.com), a pretty basic casino-hotel, or to visit the ghost town of **Goodsprings**, which hit the headlines in 1942 when Clark Gable waited for news of the plane crash that killed his wife, Carole Lombard.

Right on the Nevada–California border, **Primm** is a three-resort cluster of more modern aspect. The success of **Whiskey Pete's**, the Primm family's first casino-hotel, was so great that they followed it with two more, **Primm Valley** and **Buffalo Bill's** (1-800 386 7867, www.primmvalleyresorts.com for all three). However, the main reason to pull in here is the presence of **Fashion Outlets Las Vegas** (874 1400, www.fashionoutletlasvegas.com), a better-than-you'd-expect outlet mall that features a number of familiar brands that aren't present at either Vegas outlet enterprise.

Continuing south, the I-15 passes through stunning scenery along the northern boundary of **Mojave National Preserve** (*see p293*). The small town of **Baker**, 90 miles south of Vegas, makes a convenient gateway to this wilderness, and is home to the world's tallest thermometer, which measures 134 feet (40 metres) top to toe. West, the I-15 continues through stark desert for 60 miles until it reaches **Barstow**, a bleak town notable primarily for its location on historic Route 66. Beyond the high desert hicktown of **Hesperia**, I-15 takes you through the pine-capped wilderness of the San Bernardino Mountains until it hits the Los Angeles sprawl.

Mojave National Preserve

Covering a gigantic rectangle bordered by I-15 to the north and I-40 to the south, the 2,500-square-mile **Mojave National Preserve** is a Cinderella park: it has no honeypot attractions, low visitorship and few facilities, and is really best approached as a giant desert sampler. The meeting point of three of the four types of North American desert (Mojave, Great Basin and Sonoran), it contains a variety of terrains, features and ecosystems, including the human.

Because its protected status is relatively recent, historical relics of inhabitants and would-be conquerors, from early man right through to 20th-century ranchers, dot the landscape. Spanish explorers, western pioneers and routefinders, soldiers, navvies and settlers passed this way, leaving behind roads and railroads still in use today. The best times to visit are spring or autumn; it's brutally hot from mid May to mid September, often over 110°F (43°C). Whenever you visit, admission is free.

Mojave National Preserve has been developed only minimally: there are just four paved roads and three marked trails, and gas and lodging are available only on its borders. You can see plenty by car and on short walks, but those with four-wheel-drive vehicles will find it an off-road paradise. The numerous unpaved roads include the 140-mile east–west Mojave Road, a Native American track developed by successive users.

If you're coming from Vegas along I-15, be sure to fill up with both gas and drinking water at the aforementioned town of Baker. If you've only a few hours, a 67-mile triangular drive from Baker, via the Kelbaker Road, Kelso–Cima Road and Cima Road, to rejoin I-15 at the end of the trek, is a good introduction to the sights.

You'll pass the reddish humps of over 30 young volcanic cones before reaching **Kelso**; once a major passenger stop on the Union Pacific Railroad, it was named after a local railway worker when his name was the first one pulled from a hat by colleagues looking to christen the site. The grand, Spanish Mission-style depot, built in 1924 and closed in 1985, has been converted into a visitors' centre.

From here, you can detour to the 500-foot (150-metre) Kelso sand dunes by heading south on the Kelbaker Road and turning right after about seven miles on to a signed dirt road.

Back in Kelso, turn left towards **Cima**, passing the 7,000-foot-high (2,150-metre) Providence Mountains en route. At Cima, you can take Cima Road towards I-15 past the gently swelling Cima Dome, which has the largest stand of Joshua trees in the world. Alternatively, head along Morning Star Mine Road to Nipton Road up the Ivanpah Valley, then either take a left to I-15 or a right to tiny **Nipton**, at the preserve's northern edge. Here you'll find a railroad crossing, a town hall and the charming **Hotel Nipton** (*see below*).

If you've time, you could take the Essex Road to the **Providence Mountains State Recreation Area** (1-760 928 2586, www.parks.ca.gov), which is far cooler than the desert floor. Multi-branched cholla, spiky Mojave yucca, round barrel cactus, spindly Mormon tea and the flat pads of prickly pears share the upland slopes with juniper and piñon trees, creating a stunning geometric display. There are great views south from the visitor centre. This park within a park also houses the dramatic limestone **Mitchell Caverns**, which remain a cool and comforting 65°F (18°C) all year round. Tours of the caves ($4, $2 children) run daily during the week and thrice-daily between Labor Day and Memorial Day, and at 1.30pm daily during the rest of the year.

Another diversion from I-40 is a stretch of the old Route 66, featuring the kind of bleak desert landscapes beloved of cinematographers and the similarly iconic Americana of photogenic **Amboy**. To the east, 66 crosses I-40 and dips back into the preserve to **Goffs**, a lonely spot despite its status as 'the Desert Tortoise Capital of the World'. Further south is **Joshua Tree National Park**, worth a look in its own right.

Where to stay & eat

Lodgings within the park are limited to a pair of campgrounds. **Mid-Hills** is usually cooler than **Hole-in-the-Wall**, and always much prettier. You'll need to drive some reliable but not always comfortable dirt roads to get here; Hole-in-the-Wall is accessible on blacktop from I-40. The fee at each is $12, and pitches are distributed on a first-come, first-served basis.

On the edge of the park, Baker has a clutch of pretty basic non-chain motels as well as the rammed and rated **Mad Greek Diner** (1-760 733 4354), where fast food both Greek and American is served to starving motorists. However, the pick of the park-side lodging options is the **Hotel Nipton** (1-760 856 2335,

Trips Out of Town

www.nipton.com, rates $69), a century-old hotel in splendid desert isolation (except, that is, for its Wi-Fi access). If the main building is full, stay in one of the eco-cabins scattered behind the main building. Also here is the **Whistle Stop Oasis** (1-760 856 1045), a basic-looking shack where Bill Sarbello's food (especially the burgers) is better than it has any right to be.

Getting there

By car
Baker is 90 miles south of Las Vegas on I-15. Nipton is located on Hwy 164, accessible via I-15 or Hwy 95, 63 miles south of Las Vegas. To reach Joshua Tree, take Kelbaker Road through the Mojave National Preserve and head south via Amboy until you reach Twentynine Palms; it's 130 miles from Baker.

Tourist information

Mojave National Preserve: Kelso Visitor Center *Kelbaker Road, Kelso (1-760 733 4456/ www.nps.gov/moja).* **Open** 9am-5pm daily.
Mojave National Preserve: Hole-in-the-Wall Information Center *Essex & Black Canyon Roads, north of I-40 (1-760 928 2572/www.nps.gov/moja).* **Open** *May-Sept* 9am-4pm Fri-Sun. *Oct-Apr* 9am-4pm Wed-Sun.

Death Valley National Park

Enlarged and redesignated a national park under the 1994 Desert Protection Act, Death Valley is now the largest national park outside Alaska, covering more than 5,156 square miles. It's also, famously, one of the hottest places on the planet. The park's website calmly offers that 'Death Valley is generally sunny, dry and clear throughout the year'. True, but the word 'generally' masks a multitude of curiosities. Air temperatures regularly top 120°F (49°C) in July and August, and are 50 per cent higher on the ground; fearsome by anyone's standards.

However, while the park is usually parched, receiving fewer than two inches of rain in an average year, it's not immune from water. In August 2004, terrifying flash floods hit Death Valley, killing two tourists and destroying parts of Highway 190. Reconstruction of the road was completed a couple of years later, but the same thing could happen again at any time.

Get your bearings at the **Death Valley Visitor Center** (*see p295*) at **Furnace Creek**, where you'll find an excellent bookshop, decent exhibits, a useful orientation film and helpful staff. Stop in for advice on current weather and road conditions (some tracks are only accessible to 4WD vehicles), pay your fee of $20 per car and take the opportunity to fill up at one of the park's three expensive gas stations.

Scotty's Castle.

However, if you've entered the park on Highway 190 from Las Vegas, you'll pass two of the most amazing sights en route to Furnace Creek, and it may save time to stop at them before hitting the visitors' centre. Roughly 13 miles off the main road and standing 5,475 feet (1,669 metres) above sea level, **Dante's View** is a wonderful place from which to first survey the park's otherworldly landscape. And just three miles south of Furnace Creek lies **Zabriskie Point**, famed for the eponymous 1970 Antonioni film but recognisable to all by its ragged, rumpled appearance.

There's more to see further south of Furnace Creek. At **Golden Canyon**, there's a simple two-mile round-trip hike that's best walked in the late afternoon sunlight, when you'll see how the canyon got its name. Continuing south, the landscape gets plainer. Nine miles down the road is the **Devil's Golf Course**, a striking, scrappy landscape formed by salt crystallising and expanding; a few miles further is bleak, eerie **Badwater**, just two miles as the crow flies from Dante's View but more than 5,000 feet (1,524 metres) lower. Indeed, this is the lowest point in the Western Hemisphere, 282 feet (86 metres) below sea level. Unexpectedly, it's only 85 miles from the highest point in the US, the 14,494-foot (4,420-metre) Mount Whitney in the Sierra Nevada. An annual 'ultramarathon' race is held between the two, though it no longer extends all the way to Whitney's summit.

Heading north from Furnace Creek offers a greater variety of sights. The remains of the **Harmony Borax Works** have been casually converted into a short trail; there's a similarly simple walk, less historic but more aesthetically pleasing, at nearby **Salt Creek** (look for desert pupfish in the stream in spring). Following the road around to the left will lead you past the eerie **Devil's Cornfield**, the frolic-friendly **Sand Dunes**, which rise and dip in 100-foot (30-metre) increments, and on to the small settlement at **Stovepipe Wells**. Taking a right and driving 36 miles will lead you to the luxurious **Scotty's Castle**; built in the 1920s for Chicago millionaire Albert Johnson, it was named after Walter Scott, his eccentric chancer of a friend. Tangers tell the story on 50-minute tours (usually hourly, 9am-5pm, $11).

It's often too hot to hike, but there are plenty of trails in Death Valley, short and long. The options include the 14-mile round trip to the 11,000-foot (3,300-metre) summit of **Telescope Peak**, a good summer hike (the higher you climb, the cooler it gets). Starting at Mahogany Flat campground, you climb 3,000 feet (900 metres) for some spectacular views of Mount Whitney. In winter, only experienced climbers with ice axes and crampons should attempt it.

Where to stay & eat

Set into the hillside above Furnace Creek Wash, **Furnace Creek Inn** (1-888 297 2757, 1-760 786 2345, www.furnacecreekresort.com, closed mid May-mid Oct, double $265-$390) was built in the 1930s, and retains a cultured dignity reminiscent of the era from which it emerged. The rooms are charming and well equipped, while the landscaped gardens are picture-perfect and the pool is a refined delight. The inn's restaurant, where the upscale Californian food is far better than you might expect, is comfortably the best eating option in the area.

Elsewhere, the **Furnace Creek Ranch** (same phone & URL, $116-$193) has 200 motel-style rooms and cabins, as well as a pool, tennis courts and the world's lowest golf course, plus a pretty basic restaurant and bar. The 83-room **Stovepipe Wells Village** (1-760 786 2837, www.stovepipewells.com, double $91-$111) also has food on offer, but few other amenities. Four of the park's nine campgrounds are free, with the others costing between $12 and $18 a night. The most central, and the only one for which reservations are taken, is at **Furnace Creek** (1-877 444 6777, www.recreation.gov).

Getting there

By car

From Vegas, head south on I-15 towards LA, exit on to Blue Diamond Road (at Silverton), then head west on Hwy 160 over the Spring Mountains. A few miles after Pahrump, take Bell Vista Road to Death Valley Junction and Hwy 190 into the park (120 miles). (Returning to Vegas via Death Valley Junction, note that Bell Vista Road is labelled State Line Road.) Alternatively, take US 95 to Beatty and then head south on Hwy 374.

Tourist information

Death Valley Visitor Center *Furnace Creek, Death Valley National Park (1-760 786 3200/ www.nps.gov/deva).* **Open** 8am-5pm daily.
Scotty's Castle Visitor Center *Scotty's Castle, Death Valley National Park (1-760 786 2392/ www.nps.gov/deva).* **Open** *Summer* 9am-4.30pm daily. *Winter* 8.30am-5pm daily.

Theatre of dreams

It's not your archetypal ghost town, Death Valley Junction. It was settled not by travelling pioneers or gold-hungry prospectors but by the Pacific Coast Borax Company, which built it in the mid 1920s to house its workers. When they left, the town crumbled, until a fortysomething ballet dancer arrived from New York in 1967, took over a derelict community hall and began to fashion from it her own American dream.

Renovating the building as the **Amargosa Opera House**, Marta Becket turned coffee-cans into spotlights and filled the room with garden chairs. She even painted an audience on the walls, which made performing in an empty hall, as she often did, easier to bear. Eventually, though, word spread, and people travelled to see both Becket's theatre and her self-devised, folk art-ish performance pieces. In the early 1980s, Becket finally bought the property; audiences, fascinated by this tale of devotion and self-imposed isolation, continued to come.

Tom Willett (aka Wilget), Becket's longtime partner, died of a stroke in 2005, but the octogenarian Becket has continued without him, staging shows every Saturday night ($15, booking essential; 1-760 852 4441, www.amargosaoperahouse.com). There's nowhere quite like it.

Nevada

Would you like to see the desert menu?

Virginia City. *See p300.*

Those who claim that there's plenty more to Nevada outside Las Vegas are overstating their case a little. Those who aver that there's plenty more *of* Nevada outside Las Vegas, on the other hand, are right on the money. Although the state is the seventh largest in the Union, almost three-quarters of its residents live within 40 miles of Las Vegas, with half the remainder in the Reno-Sparks urban area. That leaves an awful lot of not very much.

Yet after Vegas, an awful lot of not very much can be just what one needs. The under-visited **Valley of Fire State Park** (*see p281*) is stunning, offering the kind of carefree escape from civilisation that **Red Rock Canyon** (*see p281*), with the city creeping ever closer to it, fails quite to provide. The drive north-west from Vegas to **Reno** on I-95 offers desert landscape alternately bleak and beautiful under skies as big as you'll ever see. The smattering of towns along it are scruffy but fascinating, all in thrall to the prospectors and chancers who established them a century ago. And then there's the **Extraterrestrial Highway**, named after the many extraordinary tales of UFO sightings and other sinister goings-on at Nevada Test Site's infamous Area 51.

The road to Reno

US 95 leaves the lights of Las Vegas behind in a hurry. As the road roars out through the city's north-western corner, the landscape visible from the driver's seat empties from urban sprawl into endless desert. Get used to the view. You'll have seen a lot like it by the time your 450-mile ride from Vegas to Reno is complete. Soon, you'll be rolling past **Mount Charleston** (*see p282*). On the right sits **Nellis Air Force Range**, a vast tract of desert that, with an area of 5,200 square miles, is slightly larger than the state of Connecticut.

From 1951 until 1995, the US government, which owns more than 80 per cent of the land in Nevada, used the **Nevada Test Site**, which is flanked on three sides by the Nellis Range, to test atomic weapons, both above ground and beneath it. Day-long tours of the site, which leave from the **Atomic Testing Museum** in Las Vegas (itself worth a visit; *see p135*), are available to those prescient enough to book two months ahead and prepared to supply all manner of information to pass security screenings. For details, see www.nv.doe.gov, or call 295 0944.

Trips Out of Town

Shortly after Indian Springs, you'll leave Clark County and enter Nye County. At 18,147 square miles, it's the third largest county in the US, but it's also one of the emptiest: the 2000 census tagged the population at 34,075. At **Amargosa Valley**, close to the junction of US 95 and SR 373 (leading towards **Death Valley**; *see p294*), an unprepossessing cluster of buildings houses a bar, a gas station and a brothel, making it perhaps America's ultimate travellers' rest area. Across the road sits a bar; nearby, on SR 373, sits Jackass Airport, named for the animal rather than the idiocy of the local pilots. And that's more or less it.

For years, the government has planned to use **Yucca Mountain**, just north of Amargosa Valley, as the repository for the country's spent nuclear waste. The Department of Energy even set a date for the site's opening: 31 March 2017. However, Nevada senator (and, as of 2007, Senate majority leader) Harry Reid has insisted that the plan will never come to pass; this one looks set to run and run. Tours of the mountain, which sits inside the Nevada Test Site, are available to those who book well in advance; call 821 8687 or see www.ocrwm.doe.gov.

Head 30 miles north-west of Amargosa Valley and you'll find **Beatty**, established – as were so many towns at the turn of the 20th century – by prospectors ambitious to make their fortunes. When word got around that Ed Cross and Frank 'Shorty' Harris had discovered a goldmine in the hills, hundreds of hopefuls descended on the area, leading Walter Beatty to set up a town on his homestead. The volunteer-run **Beatty Museum** (417 Main Street, 1-775 553 2303, www.beattymuseum.com) offers exhibits and anecdotes on these early days.

Beatty is now a ramshackle collection of casinos and bars, but at least it's still alive, which is more than can be said for nearby **Rhyolite**. An archetypal gold rush town, it sprung up after gold was found in August 1904. The first lots were sold in February 1905; by 1908, 10,000 locals were served by schools, hospitals, 50 bars, an opera house and a red light district. But by 1910, all but a few hundred had moved on to the next boomtown, leaving the town to crumble. Today, a handful of buildings sit in various states of disrepair, weather-beaten and neglected but refusing to vanish; hand-drawn street signs remind visitors that these tracks were once busy thoroughfares. It's a fascinating, melancholy place. To reach it, take SR 374 south from Beatty (towards Death Valley) for about four miles, then take a right. Also here is the **Goldwell Open Air Museum** (www.goldwellmuseum.org), a haunting spot that comprises a half-dozen works by Belgian artists who settled in the area 20 years ago.

Look out for Albert Szukalski's striking sculpture *The Last Supper*, although, to be honest, it's pretty hard to miss.

Some 50 miles north of Beatty sits **Goldfield**, another former mining town whose population surged from nothing to 10,000 between 1902 (when gold was discovered here) and 1907, and then doubled in the following three years. It didn't last, but Goldfield refused to die: a population of 500 makes it a sizeable settlement for this part of the world. If several grand stone buildings, including the Goldfield Hotel, the courthouse and the imposing former fire station, are poignant reminders of the town's heyday, the Mozart Club bar offers evidence that not everybody got lucky.

It's 26 miles from here to **Tonopah**, on US 95 at about the halfway point between Vegas and Reno. Jim Butler found silver here in 1900; over the next 15 years, almost $150 million of ore was dug from the small mines that dot the area. The **Central Nevada Museum** (1900 Logan Field Road, 1-775 482 9676, www.tonopah nevada.com, closed Mon & Tue) details this history, though you might be better off heading for the century-old buildings at the **Tonopah Historic Mining Park** (520 McCulloch Street, 1-775 482 9274, www.tonopahnevada.com, closed Mon & Tue Nov-Feb, $5).

From here, the landscape gets plainer. Settlements seem further apart – the next town of any note, **Hawthorne**, is 100 miles down the road – and there's little to engage the senses save the freedom of an open road. Until, that is, a few miles after Hawthorne, when you find US 95 narrowing and curving – quite a shock after 300 miles of mainly straight highway – as it forces its way around a sizeable body of water.

In prehistoric times, **Walker Lake** covered much of western Nevada. These days, though still 20 miles long, it's in decline: with the Walker River diverted for irrigation purposes, it's dropped 100 feet (30 metres) since 1930. While not spectacularly beautiful, the lake and the state park that frames it are popular spots for swimming, boating and camping; call the state park on 1-775 867 3001 for more details on park activities, or see http://parks.nv.gov/walk.htm.

Past **Schurz**, a town every bit as unbecoming as its name, there are several routes to Reno. The quickest is to take US 95 north to Fallon, then pick up US 50 and Alternate US 50 to the surprisingly picturesque I-80, and head west on the Interstate into Reno. A slightly slower, slightly more scenic option is to head west on US 95 at Schurz, via the pleasant town of **Yerington** and the enjoyably green **Fort Churchill Historic State Park** in Silver Springs (1-775 577 2345, www.parks.nv.gov/fc.htm, admission $4), and

Trips Out of Town

then pick up I-80 to Reno near Fernley. The slowest option is to take this latter route as far as Silver Springs, then take US 50, SR 341 and US 395 into Reno via **Virginia City** (*see p300*). Our advice? Take the speedy run into Reno, but return to Vegas via Virginia City.

Where to stay, eat & drink

In Tonopah, the large **Tonopah Station** casino (1137 S Main Street, 1-775 482 9777, www.tonopahstation.com) has a dark gaming area, rooms, a restaurant and a wonderful collection of old chrome slot machines in the basement. **El Marques** (1-775 482 3885) serves decent, good-value Mexican food.

Hawthorne has a number of motels and one casino, the **El Capitan** (540 F Street, 1-775 945 3321, www.elcapitanresortcasino.com). **Maggie's** (US 95 at E Street, 1-775 945 3908) serves burgers, salads and sandwiches.

Tourist information

For information about **Tonopah**, contact the Chamber of Commerce at 301 Brougher Avenue (1-775 482 3859, www.tonopahnevada.com).

Reno

Popular culture flags the differences. In song, Las Vegas is the town that set Elvis's soul on fire; Reno is where Johnny Cash shot a man just to watch him die. On film, Vegas always looks glamorous, stealing scenes from every actor dumb enough to compete with it. The finest Reno movie is Paul Thomas Anderson's *Hard Eight* (aka *Sydney*), a bleak, edgy tale set in the shadows of the town's gaming industry.

To visitors, Reno can't compete with Las Vegas. The casinos are smaller and shabbier, the neon less dazzling, the dining not as varied and the entertainment decidedly wearier. But to suggest that Reno is Vegas in miniature is to do it a disservice: after all, it's never attempted to compete with its glossier, more glamorous rival. Reno hardly sees itself as a gambling town at all; rather, it's a pretty little city with numerous and varied attractions, one of which is casinos.

Reno long ago made a deliberate decision not to become Las Vegas. In the 1950s, the city fathers passed a law that limited gambling to downtown Reno, then sat back and let Vegas explode in popularity, population and wealth. The 25-year law expired in 1978; since then, just enough (but not too many) casinos have opened, attracting just enough (not too many) gamblers. At the same time, Reno has diversified its economy and tourism marketing focus, growing at a controlled pace.

Locals are proud of their town and disparaging about their putative rival; there's little love lost between Renoites and Las Vegans. In truth, gambling aside, the two cities have as little in common as San Francisco and Los Angeles. Where Vegas is an anything-goes, 24-7 kind of town, Reno is slower, prettier and more conservative. The flow of the Truckee River through downtown is attractive; if the Riverwalk that's been built around it doesn't differ wildly from the formula that's been applied in countless other American cities (a few shops, a handful of restaurants), it's no less pleasant for its lack of originality.

Reno also benefits from the variety of its seasons. Winter can be cold, but you won't hear a word of complaint from the skiers who jam the slopes of the 20-plus resorts within an hour of town. Summer, meanwhile, is usually balmy, with outdoor events galore. The biggest is **Hot August Nights** (www.hotaugustnights.net), a 1950s-themed mix of classic cars and rock 'n' roll, but **Street Vibrations** in September (www.road-shows.com), the Harley-Davidson equivalent, keeps pace with it.

Sightseeing

The **Nevada Museum of Art** (160 W Liberty Street, 1-775 329 3333, www.nevadaart.org, closed Mon, $1-$10), housed in a striking black building, has a strong permanent collection, the majority of pieces from the last century, plus temporary shows: check online for details.

The **National Automobile Museum** (10 S Lake Street, 1-775 333 9300, www.automuseum. org, $3-$9) is the best museum in Reno, and one of the best in the state. The building holds more than 200 cars from a timeframe of more than a century, from an 1892 Philion Road Carriage – imagine a throne stuck on top of an outsized perambulator – to altogether less dignified Ed Roth Kustom creations. The cars, including 1940s Lincolns, a 1930s Mercedes and a divine 1957 Cadillac, are all beautifully maintained.

Reno's other attractions sit on the University of Nevada campus north of downtown. At the **Fleischmann Planetarium** (1650 N Virginia Street, 1-775 784 4811, http://planetarium.unr. edu), star shows run alongside 70mm nature films. A stone's throw away at the **Nevada Historical Society** (1650 N Virginia Street, 1-775 688 1190), there's a fine primer on the history of the state and a good bookstore.

Casinos

Though there are a handful of casinos out of the centre, notably the monstrous **Grand Sierra Resort** (formerly the Reno Hilton; 2500 E 2nd

No fear of failure

Most of us are losers. That's all there is to it. Tinhorns. Pikers. *Punters.* We keep going to casinos and keep getting ground up into chopped meat. And then we keep on playing.

Sure sure: it's about the fun, about the recreation value, about spending the same money on gambling that you might use to buy tickets to a concert or a ballgame or an amusement park. And yeah, it's about risking your bankroll for the excitement of the casino, the adrenaline of the action, and, to some extent, the dream of a once-in-a-lifetime monster run. But mostly, it's about seeing how your luck is holding up, and finding out that it's not holding up very well. Gambling is all about trying for the acute fun of winning, but fading the chronic pain of losing to do so.

There is a shrine to all us losers in Nevada, but it's not in Las Vegas, which takes itself way too seriously to even consider having a little fun at the expense of those who line its pockets. To find it, you'll have to head south on US 95 for 70 miles and then east on Highway 163 to Laughlin, a scruffy little low-rollers' haven founded in 1969 by Don Laughlin on the border with Arizona. Inside the Riverside (1-800 227 3849, www.riversideresort.com), the town's original hotel-casino, sits one of the most imaginative bars in Nevada. A lot of thought, planning, and collecting went into its decorations at the **Losers Lounge**, which dares to point out that the emperor isn't really wearing anything.

The setting is typical for a bar: a stage, a dancefloor, a balcony, bars, barstools and tables. But the decor is anything but ordinary, especially for a casino. The ornamentation pays homage to many of recent history's most famous fall guys and gals, who wound up on the wrong side of some track or another and went down in high-visibility flames.

A big presidential-campaign mirror decorates the main bar, touting 'Nixon and Agnew – a Team of Honesty and Integrity'. A photograph of John Belushi hangs on the wall; on his face is etched one of the most desperate expressions ever captured by camera. Also commemorated here are the Hindenburg, Ma Barker and her boys, General Custer, Buffalo Bill and Mike Tyson, shooting stars to a man (and woman). Movie posters commemorate the spectacular failure of the Attack movies, among them *Attack of the 50-Foot Woman* and *Attack of the Puppet People.*

On the stairs up to the balcony are displays spotlighting such notables as Timothy McVeigh, Tonya Harding, OJ Simpson and Marcia Clark (side by side) and Ted Kaczynski. The balcony walls are (dis)graced by Imelda Marcos, Ethel and Julius Rosenberg, Eddie Fisher and Debbie Reynolds (in an old poster for a movie they co-starred in), Edsel Ford, Bonnie and Clyde, and Gary Hart. You can easily spend an hour here perusing the losers. But don't be too surprised if your own photo is up there on the wall.

Street, at US 395, 1-775 789 2000, www.grand sierraresort.com) and the colourful **Peppermill** (2707 S Virginia Street, at W Grove Street, 1-866 821 9996, www.peppermillreno.com), Reno's gambling is mostly downtown. Some of the names in lights will be familiar, among them the characterless **Harrah's** (219 N Center Street, at E 2nd Street, Reno, 1-775 786 3232, www.harrahs.com) and the family-friendly **Circus Circus** (500 N Sierra Street, at W 5th Street, 1-800 648 5010, www.circusreno.com).

Other casinos, though, are unique to Reno. The **Eldorado** (345 N Virginia Street, at W 4th Street, 1-800 648 5966, www.eldoradoreno.com) is the most pleasant operation, while the upscale **Silver Legacy** (407 N Virginia Street, at W 4th Street, 1-800 687 8733, www.silverlegacy reno.com) boasts a lobby filled with treasures from Tiffany's. It's in contrast to the basic **Club Cal-Neva** (38 E 2nd Street, at N Virginia Street, 1-877 777 7303, www.clubcalneva.com).

Where to eat & drink

Stay in or near a casino, as almost all visitors to Reno do, and you'll probably eat a number of your meals there. Of the downtown spots, the Eldorado and Harrah's offer the best dining; try Roxy's at the former and the Steakhouse at the latter. The Cal-Neva Virginian attracts the bargain-hunters. Out of the centre, the Grand Sierra and the Peppermill are among the strongest for food: the Peppermill's buffet is Reno's best and its White Orchid is the finest dining in town. For all, *see above.*

Outside the casinos, find fine and messy Mexican food at **Bertha Miranda's** (336 Mill Street, at Lake Street, 1-775 786 9697), heavy traditional Basque scran at **Louie's Basque Corner** (301 E 4th Street, at Evans Avenue, 1-775 323 7203) and splendid coffee at **Java Jungle** (246 W 1st Street, at S Arlington Avenue, 1-775 329 4484). Microbrews can be sunk at the attractive, slightly tucked-away **Silver Peak** (124 Wonder Street, at Holcomb Avenue, 1-775 324 1864, www.silverpeak brewery.com), which serves upscale bar food.

Where to stay

Roughly 25,000 rooms are available in Reno, running the pricing gamut from dirt-cheap to sky-high. Prices peak in August (it's worth booking) but are cheap in winter: you can often get a room in one of the downtown casinos or motels for under $30. Note that rooms in casinos that have a sister Vegas hotel won't necessarily be in an identical mould.

Tourist information

Reno's visitor centre is in the lobby of the **National Bowling Stadium**. Alternatively, phone the information line at the Reno-Sparks CVA (1-800 367 7366, www.visitrenotahoe.com).

Around Reno

Carson City

As state capitals go, **Carson City**, 30 miles south of Reno on US 395, is not one of the more demonstrative. Still, what it lacks in pomposity it makes up for in quaintness, albeit a quaintness balanced by a string of casinos on Carson Street, the town's main drag and also US 395.

Cynics suggest that the real balance of power in Nevada is held by the casino owners in Las Vegas, but the politicos of Carson City can still pack a punch when they need to. The centres of their activity are the **Nevada State Capitol** (N Carson Street, at Musser Street), a handsome domed structure dated 1871, and the **State Legislature**, a dreary building erected nearby a century later. The Kit Carson Trail, a two-mile walk detailed on a map available from the Chamber of Commerce (1900 S Carson Street, 1-775 882 1565, www.carsoncitychamber.com), offers a decent overview of the town's history.

Most of these buildings are closed to the public, but one that isn't is the suitably grand old US Mint Building at 600 N Carson Street, which for the last 60 years has served as the eclectic **Nevada State Museum** (1-775 687 4810, www.nevadaculture.org). The state's historic railroad comes under the microscope at the **Nevada State Railroad Museum** (2180 S Carson Street, 1-775 687 6953, www.nsrm-friends.org). Rides on old trains are offered most weekends outside winter. Still, the few casinos aside, there's not much nightlife here, and Carson City's best taken in during a day-trip from Reno or Lake Tahoe.

Virginia City

A pleasant half-hour drive from Reno, south on US 395 for eight miles, then east on SR 341 for another eight miles, will take you to one of the most authentic historic mining towns in the West, where the discovery of gold and silver in nearby mines on the land of Henry Comstock sparked a furious bonanza in the 1860s. Of course, **Virginia City** is now also one of the most touristy towns in the West, its thin main drag soaked with themed bars, tatty museums – try the **The Way It Was Museum** (118 N C Street, 1-775 847 0766), which looks like the Smithsonian next to some of its neighbours – photo studios and other less easily categorisable attractions ('See the Suicide Table!').

That said, provided you avoid summer weekends, when C Street can get claustrophobic with tourists, it's great fun. If you take the time to wander off the main drag, it's even a little bit more than that. The Walking Tour, available from the town's visitor centre, takes in the town's most fascinating buildings, among them the regenerated **Piper's Opera House** (1 N B Street, 1-775 847 0433). Visitors should note that many of the town's sights close during the viciously chilly winters).

Eating and drinking options in Virginia City are hardly varied, but you can wash down your sandwich or burger with a beer or a Coke in any number of establishments. There aren't too many places to stay, reflecting Virginia City's status as a day-tripper's paradise; in fact, you're best off driving back to Reno to find a bed for the night. And if you've time, take the long way round – south on SR 341, then west on US 50 and back north on US 395 – in order to stop in at the magnificent **Chocolate Nugget** candy factory (56 SR 341, 1-775 849 0841) and pick up a couple of bags of sugar-rush.

Lake Tahoe

After driving through miles of desert, Reno's verdant trim comes as a pleasant surprise. But it's as nothing compared to **Lake Tahoe**, which sits on the California border a 45-minute drive from Reno (south on US 395 for eight miles, then west on SR 431 for 25 miles). Some 22 miles long and 12 miles wide, it's one of the world's most beautiful alpine lakes.

Tahoe's two main settlements are at either end of the lake, both within a few miles of the state line. **Incline Village**'s population of 7,000 is swelled in winter by skiers (the slopes of **Mount Rose–Ski Tahoe** and **Diamond Peak** are nearby, with **Northstar-at-Tahoe** and the well regarded **Squaw Valley USA** just across the state line), in summer by the hiking and other outdoor sports, and year-round by the socialising. Three miles west in **Crystal Bay**, on the state line, are a handful of casinos; the best of them is almost certainly the **Cal-Neva** (1-800 225 6382, www.calnevaresort.com).

South Lake Tahoe, meanwhile, also has its casinos, temptingly positioned on the Nevada edge of the state line. Among those offering accommodation are the **Montbleu** (formerly Caesars Tahoe; 1-888 829 7630, www.caesars.com), **Harrah's** (1-800 427 7247, www.harrahs.com), and its relation **Harveys** (1-800 427 8397, www.harrahs.com). On the California side sit restaurants, bars and motels. Skiers flock here in winter – **Heavenly**, **Sierra-at-Tahoe** and **Kirkwood** are the nearest slopes – while summer brings a more demure holiday-maker.

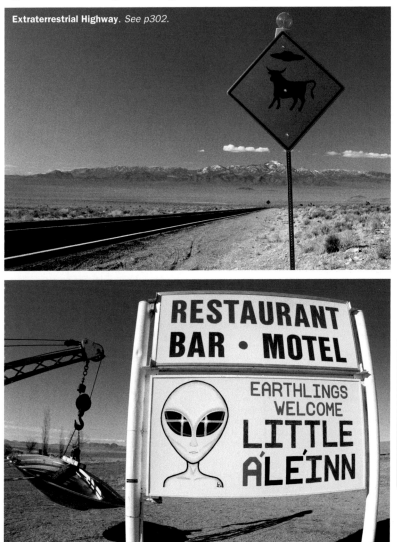

Extraterrestrial Highway. *See p302.*

Trips Out of Town

The Extraterrestrial Highway & Area 51

Of course, you won't see anything. No one ever does. And if you're thinking about walking into the desert for a closer look, think again: you may find yourself greeted by employees of the US government wielding the kind of weaponry that'll encourage you to turn around in a hurry.

Still, SR 375 continues to draw tourists year-round. A few are here to plane-spot the military aircraft that roar overhead. A handful are on their way north to Ely. But the reason most people are ploughing up and down SR 375 is its now-official nickname, and what reputedly rests just a few miles west of the road.

If you've taken US 95 north to Reno, you'll already have skirted the western edge of the Nellis Air Force Range (see p296). Well, if you take SR 375, a plain-as-day desert road that links US 93 with US 6 in central Nevada, you'll be edging along its eastern perimeter. No one gave this much thought until the 1980s, when physicist Bob Lazar, in a series of interviews with local news gadfly George Knapp, claimed he had worked at Papoose Lake inside the range on alien spaceships. He also gave details – scant, but enough to light the touchpaper of conspiracy theorists – of the previously unknown dry-bedded Groom Lake, allegedly a test site for top-secret new military aircraft and, more contentiously, the centre of government investigations into alien life. After the numbered grid square in which the base sits on maps of the test site, it's become known as Area 51; as a result of its notoriety, SR 375 has nicknamed the **Extraterrestrial Highway**.

The US government refuses to acknowledge the existence of Area 51. Rumours persist that the notoriety of the base forced the government to move its operations from here to Utah during the 1990s. Either way, sightings of UFOs near the road are predictably common, and just as predictably difficult to substantiate.

Take care: someone is watching your movements. Don't cross into the military zone: you'll be arrested, questioned and fined. Armed guards are authorised to use 'deadly force' on trespassers. The border is not marked on maps and is often hard to detect: it's defined by orange posts, some topped with silver globes, and occasional 'restricted area' signs, but no fence.

The only town on SR 375 is Rachel, a scruffy, collection of houses and huts that's home to a little under 100 people. This number is swelled by tourists staying at the **Little A'Le'Inn**, a slightly scruffy motel-bar-restaurant combo stocked with cheaply made, dearly priced alien ephemera and staffed by chatty people unafraid of engaging customers in a conversation about politics (tip: if you're a Democrat, keep your mouth shut).

Since 1995, when the military annexed more land, the only view of Area 51 is from Tikaboo Peak, 26 miles from the base. You get superb views of the desert, but even with binoculars, all you'll see of the base is a few distant buildings. It's a strenuous hike, best done in summer and early in the morning, before heat haze distorts the view. The best route is via a dirt road off US 93 at milepost 32.2, south of Alamo. It's just over 22 miles to Badger Spring and then a two-hour hike to the summit, but it's easy to get lost.

Where to stay, eat & drink

The aforementioned **Little A'Le'Inn** (1-775 729 2515, www.aleinn.com) has seven rooms in run-down trailers: you get a shared bathroom, a communal kitchen-cum-living room and UFO photos. The bar serves beer and burgers.

Getting there

By car

Take US 93 north for 107 miles to the junction with SR 375, aka Extraterrestrial Highway. Rachel is 36 miles north-west of the junction. When driving, watch not so much for aliens but for wandering cows: much of the road is an open range, and collisions occur regularly.

You're fired

To say the **Burning Man Festival** isn't really like most other events in Nevada is to say that Las Vegas isn't really like most other cities. Each year, in the week leading up to Labor Day, 30,000 people gather in the isolated Black Rock Desert to build a temporary, self-contained city, the physical, spiritual and symbolic centre of which is a 50-foot man who's set aflame at the end of the event. What goes on beforehand defies both belief and easy description, suffice to say that the event will be unlike anything you've ever experienced before. Self-expression is prized above all else (one participant pinned Burning Man as a non-stop, week-long piece of performance art) with self-reliance a close second; temperatures can range from 0°C to 40°C (32°F to 104°F). Either way, for one week you'll be part of the world's most eccentric and fascinating community. For more, see www.burningman.com.

Utah

The natural world at its most alien.

Utah will come as a culture shock after Las Vegas. It can be hard just to find a bar that serves alcohol here, or a restaurant that stays open past 9pm. If Las Vegas is a 24-hour city, then Mormon-dominated Utah, suspicious of outsiders and deeply mistrustful of its Nevada neighbours, is a 12-hour state. But southern Utah is a unique place, not to say a spectacular one. National Park follows National Recreation Area follows National Monument, and hulking rock formations give way to vistas by turns peculiar and pretty. **Zion National Park** is a bit of both.

Zion National Park

A few hours north from Las Vegas, Zion National Park is a glorious introduction to the canyon country of south-east Utah. Zion's 2,000-foot (600-metre) cliffs and towering rock formations were discovered by early Mormon travellers in the 1880s. Originally called Mukuntuweap (roughly 'like a quiver', a description of the canyon's shape), its name was changed to Zion, an ancient Hebrew word meaning 'place of refuge', when it became a national park in 1919. With more than 2.5 million visitors annually, Zion is busy all year. However, it's best avoided in winter, when snow and ice make the trails tough to negotiate, and summer, when temperatures top 110°F (43°C).

The main entrance to the park is in the south, near the pretty town of Springdale (admission $25 per car, valid for seven days). Just beyond the entrance are the park's two campgrounds (*see p304*) and visitors' centre (staff are wonderfully helpful), with the tidy new **Zion Human History Museum** a further half-mile inside the gates. From April to October, when parts of the park are off-limits to cars, visitors should leave their cars at the south entrance or in Springdale, then take a free bus into the park. The rest of the park is open to private cars, but vehicles wider than 7ft 10in (2.39m) or higher than 10ft 4in (3.15m) must be escorted through the Zion–Mount Carmel tunnel ($15/vehicle), which can lead to delays.

The majority of the park's sights and trails are accessible or visible from the six-mile dead-end **scenic drive**, which starts at the main entrance and winds through the Virgin River gorge. (It's one of the aforementioned sections of the park that's closed to private cars from April to October.) The names of the vividly coloured Navajo sandstone monoliths along the drive echo the first visitors' religious sensibilities: the **Great White Throne**, **Angel's Landing**, the **Three Patriarchs**, the **Pulpit** and the **Temple of Sinawava**. Scan the sheer rock faces and you may see the ant-like figures of climbers; routes are detailed in Eric Bjornstad's *Desert Rock: Rock Climbs in the National Parks* (Falcon), an excellent resource for any traveller wanting to go climbing in this part of the world.

There are plenty of hiking trails off the scenic drive. The busiest are the short easy routes along the valley floor, such as **Weeping Rock** (0.5 miles, 30 minutes) and the **Riverside Walk** (two miles, one and a half hours), but the best views are at the end of the **Watchman Trail** (two and a half miles, two hours; shade on the route is minimal) and the five-mile, four-hour trail to and from **Angel's Landing**. Don't even attempt the latter if you're afraid of heights: the last half-mile follows a steep, narrow ridge fitted with chains.

Perhaps the most spectacular hike is through the 16-mile **Narrows**, with canyon walls up to 2,000 feet (600 metres) high and at times only 20-30 feet apart. Be prepared to wade (or swim) through cold water and check conditions at the visitors' centre: there can be flash floods in summer. A permit ($10) is required for all hikes through the Narrows, as well as for all overnight hikes in the park.

East from Springdale and the scenic drive, you'll travel along the twisting **Zion–Mount Carmel Highway**, an engineering miracle when it was built in 1930. The impressive route leads through two long, narrow tunnels, passing scenery that is completely different from the landscapes of Zion Canyon. This is slickrock country: vast white, orange and pink rock formations, eroded into domes and buttes and marked with criss-cross patterns, loom next to the road. You can't miss the huge white monolith of **Checkerboard Mesa**.

Kolob Canyons, which is located in the park's north-western corner, has its own entrance (at exit 40 off I-15) and visitors' centre, from where a stunning five-mile drive leads into the red-rock **Finger Canyons**. There are also two hiking trails to embark on from here;

the longer trail culminates at **Kolob Arch**, which at 310 feet (95 metres) is possibly the world's largest natural arch reaching.

Where to eat & drink

Inside the park, the restaurant at **Zion Lodge** (*see below*) is open for breakfast, lunch and dinner. Reservations are recommended for the latter, especially in summer; call 1-435 772 7760.

Springdale has plenty of cafés and restaurants, but – this is Utah, folks – a shortage of bars. The closest you'll find is the **Bit & Spur** (1212 Zion Park Boulevard, 1-435 772 3498, www.bitandspur.com, main courses $12-$25), a Mexican-slanted restaurant with outdoor seating. **Oscar's Café** (612 Zion Park Boulevard, 1-435 772 3232, main courses $10-$18) serves sturdy burgers and other straightforward treats, while the family-friendly **Bumbleberry Restaurant** (897 Zion Park Boulevard, 1-435 772 3224, www.bumbleberry. com) has a nice line in breakfasts.

Where to stay

Within the park sits the rustic-style **Zion Lodge** (1-888 297 2757, 1-435 772 3213, www.zionlodge.com), built in 1925 by the Union Pacific Railroad. Accommodation at the lodge includes six suites ($171), 40 cabins ($161) and 75 motel-style rooms ($151); you'll need to book well in advance between April and October.

There are also three campgrounds inside the park. The **Watchman Campground** is open all year (rates $16-$20); reservations are taken from April to October (1-877 444 6777, http://reservations.nps.gov), with pitches allocated on a first-come, first-served basis at other times. The **South Campground** is open only from March to October and operates on a walk-up basis (rates $16). Group campgrounds are also available to organised groups of nine to 40 people by booking in advance (1-877 444 6777, http://reservations. nps.gov, rates $3).

There are many places to stay in Springdale, ranging from the cheap and friendly little **El Rio Lodge**, 995 Zion Park Boulevard, 1-888 772 3205, 1-435 772 3205, www.elrio lodge.com, double $39-$84) to the 40-room **Cliffrose Lodge & Gardens**, 281 Zion Park Boulevard, 1-800 243 8824, 1-435 772 3234, www.cliffroselodge.com, rates $139-$219 and, perhaps most appealingly, the **Desert Pearl Inn** (707 Zion Park Boulevard, 1-888 828 0898, 1-435 772 8888, www.desertpearl.com, double $143-$178). For details of other options, contact

the **Zion Canyon Visitors' Center** (*see below*); note that not all the town's hotels and motels are open in winter.

Getting there

To reach the park (164 miles from Vegas), take I-15 north, watching your speed once you leave Nevada (and being particularly careful in Arizona, where the police aren't slow to stop speeding cars). Head through the pleasant Mormon town of St George and turn right at exit 16 on to Highway 9 to Springdale. To visit the Kolob Canyons area, continue for 25 miles on I-15 until you reach exit 40.

Tourist information

Kolob Canyon Visitors' Center *3752 E Kolob Canyon Road, New Harmony (1-435 586 9548/www.nps.gov/zion).* **Open** *Spring, summer* 8am-5pm daily. *Autumn, winter* 8am-4.30pm daily.
Zion Canyon Visitors' Center *Springdale (information 1-435 772 3256/www.nps.gov/zion).* **Open** *Spring, autumn* 8am-6pm daily. *Summer* 8am-7pm daily. *Winter* 8am-5pm daily.
Zion Chamber of Commerce *1-888 518 7070/ www.zionpark.com.*

Beyond Zion

At **Mount Carmel Junction**, east of the park, Highway 9 joins up with US 89 for access to the rest of Utah and Arizona, and scenery that is arguably even more spectacular and other-worldly than in Zion.

Heading north on US 89 and then east on SR 12 takes you to **Bryce Canyon National Park** (1-435 834 5322, www.nps.gov/brca), where the landscape of vast rock hoodoos is breathtakingly odd. It's dramatically snow-soaked in winter but mild during the summer months, making it ideal for the casual hiker. Try the Tower Bridge Trail, a three-mile round-trip through some extraordinary scenery, or venture out on to the Rim Trail, which affords astonishing views of this peculiar landscape. Admission to the park is $25 for private vehicles, a pass that's valid for seven days. The website above has details on accommodation.

Travelling north up Highway 12 from Zion, through **Dixie National Forest**, brings you to the **Capitol Reef National Park** (1-435 425 3791, www.nps.gov/care). While it's by no means as spectacular as its neighbours, and doesn't offer anything like the variety of hikes that you'll find at Bryce Canyon or Zion, it's geologically fascinating and very much worth a brief diversion if you're heading this way.

Alternatively, leave Zion on US 89 south towards the **Grand Canyon** (*see pp284-291*).

Directory

Features

Adventuredome. *See p132.*

Directory

Getting Around

By air

McCarran International Airport (261 5211, www.mccarran.com) is just five minutes from the south end of the Strip, which makes the trip from airport to hotel relatively painless. The airport itself is clean and modern, and takes first (and last) tilt at the tourist dollar with halls of slot machines and video poker.

There are hundreds of internal flights to Las Vegas each week. However, direct international flights are limited; from the UK, for example, only Virgin Atlantic (from London Gatwick) and BMI (from Manchester) fly direct. Most flights to and from Europe require passengers to change at an East Coast airport or at LAX.

Public bus routes 108 and 109 run north from the airport: the 108 heads up Swenson Avenue and stops at the Las Vegas Hilton, while the 109 goes along Maryland Parkway. Shuttle buses run by **Bell Trans** (739 7990, www.bell-trans.com), **Grayline** (739 5700, www.grayline.com) and **Ritz** (889 4242, www.shuttle lasvegas.com) run to the Strip and Downtown 24 hours a day. Expect to pay $5-$7 for transport to a Strip hotel, slightly more to Downtown.

Taxis can be found outside the arrivals hall. There's a $1.20 surcharge on all fares originating at McCarran; bearing that in mind, expect to pay $10-$15 to get to most hotels on the Strip, or $15-$20 to Downtown (plus tip).

Airlines

Air Canada *1-888 247 2262/ aircanada.ca.*
Alaska Air *1-800 426 0333/ www.alaskaair.com.*
America West *1-800 235 9292/ www.americawest.com.*
American Airlines *1-800 433 7300/www.aa.com.*
BMI *UK: 0870 607 0222/ www.flybmi.com.*
Continental *domestic 1-800 523 3273/international 1-800 231 0856/ www.continental.com.*
Delta *domestic 1-800 221 1212/ international 1-800 241 4141/ www.delta.com.*
Jet Blue *1-800 538 2583/ www.jetblue.com.*
Northwest *domestic 1-800 225 2525/international 1-800 447 4747/ www.nwa.com.*
Southwest *1-800 435 9792/ www.southwest.com.*
United Airlines *domestic 1-800 864 8331/international 1-800 538 2929/www.united.com.*
US Airways *domestic 1-800 428 4322/international 1-800 622 1015/ www.usairways.com.*
Virgin Atlantic *UK: 0870 380 2007/US: 1-800 862 8621/www. virginatlantic.com.*

By road

Greyhound buses (1-800 231 2222, www.greyhound.com) arrive at the bus station on 200 Main Street, just by the Plaza. The ride from LA ($41.50 one-way, $80 round trip) takes between five and eight hours. Reservations are not required.

The **Citizens Area Transit** bus network (**CAT**, though the name may change), is run by the **Regional Transportation Commission of Southern Nevada** (**RTC**). The **Downtown Transportation Center** (**DTC**) is the transfer point for many routes. For a system map, *see p331.*

Downtown Transportation Center (DTC) *300 N Casino Center Boulevard, at E Stewart Avenue, Downtown (228 7433/www.rtc southernnevada.com). Bus Deuce & all DTC-bound buses.* **Open** *7am-5.30pm daily.* **Map** *p334 D1.*

CAT fares & tickets

Most **CAT** routes cost $1.25, or 60¢ for over-62s, 6-17s and the disabled. The exception is the Deuce route along the Strip, which costs $2 or $5 for a 24-hour pass. Use exact change; you must have a photocard (available from the DTC) to get a concessionary fare. Transfers are free, if you ask for one when you pay. A 30-day system pass costs $40.

CAT routes

Buses run 24-7 on the Deuce route along Las Vegas Boulevard, and roughly 5.30am-1.30am elsewhere. The buses are safe and relatively comprehensive in their coverage of the city. Bus stops are marked by white, green and purple signs; most have shelters.

The most useful bus for tourists is the **Deuce**: named as it's a double-decker bus, it travels the length of Las Vegas Boulevard from the DTC in the north to just by I-215 in the south, stopping in front of all major casinos. Deuces are often busy, especially at night.

Most bus routes run along the length of a single street, some with a quick turnaround at either end of the route. Buses with a route number beginning in '1' generally run north–south; those starting '2' run east–west. Below is a list of some key routes.

Deuce	Las Vegas Boulevard (south of DTC only)
103	Decatur Boulevard
105	Martin Luther King Boulevard/Industrial Road
106	Rancho Drive
107	Boulder Highway
108	Paradise Road
109	Maryland Parkway
110	Eastern Avenue
113	Las Vegas Boulevard (north of DTC only)
201	Tropicana Avenue
202	Flamingo Road
203	Spring Mountain Road/Sands Avenue/Twain Avenue
204	Sahara Avenue
206	Charleston Boulevard
207	Alta Drive/Stewart Avenue
208	Washington Boulevard

Many bus routes, among them the Deuce, 105, 107, 108, 109, 113 and 207, stop at the DTC. Throughout the listings in this book, we have used the shorthand 'DTC-bound buses' to refer to these buses.

Monorails & shuttle buses

After teething problems, the **Las Vegas Monorail** is now running a reliable service along Paradise Road and then behind the Strip. However, it hasn't displaced the numerous hotel buses and monorails.

Las Vegas Monorail
699 8200/www.lvmonorail.com.
The pricey and not wholly convenient Las Vegas Monorail runs from the **Sahara** to the **MGM Grand**, stopping at the **Las Vegas Hilton**, the **Las Vegas Convention Center**, **Harrah's**, the **Flamingo** and **Bally's**. The service runs 7am-2pm Mon-Thur, and 7am-3am Fri-Sun. The journey time from end to end is usually around 15 minutes. Single-ride tickets cost $5 and two-ride tickets go for $9, though the ten-ride package ($35) and day pass ($15) offer marginally better value.

Other monorails
Free, 24hr monorails, separate to the Las Vegas Monorail, link the **Mirage** and **TI**; and **Excalibur**, the **Luxor** and **Mandalay Bay**. For all of them, it's often quicker to walk.

Free shuttle buses
A shuttle bus connects the **Rio** with **Harrah's** on the Strip, just south of the **Aladdin**. Nearby, the **Palms**

lays on a shuttle to and from the **Fashion Show Mall** and the **Forum Shops**. The **Hard Rock** runs a shuttle that loops around from the hotel to the Forum Shops, Planet Hollywood and the MGM Grand. Shuttle buses link **Sam's Town** to Downtown and the Strip, and the **South Point** and the Strip. And there are free shuttle buses linking **Green Valley Ranch**, **Red Rock**, **Palace Station** and **Sunset Station** to both the Strip and McCarran Airport.

Taxis & limos

There are **taxi ranks** outside most hotels; restaurants and bars will be happy to call a cab for you. Technically, you're not allowed to hail a taxi from the street and most won't stop if you try, but it's usually OK to approach an empty cab with its light on if it has stopped in traffic. Meters start at $3.20, and increase by $2 per mile. If you have a complaint, note the cab number and call the **Nevada Taxicab Authority** (486 6532, www.taxi.state.nv. us). For lost property, *see p312*.

Limousines are a flash and popular way of getting around. The rides vary from the basic black stretch ($40/hr) to huge SUVs with hot tubs, disco balls and the like ($100/hr). Many limos are available for hire outside hotels and the airport. Limo drivers are not allowed to solicit passengers, but you are perfectly at liberty to approach them for a ride.

Cab companies
Yellow-Checker-Star (YCS)
873 2000/www.ycstrans.com.
Desert *386 9102.*
Whittlesea *384 6111.*

Limousine companies
Bell Trans *385 5466/ www.bell-trans.com.*
Las Vegas Limo *736 1419/ www.lasvegaslimo.com.*
Presidential *731 5577/ www.presidentiallimolv.com.*

Driving

If you're based on the Strip, a mix of buses, taxis, monorails and feet will get you to most

places. However, automobile rental is affordable in Vegas; a car is recommended if you're staying away from the Strip or are keen to visit off-Strip attractions, and essential if you're planning to visit any out-of-town destinations.

The Las Vegas streets get very congested in the morning and evening rush hours (7-9am, 4-6pm), as well as at weekends, when traffic is horrific in tourist areas after 4pm. The Strip is slow-going most of the time and turns into a virtual car park when the town is busy.

The nearby parallel streets – Industrial Road and Frank Sinatra Drive to the west, Paradise Road to the east – move faster, and provide access to several casinos. For north–south journeys longer than a block or two, it's often worth taking I-15, which runs parallel to the Strip. If you're trying to get east–west across town, take the Desert Inn arterial, a mini-expressway that runs under the Strip and over I-15 (though there are no junctions at either).

I-15 intersects with the east–west US 95 north-west of Downtown. US 95 connects to the 53-mile beltway at the edges of the valley, which leads commuters around the region. For road conditions, call 486 3116 or see www. nevadadot.com/traveler/roads.

Speed limits vary in Nevada. In general, the speed limit on freeways is 65mph; on the highway, it's either 65mph or 70mph. Limits on main urban thoroughfares (such as Tropicana Avenue) are 45mph; elsewhere, limits are 25mph, 30mph or 35mph. Look for signs in construction zones and near schools, which often enforce a reduced limit.

Unless otherwise specified, you can turn right on a red light, after stopping, if the street is clear. U-turns are not only legal (unless specified)

Directory

but often a positive necessity given the length of the blocks. In case of a car accident, call 911; do not move the cars involved in the accident until the police ask you to do so.

In Nevada, you can be arrested for driving under the influence if your blood alcohol level is 0.08 or higher (or 0.02 for under-21s. If you're pulled over, the police can give you a drink-driving test on the spot. If you refuse, you'll be taken to jail for a blood test, which will be taken by force if necessary.

Gas is far cheaper than in Europe, but pricey for the US. There are gas stations by Circus Circus and across from Mandalay Bay; stations abound on (among others) Paradise Road, Maryland Parkway, Tropicana Avenue and Flamingo Road. For mechanics and full-service gas stations, see 'Automobile repair' in the *Yellow Pages*.

The **American Automobile Association** (**AAA**) provides maps, guidebooks and other useful information. They're free if you're a member or belong to an affiliated organisation, such as the British AA. The main Vegas office, open 8.30am-5.30pm during the week, is at 3312 W Charleston Boulevard; call them on 870 9171 or see www.aaa.com for more details.

Car hire

Most car-hire agencies are at or near the airport. Call around for the best rate, booking well in advance if you're planning to visit over a holiday weekend or for a major convention. When business renters are scarce, though, you should get a good rate, and maybe – if you ask nicely – an upgrade.

Almost every firm requires a credit card and matching driver's licence; few will rent to under-25s. Prices won't include tax, liability insurance or collision damage waiver (CDW); US residents may be covered on their home policy, but foreign residents will need to buy extra insurance. UK travellers should note that while rental deals struck with the UK offices of the major firms include insurance, it's often cheaper to rent the car from the US office and rely for insurance on the good-value, year-long policy available from www.insurance4carhire.com.

Car rental companies

Alamo *US: 1-800 462 5266/ 263 8411/www.alamo.com. UK: 0870 400 4562/ www.alamo.co.uk.*
Avis *US: 1-800 331 1212/261 5595/www.avis.com. UK: 0870 606 0100/www.avis.co.uk.*
Budget *US: 1-800 527 0700/736 1212/www.budget.com. UK: 0844 581 2231/www.budget.co.uk.*
Dollar *US: 1-800 800 3665/www. dollar.com. UK: 0808 234 7524/ www.dollar.co.uk.*
Enterprise *US: 1-800 261 7331/ 365 6662/www.enterprise.com. UK: 0870 350 3000/www.enterprise.co.uk.*
Hertz *US: 1-800 654 3131/220 9700/www.hertz.com. UK: 0870 844 8844/www.hertz.co.uk.*
National *US: 1-800 227 7368/261 5391. UK: 0870 400 4581. Both: www.nationalcar.com.*
Thrifty *US: 1-800 847 4389/896 7600/www.thrifty.com. UK: 0808 234 7642/www.thrifty.co.uk.*

Motorcycle rental

Eaglerider *876 8687/www. eaglerider.com.*
Harley-Davidson of Southern Nevada *431 8500/www.lvhd.com.*

Parking

Most hotel-casinos have valet parking, which is convenient, safe and free (apart from the $2-$5 tip on your way out). If you see a sign saying the valet car park is full and you're in a luxury car, stay put: chances are the valets will find a spot for you. Hotel guests also get preferential treatment; when the attendant asks to see your room key, $5-$10 will often substitute. Self-parking is free at every Vegas resort (Downtown casinos require a validation stamp), but the convenience of lots is variable.

Cycling

In a word: don't. Some try and get away with cycling on the Strip on weekend nights, when traffic has slowed to a crawl. But it's dicey even then; and at other times, the drivers on the three- and four-lane roads in the city simply aren't looking for cyclists: you're taking your life in your hands.

Walking

Pedestrians are rarely seen off the Strip in Vegas, and even there they face danger from carefree and often careless drivers. The bridges on the Strip help, but it's still tricky. Jaywalking is so potentially deadly that police often issue citations. Laws, and physics, favour the driver: never put yourself in the path of cars that have the green light.

The safest places to cross are the overhead pedestrian bridges at several key Strip locations, bridges that (of course) guide you past the entrances of the casinos on each corner. You can find them at Tropicana Avenue, at Flamingo Road, and at Spring Mountain Road near Wynn Las Vegas. Where there are no bridges, closely follow all traffic signals and check both directions twice before stepping into the street.

It's possible to take short-cuts from one Strip hotel to the next, but you're likely to get trapped in a maze of service roads. Use our maps to guide you (*see pp333-336*) and don't underestimate the distances between resorts: the Strip is longer than it looks, and walking it end to end will take at least 90 minutes and almost certainly longer. And always factor in plenty of time to get out of the resort in which you've been staying, dining, gambling or partying: you may be as much as a 15-minute walk from the main exit.

Resources A-Z

Addresses

Written addresses follow the standard US format. The room and/or suite number usually appears after the street address (where applicable), followed by the city name and the zip code. Note that Las Vegas Boulevard South is the official name of the Strip. For more on street numbering and orientation, *see pp120-121*.

Age restrictions

Las Vegas is a carefree city of hedonism and wild abandon, but only if you're old enough.

Admission to nude clubs 18 (except Palomino).
Admission to topless clubs 21.
Buying/drinking alcohol 21.
Driving 16.
Gambling 21.
Marriage 16 (with parental consent) or 18 (without).
Sex 16 (heterosexual) or 18 (homosexual).

Attitude & etiquette

As a tourist city, Vegas is as formal or informal as you want it to be. During the warmer months, shorts and T-shirts are accepted wear along the Strip as well as on the gaming floors of most casinos, though dressing up to a minimum of smart-casual has become the norm. Some lounges and nightclubs have dress codes (sports shoes, T-shirts and jeans may be prohibited), and dining in some high-end restaurants can be formal.

Business

The climate and favourable tax structure have helped Nevada attract hundreds of companies to the city. But a stronger input into the Vegas economy comes from the six million business travellers who come to town each year for one of roughly 24,000 conventions. As a result, most major resorts offer excellent business services: faxing, copying and shipping services are standard; phone and computer hire is common, as are the presence of conference rooms; and in-room high-speed internet access is growing in popularity.

Conventions & conferences

Vegas is the convention capital of the US. Most conventions and trade fairs are held at the **Las Vegas Convention Center**, the **Sands Expo** and the convention centre at Mandalay Bay (*see p71*), with smaller shows held at other resorts and the Cashman Center near Downtown.

Las Vegas Convention Center

3150 Paradise Road, at Convention Center Drive, East of Strip (892 0711/www.lvcva.com). Bus 108, 213. **Map** p335 C5.
The largest convention facility in the US now contains 3.2 million sq ft (300,000sq m) of meeting and exhibition space, and it's soon to be expanded still further. Parking is pretty limited: if possible, either walk, take the Las Vegas Monorail or use shuttle buses.

Sands Expo & Convention Center

210 Sands Avenue, at Koval Lane, East of Strip (733 5556/www. sandsexpo.com). Bus 203, 213. **Map** p336 B6.
Second in size to the LVCC and connected to the Venetian, this facility offers the same excellent amenities, with even worse parking.

Convention dates

The LVCVA website (*see p316*) has a search engine listing the city's conventions. We've listed the town's most sizeable conventions and their approximate dates; check online for precise dates. Hotel rooms may well be hard to find during these periods, so book ahead.

Consumer Electronics Show (CES) (150,000 delegates) 4 days, early Jan.
World of Concrete (85,000 delegates) 4 days, mid-late Jan.
Nightclub & Bar Convention (40,000 delegates) 3 days, late Feb/ early Mar.
National Association of Broadcasters (140,000 delegates) 4 days, mid Apr.
World Shoe Association (35,000 delegates) 4 days, mid Feb & late July/early Aug.
Associated Surplus Dealers/ Associated Merchandise Dealers (ASD/AMD) (60,000 delegates) 5 days, mid Mar & mid Aug.
Automotive Aftermarket Products Expo (AAPEX) (130,000 delegates) 3 days, late Oct/ early Nov.
Specialty Equipment Marketing Association (SEMA) (130,000 delegates) 3 days, late Oct/early Nov.

Travel advice

For current information on travel to a specific country, including the latest news on health issues, safety and security, local laws and customs, contact your home country's government department of foreign affairs. Most have websites with useful advice for would-be travellers.

Australia
www.smartraveller.gov.au

Canada
www.voyage.gc.ca

New Zealand
www.safetravel.govt.nz

Republic of Ireland
http://foreignaffairs.gov.ie

UK
www.fco.gov.uk/travel

USA
http://travel.state.gov

Directory

Couriers & shippers

Many hotels have business centres with courier services.

DHL *1-800 225 5345/www.dhl.com.* **Credit** AmEx, DC, Disc, MC, V.
FedEx *1-800 463 3339/www.fedex. com.* **Credit** AmEx, DC, Disc, MC, V.
UPS *1-800 742 5877/www.ups.com.* **Credit** AmEx, Disc, MC, V.

Office services

Bit by Bit

221 2255/www.bit-by-bit.com. **Credit** AmEx, MC, V.
Bit by Bit rents laptops, desktop computers and other technological accoutrements. Call ahead to arrange delivery.

FedEx Kinko's

395 Hughes Center Drive, at Paradise Road, East of Strip (951 2400/http://fedex.kinkos.com). Bus 108, 213. **Open** 24hrs daily. **Credit** AmEx, Disc, MC, V. **Map** p336 C7.
The prominent chain of copy shops has five branches in the Las Vegas area; this is one of two that are open 24hrs. Services include printing, shipping and internet access. **Other locations** throughout the city.

Useful organisations

For the **Las Vegas Chamber of Commerce** and the **Las Vegas CVA**, *see p316.*

Consumer

For complaints about casinos, contact the **Gaming Control Board** (486 2000, http:// gaming.nv.gov). For general enquiries and complaints, contact the privately operated **Better Business Bureau** (320 4500, www.vegasbbb. org), which receives and investigates complaints, or the Consumer Affairs Division of the **Nevada Department of Business & Industry** (486 7355, www.fyiconsumer.org).

Customs

Travellers arriving in Vegas on an indirect international flight will go through customs and immigration at the airport in which they change planes. This involves reclaiming baggage at the transfer airport, taking it through customs and then checking it in again. Connection times should take account of this process.

On US flights, non-US citizens are given two forms – one for immigration, one for customs – which must be filled in and handed in at the appropriate desk on landing. Foreign visitors can import the following items duty-free: 200 cigarettes or 50 cigars (not Cuban; over-18s only) or 2kg of smoking tobacco; one litre of wine or spirits (over-21s only); and up to $100 in gifts ($800 for returning Americans). You must declare and maybe forfeit plants and foodstuffs. Check www.cbp.gov/xp/cgov/travel before travelling.

UK Customs & Excise allows returning travellers to bring in £145 of goods bought abroad. Citizens of other countries should check the rules in their country.

Disabled

Vegas is a disabled-friendly city. Strip resorts are fully wheelchair-accessible, from pools, spas and restrooms to gambling facilities; things are a little harder in the older Downtown properties. A few casinos offer games for sight- and hearing-impaired players. Disabled parking is found almost everywhere; buses and many taxis are adapted to take wheelchairs (though be sure to ask when you book).

The **Southern Nevada Center for Independent Living** (889 4216, www.sncil. org) offers advice, information, transport and equipment loans (including wheelchairs). The **Society of Accessible Travel and Hospitality** (1-212 447 7284, www.sath.org) can provide advice for disabled people planning trips to all corners of the US.

Drugs

The use of illegal drugs, including clubbing drugs such as ecstasy, is quite prevalent in Sin City. Dealers will approach you all over town, but take care. And always watch your drinks: illicit, hard-to-trace drugs are sometimes slipped into unattended glasses.

The local authorities have a strict zero-tolerance policy on drug use and trafficking. If you're implicated in a drug sale or purchase, you will be arrested and subject to trial, and if convicted could receive a maximum sentence of five to ten years in prison.

Electricity

The US uses a 110-120V, 60-cycle AC voltage. Except for dual-voltage flat-pin shavers, most foreign visitors will need to run appliances through an adaptor. Most US TVs and DVDs use a different frequency from those in Europe.

Embassies & consulates

The nearest foreign embassies and consulates to Las Vegas are in Los Angeles.

Australia *Suite 3150, Century Plaza Towers, 2029 Century Park East, Los Angeles, CA 90067 (1-310 229 4800/www.dfat.gov.au).* **Open** 9am-5pm Mon-Fri.
Canada *9th Floor, 550 S Hope Street, Los Angeles, CA 90071 (1-213 346 2700/http://geo. international.gc.ca).* **Open** 8.30am-4.30pm Mon-Fri.
New Zealand *Suite 600E, 2425 Olympic Boulevard, Santa Monica, CA 90404 (1-310 566 6555/ www.nzcgla.com).* **Open** 8.30am-1pm, 1.30-4.30pm Mon-Fri.
Republic of Ireland *Suite 3350, 100 Pine Street, San Francisco, CA 94111 (1-415 392 4214/ www.irelandemb.org).* **Open** 10am-noon, 2-3.30pm Mon-Fri.
South Africa *Suite 600, 6300 Wilshire Boulevard, Los Angeles, CA 90048 (1-323 651 0902/www. saembassy.org).* **Open** 9am-noon Mon-Fri.

United Kingdom *Suite 1200, 11766 Wilshire Boulevard, Los Angeles, CA 90025 (1-310 481 0031/24hr emergencies 1-877 514 1233).* **Open** 8.30am-5pm Mon-Fri.

Emergencies

In an emergency, dial **911** (free from public phones) and state the nature of the problem.

Gay & lesbian

Q-Vegas (www.qvegas.com) is the leading media resource for the GLBT community. You can pick up the monthly magazine at, among others, **Get Booked** (*see p249*), or download it from its website.

Center

Commercial Center, 953 E Sahara Avenue, between S 6th Street & S Maryland Parkway, East of Strip (733 9800/www.thecenter-lasvegas. com). Bus 109, 204. **Open** 10am-7pm Mon-Fri; 10am-3pm Sat. **Map** p333 Y2.
A support organisation for the gay, lesbian, bisexual and transgender communities, the Center organises a wild variety of social events, from miniature golf tournaments to leather nights, and is a meeting place for a variety of groups; check its website for a full calendar of events.

Health

Doctors are available around the clock in emergency rooms and at some UMC Quick Care locations, and by appointment during regular hours. Take the prescription to a licensed pharmacist (*see p206*), who'll usually be able to provide the medication within minutes.

Most hospitals accept major insurance plans, but – unless it's an emergency – you should call ahead to check. Large hotels have access to on-call doctors, at a cost.

Accident & emergency

All the hospitals listed below have a 24-hour ER, although only **Sunrise** and **UMC** have out-and-out trauma centres.

The UMC on Charleston is the only hospital that by law must treat all applicants. The ER entrance is on the corner of Hasting and Rose Streets.

Desert Springs Hospital *2075 E Flamingo Road, at Burnham Street, East Las Vegas (733 8800/www. desertspringshospital.net). Bus 202.*
North Vista Hospital *1409 E Lake Mead Boulevard, between Las Vegas Boulevard North & N Eastern Avenue, North Las Vegas (649 7711/www.northvistahospital.com). Bus 113, 210.*
St Rose Dominican Hospital *102 E Lake Mead Drive, at Boulder Highway, Henderson (564 2622/ www.strosecares.com). Bus 107, 212.*
Summerlin Hospital Medical Center *657 N Town Center Drive, at Hualapai Way, North-west Las Vegas (233 7000/www.summerlin hospital.org). No bus.*
Sunrise Hospital & Medical Center *3186 S Maryland Parkway, between E Sahara Avenue & E Desert Inn Road, East Las Vegas (731 8000/ www.sunrisehospital.com). Bus 109.*
University Medical Center *1800 W Charleston Boulevard, at Shadow Lane, West Las Vegas (383 2000/ www.umc-cares.org). Bus 206.*
Valley Hospital Medical Center *620 Shadow Lane, off W Charleston Boulevard, West Las Vegas (388 4000/www.valleyhospmedcenter.com). Bus 206.*

Complementary medicine

The city's few practitioners of complementary medicine enjoy a healthy business, as do aromatherapists and herbal healers. All of the major hotel spas include some form of aromatherapy.

Contraception & abortion

Planned Parenthood

3220 W Charleston Boulevard, between S Rancho Drive & S Valley View Boulevard, West Las Vegas (878 7776/www.pprm.org). Bus 206. **Open** (appointment only) 9am-5pm Mon, Tue, Thur; 11am-7pm Wed; 9am-4pm Fri; 9am-2pm Sat.
This non-profit organisation can supply contraception (including the morning-after pill), treat STDs, perform abortions and test for AIDS (results take a week).
Other location Suite 54, 3320 E Flamingo Road (547 9888).

Dentists

The **Nevada Dental Association** (255 4211, www.nvda.org) will make referrals to registered local dentists, including Medicaid and Medicare practitioners.

Hospitals

See above **Accident & emergency**.

Pharmacies

Both over-the-counter and prescription drugs are readily available all over town. For pharmacies, *see p206*.

STDs, HIV & AIDS

For specific information on HIV/AIDS, local resources, various support groups and free, confidential tests, contact **Aid for AIDS of Nevada**. For treatment of STDs and free AIDS tests, visit **Planned Parenthood** (*see above*). *See also below* **Helplines**.

Aid for AIDS of Nevada (AFAN) *Suite 211, Sahara Rancho Medical Center, 2300 S Rancho Drive, between W Sahara Avenue & W Oakey Boulevard, West of Strip (382 2326/hotline 842 2437/www.inside afan.org). Bus 106.* **Open** 7am-5pm Mon-Fri.

Helplines

For information on what to do in an emergency, *see above*. *See also above* **Health**.

AIDS Information Line *759 0743.*
Alcoholics Anonymous *598 1888.*
Gamblers Anonymous *385 7732.*
Narcotics Anonymous *369 3362.*
Poison Control Center *732 4989.*
Rape Crisis *366 1640.*
Suicide Prevention *731 2990.*

ID

You'll need to prove your age with a photo ID (passport, driver's licence or state ID card) when buying tobacco and alcohol, gambling, and entering strip clubs and nightclubs.

Directory

Insurance

Non-nationals should arrange comprehensive baggage, trip-cancellation and medical insurance before departure; US citizens should consider doing the same. Medical centres will ask for details of your insurance company and your policy number; keep them with you at all times.

Internet

Most hotels have high-speed connections wired into every room (around $10 per day); some have wireless access. Savvy laptoppers can link to free Wi-Fi at 12 branches of the **Coffee Bean & Tea Leaf**, among them in the Miracle Mile Shops (*see p192*; 696 0564), at the Venetian (*see p75*; 650 0734) and in the University District (4550 S Maryland Parkway, between E Flamingo Road & E Tropicana Avenue (944 5029). There's also free wireless in the **Fashion Show Mall** (*see p193*) near the Apple Store, and in the city's libraries (*see below*).

For those without a laptop, the pickings are slimmer. A few convenience stores have terminals (there's one by the Hawaiian Marketplace; *see p126*), but prices are high. Public libraries (*see below*) offer free, time-limited access; **FedEx Kinko's** (*see p310*) has paid-for access; and the display computers in the Apple Store serve as an unofficial internet café.

Left luggage

Hotel bell desks are happy to look after bags for up to 12 hours. Lockers are available in McCarran Airport; expect to pay $2-$3/hr or $8-$12/day.

Legal help

If you're arrested, call your insurance firm, your consulate or the Lawyer Referral Service on 382 0504. If you do not have a lawyer, the court will appoint one for you.

Libraries

Las Vegas–Clark County Library District

www.lvccld.org. Libraries open 9am-9pm Mon-Thur; 10am-6pm Fri-Sun.
Clark County Library *1401 E Flamingo Road, at S Maryland Parkway, University District (507 3400). Bus 109, 202.* **Map** p333 Y3.
Enterprise Library *25 E Shelbourne Avenue, at Las Vegas Boulevard South, South Las Vegas (507 3760). Bus 117.*
Green Valley Library *2797 N Green Valley Parkway, at E Sunset Road, Henderson (507 3790). Bus 114, 212.*
Las Vegas Library *833 Las Vegas Boulevard North, between E Bonanza Road & E Washington Avenue, North of Strip (507 3500). Bus 113.* **Map** p334 D1.
Rainbow Library *3150 N Buffalo Drive, at W Cheyenne Avenue, North Las Vegas (507 3710). Bus 211, 218.*
Sahara West Library *9600 W Sahara Avenue, between S Hualapai Way & S Fort Apache Road, West Las Vegas (507 3630). Bus 204.*
Spring Valley Library *4280 S Jones Boulevard, at W Flamingo Road, South-west Las Vegas (507 3820). Bus 102, 202.*
Summerlin Library *1771 Inner Circle Drive, Summerlin (507 3860). Bus 210.*
West Charleston Library *6301 W Charleston Boulevard, between S Jones & S Rainbow Boulevards, West Las Vegas (507 3940). Bus 206.*
West Las Vegas Library *951 W Lake Mead Boulevard, at N Martin Luther King Boulevard, West Las Vegas (507 3980). Bus 105, 210.*
Whitney Library & Recital Hall *5175 E Tropicana Avenue, at S Nellis Boulevard, East Las Vegas (507 4010). Bus 201.*

Lied Library

4505 S Maryland Parkway, between E Flamingo Road & E Tropicana Avenue, University District (895 3531/www.library.nevada.edu). Bus 109. **Open** 7.30am-midnight Mon-Thur; 7.30am-7pm Fri; 9am-6pm Sat; 11am-midnight Sun. **Map** p333 Y3. This $40-million facility houses 1.8 million volumes.

Lost property

Casinos all have lost and found departments. If you lose an item in a cab, call the taxi firm.

McCarran International Airport *Terminal 1 (261 5134).* **Open** 6.30am-1am daily.
Citizens Area Transit (CAT) *South Strip Transfer Terminal, 6675 S Gillespie Street, at I-215 (1-800 228 3911/228 7433). Bus Deuce, 105, 109, 212.* **Open** 7am-5.30pm Mon-Fri.

Media

Daily newspapers

The **Las Vegas Review-Journal** (50¢, or $1 in casinos; $2.50 on Sunday; www.lvrj.com) offers toothless but serviceable coverage of local and national stories. John L Smith is the must-read columnist for local politicos, a useful counterpoint to the entertainingly awful weekly columns of publisher Sherman Frederick; Norm Clarke covers gossip with tireless enthusiasm; and Mike Weatherford writes astutely about the local entertainment scene. 'Neon', the *R-J*'s pull-out entertainment guide issued each Friday, has listings for films, shows and restaurants.

The **Las Vegas Sun** (www.lasvegassun.com) once offered a populist, left-leaning alternative to the conservative *R-J*, but it's now an eight-page shadow of its former self, folded into the *R-J* each morning; however, despite this curious arrangement, the papers are run separately. The *Sun*'s news reporting has considerably more bite than the *R-J*, with Jon Ralston's column a real draw.

As well as the city's two daily papers, the **Los Angeles Times** (50¢) is widely available, and most Strip hotels will also carry the **Wall Street Journal** (75¢) and the **New York Times** ($1). International media is harder to find, though the branches of **Borders** (*see p194*) keep a pretty good stock of magazines and newspapers from abroad.

Alternative weeklies

Established in 1992 as *Scope* and purchased in 1998 by the Greenspun family, the **Las Vegas Weekly** (free, www. lasvegasweekly.com) has gone through various editorial phases, but is now very much focused on entertainment. Ironically, then, it's at its best when it looks at the broader picture of Las Vegas life, with skilled reporter Joshua Longobardy and roving columnist Liz Armstrong among the writers who are always well worth a read.

It's debatable whether Las Vegas really needs two alt-weeklies. Even so, until **Las Vegas CityLife** (www. lasvegascitylife.com) absorbed the *Las Vegas Mercury* into its pages in 2005, the city actually had three of 'em. A good deal less glossy and a touch more political than the *Weekly*, the relatively low-key *CityLife* retains a fanbase. The writing is solid and often excellent, but the design is right out of 1985.

Other magazines

Numerous freebie mags, such as **Today in Las Vegas**, **What's On** and **Las Vegas Magazine**, are distributed for free at hotels and other tourist spots. They're useful for show listings and discount coupons, but the editorial is little more than regurgitated press releases; don't stop here if you're after recommendations.

A couple of free magazines launched in 2006 and 2007, each with a different focus. The calm, cultured **Vurb** (www.vurbmagazine.com) has its eye trained firmly on Downtown, while the more raucous **Racket** (www.racket online.com) is more interested in the city's nightlife. It's the sister mag to **944** (www.944. com), which is just as shiny and celeb-oriented as long-running glossy **Vegas**.

For gaming news, check out the monthly **Las Vegas Advisor**, focused on the city, or the weekly **Gaming Today**, which has a wider remit. Other business news is covered in the monthly **Nevada Business Journal**, and two weeklies, **In Business Las Vegas** and the **Las Vegas Business Press**. And last but not least, keep an eye out for **Las Vegas Life**, a better-than-average monthly glossy that costs $3.99 on newsstands but is often found for free in hotel rooms.

Radio

FM radio in Vegas is a bland parade of hackneyed playlists and punchable DJs suitable only for splicing together ads for car sales and topless joints. The best station in town is **KNPR**, one of two National Public Radio affiliates.

On AM, news and sports dominate. All the big national shows are syndicated here, with **KXNT** 840AM bringing a particularly pungent triple-threat in the forms of fearsome conservative Rush Limbaugh (9am-noon), agony aunt Laura Schlessinger (noon-3pm) and serial controversialist Sean Hannity (3-6pm).

Radio stations
KCEP *88.1 FM/www.power88lv.com.* Urban contemporary tunes.
KNPR *88.9 FM/www.knpr.org.* News, talk and commentary from this National Public Radio affiliate.
KCNV *89.7 FM/www.classical897.org.* Classical music; another NPR station.
KUNV *91.5 FM/http://kunv.unlv.edu.* Mostly jazz, but pretty eclectic.
KOMP *92.3 FM/www.komp.com.* Mainstream rock.
KMXB *94.1 FM/www.mix941.fm.* Adult alternative and 1980s hits.
KWNR *95.5 FM/www.kwnr.com.* Country and western.
KKLZ *96.3 FM/www.963kklz.com.* Classic rock.
KXPT *97.1/www.point97.com.* More classic rock.
KLUC *98.5 FM/www.kluc.com.* Mainstream pop.
KWID *101.9 FM/www.wild102.com.* Hip hop.
KJUL *104.7 FM/www.kjul1047.com.* Your (grand)parents' favourite tunes.

KSNE *106.5 FM/www.ksne.com.* Light rock and pop.
KVGS *107.9 FM/www.area108.com.* Mainstream alternative.

Television

The Las Vegas affiliates of the four major American networks are **KVBC 3** (NBC), **KVVU 5** (Fox), **KLAS 8** (CBS) and **KTNV 13** (ABC). The city's public broadcasting affiliate is **KLVX 10**. Every hotel TV will get these stations and plenty of others; among them is **Las Vegas One**, co-run by KLAS. Most hotels will also offer subscription-based cable networks such as **CNN** (news), **ESPN** (sport) and **HBO** (movies). Daily TV listings can be found in the *R-J* and *TV Guide*.

Money

The US dollar ($) is split into 100 cents (¢). Coins run from the copper penny (1¢) to the silver nickel (5¢), dime (10¢), quarter (25¢), the less common half-dollar (50¢) and the rarely seen dollar (silver and gold). Notes ('bills') are all the same green colour and size, but come in denominations of $1, $5, $10, $20, $50 and $100. Credit cards are accepted in almost every hotel, shop and restaurant, but do keep cash on hand just in case (and, of course, for tips).

Banks & ATMs

ATMs are ubiquitous in Las Vegas: you'll find them in stores, bars, casinos and even strip clubs. ATMs accept most major credit and debit cards, but almost all will charge a usage fee. You can withdraw cash on a card without a PIN at most casinos, though you'll be charged a premium. It's cheaper to visit one of the banks scattered all over town; ask staff at your hotel for details of your nearest.

Directory

Bureaux de change

Some casinos have their own bank or bureau de change; all have a 24-7 cashier's cage where you can cash most US bank and travellers' cheques, and exchange most major currencies. Indeed, the casinos tend to offer better rates on currency than **American Express**. At non-casino hotels, you should be able to cash travellers' cheques at the front desk with photo ID.

American Express *Fashion Show Mall, 3200 Las Vegas Boulevard South, at Spring Mountain Road (739 8474/www.americanexpress.com). Bus Deuce, 205, 203.* **Open** *9am-9pm Mon-Fri; 10am-8pm Sat; 11am-6pm Sun.* **Map** *p335 & p336 A6.*

Lost/stolen credit cards

American Express *1-800 992 3404/travellers' cheques 1-800 221 7282/www.americanexpress.com.* **Diners Club** *1-800 234 6377/ www.dinersclub.com.* **Discover** *1-800 347 2683/ www.discovercard.com.* **MasterCard** *1-800 622 7747/ www.mastercard.com.* **Visa** *1-800 847 2911/www.visa.com.*

Tax

Sales tax is 7.75%; food (groceries) purchased in stores are exempt. Room tax is 9%, or 11% for Downtown properties.

Natural hazards

The most obvious hazards are the heat and the sun (*see p316*), but summer visitors should be prepared for other severe weather: flash floods are not uncommon in July and August.

Opening hours

The casinos, their bars and at least one of their restaurants or coffeeshops are open all day, every day. Many grocery stores, dry-cleaners and gas stations are also open 24-7. On a local level, however, Las

Vegas keeps small-town hours. Many eateries close at 10pm; non-chain shops may shut at 6pm and won't open on Sundays. Office hours are 9am to 5pm or thereabouts.

Police

For emergencies, *see p311*. For non-emergencies, there's a police station at 400 E Stewart Avenue, just off Las Vegas Boulevard in Downtown (795 3111).

Postal services

US mailboxes are red, white and blue. Packages weighing more than 16 ounces must be taken to a post office (*see below*). For couriers and shippers, *see p310*.

Stamps are sold in shops and from machines. For most transactions, contract stations in Albertsons stores should suffice. For your nearest post office, call 1-800 275 8777 and quote the zip code.

Main post office *1001 E Sunset Road, at Paradise Road, East of Strip (1-800 275 8777). Bus 212.* **Open** *8am-9pm Mon-Fri; 8am-4pm Sat.* **Map** *p333 Y4.*
Downtown station *201 Las Vegas Boulevard South, between E Fremont Street & F. Bonneville Avenue (1-800 275 8777). Bus Deuce & all DTC-bound buses.* **Open** *8.30am-5pm Mon-Fri.* **Map** *p334 D1.*
Strip station *3100 Industrial Road, at Stardust Way, West of Strip (1-800 275 8777). Bus Deuce, 105.* **Open** *8.30am-5pm Mon-Fri.* **Map** *p335 A5.*

Poste restante

General delivery mail (*poste restante*) can be collected from the Downtown station (to: General Delivery, Las Vegas, NV 89101). You'll need to show photo ID when you collect it.

Religion

For your nearest **Episcopal** church, call 737 9190; and for **Methodist**, 369 7055. For others, consult the phone book.

Congregation Ner Tamid *55 Valley Verde Drive, Henderson (733 6292). Bus 112.* Jewish Reform.
First Baptist Church *4400 W Oakey Boulevard, West Las Vegas (821 1234). Bus 104.*
First Presbyterian Church *1515 W Charleston Boulevard, West of Strip (384 4554). Bus 206.* **Map** *p335 B3.*
Guardian Angel Cathedral *302 Cathedral Way, at E Desert Inn Road (735 5241). Bus Deuce.* **Map** *p335 B5.* The Catholic diocese of Reno-Las Vegas.
Islamic Center of Las Vegas *3799 Edwards Avenue, North-west Las Vegas (395 7013). Bus 106.*
Latter-Day Saints Las Vegas Temple *827 N Temple View Drive, East Las Vegas (452 5011). Bus 208.* The Church of Jesus Christ of Latter-Day Saints (Mormons) only.
Temple Beth Sholom *10700 Havenwood Lane, Las Vegas (804 1333). Bus 211.* The city's oldest Jewish congregation.

Safety & security

There's less crime than you might expect in Las Vegas. Casinos have such elaborate security systems that few serious offences take place within them, and those that do occur are hurriedly swept under the carpet. However, on the streets, pickpockets and muggers strike more often than the city would like. Be careful, especially in the seedier areas of Downtown, and follow a few simple precautions.

● Only take out what you need: leave the bulk of your money in a room safe or in a safety deposit box at the hotel.
● Keep a note of the numbers and details of your passport, driving licence, travellers' cheques, cards and insurance policies, along with the phone numbers you'll need to report their loss (*see above*).
● Take the usual precautions with your wallet or handbag, especially on buses.
● If you're threatened with a weapon, give your assailants what they want. Then immediately find a phone and call the police (911).

Passport update

People of all ages (children included) who enter the US on the Visa Waiver Program (VWP; see p316) are now required to carry their own machine-readable passport, or MRP. MRPs are recognisable by the double row of characters along the foot of the data page. All burgundy EU and EU-lookalike passports issued in the UK since 1991 (and still valid) should be machine-readable. However, some of those issued outside the country may not be; in this case, holders should apply for a replacement even if the passport has not expired. Check at your local passport-issuing post office if in any doubt at all.

The US's requirement for passports to contain a 'biometric' chip applies only to those issued from 26 October 2006. All new and replacement UK passports should be compliant, following a gradual phase-in. The biometric chip contains a facial scan and biographical data.

Though it is being considered for 2008, when ID cards may be introduced, there is no current requirement for UK passports to contain fingerprint or iris data. The application process remains as it was, except for new guidelines that ensure the photograph you submit can be used to generate the facial scan in the chip.

Further information for UK citizens is available at www.passport.gov.uk or 0870 521 0410. Nationals of other countries should check well in advance of their trip whether their passport meets the requirements for the time of their trip, at http://travel.state.gov/visa and with the issuing authorities of their home country.

Smoking

In 2007, smoking was banned in most establishments that serve prepared food (casinos and strip clubs were exempt). However, many businesses flouted the law, and it remains a matter for debate whether continued enforcement is possible. Smoking is ubiquitous on casino floors, though a couple have non-smoking areas. A few hotels (such as the Four Seasons) are entirely smoke-free; most others offer non-smoking rooms.

Study

Many local colleges feed the service and gaming industry. Those looking to learn how to become a dealer or croupier must attend one of the city's specialist dealer schools.

PCI Dealers School *920 S Valley View Boulevard, Las Vegas, NV 89102 (877 4724/www.pcidealerschool.com).*

Telephones

Dialling & codes

There are two area codes for Nevada: 702 for Clark County (including Las Vegas) and 775 for the rest of the state. Within Vegas, there's no need to use 702: just dial the seven-digit number. Outside the city, calls are long distance: dial 1, then the area code, then the number. The 1-800, 1-866, 1-877 and 1-888 codes denote toll-free numbers; many are accessible from outside the US, but you'll be charged for your call. Calls to 1-900 numbers will be charged at premium rates.

Most hotels charge a flat fee of between 50¢ and $1 for calls to local and toll-free numbers. You can get around this at some hotels by using a house phone and asking the operator to connect you. Long-distance and international calls can be pricey if direct-dialled from a hotel. You're better off using a US phonecard, whether tied to a domestic account or bought as a one-off. Drugstores and convenience stores sell them in various denominations.

Mobile phones

Vegas operates on the 1900 GSM frequency. European travellers with tri-band phones will be fine; all others will need to rent a handset (see p212).

Operator services

Collect calls (reverse-charge) 0.
Local directory enquiries 411.
National directory enquiries 1 + [area code] + 555 1212 (if you don't know the area code, dial 0 for the operator).
International calls 011 + [country code] + [area code] + [number].
International country codes UK 44; New Zealand 64; Australia 61; Germany 49; Japan 81.

Public phones

Payphones are harder to find these days, though casinos still have them. To use one, check for a tone and then put in your change (35¢ for a local call; await an operator for long-distance calls). Operator and emergency calls are free. Some payphones accept credit cards.

Time

Nevada operates on Pacific Standard Time, eight hours behind GMT (London). Clocks go forward by an hour in late April, and back in late October. (Note: neighbouring Arizona has no daylight saving time.)

Tipping

Limo drivers ($10-$25 per ride), valet parking attendants ($2-$5), cocktail waitresses

($1-$2), housekeepers ($2-$4 a night) and even desk clerks ($10-$20 if you're looking for a better room) all ride the tip gravy train. For detailed information on tipping in casinos, *see pp46-47*.

Tourist information

There are many self-styled tourist offices on the Strip, but only those listed below are official. For the Nevada Commission on Tourism's contact details, *see p277*.

Las Vegas Chamber of Commerce

Hughes Center, 3720 Howard Hughes Parkway, between Sands Avenue & E Flamingo Road, East of Strip, Las Vegas, NV 89109 (735 1616/www.lvchamber.com). Bus 108, 203. **Open** 8am-5pm Mon-Fri. **Map** p336 C6.
Advice, brochures, maps and a few coupons are available if you visit in person; there's also a good phone information service, and you can write in advance for a visitor pack.

Las Vegas Convention & Visitors Authority

3150 Paradise Road, opposite Convention Center Drive, East of Strip, Las Vegas, NV 89109 (892 0711/www.visitlasvegas.com). Bus 108, 213. **Open** 8am-5pm Mon-Fri. **Map** p335 C5.
Write to the very excellent LVCVA for a visitor pack that includes lists of hotels, a brochure, a map and the regularly updated *Showguide*. In the UK, contact Cellet Travel Services for details on Vegas (01564 794999, www.visitlasvegas.co.uk).

Visas & immigration

Under the **Visa Waiver Program**, citizens of 27 countries, including the UK, Ireland, Australia and New Zealand, do not need a visa for stays in the US of less than 90 days (business or pleasure) if they have a passport valid for six months beyond the return date and a return (or open standby) ticket. Canadians and Mexicans do not need visas. All other travellers must have visas. For more information, *see p315* **Passport update**; *see also below* **Work**.
Visa application forms can be obtained from your nearest US embassy or consulate. UK travellers should check the US Embassy's website at www.usembassy.org.uk, or call its helpline on 09042 450100 (£1.20 a minute).

When to go

Though there's no off-season in Las Vegas, it's slightly quieter (and cheaper) between Thanksgiving and Christmas, and during the heat of July and August. Public holidays are always busy. If you're planning a short visit, try to avoid busy, pricey weekends. The convention schedule (*see p309*) has a major effect on hotel prices and availability.

Climate

Las Vegas has blue skies and little rain all year round. In July and August, it can get absurdly hot during the day, with temperatures soaring to more than 110°F (43°C). Drink lots of water and wear a hat, sunglasses and sunscreen. Conversely, winter nights can dip below freezing.

Public holidays

1 Jan New Year's Day; **3rd Mon in Jan** Martin Luther King Jr Holiday; **3rd Mon in Feb** Presidents' Day; **Mar/Apr** Easter Sunday; **last Mon in May** Memorial Day; **4 July** Independence Day; **1st Mon in Sept** Labor Day; **last Fri in Oct** Nevada Day; **2nd Mon in Nov** Veterans' Day; **4th Thur in Nov** Thanksgiving; **25 Dec** Christmas Day.

Women

Las Vegas is an interesting contradiction in feminist politics. On the one hand, women are objectified in the entertainment industry; on the other, they fare well in the job market. There's no women's centre; the **UNLV Women's Studies Office** (895 0837) is a good first contact.

Work

To work, non-nationals must be sponsored by a US company and get an H-1 visa. They also have to convince immigration that no American is qualified to do the job. Contact your US embassy for details.

Climate

	Ave high	Ave low	Ave rainfall
January	57°F (14°C)	37°F (3°C)	0.59in (1.5cm)
February	63°F (17°C)	41°F (5°C)	0.69in (1.8cm)
March	69°F (21°C)	47°F (8°C)	0.59in (1.5cm)
April	78°F (26°C)	54°F (12°C)	0.15in (0.4cm)
May	88°F (31°C)	63°F (17°C)	0.24in (0.6cm)
June	99°F (37°C)	72°F (22°C)	0.08in (0.2cm)
July	104°F (40°C)	78°F (26°C)	0.44in (1.1cm)
August	102°F (39°C)	77°F (25°C)	0.45in (1.1cm)
September	94°F (34°C)	69°F (21°C)	0.31in (0.8cm)
October	81°F (27°C)	57°F (14°C)	0.24in (0.6cm)
November	66°F (19°C)	44°F (7°C)	0.31in (0.8cm)
December	57°F (14°C)	37°F (3°C)	0.40in (1cm)

Average sunshine: 294 days per year (211 clear, 83 partly cloudy)

Further Reference

Books

Non-fiction

Al Alvarez
The Biggest Game in Town
It's more than two decades old, but
Alvarez's account of the World Series
of Poker still fascinates.

**Fred E Basten & Charles
Phoenix** *Fabulous Las Vegas in
the 50s: Glitz, Glamor & Games*
A nostalgic full-colour collection of
photographs, menus and postcards
from the lost glory days of Vegas.

Susan Berman *Easy Street*;
*Lady Las Vegas: The Inside Story
Behind America's Neon Oasis*
Written by the daughter of a Mob
insider, and made all the more
creepy by her murder in 1999.

Eric Bjourstad *Desert Rock:
Rock Climbs in the National Parks*
A useful desert companion.

Jeff Burbank *License to Steal*
A detailed exposition of the legal side
of Nevada gaming control and how it
participated in building Las Vegas.

Deke Castleman
*Whale Hunt in the Desert: The Secret
Las Vegas of Superhost Steve Cyr*
A fascinating glimpse into the world
of the high roller, via one of the
town's most powerful casino hosts.

Su Kim Chung
Las Vegas Then and Now
Vintage photographs of Las Vegas,
printed alongside images of the same
locations in the 21st century. A nice
idea, executed well.

Sally Denton & Roger Morris
*The Money and the Power: The
Making of Las Vegas and Its Hold
on America*
This investigative history of how
Vegas was shaped and corrupted
is perhaps the best single-volume
history of the city.

Pete Early *Super Casino:
Inside the 'New' Las Vegas*
A fizzing journalistic account of the
1990s revolution in resort-building.

William L Fox
In the Desert of Desire
The nature of culture and the culture
of nature in Las Vegas.

Jeff German
*Murder in Sin City: The Death
of a Las Vegas Casino Boss*
Reporter German explores the
1998 death of Ted Binion.

**Mark Gottdiener, Claudia C
Collins & David R Dickens**
*Las Vegas: The Social Production
of an All-American City*
A fascinating look at the social
phenomenon of Vegas, from how a
city grows in the desert to what it
means to live off the tourist dollar.

AD Hopkins & KJ Evans (eds)
*The First 100: Portraits of the Men
and Women Who Shaped Las Vegas*
A thought-provoking, well-written
encyclopaedia.

Joan Burkhart Whitely
*Young Las Vegas 1905-1931:
Before the Future Found Us*
A photographic essay on the city's
early years.

**The story of the city's
Shaun Levy** *Rat Pack Confidential*
A modern, funky appraisal of the Rat
Pack years and beyond.

Andrès Martinez
*24/7: Living It Up and Doubling
Down in the New Las Vegas*
An attorney and journalist spends
his $50,000 advance in this modern-
day *Fear and Loathing*.

Robert D McCracken *Las Vegas:
The Great American Playground*
A mix of history and commentary,
and a great read to boot.

James McManus *Positively Fifth
Street: Murders, Cheetahs, and
Binion's World Series of Poker*
McManus was sent on assignment to
cover the 2000 World Series of Poker,
but ended up taking part. Great fun.

**Eugene P Moehring
& Michael S Green**
Las Vegas: A Centennial History
The best of the centennial books.

Dick Odessky
*Fly on the Wall: Recollections of Las
Vegas' Good Old, Bad Old Days*
Very readable first-person tales of
1950s and '60s Vegas.

William F Roemer
*The Enforcer: Spilotro – The Chicago
Mob's Man over Las Vegas*
Vegas attorney Oscar Goodman kept
Tony 'The Ant' Spilotro out of jail for
a decade. Now Goodman is mayor
and Spilotro is dead, beaten to death
and buried in an Indiana cornfield.

Hal Rothman *Neon Metropolis: How
Las Vegas Started the 21st Century*
Late UNLV history professor
deconstructs Las Vegas's myth.

**Hal Rothman & Mike Davis
(eds)** *The Grit Beneath the Glitter:
Tales from the Real Las Vegas*
A spotty but often fascinating
collection of essays about the city.

Geoff Schumacher
*Sun, Sin and Suburbia: An Essential
History of Modern Las Vegas*
The former editor of *Las Vegas
CityLife* surveys the last few decades
in readable fashion.

Cathy Scott *Murder of a Mafia
Daughter: The Life and Tragic
Death of Susan Berman*
Journo investigates the murder of the
mafia daughter-turned-author.

John L Smith *No Limit: The
Rise and Fall of Bob Stupak & Las
Vegas' Stratosphere Tower*; *Running

*Scared: The Life and Treacherous
Times of Las Vegas Casino King
Steve Wynn*; *Of Rats and Men: Oscar
Goodman's Life from Mob Mouthpiece
to Mayor of Las Vegas*; *Sharks in the
Desert: The Founding Fathers and
Current Kings of Las Vegas*
Preposterously prolific *R-J* columnist
dishes the dirt on two major casino
players, the current mayor and the
men who shaped the town.

Lyle Stuart
Howard Hughes in Las Vegas
This history of a Vegas maverick
gets behind the legend.

David Thomson *Into Nevada*
Musings on Nevada – its mining,
nuclear and gambling history – by an
expat Brit-Californian.

Nick Tosches *Dino*
Scorching biog of the Rat Packer.

Mike Tronnes (ed)
Literary Las Vegas
An excellent anthology of journalism
from 1952 to the late 1990s.

**Robert Venturi, Steven Izenour
& Denise Scott Brown** *Learning
from Las Vegas: The Forgotten
Symbolism of Architectural Form*
Fascinating study of the auto-driven
architecture of the Strip.

Mike Weatherford *Cult Vegas:
The Weirdest! The Wildest!
The Swingin'est Town on Earth*
Offbeat movies, ornery characters,
unforgettable trivia, all explained in
gossipy detail by an *R-J* columnist.

Fiction

Larry McMurtry *Desert Rose*
The *Terms of Endearment* writer
turns his attention to the portrayal of
a washed-up showgirl.

John O'Brien *Leaving Las Vegas*
Love, loneliness and alcoholism in
the city of fun. Better than the film.

Wendy Perriam *Sin City*
Personal drama played out against an
impersonal city.

Nicholas Pileggi *Casino:
Love and Honour in Las Vegas*
Book of the film: a cracking read.

Tim Powers *Last Call*
A fantasia on the Las Vegas myth,
in which Bugsy Siegel is the Fisher
King and tarot cards the deck of
choice at the Flamingo's poker tables.

Mario Puzo *Fools Die*
The *Godfather* author returns with
another 'sweeping epic'.

Hunter S Thompson
Fear and Loathing in Las Vegas
The drug-crazed classic is always
worth re-reading.

Michael Ventura
The Death of Frank Sinatra
Cracking private-eye story set among
the implosions of the early 1990s.

Gambling

Gambling guides are many and varied, but a sizeable number are poorly researched and dangerously misleading. We recommend ordering material direct from renowned gambling experts **Huntington Press** (1-800 244 2224, www.huntingtonpress.com), which publishes all the books listed below.

Ian Andersen *Burning the Tables in Las Vegas: Keys to Success in Blackjack and in Life*
A high-stakes blackjack player reveals how he gets away with it.
Bob Dancer
Video Poker for Winners
Software tutor (download, PC only) on proper strategies for video poker. A must for players.
Max Rubin *Comp City: A Guide to Free Gambling Vacations*
Classic text on casino comps, now in its second edition. A hilarious read.
Jean Scott *The Frugal Gambler*
How to get the most from the least. A classic text.
Olaf Vancura & Ken Fuchs
Knock-Out Blackjack: The Easiest Card-Counting System Ever Devised
This former astrophysicist's 'unbalanced' count eliminates most of the mental gymnastics of other systems. Not easy, but doable.

Film

In addition to these movies, recent TV shows worth catching (either on TV or on tape) include **American Casino, Casino, CSI: Las Vegas** and **The Real World: Las Vegas**.

America's Sweethearts (2001)
Filmed in Lake Las Vegas. Stars Billy Crystal. Abysmal.
Bugsy (1991)
Witty script (James Toback), classy direction (Barry Levinson) and great performances (Beatty, Bening).
Casino (1995)
Martin Scorsese's three-hour mishmash of gambling and the Mob, voiceovered to death.
The Cooler (2004)
Set in Vegas (but filmed mostly in Reno). William H Macy stars.
Diamonds Are Forever (1971)
Bond (Connery, this time) in Vegas. Silly gadgets abound.
Fear and Loathing in Las Vegas (1998)
This relentless adaptation of the Thompson classic was a cult movie before it was even released.
Go (1999)
Doug Liman's follow-up to *Swingers* seems a little forced, but there are some good bits of business.
Honeymoon in Vegas (1992)
Nicolas Cage in engagingly oddball comedy mode.

Leaving Las Vegas (1995)
This Mike Figgis masterpiece stars Cage as a self-destructive alcoholic.
Meet Me in Las Vegas (1956)
Problem gambler hooks up with Strip dancer in a familiar plot, brightened by Cyd Charisse as the dancer.
Ocean's 11 (1960)
With all the Rat Pack present, this kitschy, corny film has become the de facto video history of a romantic Vegas era. Soderbergh's 2001 *Ocean's Eleven* deploys George Clooney and chums in a surprisingly vigorous high-tech remake.
One From the Heart (1980)
Coppola's Vegas love story, flawed but still somehow winning. Tom Waits and Crystal Gayle (duetting!) provide the beautiful soundtrack.
Rain Man (1988)
Dustin Hoffman's autistic Raymond – and brother Charlie (Tom Cruise) – finds his ability to remember numbers comes in handy in Vegas.
Showgirls (1995)
Some films that are universally panned on release benefit from a later reappraisal. Paul Verhoeven's Vegas misadventure still isn't one of them.
Swingers (1996)
First feature by Doug Liman: 90 minutes learning how not to pick up girls. Vince Vaughn is still trading off the kudos.
Viva Las Vegas (1963)
Fun film for those nostalgic for the old, swanky Vegas and the young, svelte Elvis. Ann-Margret co-stars.

Music

Crystal Method *Vegas*
This techno duo studied at UNLV.
David Holmes *Ocean's Eleven*
Funky, spunky soundtrack to the Steven Soderbergh remake of the Rat Pack classic.
The Killers *Hot Fuss*
Indie-rock from Vegas; the first band from the town to make it big in aeons.
Wayne Newton
Wild, Cool and Swingin'
Back when he still had a voice.
Panic! At the Disco
A Fever You Can't Sweat Out
Theatrical indie rockers straight out of Summerlin.
Elvis Presley *Live in Las Vegas*
As Elvis got fatter, his shows got glammier. This box set is all the fat Elvis you'll ever need, and then some.
Louis Prima *Collectors Series*
Glorious, hard-swingin' lounge stuff from the 1950s.
Frank Sinatra *Sinatra at the Sands*
Classic recording of Frank backed by the Count Basie Orchestra.
Various Artists
The Rat Pack: Live at the Sands
The definitive audio record of Dino (on top form), Sammy and the Chairman of the Board.

Websites

www.bj21.com
Head here for the invaluable monthly *Current Blackjack News*, which details current playing conditions at every casino in the city.
www.cheapovegas.com
An excellent guide to Vegas casinos, slanted towards cash-poor travellers but with enough useful information (and fine writing) for all. Run by Big Empire, which supplements it with a guide to Vegas on 25¢ a day (www.bigempire.com/vegas).
http://crecon.com/vintagevegas
Nothing here but images of classic Vegas matchbooks, postcards and gambling chips. Isn't that enough?
www.firstfriday-lasvegas.org
Information on Vegas's highly successful monthly cultural event.
www.intercomm.com/koala
The Nevada Movie Page is a wide-ranging look at the more than 500 movies made in or about the state.
www.knpr.org
Run by the local NPR affiliate, this site has a great programming archive with transcripts and audio files.
www.lasvegas.com
Links to local news, event listings and other resources.
www.lasvegasadvisor.com
The online version of the gambling bible has all the latest gambling tips, advice on how to make the most of your cash, and an always-interesting 'Question of the Day' section.
www.lvrj.com
Your first stop for Vegas news. The weekly eNeon newsletter is a useful entertainment resource.
www.nextshooter.com/vegas
The latest news on craps in Vegas: where to play and where to avoid.
www.vegas.com
This portal includes reviews of bars and restaurants, and listings of shows, films and nightlife. A useful resource, even if the reviews sometimes read a little like PR copy.
www.vegastodayandtomorrow. com
The design is a little loud and rather 1999, but don't be fooled: Mark Adams' labour of love, documenting the extraordinary wave of construction in the city with maps, features and hearsay, is perhaps the city's most vital website right now.
www.visitlasvegas.com
The official consumer website of the Las Vegas Convention & Visitors Authority has all sorts of information.
www.weddinginvegas.com
Planning to get hitched in Vegas? Find information and ideas here.
http://wizardofodds.com
A phenomenally detailed survey of casino games, including incisive tips on where to find the best odds in Vegas. An excellent site.

Directory

Index

Note: Page numbers in **bold** indicate section(s) giving key information on a topic; *italics* indicate photographs.

Index

Advertisers' Index

Please refer to the relevant pages for contact details

Major sight or landmark	▢
Major casino & hotel	▢
Park or forest	▢
Pedestrianised street	▨
One-way street	→
Interstate highway	⑧⓪
US highway	⑨⑤
State or provincial highway	⑦⑤

Maps

Trips Out of Town

0   40   80 miles
0   100 km
© Copyright Time Out Group 2007

Pyramid Lake

RENO (p298)
395

Virginia City (p300)
Fallon

Lahontan Lake

50

Carson City (p300)
95

Lake Tahoe (p300)

ALT 95

Schurz

Yerington

N E V

50

505

80

SACRAMENTO

361

376

Walker Lake

SAN FRANCISCO

580

Hawthorne
359

95

167

Mono Lake

Tonopah
6 95

280

MODESTO

120

Yosemite National Park

395

6

Goldfield
95

41

Bishop

Scotty's Junction
267

Monterey

Salinas

FRESNO

Kings Canyon National Park

180

Death Valley National Park

Rhyolite

374

Stovepipe Wells
190

P A C I F I C   O C E A N

Mt Whitney (14,494ft)

Furnace Creek

Badwater (-282ft)

C A L I F O R N I A

198

Ballarat

46

395

178

BAKERSFIELD

M O J A V E

Barstow

5

15

Hesperia

San Bernardino Mtns

10

LOS ANGELES

215

CANADA

Vancouver   Calgary
Seattle   Regina   Winnipeg

Québec
Montreal
Ottawa

Minneapolis

Salt Lake City

Detroit   Buffalo   Boston
Chicago   Pittsburg   New York
   Philadelphia
Washington

San Francisco

Denver   Kansas City   St Louis

Las Vegas
Los Angeles
Phoenix

U S A

Oklahoma City   Memphis
    Atlanta

San Diego

Dallas

Charleston

Houston   New Orleans

Miami

MEXICO

CUBA

NEVADA

50 Austin
93

50

Great Basin
National Park

UTAH

6

15

70

Warm
Springs

Extraterrestrial
Highway
(p302)

Rachel

Caliente

93

89

Bryce Canyon
National Park

Zion
National Park
(p303)

Lake
Powell

Nellis
Air Force
Base

375

93

Nevada
Test
Site

Nellis
Air Force
Base

St George

15

9

Springdale

89

Beatty

Amargosa
Valley

160

95

Spring Mtns
Recreation
Area

Death Valley
Junction

Pahrump

LAS
VEGAS

See p330

Grand Canyon
National Park
(p284)

67

North Rim
Village

89

Supai

Death
Valley
National
Park
(p294)

127

Lake

Mead

National

Recreation

Area

Grand Canyon
Village

Tusayan

180

Jean

95

Primm

160

93

66

64

180

Seligman

Williams

Flagstaff

15

Nipton

Baker

Mojave
National
Preserve
(p293)

40

DESERT

Zzyzx

Kelso

Providence
Mtns State
Rec Area

Laughlin
(p299)

Kingman

40

ARIZONA

89

Amboy

93

Twentynine
Palms

Colorado River

60

Palm
Springs

Joshua Tree
National Park

10

PHOENIX

Salton
Sea

Day Trips

Towards Utah

Overton

169

Valley of Fire State Park (p281)

Visitor Centre

Overton Beach

169

Echo Bay

Temple Bay

Lake Mead (p279)

167

NORTHSHORE SCENIC ROUTE

A R I Z O N A

93

Lake Mead National Recreation Area

167

Callville Bay

Las Vegas Bay

Hoover Dam (p278)

166

Lake Mead Marina

Boulder City (p279)

Visitor Centre

95

95

To Laughlin

147

146

93

N E V A D A

15

93

93

Henderson

95

LAS VEGAS

515

See p333

Las Vegas Beltway

Floyd Lamb State Park (p283)

95

Desert National Wildlife Refuge

215

Blue Diamond

Bonnie Springs Old Nevada

159

Scenic Loop

Visitor Centre

15

Goodsprings

To Los Angeles

Jean

Nellis Air Force Base

156

Spring Mountains

157

National Recreation

158

Area

Red Rock Canyon National Park (p281)

Spring Mountain State Park

160

15 miles

20 km

To Los Angeles

Goodsprings

Mount Charleston (11,918ft) (p282)

© Copyright Time Out Group 2007

0

0

CALIFORNIA

95

To Death Valley & Reno

330 Time Out Las Vegas

Transit|map

N Map not to scale

Time Out Las Vegas 331

Street Index

Central Las Vegas

X **Y** **Z**

W Lake Mead Boulevard

58 Texas Station

Vegas Drive

N Rancho Drive

W Washington Avenue

Lorenzi Park

Nevada State Museum

111

W Bonanza Road

Las Vegas Springs Preserve

Alta Drive

To Arizona Charlie's →

See p335

W Charleston Boulevard

W Oakey Boulevard

Stratosphere

589

114 Palace Station

Circus Circus

"The Strip"

Las Vegas Hilton

Riviera

Site of Echelon Place

Sahara

Las Vegas Country Club

Las Vegas Convention Center

Fashion Show Mall

Wynn Las Vegas

Palazzo

Venetian

Monorail

Spring Mountain Road

112 **118**

TI

Mirage

Harrah's

Imperial Palace

Flamingo

Sands Avenue

Gold Coast

33 **96**

122 **25**

56

Rio

Caesars Palace

Palms

32 **92** **94** **95**

97 **23** **24**

Bellagio

Site of CityCenter

Bally's

Paris LV

Planet Hollywood

Monte Carlo

New York New York

Harmon Ave

Showcase Mall

MGM Grand

Hard Rock

To Orleans ←

593

55 **52** **43**

Excalibur

Tropicana

Hooters

Luxor

Mandalay Bay

Las Vegas Boulevard South

McCarran International Airport

See p336

15

604

E Sunset Road

45

562

W Owens Avenue

604

15

Las Vegas Motor Speedway

Moulin Rouge

Lied Discovery Children's Museum

Old LV Mormon Fort Historic Park

E Washington Avenue

1

Cashman Field

LV Natural History Museum

Las Vegas Boulevard

Main Street

Grand Central Pkwy

Las Vegas Premium Outlets

Downtown

Arts Factory

See p334

159

Fremont Street

E Wyoming Avenue

S Maryland Parkway

E Oakey Boulevard

Main St

2

93

Fremont Street

Boulder Hwy

515

95

E Sahara Avenue

74

Commercial Center

89 **90**

To Sam's Town & Boulder Station

E Desert Inn Road

41

39

Las Vegas Hilton Country Club

115

To Henderson, Lake Mead, Boulder City & Laughlin

Sandhill Road

Paradise Road

Swenson St

Koval Avenue

Paradise Road

E Flamingo Road

116

44

117

77

UNLV

43

Thomas & Mack Center

40

E Tropicana Avenue

113

E Harmon Avenue

S Maryland Parkway

S Eastern Avenue

McLeod Drive

S Pecos Road

Sandhill Road

42

Liberace Museum

3

Desert Pines Golf Course

Eastern Avenue

S Pecos Road

1

Las Vegas Springs

515

95

❶ Casinos & Hotels pp63-118
❶ Restaurants & Buffets pp152-177
❶ Bars & Lounges pp178-188

0   1 mile

0   1 km

© Copyright Time Out Group 2007

To Sunset Station

Sunset Park

Time Out Las Vegas **333**

The Strip (North)

A   **B**   **C**

MAIN STREET

PINTO LANE

S 1ST ST

S CASINO CENTER

To Downtown

TONOPAH DRIVE
GOLDRING AVENUE

MARTIN L KING BLVD

DESERT LANE

0   700 m
0   700 yds

© Copyright Time Out Group 2007

2

W CHARLESTON BOULEVARD   **CHARLESTON BOULEVARD**

93

S COMMERCE STREET

CALIFORNIA AVE

99

107

COLORADO AVE

4TH STREET

S 3RD STREET

BOULEVARD SOUTH

44

42
37

WESTWOOD DRIVE

❶ Casinos & Hotels pp63-118
❶ Restaurants & Buffets pp152-177
❶ Bars & Lounges pp178-188

PARK CIRCLE

WALDMAN AVENUE

BANNIE AVENUE

SILVER AVENUE

HIGHLAND DRIVE

15

IMPERIAL AVENUE

UTAH AVENUE

S MAIN STREET

S CASINO CENTER BLVD

S LAS VEGAS BLVD

71

72
26
23
69

3

Little White Wedding Chapel

CAHLAN AVE
STRONG DRIVE

BRYANT AVE

GILMARY AVE

PINE STREET

SILVER AVENUE

W WYOMING AVENUE

W OAKEY BOULEVARD

RANCHO DRIVE

LA SOLANA WAY

VILLA DE CONDE

BONNIE BRAE AVE

KIRKLAND AVE

WESTERN AVENUE

NEW YORK AVENUE

W CHICAGO AVENUE

PHILADELPHIA AVE

REXFORD AVE

BARBARA WAY

E OAKEY BLVD

Bob Baskin Park

FULANO WAY

WESTLUND DRIVE

GLEN HEATHER WAY

HIGHLAND DRIVE

S INDUSTRIAL ROAD

W ST LOUIS AVE

W BOSTON AVE

25 70

Stratosphere

PARADISE ROAD

SANTA CLARA DRIVE
SANTA PAULA STREET

BONITA AVE

ST LOUIS AVENUE

SIDONIA AVENUE

LOURDES AVENUE

W BALTIMORE AVE

W CLEVELAND AVE

FAIRFIELD AVE

Bonanza

SANTA RITA DR
SANTA INEZ ST

SANTA ROSA DRIVE
VAN PATTEN DRIVE

W SAHARA AVENUE   91   W CINCINNATI AVE   **E SAHARA AVENUE**   **4**

ALCOA AVE

MERRITT AVE

Palace Station 57

43 22

24   Sahara

LYNNWOOD ST

VAN PATTEN ST

KINGS WAY

WESTWOOD DRIVE

HIGHLAND DRIVE

WESTERN LANE

KAREN AVENUE

TAM O'SHANTER WEST

JAMESTOWN WAY
MILO WAY

KINGS WAY

'THE STRIP'

OAKMONT AVE

Las Vegas Country Club

OAKMONT DRIVE

MEADE AVE

RANCHO DRIVE

WESTWOOD DRIVE

CIRCUS CIRCUS DRIVE

20 18
7

Circus Circus

JOE W BROWN DRIVE

Scandia

HIGHLAND DRIVE

RIVIERA BOULEVARD

Las Vegas Hilton

31 20

Riviera
23

Las Vegas Convention & Visitors Authority

5

Site of Echelon Place (open 2010)

13

CONVENTION CENTER DRIVE

Las Vegas Convention Center

STARDUST ROAD

Guardian Angel Cathedral

Monorail

15

DESERT INN ROAD

Trump International   29

41   **E DESERT INN ROAD**

WESTERN AVE

LEXINGTON ST

Encore (open 2008)

75
36

COUNTRY CLUB LANE

SIERRA VISTA DRIVE

OLYMPIC AVENUE

Fashion Show Mall

10 30 36

Wynn Las Vegas

7 20 26 27
32 43 67 12

Wynn Golf & Country Club

PARADISE ROAD

EDISON CIRCLE

SPRING MOUNTAIN RD

T I

17 52 54
58 10

ELM DRIVE

ROYAL CREST CIR

6

Palazzo

Venetian

S INDUSTRIAL ROAD

Mirage

4 17 24
50 55 15

F 19

Casino Royale

6 14 29 41
49 60 61 68 18

SANDS AVENUE

Sands Expo

COUNTRY CLUB LANE

Encore (open 2008)

A **B** **C**

Fashion Show Mall
10 30 36

SPRING MOUNTAIN RD

Wynn Las Vegas
7 20 26 27
32 43 61 67 12

Wynn Golf & Country Club

T 1
17 52 54
58 10

Palazzo

SANDS AVENUE

COUNTRY CLUB LANE

Mirage
4 17 24
50 55 15

Venetian

Casino Royale
19

Sands Expo

6 14 29 41
49 60 68 18

WESTCHESTER DRIVE

PARADISE ROAD

TWAIN AVENUE

CASSELLA DRIVE

EDISON CIRCLE

ELM DRIVE

10 8 47

Harrah's
Imperial Palace
11 16

Forum Shops

Caesars Palace
2 3 4 9 16 42
46 48 53 62 17

O'Sheas

9 Flamingo

IDA AVENUE

80

W FLAMINGO ROAD

18 Bill's Gamblin'
Hall & Saloon

34

E FLAMINGO ROAD

83

Bellagio

8 120 51

Bally's

35 78

1 8 12 15 51
39 40 47 63 66
121 2 6 50

Paris Las Vegas
5 33 38
124 11 46

16 13 59

ROCHELLE AVENUE

DECKOW LN
LA CIENEGA ST
SADIE ST
SALTON ST
KISHNER DRIVE

CHARLOTTE DRIVE

40

"THE STRIP"

AUDRIE STREET

Monorail

LANA AVENUE

Hard Rock
30 73 76 79
85 83 21

Planet Hollywood

E HARMON AVENUE

39

Site of CityCenter (open 2010)

14 Monte Carlo

Showcase Mall

KOVAL LANE

37

84

HARMON AVE
82

NAPLES 19 DR

PARADISE ROAD

TOMPKINS AVE

MGM Grand

13 7 11 23 23
25 28 35 44 51
57 65 3

DECKOW LANE

New York New York
15 1 1
4 5 45

W TROPICANA AVENUE

E TROPICANA AVENUE

Excalibur
21

26 48

Hooters

22

DUKE ELLINGTON WAY

Tropicana

RENO AVENUE

RENO AVENUE

Luxor
12

GILES STREET

ALI BABA LANE

KOVAL LANE

HACIENDA AVENUE

HACIENDA AVENUE

McCarran International Airport

LAS VEGAS BOULEVARD SOUTH

S INDUSTRIAL ROAD

3 28 2
5 19 34
37 56 64
119 14 49

Mandalay Bay

Four Seasons
27 6 21

Little Chapel of the West

HAVEN STREET

DIABLO DRIVE

0   700 m

0   700 yds

© Copyright Time Out Group 2007

DEWEY DRIVE

1 Casinos & Hotels pp63-118
1 Restaurants & Buffets pp152-177
1 Bars & Lounges pp178-188

**The Strip
(South)**

RUSSELL ROAD